THE ROUGH GUIDE TO

Paris

This fifteenth edition updated by

Ruth Blackmore and Samantha Cook

ROUGH
GUIDES

roughguides.com

Contents

OPPOSITE PLACE DU TERTRE AND SACRE-COEUR **PREVIOUS PAGE** JARDIN DES TUILERIES

Introduction to
Paris

Paris has an awesome emotional pull: Parisians rarely want to escape, while most visitors find themselves yearning to return. Its power derives from the city's rare beauty, of course, and its celebrated style and romanticism, but also from its unique history as the beating cultural heart of Europe over much of the last thousand years. For all the passions the city arouses, its actual fabric can feel inhumanly magnificent, its monuments encompassing the grandeur of the Panthéon, the industrial chic of the Eiffel Tower and the almost spiritual glasswork of the Louvre pyramid. Yet the real Paris operates on a very human scale, with exquisite, secretive little nooks and defined communities revolving around the local boulangerie and café. And even as Paris's culture has been transformed by its large immigrant and gay populations, even as extravagant new buildings are commissioned and erected, many of the city's streets, cafés and restaurants remain defiantly unchanged.

In the great local tradition of the *flâneur*, or thoughtful urban wanderer, Paris is a wonderful city for aimless exploration. Quarters such as the charming Marais, elegant St-Germain and romantic Montmartre are ideal for strolling, browsing the shops and relaxing in cafés, and the city's lack of open space is redeemed by some beautiful formal gardens and the pathways that run beside the River Seine.

There are nearly 150 **art galleries** and **museums** on offer, and few are duds. **Places to eat and drink** line the streets and boulevards, ranging from chic temples of gastronomy and grandly mirrored brasseries down to tiny, chef-owned *bistrots* and bustling Vietnamese diners. After dark, the city's theatres, concert halls and churches host world-leading productions of **theatre, dance and classical music**, and there is no better place in the world for **cinema**. The live music and clubbing scene is impassioned, and this is also a great place to explore jazz, world music and the home-grown singer-songwriter genre of *chanson*.

ABOVE LOUIS VUITTON, CHAMPS-ELYSEES; STALL AT THE MARCHE BIO; *LE BARON ROUGE* WINE BAR

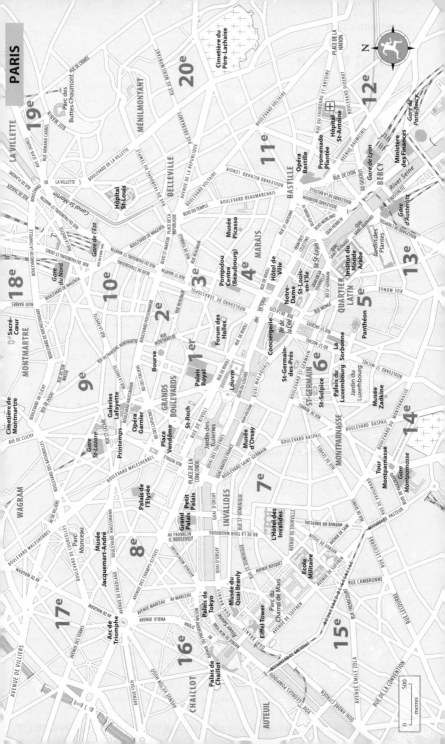

What to see

The now-demolished ring of fortifications that once encircled the city and was replaced by the *boulevard périphérique* still defines the boundary between Paris and its suburbs. At its widest point, the city is only about 12km across – roughly two hours' walk. At the hub of the circle, in the middle of the **River Seine**, is the island from which all the rest grew: the **Ile de la Cité**, defined by its Gothic cathedral of **Notre-Dame**.

The city is divided into twenty **arrondissements**. Centred on the royal palace and museum of the **Louvre**, they spiral outwards in a clockwise direction. On the north or **Right Bank** (*rive droite*) of the Seine, which is the more business-focused and fashionable of the city's two halves, the longest and grandest vista of the city runs west from the Louvre: this is **La Voie Triomphale** – comprising the Tuileries gardens, the grand avenue of the **Champs-Elysées** and the Arc de Triomphe. North of the Louvre is the commercial and financial quarter, where you can shop in the department stores on the broad **Grands Boulevards**, in the little boutiques of the glass-roofed **passages**, or in the giant, underground mall of **Les Halles**. East of the Louvre, the enchanting **Marais** and vibrant **Bastille** quarters are alive with trendy shops, cafés and bars. Further east, the **Canal St-Martin** and **Ménilmontant** are good places to go for cutting-edge bars and nightlife.

The south bank of the river, or **Left Bank** (*rive gauche*), is quieter. The **Quartier Latin** is the traditional domain of the intelligentsia – from artists to students – along with **St-Germain**, which becomes progressively more chichi until it hits the grand district of ministries and museums that surrounds the **Eiffel Tower**. As you move south towards **Montparnasse** and the southern swathe of the Left Bank, high-rise flats start to alternate with charming bourgeois neighbourhoods.

Back on the Right Bank, many of the outer arrondissements were once outlying villages. Hilly **Montmartre**, with its rich artistic associations and bohemian population, is the most picturesque, but **Belleville** and **Passy** have also retained village-like identities – working-class in the east, wealthy in the west.

THE SEINE

Referred to by some as Paris's main avenue or the city's 21st arrondissement – and by others as a murky, polluted waterway – the **Seine** is integral to Paris, sashaying through its centre in a broad arc, taking in the capital's grandest monuments. It even makes its way into the city's coat of arms, which depicts a ship sailing on choppy waters accompanied by the words *fluctuat nec mergitur* – "it is tossed about but does not sink", a singularly apt motto for a city that has weathered events as turbulent as the French Revolution and the Commune.

The Seine brought the city into being and was for centuries its lifeblood, a major conduit of **trade** and **commerce**. Floods, however, have always been a regular hazard, sometimes sweeping away bridges, houses and lives. One of the worst recorded was in 1176, when the city was almost completely engulfed. The construction of the **quais** in the nineteenth century helped to alleviate the problem, and these tree-lined walkways have today become one of Paris's major assets – attractive and leafy havens away from the city's bustle. More and more of the riverbank is being **reclaimed** for pedestrians and cyclists. Cars are now completely banned from a stretch of the Left Bank (the Berges de Seine) and, in summer, tonnes of sand are imported to create a kind of Paris-sur-Mer, complete with palm trees and deckchairs.

WALLACE'S FOUNTAINS

Moved by the suffering that Parisians had endured during the Siege of Paris in 1870–71 (see box, p.186), which had deprived the citizens of running water, a wealthy British resident of the city called **Richard Wallace** came up with the perfect gift. In 1872, Wallace gave the city fifty cast-iron drinking fountains, each topped with a kind of miniature temple designed by the sculptor Charles-Auguste Lebourg, its roof supported by four caryatids representing Simplicity, Temperance, Charity and Goodness. More fountains were added in later years, and today some 67 still stand in the city. Painted in lustrous green, their usefulness is limited these days by the loss of the cups once permanently attached to them, but they still work (from mid-March to mid-Nov only, because of the risk of damage from ice in winter) and the water's good to drink – it's the same water that flows through all the city's taps, although a recent study showed that only around thirty per cent of Parisians actually use them. All the same, *les fontaines Wallace* remain quintessential symbols of Paris. Curiously, the fountains have an unusual status in the French language, too, being one of the few French words to begin with "w"; like *le whisky, le weekend* and *le wi-fi, les fontaines Wallace* are something of a linguistic collector's item.

Central Paris has lots of wonderful gardens, notably the **Jardin du Luxembourg**, **Jardin des Tuileries** and **Jardin des Plantes**, offering a welcome escape from the urban hustle and bustle. For something a little wilder and more expansive, the best big parks are the **Bois de Vincennes** and the **Bois de Boulogne**, at the eastern and western edges of the city, respectively. Smaller pockets of green crop up all over Paris: try the **square du Vert-Gallant**, **place des Vosges**, **Les Halles** and the **gardens** at any number of institutions, including the Petit Palais, Palais Royal, Musée Rodin, Musée du Quai Branly, Musée de Montmartre and Musée de l'Histoire de France.

The region surrounding the capital, beyond the **boulevard périphérique ring road**, is known as the **Ile de France**, and is dotted with cathedrals and châteaux. Sights such as the Gothic cathedral at **St-Denis** and the astonishing royal palace at **Versailles** are easy to get to, while full day-trip destinations include the stunning cathedral town of **Chartres** and Monet's lovely garden at **Giverny**. An equally accessible outing from the capital is that most un-French of French attractions, **Disneyland Paris**.

When to go

In terms of climate (see p.33), **spring** is deservedly the classic time to visit, with bright days balanced by rain showers. Paris in high **summer** is usually hot and can be uncomfortably humid, especially between mid-July and the end of August, when many Parisians flee south, leaving the city to the tourists. In **autumn**, things can be pleasingly mild and gratifyingly uncrowded (except during the autumn fashion show and trade-fair season, when hotels fill up early), but on overcast days – all too common – it can feel very melancholy. **Winter** can be harsh, with icy winds cutting down the boulevards and snow not uncommon; the winter sun, on the other hand, is the city's most flattering light.

Author picks

Our authors have explored every corner of Paris in order to uncover the very best it has to offer. Here are some of their favourite things to see, do, sip and savour.

Divine croissants It's futile to resist the croissants made by *Sébastien Gaudard* (p.335), *Du Pain et des Idées* (p.334) – try the rosewater and green tea flavours – or *Le Grenier à Pain* (p.334).

People-watching The quintessential Parisian pastime. Try the *terrasse* of *Les Philosophes* (p.280), *Café Charlot* (p.278), *Café de la Paix* (p.275), the Jardin du Luxembourg (p.140), *Aux Folies* (p.301), *Café St-Régis* (p.271) or *Bar du Marché* (p.284).

Foodie heaven Our favourite places to go food shopping are Richard Lenoir market (p.199), Marché des Enfants Rouges (p.104), Marché d'Aligre (p.113), Marché Edgar-Quinet (p.164) and the St-Germain *quartier* (p.134).

Compelling stories Hunt down these lesser-known corners for insights into the capital's turbulent past: the French Revolution section in the Musée Carnavalet (p.96), the Conciergerie (p.45), the Mémorial de la Shoah museum (p.106) and the Musée Nissim de Camondo (p.68).

Perfect apéros Sipping a *pastis* or a *kir* in a Paris bar – life doesn't get much better. Try *Le Progrès* (p.290), *Au Chai de l'Abbaye* (p.285), *La Palette* (p.285) or *Rosa Bonheur sur Seine* (p.288).

Blissful sunsets You're spoilt for choice: head for the Parc de Belleville (p.209), the top of the Arc de Triomphe (p.63), the rooftop terrace of *Le Perchoir* (p.301) or sit by the pond in the Jardin des Tuileries (p.70).

Live music There are many wonderful places to hear live music in Paris; we love Hungarian gypsy music at *La Bellevilloise* (p.305), *chanson* at *Au Limonaire* (p.306), the eclectic mix at *Social Club* (p.302), jazz at *New Morning* (p.307) and grand symphonic concerts at the new Philharmonie de Paris (p.375).

> Our author recommendations don't end here. We've flagged up our favourite places – a perfectly sited hotel, an atmospheric café, a special restaurant – throughout the Guide, highlighted with the ★ symbol.

FROM TOP BREAKFAST AT A PARISIAN CAFE; JARDIN DU LUXEMBOURG; *BAR DU MARCHE*

20

things not to miss

It's not possible to see everything Paris has to offer on a short trip – and we don't suggest you try. What follows is a subjective selection of the city's highlights, in no particular order, ranging from the Sainte-Chapelle to *chanson* concerts, which will help you find the very best things to see, do and experience. Each highlight has a page reference to take you straight into the Guide, where you can find out more. Coloured numbers refer to chapters in the Guide section.

1 JARDIN DU LUXEMBOURG

Page 140

The oasis of the Left Bank: students hang out on the lawns, old men play chess under the trees and children sail toy yachts around the pond.

2 MUSEE RODIN

Page 155

Elegance matched with passion: Rodin's powerful works are shown off to their best advantage in the sculptor's beautiful, recently renovated, eighteenth-century mansion.

3 PUCES DE ST-OUEN

Page 223

It's easy to lose track of an entire weekend morning browsing the acres of fine antiques, covetable curios and general bric-a-brac at St-Ouen, the mother of Paris's flea markets.

18

19

20

Itineraries

Paris is made for wandering on foot. The following itineraries take in some of the capital's most famous sights as well as some lesser-known districts.

TWO DAYS IN PARIS

Day 1

Ile de la Cité Begin at the beginning, on the island where Paris was founded by early Celtic tribes. **See p.42**

Notre-Dame cathedral Visit the magnificent Gothic cathedral of Notre-Dame, which graces the very centre of Paris. **See p.46**

Pont-Neuf Walk across the oldest bridge in the city to the Left Bank, and the fashionable St-Germain *quartier*. **See p.43**

Lunch Enjoy a lunch of the finest produce and a glass of natural wine at *La Grande Crèmerie*. **See p.286**

Jardin du Luxembourg Wander through elegant place St-Sulpice to the Jardin du Luxembourg, the green heart of the Left Bank. **See p.140**

Musée d'Orsay The world-beating Impressionist collection is housed in a dramatically converted railway station. **See p.144**

The Eiffel Tower Unmissable, especially at sunset. **See p.148**

Dinner Linger by the river and enjoy an aperitif or meal at *Rosa Bonheur sur Seine*, or make for *David Toutain* to sample some of the most innovative and exciting food in Paris. **See p.288**

Day 2

Pompidou Centre This radical building is home to one of the world's best collections of modern art. **See p.86**

The Marais Explore the elegant Marais *quartier*, full of handsome Renaissance mansions and fascinating museums. **See p.93**

Lunch Set in an excellent foodie market, *L'Estaminet* makes an atmospheric lunch spot. **See p.280**

Musée Picasso The recently revamped Picasso museum displays an extraordinary collection of works by this restlessly inventive artist. **See p.102**

Place des Vosges Arguably the city's most beautiful square, with art galleries and cafés under the arches, and buskers playing jazz and classical favourites. **See p.95**

Canal St-Martin Take a stroll along the tree-lined canal, with its attractive iron-work bridges, arty shops and cafés. **See p.197**

Dinner and drinks Soak up the canalside vibe at locals' favourite *Chez Prune*, then head for dinner at *Le Verre Volé*. **See p.293 & p.294**

PARIS ON A BUDGET

Despite Paris's reputation as an expensive city, there are many treats to be enjoyed for free, and many restaurants where you can sample its wonderful food without breaking the bank.

Musée d'Art Moderne de la Ville de Paris, Palais de Tokyo A choice collection of modern art, including works by Chagall, Matisse and Modigliani, without the crowds and queues of the Pompidou Centre – and it's free. **See p.158**

ABOVE ILE ST-LOUIS **OPPOSITE** MUSEE D'ORSAY

Bus ride Hop on the #63 near the Pont de l'Alma and enjoy an inexpensive sightseeing ride along the Left Bank, taking in Les Invalides and the Musée d'Orsay. **See p.26**

Lunch Alight at the Maubert-Mutualité métro stop in the Quartier Latin and head down rue Mouffetard to *Le Verre à Pied*, an old market bar, where you'll get a good *entrecôte* or *saucisson* for around €12. **See p.283**

Pompidou Centre Check out the centre's new Galerie de Photographies, which stages free photography exhibitions taken from its extensive archive. **See p.87**

Vintage buys Wander through the Marais, browsing for bargains in the many vintage and secondhand clothes shops. **See p.328**

Dinner *Chez Hanna*, in the Marais, is a favourite with locals, who come for its reasonably priced Middle Eastern and Jewish delicacies. **See p.280**

Catch a movie The Cinémathèque, a half-hour walk or short métro ride away in Bercy, is the city's best venue for cinephiles, showing more than twenty films a week (many rarely screened) at low prices. **See p.116**

RIVERSIDE PARIS

The elegant riverbanks and bridges of the Seine provide some of Paris's finest vistas. Take a waterside day to enjoy some of the city's most memorable experiences.

Boat ride The classic way to enjoy the Seine is on a boat ride. The popular Bateaux-Mouches leave from the Pont de l'Alma. **See p.28**

Riverside Cross over the Pont de l'Alma to check out what's happening on the Left Bank

Berges de Seine; there are often free workshops, food festivals and concerts, and it's a good place for a picnic. **See p.152**

Musée d'Orsay Walk along the riverbank to the Musée d'Orsay and track down paintings of the Seine by the Impressionists Renoir, Sisley, Pissarro and Monet. The chic *Café Campana*, with its huge clock window looking out onto the river and summer terrace, is a great spot for a drink or bite to eat. **See p.144**

Bouquinistes All along the riverbank from the Musée d'Orsay to the Quai de la Tournelle you'll see the distinctive green stalls of the *bouquinistes*; selling secondhand books, posters and postcards, they're always good for a browse. **See p.121**

Pont des Arts The pedestrian Pont des Arts enjoys classic views of the Ile de la Cité and the Louvre. **See p.134**

River islands The graceful Pont-Neuf will take you across to the Ile de la Cité and the Ile St-Louis. The latter is especially good for a waterside stroll, with its tranquil, leafy *quais*. **See p.42**

Right Bank Opposite the river islands on the Right Bank, the pedestrian-friendly *quai* between the Hôtel de Ville and Port de l'Arsenal is lovely on Sundays, when cars are banned completely. **See p.89**

Péniche Le Marcounet For a chilled end to the day head to *Le Marcounet*, a canal barge moored on the Quai de l'Hôtel de Ville by the Pont Marie, where you can enjoy an *apéritif* on deck and then a jazz or blues concert down below. **See p.306**

CANAL DE L'OURCQ, PARC DE LA VILLETTE

Basics

Getting there

Paris has direct connections with airports all over the world, and ultra-high-speed rail links to much of Western Europe – London can now be as little as 2hr 20min away by the Eurostar train link. Airfares usually depend on the season, with the highest being around early June to the end of August; the lowest prices are available from November to March (excluding Christmas and New Year).

By Eurostar from the UK and Ireland

The most enjoyable way to reach Paris from Britain is the **Eurostar** train service (☎03432 186186, ⓦeurostar.com). It's competitively priced, and can be far quicker than the plane if you live in the southeast: flying time from London is around 1hr 10min, but once you've added travel to and from airports, extended check-in times and ever more frequent delays, any journey time saved is negligible. The train is far less carbon-intensive, too. The Eurostar takes 2hr 20min–2hr 45min from London St Pancras to **Paris Gare du Nord**, with a few services stopping at Ebbsfleet International or Ashford International stations, in Kent.

Prices of Eurostar tickets depend on how far in advance you book and how much flexibility you need. The lowest fares are almost always for early-morning trains, especially those departing midweek. It's possible to find tickets for as little as £35 single/£69 return, but you could pay double that. A number of **discounted seats** are set aside on each train for young people aged 12–25 and for the over-60s; the further in advance you book, the better your chances are of securing one. Fares for children aged 4–11 start at £49 return.

Eurostar tickets can be bought online or over the phone. If you're coming from outside London, it usually pays to buy a through ticket – available from any mainline station.

Eurostar's **monopoly** came to an end in 2010 and "open access" laws on the route came into effect. At the time of research, a number of companies, including Deutsche Bahn, had stated their interest in running services, which may result in lower fares in the future. Check ⓦseat61.com for more details on train travel throughout Europe.

Flights from the UK and Ireland

The most competitive airfares from the UK and Ireland tend to be with **no-frills airlines** such as **easyJet** and **Ryanair**, as well as a number of other operators on regional routes – **Flybe** serves Paris from Belfast, Birmingham, Cardiff, Dublin, Edinburgh, Exeter, Glasgow and Manchester, among other cities, while **Jet2** flies from Leeds-Bradford and **CityJet** from London City, Stansted and Cardiff. Once you've added airport tax, **fares** typically work out at around £90–120 return, though you can pick up tickets for less if you book well in advance and travel off-peak. National carriers **British Airways**, **Air France**, **KLM** and **Aer Lingus** may often be only slightly more expensive than the low-cost airlines, and often have special offers; students and people under 26 should enquire about discounts on scheduled flights. The airports they serve may be more convenient too. **Roissy-Charles de Gaulle** (CDG) and **Orly** (ORY) are both handy airports at which to arrive; **Paris Beauvais** (BVA), however, served by Ryanair, is a good 80km north of the city.

Flights from the US and Canada

The widest choice of flights to Paris is offered by Air France, with regular nonstop scheduled services to Paris CDG from across the **US**. American Airlines and Delta may be slightly cheaper, though you may have to stop off en route from smaller cities. The least expensive deals of all may be found with non-French European carriers, including British Airways and Lufthansa, though you'll probably have to change flights in their hub city within Europe. While you can get deals from around US$500 return from New York or Washington DC, typical midweek **fares** range from around US$700 in low season to US$1200 in high season; they're higher, of course, the further west you leave from.

Air France and Air Canada both fly nonstop to Paris from all the major cities in **Canada**. Return flights from Montréal, Québec and Toronto tend to start at around Can$800 in low season; high-season **fares** can top Can$2000, but with a little flexibility over dates it's usually possible to pay around half that. Equivalent fares from Vancouver are generally about Can$200 higher. In addition, Air Transat offers good-value charter flights from Calgary, Montréal, Québec, Toronto and Vancouver, for similar prices.

Flights from Australia, New Zealand and South Africa

There are scheduled flights to Paris from **Auckland**, **Brisbane**, **Cairns**, **Melbourne**, **Perth** and **Sydney**, but you can find a wider range of options by flying to another European capital – usually London – and making a connection from there. The best deals from Australia or New Zealand to Europe are routed via Asia or the Middle East, often with a transfer or overnight stop in the airline's home city. Flights via the US are usually slightly more expensive. From Australia, you should be able to find scheduled **fares** to Paris for around Aus\$1400–1600 in low season (roughly Nov–March, excluding Christmas and New Year), and more like Aus\$1800–2000 in high season. **From New Zealand** you might pay from NZ\$2000 right up to NZ\$3000-plus in peak season. Flight times vary considerably depending on the route, but it's roughly 30hr from Sydney or Auckland to Paris.

From **South Africa**, Johannesburg is the best place to start, with Air France flying direct to Paris from around ZAR7000 return. BA, flying via London, is pricier, with low-season fares from around ZAR10,000 from Cape Town and ZAR9000 from Johannesburg, each rising by ZAR2000–3000 in high season. Flight times are around 10hr from Johannesburg to Paris, and 14hr from Cape Town including a stopover in Amsterdam (Air France code-shares with KLM).

By car, ferry and coach from the UK and Ireland

The most convenient way of taking a **car** across to France is to drive down to the Channel Tunnel, load it on **Eurotunnel**'s frequent train shuttle service, and be whisked under the Channel in 35min to Sangatte on the French side, just outside Calais. The British tunnel entrance is off the M20 at junction 11A, just outside Folkestone. You can simply buy a ticket at one of the booths and drive straight on, as there are departures roughly every 15min (or hourly midnight–6am), but it's cheaper to

book in advance. Expect to pay in the region of £25–160 per car each way, depending on the time of year and how far ahead you book, and how much flexibility you need. In summer and around Easter you should definitely book in advance to avoid queues and higher tariffs – don't worry if you miss your departure, though, as you can usually just roll onto the next available train. Once on the French side, it's little more than a 3hr drive to Paris on the fast autoroutes A26 and A1 (tolls payable).

The car **ferries** from Dover to Calais (1hr 30min) or Dunkerque (2hr) – from where the drive to Paris takes just over 3hr – are slower but less expensive than Eurotunnel. P&O and My Ferry Link run regular services on the former route, DFDS on both; P&O also offers services from Hull to Zeebrugge (3hr 30min drive to Paris) and Rotterdam (5hr drive to Paris), while DFDS also offers ferries from Newhaven to Dieppe (4hr; 2hr 30min drive to Paris). **Fares** vary according to season (school and bank holidays being the most expensive), and, on certain routes, depending on how many passengers there are. Lower fares are usually available if you can avoid travelling out on Fridays and Saturdays. While you can find deals for as little as £45 return on a ferry, you should normally expect to pay £75–180.

Given the competitive prices and relative speed of the Eurostar, it is generally not worth the hassle to travel from the UK to Paris by **coach**, though it can be cheaper in high season. **Eurolines** runs **bus-and-ferry** services from London's Victoria coach station to Paris's CDG Airport and Bagnolet in eastern Paris. Off-peak return fares can be as low as £30, if you book well in advance, but it's usually more like £40–45, and the journey takes a tedious 7–10hr. **Megabus** runs a similar service, stopping in Paris in a more central location a couple of métro stops from the Arc de Triomphe. **iDBUS**, part of the French national train company, SNCF, runs coaches from London to CDG and Bercy; if you're planning ahead this is generally a pricier option, with single fares between £20 and £45, but can be cheaper than the other bus companies if you're booking at the last minute.

A BETTER KIND OF TRAVEL

At Rough Guides we are passionately committed to travel. We believe it helps us understand the world we live in and the people we share it with – and of course tourism is vital to many developing economies. But the scale of modern tourism has also damaged some places irreparably, and climate change is accelerated by most forms of transport, especially flying. All Rough Guides' flights are carbon-offset, and every year we donate money to a variety of environmental charities.

AIRLINES

Aer Lingus Ⓦ aerlingus.com.
Air Canada Ⓦ aircanada.com.
Air France Ⓦ airfrance.com.
Air Transat Ⓦ airtransat.ca.
American Airlines Ⓦ aa.com.
British Airways Ⓦ britishairways.com.
CityJet Ⓦ cityjet.com.
Delta Ⓦ delta.com.
easyJet Ⓦ easyjet.com.
flybe Ⓦ flybe.com.
Jet2 Ⓦ jet2.com.
KLM Ⓦ klm.com.
Lufthansa Ⓦ lufthansa.com.

FERRY, EUROTUNNEL, BUS AND RAIL CONTACTS

DFDS Seaways UK ☎ 0871 574 7235, Ⓦ dfdsseaways.com. Dover to Calais and Dover to Dunkerque ferries, plus Newhaven to Dieppe.
Eurodrive UK ☎ 0844 371 8021, Ⓦ eurodrive.co.uk. Discount agent for ferry and Eurotunnel tickets.
Eurolines UK ☎ 0871 781 8178, Ⓦ eurolines.co.uk. International coach company.
Eurotunnel UK ☎ 0844 335 3535, Ⓦ eurotunnel.com. Folkestone to Calais car-loading train service through the Channel Tunnel.
Ferrysavers UK ☎ 0844 371 8021, Ⓦ ferrysavers.co.uk. Discount agent for the major ferry companies.
iDBUS ☎ 0844 369 0379, Ⓦ idbus.com. European coach company.
Man in Seat 61 Ⓦ seat61.com. Excellent and detailed advice on travel by train.
Megabus ☎ 0141 352 4444, Ⓦ uk.megabus.com. Coaches throughout Europe.
My Ferry Link UK ☎ 0844 248 2100, Ⓦ myferrylink.com. Dover to Calais ferries.
P&O Ferries UK ☎ 0871 664 6464, Ⓦ poferries.com. Dover to Calais; Hull to Rotterdam and Zeebrugge.
SNCF France Ⓦ sncf.com. The French national rail company.
Transilien Ⓦ transilien.com. Information on suburban train lines.
Voyages-SNCF ☎ 0844 848 5848, Ⓦ uk.voyages-sncf.com. Tickets, passes and information about SNCF and other European trains.

AGENTS AND OPERATORS

Even if you're not interested in a package tour, if you're aiming to stay in three- or four-star hotels it's worth considering booking a **hotel-and-flight package**, as these can save you considerable sums. The drawback is that the hotels on offer tend to lack character, and of course you're more restricted in your choice than if you book independently.

Abercrombie & Kent US ☎ 1 800 554 7016, Ⓦ abercrombiekent .com. An upmarket travel agency running a variety of guided tours to France, some of which include days in Paris. An eleven-day river cruise taking in Paris, Burgundy and the South of France, for example, starts at US$5795.

Co-op Travel UK ☎ 01733 224 804, Ⓦ co-operativetravel.co.uk. Flights and holidays, with some inexpensive flight/accommodation packages in Paris.
Eurostar UK ☎ 0843 218 6186; from France ☎ +44 1233 617575, Ⓦ eurostar.com. The website puts together rail-and-hotel packages which can represent significant savings on doing it yourself – though its choice of hotels is relatively limited.
French Travel Connection Australia ☎ 1300 858 304, Ⓦ www.frenchtravel.com.au. Specialists in French travel, offering everything from cooking classes and barge holidays to Paris accommodation and packages.
Martin Randall Travel UK ☎ 020 8742 3355, Ⓦ martinrandall .com. High-quality, small-group cultural and wine/gastronomic tours, led by experts in their field. Some, such as "History of Impressionism" or "Ballet in Paris", concentrate on a specific detail of the capital; these include tickets, hotels, travel and the attentions of an art curator and a dance curator respectively.
North South Travel UK ☎ 01245 608291, Ⓦ northsouthtravel .co.uk. Friendly travel agency, offering discounted air fares – profits are used to support projects in the developing world, especially the promotion of sustainable tourism.
STA Travel UK ☎ 0333 321 0099, Ⓦ statravel.co.uk; US ☎ 1 800 781 4040, Ⓦ statravel.com; Australia ☎ 134 782, Ⓦ statravel.com .au; South Africa ☎ 0861 781 781, Ⓦ statravel.co.za. Worldwide specialists in low-cost flights and tours for students and under-26s, though also welcomes other customers.
Trailfinders UK ☎ 020 7368 1200, Ⓦ trailfinders.com. One of the best-informed and most efficient agents for independent travellers.

Arrival

Many British travellers to Paris arrive by Eurostar at the central Gare du Nord train station, while visitors from more far-flung starting points are likely to land at one of Paris's airports: Roissy-Charles de Gaulle, Orly and Beauvais. Trains from other parts of France or continental Europe draw in at one of the six central mainline stations.

By train

Paris has six mainline train stations. **Eurostar** (see p.21) terminates at **Gare du Nord**, rue Dunkerque, in the northeast of the city – a bustling convergence of international, long-distance and suburban trains, the métro, RER and several bus routes. Coming off the train, turn left for the métro and the RER, right for the taxi rank (a sample price would be €10–15 to a hotel in the 4ᵉ) – avoid the touts who approach you directly and wait in line in the specified spot. The station also has **left luggage** facilities (*consignes*; daily 6.15am–11.15pm; €5.50–9.50 for the first 24hr, depending on locker size, and then €5/24hr after that), and shower facilities (€6) in the public toilets (daily 6am–midnight; €0.70) at the bottom of the métro escalators. There are a couple of information desks too (Mon–Fri 6.10am–9.30pm, Sat 7.30am–3pm, Sun 2–9.30pm). Gare du Nord is also the arrival point for trains from Calais and other north European countries. The station isn't dangerous but keep your wits about you, and avoid scammers offering to "help" with tickets or taxis.

Nearby, **Gare de l'Est** (place du 11-Novembre-1918, 10e) serves eastern France and central and eastern Europe. **Gare St-Lazare** (place du Havre, 8e), serving the Normandy coast and Dieppe, is the most central, close to the Madeleine and the Opéra Garnier. Still on the Right Bank but towards the southeast corner is **Gare de Lyon** (place Louis-Armand, 12e), with trains from Italy and Switzerland and TGV lines from southeast France. South of the river, **Gare Montparnasse** on boulevard de Vaugirard, 15e, is the terminus for Chartres, Brittany, the Atlantic coast and TGV lines from southwest France. **Gare d'Austerlitz**, on boulevard de l'Hôpital, 13e, serves the Loire Valley and the Dordogne. The motorail station, **Gare de Paris-Bercy**, is down the tracks from the Gare de Lyon on boulevard de Bercy, 12e.

All the stations are equipped with cafés, restaurants, *tabacs*, ATMs and bureaux de change (long waits in season), and all are connected with the métro system; most also offer free wi-fi. The tourist offices at the Gare du Nord, Gare de l'Est and Gare de Lyon can also book same-day accommodation (see p.40). Secure, but limited, **left luggage** facilities are available at all except St-Lazare and Paris-Bercy.

By plane

The two main Paris **airports** (W aeroportsdeparis.fr) that deal with international flights are Roissy-Charles de Gaulle and Orly, both well connected to the centre. A third airport, Beauvais, is used by some low-cost airlines.

Roissy-Charles de Gaulle airport

Roissy-Charles de Gaulle airport (W aeroportsde paris.fr), usually referred to as **Charles de Gaulle** and abbreviated to CDG or Paris CDG, is 26km northeast of the city. The airport has three terminals: CDG 1, CDG 2 and CDG 3. A TGV station links CDG 2 with a number of French cities and with Brussels.

The cheapest way to get to the centre of Paris – if you book well in advance – is on the new **easyBus shuttle** (daily 5am–midnight; every 30min; 45min–1hr; from €2; W easybus.co.uk) to the Palais Royal in the 1er. As with easyJet flights, all places must be booked in advance online, and prices vary according to when you book. Priority is given to easyJet travellers and buses are small, so they can fill fast.

Otherwise, the quickest and easiest way to get into town is on the **Roissyrail** train link that runs on RER line B (daily 5am–11.50pm; every 10–15min; 25–50min; €10 one way). You can pick it up direct from CDG 3 and most parts of CDG 2; from CDG 1 a light rail runs to the RER station, while from some parts of CDG 2 you will need to hop on a shuttle bus (*navette*). The train stops at Gare du Nord, Châtelet-Les Halles, St-Michel and Denfert-Rochereau, all of which have métro stations for onward travel. A number of regular **RER stopping trains** also serve the airport; these only take about five minutes more than the Roissyrail to get to the centre, though they aren't designed to accommodate luggage.

Various bus companies provide services from Charles de Gaulle direct to a number of city-centre locations, but they're slightly more expensive than Roissyrail and may take longer. The **Roissybus**, for instance, connects the three terminals with the Opéra Garnier (corner of rues Auber and Scribe; W Opéra/RER Auber; daily 6am–12.30am; every 15–20min; 1hr; €11 one way). There are also two **Air France buses** (daily 5am–11.40pm; every 20–30min; W lescarsairfrance.com) from CDG 1 and 2: the green-coded line 2 stops outside Charles-de-Gaulle-Etoile RER/métro (1hr; €17 one way, €29 return) while the orange-coded line 4 stops at Gare de Lyon before terminating near Gare Montparnasse (1hr 15min; €17.50 one way, €30 return).

Taxis into central Paris from CDG cost around €50–70, more at night, and should take about 1hr. Slightly less expensive is the **minibus door-to-door service**, Paris Blue, which costs from €39 for two people, with no extra charge for luggage. It operates round the clock but bookings must be made at least 24hr in advance on T 01 30 11 13 00 or via W paris-blue-airport-shuttle.fr.

If your flight gets in after midnight, the options are a taxi, the minibus, or the Noctilien buses #N140 and #N143, which link the airport to Gare du Nord and Gare de l'Est every 30min until 4.30am (€8); for timetable and pick-up points, see W ratp.fr.

Orly airport

Orly airport (W aeroportsdeparis.fr), 14km south of Paris, has two terminals, Orly Sud (south, for international flights) and Orly Ouest (west, for domestic flights), linked by shuttle buses but easily walkable. One of the easiest ways into the centre is the fast **Orlyval train shuttle** link to the RER line B station Antony (daily 6am–11pm; every 4–7min; €12.05 one way), followed by métro connection stops at Denfert-Rochereau, Châtelet-Les Halles and Gare du Nord.

Two other services are also worth considering: the **Orlybus**, which runs to Denfert-Rochereau RER/métro station in the 14ᵉ (6am–midnight; every 15–20min; around 30min; €7.70 one way); and **tram T7**, which runs to métro Villejuif-Louis-Aragon, on métro line 7 (daily 5.30am & 12.30am; every 8–15min; 45min; €1.80). Finally, the **Air France bus** on line 1 (purple) runs to Charles de Gaulle/Etoile, stopping at Gare Montparnasse and Invalides (6am–11.40pm; every 15–30min; about 35min; €12.50 one way, €21 return; ⓦ lescarsairfrance.com). Leaving Paris, the Air France bus can be caught from 1 avenue Carnot near Place Charles de Gaulle, and from Montparnasse on rue du Commandant Mouchotte.

Taxis take about 35min to reach the centre of Paris and cost around €45.

Beauvais airport

Beauvais airport (ⓦ aeroportbeauvais.com), 80km northwest of Paris, is served by Ryanair from Dublin and Manchester. It's sometimes called Paris Beauvais-Tillé. **Coaches** (€17 one way, €15.90 if reserved online) shuttle between the airport and Porte Maillot in the 17ᵉ arrondissement, where you can pick up métro line 1 to the centre. The journey takes about 1hr 15min in all. The coach leaves around 20min after the flight has arrived and 3hr before the flight departs on the way back. Tickets can be bought online, at Arrivals, or at the Pershing bus station, near the Porte Maillot terminal.

By bus and car

Almost all the **buses** coming into Paris – whether international or domestic – arrive at the main **gare routière** at 28 avenue du Général-de-Gaulle, Bagnolet, at the eastern edge of the city in the 20ᵉ; métro Gallieni (line 3) links it to the centre. If you're **driving** into Paris yourself, don't try to go straight across the city to your destination unless you know what you're doing. Use the ring road – the **boulevard périphérique** – to get around to the nearest "porte". Apart from during rush hour, it's very quick – sometimes frighteningly so – and relatively easy to navigate.

Getting around

A combination of walking, cycling and public transport is undoubtedly the best way to discover Paris. The bike rental service, Vélib', is hugely useful for visitors, and the city's integrated public transport system of bus, métro and RER trains – the RATP (Régie Autonome des Transports Parisiens) – is cheap, fast and meticulously signposted. There are various tickets and passes available.

Free **maps** of varying sizes and detail are available at most métro stations: the largest and most useful is the *Grand Plan de Paris avec rues (numéro 2)*, which overlays the métro, RER and bus routes on a city plan so you can see exactly how transport lines and streets match up; you may find these on the walls of the stations, along with interactive touchscreens to aid journey planning, but it can be difficult to get a hard copy from the ticket offices, who are far more likely to hand you a *Plan des lignes (numéro 1)*, a simplified but useful pocket-sized métro/RER/bus map showing all the routes. Some RATP information leaflets, available at stations, do include the *Grand Plan*, and you can view it online (ⓦ ratp.fr).

By métro and RER

The **métro** (underground) combined with the five **RER** (Réseau Express Régional) suburban express lines, is the simplest way of moving around the city and also one of the cheapest – €1.80 for a single journey anywhere in the centre (children aged 4 to 10 travel half-price; kids under 4 travel free). Both the métro and the RER run from 5.30am to around 1am (the métro runs even later on Fridays and Saturdays, with fewer services on Sundays).

Many of the métro lines follow the streets that run above them; line 1, for example, shadows the Champs-Elysées and rue de Rivoli. **Stations** (abbreviated: ⓜ Concorde, RER Luxembourg, etc) are evenly spaced and you'll rarely find yourself more than 500m from one in the centre, though the interchanges at big stations can involve a lot of legwork. Train lines are colour-coded and designated by numbers for the métro and by letters (A–E) for the RER. You also need to know the **direction in which you want to travel** – signposted using the names of the terminus: for example, travelling from Montparnasse to Gare du Nord on métro line 4, you follow the sign "Direction Porte de Clignancourt"; from Gare d'Austerlitz to Maubert Mutualité on line 10 you follow "Direction

Boulogne–Pont de St-Cloud". The numerous interchanges (*correspondances*) make it possible to cover most of the city in a more or less straight line.

For RER journeys beyond the city, make sure that the station you want is illuminated on the platform display board.

By bus and tram

Buses are often rather neglected in favour of the métro, but can be very useful where the métro journey doesn't quite work. They aren't difficult to use and naturally you see much more, with bus lanes making journeys relatively unproblematic. Generally, buses run from Monday to Saturday from 7am to 8.30pm with some services continuing to 12.30am, and a restricted night bus service, Noctilien, taking over between 12.30 and 5.30am. Around half the lines also operate on Sundays and holidays – bus maps list those that do. Every bus stop displays the numbers of the buses that stop there, a map showing all the stops on the route, and some form of timetable; you need to hail the driver if you want the bus to stop. You can buy a single **ticket** (€1.80) from the driver, or use a pre-purchased **carnet** of ten tickets or a pass (see opposite). Press the red button to request a stop. All Paris bus lines are accessible for wheelchairs and prams.

On Sundays and holidays from mid-April to mid-September, a special **Balabus** service – not to be confused with Batobus (see p.28) – passes all the major tourist sights between the Grande Arche de la Défense and the Gare de Lyon, including the Eiffel Tower and the Louvre (1.30–8.30pm from the Gare de Lyon, 12.30–8pm from La Défense; every 15–30min; full circuit 1hr). The bus uses ordinary bus stops, indicated with a "Balabus" or "Bb" sign,

and you'll need one to three bus tickets, depending on the length of your journey: check the information at the bus stop or ask the driver. The Paris Visite, Mobilis and Navigo passes (see opposite) are all valid on the Balabus.

Paris's **tram** lines are mostly concentrated in the outer reaches of town – however, the T3a line, from Pont du Gagliano in the west to Porte du Vincennes in the east, is useful for getting from east to west in the south of the city, and convenient for Parc Montsouris (see Ⓦ ratp.fr for maps and schedules).

Tickets and passes

Greater Paris's integrated transport system (Ⓦ ratp .fr) is divided into five **zones**; the métro system more or less fits into zones 1 and 2. The same **tickets** are valid for bus, métro and, within the city limits and immediate suburbs (zones 1 and 2), the RER express rail lines, which also extend far out into the Ile-de-France. Only one ticket is ever needed on the métro system, and within zones 1 and 2 for any RER or bus journey, but you can't switch between bus and métro/RER on the same ticket. For **RER journeys** beyond zones 1 and 2 you must buy an RER ticket; visitors often get caught out, for instance, when they take the RER to La Défense using a métro ticket. Be sure to keep your ticket until the end of the journey as you'll be fined on the spot if you can't produce one; you'll also need it to exit the RER.

Individual **tickets** cost €1.80, so for a short stay it saves money (and time) to buy a **carnet** of ten tickets (€14.10), available from self-service machines and ticket offices at the stations or from any *tabac*. (**Eurostar** travellers can also buy *carnets* from the information desk in the St Pancras International departure lounge, or from the buffet car on the

---

SEEING THE CITY BY BUS

One good way to take in the city sights is to hop on a public **bus**. Bus #20 from the Gare de Lyon follows the Grands Boulevards and does a loop through the 1er and 2e arrondissements. Bus #24 between Bercy and Gare St-Lazare follows the left bank of the Seine from the Gare d'Austerlitz to the Pont de la Concorde. Bus #29 is one of the best routes for taking in the city: it ventures from the Gare St-Lazare past the Opéra Garnier, the Bourse and the Centre Pompidou, through the heart of the Marais and past the Bastille to the Gare de Lyon. For the Champs-Elysées, take a trip on bus #73 between La Défense and the Assemblée Nationale, while bus #63 drives a scenic route along the Seine from the Assemblée Nationale on the Rive Gauche, then crosses the river and heads up to Trocadéro, where there are some wonderful views of the Eiffel Tower. Many more bus journeys – outside rush hours – are worthwhile trips in themselves: take a look online at Ⓦ ratp.fr or get hold of a map from a métro station and check out routes #38, #42, #48, #64, #67, #68, #69, #82, #87 and #95.

PERFECT PARIS VIEWS

Few cities present such a harmonious skyscape as Paris. Looking down on the ranks of seven-storey apartment buildings from above, it's easy to imagine the city as a lead-roofed plateau split by the leafy canyons of the boulevards and avenues. Spires, towers and parks – not to mention multicoloured art museums and glass pyramids – stand out all the more against the solemn grey backdrop. Fortunately, many of Paris's tall buildings provide access to wonderful rooftop views. The following are some of the best in town:

Arc de Triomphe Look out over an ocean of traffic and enjoy impressive vistas of the Voie Triomphale. See p.63

Eiffel Tower It's worth battling the queues for the unrivalled panorama of the city. Best at night. See p.148

Institut du Monde Arabe The ninth-floor restaurant has a panoramic view overlooking the Seine, or you could simply check out the observation deck. See p.132

Notre-Dame Perch among the gargoyles for a spot of waterside contemplation and a clear view of the Panthéon dome. See p.46

Nüba, Cité de la Mode et du Design Kick back and enjoy a cocktail – or a daytime coffee – at *Nüba*, where the huge rooftop

deck offers amazing views of the river and the Right Bank. See p.304

Parc André-Citroën A tethered balloon rises 150m above this modern park. See p.174

Parc de Belleville Verdant and peaceful little park where you can watch the sun set over the city's skyline. See p.209

Pompidou Centre An arty backdrop for rooftop ogling. See p.86

Sacré-Coeur Paris's second-highest point, where on a clear day you can sit on the basilica steps and marvel at an unobstructed view of the city. Be warned – it's a popular spot at sunset. See p.185

Tour Montparnasse The only panoramic view in Paris that takes in the Eiffel Tower too. Stunning. See p.161

train.) If you're making a number of journeys in one day, it might be worth getting a **Mobilis day-pass** (from €7 for zones 1 and 2 to €16.60 for zones 1 to 5), which offers unlimited access to the métro, buses and, depending on which zones you choose, the RER – note that this is a day- rather than a 24hr pass, so it pays to buy it in the morning.

If you've arrived early in the week, are staying more than three days and plan to use public transport a lot, it might be more economical to buy a swipeable **Navigo Découverte** pass (Ⓦnavigo.fr). A weekly pass costs €21.25 for zones 1 and 2, and is valid for an unlimited number of journeys on all modes of transport from Monday morning to Sunday evening. You can only buy a ticket for the current week until Wednesday; from Thursday you can buy a ticket to begin the following Monday. Monthly passes are also available (€70 for zones 1 and 2). You need to factor in the initial one-off purchase of the Navigo swipe card itself (€5, unrefundable); you'll also need a passport photo.

Paris Visites, passes that cover one, two, three or five consecutive days, either in the central zones or extending as far as the suburbs and the airports (€11.15–61.25), are not as good value as the Navigo and Mobilis passes, but they do give reductions on certain tourist attractions.

By taxi

The best place to get a **taxi** is at a rank (*arrêt taxi*) – which is usually more effective than hailing from the street. Bear in mind that finding a taxi at lunchtime, during rush hour or after 7pm can be difficult; give yourself time if you're aiming to get somewhere on time. The green light on top of the vehicle signals the taxi is free and the red light means it's in use. If there are no taxis waiting at the rank you can call for one on ☎01 45 30 30 30. You can also call a company such as Taxis G7 (☎01 41 27 66 99 for an English-speaking operator, Ⓦtaxisg7.fr), Taxis Bleus (☎3609, Ⓦtaxis-bleus.com) or Alpha Taxis (☎01 45 85 85 85, Ⓦwww.alphataxis.fr) – note, though, that calling a taxi out will cost more than picking one up on the street.

Taxis are metered and **charges** are fairly reasonable: between €7 and €15 for a central daytime journey if you hail one on the street. Rates vary from €1.04–1.54/km depending on when you travel and whether you are in the centre or outside the *périphérique*. There's a minimum charge of €6.90, a pick-up charge of €2.60, and a charge of €1 per item if more than one piece of (bulky) luggage is carried. Taxi drivers do not have to take more than three passengers (they don't like people sitting in the front); if a fourth passenger is accepted, an extra €3 will be added. A **tip** of ten percent, while optional, is generally expected.

By boat

The **Batobus** river bus (April–Aug every 10–20min 10am–9.30pm; Sept–March every 15–25min 10am–7pm; ⓦbatobus.com) provides a thrilling way to get around Paris, stopping at eight points along the Seine between the Eiffel Tower at Port de la Bourdonnais in the west (ⓂBir Hakeim/Trocadéro) and Champs-Elysées in the east (ⓂChamps-Elysées). The total journey time for a one-way, straight-through trip is around 1hr 30min. A hop-on, hop-off day-pass costs €16 and a two-day (consecutive) pass €18. You can buy tickets online, at Batobus stops and at the tourist offices (see p.40).

By car

Travelling around **by car** – in the daytime at least – is hardly worth it, not least because of the difficulty of finding parking spaces. Drivers are better off finding a motel-style place on the edge of the city and using public transport to get around. But if you're determined to use the pay-and-display parking system, note that the meters don't take cash. You need to buy a **Paris Carte** (like a phonecard) worth €10–30 from a *tabac*, then look for the blue "P" signs alongside grey parking meters. Introduce the card into the meter and it gives you a ticket while automatically deducting the appropriate value from the card – €1.20–3.60 an hour depending on location, for a maximum of two hours. Parking is generally free on Sundays and from 7pm to 9am.

Alternatively, make for one of the many underground **car parks**, which cost up to €2.50 per hour, or from around €20 for 24 hours. Whatever you do, don't park in a bus lane or the Axe Rouge express routes (marked with a red square). Should you be towed away, you'll find your car in the pound (*fourrière*) belonging to that particular arrondissement. The website ⓦparkingsdeparis.com locates dozens of public car parks and lets you pre-book discounted spaces. The associated book *Parkings de Paris*, handy to keep in the car, has even more information on the city's 215 car parks – it's available at bookstores or on the website for €15.

BOAT TRIPS

Seeing Paris from a **boat** is one of the city's most enduring experiences – and a lot of fun. The **Batobus** riverbus (see above) is the easiest option, but there a number of alternatives if you want to enjoy a more leisurely cruise.

BATEAUX-MOUCHES

Bateaux-Mouches Trips start from the Embarcadère du Pont de l'Alma, on the Right Bank in the 8ᵉ ☎01 42 25 96 10, ⓦbateaux-mouches.fr; ⓂAlma-Marceau. Many a romantic evening stroll along the quais has been rudely interrupted by the sudden appearance of a Bateau-Mouche, with its dazzling floodlights and blaring commentaries. One way of avoiding the annoyance is to get on one yourself. You may not be able to escape the noisy narration, but you'll certainly get a glamorous close-up view of the classic buildings along the Seine (daily: April–Sept every 20–45min 10.15am–10.30pm; Oct–March 10.15am–9.20pm; €13.50, €5.50 children 4–12). You're probably best off avoiding the overpriced lunch and dinner trips, for which "correct" dress is mandatory (€55 for lunch, from €99 for dinner).

OTHER RIVER-BOAT TRIPS

River cruise companies The main competitors to the Bateaux-Mouches are: Bateaux Parisiens, from the Eiffel Tower or Notre-Dame (ⓦbateauxparisiens.com); Vedettes de Paris, from the Eiffel Tower (ⓦvedettesdeparis.fr); and Bateaux-Vedettes du Pont-Neuf, from the Pont-Neuf (ⓦvedettesdupontneuf.com). They're all much the same, with hour-long cruises from around €14.

CANAL TRIPS

Canauxrama ⓦcanauxrama.com. Less overtly touristy than the river trips, Canauxrama boats offer a number of narrated cruises on the St-Martin, Ourcq and St-Denis canals, the Seine and the River Marne. Options include a romantic 2hr trip between the Port de l'Arsenal and Bassin de La Villette; at the Bastille end is a long, spooky tunnel, complete with light installation (reservations essential; 9.45am & 2.30/2.45pm departures in summer, fewer at other times; €17, students/over-60s €13 Mon–Fri, under-12s €9, under-4s free). **Paris-Canal** ☎01 42 40 96 97, ⓦen.pariscanal.com. Catamaran tours of the Canal St-Martin, between the Musée d'Orsay (quai Anatole-France by the Pont Solférino, 7ᵉ; ⓂSolférino) and the Parc de la Villette (La Folie des Visites du Parc, on the canal by the bridge between the Grande Salle and the Cité des Sciences, 19ᵉ; ⓂPorte de Pantin). Cruises last 2hr 30min and run from February to mid-November (from Musée d'Orsay 9.45am & 2.25pm; from Parc de la Villette 10.30am & 2.30pm; €20, 12–25-year-olds and over-65s €17, 4–11s €13).

CHAUFFEUR-DRIVEN TOURS: PARISIAN STYLE

A number of companies now offer tours in the nimble little **Citroën 2CV**. The classic, open-top "deux chevaux" was originally designed as an economy vehicle for farmers, but has since become a beloved symbol of French identity. The original and still most adaptable company is **4 Roues Sous 1 Parapluie** ("4 Wheels under an Umbrella"), which offers a range of tours, from a thirty-minute zip around the Champs-Elysées, with an English-speaking driver suggesting places to which you might want to return, to a two-hour movie tour or a ninety-minute tour focused on the Impressionists or on André Citroën, the car's inventor (from €20; maximum of three people in each car; ☎01 58 59 27 82, ⊛4roues-sous-1parapluie.com).

The French **drive on the right** – if your car is right-hand drive, you must (by law) adjust your headlights to dip to the right before you go; this is most easily done by sticking on black glare deflectors. Remember also that you have to be 18 to drive in France, regardless of whether you hold a licence in your own country.

In the event of a **breakdown**, call Dan Dépann (☎01 40 06 09 64, ⊛dandepann.fr) or ask the police (see p.35) for advice. For **traffic conditions** in Paris tune in to 105.1 FM (FIP).

Car and scooter rental

If you're intending to rent a car for a short time in Paris your cheapest option is the city's pioneering **electric car rental scheme**, Autolib' (⊛autolib.eu), which operates on a similar model to the successful bike rental scheme Velib'. Around 1750 electric cars are currently available to rent from around a thousand stands (700 in central Paris itself) dotted all over the greater Paris region. Cars can be picked up at one station and deposited at another. Users need to buy a subscription card first, either online, from one of the subscription kiosks around central Paris, or in the Autolib' showroom at 5 rue Edouard VII, 9ᵉ (⊛Opéra). You will simply need your driving licence, a valid ID and a credit card. The subscription fee depends on the type of subscription you're buying: free if you're only subscribing for a day, €10 for the week, €25 for the month and €120 for the year. You are then charged rental based on the amount of time you are in the car. The first 20min are free, then the cost depends on your subscription – ranging from €5.50/30min if you have a yearly subscription to €9/30min for the daily option. You can reserve a car up to 30min beforehand by phone (☎0800 942 000), online, or directly from one of the car rental points.

The big international rental companies, including Avis, Budget, Europcar and Hertz, have offices at the airports and at several locations in the city; the best deals will be found online, particularly if you're renting for several days. One **local company** worth checking out is Locabest (⊛locabest.fr).

North Americans and Australians in particular should be aware that it's difficult to rent a car with automatic transmission in France; if you can't drive a manual/stickshift, try and book an **automatic** (*voiture à transmission automatique*) well in advance, and be prepared to pay a much higher price for it.

Renting a **scooter** in Paris is also viable, with a number of outfits offering 50cc/125cc Vespas for quick – and stylish – jaunts. Freescoot (⊛scooter-rental-paris.com) has 50ccs from €45/day, while **Paris by Scooter** (⊛parisbyscooter.com), which rents Vespas from €69/day, also offers customizable private scooter tours, ranging from three hours to a full day – including an *Amélie* movie-themed jaunt, and a trip to Versailles – from €149. Costs include the bike being delivered and picked up from your hotel.

By bike

Paris has 700km of **cycle lanes**, mostly along the busier roads; the volume of traffic means you need to keep your wits about you. The smaller, quieter roads have no cycle lanes and many are one way. You can pick up a free **map** of the routes, *Paris à Vélo*, from the tourist office or bike rental outlets, or download it from ⊛paris.fr – click on the "Paris Pratique" link, then "Déplacements" and "Vélos"; the page also has the latest news and information about cycling in the city.

PEDESTRIAN CROSSINGS

Pedestrian/zebra crossings, marked with horizontal white stripes on the road, have a different meaning from those back home: they're simply there to suggest a good place to cross, but certainly won't give you priority over cars. It's very dangerous to step out onto one and assume drivers will stop. Take just as much care as you would crossing at any other point.

BIKE TOURS

Zipping around on a Vélib' is a splendid way to take a short hop around Paris, but if you want to go deeper, it is well worth considering a **cycling tour**. Bike tours also provide good exercise and cheerful camaraderie for people of all ages looking to explore Paris but who don't want to go it alone.

Blue Bike Tours ☎ 06 49 32 36 49, 🌐 bluebiketours.com. Small-group cycle tours, setting off from place St-Michel in St Germain (6ᵉ), with local, English-speaking guides. Options include an evening tour, a trip to Versailles and a "hidden secrets" tour that takes you beyond the major sights. Prices start at €29 per person and reservations are required – book well in advance if you can.

Fat Tire Bike Tours 24 rue Edgar Faure, 15ᵉ ☎ 01 56 58 10 54, 🌐 fattirebiketours.com/paris; Ⓜ Dupleix. Friendly, Anglo-run agency offering 3hr 30min–4hr 30min guided bicycle trips in English, with a choice of day and night tours (€32), and full-day tours to Versailles and Monet's gardens (including train travel). Also offers electric Segway tours (🌐 paris.citysegwaytours.com). Reservations are recommended for the standard tours and required for Versailles and Monet gardens options; online deals can cut costs.

Paris à Vélo C'est Sympa 22 rue Alphonse Baudin, 11ᵉ ☎ 01 48 87 60 01, 🌐 parisvelosympa.com; Ⓜ Richard Lenoir. One of the least expensive (€25 for a weekend, or €60 for a tandem)

and most helpful bike rental companies. Their excellent 3hr tours of Paris take a different angle – including "Unusual Paris" and "Paris Contrast", combining modern architecture with green spaces. €35, €29 for under-26s. Reservations required.

Paris Bike Tour 13 rue Brantôme, 3ᵉ ☎ 01 42 74 22 14, 🌐 parisbiketour.net; Ⓜ Rambuteau/Hôtel-de-Ville. Bike rental (€15/day, €16 at the weekend, €30 for a whole weekend; bike delivery and pick-up extra) and a range of relaxed tours (from €32), including a "tasting tour" with a stop at a covered market. Reservations required.

Paris Charms and Secrets Place Vendôme, 1ᵉʳ ☎ 01 40 29 00 00, 🌐 parischarmssecrets.com. Something different – an electric bike tour (covering a lot of ground and taking the effort out of pedalling) that explores the city's little corners and secret places, as well as its major sights – raincoats and gloves are provided in bad weather, and they can even rent you a heated jacket (Mon–Sat 9.30am, 2.30pm & 8pm, Sun 8.30am, 2.30pm & 8pm; 3–4hr; reservations required; €45).

The easiest way to **rent a bike** is to get hold of one of the city's 20,000 **Vélib'** machines (🌐 velib .paris.fr). These three-gear municipal bikes, available to anyone aged over 14, can be picked up from any one of the 1800 stations (found every 300m or so across Paris, and mapped on the Vélib' website), and deposited at any other. One-day (€1.70), seven-day (€8) and one-year (€29/€39) tickets are available. One- and seven-day tickets are sold at the bike stations (follow the instructions on screen) or up to two weeks in advance online. You can then use a bike as many times as you like during that period simply by entering your number each time you pick one up. The first 30min of each journey in that period is free; after that you have to pay a €1 supplement for the second half-hour, €2 for the third, and €4 per half-hour thereafter. The city's **P'tit Vélib'** scheme, offering bike rental for kids, can be great fun for families wanting a day out (see p.352).

Many **bike tour** operators (see box above) also rent bikes, which may work out cheaper if you want a whole day of cycling. Prices depend on the type of bike; you have to leave a variable *caution* (deposit) or your credit card details.

Note that during the so-called **Paris Respire** scheme, on Sundays and public holidays from 9am

to 5pm, all the riverside expressways and many other city streets are **closed to cars**. If you want a bike on one of those days, when it feels like all of Paris takes to the *quais*, it's best to book in advance.

For more on **recreational cycling**, turn to the "Activities and sports" chapter (see p.341).

The media

Despite hefty state subsidies the traditional French press is currently in something of a crisis – circulation is low and print costs some of the highest in Europe. Meanwhile many believe that the fact that the majority stakeholders of practically all the major newspapers now come from big business is inevitably compromising political neutrality. Things are slightly healthier in TV, though the quality of programmes isn't generally very high, with lots of light entertainment and dubbed foreign soaps. Some serious programmes, such as political and philosophical debates do exist, though, and these make no attempt to dumb down.

Newspapers and magazines

British newspapers, as well as the *Washington Post*, *New York Times* and the *International Herald Tribune* are widely on sale in the city on the day of publication. *FUSAC* (France USA Contacts; Ⓦfusac.fr), a free American fortnightly available in cafés, restaurants, shops and colleges, is useful for flats, jobs and entertainment news.

Of the quality **French daily papers**, the centre-left *Le Monde* (Ⓦlemonde.fr) is the most intellectual; it is widely respected, though somewhat austere. *Libération* (Ⓦliberation.fr), founded by Jean-Paul Sartre in the 1960s, is slightly more colloquial and choosy in its coverage. *Le Figaro* (Ⓦlefigaro.fr) is the most respected right-wing national. The best-selling tabloid is *Le Parisien* (Ⓦleparisien.fr; published as *Aujourd'hui en France* outside Paris), good on local news and events, while for sports news the paper of choice is *L'Equipe*.

News weeklies include the wide-ranging and socialist-inclined *L'Obs* (Ⓦtempsreel.nouvelobs .com; formerly *Le Nouvel Observateur* but now part of the *Le Monde* group), the right-centrist *L'Express* (Ⓦexpress.fr) and staunchly republican *Marianne* (Ⓦmarianne.net). The best investigative journalism is to be found in the satirical weekly *Le Canard Enchaîné* (Ⓦlecanardenchaine.fr), a sort of *Private Eye* equivalent. *Charlie Hebdo* (Ⓦcharliehebdo.fr), meanwhile, the satirical weekly that hit the world's headlines in January 2015 (see p.376) continues – despite huge stress and tension in the ranks – to publish its transgressive cartoons, poking fun at everything from religion to politicians.

TV and radio

Viewers in France can access a variety of free French **TV channels**, providing they have a decoder or are hooked up to satellite or cable. The main public channels are **France 2** (Ⓦfrance2.fr), and slightly more highbrow **France 3** (Ⓦfrance3.fr), which serves up drama, debates and arts programmes; **Arte** (Ⓦarte-tv.com) is a cultural channel, with lots of documentaries and subtitled films. The two main commercial channels are **TF1** (Ⓦtf1.fr), with dubbed American series and reality shows, and **M6** (Ⓦm6.fr), which specializes in reality shows, cooking and chat shows and kids' TV. The main French **news broadcasts** are at 8pm on F2 and TF1. The main cable channel is **Canal Plus** (Ⓦcanalplus.fr), good for films, drama and sports. France also has its own rolling news station, **France 24** (Ⓦfrance24.com), which puts across a French

outlook on world affairs. It broadcasts in both English and French, and has an Arabic service. As well as politics, it covers arts and culture.

For **radio news** in French, there's the state-run France Inter (Ⓦfranceinter.fr; 87.8FM), Europe 1 (Ⓦeurope1.fr; 104.7FM), or round-the-clock news on France Info (Ⓦfranceinfo.fr; 105.5FM).

Living in Paris

Work

Although EU nationals and Swiss citizens are free to move to France without a special permit, and can look for work on the same basis as French citizens, it's worth noting that casual work in Paris is hard to come by and generally poorly paid. And for visitors from North America or Australasia arriving without a prearranged job offer, the chance of finding legal paid employment is practically nil. Most nationalities need authorization from a prospective employer in order to apply for a visa/residency permit or, if the work period is less than ninety days, for a short-stay work visa. There are a number of different permits available; check with the French consulate in your home country as to the latest regulations.

EU nationals are legally entitled to the same pay, conditions and union rights as French nationals. The French **minimum wage** (SMIC – *Salaire Minimum Interprofessionnel de Croissance*), indexed to the cost of living, is currently around €9.60 an hour (for a maximum 152-hour month). Employers, however, are likely to pay lower wages to temporary foreign workers who don't have easy legal resources, and may make them work longer hours.

If you're looking for secure employment, it's important to begin planning before you leave home. A couple of **books** that might be worth consulting are *Work Your Way Around the World* by Susan Griffith, updated yearly, and *Summer Jobs Worldwide*, both published by Vacation Work, an imprint of Crimson Publishing (Ⓦcrimson publishing.co.uk).

For **temporary work** check the ads in *FUSAC* (see above) or at *Paris Voice*, an online mag for English-speaking expats (Ⓦparisvoice.com). You could also try the notice boards at CIDJ or CROUS (see p.32), youth information agencies that advertise some temporary jobs for foreigners.

The national employment agency, **Pôle Emploi** (Ⓦpole-emploi.fr), advertises temporary jobs in all fields and, in theory, offers a whole range of services to job-seekers; though it's open to all EU citizens, it is not renowned for its helpfulness to foreigners. If your French is up to par, take a look at Keljob (Ⓦkeljob.com), an informative site that can help with your CV, interview questions and other job-seeking issues.

Other possible sources include the "Offres d'Emploi" (Job Offers) in *Le Monde*, *Le Figaro* and the *International Herald Tribune*, and notice boards at English bookshops. The American/Irish/British **bars and restaurants** sometimes have vacancies. You'll need to speak French, look smart and be prepared to work very long hours. Obviously, the better your French, the better your chances are of finding work.

Teaching

Finding a **teaching job** is best done in advance, usually in late summer. In Britain, jobs are often advertised in the *Times Educational Supplement* (Ⓦtes.co.uk). You don't need fluent French to get a post, but a degree and a TEFL (Teaching English as a Foreign Language) qualification are usually required. The TEFL site (Ⓦtefl.org.uk) is a useful resource, as is the British Council's website (Ⓦbritishcouncil.org), which has a list of English-teaching vacancies. If you apply for jobs from home, most schools will fix up the necessary papers for you. EU nationals don't need a work permit, but getting social security can still be tricky should employers refuse to help. For addresses of schools, look under "Cours de langues" in the *Yellow Pages* (Ⓦpagesjaunes.fr). If you offer **private lessons** (via university notice boards or classified ads), you'll have lots of competition.

Au pair work

Although **working as an au pair** can be set up online via dedicated sites such as Ⓦaupair-world .net or Ⓦaupair.com, this sort of work can be misery if you end up with an unpleasant employer. If you're determined to try – and it can be a very good way of learning the language – it's better to apply once in France, where you can at least meet the family first and check things out. Again, FUSAC (see p.31) is a good resource, with a classified ads section dedicated to childcare. Conditions vary, but you should expect board, lodging and pocket money, along with some sort of travel pass. Working hours are officially capped at 30hr a week, plus two or three evenings' babysitting.

Claiming benefit

Any EU citizen who has been signing on for **unemployment benefit** at home, and intends to try and continue doing so in Paris, needs a letter of introduction from their own social security office, plus a U2 certificate of authorization (be sure to give them plenty of warning to prepare this). You must pre-register with the Pôle Emploi office (see p.31) within seven days of your arrival in France – either online or by phone (☎39 49) – to make an appointment to register at their offices.

It's possible to claim benefit for up to three months while you look for work, but it can often take that amount of time for the paperwork to be processed. Pensioners can arrange for their **pensions** to be paid in France, but cannot receive French state pensions.

Study

It's relatively easy to be a **student** in Paris. Foreigners pay no more than French nationals to enrol on a course, and the only problem then is how to support yourself, though you'll be eligible for subsidized accommodation, meals and all the student reductions. Few people want to do undergraduate degrees abroad, but for higher degrees or other diplomas, the range of options is enormous. Strict entry requirements, including an exam in French, apply only for undergraduate degrees. For a comprehensive rundown on studying in France, including a list of programmes and courses, information on how to apply and possible grants, check Ⓦcampusfrance.org.

Courses at the non-profit-making **Alliance Française** (101 bd Raspail, 6ᵉ; Ⓦalliancefr.org; Ⓜ St-Placide) are quite reasonably priced (from €90/week for 9hr of classes) and well regarded, while the **Sorbonne** (Ⓦccfs-sorbonne.fr) has special short courses aimed at foreigners. US students could also get in touch with the **CIEE** (Council on International Educational Exchange; Ⓦciee.org), which can arrange gap-year and study programmes in Paris.

STUDENT/YOUTH ORGANIZATIONS

Student information (CROUS) 39 av Georges-Bernanos, 5ᵉ Ⓦ crous-paris.fr; RER Port-Royal. The University of Paris student organization, providing help with student accommodation and other services.
Youth information (CIDJ) (Centre d'Information et de Documentation de la Jeunesse) 101 quai Branly, 15ᵉ Ⓦ cidj.com; Ⓜ Bir-Hakeim. Provides all sorts of information for young people and students, for example on studying in France and finding somewhere to live. Tues–Fri 1–6pm, Sat 1–5pm.

Travel essentials

Addresses

Paris is divided into twenty districts, or **arrondisse-ments**. The first arrondissement, or "1er" is centred on the Louvre, in the heart of the city. The rest wind outward in a clockwise direction like a snail's shell: the 2e, 3e and 4e are central; the 5e, 6e and 7e lie on the inner part of the Left (south) Bank; while the 8e–20e make up the outer districts. Parisian addresses generally quote the arrondissement, along with the nearest métro station, or stations, too. The **postcode** in Parisian addresses consists of the generic 750 plus the number of the arrondissement: so, for example, the 14e becomes 75014 Paris. Bis and ter (as in 4bis rue de la Fontaine) are the equivalent of "a" and "b".

Climate

Paris's **climate** is fairly stable, with longish stretches of sunshine (or rain) year round. Summer can get hot, with temperatures occasionally reaching as high as 38ºC (100ºF), and humidity high. It can rain at any time of year: summer sees fewer heavy showers, while at other times there's a tendency to drizzle. Spring sees its fair share of showers, but is characterized by bright, sunny days, and autumn can be very rewarding, weather-wise. Winter is cold, but the light is beautiful.

Costs

Paris has the potential to be very expensive, certainly more so than the rest of France, particularly for visitors from outside the eurozone. However, transport prices (see p.26) compare favourably with other north-European capitals, and although accommodation prices are high, if you are one of two people sharing a comfortable central hotel room, you can get by happily on around €125 per person per day. At the bottom line, by watching the pennies, staying at a hostel and visiting monuments and museums on free entry days (see box, p.34), you could survive on as little as €65 a day, including one restaurant meal.

In budget **hotels**, simple doubles with shower can be had from as little as €70 (without shower around €10–15 less), but for more comfort, prices start at around €90. Single rooms are often available, starting at around €40 in a cheap hotel. At most hotels breakfast costs an extra €7–14; it will usually be cheaper to eat in a local café.

Eating out in restaurants can be expensive. Prices vary of course, but typically, a three-course evening set menu might cost around €28 and upwards. The lunchtime menu will be cheaper (from around €16) and you can generally get a filling midday plat du jour (dish of the day) of hot food for around €12. **Drinks** in cafés and bars can easily mount up; in many cafés it's cheaper to stand at the bar than sit at a table, and some places charge a premium for outside seating on the terrasse. A black espresso coffee (un café) is the cheapest drink (around €2); a café crème ranges from around €2.60 at the bar to anything up to €9 on a terrasse in the more touristy areas. Glasses of wine cost from around €4, but draught lager tends to be a bit more expensive. Mixed drinks or cocktails generally cost €8–16.

Discounts

Institutions have different policies, but at the time of writing, national museums are free to all under-18s, plus all EU nationals (as well as students studying in the EU who can prove it) under the age of 26. All public monuments are free for under-12s. Under-4s usually go free everywhere, under-8s less often. Privately owned sights usually offer half-price or reduced admission to 5- to 18-year-olds, though more commercial places charge adult rates at age 12.

If you are a full-time **student**, it's worth carrying the **ISIC** (International Student Identity Card; ⓦisic .org) to gain entrance reductions (usually about a

PARIS CLIMATE												
	Jan	Feb	Mar	Apr	May	Jun	Jul	Aug	Sep	Oct	Nov	Dec
AVERAGE DAILY TEMPERATURE												
Max/min (°F)	43/34	45/34	54/40	61/43	68/50	72/55	77/59	75/57	70/54	61/46	50/41	45/36
Max/min (°C)	6/1	7/1	12/4	16/6	20/10	23/13	25/15	24/14	21/12	16/8	10/5	7/2
AVERAGE RAINFALL												
mm	56	46	35	42	57	54	59	64	55	50	51	50

PARIS ON A BUDGET

Paris is a pricey destination, but there are a few tips to bear in mind that will make it easier to keep control of your spending.

MUSEUM ENTRY

The permanent collections at all municipal museums are **free all year round**. These are: Maison de Balzac (see p.219); Maison de Victor Hugo (see p.95); Musée Bourdelle (see p.164); Musée Carnavalet (see p.96); Musée Cernuschi (see p.168); Musée Cognacq-Jay (see p.98); Musée d'Art Moderne de la Ville de Paris (see p.158); Musée de la Vie Romantique (see p.191); Musée Jean-Moulin (see p.164), and Petit Palais/Musée des Beaux-Arts de la Ville de Paris (see p.67). In addition, the national museums are **free on the first Sunday of the month**: Cité de l'Architecture et du Patrimoine (see p.156); The Louvre (see p.49; Oct–March only); Musée d'Orsay (see p.144); Musée de l'Orangerie (see p.71); Musée du Moyen Âge (see p.125); Musée du Quai-Branly (see p.152); Musée Gustave-Moreau (see p.192); Musée National d'Art Moderne at the Pompidou (see p.87); Musée National Eugène Delacroix (see p.139), and Musée Rodin (see p.155).

FREE ATTRACTIONS

Churches, **cemeteries** and, of course, **markets** (except for some specialist annual antique and book markets) are free. Most **parks** are free but some gardens within have small entry charges, usually around €1.50. **Libraries** and the cultural centres of different countries often put on films, shows and exhibitions for next to nothing – check details in the listings mags (see p.40).

ENTERTAINMENT

Discounted theatre tickets are available online at ⓦ billetreduc.com. Cinema tickets will be much cheaper at the smaller independent cinemas, particularly those around the student area in the 5e. Regular **free festivals** (see p.320) and **cultural offerings**, from bands in the streets to firework shows, come courtesy of the Mairie de Paris and are publicized throughout Paris. It's well worth checking out what's on before you arrive (ⓦ paris.fr).

third off). The card is universally accepted as ID, while the student card from your home institution is not. Travellers aged 30 or younger qualify for the **International Youth Travel Card** – these offer similar discounts to the ISIC and are available via ⓦ isic.org. For anyone over 60 or 65 (depending on the institution), reductions are only patchily available; carry your passport with you as proof of age.

Whatever your age, if you are going to visit a lot of museums, it's worth considering the **Paris Museum Pass** (€42 two-day, €56 four-day, €69 six-day; ⓦ parismuseumpass.com). Available from the tourist offices, Fnac stores and museums, the pass is valid for more than thirty museums and monuments, including the main ones (though not special exhibitions), in Paris, and twenty in the surrounding area. It also allows you to bypass ticket queues (though not the security checkpoints). Before splashing out, though, if you're going to be in Paris on the first Sunday of the month, and plan to do a lot of sightseeing, bear in mind that some museums open their doors for free on those days (see above).

Crime and personal safety

Petty **theft** is as common in the crowded hangouts of the capital as in most major cities; the métro, train stations and Les Halles are notorious pickpocketing grounds. Take the usual precautions, and if you need to report a theft, immediately go to the *commissariat de police* of the arrondissement in which the theft took place. They will fill out a *constat de vol*; the first thing they'll ask for is your passport, and vehicle documents if relevant. Although the police are not always as cooperative as they might be, it is their duty to assist you if you've lost your passport or all your money. If you've lost something less serious, you could try the **lost property office** (see p.37).

Should you be **arrested**, you have the right to contact your consulate (see opposite). **Drug use** is as risky and as severely punished in France as anywhere else in Europe – and no allowances are made for people who are on holiday.

Travellers of North African or Arab appearance may occasionally encounter excessive police interest, or sometimes outright hostility. Carrying your passport

---

EMERGENCY NUMBERS

Fire brigade/Paramedics (sapeurs-pompiers) ☎ 18
Medical emergencies See p.36
Police ☎ 17
Rape crisis (SOS Viol) ☎ 08 00 05 95 95

---

at all times is a good idea (everyone is legally required to have some identification on them in any case). There are occasional reports of hotels or restaurants claiming to be fully booked, or clubs refusing entry, but racist incidents involving tourists are fairly rare.

French **police** (in popular slang, *les flics*) are barely polite at the best of times, and can be extremely unpleasant if you get on the wrong side of them. You can be stopped at any time and asked to **produce ID**. The two main types of police – the Police Nationale and the Gendarmerie Nationale – are for all practical purposes indistinguishable. The CRS (Compagnies Républicaines de Sécurité), on the other hand, are an entirely different proposition. They are a mobile force of paramilitary heavies, used to guard sensitive embassies, control demonstrations and keep the peace during highly sensitive situations – following the Charlie Hebdo attacks in 2015, for example.

Free legal advice over the phone (in French) is available from SOS Avocats (Mon–Fri 7–11.30pm; closed mid-July to Sept 1; ☎ 08 25 39 33 00; €0.15/minute).

Electricity

France uses double, round-pin wall sockets that supply 220V. If you haven't bought the appropriate adaptor (*adapteur*) or transformer (*transformateur* – for US appliances) before leaving home, try the electrical section of a large department store like BHV (see p.324).

Entry requirements

Citizens of EU countries, and various other countries, including Canada, the US, Australia and New Zealand, do not need any sort of visa to enter France for a stay of up to ninety days. Citizens of all other countries must obtain a visa before arrival.

Two types of tourist **visa** are currently issued: a short-stay (*court séjour*) visa, valid for multiple stays of up to ninety days in a six-month period, including transit through a French airport if required. All non-EU citizens who wish to remain

longer than ninety days must apply for a long-stay (*long séjour*) visa, for which you'll have to show proof of – among other things – a regular income, or sufficient funds to support yourself, and medical insurance. Note that you can't change your visa to long-stay if you've already arrived in France on a short-stay visa. Always check the current regulations with your embassy or consulate, well in advance of travelling. A complete list of all French government websites, including **embassies** and **consulates**, can be found at ⓦ gksoft.com/govt/en/fr.html.

FOREIGN EMBASSIES AND CONSULATES IN PARIS

Australia 4 rue Jean-Rey, 15ᵉ; Ⓜ Bir-Hakeim (☎ 01 40 59 33 00, ⓦ www.france.embassy.gov.au).

Canada 35 av Montaigne, 8ᵉ; Ⓜ Franklin-D.-Roosevelt (☎ 01 44 43 29 00, ⓦ amb-canada.fr).

Ireland 4 rue Rude, 16ᵉ; Ⓜ Charles-de-Gaulle-Etoile (☎ 01 44 17 67 00, ⓦ embassyofireland.fr).

New Zealand 103, rue de Grenelle, 7ᵉ; Ⓜ Varenne (☎ 01 45 01 43 43, ⓦ nzembassy.com/france).

South Africa 59 quai d'Orsay, 7ᵉ; Ⓜ Invalides (☎ 01 53 59 23 23, ⓦ afriquesud.net).

UK 35 rue du Faubourg-St-Honoré, 8ᵉ; Ⓜ Concorde (☎ 01 44 51 31 00, ⓦ ukinfrance.fco.gov.uk).

US 2 av Gabriel, 1ᵉʳ; Ⓜ Concorde (☎ 01 43 12 22 22, ⓦ france.usembassy.gov).

Health

Citizens of all EU countries are entitled to take advantage of French health services under the same terms as residents, provided they have the correct documentation. For British citizens, this means the European Health Insurance Card (**EHIC**), which can be applied for, free of charge, at UK post offices or online at ⓦ nhs.uk. Non-EU citizens have to pay for most medical attention and are strongly advised to take out some form of travel insurance.

Under the French Social Security system, every hospital visit, doctor's consultation and prescribed medicine incurs a charge, which you have to pay upfront. Although all EU citizens with the correct documents are entitled to a **refund** of around 70–80 percent of the standard fee for medical and dental expenses (the refund is lower when it comes to the cost of prescribed medicines) – providing the doctor is a *médecin conventionné* (government-registered and providing state rather than private care) – this can still leave a hefty shortfall, especially after a stay in hospital. Present your EHIC card when dealing with any medical service, and keep the

MEDICAL EMERGENCY NUMBERS

Paramedics/Fire brigade (sapeurs-pompiers) ☎ 18

SAMU Service d'Aide Médicale d'Urgence; serious medical emergencies/ambulance ☎ 15

SOS Médecins Doctor call-out ☎ 01 47 07 77 77

SOS Dentaire Emergency dental care ☎ 01 43 37 51 00

treatment form (*feuille de soins*), plus all receipts, prescriptions and any paperwork, in order to claim any reimbursements. Reimbursements should be claimed from the local CPAM (Caisse Primaire d'Assurance Maladie) office in Paris; you will need to present your bank details, including IBAN and BIC.

In **emergencies** you will always be admitted to the nearest hospital (*hôpital*), either under your own power or by ambulance, which even French citizens must pay for. Far better to call the fire brigade (*sapeurs-pompiers*) instead; acting as paramedics, they are equipped to deal with medical emergencies and are the fastest and most reliable emergency service.

If you prefer to go private you could try one of two English-speaking **private hospitals**: the American Hospital of Paris at 63 bd Victor-Hugo, Neuilly-sur-Seine (Ⓜ Porte Maillot; ☎ 01 46 41 25 25, Ⓦ american-hospital.org), and the Hertford British Hospital at 4 rue Kléber (Ⓜ Kléber; ☎ 01 47 59 59 59, Ⓦ british-hospital.org). Note that any costs incurred for private health care are not refundable.

To find a **doctor**, ask at any *pharmacie*, local police station, tourist office or your hotel. Alternatively, look under "Médecins" in the *Yellow Pages* or search for healthcare providers near you on Ⓦ ameli-direct.ameli.fr. An average consultation fee should be between €20 and €30. You will be given a *feuille de soins* (statement of treatment) for later

insurance claims. Prescriptions (*ordonnances*) should be taken to a *pharmacie* and must be paid for; the medicines will have little stickers (*vignettes*) attached to them, which you should remove and stick to your *feuille de soins*, together with the prescription itself.

Pharmacies, signalled by an illuminated green cross, can give advice on minor complaints and are also equipped to provide first aid on request (for a fee). Most pharmacies will have at least one chemist who speaks English. They tend to open from Monday to Saturday – many are closed on Sundays, though there are plenty in central areas such as the Marais that open – from roughly 8am–8pm; at night, details of the nearest open pharmacy are posted in the windows. To find your nearest duty pharmacy call ☎ 32 37 or search on Ⓦ 3237.fr (though note that not all of the city's pharmacies are listed there).

For a list of pharmacies that are open on particular nights, check Ⓦ pharmaciesdegarde.fr.

Insurance

Even though EU healthcare privileges apply in France, you'd do well to take out an **insurance policy** before travelling to cover against theft, loss and illness or injury. Many policies can be chopped and changed to exclude coverage you don't need – for example, sickness and accident benefits can often be excluded or included at will. If you do take **medical coverage**, check whether benefits will be paid as treatment proceeds or only after you return home, and whether there is a 24-hour medical emergency number. When securing **baggage cover**, make sure that the per-article limit – typically under £500 – will cover your most valuable possession. If you need to make a claim, you should keep **receipts** for medicines and medical treatment (see above), and in the event you have anything stolen you must obtain an official statement from the police (called a *constat de vol*).

ROUGH GUIDES TRAVEL INSURANCE

Rough Guides has teamed up with WorldNomads.com to offer great travel insurance deals. Policies are available to residents of over 150 countries, with cover for a wide range of adventure sports, 24hr emergency assistance, high levels of medical and evacuation cover and a stream of travel safety information. Roughguides.com users can take advantage of their policies online 24/7, from anywhere in the world – even if you're already travelling. And since plans often change when you're on the road, you can extend your policy and even claim online. Roughguides.com users who buy travel insurance with WorldNomads.com can also leave a positive footprint and donate to a community development project. For more information, go to Ⓦ roughguides.com/travel-insurance.

Internet

Though most hotels have free **wi-fi** (with variable reception), US and UK visitors will find that in general free wi-fi access in cafés and bars is not as widespread as in their home countries. Your best bet is to follow the bobo (bourgeois-bohemian) trail to Marais, Montmartre, Belleville and the Canal St-Martin, for example – though note that some of the new breed of hipster coffee bars actively ban computers and tablets. More conveniently, you can connect to the city's free wi-fi network from more than 260 **parks, museums and libraries**; these are all clearly marked with a "Paris Wi-Fi" logo, and the municipal website, Ⓦ paris.fr/wifi, lists all the hot spots. Some train stations also offer free wi-fi. Internet cafés are becoming harder to find. A small chain, Milk, has two branches, both open 24/7 (Ⓦ milklub.com): the most central is by Les Halles at 31 bd Sébastopol, 1er, and the other is in Montparnasse at 5 rue d'Odessa, 14e.

Laundry

You shouldn't have any trouble finding a **laundry** in Paris. If you can't spot one near your hotel, look in the phone book under "Laveries Automatiques". They're often unattended, so bring small change with you. Hours vary, but generally self-service laundries open at 7/8am and close between 7pm and 10pm. The alternative *blanchisserie*, or pressing services, are likely to be expensive, and hotels in particular charge high rates. If you're doing your own washing in hotels, keep quantities small, as most places forbid doing any laundry in your room.

Lost property

The **lost property office** (Bureau des Objets Trouvés) is located at the Préfecture de Police, 36 rue des Morillons, 15e; Ⓜ Convention (Mon–Thurs 8.30am–5pm, Fri 8.30am–4.30pm; ☎ 08 21 00 25 25). For property lost on public transport, phone the RATP on ☎ 3246. If you lose your passport, report it to a police station and then your embassy (see p.35).

Mail

French **post offices** (*bureaux de poste* or *PTTs*; Ⓦ laposte.fr) – look for bright yellow-and-blue La Poste signs – also offer money exchange, photocopying and phone services. They are generally open 8am until 7pm Monday to Friday, and 8am till noon on Saturdays. However, **Paris's main office**, at 52 rue du Louvre, 1er (Ⓜ Etienne-Marcel), is open (for postal services) Monday to Saturday from midnight until 6am and from 7.30am till midnight, plus 10am till midnight on Sundays (the other services are daytime only, as in all post offices).

Standard airmail letters (20g or less) and postcards within France and to European Union countries cost €0.95 and to North America, Australia and New Zealand €1.20. Remember that you can also buy **stamps** from *tabacs*.

To post your letter on the street, look for the bright yellow **post boxes**.

Maps

The **maps** in this Guide and the free *Paris Map* available from the tourist offices (see p.40) should be adequate for a short sightseeing stay, but for a more detailed map your best bet is the pocket-sized *L'Indispensable Plan de Paris* 1:15,000, published by Atlas Indispensable; it comes in a robust plastic cover, and gives full A–Z street listings.

Money

France's currency is the euro (€), which is split into 100 cents. There are seven euro notes – in denominations of 500, 200, 100, 50, 20, 10 and 5 (though many vendors are reluctant to accept the 500 and 200 euro notes) – and eight different coin denominations, from 2 euros down to 1 cent. For the most up-to-date exchange rates, consult the currency converter website Ⓦ oanda.com.

The easiest way to access your funds while away is with a **debit or credit card** – but it's not necessarily the cheapest option, with many UK banks levying charges totalling around 5 percent on foreign withdrawals. Added to the French bank's transaction charges, these can really add up. Depending on your bank, it may be necessary to contact them before leaving to let them know you'll be abroad, so they won't block your funds for security reasons. Most foreign cards will work in a French ATM/cash machine (called a *distributeur* or *point argent*). Credit cards are widely accepted but it's always worth checking first that restaurants and hotels will accept your card – American Express cards can sometimes be a bit tricky, and some smaller places won't accept them, even if they have a sign suggesting that they do. And note that some machines don't recognize foreign cards at all – transport vending machines and automatic petrol pumps, especially those at major supermarkets, are particularly problematic, but it can happen in restaurants and hotels, too. North American credit cards, for example, are not accepted at RATP/SNCF machines. French cards use the **chip-and-pin system**.

To cancel **lost or stolen** cards, call the following 24-hour numbers: American Express (☎+44 1273 696 933); MasterCard (☎0800 90 13 87); Visa (☎0800 90 11 79).

Changing money and banking hours

Exchange rates and **commission fees** charged by banks and bureaux de change vary considerably. On the whole, the best exchange rates are offered by **banks**, though there's always a commission charge on top (a 2–4 percent commission on cash). **Bureaux de change** can give terrible rates, though the ones at the airports and those on the Champs-Elysées, near *McDonald's*, are usually pretty reputable.

Standard **banking hours** are Monday to Friday or Tuesday to Saturday from 9am till 5pm. Some banks close at lunchtime (usually 12.30–2pm). All are closed on Sunday and public holidays. Money-exchange bureaux stay open longer, tend not to close for lunch and may even open on Sundays in the more touristy areas.

Avoid the **automatic exchange machines** at the airports and train stations and outside many money-exchange bureaux, except in emergencies. They offer a very poor rate of exchange.

Opening hours and public holidays

Most shops, businesses, information services, museums and banks in Paris stay open all day. The exceptions are the smaller shops and enterprises, which may close for lunch sometime between 12.30pm and 2.30pm. Although France recently eased its Sunday trading restrictions, with shops in the more touristy areas allowed to stay open (see p.324), basic **hours of business** are from 8 or 9am to 6.30 or 7.30pm Monday to Saturday. Big department stores will also have a "*nocturne*" each week – a night where they stay open late. You can always find boulangeries and food shops that stay open on days when others close – on Sunday normally until noon (but note that many boulangeries also have a day or a couple of days each week when they close). Most shops – large and small – open on Sundays in December.

Museums generally open at 9/10am and close at 5/6pm. Summer hours may differ from winter

hours. Don't be caught out by museum **closing days** – usually Monday or Tuesday and sometimes both.

Many restaurants and shops take a **holiday** between the middle of July and the end of August (see p.270) and over Easter and Christmas.

France celebrates eleven **national holidays** (*jours fériés* or j.f.) – not counting the two that fall on a Sunday anyway. Throughout the Guide, opening hours given for Sundays also apply to public holidays. With three, and sometimes four, holidays, **May** is a particularly festive month. It makes a peaceful time to visit, as people clear out of town over several weekends, but many businesses will have erratic opening hours. Just about everything, including museums, will be closed on May 1. July 14 heralds the beginning of the French holiday season and people leave town en masse between then and the end of August.

NATIONAL HOLIDAYS

January 1 (New Year's Day) Le Jour de l'an
Easter Sunday Pâques
Easter Monday Lundi de Pâques
May 1 (May Day) La Fête du travail
May 8 (VE Day) La Fête de la Victoire 1945
Ascension Day (40 days after Easter: mid-May to early June) L'Ascension
Whitsun (7th Sun after Easter: mid-May to early June) La Pentecôte
Whit Monday (7th Mon after Easter: mid-May to early June) Lundi de Pentecôte
July 14 (Bastille Day) La Fête nationale
August 15 (Feast of the Assumption) L'Assomption
November 1 (All Saints' Day) La Toussaint
November 11 (Armistice Day) L'Armistice 1918
December 25 (Christmas Day) Noël

Phones

Most foreign mobile/cell phones automatically connect to a local provider as soon as you arrive in France. Make sure you know what your provider's call charges are in advance – they can be exorbitant, and you are usually charged to take calls as well as make them. Be wary, too, of data roaming charges, which have traditionally been extortionate – however, within the EU these look set to be reduced significantly after April 2016, and by 2017 they should be abolished entirely.

France operates on the European GSM standard, so US **cell phones** won't work unless you've got a tri-band phone. If you're making a lot of calls,

INTERNATIONAL CALLS

To **call France from abroad**, use the international dialling code for your country (00 or 011 in most cases) followed by the French country code (33), then the local number minus the initial "0". So to call Paris from the UK, Ireland and New Zealand dial ⓣ00 33 1 then the nine-digit number; from the US, Canada and Australia, dial ⓣ011 33 1.

CALLING HOME FROM PARIS

UK 00 + 44 + area code (minus initial zero) + number
US & Canada 00 + 1 + area code + number
Ireland 00 + 353 + area code (minus initial zero) + number
Australia 00 + 61+ area code (minus initial zero) + number
New Zealand 00 + 64 + area code (minus initial zero) + number
South Africa 00 + 27 + area code + number

consider buying a local SIM card or a pre-pay (*mobicarte*) package once in Paris. These are sold in mobile phone shops, Fnac stores (see p.332) and some supermarkets.

Prepaid phonecards (*télécartes*) for use in phone booths or hotel phones are also available – these are sold in post offices, tourist offices, *tabacs*, newsstands and some supermarkets. Expect to pay around €10–15.

For **calls within France** – local or long-distance – dial all ten digits of the number. Paris and Ile-de-France numbers start with ⓣ01. Numbers beginning with ⓣ080 up to ⓣ08 05, ⓣ30 and ⓣ31 are free to call; ⓣ081 is charged at local rates, no matter where you're calling from; all other ⓣ08 numbers, and ⓣ118 numbers are premium rate and can't be accessed from outside France. Numbers beginning with ⓣ06 or ⓣ07 are **mobile** and therefore expensive to call.

Sales tax

VAT (Value Added Tax) is referred to as **TVA** in France (*taxe sur la valeur ajoutée*). The standard rate in France is currently 20 percent; it's higher for luxury items and lower for essentials, but there are no exemptions. However, non-EU residents who have been in the country for less than six months are entitled to a refund (*détaxe*) of some or all of this amount (but usually around fourteen percent) if you spend at least €175 in a single trip to one shop. Not all stores participate in this scheme, though, so ask first. The procedure is rather complicated: present your passport to the shop when you pay and ask for the *bordereau de vente à l'exportation* form. At this stage you need to tell them whether you want to reclaim your refund from a reimbursement window, if there is one at your departure point, or, somewhat easier, via bank transfer. If you choose the former, when you leave France the easiest thing to do is scan your form at a PABLO barcode reader, which are located near the Customs offices; once it's validated and approved you can obtain your refund. If there is no barcode reader, you can approach Customs directly. For more information on the *détaxe* and other customs-related questions, check with the Centre de Renseignements des Douanes (ⓣ08 11 20 44, ⓦdouane.gouv.fr).

Smoking

Smoking is officially banned in public places in France, but don't be surprised to find yourself occasionally surrounded by cigarette smoke if you're dining on a *terrasse* – even if it's covered.

Time

Paris, and all of France, is in the Central European Time Zone (GMT+1): 1hr ahead of the UK, 6hr ahead of Eastern Standard Time and 9hr ahead of Pacific Standard Time. France is 8hr behind all of eastern Australia and 10hr behind New Zealand from April to October (but 10hr behind southeastern Australia and 12hr behind New Zealand from November to March).

Toilets

Paris's automatic public toilets, known as "*sanisettes*", are free to use. Elsewhere, ask for *les toilettes* or look for signs for the WC (pronounced "vay say"); when reading the details of facilities outside hotels, don't confuse *lavabo*, which means washbasin, with lavatory. French toilets in some of the cheapest and most old-fashioned bars are still occasionally of the hole-in-the-ground variety, and often lack toilet paper. Standards of cleanliness aren't always high. Toilets in railway stations and department stores are commonly staffed by attendants who will expect a bit of spare change.

Tourist information

The main **Paris tourist office** is at 25 rue des Pyramides, 1er (daily: May–Oct 9am–7pm; Nov–April 10am–7pm; Ⓦ paris-info.com; Ⓜ Pyramides/RER Auber). There are **branch offices** in the various terminals at CDG (hours vary but most are open daily 7.15am–10pm) and Orly (daily 7.15am–9.45pm) airports; at the Gare du Nord (daily 8am–6pm), Gare de Lyon (Mon–Sat 8am–6pm) and Gare de l'Est (Mon–Sat 8am–7pm); and opposite 72 bd Rochechouart, 9e (daily 10am–6pm; Ⓜ Anvers). In addition to giving out general information, the offices can help with booking accommodation and sell public transport tickets, tour tickets and the Paris Museum Pass (see p.34). All the tourist offices should have copies of the free Paris Map – this might be behind the counter, so you'll need to ask.

The website has a **hotel booking service**, with many hotels offering discounted stays, and it also allows you to buy advance tickets online for some of the most popular sights, such as the Arc de Triomphe and the Sainte-Chapelle, enabling you to bypass long queues.

Another useful resource is Ⓦ nouveau-paris-ile-de-france.fr, which has information on attractions and activities in Paris and the surrounding area.

For detailed **what's-on information** you'll need to buy one of Paris's weekly **listings magazines**, Pariscope (€0.70) or L'Officiel des Spectacles (Ⓦ offi.fr; €0.70), available from all newsagents and kiosks. Pariscope, in particular, has a huge section on films. You could also keep a lookout for the free weekly listings paper, A nous Paris (Ⓦ anousparis.fr), which comes out on Mondays and is available from métro stations. In addition, a number of free pocket independent nightlife guides (Lylo is a good one; Ⓦ lylo.fr) can be picked up in stores and cafés all over the city.

Travellers with disabilities

Paris has never had a particularly good reputation for **access facilities**, though there have been signif-icant improvements, especially to the bus network,

and the city's public toilets (sanisettes) are fully accessible to wheelchair users.

The tourist board website, Ⓦ parisinfo.com, includes a section dedicated to disabled travellers. In addition to featuring possible itineraries, their Accessible Paris guide lists museums that are either accessible or offer **guided visits and activities** for disabled people. Meanwhile, Ⓦ accesculture.org has a list of **theatres** where audio descriptions or surtitles are provided for the visually impaired or deaf/hard-of-hearing. Admission to most **museums** is free for blue badge holders and one companion.

Eurostar offers a good deal for wheelchair users. There are two spaces in the first-class carriages for wheelchairs, each with an accompanying seat for a companion. Fares for all four are fixed at the lowest standard-class fare (with semi-flexible conditions), and you will normally get the first-class meal as well. You need to reserve well in advance and arrange the special assistance that Eurostar offers at either end. Companions travelling on Eurostar with visually and hearing impaired travellers – who pay the normal fare – can travel at the same price as a wheelchair user's companion by calling ☎ 08432 186 186.

Getting around

G7 Horizon (English-speaking operator on ☎ 01 41 27 66 66, Ⓦ taxis-g7.fr) offers fully adapted **taxis** and drivers trained to take care of physically disabled and sight-impaired travellers. Fares are the same as for classic taxis; you just need to reserve four hours in advance.

Bus lines are accessible for wheelchairs, with mechanical ramps for getting on and off and a designated wheelchair space in the bus. Not all **RER** stations are accessible, however, and most require an official to work the lift for you. The Météor **métro** line (14), and the RER line E are designed to be easily accessible by all.

For travel on the buses, métro or RER, the RATP offers **accompanied journeys** for disabled people – Les compagnons du voyage (Ⓦ compagnons.com) – which costs €31.50 an hour (€21 for over-60s) and is available round the clock. You have to book online or on ☎ 01 58 76 08 33 (Mon–Fri 7am–7pm) at least a day in advance.

You can download a guide to disabled access on the bus, métro and RER at Ⓦ ratp.fr, though it is more of a PR information document than a useful manual.

Cars with hand controls can be rented from Hertz, usually with 24 hours' advance notice.

RESOURCES FOR DISABLED TRAVELLERS

Ⓦ **accessinparis.org** Thoroughly researched and nicely put together guide which, although last updated in 2008, still has a lot of good detail on what it is like to travel in Paris, with sections on transport, accommodation and loos, among others.

APF (Association des Paralysés de France) Ⓦ apf.asso.fr. National organization providing information and support for disabled people.

Handitourisme One of the best sources of information for travellers with disabilities in France (with a large section on Paris), published by Petit Futé (Ⓦ petitfute.fr; €16.95/€12 in digital format). Written in French, and regularly updated, the guide lists hundreds of sites, museums, hotels and restaurants with full accessibility to handicapped travellers.

Ⓦ **infomobi.com** Useful source of information on getting around Paris, with English translations and a helpline.

Ⓦ **jaccede.com** Handy website (in French only) giving a list of museums, monuments and other public places in Paris that are wheelchair accessible.

Paris comme sur des roulettes A guide detailing how to get about by wheelchair in Paris; available at Fnac, Gibert Jeune and other large bookstores.

PONT-NEUF

The islands

There's no better place to start a tour of Paris than the two river islands at its centre, the Ile de la Cité and the Ile St-Louis. The former is the core from which the rest of Paris grew and harbours the cathedral of Notre-Dame, a superb example of Gothic grandeur and harmony, and the stunning Sainte-Chapelle, preserved within the precincts of the Palais de Justice. Linked to the Ile de la Cité by a footbridge, the smaller Ile St-Louis has no heavyweight sights, but possesses a beguiling charm of its own, with its tall, austerely beautiful houses on single-lane streets, tree-lined *quais*, a church and assorted restaurants, cafés and shops. The island feels removed from the rest of Paris, an oasis little touched by the city's turbulent years of revolution and upheaval. Inhabitants of the island even have their own name: "Louisiens".

Ile de la Cité

Ⓜ Cité/St-Michel/Pont-Neuf

1

The **Ile de la Cité** is where Paris began. It was settled in around 300 BC by a Celtic tribe, the Parisii, and in 52 BC was overrun by the Romans, who built a palace-fortress at the western end of the island. In the tenth century, the Frankish kings transformed this into a splendid palace, of which the **Sainte-Chapelle** and the **Conciergerie** prison survive today. At the other end of the island they erected the great cathedral of **Notre-Dame**. By the twelfth century the small Ile de la Cité teemed with life, somehow managing to accommodate twelve parishes plus numerous chapels and monasteries. It was all too much for the monks at St-Magloire, who moved out in 1138 to quieter premises on the Right Bank.

It takes some imagination today – or a visit to the Crypte Archéologique near Notre-Dame (see p.47) – to picture what the medieval city must have looked like, as most of it was erased in the nineteenth century by Baron Haussmann, Napoléon III's Préfet de la Seine (equivalent to mayor of Paris), displacing 25,000 people and destroying ninety streets – which had, admittedly, become squalid and dangerous. In their place were raised four imposing Neoclassical edifices, largely given over to housing the law and police. The few corners of the island untouched by Haussmann include the tranquil **square du Vert-Galant**, **place Dauphine** and the medieval streets **rues Chanoinesse**, **des Ursins** and **de la Colombe**, north of the cathedral.

Pont-Neuf

Ⓜ Pont-Neuf

A popular approach to the Ile de la Cité is via the graceful, twelve-arched **Pont-Neuf**, which, despite its name ("New Bridge"), is Paris's oldest surviving bridge, built by Henri IV, who is commemorated with a statue halfway across. Made of stone and free of the usual medieval complement of houses, it was a radical departure from previous structures, hence its name. Henri IV, one of the capital's first great town planners, took much interest in the Pont-Neuf's progress and would sometimes come to inspect it, delighting the workmen on one occasion by taking a flying leap over an incomplete arch.

So impressive was the bridge in scale and length that it soon became symbolic of the city itself, drawing large crowds; peddlers, secondhand book- and flower-sellers, dog-barbers and tooth-pullers set up stalls, while acrobats and actors entertained passers-by.

Square du Vert-Galant

Ⓜ Pont-Neuf

The **square du Vert-Galant** is enclosed within the triangular stern of the island, and reached via steps leading down behind the statue of Henri IV on the Pont-Neuf. "Vert-Galant", meaning a "green" or "lusty" gentleman, is a reference to the king's legendary amorous exploits, and he would no doubt have approved of this tranquil, tree-lined garden, a popular haunt of lovers – the prime spot to occupy is the knoll dotted with trees at the extreme point of the island. From here you can also hop onto one of the river boats that dock on the north side of the square (see p.28).

Place Dauphine

Ⓜ Pont-Neuf

On the eastern side of the Pont-Neuf, across the street from the Henri IV statue, red-brick seventeenth-century houses flank the entrance to **place Dauphine**, one of the city's most secluded and attractive squares. The traffic noise recedes, often replaced by nothing more intrusive than the gentle tap of boules being played in the shade of the chestnuts. At the eastern end is the hulking facade of the **Palais de Justice**, which swallowed up the palace that was home to the French kings until Etienne Marcel's bloody revolt in 1358 frightened them off to the greater security of the Louvre.

1

Sainte-Chapelle

Palais de Justice, 4 bd du Palais, 1ᵉʳ • Daily: March–Oct 9.30am–6pm, mid-May to mid-Sept also Wed till 9pm; Nov–Feb 9am–5pm •
€8.50, combined admission with the Conciergerie €13.50 • ☎ 01 53 40 60 80 • Ⓜ Cité

The only part of the Ile de la Cité's old palace that remains in its entirety is the
Sainte-Chapelle, its fragile-looking spire soaring above the Palais buildings and its
excessive height in relation to its length giving it the appearance of a lopped-off
cathedral choir. Though damaged in the Revolution, during which it was used as a flour
warehouse, it was sensitively restored in the mid-nineteenth century, and remains one of
the finest achievements of French High Gothic, renowned for its exquisite stained-glass
windows. It was built by Louis IX in 1242–48 to house a collection of holy relics
bought at an extortionate price – far more than it cost to build the Sainte-Chapelle –
from the bankrupt Byzantine Empire. The relics, supposedly Christ's crown of thorns
and fragments of the True Cross and a nail of the Crucifixion, are now in Notre-Dame's
treasury, displayed only on certain days, including Good Friday.

The upper and lower chapels

The Sainte-Chapelle actually consists of two chapels: the simple **lower chapel** was
intended for the servants, and the **upper chapel**, reached via a spiral staircase, was
reserved for the court. The latter is dazzling, its walls made almost entirely of stained
glass held up by powerful supports, which the medieval builders cleverly crafted to
appear delicate and fragile by dividing them into clusters of pencil-thin columns.
When the sun streams through, the glowing blues and reds of the stained glass dapple
the interior and you feel like you're surrounded by myriad brilliant butterflies. There
are 1113 glass panels, two-thirds of which are original (the others date from the
nineteenth-century restoration); they tell virtually the entire story of the Bible,
beginning on the north side with Genesis, continuing with the Passion of Christ
(east end) and the history of the Sainte-Chapelle relics (on the south side), and ending
with the Apocalypse in the rose window. The chapel is used for classical **concerts** almost
daily – buy tickets a day or so in advance to avoid long queues.

ILE DE LA CITÉ AND ILE ST-LOUIS

CAFÉS AND WINE BARS
Berthillon — 4
Café St-Régis — 2
Taverne Henri IV — 1

RESTAURANT
Mon Vieil Ami — 3

Conciergerie

Palais de Justice, 2 bd du Palais, 1ᵉʳ • Daily 9.30am–6pm • €8.50, combined ticket with Sainte-Chapelle €13.50 • ☎ 01 53 40 60 80 • Ⓜ Cité

The **Conciergerie** is one of the few remaining vestiges of the old medieval Palais de Justice and is Paris's oldest prison, where Marie-Antoinette and the leading figures of the Revolution were incarcerated before execution. Inside are several splendid, vaulted Gothic halls, including the Salle des Gens d'Armes, built in 1301–15. The far end is separated off by an iron grille; during the Revolution this area was reserved for the *pailleux*, prisoners who couldn't afford to bribe a guard for their own cell and had to sleep on straw (*paille*).

Beyond is a corridor where prisoners were allowed to wander freely. There are a number of reconstructed rooms here, such as the "salle de toilette", where the condemned had their hair cropped and shirt collars ripped in preparation for the guillotine. On the upper storey is a mock-up of **Marie-Antoinette's cell** in which the condemned queen's crucifix hangs forlornly against peeling fleur-de-lys wallpaper.

Tour de l'Horloge

Ⓜ Cité

Outside the Conciergerie is the **Tour de l'Horloge**, a tower built around 1350, and so called because it displayed Paris's first public clock. The ornate face, set against a background of vivid blue and gold, is flanked with statues representing Law and Justice, added in 1585. The clock tower's bell, which would once have rung out to mark special royal occasions, sounding during the St Bartholomew's Day massacre (see p.365), was melted down during the Commune (see p.186).

Place Lépine

Ⓜ Cité

East from the Conciergerie is **place Lépine**, named after the police boss who gave Paris's coppers their white truncheons and whistles. The police headquarters, known popularly

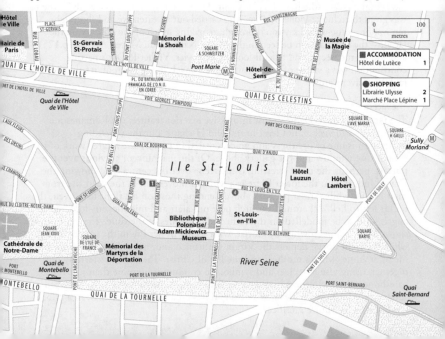

1

as the Quai des Orfèvres (as readers of Georges Simenon's Maigret novels will know), stands on one side of the square, though the police are set to move to new modern offices before long. Livening up the square on the other side is a daily **flower market**, which is augmented by a chirruping bird market on Sundays. Following a state visit by the British queen in 2014, the market officially changed its name to Marché aux Fleurs Reine-Elizabeth-II, but nobody uses its full name.

Cathédrale de Notre-Dame

Place du Parvis Notre-Dame, 4ᵉ • **Cathedral** Mon–Fri 8am–6.45pm; Sat & Sun 8am–7.15pm; guided tours 1hr–1hr 30min in English (Wed & Thurs 2pm, Sat 2.30pm) and French (Mon–Fri – though not first Fri of the month or any Fri during Lent – 2pm & 3pm, Sat & Sun 2.30pm) • Free • ☎ 01 42 34 56 10, ⓦ cathedraledeparis.com • **Towers** April, May, June & Sept daily 10am–6.30pm; July & Aug Mon–Thurs & Sun 10am–6.30pm, Fri & Sat 10am–11pm; Oct–March daily 10am–5.30pm • €8.50 • ⓦ notre-dame-de-paris.monuments -nationaux.fr • **Trésor** Daily 9.30am–6pm • €3 • Ⓜ St-Michel/Cité

A Gothic masterpiece, the **Cathédrale de Notre-Dame** rears up from the Ile de la Cité like a great ship moored by huge flying buttresses. Built on the site of the Merovingian cathedral of St-Etienne, itself sited on the old Roman temple to Jupiter, Notre-Dame was begun in 1160 under the auspices of Bishop de Sully and completed around 1345. The cathedral's seminaries became an ecclesiastical powerhouse, churning out six popes during the thirteenth and fourteenth centuries, though it subsequently lost some of its pre-eminence to other sees, such as Rheims and St-Denis. The building later fell into decline, and during the Revolution the frieze of Old Testament kings on the facade was damaged by enthusiasts who mistook them for the kings of France. Napoleon restored some of the cathedral's prestige, crowning himself emperor here in 1804, though the walls were so dilapidated they had to be covered with drapes to provide a sufficiently grand backdrop.

In the 1820s Notre-Dame was given a much-needed **restoration**, largely thanks to a petition drawn up by Victor Hugo. Hugo had stirred public interest through his novel *Notre-Dame de Paris*, in which he lamented the building's sorry state (Gothic architecture was particularly favoured by Romantic novelists, who deemed the soaring naves of the great cathedrals singularly suited to sheltering "tormented souls"). The task was given to architect **Viollet-le-Duc**, who carried out an extensive and thorough renovation, some would say too thorough, remaking much of the statuary on the facade – the originals can be seen in the Musée National du Moyen Age (see p.125) – and adding the steeple and baleful-looking gargoyles. Viollet-le-Duc's parting contribution was a statue of himself among the angels lining the roof: it's the only one looking heavenwards.

The facade

The **facade** is Notre-Dame's most impressive exterior feature; the Romanesque influence is still visible, not least in its solid H-shape, but the overriding impression is one of lightness and grace, created in part by the filigree work of the central rose window and the gallery above. Of the magnificent **carvings over the portals**, perhaps the most arresting is the scene over the central one showing the Day of Judgement: the lower frieze is a whirl of movement as the dead rise from their graves, while Christ presides above, sending those on his right to heaven, those on his left to hell. All around the arch peer out alert and mischievous-looking angels, said to be modelled on the cathedral choirboys of the time. The left portal shows Mary being crowned by Christ, with scenes of her life in the lower friezes, while the right portal depicts the Virgin enthroned and, below, episodes from the life of St Anne (Mary's mother) and the life of Christ. These are masterfully put together, using visual devices and symbols to communicate more than just the bare-bones story – in the nativity scene, for example, the infant Christ is placed above Mary to show his elevated status and lies on an altar rather than in a crib, symbolizing his future sacrifice.

The towers

If you climb the **towers** (access to which is around the side of the cathedral), you can see Viollet-le-Duc's gargoyles and angels up close, as well as the great 13-tonne Emmanuel Bell in the south tower. One of the largest and oldest bells in Europe, the Emmanuel Bell was forged in 1685 and spared during the 1789 Revolution (unlike Marie, the large bell in the north tower, which was destroyed and melted down). It is only rung at Christmas and other special occasions, or in times of mourning, such as the day after the Charlie Hebdo attacks in 2015. The cathedral's other nine bells, which had become badly out of tune, were replaced in 2013. Note there are 387 **steps** to the top of the South Tower.

The interior

Inside Notre-Dame, you're struck immediately by the dramatic contrast between the darkness of the nave and the light falling on the first great clustered pillars of the choir. It is the end walls of the transepts, nearly two-thirds glass, including two magnificent rose windows coloured in imperial purple, that admit all this light. These, the vaulting and the soaring shafts reaching to the springs of the vaults, are all definite Gothic elements, while there remains a strong influence of Romanesque in the stout round pillars of the nave and the general sense of four-squareness. The **trésor** is unlikely to appeal unless ornate nineteenth-century monstrances and chalices are your thing.

Your best bet if you want to avoid the crowds is to visit between 8 and 9am or in the evening. To join a free **tour**, meet at the welcome desk near the entrance. Free **organ recitals** are also held regularly; the instrument, crafted by the great nineteenth-century organ-maker Aristide Cavaillé-Coll, is one of France's finest, with more than six thousand pipes.

Kilomètre zéro

Ⓜ Cité

Notre-Dame, at the heart of Paris, is also the symbolic heart of France: outside on the pavement by the cathedral's west side is a bronze star, known as **kilomètre zéro**, from where all main-road distances in France are calculated. The large square in front of the cathedral, built by Haussmann in the 1860s, is known as the **Parvis** (from "paradise") **Notre-Dame**. Paving stones show the outlines of the small streets and buildings that stood here in medieval times.

Crypte Archéologique

Parvis Notre-Dame, 4ᵉ • Tues–Sun 10am–6pm • €7; free tours on Sat • ☎ 01 55 42 50 10, Ⓦ crypte.paris.fr • Ⓜ Cité/St-Michel

At the far end of the Parvis Notre-Dame is the entrance to the **Crypte Archéologique**. This large, well-presented excavated area holds the remains of the original cathedral (St-Etienne) plus vestiges of the streets and houses that once clustered around Notre-Dame; most are medieval, but some date as far back as Gallo-Roman times and

---

SCHOOL FOR SCANDAL

On rue Chanoinesse, the cathedral school of Notre-Dame, forerunner of the Sorbonne, once flourished. Around the year 1200, one of the teachers was **Peter Abélard**. A philosophical whizz kid and cocker of snooks at establishment intellectuals, he was very popular with students but not with the authorities, who thought they caught a distinct whiff of heresy. Forced to leave the school, he set up shop on the Left Bank with his disciples, in effect founding the University of Paris. Less successful was the story of his love life. While living near the rue Chanoinesse, he fell passionately in love with his landlord's niece, **Héloïse**, and she with him. She gave birth to a baby, her uncle had Abélard castrated, and the story ended in convents, lifelong separation and lengthy correspondence. They were reunited in death, however, and lie side by side in Père-Lachaise cemetery (see p.210).

1

include parts of the city's Roman quay and its thermal baths. Digital technology, including touchscreens on which you can explore the cathedral – and the city – from every angle during four stages of its development, give context to what might otherwise be little more than an evocative set of stones, while excellent captions go deeper into the history of everything from Paris's lost topography to the many myths that have gone into writing about Lutetia, the Roman city.

Mémorial des Martyrs de la Déportation

Square de l'Ile de France, 4ᵉ • Tues–Sun: April–Sept 10am–7pm; Oct–March 10am–5pm • Free • ☎ 01 46 33 87 56 • Ⓜ St-Paul/ Maubert Mutualité

At the eastern tip of the Ile de la Cité is the stark and moving symbolic tomb of the 200,000 French who died in Nazi concentration camps – among them Resistance fighters, Jews and forced labourers. The **Mémorial des Martyrs de la Déportation** is easily missed and barely visible above ground; stairs hardly shoulder-wide descend into a claustrophobic underworld reminiscent of a prison yard, and off here is a stifling, narrow crypt, its walls lined with thousands of illuminated quartz pebbles representing the dead. Barred cells sit on either side, and it ends in a dark, raw space with a single naked bulb hanging in the middle. Above the exit are the words "Pardonne. N'oublie pas" ("Forgive. Do not forget").

Ile St-Louis

Ⓜ Pont Marie/Sully-Morland

The **Ile St-Louis** is arguably the most romantic part of Paris. For centuries this was nothing but swampy pastureland, a haunt of lovers, duellists and miscreants on the run, until in the seventeenth century developer Christophe Marie chose to fill it with elegant mansions; by 1660 the island was transformed. Unlike its larger neighbour, the Ile St-Louis has no sights as such, save for three tiny "**museums**" in the Bibliothèque Polonaise at 6 quai d'Orléans: a room devoted to Frédéric Chopin, another to Boleslas Biegas – sculptor, painter, playwright of the Viennese Secession – and a museum to Romantic Polish poet **Adam Mickiewicz** (all Tues–Fri 2.15–6pm; €5; ☎ 01 55 42 83 83; Ⓜ Pont Marie).

Hôtel Lauzun

17 quai d'Anjou, 4ᵉ • Not open to the public • Ⓜ Pont Marie/Sully Morland

One of the most elegant mansions on Ile St-Louis, the **Hôtel Lauzun** was built in 1657 by Versailles architect Le Vau. Its most famous inhabitant was the poet Baudelaire who lived in a small apartment on the second floor from 1843 to 1845. He wrote much of *Les Fleurs du mal* here and hosted meetings of the Haschischines club, attended by bohemian writers and artists, including Manet, Balzac and Delacroix, and during which, as the name suggests, hashish was handed round – apparently in the form of a green jelly. Flutes of champagne are probably as heady as things get these days, as the mansion is often used for government receptions.

Southern quais

A visit to the island wouldn't be complete without a stop at *Berthillon* on rue St-Louis-en-l'Ile (see p.271); eating one of its exquisite ice creams while strolling the streets is a tradition. For seclusion, head for the **southern quais**, or head to the garden across boulevard Henri-IV to reach Paris's best sunbathing spot. The island is particularly atmospheric in the evening, when an arm-in-arm stroll along the *quais* is a must on any lovers' itinerary.

THE LOUVRE AT NIGHT

The Louvre

The Louvre – catch-all term for the palace and the museum it houses – cuts a grand Classical swathe through the centre of the city, running west along the right bank of the Seine from the Ile de la Cité towards the Champs-Elysées. Even if you don't venture inside, the sheer bravado of the architectural ensemble is thrilling. If you do, you'll find a truly astonishing museum. Its paintings, sculptures and decorative arts cover everything from the Middle Ages to the beginnings of Impressionism, while the collection of antiquities from Egypt, the Middle East, Greece and Rome is unrivalled. The hoard of Italian Renaissance paintings is priceless, and the French collection acts as the gold standard of the nation's artistic tradition. Separate from the Louvre proper, but still within the palace are three design museums dedicated to fashion and textiles, decorative arts and advertising.

The original **Palais du Louvre** was little more than a feudal fortress, begun by Philippe-Auguste in the 1190s. Charles V was the first French king to make the castle his residence, in the 1360s (the ground plan of his new palace can be seen traced on the pavement of the **Cour Carrée**). It wasn't until 1546, the year before the death of François I, that the first stones of the Louvre we see today were laid by the architect, Pierre Lescot. Henri II continued François I's plans, building the two graceful wings that now form the southwestern corner of the Cour Carrée. It's still possible to imagine how extraordinary the building would have looked, a gleaming example of the new Renaissance style surrounded by the late Gothic of Charles V's day.

When Henri IV took charge in 1594, he set about linking the Louvre with Catherine de Médicis' Palais des Tuileries (see box, p.70), building the long, riverside Grande Galerie. Louis XIII and Louis XIV contented themselves with merely completing the Cour Carrée in a style copied from Lescot's original facade, and the only architectural intrusion of this era was Claude Perrault's sober **Classical colonnade** facing rue de l'Amiral de Coligny, which tragically beat Bernini's stunning Baroque design (occasionally on display in the department of Prints and Drawings) for the same contract. Napoléon III's main contributions – the courtyard facades of the nineteenth-century Richelieu and Denon wings – repeated the basic theme of the Cour Carrée, with typical conservatism.

Brief history of the collections

The **Musée du Louvre** began as the personal art collection of François I who, in 1516, summoned Leonardo da Vinci from Milan. Leonardo brought his greatest works with him across the Alps, and later kings set up "cabinets" of artworks and antiquities in the Louvre, but these were all very much private collections. Artists and

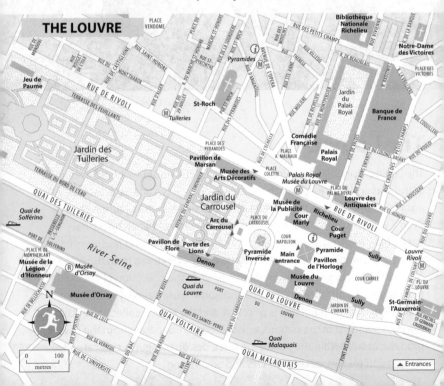

academics – as well as prostitutes – lived in the palace under Louis XIV, and a royal arts academy mounted exhibitions here, known as *salons*, as early as 1725. But the plan for a public museum was only conceived in the 1740s, and it wasn't until 1793, the year of Louis XVI's execution, that the gallery actually opened. Within a decade, Napoleon's wagonloads of war booty – not all of which has been returned – transformed the Louvre's art collection into the world's largest. Since then, various projects, notably the Grand Louvre project in the 1980s (see below), have concentrated on expanding the museum's exhibition space and exporting the Louvre to other sites. In 2012, the Musée du Louvre-Lens was opened in the former coal-mining town of Lens, in northern France, while the end of 2015 saw the opening of the "Louvre Abu Dhabi" annexe, which will borrow works from the main collection. The projects are described by the Louvre as generous attempts to decentralize the arts and make the museum's works accessible to more people, though others have accused the museum of more cynical economic motives.

The great 1980s makeover

For all its many additions and alterations, the palace remained a surprisingly harmonious building, its grandeur and symmetry soberly suited to this most historic of Parisian landmarks. Then, in 1989, I.M. Pei's controversial glass **Pyramide** erupted from the centre of the Cour Napoléon like a visitor from another architectural planet. (Just for the record, the pyramid has 673 panes of glass, not the fabled 666.) It was the centrepiece of President Mitterrand's "**Grand Louvre**" makeover, along with the basement Carrousel du Louvre shopping complex and fashion arena, the weird, downward-pointing **Pyramide Inversée** (which later found a starring role in *The Da Vinci Code*) and the dramatic glazing over of the courtyards of the Richelieu wing – from which the Finance Ministry was ejected. The Pyramide has since found a place in the hearts of even the most conservative Parisians, outstaging even Napoleon's pink marble **Arc du Carrousel**. Perhaps emboldened by this success, the Louvre completed another daring project in 2012 when a stunning metal-and-glass roof – by the Franco-Milanese architectural team of Mario Bellini and Rudy Ricciotti – was installed in the **Cour Visconti** (home of the new Islamic art collection).

INFORMATION

Opening hours Permanent collection: Mon & Wed–Sun (closed Jan 1, May 1, July 14 and Dec 25) 9am–6pm, Wed & Fri till 9.45pm. Doors shut 30min before the museum closes. Almost a quarter of the museum's rooms are closed one day a week on a rotating basis, so if you're interested in one of the less popular sections it's worth checking the schedule online.

Admission €12, €16 with entry to temporary exhibitions; free to all under-18s and EU residents aged 18–26; free to under-26s from any country on Fri after 6pm, and to all on the first Sun of each month from October to March, as well as July 14. Tickets can be bought at the museum, from branches of Fnac (see p.332) or online in France via ⓦticketnet.fr, or in the US (in US dollars) via ⓦticketweb.com.

Contact details ☎01 40 20 53 17, ⓦlouvre.fr

Métro ⓜPalais Royal-Musée du Louvre

Access The main entrance is via the Pyramide, but you'll find shorter queues at two different entrances: the one near the Arc du Carrousel (which can also be accessed from 99 rue de Rivoli and from the line #1 platform of the Palais-Royal-Musée-du-Louvre métro stop); and at the Porte des Lions entrance, just east of the Pont Royal (though this is sometimes closed, so it's best to phone ahead to check). If you've already got a ticket or a museum pass (see p.34) you can join a fast-track queue at the Pyramide. Disabled access is via the futuristic sinking column in the middle of the Pyramide; entry is free to registered disabled visitors and to one companion. Once you've entered the museum, you'll then need to queue to have your bags checked, and if you haven't already got a ticket, you'll also need to queue at a machine or ticket desk; it sounds daunting, but things usually move pretty quickly. Queues and congestion should start reducing in 2016 with the reconfiguration of the main entrance, the Hall Napoléon. The work was undertaken in order to cope with the increasing numbers of visitors (nearly ten million in 2014).

Maps A map, freely available from information booths in the Hall Napoléon under the Pyramide, shows exactly what is where.

Tours and guides Ninety-minute guided tours in English of the masterpieces run every day at 11.15 and 2pm (€10;

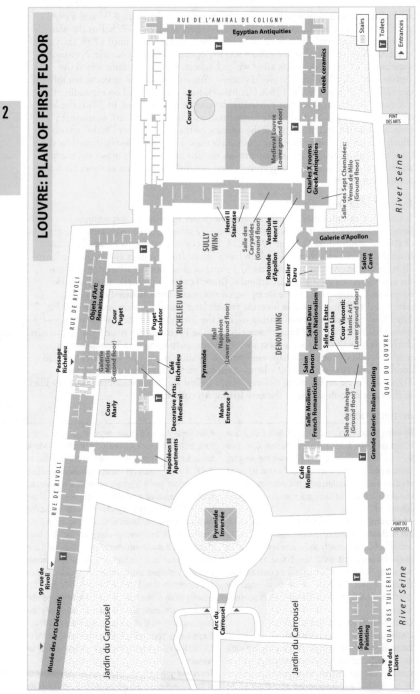

LOUVRE: PLAN OF FIRST FLOOR

RUE DE L'AMIRAL DE COLIGNY

Egyptian Antiquities

Greek ceramics

Cour Carrée

Medieval Louvre (Lower ground floor)

Charles X rooms; Greek Antiquities

Salle des Sept Cheminées; Venus de Milo (Ground floor)

River Seine

PONT DES ARTS

Henri II Staircase

SULLY WING

Salle des Caryatides (Ground floor)

Vestibule Henri II

Rotonde d'Apollon

Escalier Daru

Galerie d'Apollon

RICHELIEU WING

Objets d'Art: Renaissance

Cour Puget

Puget Escalator

Galerie Médicis (Second floor)

Café Richelieu

Passage Richelieu

RUE DE RIVOLI

Pyramide

Hall Napoléon (Lower ground floor)

Main Entrance ▲

DENON WING

Salon Carré

Salon Denon

Salle Daru: French Nationalism

Salle des Etats: Mona Lisa

Cour Visconti: Islamic Art (Lower ground floor)

QUAI DU LOUVRE

Decorative Arts: Medieval

Cour Marly

Napoléon III Apartments

RUE DE RIVOLI

Salle Mollien: French Romanticism

Salle du Manège (Ground floor)

Grande Galerie: Italian Painting

Café Mollien

PONT DU CARROUSEL

Jardin du Carrousel

Pyramide Inversée

99 rue de Rivoli

Musée des Arts Décoratifs

RUE DE RIVOLI

Arc du Carrousel

Jardin du Carrousel

QUAI DES TUILERIES

River Seine

Spanish Painting

Porte des Lions

2

Stairs

T Toilets

▲ Entrances

LOUVRE SURVIVAL TIPS

Tales of queues outside the Pyramide, miles of corridors and paparazzi-style jostles in front of the *Mona Lisa* can leave you feeling somewhat intimidated by the Louvre before you've even set foot in the place. Don't attempt to see too much – even if you spend the entire day here you'll only see a fraction of the collection. Arrive early or come for the evening openings; Thursday tends to be relatively quiet, though more sections than usual tend to close on this day. If you want to avoid the crowds, stay away from the busy Denon wing; after all, the Louvre is much more than just the Italian Renaissance and the *Mona Lisa*. Note also that **pickpocketing** is a significant problem, so be careful about how you carry your money and watch out for people trying to distract you, especially at the ticket machines.

---

not bookable in advance). Thematic trails for adults and children are available on request or can be downloaded and printed in advance from the website. Nintendo 3DS audioguides, with an interactive map, can be rented for €5 (ID required), or you can download the official Louvre Audioguide app (€1.79) onto your smartphone.

Eating The elegant *Café Richelieu* (first floor, Richelieu) has a wonderful summer-only terrace with a view of the Pyramide. *Café Mollien* (first floor, Denon) is the busiest and also has a summer terrace. *Café Denon* (lower ground floor, Denon) is cosy and classy. The various cafés and restaurants under the Pyramide itself are mostly noisy and unpleasant.

ORIENTATION

The Louvre has **three named wings**, each accessible from under the great pyramid: Denon (south), Richelieu (north) and Sully (east, around the giant quadrangle of the Cour Carrée). The exhibits are arranged in **themed sections**: Antiquities (Near Eastern, Egyptian and Greek/Roman); Painting; Sculpture; Decorative arts; Prints and drawings (exhibited on a temporary, rotational basis); Islamic art; and the Medieval Louvre. Some sections spread across two wings, or two floors of the same wing. Most visitors head straight to the **Denon wing**, whose first floor contains the *Mona Lisa* and Italian paintings, plus the great French nineteenth-century canvases and the stunning, gilded Galerie d'Apollon; its lower floors house the sublime Classical sculpture collection. Denon is the busiest part of the museum; a relatively peaceful alternative would be to focus on the grand chronologies of French painting and sculpture in the **Richelieu wing**, starting on the second floor. It's in Richelieu, too, that you'll find the dramatic, glazed-over courtyards, and the superb Decorative Arts section (first floor). Few visitors begin with the **Sully wing**, though it's well worth seeing the foundations of Philippe-Auguste's twelfth-century fortress on the lower ground floor, and there are also some rooms preserved from the original palace (see box, p.60).

Painting

The largest section by far is **Painting**. The Richelieu side of the museum houses the main French and Northern European painting collections, while the Italian, Spanish and large-scale nineteenth-century French works are found in Denon. Interspersed throughout are rooms dedicated to the Louvre's impressive collection of **prints and drawings**; these are exhibited in rotation, because of their vulnerability to the light.

French painting

The main chronological circuit of **French painting** begins on the second floor of the Richelieu wing, and continues right round the Cour Carrée in the Sully wing. It traces the extraordinary development of French painting from its edgy, pre-Renaissance beginnings through to Corot, whose airy landscapes anticipate Impressionism.

Medieval and Renaissance

Surprisingly few works predate the Renaissance. There are some intriguing portraits of French kings, notably the Sienese-style *Portrait of John the Good*, Jean Fouquet's pinched-looking *Charles VII* and Jean Clouet's two noble portraits of *François I*, the king who attracted numerous Italian artists to his court. Look out for the strange atmosphere of the two **Schools of Fontainebleau** (rooms 9 and 10), which were heavily influenced by Italian Mannerist painting. Two portraits of royal mistresses are provocatively erotic: from the First School of Fontainebleau (1530s), Henri II's mistress, Diane de Poitiers, is depicted semi-nude as the huntress Diana, while in a Second School piece from the 1590s, Gabrielle d'Estrées, the favourite of Henri IV, is shown sharing a bath with her sister, pinching her nipple as if plucking a cherry.

Classicism

It's not until the seventeenth century (rooms 12–16), when Poussin breaks onto the scene, that a definitively French style emerges. As the undisputed master of **French Classicism**, Poussin's grand themes, taken from antiquity and the Bible, were to influence generations of artists to come. *The Arcadian Shepherds*, showing four shepherds interpreting the inscription "Et in arcadia ego" ("I, too, in Arcadia"), has been taken to mean that death exists even in paradise. You'll need a healthy appetite for Classicism in the next suite of rooms, but there are some arresting portraits by Hyacinthe Rigaud, whose *Louis XIV* shows all the terrifying power of the king, and Philippe de Champaigne, whose portrait of his patron Cardinal Richelieu is even more imposing. The paintings of Georges de la Tour (rooms 28 and 29) and the three Le Nain brothers (look out for their *Denial of St Peter*, an intense work which was only acquired by the Louvre in 2010) are more idiosyncratic. De la Tour's *Card Sharp* is compelling for its uneasy poise and strange lack of depth, though his *Christ with Joseph in the Carpenter's Shop* is a more representative work, mystically lit by a single candle.

Rococo to Realist

After the Classical bombast of the likes of Le Sueur and Le Brun, the more intimate or movement-filled eighteenth-century **Rococo** paintings of Watteau come as a relief, as do Chardin's intense still lifes – notably *The Skate* – and the inspired sketches by

---

THE LOUVRE AS PALACE: AN ALTERNATIVE GUIDE

The Louvre is more than an art gallery: it is one of the greatest of France's royal palaces. To tour its historic rooms and galleries, many of which are stunningly decorated, take the entrance marked "**Sully**" in the Hall Napoléon. On the lowest level of the Sully wing you can continue through to the Louvre's medieval foundations (see p.601), or take the Henri II staircase – with its intertwined monograms H and D, for Henri and his mistress, Diane de Poitiers – up to the Renaissance Salle des Caryatides (see p.60) on the ground floor.

Up again, on the first floor, there's a succession of **finely decorated rooms**: the Vestibule Henri II, where the gilded, sixteenth-century ceiling is graced with George Braque's simple but stirring *The Birds* (room 33); the Salle des Bronzes (room 32), its huge ceiling painted a dazzling blue by Cy Twombly in 2010; the Salle des Sept Cheminées, once the royal bedroom (room 74); and the Rotonde d'Apollon (off room 34), built for Louis XIV by Le Vau, the architect of Versailles. Most stunning of all is the golden Galerie d'Apollon (room 66), its utterly splendid decor conceived by Charles Le Brun in 1661. It represents Louis XIV (the Sun King) as Apollo (the sun god); Eugène Delacroix added his *Apollo Slaying the Serpent Python* to the central medallion of the ceiling in 1851. It's particularly atmospheric at night. From here you can skirt the grand Escalier Daru (see p.56) to enter the Italian painting section, passing through the lofty Salon Carré (see p.56) on your way to the Grande Galerie (rooms 5, 8 and 12), which were originally built to link the Louvre and Tuileries palaces.

For **architectural gems** from the grand Third Empire remodelling, seek out the Salle du Manège on the ground floor of Denon (room A), and the Appartements Napoléon III on the first floor of Richelieu. For the lavish museum established for Charles X in the 1820s, visit the first floor of Sully (rooms 33–44); room 40, the Salle des Colonnes, has a fine mosaic floor and Neoclassical ceiling paintings of French monarchs by Antoine-Jean Gros. The highlights of I.M. Pei's 1980s makeover are the Pyramide and its strange twin, the Pyramide Inversée in the Carrousel du Louvre shopping complex; the two glazed-over courtyards of the Richelieu wing; and the magnificent escalator climbing alongside the Cour Puget. Don't miss the Cour Visconti, either, with its sinuous, new glass roof.

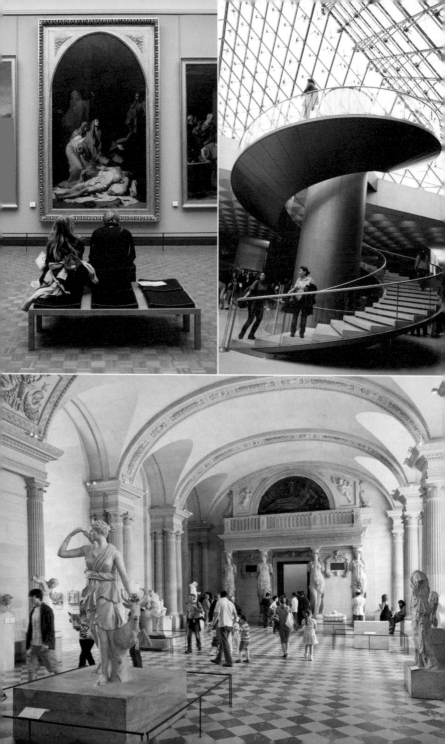

Fragonard known as the *Figures of Fantasy*, traditionally thought to have been completed in just one hour. From the southern wing of Sully to the end of this section, the chilly wind of **Neoclassicism** blows through the post-Revolution paintings of Gros, Gérard, Prud'hon, David and Ingres, contrasting with the more sentimental style that begins with Greuze, and continues into the **Romanticism** of Géricault and Delacroix, which largely supplanted the Neoclassical style from the 1820s onwards. Ingres' glassily exquisite portraits were understandably much in demand in his day, but modern visitors are much taken with his nudes: the bathers from 1808 and 1828, and the *Turkish Bath* (room 60), a painting at once sensuous and abstracted. The final set of rooms takes in Millet, Corot and the **Barbizon School** of painting, the precursor of Impressionism. For anything later than 1848, you'll have to head over to the Musée d'Orsay (see p.144).

Northern European painting

The western end of Richelieu's second floor is given over to a relatively selective collection of **German**, **Flemish** and **Dutch** paintings, though the seventeenth-century Dutch suite is strong, with no fewer than twelve paintings by Rembrandt – look out for *Bathsheba* and *The Supper at Emmaus* in room 31 – and two serene canvases from Vermeer, *The Astronomer* and *The Lacemaker*, in room 37. An awesome set of two dozen works by Rubens can be found in the **Galerie Médicis** (room 18), a stripped-down modern replica of a room originally in the Palais du Luxembourg (see p.140). The cycle is dedicated to the glory of Queen Marie de Médicis, as commissioned by herself. Rubens painted the entire 300 square metres of canvas himself, and his swirling colours and swathes of flapping cloth were to influence French painters from Fragonard to Delacroix.

Italian painting

The staggering **Italian collection** spreads across the first floor of the Denon wing, at the head of the Escalier Daru. Things begin well with two exquisite Botticelli frescoes painted for the Villa Lemmi near Florence. Next, the high-ceilinged **Salon Carré** (room 3) was used to exhibit contemporary paintings from the first exhibition or "salon" of the Académie Royale in 1725; it now displays the so-called Primitives, with thirteenth- to fifteenth-century works from Italian painters such as Giotto, Cimabue and Fra Angelico, as well as one of Uccello's bizarrely theoretical panels of the Battle of San Romano.

To the west of the Salon, the **Grande Galerie** stretches into the distance, a ribbon of pale, perfect parquet. On its walls, it parades all the great names of the Italian Renaissance, kicking off with Mantegna's opulent *Madonna of Victory* and his meticulous miniature of the Crucifixion, and continuing through Giovanni Bellini, Filippo Lippi, Raphael, Coreggio and Titian, in the first part of the gallery alone. Leonardo da Vinci's *Virgin of the Rocks*, *St John the Baptist* and *Virgin and Child with St Anne* are on display just after the first set of pillars, normally untroubled by crowds. The restored **Salle des Etats** (room 6) is the noisy, bustling setting for Leonardo da Vinci's **Mona Lisa** (see box opposite), as well as Paolo Veronese's vast *Marriage at Cana*, which once hung in the refectory of Venice's island monastery of San Giorgio Maggiore. Sadly, there's little chance to enjoy the other Venetian works nearby in peace, but you can walk through to the twin galleries of French Nationalism and Romanticism. A little further down the Grande Galerie, the Mannerists make their entrance with a wonderfully weird *St Anne with Four Saints* by Pontormo and a Rosso Fiorentino *Pietà*. From here on, the quality falls off.

Spanish painting

The relatively small **Spanish collection** is relegated to the far end of the Grande Galerie. There are a few gems, however, notably Murillo's tender *Beggar Boy*, and the *Marquise de Santa Cruz* among the Goya portraits. Zurbarán's *St Bonaventure Lying in State*

THE MONA LISA

The **Mona Lisa** receives some six million visitors a year. Reason enough to smile, maybe, but how did a small, rather dark sixteenth-century portrait acquire such unparalleled celebrity? It can't be Leonardo da Vinci's sheer excellence, as other virtuoso works of his hang nearby, largely ignored. Nor the painting's famously seductive air – even if Napoleon was so captivated that he had the picture hung in his bedroom in the Tuileries, there are other, far sexier portraits in the Louvre. (Sadly, the nude version Leonardo apparently painted has been lost for centuries, and is known only from early copies.) Instead, the answer lies in the painting's own story.

The English title is a corruption of *Monna* ("milady") Lisa, the title of the painting's (probable) subject, **Lisa Gherardini**. She was the wife of one Francesco del Giocondo. It's from his surname that the Italians get their name for the painting, *La Gioconda*, and the French their *La Joconde*, and it may even explain the *Mona Lisa*'s "smile", as *giocondo* means "light-hearted" in Italian. It is said that Lisa smiled because Leonardo employed singers and jesters to keep her happy while he painted.

The *Mona Lisa* probably came to France along with Leonardo himself, when he joined the service of François I. It remained largely neglected, however, until the mid-nineteenth century, when the poet Théophile Gautier described how the painting "mocks the viewer with such sweetness, grace and superiority that we feel timid, like schoolboys in the presence of a duchess". Then the English critic **Walter Pater** famously gushed that she is "expressive of what in the ways of a thousand years men had come to desire… She is older than the rocks among which she sits; like the vampire, she has been dead many times, and learned the secrets of the grave; and has been a diver in deep seas, and keeps their fallen day about her; and trafficked for strange webs with Eastern merchants … and all this has been to her but as the sound of lyres and flutes, and lives only in the delicacy with which it has moulded the changing lineaments, and tinged the eyelids and hands".

Pater made her famous, but the *Mona Lisa* only really went stellar when she was **stolen** by an Italian chancer and self-professed nationalist in August 1911. By the time the painting was recovered, in December 1913, that face had graced the pages of countless newspapers. Since then, celebrity has fed on itself, despite the complaints of art critics. Bernard Berenson, for example, decided she was "watchful, sly, secure, with a smile of anticipated satisfaction and a pervading air of hostile superiority"; Roberto Longhi called her a "wan fusspot". Still, she now faces more cameras every day than a well-dressed starlet on Oscar night.

Visitors today are sometimes unimpressed. The painting is surprisingly small (53x76cm, or 21x30 inches, to be exact) and fogged by filth – no art restorer has yet dared to propose actually working on the picture. Eventually, time may force the museum's hand, as the thin poplar panel the image is painted on is reported to be slowly warping. The new, air-conditioned glass frame – designed, appropriately, by a Milanese firm – may help. Meanwhile, if you can struggle past the crowds, the patina of fame and the dirt of centuries, you might just discover a strange and beautiful painting. If not, try the Leonardo portrait known as *La Belle Jardinière*, in the Grande Galerie, adjacent.

splendidly betrays the artist's obsession with cloth, and it's hard not to be beguiled by De Ribera's bittersweet portrait of *The Clubfoot*; the overwrought genius of El Greco's *Crucifixion*, meanwhile, is simply mind-blowing. From room 32, stairs lead down to the ground floor and the collection of art from Africa, Asia, Oceania and the Americas.

French Nationalism

Running parallel to the Grande Galerie are two giant rooms dedicated to post-Revolution **French Nationalism** and early to mid-nineteenth-century Romanticism. The plan labels this section "large-format French paintings", and it features some of the best-known French works. The Salle Daru (room 75) boasts David's epic *Coronation of Napoleon I*, in which Napoleon is shown crowning himself with a rather crestfallen clergy in the background; almost unbelievably, David conceived this work as part of a much larger composition. Nearby are some fine portraits of women, including Prud'hon's Leonardo-like *Josephine in the Park at Malmaison*, and some compellingly perfect canvases by Ingres.

Romanticism

Romanticism is heralded in the Salle Mollien (room 77) by Géricault's dramatic *Raft of the Medusa*, based on a notorious incident off the coast of Senegal in 1816. The survivors are seen despairing as a ship disappears over the horizon – as a survivor described it, "from the delirium of joy we fell into profound despondency and grief". The fifteen shown here were the last of 150 shipwrecked sailors who had escaped on the raft – thirst, murder and cannibalism having carried off the rest. The dead figure lying face down with his arm extended was modelled by Delacroix, whose *Liberty Leading the People* also hangs in this room; Delacroix's work is a famous icon of revolution, though you can tell by the hats that it depicts the 1830 revolution, which brought in the "bourgeois king" Louis-Philippe, rather than that of 1789. On seeing the painting, Louis-Philippe promptly ordered it to be kept out of sight so as not to give anyone dangerous ideas.

Sculpture

French sculpture fills the lowest two levels of the Richelieu wing, including the twin, glass-roofed courtyards. Cour Marly shelters the four triumphal Marly Horses, which once stood in the park at Marly-le-Roi: two were done by Coysevox for Louis XIV (the ones at the top of the stairs), and two by Costou for Louis XV. Cour Puget has Pierre Puget's dynamic *Milon de Crotone* as its agonizing centrepiece, the lion's claws tearing into Milon's apparently soft flesh.

The surrounding rooms trace French sculpture from painful Romanesque Crucifixions through to the lofty nineteenth-century works of David d'Angers. Don't miss the Burgundian *Tomb of Philippe Pot*, borne by hooded mourners known as *pleurants*, Michel Colombe's Italianate relief of *St George Slaying the Dragon*, or the distinctively French and strangely liquid bas-reliefs sculpted by Jean Goujon in the 1540s, at around the same time as he was working on Lescot's facade for the Cour Carrée. After a while, however, you may find yourself crying out for an end to all the gracefully perfect nudes and grandiose busts of noblemen. François Rude's charming *Neapolitan Fisherboy* provides some respite, but really the best antidote to all this is Rodin – and, unfortunately, his career postdates the Louvre's self-imposed 1848 cut-off, so you'll have to visit the Musée d'Orsay (see p.144) or Musée Rodin (see p.155) to explore his work.

Italian sculpture

The small, intense **Italian sculpture** section fills the long Galerie Michel Ange (room 4), on the ground and basement floors of Denon. Here you'll find such bold masterpieces as two of Michelangelo's torturedly erotic *Slaves*, Giambologna's airy *Flying Mercury*, the anonymous *Veiled Woman* and Canova's irresistible *Cupid and Psyche*. At the gallery's western end, the grand Escalier Mollien leads up towards the main Painting section (see p.53) while, immediately below, in the old stables on the lower ground floor (room 1), you'll find early Italian sculpture, notably Duccio's virtuoso *Virgin and Child Surrounded by Angels*, and the **Tactile Gallery**, where you can run your hands over copies of some of the most important sculptures from the collection. In the small adjacent rooms A to C you can seek out some severe but impressive **Gothic Virgins** from Flanders and Germany.

Decorative arts

The vast **Decorative arts** section (not to be confused with the separate **Les Arts Décoratifs** museum in the Louvre's westernmost wing; see p.60), on the first floor of the Richelieu wing, presents the finest tapestries, ceramics, jewellery and furniture commissioned by France's most wealthy and influential patrons, beginning with an exquisite little equestrian sculpture of Charlemagne (or possibly Charles the Bald) and continuing through 81 relentlessly superb rooms to a salon decorated in the style of

Louis-Philippe, the last king of France. Walking through the entire chronology gives a powerful sense of the evolution of aesthetic taste at its most refined and opulent, and numerous rooms have been partially re-created in the style of a particular epoch, so it's not hard to imagine yourself strutting through a Renaissance chamber or gracing an eighteenth-century salon, especially as whole suites are often devoid of other visitors. Towards the end, the circuit passes through the breathtaking **apartments** of Napoléon III's Minister of State (room 87), full of plush upholstery, immense chandeliers and dramatic ceiling frescoes, in true Second Empire style.

Antiquities

The enormous **Antiquities** collection offers an embarrassment of riches. The superb Egyptian and Near Eastern collections reflect the long-standing French fascination with both regions, while the outstanding Greek and Roman collections date back to the eager acquisitions of François I, Richelieu and Mazarin.

Near Eastern antiquities

Near Eastern antiquities (Richelieu wing, ground floor) covers the Mesopotamian, Sumerian, Babylonian, Assyrian and Phoenician civilizations, plus the art of ancient Persia. The highlight is the boldly sculpted stonework, much of it in relief. Watch out for the statues and busts depicting the young Sumerian prince Gudea, and the black, 2m-high Mesopotamian Code of Hammurabi, which dates from around 1800 BC. Standing erect like a warning finger, a series of royal precepts (the "code") is crowned with a stern depiction of the king meeting the sun god Shamash, dispenser of justice. The Cour Khorsabad, adjacent, is dominated by two giant Assyrian winged bulls (one is a reproduction) that once acted as guardians to the palace of Sargon II, from which many treasures were brought to the Louvre.

Egyptian antiquities

Jean-François Champollion, who translated the hieroglyphics of the Rosetta Stone, began collecting **Egyptian antiquities** for France, and the collection is now second only to Cairo's. Starting on the ground floor of the Sully wing, the thematic circuit leads up from the atmospheric crypt of the Sphinx (room 1) to the Nile, source of all life in Egypt, and takes the visitor through the everyday life of pharaonic Egypt by way of cooking utensils, jewellery, the principles of hieroglyphics, musical instruments, sarcophagi and a host of mummified cats. Upstairs, on the first floor, the chronological circuit keeps the masterpieces on the right-hand side, while pots and statuettes of more specialist interest are displayed to the left. Look out for the *Great Sphinx*, carved from a single block of pink granite; the polychrome statue *Seated Scribe*; the striking, life-size wooden statue of Chancellor Nakhti; a bust of Amenophis IV; and a low-relief sculpture of Sethi I and the goddess Hathor.

Greek and Roman antiquities

The magnificent collection of **Greek and Roman antiquities** brings together everything from the stylized Cycladic *Woman's Head* of around 2700–2300 BC, to the finest Roman marbles. On the ground floor of Denon, the handsomely vaulted **Salle du Manège** (room A) was built as a riding school for the short-lived son of Napoléon III, but now houses Italian Renaissance copies and restorations of antique sculptures. To the east of the adjoining vestibule, the grand **Galerie Daru** (room B) kicks off with the poised energy of Lysippos's *Borghese Gladiator*. At the eastern end of the gallery, Lefuel's imperial **Escalier Daru** rises triumphantly under the billowing, famous feathers of the recently restored *Winged Victory of Samothrace* towards the Italian painting section and the Grande Galerie. Skirting the staircase will take you to the **Etruscan and Roman** collections, with their beautiful mosaics and stunning, naturalistic frescoes.

2

Beyond, in the Sully wing, you enter Pierre Lescot's original sixteenth-century palace. In the **Salle des Caryatides** (room 17), which houses Roman copies of Greek works, the musicians' balcony is supported by four giant caryatids, sculpted in 1550 by Jean Goujon. Beyond, in the main Greek section of Sully, you'll find the graceful marble head known as the *Tête Kaufmann* (room 16) and the delightful *Venus of Arles* – both early copies of the work of the great sculptor Praxiteles. Up on the first floor, the gorgeous marble-and-gilt decor of rooms 32 to 44 dates from a museum created here for Charles X (see box, p.54). The works are primarily a daunting run of terracotta and ceramics.

Islamic art

In 2012, an entirely new section of the museum was opened in the central Cour Visconti – the **Islamic art collection**, the Louvre's eighth department, partly funded by Prince Alwaleed bin Talal of Saudi Arabia. In the museum's most daring architectural project since I.M. Pei's pyramid, the Cour Visconti has been covered over with an undulating, gold-filigree glass roof that seems to float in midair (it is supported by just eight slender columns). Suggesting for some the shimmering wings of an insect, for others a bedouin tent, a flying carpet or sand dunes, the roof is a fittingly stunning "crown" to the beautiful artworks below. Some three thousand objects are on display (out of an archive of 18,000 and many never before seen by the public), ranging from early Islamic inscriptions to intricate Moorish ivories, and from ninth-century Iraqi moulded glass to exquisite miniature paintings from the courts of Mughal India.

The collection is arranged on **two floors**: the ground floor, directly under the roof, which covers the seventh to eleventh centuries, and the rather darker lower floor ("*parterre*"), which continues up to the nineteenth century. Some of the objects challenge the usual clichés about Islamic art: for example, an exquisite ivory box, from tenth-century Spain, carved with hunting scenes and people collecting eggs and picking dates, disproves the popular belief that figurative depictions are forbidden in Islamic art, as do a nearby copper peacock vase from the same period and an elegant, twelfth-century bronze lion that would have served as a fountainhead in an Andalusian palace garden. Elsewhere there is evidence of the diversity of cultures that co-existed under Islamic rule: a wooden portal from Cairo, for example, bears Hebrew inscriptions, while a flabellum, or ceremonial fan, from twelfth-century Egypt depicting the Virgin and Child, would have been used by a Christian congregation.

The Medieval Louvre

For a complete change of scene, descend to the **Medieval Louvre** section, on the lower ground floor of Sully. The dramatic stump of Philippe-Auguste's keep soars up towards the enormous concrete ceiling like a pillar holding up the entire modern edifice, while vestiges of Charles V's medieval palace walls buttress the edges of the vast chamber. A similar but more intimate effect can be felt in the adjacent Salle St-Louis, with its carved pillars and vaults cut short by the modern roof.

Les Arts Décoratifs

Entrance at 107 rue de Rivoli, 1ᵉʳ • Tues, Wed & Fri–Sun 11am–6pm, Thurs 11am–9pm (late opening during exhibitions only) • €11; free to all under-18s and under-26s from (or studying in) most European countries • ☎ 01 44 55 57 50, ⓦ lesartsdecoratifs.fr

The westernmost wing of the Palais du Louvre, on the north side, houses a second, entirely separate museum called, simply, **Les Arts Décoratifs**. It's an umbrella for three separate museums: the revamped **Musée des Arts Décoratifs** focuses on "the art of design" or, more prosaically, the "applied arts", while fashion and advertising are showcased in the **Musée de la Mode et du Textile** and **Musée de la Publicité**.

Musée des Arts Décoratifs

The **Musée des Arts Décoratifs** centres on its grand "nave" on the first floor – an original feature of the building, which dates from the 1870s. It's used for temporary exhibitions. The second floor of the museum is occupied by a quartet of themed galleries. The **toys gallery** runs from wooden soldiers and china dolls to *Star Wars* figures and (playable) computer games. **Jewellery** focuses on twentieth-century designs, notably from the Art Nouveau jeweller René Lalique. A third gallery contains paintings by the "outsider" artist **Jean Dubuffet** (1901–85), while the **Galerie d'Etudes** houses clever, themed exhibitions – recent shows have included the use of trompe l'oeil in paintings, and the vogue for chinoiserie in the nineteenth century.

Medieval to Renaissance

At the museum's heart is the grand chronology of French furnishings, which begins on the third floor, with the rooms dedicated to furnishings and tapestries of the **Middle Ages** and **Renaissance**. The highlight is a reconstruction of a late fifteenth-century bedchamber, complete with original wall panelling, canopied bed, chairs and benches – even the door, fireplace and windows date from the period. The rooms covering the **seventeenth, eighteenth and nineteenth centuries** may represent the glory years of French furniture design, but the endless gilt cabinets, commodes and consoles can get a little wearisome. Look, again, for the reconstructed rooms. One shows off panelling installed in the Hôtel de Verrue in the 1720s, when the fashion for *singeries*, or frescoes themed around monkeys dressed in human clothing, was in full swing. Another, found on the terrace level overlooking the nave, is a reconstruction of the splendid panelling from the aptly named "golden study" of the Hôtel de Rochegude, at Avignon.

Art Nouveau to Philippe Starck

In the early twentieth century, French designers shaped the tastes of the world, and in this section of the museum (first, third and fourth floors, at the far end of the nave) it's easy to see why. There's a complete 1903 bedroom by Hector Guimard (the Art Nouveau designer behind the original Paris métro stations), a 1925 study by Pierre Chareau and an entire apartment created in the early 1920s by Armand-Albert Rateau for the *couturière* Jeanne Lanvin. On the first floor, the **Salon des Boiseries** shows off the best in French wood-panelling; check out, too, the **Salon du Bois**, a huge drawing room made for the 1900 Universal Exhibition by Georges Hoentschel.

The final part of the chronology takes you through a suite of interlinked rooms stacked inside the lofty **Pavillon Marsan** (with stunning views down the rue de Rivoli and over the Tuileries). You begin on the ninth floor with the 1940s, and end many, many designer chairs later on the fifth floor, with the contemporary collections. On the sixth floor, you'll find the original carriage design for the TGV high-speed train, and various podiums devoted to individual designers of the 1980s and 90s. **Philippe Starck**, for instance, is represented by five hyper-cool chairs, a stool, a mirror and a lampshade.

Musée de la Mode et du Textile and Musée de la Publicité

The eastern half of the museum, to the left of the main entrance, puts on exhibitions dedicated to fashion and advertising. These can be among the city's most innovative, as most shows are curated by industry professionals rather than state museum administrators. On the first and second floors, the **Musée de la Mode et du Textile** holds high-quality temporary exhibitions drawn from the large permanent collection. Recent shows have included "Fashion Unbuttoned", featuring some three thousand buttons by famous designers and artists. On the third floor, directly above, the **Musée de la Publicité** shows off its collection of advertising posters and video through cleverly themed, temporary exhibitions, which might feature, for example, Henri de Toulouse-Lautrec's posters of Montmartre nightlife. The space is appropriately trendy – exposed brickwork and steel panelling meets crumbling Louvre finery – and you can access the digital archive too.

ARC DE TRIOMPHE

The Champs-Elysées and around

Synonymous with glitz and glamour and studded with luxury hotels and high-end fashion boutiques, the Champs-Elysées sweeps through one of the city's most exclusive districts. The avenue in turn forms part of a grand 9km axis, extending from the Louvre at the heart of the city to the business district of La Défense in the west. With impressive vistas along its length, this axis, sometimes referred to as the Voie Triomphale (Triumphal Way), incorporates some of the city's most famous landmarks – the place de la Concorde, Tuileries gardens and the Arc de Triomphe. The whole ensemble is so regular and geometrical it looks as if it were laid out by a single town-planner rather than successive kings, emperors and presidents, all keen to add their stamp and promote French power and prestige.

Last to join the list was President Mitterrand (whose *grands projets* for the city outdid even Napoleon's) – his glass pyramid entrance to the Louvre (see p.51) and immense marble-clad cubic arch at La Défense (see p.229) effectively mark each end of the historic axis. The two great constructions echo each other in scale and geometry, with both aligned at the same slight angle away from the axis; certainly in the case of the Grande Arche, this was more pragmatic than aesthetic, its foundations having to be laid in an area riddled with tunnels for the métro and RER.

The Arc de Triomphe

Daily: April–Sept 10am–11pm; Oct–March 10am–10.30pm • €9.50 • ⓜ Charles-de-Gaulle-Etoile

The **Arc de Triomphe** towers up in the middle of place Charles-de-Gaulle, better known as place de l'Etoile, essentially a giant roundabout. The arch is modelled on the ancient Roman triumphal arches and is impressive in scale, memorably likened by Guy de Maupassant in his novel *Bel Ami* to "a shapeless giant on two monstrously large legs, that looks as if it's about to stride off down the Champs-Elysées". The arch was begun by Napoleon in 1806 in homage to his Grande Armée, but only completed in 1836 by Louis-Philippe, who dedicated it to the French army in general. Later, victorious German armies would make a point of marching through the arch to compound French humiliation. After the Prussians' triumphal march in 1871, Parisians lit bonfires beneath the arch and down the Champs-Elysées to eradicate the "stain" of German boots. Still a potent symbol of the country's military might, the arch is the starting point for the annual Bastille Day procession, a bombastic march-past of tanks, guns and flags.

Access to the arch is via underground stairs on the north corner of the Champs-Elysées. The names of 660 generals and numerous French battles are engraved on its inside, while reliefs adorn the exterior; the best is François Rude's extraordinarily dramatic *Marseillaise*, in which an Amazon-type figure personifying the Revolution charges forward with a sword, her face contorted in a fierce rallying cry. Climbing the 280 twisty, narrow steps to the top (there is a lift you can ask to use) rewards you with panoramic views, at their best towards dusk on a sunny day when the marble of the Grande Arche de la Défense sparkles in the setting sun and the Louvre is bathed in warm light. A **mini-museum** at the top of the arch screens relevant historical footage, including extraordinary images of Victor Hugo's funeral in 1885, when more than half the population of Paris turned out to pay their respects to the poet, his coffin mounted on a huge bier beneath the arch, draped in black velvet for the occasion.

The Champs-Elysées

Twelve avenues radiate out from place de l'Etoile (*étoile* meaning "star"), of which the best known is the **Champs-Elysées** ("Elysian Fields"). Tree-lined and broad, it sweeps down from the Arc de Triomphe towards the place de la Concorde. Close up it can be

---

THE TOMB OF AN UNKNOWN SOLDIER

A poignant ceremony is conducted every evening at 6.30pm at the foot of the Arc de Triomphe, when war veterans stoke up the flame at the **tomb of an unknown soldier**, killed in the Great War. Not even the Nazi occupation of Paris on June 14, 1940, could interrupt this sacred act. At 6.30pm that day, German troops gathering around the Arc de Triomphe were astonished to see two elderly French soldiers marching towards them in full dress uniform. The Germans instinctively stood to attention while Edmond Ferrand, the guardian of the Eternal Flame, and André Gaudin, a member of the flame's committee, solemnly saluted the tomb; the Germans, somewhat disconcerted, apparently followed suit.

a little disappointing, with its constant stream of traffic, its fast-food outlets and chain stores, though it has recently regained something of its former cachet. The avenue's renaissance started with a facelift in the mid-1990s, when the rows of trees the Nazis removed during World War II were replanted and pavements were refurbished. Luxury hotels subsequently moved in, and formerly dowdy shops underwent stylish makeovers. Now major fashion brands – including Banana Republic, Levi's, H&M and Marks and Spencer – have their flagship stores on the avenue. The southern side, where Louis Vuitton, Lanvin and the like flaunt their wares, is more sought after than the northern side. The area bounded by the Champs-Elysées and, to the south, avenue Montaigne and rue François 1er, is nicknamed the **Triangle d'Or** (Golden Triangle) on account of its high concentration of luxury hotels and flagship designer stores.

THE CHAMPS-ELYSÉES AND AROUND

● SHOPPING	
Le 66	11
Artcurial	14
Les Caves Augé	
Fnac	10
Fromagerie Alléosse	2
Hermès	6
Ladurée	13
Lanvin	7/8
Louis Vuitton	12
Marché aux Timbres	9
Marché Place des Ternes	3
Saint Laurent	5
Sonia Rykiel	4

■ BARS	
Pershing Lounge	4
Sir Winston	2
■ CLUBS	
Showcase	5
Zig Zag Club	3
■ LGBT CLUB	
Queen	1

■ ACCOMMODATION	
Le 123	5
Hôtel d'Albion	3
Hôtel Arioso	1
Le Bristol	4
Hôtel Lancaster	6
Hôtel Le Lavoisier	2
Hôtel de Sers	7

● CAFÉS AND WINE BARS	
Aubrac Corner	5
Le Café Jacquemart-André	
Le Fouquet's	4
● RESTAURANTS	
Al Ajami	7
Lasserre	9
La Maison de l'Aubrac	5
Mini Palais	10
Miss Kô	6
Pierre Gagnaire	3
Le Relais de l'Entrecôte	8
Taillevent	2

Brief history

The Champs-Elysées began life as a leafy promenade, an extension of the Tuileries gardens. It became fashionable during the Second Empire when the *haute bourgeoisie* built splendid mansions along its length and high society came to stroll and frequent the cafés and theatres. Most of the mansions finally gave way to office blocks and the *beau monde* moved elsewhere, but remnants of the avenue's heyday live on at the *Lido* cabaret, *Fouquet's* café-restaurant (see p.272), the perfumier Guerlain's shop, occupying an exquisite 1913 building, and the former *Claridges* hotel, now a swanky shopping arcade, the Galerie du Claridge. One of the most opulent of the mid-nineteenth-century mansions also survives: *La Paiva* restaurant at no. 25 was once home to the famous courtesan, La Païva, whose bathroom alone, it is said, was worthy of a Sultana in the *Arabian Nights*.

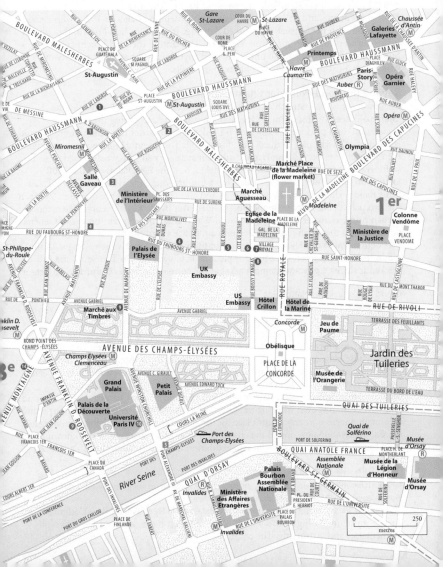

The Champs-Elysées occupies an important place in the national psyche and is a rallying point at times of crisis and celebration; crowds thronged here to greet Général de Gaulle as he walked down the avenue just after the Liberation in May 1944 and many turned out to support him again in 1968 in the wake of the student riots; while around a million Parisians congregated here in 1998 after France won the World Cup.

Théâtre des Champs-Elysées

15 av Montaigne • ☎ 01 49 52 50 50, ⓦ theatrechampselysees.fr • Ⓜ Alma-Marceau

At the bottom of avenue Montaigne is the **Théâtre des Champs-Elysées**, one of the city's premier concert halls (see p.318). Erected in 1913, it was among the first buildings in Paris to be made of reinforced concrete, its exterior softened with marble reliefs by the sculptor Bourdelle, a student of Rodin. The theatre has seen a number of notable premieres and debuts, including that of Josephine Baker in 1925, who created a sensation with her sensual, abandoned dancing. It's perhaps best known, though, for being the scene of great uproar on May 29, 1913, during the world premiere of Stravinsky's *Rite of Spring*, the unprecedented rhythmic and harmonic ferocity of which provoked loud catcalls and fights in the stalls.

Beyond the Rond-Point des Champs-Elysées

The lower – eastern – stretch of the Champs-Elysées between the **Rond-Point des Champs-Elysées** (whose Lalique glass fountains disappeared during the German occupation) and place de la Concorde is bordered by chestnut trees and flowerbeds, and is the most pleasant part of the avenue for a stroll. The gigantic building with grandiose Neoclassical exterior, glass roofs and exuberant statuary rising above the greenery to the south is the **Grand Palais**, created with its neighbour, the **Petit Palais**, for the 1900 **Exposition Universelle**. The Petit Palais has a fine arts museum, while the Grand Palais hosts major exhibitions and special events and also contains a science museum. Between the two palaces lies **place Clemenceau**, presided over by statues of Georges Clemenceau, French prime minister at the end of World War I, and a more recent bronze of Général de Gaulle. To the north of place Clemenceau, police guard the high walls around the presidential **Palais de l'Elysée** and the line of ministries and embassies ending with the US in prime position on the corner of place de la Concorde. On Thursdays and at weekends there's a **postage-stamp market** at the corner of avenues Gabriel and Marigny.

Grand Palais: Galeries Nationales

Av Winston Churchill, 8ᵉ; Galeries Nationales entry at 3 av du Général-Eisenhower • Opening times vary, but usually Mon, Thurs, Sat & Sun 10am–8pm, Wed & Fri 10am–10pm • Usually €12–13, though prices vary • ☎ 01 44 13 17 17, ⓦ grandpalais.fr • Ⓜ Champs-Elysées-Clemenceau

The 45m-high glass cupola of the **Grand Palais** can be seen from most of the city's viewpoints and forms the centrepiece of the *nef* (nave), a huge, impressive exhibition space, whose glass-and-steel ceiling allows light to flood the interior. After a lengthy restoration project (due for completion in 2017), the *palais* has resumed its role as the city's premier special-events venue, hosting music festivals and art exhibitions – including the prestigious annual art fair, **FIAC** (ⓦ fiac.com), in October – as well as trade fairs and fashion shows; while its restaurant, the *Mini Palais* (see p.274), with its grand colonnaded terrace, is an elegant place for dinner. In the west wing of the building are the **Galeries Nationales**, one of the city's major exhibition spaces and well known for its blockbuster shows, such as the Picasso exhibition in 2016 (book online in advance).

Grand Palais: Palais de la Découverte

Av Franklin D. Roosevelt, 8ᵉ • Tues–Sat 9.30am–6pm, Sun 10am–7pm • €9, combined ticket with planetarium €12 • ☎ 01 56 43 20 20, ⓦ palais-decouverte.fr • Ⓜ Champs-Elysées-Clemenceau/Franklin-D.-Roosevelt

The Grand Palais' eastern wing houses the **Palais de la Découverte**, Paris's original science museum, dating from 1937. It covers physics, biology, chemistry, geography, mathematics and astronomy. The emphasis is, as the name suggests, very much on discovery and experiment; there are plenty of interactive exhibits and working models to help you explore the properties of electromagnets, for example, or find out how ants and spiders communicate, and around forty live experiments are conducted throughout the day. There are also engaging temporary exhibitions on subjects as diverse as dinosaurs, clay and climate change, as well as an excellent **planetarium**.

Petit Palais: Musée des Beaux Arts de la Ville de Paris

Av Winston Churchill, 8ᵉ • Tues–Sun 10am–6pm; monthly concerts 12.30pm (arrive 30min beforehand to collect your free ticket) • Free • ☎ 01 53 43 40 00, ⓦ petitpalais.paris.fr • Ⓜ Champs-Elysées-Clemenceau

The **Petit Palais**, facing the Grand Palais on avenue Winston Churchill, holds the **Musée des Beaux Arts de la Ville de Paris**. It's hardly "petit", but it's certainly palatial, with its highly decorated Neoclassical exterior, interior garden with Tuscan colonnade, beautiful spiral wrought-iron staircases and a grand gallery on the lines of Versailles' Hall of Mirrors. The museum's extensive holdings of paintings, sculpture and decorative artworks are displayed on two floors and range from the ancient Greek and Roman period up to the early twentieth century. At first sight it looks like it's mopped up the leftovers after the city's other galleries have taken their pick, but there are some real gems here, such as Monet's *Soleil couchant sur la Seine à Lavacourt*, Courbet's provocative *Demoiselles du bord de la Seine* and Pissarro's delicate *Le Pont Royal et le Pavillon de Flore*, painted a few months before he died. Decorative arts feature strongly, especially eighteenth-century furniture and porcelain, including a whimsical clock decorated with a monkey orchestra in Meissen china. There's also fantasy Art Nouveau jewellery, an elegant pear-wood dining room designed by Hector Guimard (who also designed the original Paris métro stations), Russian icons and a fine collection of seventeenth-century Dutch landscape painting. Changing exhibitions allow the museum to display works from its vast reserves. There's a smart **café** which opens out onto the interior garden, plus free monthly classical music **concerts** on a Thursday lunchtime (see website).

South of the Arc de Triomphe

Heading **south of the Arc de Triomphe** down avenues Kléber or d'Iéna, both lined with imposing mansion blocks, will take you to the Trocadéro quarter (see p.156). En route you could take in one or two smaller sights such as the **Musée Dapper** and the **Galerie-Musée Baccarat**.

Musée Dapper

35 rue Paul-Valéry, 16ᵉ • Mon, Wed & Fri–Sun 11am–7pm • €6 • ☎ 01 45 00 91 75, ⓦ dapper.fr • Ⓜ Victor Hugo/Kléber

The small and intimate **Musée Dapper**, specializing in tribal art from sub-Saharan Africa, puts on well-thought-out and fascinating exhibitions on themes such as initiation ceremonies, carnivals, and rites and traditions associated with eating and drinking. Masks, wooden sculptures and other artefacts, usually accompanied by videos, are well displayed in darkened rooms. Exhibitions usually run from mid-October to mid-July (the museum is closed between exhibitions). The downstairs café and bookshop are also worth a detour.

Galerie-Musée Baccarat

11 place des Etats-Unis, 16ᵉ • Mon & Wed–Sat 10am–6.30pm • €7 • ☎ 01 40 22 11 00, ⓦ baccarat.fr • Ⓜ Boissière

The **Galerie-Musée Baccarat** is a small museum displaying some exquisite examples of Baccarat crystal glassware. It occupies the first floor of a grand mansion, once owned by Vicomtesse de Noailles, renowned patron of the Surrealists, and now the headquarters of the Maison Baccarat. An air of opulence reigns in the red-carpeted entrance hall and upstairs rooms, redesigned by Philippe Starck in Neo-Rococo style. The items on display include Art Deco perfume bottles, ornate glassware commissioned for Tsar Nicholas ll, sketches of designs for elaborate candelabras and chandeliers, and items made for the Universal Exhibitions of the 1860s and 70s, such as an elephant-shaped decanter. You can also peek into the adjoining restaurant, *Le Cristal Room*, to admire the lavish decor.

Quartier Monceau

North of the Arc de Triomphe, the 16^e and 17^e arrondissements are somewhat cold and soulless, their huge, fortified apartments empty much of the time. Further east, however, the **Quartier Monceau** has more to offer, with its attractive park and honey-coloured stone mansions, ornamented with pilasters, caryatids and elaborate mouldings. These aristocratic buildings are the legacy of the building boom in the 1860s – for the Second Empire's newly rich financiers and property developers, the ultimate status symbol was a mansion on the plaine de Monceau. As much money was lavished on the interiors, with many amassing fine collections of furniture and art – some of these collections have been preserved and now make for rewarding museums: the **Musée Cernuschi**, the **Musée Nissim de Camondo** and, most magnificent of all, the **Musée Jacquemart-André**.

Parc Monceau

Ⓜ Monceau • Daily: May–Aug 7am–10pm; Sept–April 7am–8pm

Surrounded by grand houses, **Parc Monceau** is an informal, English-style park, with undulating lawns, rock gardens, a moss-grown, mock-Classical colonnade and statues of brooding, French Romantic poets. It also has a children's playground and makes a nice spot for a picnic.

Musée Cernuschi

7 av Velásquez, 8e • Tues–Sun 10am–6pm • Free • ☏ 01 53 96 21 50, Ⓦ cernuschi.paris.fr • Ⓜ Monceau/Villiers

The **Musée Cernuschi** houses a small collection of Far Eastern art, mainly ancient Chinese, bequeathed to the state by the banker Cernuschi, who nearly lost his life for giving money to the insurrectionary Commune of 1871, and in whose elegant mansion the museum is housed. A grand staircase takes you up to the permanent collection on the first floor, where there are some exquisite pieces, including a selection of ceremonial jade objects dating from 3000 BC, highly worked bronzes from the Shang era (1550–1005 BC) and some unique ceramics detailing everyday life in ancient China. On the mezzanine, among a collection of Buddhas and other statuary, a beautiful, sinuous figure playing a lute, dating from the Wei dynasty, stands out.

Musée Nissim de Camondo

63 rue de Monceau, 8e • Wed–Sun 10am–5.30pm • €9 • ☏ 01 45 63 26 32 • Ⓜ Monceau/Villiers

Beside the Musée Cernuschi, the **Musée Nissim de Camondo** has an impressive collection of eighteenth-century decorative art and painting, built up by Count Moïse de Camondo, son of a wealthy Sephardic Jewish banker who emigrated from Istanbul to Paris in the late nineteenth century. To provide a showcase for his treasures, the count commissioned a mansion in eighteenth-century style, modelled on Versailles' Petit Trianon. The **ground-floor rooms** overflow with Gobelin tapestries, paintings of pastoral scenes by Huet and Vigée-Lebrun, gilded furniture and delicate Sèvres porcelain; an excellent free audioguide helps you get the most out of the exhibits. The **upper-floor rooms**, where the family spent most of their time, are more homely; here and there some of the anachronistic mod-cons of an early twentieth-century aristocratic home surface, such as the count's well-appointed bathroom. These rooms take on a progressively melancholy air, however, as you learn more about the Camondos and their fate: after a few years of marriage Moïse's wife left him for the head groom; his beloved son, Nissim, after whom the museum is named, died on a flying mission in World War I, while his remaining child, Béatrice, perished together with her children in the concentration camps in World War II.

Musée Jacquemart-André

158 bd Haussmann, 8ᵉ • Daily 10am–6pm • €12 • ☎ 01 45 62 11 59, 🖥 musee-jacquemart-andre.com • Ⓜ Miromesnil/St-Philippe-du-Roule

A few blocks south of the Parc de Monceau stands the lavishly ornamented palace of the nineteenth-century banker and art-lover Edouard André and his wife, society portraitist Nélie Jacquemart. Built in 1870 to grace Baron Haussmann's grand new boulevard, the Hôtel André is now the **Musée Jacquemart-André**, housing the couple's impressive art collection and a fabulous *salon de thé* (see p.272). Bequeathed to the Institut de France by Edouard's widow, the Hôtel André deploys the couple's collection exactly as they ordained. Nélie painted Edouard's portrait in 1872 – on display in what were their private apartments on the ground floor – and nine years later they were married, after which Nélie gave up her painting career and the pair devoted their spare time to collecting art. Their preference for **Italian art** is evident in the stunning collection of fifteenth- and sixteenth-century genius, including the works of Tiepolo, Botticelli, Donatello, Mantegna and Uccello, which form the core of the collection. Almost as compelling as the interior and art collection is the insight gleaned into an extraordinary marriage and grand nineteenth-century lifestyle, brought to life by the fascinating narration on the free audioguide.

Ground floor

In Room 1, mostly eighteenth-century French paintings are displayed, including several portraits by **Boucher**, in addition to two lively paintings of Venice by Canaletto. Room 2, the reception area, has specially constructed folding doors which, when opened, transformed the space into a ballroom large enough to hold a thousand guests. Room 3 contains three huge tapestries depicting Russian scenes that capture the fashion for Slav exoticism of the mid-eighteenth century. Room 6, formerly the library, focuses on Dutch and Flemish paintings, including three by **Van Dyck** and two by **Rembrandt**. Room 7 is the Salon de Musique (and the other half of the ballroom), its dramatic high ceiling decorated with a mural by Pierre Victor Galant; the musicians would play from the gallery, and you're treated to a mini-concert on the audioguide as you gaze at the ceiling. In Room 8, a huge, animated fresco by **Tiepolo**, depicting the French king Henri III being received by Federico Contarini in Venice, graces the extraordinary marble, bronze and wrought-iron, double spiral staircase that leads from an **interior garden** of palm trees up to the musicians' gallery. Room 9, once the smoking room, where the men would retreat after dinner, is hung with the work of eighteenth-century English portraitists, among them **Joshua Reynolds**.

First floor

Leading off the music gallery, **on the first floor**, are the rooms in which the couple displayed their **early Italian Renaissance collection**. The first, a sculpture gallery, its walls covered in low-relief carvings, includes three bronzes by **Donatello**. The Florentine room next door includes a wonderful, brightly coloured *Saint George Slaying the Dragon* (1440) by **Uccello**, a **Botticelli** *Virgin and Child* (1470) depicted with touching fragility, and an exquisite, sixteenth-century inlaid choir-stall. Adjacent is the Venetian room, with paintings by **Bellini** and **Mantegna** among others.

Place de la Concorde

At the eastern end of the Champs-Elysées lies the grand, pleasingly harmonious **place de la Concorde**, marred only by its constant stream of traffic. Its centrepiece is a gold-tipped obelisk from the temple of Ramses at Luxor, given by Mohammed Ali to Louis-Philippe in 1831, and flanked by two ornate bronze fountains, modelled on those in St Peter's Square, Rome. The square's history is much less harmonious than its name "Concorde" suggests. The equestrian statue of Louis XV that formerly stood at the centre of the

was toppled in 1792, and between 1793 and 1795, 1300 people died here
the revolutionary guillotine, including Louis XVI, Marie-Antoinette, Danton
Robespierre. When deciding later what to put in place of Louis XV's statue,
Louis-Philippe thought the obelisk would be ideal – having no political message, it
wasn't likely ever to be demolished or become the focus of popular discontent. It was
erected with much pomp in October 1836 in the presence of 200,000 spectators, while
an orchestra played tunes from Bellini's *I Puritani*.

From the centre of the square there are magnificent views of the Champs-Elysées and
Tuileries, and you can admire the symmetry of the Assemblée Nationale, on the far side
of the Seine, with the church of the Madeleine at the end of rue Royale to the north.
The Neoclassical *Hôtel Crillon* and its twin, the Hôtel de la Marine, housing the
Ministry of the Navy, flank the entrance to rue Royale, which meets the Champs-
Elysées at a right angle.

3 Jardin des Tuileries

Extending for around 1km from the place de la Concorde to the Louvre, the **Jardin des
Tuileries** is the formal French garden *par excellence*. The grand central alley is lined
with clipped chestnuts and manicured lawns, and framed by ornamental ponds.
Surrounding these is an impressive gallery of statues (by the likes of Rodin, Coustou
and Coysevox), many brought here from Versailles and Marly (Louis XIV's retreat from

THE LOST PALAIS DES TUILERIES

For much of its life, the Louvre stood facing a twin sister, the **Palais des Tuileries**. Built in 1559
for **Catherine de Médicis** shortly after the accidental death of her husband, Henri II, it was a
place where she could maintain her political independence while wielding power on behalf of
her sickly son, François II. It was apparently Catherine herself who conceived the idea of linking
the two palaces with a *grande galerie* running along the right bank of the Seine, but in 1572
she abandoned the entire project. Tradition has it that she was warned by a soothsayer to
"beware of St-Germain" if she wanted to live into old age – and the Tuileries lay in the parish of
St-Germain l'Auxerrois. It's more likely that the palace's location just outside the protection of
the city walls was the problem, as 1572 was a dangerous year: on August 24, the bells of
St-Germain l'Auxerrois rang out according to a prearranged signal, whereupon radical
Catholics set about the murder of some three thousand Parisian Protestants, possibly under
the secret orders of Catherine herself.

It wasn't until forty years after the St Bartholomew's Day Massacre that the two palaces
were finally linked, in the reign of Henri IV. Louis XIV moved across from the Louvre in 1667,
but the court soon departed for Versailles, and the Tuileries remained largely empty until the
Revolution, when Louis XVI was kept under virtual house arrest there by the revolutionary mob
until the *sans-culottes* finally lost patience on June 20, 1792, breaking in and forcing the king to
don the revolutionary red bonnet. The Tuileries was revived under Napoleon, who built the
Arc du Carrousel facing its central pavilion, and its status grew still greater under his nephew,
Napoléon III, who finally united both royal palaces around a single gigantic courtyard, the
whole complex being dubbed the Cité Impériale. This glorious perfection didn't last long:
the Tuileries was set alight by the revolutionary Communards as they lost control of the city in
May 1871 (see p.186).

The ruins of the Tuileries were cleared away and replaced by the **Jardin du Carrousel**. A
recent campaign to rebuild the Tuileries palace attracted frenzied press attention, but so far
has drawn a rather negative response from the Ministry of Culture. It isn't just the estimated
€350 million cost that's the problem, nor rebuilding a sixteenth-century palace to a high
enough standard, nor how such a building would "traumatize" the architectural setting which
has been created in the last hundred years, blocking off the grand axis which extends all the
way from the Pyramide to La Défense. The true problem is undoubtedly the political
awkwardness of resurrecting such a powerful royalist symbol.

Versailles, no longer in existence), though a number are copies, with the originals in the Louvre. The much-sought-after chairs strewn around the ponds make good bases for admiring the surroundings, and there are also a number of cafés nestling among the trees. Flanking the garden at the western Concorde end, are two Neoclassical buildings: the **Musée de l'Orangerie** art gallery, by the river, and the **Jeu de Paume**, the city's premier photographic exhibition space, by the rue de Rivoli. At the eastern end of the gardens in front of the Louvre is the **Jardin du Carrousel**, a raised terrace where the **Palais des Tuileries**, burnt down by the Communards in 1871, once stood (see box opposite). It's now planted with yew hedges, interspersed with bronzes of buxom female nudes by Maillol.

Brief history

The garden originated in the 1570s when **Catherine de Médicis** had the site cleared of the medieval warren of tile manufacturers (*tuileries*) that stood here to make way for a palace and grounds (see box opposite). The Palais des Tuileries, as it became known, was surrounded by formal vegetable gardens, a labyrinth and a chequerboard of flowerbeds. The present layout, however, is largely the work of the landscape architect **Le Nôtre**, who was commissioned by Louis XIV a hundred years later to redesign the gardens on a grander scale. Employing techniques he later perfected at Versailles, Le Nôtre took the opportunity to indulge his passion for symmetry, straight avenues, formal flowerbeds and splendid vistas. During the eighteenth century, the gardens were where chic Parisians came to preen and party, and in 1783 the Montgolfier brothers, Joseph and Etienne, launched the first successful hot-air balloon here. Serious replanting was carried out after the Revolution, and in the nineteenth century rare species were added to the garden, which was by now dominated by chestnut trees.

Jeu de Paume

1 place de la Concorde, 1ᵉʳ • Tues 11am–9pm, Wed–Sun 11am–7pm • €10 • ☎ 01 47 03 12 50, ⓦ jeudepaume.org • Ⓜ Concorde

The **Jeu de Paume** was once a royal (indoor) tennis court and the place where French Impressionist paintings were displayed before being transferred to the Musée d'Orsay. Since 2004 it's been a major exhibition space dedicated to photography and video art. It's not as well lit as you might expect from the soaring, light-filled foyer, but it's one of the top venues for major retrospectives of photographers such as Martin Parr and Edward Steichen. There's also a small café and a good bookshop.

Musée de l'Orangerie

Jardin des Tuileries, 1ᵉʳ • Mon & Wed–Sun 9am–6pm • €9; book in advance as queues can be long • ☎ 01 44 77 80 07, ⓦ musee-orangerie.fr • Ⓜ Concorde

Opposite the Jeu de Paume is the **Musée de l'Orangerie**, an elegant, Neoclassical-style building, originally designed to protect the Tuileries' orange trees, and now housing a private art collection including eight of **Monet**'s giant water lily paintings. Displayed in two oval rooms, flooded with natural light, these vast canvases were executed in the last years of the artist's life, when he almost obsessively painted the pond in his garden at Giverny, attempting to capture the fleeting light and changing colours.

On the lower floor is a rather fine collection of paintings by Monet's contemporaries. Highlights include some **Cézanne** still lifes, portraits and landscapes, including *Le Rocher rouge*, in which the intense colours seem to vibrate and shimmer. **Renoir** is represented by some sensuous nudes and touching studies of children, such as *Jeunes filles au piano*, the two girls' rapt concentration on the music wonderfully conveyed. There are fine works by **Picasso** and **Matisse**; the latter's *Les Trois Soeurs* stands out for its striking portrayal of three women, the simplicity of line and colour reminiscent of a Japanese print. Space is also devoted to works by **Derain**, including some iridescent nudes and vibrant landscapes, and **Soutine**'s more expressionistic canvases.

3

GALERIE VIVIENNE

The Grands Boulevards and *passages*

Built on the site of the city's old ramparts, the Grands Boulevards stretch from the Madeleine in the west to the Bastille in the east. Once fashionable thoroughfares where "le tout Paris" came to seek entertainment, they're still a vibrant part of the city, with their brasseries, theatres and cinemas. The streets off the Grands Boulevards constitute the city's main commercial and financial district, incorporating the solid institutions of the Banque de France and the Bourse, while to the northwest is the glittering Opéra Garnier. Well-heeled shopping is concentrated on rue St-Honoré and around place Vendôme, and to the south, the Palais Royal gardens provide a retreat from the traffic. Threading their way throughout the district are the *passages* – delightful shopping arcades, full of old-fashioned charm.

The Grands Boulevards

The **Grands Boulevards** is the collective name given to the eight streets that form one continuous thoroughfare running from the Madeleine to République, then down to the Bastille. Lined with classic nineteenth-century apartment blocks, imposing banks, cinemas, theatres, brasseries and neon-lit fast-food outlets, the Grands Boulevards are busy and vibrant. They are not, however, the most alluring or fashionable parts of Paris – though this was not always so. As recently as the 1950s, a visitor to Paris would, as a matter of course, have gone for a stroll along the Grands Boulevards to see "*Paris vivant*". Something of this tradition still survives in the brasseries, cafés, theatres and cinemas, including the Max Linder and Rex, the latter an extraordinary building inside and out (see p.311).

Brief history

The **western section** of the Grands Boulevards, from the Madeleine to Porte St-Denis, follows the rampart built by Charles V in the mid-fourteenth century. When its defensive purpose became redundant with the offensive foreign policy of Louis XIV in the seventeenth century, the walls were pulled down and the ditches filled in, leaving a wide promenade. However, it wasn't until the nineteenth century that the boulevards became a fashionable place to be seen; Parisians came in droves to stroll and frequent the numerous cafés. The chic café customers of the west-end **boulevard des Italiens** set the trends for all of Paris in terms of manners, dress and conversation, and it was a hotbed of intellectual debate and ferment.

The **eastern section** developed a more colourful reputation, derived from its association with street theatre, mime artists, jugglers, puppet shows and cafés of ill repute, earning itself the nickname the "*boulevard du Crime*", immortalized in the 1945 film *Les Enfants du Paradis*. Some of this area was swept away in the latter half of the nineteenth century by Baron Haussmann's huge place de la République (see p.198).

It was at **14 boulevard des Capucines**, in the Grand Café (now the *Hôtel Scribe*), in 1895, that Paris saw its first film, or animated photography, as the **Lumière brothers'** invention was called. Some years earlier, in 1874, another artistic revolution had taken place at **no. 35** in the former studio of photographer Félix Nadar – the first **Impressionist exhibition**, greeted with outrage by the art world; one critic said of Monet's *Impression, soleil levant* ("Impression: sunrise"), "it was worse than anyone had hitherto dared to paint".

Grévin

10 bd Montmartre, 9ᵉ • Hours vary, but usually Mon–Fri 10am–6.30pm, Sat & Sun 10am–7pm; last admission 1hr before closing • €23.50, children €16.50; see website for special offers • ☎ 01 47 70 85 05, ⓦ grevin.com • Ⓜ Grands Boulevards

A remnant from the fun-loving times on the Grands Boulevards is the waxworks museum, the **Grévin**. You can have your photo taken next to Isabelle Adjani, Omar Sy, Zlatan Ibrahimovic and many other French and international celebrities, but perhaps the best thing about the museum is its rooms: the magical Palais des Mirages (Hall of Mirrors), built for the Exposition Universelle in 1900; the theatre with its sculptures by Bourdelle; and the 1882 Baroque-style Hall of Columns.

Opéra Garnier

Cnr rues Scribe and Auber, 9ᵉ • **Interior** Available for visits daily 10am–5pm • €10 • **Performances** See p.319 • ⓦ operadeparis.fr • Ⓜ Opéra

Set back from boulevard des Capucines is the dazzling Opéra de Paris – usually referred to as the **Opéra Garnier** to distinguish it from the newer opera house at the Bastille (see p.109). Constructed between 1865 and 1872 as part of Napoléon III's vision for Paris, it crowns the long, rather monotonous avenue de l'Opéra. The architect, Charles Garnier, whose golden bust by Carpeaux can be seen on the rue Auber side, drew on a number of existing styles and succeeded in creating a fantastically ornate building the like of which Paris had never seen before – when the Empress Eugénie asked in bewilderment what style it was, Garnier replied that it was "Napoléon III style". Certainly, if any building can be said to exemplify the Second Empire, it is this – in its show of wealth,

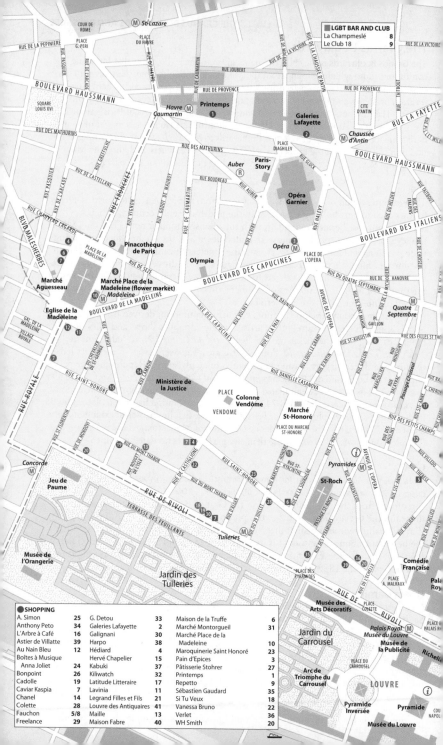

LGBT BAR AND CLUB
La Champmeslé 8
Le Club 18 9

SHOPPING

A. Simon	25	G. Detou	33	Maison de la Truffe	6
Anthony Peto	34	Galeries Lafayette	2	Marché Montorgueil	31
L'Arbre à Café	16	Galignani	30	Marché Place de la
Astier de Villatte	39	Harpo	38	Madeleine	10
Au Nain Bleu	12	Hédiard	4	Maroquinerie Saint Honoré	23
Boîtes à Musique		Hervé Chapelier	15	Pain d'Epices	3
Anna Joliet	24	Kabuki	37	Pâtisserie Stohrer	27
Bonpoint	26	Kiliwatch	32	Printemps	1
Cadolle	19	Latitude Litteraire	17	Repetto	9
Caviar Kaspia	7	Lavinia	11	Sébastien Gaudard	35
Chanel	14	Legrand Filles et Fils	21	Si Tu Veux	18
Colette	28	Louvre des Antiquaires	41	Vanessa Bruno	22
Fauchon	5/8	Maille	13	Verlet	36
Freelance	29	Maison Fabre	40	WH Smith	20

THE GRANDS BOULEVARDS AND PASSAGES

■ ACCOMMODATION
Hôtel Brighton	7
Hôtel Chopin	1
Costes	4
Hôtel Crayon	9
Hôtel Edgar	3
Le Relais Saint-Honoré	6
Hôtel Thérèse	5
Hôtel Tiquetonne	8
Hôtel Vivienne	2

■ BARS
Bar Costes	7
La Conserverie	4
Delaville Café	2
Lockwood	6

■ CLUBS
Rex Club	3
Social Club	5

■ LIVE MUSIC
Au Limonaire	1
Social Club	5

● CAFÉS AND WINE BARS
Angélina	19
Le Café des Initiés	21
Café de la Paix	3
Floquifil	1
Frenchie Bar à Vins	8
Frenchie To Go	10
Ladurée	14
Legrand Filles et Fils	7
A Priori Thé	11
Racines	2
Le Rubis	15
Verlet	20

● RESTAURANTS
L'Ardoise	13
Bistrot des Victoires	17
Drouant	6
L'Epi d'Or	22
Frenchie	9
Gallopin	5
Higuma	12
Aux Lyonnais	4
Le Meurice	18
Verjus	16

ambition and hint of vulgarity. In the event, however, it was only completed in 1875 after the Empire had been swept away by the Third Republic, and even Garnier had to pay for his ticket on the opening night. Part of the reason construction took so long – fourteen years in all – was the discovery of a water table which had to be drained and replaced by a huge concrete well, giving rise to the legend of an underground lake, popularized by Gaston Leroux's 1910 novel *Phantom of the Opera*.

The theatre's **facade** is a fairy-tale concoction of white, pink and green marble, colonnades, rearing horses, winged angels and gleaming gold busts of composers. The group sculpture on the right of the entrance, Carpeaux's *La Danse* (the original is now in the Musée d'Orsay), caused a stir upon unveiling for its frank sensuality; one outraged protestor went as far as to throw black ink over the fleshy thighs of the two female nude dancers. Perhaps more audacious to modern eyes is the recently added **restaurant** on the rue Halévy side, featuring shocking-red decor and a sinuous glass structure that encloses the Rotonde du Glacier, where patrons would once have driven up in their carriages.

The interior

You can **visit** the opulent **interior**, including the auditorium, as long as there are no rehearsals; your best chance is between 1 and 2pm. With its spacious gilded-marble and mirrored lobbies, the building was intended to give Second Empire society suitably grand spaces in which to meet and be seen. The auditorium itself is all red velvet and gold leaf, hung with a six-tonne chandelier; the colourful ceiling was painted by Chagall in 1964 and depicts scenes from well-known operas and ballets jumbled up with famous Parisian landmarks. Your entry ticket includes the **Bibliothèque-Musée de l'Opéra**, containing exquisite model sets, dreadful nineteenth-century paintings and rather better temporary exhibitions on operatic themes. Amid the postcards and memorabilia in the **shop** is one of the city's most unusual souvenirs – honey collected from hives on the vast copper and zinc roof of the opera house; some 125,000 bees seek out nectar from parks, cemeteries and window boxes and produce up to 300kg of honey a year.

Paris-Story

11bis rue Scribe, 9ᵉ • Daily with 50min shows on the hour 10am–6pm • €11 • ☎ 01 42 66 62 06, ⓦ paris-story.com • Ⓜ Opéra

On the western side of the Opéra is the **Paris-Story** multimedia show, a partial and highly romanticized history of Paris "narrated" by Victor Hugo, with simultaneous translation in English. The film uses a kaleidoscope of computer-generated images and archive footage, set against a luscious classical-music soundtrack.

Printemps and Galeries Lafayette

Bd Haussmann, 9ᵉ • Ⓜ Chaussée d'Antin/Havre Caumartin

Just to the north of the Opéra you'll find two of the city's big department stores, **Printemps** and **Galeries Lafayette** (see p.324). Built at the beginning of the twentieth century, they may have lost their grand central staircases, but they still sport their

---

BEAUTIFUL BANKS

Following in the wake of the Printemps and Galeries Lafayette department stores on boulevard Haussmann, a number of **imposing banks** were built in the area. The Crédit Lyonnais at 19 boulevard des Italiens, south of boulevard Haussmann, is perhaps the most impressive, its grand pavilion echoing that of the Louvre and its huge gold clock flanked by gigantic caryatids. Across the road at no. 20 the Banque Nationale de Paris occupies another striking building, with gilded wrought-iron balconies and finely sculpted friezes depicting hunting scenes. It used to be the *Maison Dorée*, a restaurant from the 1840s, where you might have bumped into Balzac, Hugo, Flaubert and Nerval, among other literary figures. At no. 16 is the bank's main building – a sleek 1930s Art Deco edifice. As you cross over rue Laffitte to reach it, you get a wonderful view of Notre-Dame de Lorette, with the Sacré Coeur rearing up in the background.

proud Art Nouveau stained-glass domes. Printemps' dome is particularly splendid, in glowing hues of green and blue, best appreciated from the brasserie beneath.

Eglise de la Madeleine and around

Place de la Madeleine, 8ᵉ • Ⓜ Madeleine

South of boulevard Haussmann, occupying nearly the whole of the place de la Madeleine, is the imperious-looking **Eglise de la Madeleine**, a favourite venue for society weddings. Modelled on the Parthenon, the building is surrounded by 52 Corinthian columns and fronted by a huge pediment depicting the Last Judgement; its facade is a near mirror image of the Assemblée Nationale, which lies directly opposite, just across the river, on the far side of the place de la Concorde – a fine vista best appreciated from the top of the Madeleine steps. Originally intended as a monument to Napoleon's army – a plan abandoned after the French were defeated by the Russians in 1812 – the building narrowly escaped being turned into a railway station before finally being consecrated to Mary Magdalene in 1845.

Inside, a theatrical stone sculpture of the Magdalene being swept up to heaven by two angels draws your eye to the high altar. The half-dome above is decorated with a fresco by Jules-Claude Ziegler (1804–56), a student of Ingres; entitled *The History of Christianity*, it commemorates the concordat signed between the Church and State after the end of the Revolution, and shows all the key figures in Christendom, with Napoleon centre stage, naturally. The church's interior is otherwise rather gloomy, heavy with gilt-edged marble. If you're lucky, the sombre atmosphere may be broken by the sound of the organ, reckoned to be one of Paris's best – the church is a regular venue for recitals and choral concerts. Illustrious former organists include Saint-Saëns and Fauré, whose famous *Requiem* was premiered at the Madeleine in 1888 – to be heard here again at the composer's own funeral 36 years later.

Place de la Madeleine

Ⓜ Madeleine

If the Madeleine caters to spiritual needs, much of the square around it is given over to nourishment of a rather earthier kind, for this is where Paris's top **gourmet food stores**, Fauchon and Hédiard (see box, p.334), are located. Their remarkable displays are a feast for the eyes, and both have fine restaurants. East of the church is one of the city's oldest flower markets dating back to 1832, open every day except Monday, while nearby some rather fine Art Nouveau public toilets, built in 1905, are definitely worth inspecting.

Pinacothèque de Paris

28 place de la Madeleine and 8 rue Vignon, 8ᵉ • Daily except Tues 10.30am–6.30pm, plus exhibitions Wed & Thurs till 8.30pm • Exhibitions €13, permanent collection €8 • ☎ 01 42 68 02 01, Ⓦ www.pinacotheque.com • Ⓜ Madeleine

The privately run **Pinacothèque de Paris** stages very popular temporary art exhibitions at its main site on the place de la Madeleine, while round the corner at 8 rue Vignon, you can see a fine permanent collection of around one hundred paintings on loan from forty private individuals; they include works by Rembrandt, Ghirlandaio, Picasso, Vuillard, Bonnard and Pollock, many rarely or never seen before. What also makes this collection unusual is the way in which the artworks are hung – not by artist or school, but by theme, such as "landscape" or "intimacy", rather in the manner a private collector might display their paintings. The museum's pioneering owner, Marc Restellini, takes the same approach with his temporary exhibitions, which have recently included works by Klimt, Goya and Munch.

Place Vendôme and around

Ⓜ Pyramides/Opéra

A short walk east of place de la Madeleine lies **place Vendôme**, one of the city's most impressive set-pieces, built by Versailles architect Hardouin-Mansart during the final

4

years of Louis XIV's reign. It's a pleasingly symmetrical, eight-sided *place*, enclosed by a harmonious ensemble of elegant mansions, graced with Corinthian pilasters, mascarons and steeply pitched roofs. Once the grand residences of tax collectors and financiers, they now house such luxury establishments as the newly renovated *Ritz* hotel (from where Di and Dodi set off on their last journey), Cartier, Bulgari and other top-flight jewellers, lending the square a decidedly exclusive air. The Ministry of Justice is also sited here, on the west side; its facade still has the marble plaque showing a standard metre put here in 1795 in order to familiarize Parisians with the new unit of measure. No. 12, on the opposite side, now occupied by Chaumet jewellers, is where Chopin died, in 1849.

Colonne Vendôme

Somewhat out of proportion with the rest of place Vendôme, the centrepiece is the newly restored **Colonne Vendôme**, a towering triumphal column modelled on Trajan's column in Rome, and surmounted by a statue of Napoleon dressed as Caesar. It was raised in 1806 to celebrate the Battle of Austerlitz – bronze reliefs of scenes of the battle, cast from 1200 recycled Austro-Russian cannons, spiral their way up the column. The column that stands here today is actually a replica of the original, brought crashing down during the Commune in 1871 – the main instigator behind this act was the artist Gustave Courbet, who was imprisoned and ordered to pay for the column's restoration; he was financially ruined and lived the rest of his life in exile in Switzerland.

Rue St-Honoré

Ⓜ Pyramides/Madeleine/Palais-Royal-Musée-du-Louvre

You'll need a healthy bank balance if you intend to do more than window-shop in the streets around place Vendôme, especially ancient **rue St-Honoré**, the preserve of top fashion designers and art galleries. All the classic designers such as Hermès, Yves Saint Laurent and Christian Lacroix are here – along with the Colette concept store at no. 213 (see p.327).

East of place Vendôme, on rues **St-Roch** and **Ste-Anne**, in particular, the Japanese community has established a mini-enclave; you'll find some good noodle and sushi bars here, such as *Higuma* (see p.277).

Eglise St-Roch

296 rue St-Honoré, 1ᵉʳ • Ⓜ Pyramides

On the corner of rue St-Roch and rue St-Honoré stands the **Eglise St-Roch**, begun in 1653 but not completed until 1740, as money kept running out. Its handsome honey-coloured classical facade was recently scrubbed clean and shows little sign of the battering it received in 1795 when the young Napoleon dispersed a Royalist uprising with cannon (or a "whiff of grapeshot", as he famously put it), and was rewarded with promotion to the rank of general. The St-Roch *quartier* used to be much more densely populated than it is now and boasted many illustrious parishioners, some of whom – Corneille, Diderot and Le Nôtre (who landscaped the Versailles and Tuileries gardens) among them – are buried in the church. The nave is very long, filled with light and flanked with numerous chapels richly decorated with paintings and sculpture by Coysevox and Coustou, and other leading artists of the day. A free leaflet detailing the works is available from the welcome desk. The church is also a venue for evening concerts, and holds free lunchtime song and chamber music recitals most Tuesdays from 12.30 to 1.15pm.

Palais Royal

Place du Palais Royal, 1ᵉʳ • Ⓜ Palais-Royal-Musée-du-Louvre

There are two main parts to the handsome **Palais Royal** complex: the palace itself and, beyond it, galleries surrounding gardens on three sides. The palace, a fine colonnaded building, dates back to 1624, though it has been much modified and renovated since.

It was built for Cardinal Richelieu, who left it to the king, Louis XIV, then just a boy; he and his mother lived here for a time. The palace later passed to his brother, the duc d'Orléans, and provided sanctuary to Henrietta Maria, widow of executed English king, Charles I. It is now occupied by various government departments and is rarely open to the public; an annexe to the side houses the **Comédie Française**, long-standing venue for the classics of French theatre (see p.314).

The gardens and arcades

Beyond the palace lie sedate **gardens** lined with stately **arcaded buildings**, put up in the 1780s by Philippe-Egalité, a descendant of the duc d'Orléans. Desperate to pay off his debts, he let out the spaces under the arcades to shops. One of them, Guillaumot, founded in 1785 and selling antiquarian books mostly on genealogy and heraldry (153 Galerie de Valois), is still there today. Many of the other shops also specialize in antiques or quirky collectors' items, such as lead soldiers and Légion d'Honneur medals. At no. 142 Galerie de Valois is an exquisite purple-panelled *parfumerie*, Les Salons du Palais Royal Shiseido, while the bright-red decor at Didier Ludot's La Petite Robe Noire (no. 125) sets off to advantage his wonderful collection of new and vintage little black dresses.

Former residents of the desirable flats above the arcades include Jean Cocteau and Colette – the latter enjoyed looking out over the gardens when she was too crippled with arthritis to walk. It's certainly an attractive and peaceful oasis, with avenues of limes, fountains and flowerbeds. You'd hardly guess that for many years this was a site of gambling dens, funfair attractions and brothels (it was to a prostitute here that Napoleon lost his virginity in 1787). The clearing of Paris's brothels in 1829–31 and the prohibition on public gambling in 1838, however, put an end to the fun; later, the Grands Boulevards took up the baton. Folly, some might say, has returned – in the form of Daniel Buren's black-and-white-striped **pillars**, rather like sticks of Brighton rock, all of varying heights, dotted about the main courtyard in front of the palace. Installed in 1986, they're rather disconcerting, but certainly popular with children and rollerbladers, who treat them as an adventure playground and obstacle course respectively.

The *passages* and around

The 2^e arrondissement is scattered with around twenty **passages**, or shopping arcades, that have survived from the early nineteenth century. In 1840 more than a hundred existed, but most were later destroyed to make way for Haussmann's boulevards. After decades of neglect, some have now been restored, with a number of chic boutiques moving in. The overall atmosphere, however, is one of charm and nostalgia, as most of the shops, selling old-fashioned toys, prints, secondhand books, postcards and stamps, hark back to another age. Their entrances are easy to miss and where you emerge at the other end can be quite a surprise. Most are closed at night and on Sundays.

Galerie Véro-Dodat
Between rues Croix-des-Petits-Champs and Jean-Jacques Rousseau, 1er • Ⓜ Palais-Royal-Musée-du-Louvre

The most homogeneous and aristocratic of the *passages*, with painted ceilings and panelled mahogany shop fronts divided by faux marble columns, is the elegant **Galerie Véro-Dodat**, named after the two butchers who set it up in 1824. It's been largely colonized by design shops, fashion boutiques (such as Christian Louboutin) and art galleries, though some older businesses, such as R.F. Charle, at no. 17, specializing in the repair and sale of vintage stringed instruments, remain.

The **Banque de France** lies a short way northwest. Rather than negotiating its massive bulk to reach the *passages* further north, it's more pleasant to walk through the garden of the Palais Royal via place de Valois. Rue de Montpensier, running alongside the

4

gardens to the west, is connected to rue de Richelieu by several tiny *passages*, of which Hulot brings you out at the statue of Molière on the junction of rues Richelieu and Molière. A certain charm also lingers about rue de Beaujolais, bordering the northern end of the gardens, with its corner café looking out on the Théâtre du Palais-Royal, and with glimpses into the venerable *Le Grand Véfour* restaurant, plus more short arcades leading up to rue des Petits-Champs.

Galerie Vivienne
Ⓜ Bourse • Ⓦ galerie-vivienne.com

The flamboyant Grecian and marine motifs in elegant **Galerie Vivienne**, linking rue Vivienne with rue des Petits-Champs, create the perfect ambience in which to buy Jean Paul Gaultier gear. Alternatively, you could browse in the antiquarian bookshop, Librairie Jousseaume, dating back to the *passage*'s earliest days, or check out the delightful wooden toys at Si Tu Veux toy shop (see p.356), before taking a tea break in *A Priori Thé* (see p.276). Close by is **Galerie Colbert**, linking rue des Petits-Champs and rue Vivienne. Owned by the Institut National d'Histoire d'Art, it has no shops, but is worth seeing for its elegant decor and beautiful glass rotunda.

Place des Victoires
At the eastern end of rue des Petits-Champs rears up a grand equestrian statue of Louis XIV, at the centre of attractive **place des Victoires**, surrounded by elegant seventeenth-century townhouses. Designer fashion boutiques, such as Kenzo and Cacharel, occupy most of the shops here. Adjoining the square to the north is the appealingly asymmetrical place des Petits-Pères, once the courtyard of the monastery of the Petits-Pères, closed during the Revolution. Its church, **Notre-Dame des Victoires** (daily 8.30am–7.30pm), survives, and is notable for its collection of paintings by Carl Van Loo and also contains the tomb of Jean-Baptiste Lully, Louis XIV's favourite composer. Across the street at no. 10 is Au Moulin de la Vierge, a lovely Art Nouveau boulangerie dating from 1896. The large isolated building on the west side of the square (no. 1) once housed, as a plaque testifies, the notorious French Commissariat for Jewish Affairs (1941–44), which more than willingly collaborated in rounding up the city's Jews for deportation to German concentration camps.

Bibliothèque Nationale
58 rue de Richelieu, 2ᵉ; temporary entrance during renovation work: 5 rue Vivienne • Times vary for temporary exhibitions • Admission prices vary, depending on the exhibition • ☎ 01 53 79 59 59, Ⓦ bnf.fr • Ⓜ Bourse

Across from the Palais Royal, on the other side of rue des Petits-Champs, looms the forbidding wall of the **Bibliothèque Nationale**, part of whose enormous collection has been transferred to the new François Mitterrand site in the 13ᵉ (see p.178). It's currently undergoing major renovation work to improve the conditions in which the library's twenty million documents are kept, and to open up more of the building to the public. Work is due to finish in 2019. Parts of the library will remain open during this period for exhibitions, though it's best to check the website for the latest updates.

The library's origins go back to the 1660s, when Louis XIV's finance minister Colbert deposited a collection of royal manuscripts here, and it was first opened to the public in 1692. There's no restriction on entering, nor on peering into the atmospheric reading rooms, such as the huge Salle Ovale and the Salle Labrouste, with its slender iron columns supporting nine domes, a fine example of the early use of iron frame construction.

Cabinet des Monnaies, Médailles et Antiques
Bibliothèque Nationale, 58 rue de Richelieu, 2ᵉ • Mon–Fri 1–5.45pm, Sat & Sun noon–6pm • Free • Ⓜ Bourse

Installed on the first floor of the Bibliothèque Nationale, the **Cabinet des Monnaies, Médailles et Antiques** is a fine collection of coins and ancient treasures built up by

FROM TOP OPÉRA GARNIER (P.73); CARTIER AT PLACE VENDÔME (P.77) >

successive kings from Philippe-Auguste onwards. Exhibits include Etruscan bronzes, ancient Greek jewellery and some exquisite medieval cameos. One of the highlights is Charlemagne's ivory chess set, its pieces malevolent-looking characters astride elephants. In 2016 the cabinet is due to be transferred to grander rooms in the building as part of the library's extensive revamp.

Passage Choiseul
Ⓜ Pyramides/Quatre-Septembre

West of Galerie Vivienne along rue des Petits-Champs lies one of the longest of the arcades, **passage Choiseul**. This once dark and dingy arcade is now flooded with light once more after its glass roof was repaired in 2013 and the ugly netting removed. It was here, in the early 1900s, that the author Louis-Ferdinand Céline lived as a boy, and judging by his account of it in his autobiographical *Death on Credit*, it was none too salubrious: "The gas lamps stank so badly in the stagnant air of the *passage* that towards evening some women would start to feel unwell, added to which there was the stench of dogs' urine to contend with." Nowadays the only aromas likely to assail you come from the takeaway food shops, which keep company with discount clothes and shoe stores, jewellery shops, galleries and well-known supplier of artists' materials, Lavrut (no. 52). Also here is an entrance to the Théâtre des Bouffes Parisiens, where in 1858 Offenbach conducted the first performance of *Orpheus in the Underworld*.

The Bourse and around
Rue Notre-Dame des Victoires, 2ᵉ • Ⓜ Bourse

4 A little to the north of the Bibliothèque Nationale stands the **Bourse**, the Paris stock exchange, an imposing Neoclassical edifice built under Napoleon in 1808 and enlarged in 1903 with the addition of two side wings. With trading taking place online these days, the building is now chiefly used for conferences and trade fairs. Overshadowing the Bourse from the south is the antennae-topped building of AFP, the French news agency. Rue Réaumur, running east from here, used to be the Fleet Street of Paris, but all the newspapers (as in London) have now moved elsewhere.

Passage des Panoramas
Ⓜ Grands Boulevards/Bourse

The grid of arcades north of the Bourse, just off rue Vivienne, is known as the **passage des Panoramas**, named after two large rotundas that once stood here showing huge panoramic paintings of cities and battle scenes. It was also around here, in 1817, that the first Parisian gas lamps were tried out. A little shabby, but full of charm, the *passage* combines old-fashioned chic and workaday atmosphere. It's long been a favourite with philatelists, who frequent the many stamp dealers, and has also become a foodie destination, with a number of popular wine *bistrots*, such as *Racines* (see p.276), elbowing in among the Vietnamese and Indian takeaways. *L'Arbre à Cannelle* restaurant at no. 57 is worth a look for its beautiful carved-wood ornamentation dating from the 1900s, as is at no. 47, which used to house the printshop Stern and has preserved the original decor dating from 1834.

LE CROISSANT

Just east of the Bourse, on the corner of rue du Croissant and rue Montmartre, **Le Croissant**, now a *bistrot* but once a popular drinking den, was the scene of the assassination on July 31, 1914, of **Jean Jaurès**, the Socialist leader. He was shot by young French nationalist Raul Vilain, protesting at Jaurès's pacifism. Even if he had survived it seems unlikely that Jaurès could have held back the slide to war: just three days later Germany declared war on France. The table at which Jaurès was drinking when he was shot can still be seen.

Passages Jouffroy and Verdeau

Ⓜ Grands Boulevards

On the other side of boulevard Montmartre from the passage des Panoramas, **passage Jouffroy** is full of the kind of stores that make shopping an adventure. One of them, M & G Segas, sells eccentric walking canes and theatrical antiques; opposite is Pain d'Epices (see p.356), which stocks every conceivable fitting and furnishing for a doll's house. Near the romantic *Hôtel Chopin* (see p.258), La Librairie du Passage's art books spill out into the arcade. Crossing rue de la Grange-Batelière, you enter equally enchanting **passage Verdeau**, sheltering antiquarian books, old prints and galleries.

Passage des Princes

Ⓜ Richelieu-Drouot

At the top of rue de Richelieu, near Richelieu-Drouot métro, the tiny **passage des Princes**, with its beautiful glass ceiling, stained-glass decoration and elegant globe lamps, has been taken over by the toy emporium JouéClub. Its erstwhile neighbour, the passage de l'Opéra, described in Surrealist detail by Louis Aragon in his 1926 *Paris Peasant*, was eaten up with the completion of Haussmann's boulevards.

Hôtel Drouot

9 rue Drouot • Viewing possible 11am–6pm on the eve of the sale, 11am–noon on the day of the sale • Ⓦ drouot.fr • Ⓜ Le Peletier/Richelieu-Drouot

While in the area of the passage des Princes, you could take a look at what's up for sale at auction house **Hôtel Drouot**. You can simply wander around looking at the goods before the action starts – auctions are announced in the press, under "Ventes aux Enchères". You'll find details, including photos of pieces, in the widely available weekly *Gazette de l'Hôtel Drouot* or on their website.

Sentier and around

Ⓜ Sentier/Etienne Marcel

At the heart of the 2ᵉ arrondissement lies the buzzy **Sentier** *quartier*, traditionally the centre of Paris's rag trade, though these days much of the business tends to be at the haute couture end. The deliveries of cloth and the general to-ing and fro-ing make a lively change from the office-bound districts further west. Just to the northeast of Sentier métro lies **place du Caire**; here, beneath an extraordinary pseudo-Egyptian facade of grotesque Pharaonic heads (a celebration of Napoleon's conquest of Egypt), an archway opens onto a series of arcades, the **passage du Caire**. Entirely monopolized by wholesale clothes shops (not open to the public), it is very dilapidated and little frequented these days, though it's actually the oldest (and longest) of the *passages*, built in 1798.

Tour Jean Sans Peur

20 rue Etienne Marcel • Mid-April to mid-Nov Wed–Sun 1.30–6pm • €5 • ☏ 01 40 26 20 28, Ⓦ tourjeansanspeur.com • Ⓜ Etienne Marcel

Bordering the Sentier district to the south is rue Etienne Marcel, which is roughly where the old medieval city wall used to run. At no. 20 a rare vestige from this period survives: the **Tour Jean Sans Peur**, a fine Gothic tower, the sole remnant of a grand townhouse that used to straddle the old wall. It was built by Jean Sans Peur, the duc de Bourgogne, who had the tower erected as a place of refuge; he feared reprisal after having assassinated Louis d'Orléans, the king's brother – a murder that kicked off a thirty-year war between the Armagnacs and Burgundys. A spiral stone staircase (138 steps) inside the tower ends with a beautiful vaulted roof decorated with stone carvings of oak leaves, hawthorn and hops, symbols of the Burgundy family. The rooms off the staircase contain information (in English) on the tower, while temporary exhibitions focus on aspects of medieval life.

Passage du Grand-Cerf

Ⓜ Etienne Marcel

Between rue St-Denis and rue Dussoubs arches the lofty, three-storey **passage du Grand-Cerf**, one of the most attractive of all the arcades. The wrought-iron work, glass roof and plain-wood shop fronts have all been restored, attracting chic arts, craft and design shops. There's always something quirky and original on display in the window of Le Labo (no. 4), specializing in lamps and other lighting fixtures made from recycled objects, while As'Art, opposite, is a treasure-trove of home furnishings and objects from Africa.

Rue St-Denis and rue Réaumur

Ⓜ Etienne Marcel

The northern stretch of **rue St-Denis**, beyond rue Etienne Marcel, is the city's centuries-old red-light area, where weary women still wait in doorways between strip clubs and sex shops. The area is changing, however, and some of the older outlets are closing down, partly because sex megastores have taken some of their business and partly because the 2ᵉ arrondissement *mairie* is attempting to clean up the area by encouraging new businesses to move in. Bisecting rue St-Denis, **rue Réaumur** is interesting to wander for its numerous Art Nouveau buildings, such as no. 124 whose facade is almost entirely made of glass and metal, and no. 39 with its striking caryatids.

Rue Montorgueil and around

Ⓜ Etienne Marcel

4

The emphasis on rues Montmartre, Montorgueil and Turbigo, all south of rue Réaumur, is firmly on food as they approach the Les Halles complex. Worth lingering over in particular is the picturesque, pedestrianized market street **rue Montorgueil**, where grocers, delicatessens and fishmongers ply their trade alongside cafés and traditional restaurants, such as *L'Escargot*, serving snails since 1832. Don't miss Stohrer's pâtisserie, in business since 1730, with its exquisite cakes, and beautiful decor by Paul Baudry (1864).

Rue Montmartre is characterized by excellent kitchenware shops, such as A. Simon (see p.338), MORA and Bovida, stocking all the essential utensils for rustling up a perfect *tarte tatin* or *coq au vin*.

THE POMPIDOU CENTRE

Beaubourg and Les Halles

Straddling the third and fourth arrondissements, the Beaubourg *quartier* hums with cafés, shops and galleries, and has the popular Pompidou Centre at its heart. The groundbreaking architecture of this huge arts centre provoked a storm of controversy on its opening in 1977, but has since won over critics and the public alike, becoming one of the city's most recognizable landmarks and drawing large numbers to its modern art museum and high-profile exhibitions. By contrast, nearby Les Halles, an underground shopping complex built at around the same time as the Pompidou Centre, was probably the least inspired of all the capital's late twentieth-century developments; however, it is just coming out of a major revamp, which should make it a more attractive and inviting space.

5

The Pompidou Centre

Rue St-Martin, 4e • ⓦ centrepompidou.fr • Ⓜ Rambuteau/Hôtel-de-Ville

Attracting more than five million visitors a year to its blockbuster art exhibitions, dance performances, films and concerts, the **Pompidou Centre**, known locally as Beaubourg, would seem to have fulfilled its founder Georges Pompidou's vision of a world-class modern art museum and multidisciplinary arts centre. When the centre first opened, however, it met with a very mixed reception, with one critic dubbing it an oil refinery.

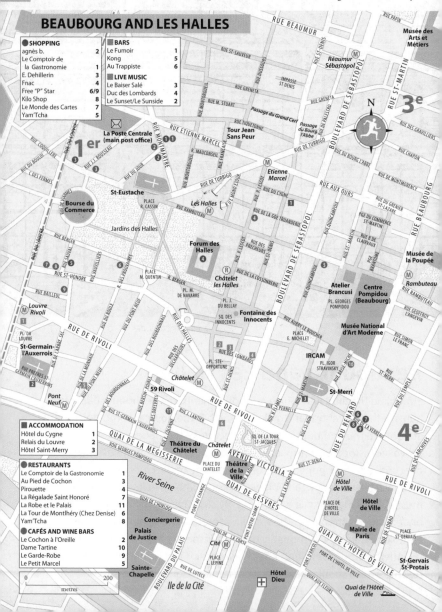

BEAUBOURG AND LES HALLES

● SHOPPING	
agnès b.	2
Le Comptoir de la Gastronomie	1
E. Dehillerin	3
Fnac	4
Free "P" Star	6/9
Kilo Shop	8
Le Monde des Cartes	7
Yam'Tcha	5

■ BARS	
Le Fumoir	1
Kong	5
Au Trappiste	6
■ LIVE MUSIC	
Le Baiser Salé	3
Duc des Lombards	4
Le Sunset/Le Sunside	2

■ ACCOMMODATION	
Hôtel du Cygne	1
Relais du Louvre	2
Hôtel Saint-Merry	3

● RESTAURANTS	
Le Comptoir de la Gastronomie	1
Au Pied de Cochon	3
Pirouette	4
La Régalade Saint Honoré	7
La Robe et le Palais	11
La Tour de Montlhéry (Chez Denise)	6
Yam'Tcha	8

● CAFÉS AND WINE BARS	
Le Cochon à l'Oreille	2
Dame Tartine	10
Le Garde-Robe	9
Le Petit Marcel	5

0 — 200
metres

The building's design is certainly radical. The architects, Renzo Piano and Richard Rogers, wanted to move away from the idea of galleries as closed treasure-chests to create something more open and accessible, so they stripped the "skin" off the building and made all the "bones" visible. The infrastructure was put on the outside: escalator tubes and utility pipes, colour-coded according to their function, climb around the exterior, giving the building its crazy snakes-and-ladders appearance.

The centre's main draw is its outstanding modern art museum, the **Musée National d'Art Moderne**, the largest in Europe, with some 100,000 works. Only a small fraction of the artworks can be displayed at any one time, though with the opening in 2010 of its sister gallery, the Pompidou Metz, and a new "pop-up" gallery in Málaga, Spain, many more can now be enjoyed by the public. The collection is displayed on the fourth and fifth floors, with temporary exhibitions on the sixth, first and basement levels. One of the added treats of visiting the upper levels is that you get to ascend the transparent escalator on the outside of the building, affording superb views over the city. Equally good is the vista from the sleek sixth-floor restaurant *Georges*. If you just want to go up the escalator and see the **view**, you can buy a "Vue de Paris" ticket for €3 on the ground floor.

On the lower floors there are cinemas, a performance space, café, a bookshop, design boutique and the BPI, or **Bibliothèque publique d'information** (Mon, Wed–Fri noon–10pm, Sat & Sun 11am–10pm; free; separate entrance on rue Beaubourg; ☎01 44 78 12 75, ⓦbpi.fr), a public reference library, which has an impressive collection of periodicals, including international press, an extensive sound and film archive and free internet access. Also worth checking out is the new **Galerie de Photographies** (free) on the basement level, which organizes three exhibitions a year drawn from the centre's archive of photographs, particularly strong on the 1920s and 30s and including Man Ray, Brassaï etc.

If you're travelling with children you should see what's going on at the excellent **galerie des enfants** on the first floor, which stages regular exhibitions and workshops. The **piazza** itself, in front of the main entrance, is also something of an attraction in its own right, as it draws mime artists, buskers, jugglers and acrobats.

Musée National d'Art Moderne

Pompidou Centre • Daily except Tues 11am–10pm (last entry 8pm) • Museum and exhibitions €11–13; under-18s free; museum (but not temporary exhibitions) free to EU residents aged 18–25, and to all first Sun of the month; tickets can be bought online; audioguides are available from the ticket office for €5 • ☎ 01 44 78 12 33, ⓦ centrepompidou.fr

Thanks to an astute acquisitions policy and some generous gifts, the **Musée National d'Art Moderne** is a near-complete visual essay on the history of twentieth-century art. The fifth floor covers 1905 to roughly the years 1970–1980, while the fourth floor takes up where the fifth floor leaves off and concentrates on contemporary art. Although works are frequently rotated, the fifth-floor layout doesn't tend to change much. The fourth-floor collection is much more fluid and undergoes a major rehang every two years. Note that the collections can be closed for a few weeks while they're undergoing a rehang; check online in advance. You might also consider downloading the museum's free app, which includes tours and commentaries on some of the works.

Your ticket is valid for a single visit only; you can't, for example, pop out for a break in one of the centre's cafés and re-enter. The collection is densely and efficiently organized, so, unlike many of the more unwieldy museums in Paris, half a day is probably enough for a rewarding visit. Queues to get in can be long; it's often quieter later in the day.

Fauvism

The collection on floor five is organized more or less chronologically and starts in a blaze of colour with the **Fauvists** – **Braque**, **Derain**, **Vlaminck** and **Matisse**. Their vibrant works reflect the movement's desire to create form rather than imitate nature. Colour becomes a way of composing and structuring a picture, as in Braque's *L'Estaque* (1906), where trees and sky are broken down into blocks of vivid reds and greens. Matisse's

5

series of *Luxe* paintings also stands out, the colourful nudes recalling the primitive figures of Gauguin.

Cubism

After the Fauvists, shape is broken down even further in Picasso's and Braque's early **Cubist paintings**. Highlights include **Picasso**'s portrait of his lover, Fernande (*Femme assise dans un fauteuil*; 1910), in which different angles of the figure are shown all at once, giving rise to complex patterns and creating the effect of movement. Hung alongside Picasso's works, and almost indistinguishable from them, are a number of **Braque**'s works, such as *Nature morte au violon* (1911) and *Femme à la guitare* (1913). The juxtaposition of these paintings illustrates the intellectual and artistic dialogue that went on between the two artists, who lived next door to each other at the Bateau-Lavoir in Montmartre.

Another artist heavily influenced by the new Cubism was **Fernand Léger**. In paintings such as *Femme en rouge et vert* (1914) and *Contraste de formes* (1913) Léger creates his own distinctive form of Cubism based on tubular shapes, inspired by the modern machinery of World War I, in which he fought.

Dadaism

Reaction to the horror of the 1914–18 war gave rise to the nihilistic **Dada movement**, a revolt against petty bourgeois values; leading members included **Marcel Duchamp**, who selected everyday objects ("ready-mades") such as the *Hat Rack* (1917), and elevated them, without modification, to the rank of works of art, simply by taking them out of their ordinary context and putting them on display. As well as the *Hat Rack*, you can inspect Duchamp's most notorious ready-made – a urinal that he called *Fontaine* and first exhibited in New York in 1917.

Abstract art

The museum holds a particularly rich collection of **Kandinsky's abstract paintings**. His series entitled *Impressions, Improvisations and Compositions* consists of non-figurative shapes and swathes of colour, and heralds a move away from an obsession with subject towards a passion for the creative process itself. Fellow pioneering abstract artists **Sonia and Robert Delaunay** set the walls ablaze with their characteristically colourful paintings. In Sonia Delaunay's wonderfully vibrant *Marché de Minho* (1916), the juxtaposition of colours makes some appear to recede and others come forward, creating a shimmering effect.

Surrealism and abstract expressionism

Surrealism, an offshoot of the Dada movement, dominates in later rooms with works by Magritte, Dalí and Ernst. Typical of the movement's exploration of the darker recesses of the mind, **Ernst**'s disturbing *Ubu Imperator* (1923) depicts a figure that is part man, part Tower of Pisa and part spinning top, and would seem to symbolize the perversion of male authority. A more ethereal, floating world of abstract associations is depicted in **Joan Miró**'s and **Jean Arp**'s canvases. **Matisse**'s later experiments with form and colour are usually on display. His technique of *découpage* (creating a picture from cut-out coloured pieces of paper) freed colour from drawing and line, and is perfected in his masterpiece *La Tristesse du roi* (1952), in which a woman dances while an elderly king plays a guitar, mourning his lost youth.

American **abstract expressionists** are also represented, including **Jackson Pollock** and **Mark Rothko**. In Pollock's splattery *No. 26A, Black and White* (1948), the two colours seem to struggle for domination; the dark bands of colour in Rothko's large canvas *No. 14 (Browns over Dark)*, in contrast, draw the viewer in.

Contemporary art

The fourth floor is given over to **contemporary art**, featuring installations, photography and video art, as well as displays of architectural models and contemporary design.

Established French artists such as Annette Messager, Sophie Calle, Christian Boltanski, Daniel Buren and Dominique Gonzalez-Foerster often feature, alongside newer arrivals such as Anri Sala. The current exhibition has a global slant, with artists from 55 countries presented.

Atelier Brancusi

Pompidou Centre piazza • Daily except Tues 2–6pm • Free • ☎ 01 44 78 12 33, ⓦ centrepompidou.fr • Ⓜ Rambuteau

On the northern edge of the Pompidou Centre, down some steps off the piazza in a small, separate one-storey building, is the **Atelier Brancusi**. Upon his death in 1956, the sculptor **Constantin Brancusi** bequeathed the contents of his 15^e arrondissement studio to the state, on the condition that it be reconstructed exactly as it was found. The artist had become obsessed with the spatial relationship of the sculptures in his studio, going so far as to supplant each sold work with a plaster copy, and the four interconnected rooms of the studio faithfully adhere to his arrangements. Studios one and two are crowded with fluid sculptures of highly polished brass and marble, his trademark abstract bird and column shapes, stylized busts and objects poised as though they're about to take flight. Unfortunately, the rooms are behind glass, adding a feeling of sterility and distance. Perhaps the most satisfying rooms are ateliers three and four, his private quarters, where his tools are displayed on one wall almost like works of art themselves.

Quartier Beaubourg

Ⓜ Rambuteau/Hôtel-de-Ville

The lively **quartier Beaubourg** around the Pompidou Centre offers much in the way of visual art. The colourful moving sculptures and fountains in the pool in front of Eglise St-Merri on **place Igor Stravinsky**, on the south side of the Pompidou Centre, were created by Jean Tinguely and Niki de Saint Phalle; the squirting waterworks pay homage to Stravinsky – each fountain corresponds to one of his compositions (*The Firebird*, *The Rite of Spring*, and so on) – but show scant respect for passers-by. Stravinsky's music in many ways paved the way for the pioneering work of **IRCAM** (Institut de la Recherche et de la Coordination Acoustique/Musique), whose entrance is on the west side of the square. Founded by the composer Pierre Boulez and now under the umbrella of the Pompidou Centre, it's a research centre for contemporary music and a concert venue (see p.318), much of it underground, with an overground extension by Renzo Piano. To the north of the Pompidou Centre numerous commercial art galleries and the odd bookshop and *salon de thé* occupy the attractive *hôtels particuliers* of narrow, pedestrianized **rue Quincampoix**. Towards the bottom of the street on the right is the charming, cobbled **passage Molière**, with some unusual shops such as Librairie Scaramouche, specializing in rare cinema posters.

Musée de la Poupée

Impasse Berthaud, 3e • **Museum** Daily except Mon 10am–6pm • €8, children €4 • **Workshops** Wed 2.30pm • €14; book in advance • ☎ 01 42 72 73 11, ⓦ museedelapoupeeparis.com • Ⓜ Rambuteau

Off rue Beaubourg is the **Musée de la Poupée**, a doll museum certain to appeal to small children. In addition to the impressive collection of antique dolls, there are displays of finely detailed tiny irons and sewing machines, furniture, pots and pans, and other minuscule accessories. There are fun **workshops** for children on Wednesday afternoons.

Hôtel de Ville

Place de l'Hôtel de Ville, 4^e • **Guided tours** Once a week (days and times vary); book ahead on ☎ 01 42 76 50 49 or at the Salon d'Accueil, 29 rue de Rivoli • **Exhibitions** Entrance usually at 5 rue de Lobau • Mon–Sat 10am–7pm • Free • Ⓜ Hôtel-de-Ville

South of the Pompidou Centre, rue du Renard runs down to the **Hôtel de Ville**, the seat of the city's government and a mansion of gargantuan proportions in florid neo-Renaissance style. It was built in 1882 and modelled pretty much on the previous building burned

5

down in the Commune in 1871. Weekly guided tours allow you to see some of the lavish reception rooms, decorated with murals by the leading artists of the day, such as Puvis de Chavannes and Henri Gervex. The Hôtel de Ville also stages regular free **exhibitions** on Parisian themes.

An illustrated history of the building is displayed along the platform of Châtelet métro station on the Neuilly–Vincennes line. Those opposed to the establishments of kings and emperors created their alternative municipal governments in this building: the Revolutionaries installed themselves in 1789, the poet Lamartine proclaimed the Second Republic here in 1848, and Gambetta the Third Republic in 1870. But, with the defeat of the Commune in 1871, the conservatives, in control once again, concluded that the Parisian municipal authority had to go if order was to be maintained and the people kept in their place. Thereafter Paris was ruled directly by the ministry of the interior until eventually, in 1977, the city was allowed to run its own affairs and Jacques Chirac was elected mayor.

Place de l'Hôtel de Ville and the riverside

The **Place de l'Hôtel de Ville**, the large square in front of the Hôtel de Ville, is the location of a popular **ice rink** in winter (Dec–Feb Mon–Fri noon–10pm, Sat & Sun 9am–10pm; skate rental €6); it also stages occasional open-air concerts and screens live sporting events. Formerly known as place de la Grève, the square used to be a shingly beach (*grève*), where boats bringing in food and supplies for the city would have docked. It was also a notorious execution site from the Middle Ages up to 1830, and witnessed many a guillotining during the Revolution.

The connection with the river has been re-established; you can walk along a renovated stretch of the riverbank between the Hôtel de Ville and the Port de l'Arsenal. Pavements have been widened, and traffic is regulated. On Sundays – when cars are banned completely – the **promenade** is a delight; Parisians head out here for cycle rides and leisurely strolls, enjoying the views of the Ile St-Louis. A stretch of the Left Bank, the Berges de Seine, has also been opened up to pedestrians (see p.152).

Les Halles

Ⓜ Les Halles/Châtelet/RER Châtelet-Les-Halles

Located right at the heart of the city is the sprawling underground shopping and leisure complex, gardens and métro interchange of **Les Halles** (pronounced "lay al"), currently being given a much-needed revamp, much of which will be complete by 2016. The most striking feature of the facelift is the **Canopée** ("canopy") – a vast, undulating, metal-and-glass roof, suspended over the entrance to the complex and designed to let more light flood into the underground **Forum des Halles** shopping mall. The new development will also include a **hip-hop centre**, La Place, with performance space and studios; the first of its kind in the capital, it's in part an acknowledgement of the popularity of Les Halles with the *banlieusards*, the young people who come in from the housing estates in the suburbs.

THE BELLY OF PARIS

Described by Zola as *le ventre de Paris* ("the **belly of Paris**"), the original Les Halles was Paris's main **food market** for more than eight hundred years until it was moved out to Rungis in the suburbs in 1969; its departure is still widely mourned today. Victor Baltard's elegant nineteenth-century iron pavilions were destroyed (two were saved – one is in Nogent-sur-Marne, the other in Yokohama, Japan) to make way for the ugly **Forum des Halles** glass-and-steel shopping mall and huge métro station, the biggest in Europe. The working-class quarter, with its night bars and *bistrots* for the market traders, was largely swept away, and though much of the area above ground was landscaped, the gardens developed an unsavoury reputation as the preferred hangout of drug dealers. Hopefully the renovation of the site (see above) will make it a much more inviting space.

5

Overground, architect and urban planner David Mangin is redesigning the **gardens**, creating wide promenades and adding more greenery and flowerbeds, as well as playgrounds and pétanque courts. His plan was chosen as the most sensitive to local needs, though it's hard not to feel an opportunity was missed to go for something really exciting and ambitious (star architect Jean Nouvel, for example, put in a proposal for an enormous hanging garden, complete with a 100m open-air swimming pool).

Forum des Halles
Ⓜ Les Halles/Châtelet/RER Châtelet Les Halles

The Forum is spread over four levels. The bottom level is the métro/RER station, where five métro lines and three suburban lines intersect, used by some 800,000 commuters a day. The other levels accommodate numerous shops, mostly high-street fashion chains (H&M, Zara, Muji and Gap, to name a few), though there's also a decent Fnac bookshop. Leisure facilities include a swimming pool (see p.346) and a number of cinemas, including the **Forum des Images** (Tues–Fri 1–10pm, Sat & Sun 2–9pm; ☏01 44 76 63 00, ⓦforumdesimages.fr; Ⓜ Les Halles/Châtelet), which houses five screens and an archive of some seven thousand films, all connected with Paris and any of which you can watch in your own private booth (from €6).

St-Eustache
2 impasse St-Eustache, 1ᵉʳ • Ⓜ Les Halles

For an antidote to the Forum des Halles's steel-and-glass troglodytism, head for the soaring vaults of the beautiful church of **St-Eustache**, on the north side of the gardens. Built between 1532 and 1637, the church is Gothic in structure, with lofty naves and graceful flying buttresses, and Renaissance in decoration – all Corinthian columns and arcades. Molière, Richelieu and Madame de Pompadour were baptized here, while Rameau and Marivaux were buried here. The side chapels contain some minor works of art, including, in the tenth chapel in the ambulatory, an early Rubens (*The Pilgrims at Emmaus*), and, in the sixth chapel on the north side, Coysevox's marble sculpture over the tomb of Colbert, Louis XIV's finance minister. In the Chapelle St-Joseph there is a naive relief by British artist Raymond Mason, *The Departure of Fruit and Vegetables from the Heart of Paris, 28 February 1969*, showing a procession of market traders, resembling a funeral cortege, leaving Les Halles for the last time. The church has a long and venerable musical tradition and is a popular venue for concerts and organ recitals (held every Sun 5.30–6pm); the *grand orgue* is reputedly the largest in France, with eight thousand pipes.

Fontaine des Innocents
Place Joachim du Bellay, 1ᵉʳ • Ⓜ Les Halles

Looking slightly marooned amid the fast-food joints, tattoo parlours and shoe shops of place Joachim du Bellay is the perfectly proportioned Renaissance **Fontaine des Innocents** (1549), adorned with reliefs of water nymphs. It's in a rather sorry state, but happily is soon to be restored. On warm days shoppers sit on its steps, drawn to the coolness of its cascading waters. It takes its name from the cemetery that used to occupy this site, the Cimetière des Innocents, which was closed in 1786 and its contents transferred to the catacombs in Denfert-Rochereau.

Châtelet and around
Ⓜ Châtelet

The labyrinth of tiny streets heading southeast from Les Halles to **place du Châtelet** teems with jazz bars, clubs and restaurants, and is far more crowded at 2am than at 2pm. One of these streets, narrow little rue de la Ferronnerie, was the scene of Henri IV's assassination in 1610. A plaque at no. 11 marks the spot where Henri's

5

carriage came to a standstill, caught in the seventeenth-century equivalent of a traffic jam, giving his assassin, religious fanatic Ravaillac, the chance to plunge his dagger into the king's breast.

Théâtre du Châtelet and Théâtre de la Ville

Place du Châtelet, 1ᵉʳ • ⓂChâtelet

Place du Châtelet was once the site of a notorious fortress prison and is now a maelstrom of traffic overlooked by two of the city's most prestigious theatres, the **Théâtre du Châtelet** (see p.314) and the **Théâtre de la Ville** (see p.316), built in the 1860s during Haussmann's *grands travaux*. The latter was formerly known as the Théâtre Sarah Bernhardt (changed to Théâtre des Nations during the German occupation on account of Bernhardt's Jewish origins) after the great actress bought it and regularly performed on stage here until her death in 1923.

Tour St-Jacques

Rue de Rivoli, 1ᵉʳ • ⓂChâtelet

One block north of the place du Châtelet stands the **Tour St-Jacques**. Built in Flamboyant Gothic style and dating from the early sixteenth century, it's all that remains of the Eglise St-Jacques-de-la-Boucherie, built by butchers from nearby Les Halles and destroyed in the Revolution. The church used to be an important stopping point for pilgrims on their way to Santiago de Compostela. At the base of the tower a statue commemorates Blaise Pascal, who carried out experiments on atmospheric pressure here in the seventeenth century. The tower is now used as a weather station and monitors pollution and air quality. For the last few years it has opened to the public for a few weeks in the summer, leading to hopes that it might open permanently and allow everyone to enjoy the wonderful views from the top – there's no sign of that as yet, however.

59 Rivoli

59 rue de Rivoli, 1ᵉʳ • Daily except Mon 1–8pm • Free • ☎01 44 61 08 31, Ⓦ59rivoli.org • ⓂChâtelet

West of the Tour St-Jacques lies busy rue de Rivoli, dominated by high-street clothing stores. No. 59, however, shelters the famous **artists' squat, 59 Rivoli**. The building, which had been left empty by its owners Crédit Lyonnais, was occupied by artists in 1999 and fast became one of the capital's most important contemporary art spaces; the Paris authorities agreed to buy and renovate it and the building reopened in 2009. Some thirty artists live and work in this "aftersquat", and you're free to wander around their studios, spread over six floors, and see them at work. Graffiti, slogans and murals cover nearly every surface, canvases and all sorts of *objets* are stacked up higgledy piggledy, and the smell of paint, varnish and coffee permeates everywhere. Regular exhibitions and concerts are held on the ground floor.

The Samaritaine and quai de la Mégisserie

Rue de Rivoli, 1ᵉʳ • ⓂPont-Neuf

The grand **Samaritaine** building was built in 1903 in pure Art Nouveau style. This famous department store was declared a fire risk in 2005 and suddenly shut down, an event that sent ripples of dismay throughout the capital; it's due to reopen in 2017 as a luxury hotel and shopping complex. The quayside behind the Samaritaine is known as **quai de la Mégisserie** ("mégisserie" is the tanning of hides), a reference to the treatment of animal skins in medieval times when this was an area of abattoirs; nowadays there are plants and pets for sale all along this stretch up to the Pont au Change.

The Marais

The Marais is one of the most seductive areas of central Paris, known for its sophistication and artsy leanings, and for being the neighbourhood of choice for gay Parisians. Largely untouched by Baron Haussmann and modern development, it preserves its enchanting narrow streets and magnificent Renaissance *hôtels particuliers* (mansions). Some of these mansions have become chic flats, boutiques and commercial art galleries, while others provide splendid settings for a number of excellent museums, not least among them the splendidly revamped Musée Picasso, the Musée Carnavalet history museum and the Musée d'Art et d'Histoire du Judaïsme. As the Marais is one of the few areas of the city where places open on a Sunday, many Parisians come here for brunch and a leisurely afternoon's shopping.

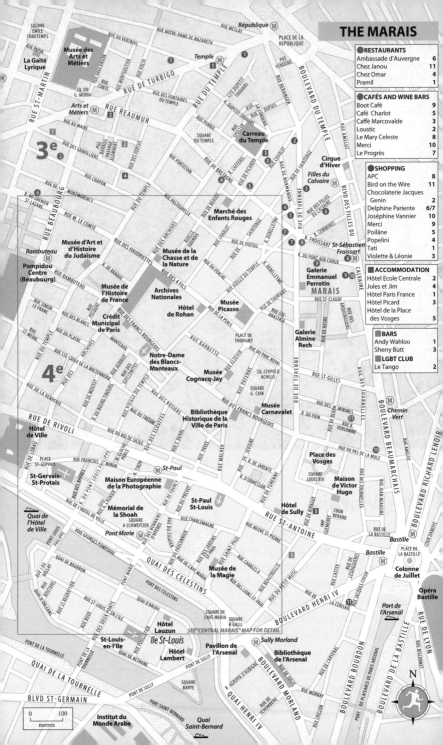

The area was little more than a riverside swamp (*marais*) up until the thirteenth century, when the Knights Templar (see p.105) moved into its northern section and began to drain the land. It became a magnet for the aristocracy in the early 1600s after the construction of the place des Vosges by Henri IV in 1605. This golden age was relatively short-lived, however, for the aristocracy began to move away after the king took his court to Versailles in the latter part of the seventeenth century, leaving their grand houses to the trading classes, who were in turn displaced during the Revolution. From this point on, the mansions became slum tenements and the streets degenerated into squalor. It was only in the 1960s, with its designation as a *secteur sauvegardé* (a conservation area), that efforts were made to smarten up the area and improve living conditions.

6

The main artery running through the Marais, dividing it roughly north and south, is the busy **rue de Rivoli** and its continuation to the Bastille, rue St-Antoine. South of this line is the **quartier St-Paul**, with its antique shops and atmospheric backstreets. To the north lies the beautiful place des Vosges; the old Jewish quarter centred on rue des Rosiers; and the Marais' other main street, **rue des Francs-Bourgeois**, lined with aristocratic mansions and chic fashion and interior-design boutiques. Other streets worth exploring are rue Vieille du Temple, with its terraced cafés and bars, and the streets further north in the trendy **Haut Marais**, home to young designers and contemporary art galleries.

Place des Vosges and around

Ⓜ Bastille/Chemin-Vert/St-Paul

Whether you approach via the narrow streets from Bastille or from the north or west, nothing quite prepares you for the size and grandeur of the **place des Vosges**, a magnificent square bordered by arcaded pink-brick and stone mansions, with a formal garden at its centre. A masterpiece of aristocratic elegance and the first example of planned development in the history of Paris, the square was commissioned in 1605 by Henri IV, and was inaugurated in 1612 for the wedding of Louis XIII and Anne of Austria; it is Louis' statue – or, rather, a replica of it – that stands hidden by chestnut trees in the middle of the gardens. Originally called place Royale, it was renamed Vosges in 1800 in honour of the *département*, the first to pay its share of the expenses of the revolutionary wars.

A royal palace, the Hôtel des Tournelles, stood on what is now the north side of the square until 1559, when it was demolished by Catherine de Médicis after her husband Henri II was killed here during a joust. The vacant space became a huge weekly horse market, trading between one and two thousand horses. So it remained until Henri IV decided on the construction of his place Royale.

Through all the vicissitudes of history, the *place* has never lost its cachet as a smart address. Today, the **arcades** harbour upmarket art, antique and fashion shops, as well as a number of restaurants and cafés. Buskers play classical music and jazz, and in the garden toddlers play in the sandpits and families picnic on the grass; this is one of the few Parisian gardens where the *pelouse* is not *interdite*.

Maison de Victor Hugo

6 place des Vosges, 4ᵉ • Tues–Sun 10am–6pm; closed hols • Free • ☏ 01 42 72 10 16 • Ⓜ Bastille

Among the many celebrities who made their homes in the place des Vosges was Victor Hugo; the second-floor apartment at no. 6, where he lived from 1832 to 1848 and wrote much of *Les Misérables*, is now a museum, the **Maison de Victor Hugo**. Hugo's life, including his nineteen years of exile in Jersey and Guernsey, is evoked through a somewhat sparse collection of memorabilia, portraits, photographs and first editions of his works. What you do get, though, is an idea of the writer's prodigious creativity: as well as being a prolific author, he drew – a number of his ink drawings are exhibited – and designed his own Gothic-style furniture, in which he let his imagination run riot, as seen in some of the pieces displayed. He even put together the extraordinary Chinese-style dining room, originally designed for the house of his lover, Juliette Drouet, in Guernsey, re-created in its entirety here. Among the family portraits is one by Auguste de Châtillon of Hugo's daughter, Léopoldine, shown holding a Book of Hours open at the Dormition of the Virgin – a poignant detail, given that eight years later at the age of 19 she drowned, along with her husband of just six months. Her loss inspired some of Hugo's most moving poetry, including the well-known *Demain dès l'aube*.

6

Hôtel de Sully

62 rue St-Antoine, 4ᵉ • Ⓜ St-Paul/Bastille

From the southwest corner of the place des Vosges, a door leads through to the formal château garden, orangerie and exquisite Renaissance facade of the **Hôtel de Sully**. The garden, with its park benches, makes for a peaceful rest stop; it's also a handy shortcut through to rue St-Antoine. The *hôtel* is the headquarters of the Centre des Monuments Nationaux, which manages more than a hundred national monuments and publishes numerous books and guides, many of which are on sale in the excellent ground-floor bookshop near the rue St-Antoine entrance; it's also worth a look for its fine seventeenth-century painted beamed ceiling.

A short distance back to the west along rue St-Antoine, almost opposite the sixteenth-century **church of St-Paul-St-Louis**, which was inaugurated by Cardinal Richelieu, you'll find another square. A complete contrast to the imposing formality of the place des Vosges, the tiny **place du Marché Ste-Catherine**, with its trees and little restaurant terraces, is intimate and irresistibly charming.

Rue des Francs-Bourgeois and around

Ⓜ St-Paul/Rambuteau

Running west from the place des Vosges, the main lateral street of the northern part of the Marais is the narrow **rue des Francs-Bourgeois**. Beatnik Jack Kerouac translated it as "the street of the outspoken middle classes", which is a fair description of the contemporary residents, though the name in fact means "people exempt from tax", referring to the penurious inmates of a medieval almshouse that once stood on the site of no. 34.

Along or just off this street lie some of the Marais' finest mansions, including the superb **Musée Carnavalet**, tracing the history of Paris; the bijou **Musée Cognacq-Jay**, devoted to eighteenth-century art and decorative arts; the engaging **Musée d'Art et d'Histoire du Judaïsme**; and the **Musée de l'Histoire de France**, the state archives museum, housed in one of the grandest mansions of all.

Musée Carnavalet

23 rue de Sévigné, 4ᵉ • Tues–Sun 10am–6pm • Free; entry to special exhibitions varies • ☎ 01 44 59 58 58, Ⓦ carnavalet.paris.fr • Ⓜ St-Paul

The fascinating **Musée Carnavalet** charts the history of Paris from its origins up to the *belle époque* through an extraordinary collection of paintings, sculptures, decorative arts and archeological finds. The museum's setting alone, in two beautiful Renaissance mansions (Hôtel Carnavalet and Hôtel Le Peletier) surrounded by attractive gardens, makes a visit worthwhile. There are 140 rooms in all, probably too much to see in one go.

The ground floor

The **ground floor** displays nineteenth- and early twentieth-century shop and inn signs and engrossing models of Paris through the ages, along with maps and plans showing how much Haussmann's boulevards changed the face of the city. The **orangerie** houses a significant collection of Neolithic finds, including a number of wooden pirogues unearthed during the redevelopment of the Bercy riverside area in the 1990s.

The post-Revolution and **Napoleonic period** is also covered on the ground floor, in rooms 115–121; look out for Napoleon's favourite canteen, which accompanied him

CENTRAL MARAIS

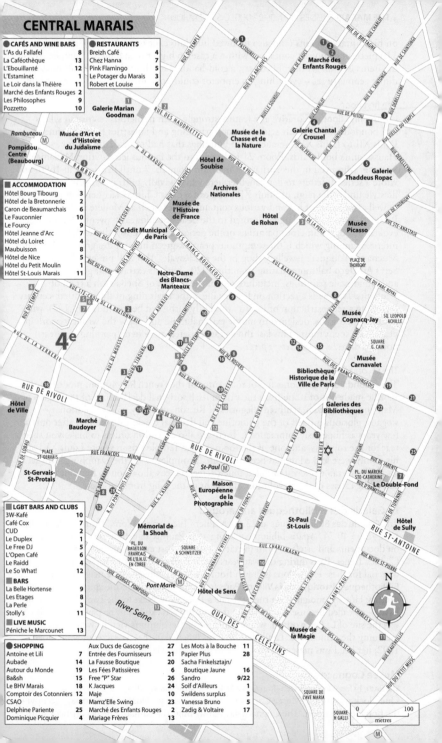

CAFÉS AND WINE BARS

L'As du Fallafel	8
La Caféothèque	13
L'Ebouillanté	12
L'Estaminet	1
Le Loir dans la Théière	11
Marché des Enfants Rouges	2
Les Philosophes	9
Pozzetto	10

RESTAURANTS

Breizh Café	4
Chez Hanna	7
Pink Flamingo	5
Le Potager du Marais	3
Robert et Louise	6

ACCOMMODATION

Hôtel Bourg Tibourg	3
Hôtel de la Bretonnerie	2
Caron de Beaumarchais	6
Le Fauconnier	10
Le Fourcy	9
Hôtel Jeanne d'Arc	7
Hôtel du Loiret	4
Maubuisson	8
Hôtel de Nice	5
Hôtel du Petit Moulin	1
Hôtel St-Louis Marais	11

LGBT BARS AND CLUBS

3W-Kafé	10
Café Cox	7
CUD	2
Le Duplex	1
Le Free DJ	5
L'Open Café	6
Le Raidd	4
Le So What!	12

BARS

La Belle Hortense	9
Les Etages	8
La Perle	3
Stolly's	11

LIVE MUSIC

Péniche le Marcounet	13

SHOPPING

Antoine et Lili	7	Les Mots à la Bouche	11
Aubade	14	Papier Plus	28
Autour du Monde	19	Sacha Finkelsztajn/	
Ba&sh	15	Boutique Jaune	16
Le BHV Marais	18	Sandro	9/22
Comptoir des Cotonniers	12	Soif d'Ailleurs	1
CSAO	9	Swildens surplus	3
Delphine Pariente	25	Vanessa Bruno	5
Dominique Picquier	4	Zadig & Voltaire	17
Aux Ducs de Gascogne	27		
Entrée des Fournisseurs	21		
La Fausse Boutique	20		
Les Fées Patissières	6		
Free "P" Star	26		
K Jacques	24		
Maje	10		
Mamz'Elle Swing	23		
Marché des Enfants Rouges	2		
Mariage Frères	13		

on his military exploits (and also followed him into exile on St Helena), consisting of 110 pieces ingeniously contained within a case no bigger than a picnic hamper. Among the items is a full set of gold cutlery, a gold-handled toothbrush, two candelabras and a dinky geometry set – everything an emperor could possibly need while on campaign.

The first floor

On the **first floor**, decorative arts feature strongly, with numerous re-created salons and boudoirs full of richly sculpted wood panelling and tapestries from the time of Louis XII to Louis XVI, rescued from buildings that had to be destroyed for Haussmann's boulevards. Room 21 is devoted to the famous letter-writer **Madame de Sévigné**, who lived in the Carnavalet mansion from 1677 until her death in 1696, and wrote a series of letters to her daughter here which vividly portray her privileged lifestyle under the reign of Louis XIV. You can see her Chinese lacquered writing desk, as well as portraits of her and various contemporaries, such as Molière and Corneille. Rooms 128 to 148 are largely devoted to the **belle époque** (early twentieth century), evoked through numerous paintings of the period and some wonderful **Art Nouveau** interiors, among which is the sumptuous peacock-green interior designed by Alphonse Mucha for Fouquet's jewellery shop in the rue Royale. Also well preserved is José-Maria Sert's **Art Deco** ballroom, dating from the 1920s, with its extravagant gold-leaf decor and grand-scale paintings, including one of the Queen of Sheba with a train of elephants. Nearby is a section on literary life at the beginning of the twentieth century, including a reconstruction of Proust's modestly furnished bedroom (room 147), with its cork-lined walls, designed to muffle external noise and allow the writer to work in peace – he spent most of his last three years closeted away here, penning his great novel, *A la recherche du temps perdu*.

The second floor

The **second floor** has rooms full of mementos of the **French Revolution**: models of the Bastille made out of stone from the prison itself, original declarations of the Rights of Man and the Citizen, sculpted allegories of Reason, crockery with revolutionary slogans, glorious models of the guillotine and decimal clocks (abandoned after only a few years as hopelessly impractical). There are also execution orders to make you shed a tear for the royalists, and one of the rooms of the Temple prison where Louis XVI and his family were locked up has been re-created, complete with the Dauphin's lotto set and billiards table. Newly installed touch-screen videos allow you to find out more about the causes of the Revolution, the flight of the king from Paris, etc.

La Galerie des Bibliothèques and around

The **Galerie des Bibliothèques** at 22 rue Malher (Tues–Sun 1–7pm, Thurs till 9pm; €6; ☏01 72 63 40 74, ⊚paris-bibliotheques.org; ⓂSt-Paul) is an exhibition space that draws on documents and artefacts from the city's libraries. Past exhibitions have included Charles Trenet, Paris during the war years and the great flood of 1910. Much of the material for these exhibitions is drawn from the huge archives of the neighbouring **Bibliothèque Historique de la Ville de Paris** (see p.344), housed in the splendid sixteenth-century Hôtel Lamoignon on rue des Francs-Bourgeois. Next to the Lamoignon on rue Pavée – so called because it was among the first of Paris's streets to be paved, in 1450 – was the site of **La Force prison**, where many of the Revolution's victims were incarcerated, including the Princesse de Lamballe, who was lynched in the massacres of September 1792; her head was presented on a stake to her friend Marie-Antoinette.

Musée Cognacq-Jay

8 rue Elzévir, 4ᵉ • Tues–Sun 10am–5.40pm • Free • ☏ 01 40 27 07 21 • ⓂSt-Paul/Chemin-Vert

One block west of the Musée Carnavalet lies the intimate **Musée Cognacq-Jay**, occupying the fine Hôtel Donon. The Cognacq-Jay family built the Samaritaine department store, now closed (see p.92), and were noted philanthropists, as well as lovers of eighteenth-century European art. Their small collection of pieces on show includes a handful of works by Canaletto, Fragonard, Rubens and Quentin de la Tour, as well as an early Rembrandt and an exquisite still life by Chardin, displayed in beautifully carved wood-panelled rooms filled with Sèvres porcelain and Louis XV furniture.

Musée de l'Histoire de France

60 rue des Francs-Bourgeois, 4ᵉ • Mon, Wed–Fri 10am–5.30pm, Sat & Sun 2–5.30pm • €3–6 • ☏ 01 40 27 60 96, ⓦ archives-nationales .culture.gouv.fr • Ⓜ Rambuteau/St-Paul

At the western end of the rue des Francs-Bourgeois there once stood a magnificent, early eighteenth-century palace complex, filling the entire block from rue des Quatre Fils to rue des Archives, and from rue Vieille-du-Temple to rue des Francs-Bourgeois. Only half remains today, but it is utterly splendid, especially the grand colonnaded courtyard of the **Hôtel de Soubise**, with its fabulous Rococo interiors, paintings by Boucher and vestigial fourteenth-century towers on rue des Quatre Fils. A stroll through the adjoining, rather charming **gardens** allows you to admire the setting all the more.

The Hôtel de Soubise houses a large number of the city archives, dating from the period before 1790, and the **Musée de l'Histoire de France**, which mounts changing exhibitions drawn from its extensive holdings; its fascinating haul includes Joan of Arc's trial proceedings, with a doodled impression of her in the margin, and a Revolutionary calendar, where "J" stands for Jean-Jacques Rousseau and "L" for "labourer". The *hôtel*'s ground-floor Chambre du Prince is the scene of **chamber music recitals** (€13), held here most Saturdays, usually at 6pm.

The **Hôtel de Rohan**, next to the Musée de l'Histoire de France, is part of the archives complex and is sometimes used when there are large exhibitions. Its fine interiors include the Chinese-inspired Cabinet des Singes, whose walls are painted with monkeys acting out various aristocratic scenes.

Crédit Municipal de Paris

55 rue des Francs-Bourgeois, 4ᵉ • La Galerie du Crédit Municipal: Mon–Fri 9am–6pm, Sat 9am–5pm, closed between exhibitions • Free • ☏ 01 44 61 64 00, ⓦ creditmunicipal.fr • Ⓜ Rambuteau/St-Paul

Opposite the Hôtel de Soubise stands the **Crédit Municipal de Paris**, formerly the Mont-de-Piété, a kind of state-run pawn shop (now with normal banking facilities too), in existence since 1637; any items that are not redeemed are sold at auction. It's started hosting free exhibitions on a range of interesting themes, well worth checking out, such as a recent one on Paris street art.

Further east, beyond several more imposing facades, you can admire the delicate filigree ironwork of the balcony above the main entrance to the **Hôtel d'Albret** (no. 31), built in 1740, its stately courtyard a delightful setting for occasional concerts in summer.

Musée de la Chasse et de la Nature

62 rue des Archives, 3ᵉ • Tues–Sun 11am–6pm, Wed till 9.30pm • €8, free for under-18s and to everyone first Sun of the month • ☏ 01 53 01 92 40, ⓦ chassenature.org • Ⓜ Rambuteau

Housed in the beautiful Hôtel Guénégaud and the neighbouring Hôtel Mongelas, the **Musée de la Chasse et de la Nature** largely explores the theme of hunting, especially animals of the hunt. The museum starts with a series of rooms each devoted to a particular animal, such as the wild boar, wolf and dog. A "cabinet of curiosities" invites you to pull open drawers and discover miscellaneous bits and bobs, such as paw prints, animal droppings and drawings, and you can look through eyeglasses and watch a video of the animal in its natural habitat – all quite appealing to children in particular. The rest of the collection includes a formidable array of stuffed animals, including a giant polar bear, weapons ranging from prehistoric stone arrowheads to highly decorative crossbows and guns, and paintings by French artists, such as Desportes, romanticizing the chase.

Musée d'Art et d'Histoire du Judaïsme

71 rue du Temple, 3ᵉ • Mon–Fri 11am–6pm, Sun 10am–6pm • €8 • ☎ 01 53 01 86 53, ⓦ mahj.org • Ⓜ Rambuteau

Two blocks west of the Musée de la Chasse et de la Nature stands the attractively restored Hôtel de St-Aignan, home to the **Musée d'Art et d'Histoire du Judaïsme**. The museum traces the culture, history and artistic endeavours mainly of the **Jews in France**, though there are also many artefacts from the rest of Europe and North Africa. The result is a very comprehensive collection, as educational as it is beautiful. Free audioguides in English are available and worth picking up if you want to get the most out of the museum.

6

The medieval period to the nineteenth century

Highlights of the museum's holdings from the **medieval period to the nineteenth century** include a Gothic-style Hanukkah lamp, one of the very few French-Jewish artefacts to survive from the period before the expulsion of the Jews from France in 1394; an Italian gilded circumcision chair from the seventeenth century; and a completely intact, late nineteenth-century Austrian *sukkah*, "a temporary dwelling built for the celebration of the Harvest, decorated with paintings of Jerusalem and the Mount of Olives". Other artefacts include Moroccan wedding garments, highly decorated marriage contracts from eighteenth-century Modena and gorgeous, almost whimsical, spice containers.

THE DREYFUS AFFAIR

The **Dreyfus Affair** was one of the biggest crises to rock the Third Republic. It centred on Alfred Dreyfus, a captain in the French army and a Jew, who was arrested and **convicted of spying** for the Germans in 1894 on the flimsiest of evidence – his handwriting was said to resemble that on documents detailing French armaments found in the German embassy. In a humiliating public ceremony of "*dégradation*" in the courtyard of the Ecole Militaire, his epaulettes were torn from his uniform and his sword broken, while anti-Semitic slogans were chanted by crowds outside. He was then sent to the notorious penal colony of Devil's Island, off Guyana. His family, convinced of his innocence, began campaigning for a retrial. Two newspapers, *L'Eclair* and *Le Matin*, questioned the evidence and in 1897 Colonel Georges Picquart, the new head of the Statistical Section, discovered a document which suggested that the true culprit was Major Ferdinand Walsin-Esterhazy. Esterhazy was perfunctorily tried by the Ministry of War, and let off. The government, keen to uphold the army's authority and reputation, acquiesced to the verdict, and Colonel Picquart was packed off to Tunisia.

However, a storm broke out when shortly afterwards writer **Emile Zola** published his famous open letter, titled *J'accuse…!*, to the President of the Republic in the *Aurore* newspaper on January 13, 1898. In it he denounced the army and authorities and accused them of a cover-up. Zola was convicted for libel and sentenced to a year's imprisonment, which he avoided by fleeing to England. The article triggered a major outcry and suddenly the *affaire* was the chief topic of conversation in every café in France. French society divided into two camps: Dreyfusards and anti-Dreyfusards. The former, convinced the army was guilty of a cover-up, comprised republicans committed to equal rights and the primacy of parliament and included many prominent intellectuals and left-wing figures such as Jean Jaurès, Anatole France, Léon Blum, Georges Clemenceau and Marcel Proust. Ranked among the anti-Dreyfusards were clerics, anti-Semitic newspapers such as *La Libre Parole*, monarchists and conservatives, all suspecting a Jewish conspiracy to tarnish the army's reputation. The former clamoured for justice, while the latter called for respect and order.

In June 1897, the secret dossier that convicted Dreyfus was finally re-examined; there was a retrial and, again, Dreyfus was convicted of treason, but was quickly pardoned by President Loubet, desperate to draw a line under the whole affair. Finally, in 1906, Dreyfus, his health broken by hard labour, was granted a **full pardon** and awarded the *Légion d'honneur*. The matter was formally closed, but the repercussions of the affair were deep and long-lasting; it had revealed fundamental divisions in French society, and split the country along lines that would determine France's development in the twentieth century.

The Dreyfus archives

The **Dreyfus archives**, donated to the museum by Dreyfus's grandchildren, document the notorious **Dreyfus affair** (see box opposite) through letters, photographs and press clippings; you can read Emile Zola's famous letter "*J'accuse…!*" in which the novelist defends Dreyfus's innocence, and the letters Dreyfus sent to his wife from prison on Devil's Island in which he talks of *épouvantable* ("terrible") suffering and loneliness.

The twentieth century

The museum also hosts a significant collection of paintings and sculpture by **Jewish artists** – Marc Chagall, Samuel Hirszenberg, Chaïm Soutine and Jacques Lipchitz – who came to live in Paris at the beginning of the twentieth century. The Holocaust is only briefly touched on, since it's dealt with in depth by the Musée de la Shoah (see p.106). The main reference is an installation by contemporary artist Christian Boltanski: one of the exterior walls of a small courtyard is covered with black-bordered death announcements printed with the names of the Jewish artisans who once lived in the building, a number of whom were deported.

The Jewish quarter: rue des Rosiers

Ⓜ St-Paul

One block south of the rue des Francs-Bourgeois, the area around narrow, pedestrianized **rue des Rosiers** has traditionally been the **Jewish quarter** of the city since the twelfth century. However, soaring property prices and the area's burgeoning popularity with tourists have forced many of the traditional grocers, bakers, bookshops and cafés to close, and the area is in real danger of losing its identity. The hammam (no. 4) now houses a clothing store, as does *Jo Goldenberg* (no. 7), once the city's most famous Jewish restaurant. Despite these changes, the area still retains a Jewish flavour, with a number of kosher food shops and Hebrew bookstores. There's also a distinctly Mediterranean feel in the *quartier*; on Sunday lunchtimes the street fills with people who come to pick up a falafel wrap from one of the handful of Middle Eastern cafés. This development is testimony to the influence of the **North African Sephardim**, who, since the end of World War II, have sought refuge here from the uncertainties of life in the French ex-colonies. They have replenished Paris's Jewish population, depleted when its Ashkenazim, having escaped the pogroms of Eastern Europe, were rounded up by the Nazis and the French police and transported back east to concentration camps. Another vestige of the strong Yiddish community that once lived here is the lovely Art Nouveau **synagogue** designed by Hector Guimard on nearby rue Pavée.

The Haut Marais

Ⓜ Filles du Calvaire/St-Sebastien Froissart

The northern part of the Marais, known as the **Haut Marais** (the "upper Marais"), encompasses the old **Quartier du Temple**, named after the Knights Templar's stronghold that once stood at its heart, and the city's original **Chinatown**, concentrated on the upper end of rue du Temple and the streets west. Here the aristocratic stone facades of the lower Marais give way to the more humble, though no less attractive, stucco, paint and thick-slatted shutters of seventeenth- and eighteenth-century streets. Some bear the names of old rural French provinces: Beauce, Perche, Saintonge, Picardie. Formerly a quiet backwater, the area now attracts an arty crowd, who come to browse the many contemporary art galleries (see box, p.102), interior design shops and boutiques of young fashion designers concentrated on **rue Charlot**, rue de Poitou, rue Vieille du Temple and around. The area's chief visitor attractions are the newly revamped **Musée Picasso**, the absorbing **Musée des Arts et Métiers** and the state-of-the-art **Gaîté Lyrique** digital arts centre.

6

Musée Picasso

5 rue de Thorigny, 3ᵉ • Tues–Fri 11.30am–6pm, Sat & Sun 9.30–6pm, last entry 5.15pm; every third Fri of the month till 9pm • €11; free to under-18s and under-26s from (or studying in) the EU; free to everyone first Sun of the month • ☎ 01 85 56 00 36, ⓦ museepicassoparis.fr • Ⓜ Chemin-Vert/St-Paul

On the northern side of rue des Francs-Bourgeois, rue Payenne leads up to the lovely gardens and houses of **rue du Parc-Royal** and on to **rue de Thorigny**. Here, at no. 5, the magnificent classical facade of the seventeenth-century **Hôtel Salé**, built for a rich salt-tax collector, conceals the **Musée Picasso**, which in 2014 emerged from a major five-year renovation. The museum now has three times as much exhibition space available to display its five thousand paintings, drawings, ceramics, sculptures and photographs – one of the largest collections of Picasso's work anywhere, representing almost all the major periods of the artist's life from 1905 onwards. Many of the pieces were owned by Picasso and on his death in 1973 were donated to the state by his family in lieu of taxes owed. The result is an unedited body of work, which, although not including the most recognizable of Picasso's masterpieces, nevertheless provides a sense of the artist's development and an insight into the person behind the myth.

The museum is very popular and it's definitely worth thinking about reserving tickets in advance to avoid the long queues. The free museum map provides a fair amount of information on the works displayed, but to really get the most out of your visit you might want to reserve a "visioguide" (€4) with your ticket online or download the same as an app. The small, new *Café sur le Toit*, with an outside terrace, is a nice spot for a restorative cuppa.

The collection

The collection, spread over four floors, level –1 to floor 2, includes **paintings** from the artist's Blue Period, studies for the *Demoiselles d'Avignon*, experiments with Cubism and

---

PRIVATE ART GALLERIES IN THE MARAIS

The Marais, and the Haut Marais in particular, is where most of the city's private **commercial art galleries** are concentrated. Many occupy handsome old mansion houses, which are set back from the road and reached via cobbled courtyards. Below are some of the highlights; all are free to visit. A handy **guide** to the best galleries is the *Galeries mode d'emploi*, usually available in the galleries themselves, and downloadable online from ⓦ www.fondation-entreprise-ricard.com or available as an app.

Galerie Almine Rech 64 rue de Turenne, 3ᵉ ☎ 01 45 83 71 90, ⓦ alminerech.com; Ⓜ St-Sébastien-Froissart; map p.94. Recently installed in this elegant gallery, Rech represents around fifty artists, including Ugo Rondinone and James Turrell. Tues–Sat 11am–7pm.

Galerie Chantal Crousel 10 rue Charlot, 3ᵉ ☎ 01 42 77 38 87, ⓦ crousel.com; Ⓜ Filles-du-Calvaire; map p.97. Around since 1980, this gallery (which also has an annexe in the 10ᵉ at 11F rue Léon Jouhaux) represents mostly foreign and some French artists, such as Thomas Hirschhorn and Mona Hatoum, working in a variety of media. It also promotes the work of video artists, such as Pierre Huyghe. Tues–Sat 11am–1pm & 2–7pm.

Galerie Emmanuel Perrotin 76 rue de Turenne, 3ᵉ ☎ 01 42 16 79 79, ⓦ perrotin.com; Ⓜ St-Sébastien-Froissart; map p.94. One of the most influential galleries on the French contemporary art scene, Perrotin has exhibited French artists like Sophie Calle as well as inter-national names such as Takashi Murakami and Maurizio Cattelan. Tues–Sat 11am–7pm.

Galerie Marian Goodman 79 rue du Temple, 3ᵉ ☎ 01 48 04 70 50, ⓦ mariangoodman.com; Ⓜ Rambuteau; map p.97. This offshoot of the famed New York gallery recently exhibited Tacita Dean, Steve McQueen and Rineke Dijkstra. Tues–Sat 11am–7pm.

Galerie Thaddeus Ropac 7 rue Debelleyme, 3ᵉ ☎ 01 42 72 99 00, ⓦ ropac.net; Ⓜ Filles-du-Calvaire; map p.97. Recent exhibitions at this well-established gallery have included Ilya and Emilia Kabakov and Joseph Beuys. Also well worth a visit is Ropac's enormous outpost in Pantin, near La Villette, sited in a former factory and ideal for showing large-scale installations and sculptures by the likes of Anselm Kiefer and Georg Baselitz. Tues–Sat 10am–7pm.

Surrealism, as well as larger-scale works on themes of war and peace (eg, the chilling *Massacre in Korea*, 1951) and his later preoccupations with love and death, reflected in his Minotaur and bullfighting paintings. Perhaps some of the most engaging works are the most personal – the portraits of the artist's lovers, Dora Maar and Marie-Thérèse, show how the two women inspired him in different ways: Dora Maar is painted with strong lines and vibrant colours, suggesting a vivacious personality, while Marie-Thérèse's muted colours and soft contours convey serenity and peace.

The numerous **engravings**, **ceramics** and **sculpture** on display reflect the remarkable ease with which the artist moved from one medium to another. Some of the most arresting sculptures are those Picasso created from recycled household objects, such as the endearing *La Chèvre* (Goat), whose stomach is made from a basket, its udders from terracotta pots; and the *Tête de taureau*, an ingenious pairing of a bicycle seat and handlebars. Also fascinating to see are the paintings Picasso bought or was given by contemporaries such as Matisse and Cézanne; his collection of African masks and sculptures; and photographs taken by Dora Maar and Brassaï of Picasso in his studio, including one of him painting *Guernica*, cigarette in one hand, paintbrush in the other.

Marché des Enfants Rouges
39 rue de Bretagne, 3ᵉ • Tues–Sat 8.30am–2pm & 4–7.30pm, Sun 8.30am–2pm • Ⓜ Filles-du-Calvaire

Just west of rue Charlot, a little short of the vibrant rue de Bretagne, is the easily missed entrance to the **Marché des Enfants Rouges**, one of the smallest and oldest food markets in Paris, dating back to 1616, its name a reference to the red uniforms once worn by children at the orphanage that stood nearby. It has a very lively atmosphere and outdoor tables where you can eat takeaway soups, couscous, sushi and much else. **Rue de Bretagne** itself is full of traditional food shops such as cheesemongers, bakeries and coffee merchants, as well as some popular cafés such as *Café Charlot* (see p.278) and *Le Progrès*.

Carreau du Temple
4 rue Eugène Spuller, 3ᵉ • ☎ 01 83 81 93 30, ⓦ carreaudutemple.eu • Ⓜ Temple

A former market pavilion, the **Carreau du Temple** has recently been converted into an arts and sports centre. The shell of the nineteenth-century brick, glass and iron-frame

---

THE TEMPLE AND LOUIS XVII

Louis XVI, Marie-Antoinette, their two children and immediate family were all **imprisoned** in the keep of the Knights Templar's ancient fortress in August 1792 by the revolutionary government. By the end of 1794, when all the adults had been executed, the two children – the teenage Marie-Thérèse and the 9- or 10-year-old Dauphin, now, in the eyes of royalists, **Louis XVII** – remained there alone, in the charge of a family called Simon. Louis XVII was literally walled up, allowed no communication with other human beings, not even his sister, who was living on the floor above (Marie-Thérèse, incidentally, survived, went into exile in 1775, and returned to France in 1814 with the Bourbon restoration). He died of tuberculosis in 1795, a half-crazed imbecile, and was buried in a public grave.

For many years afterwards, however, **rumours** circulated that Louis XVII was in fact alive. The doctor, for example, who certified the child's death kept a lock of his hair, but it was later found not to correspond with the colour of the young Louis XVII's hair, as remembered by his sister. Furthermore, Mme Simon confessed on her deathbed that she had substituted another child for Louis XVII, giving rise to the theory that the real Louis had died early in 1794 and been replaced with another child, in order to provide Robespierre with a hostage he could use against internal and foreign royalist enemies.

Taking advantage of this atmosphere of uncertainty, 43 different people subsequently claimed to be Louis XVII. After nearly two centuries of speculation, all rumours were put to rest in 2000 when **DNA** from the child who died of TB was found to match samples obtained from locks of Marie-Antoinette's hair, and also that of several other maternal relatives.

structure has been preserved to create a wonderfully light and elegant space for all kinds of events from cocktail-tasting to jazz concerts, salons, plays and fashion shows. The lower floor has dance studios and a gym, and there's also a stylish bar-restaurant, *Le Jules*. On the lower floor you can see vestiges of the old **Temple keep**, a 50m-high turreted building that used to stand on this site; this was where Louis XVI and the royal family were imprisoned before their execution (see box opposite).

The Carreau and the nearby **Square du Temple** gardens stand on what was once the Enclos du Temple, or Temple precinct, the stronghold of the **Knights Templar**, a military order established in Jerusalem at the time of the Crusades to protect pilgrims to the Holy Land. Its members were exceedingly rich and powerful, with some nine thousand commands spread across Europe. They came to a sticky end early in the fourteenth century, however, when King Philippe le Bel, alarmed at their growing power, and in alliance with Pope Clement V, had them tried for sacrilege, blasphemy and sodomy. Fifty-four of the order's members were burnt, and the order abolished. The Temple buildings survived until they were demolished in 1808 by Napoleon.

6

Rue du Temple

Ⓜ Arts-et-Métiers/Temple

A couple of blocks to the west of the Carreau du Temple, on and around the top end of **rue du Temple**, lies Paris's original **Chinatown**. The area was settled during World War I when Chinese immigrants came over to fill the gap in the workforce left by the departure of French troops for the front. Rue du Temple, lined with many beautiful houses dating back to the seventeenth century, is full of Chinese-run wholesale businesses trading in leather and fashion accessories, as well as jewellers' shops, a hangover from the times when this formed part of the Temple precinct, the inhabitants of which were accorded special privileges such as tax exemption and the exclusive right to make costume jewellery.

The streets to the west of rue du Temple are narrow, dark and riddled with passages, the houses half-timbered and bulging with age. No. 51 rue Montmorency is Paris's oldest house, built in 1407 for the alchemist Nicolas Flamel, whose name will ring a bell with Harry Potter fans; the building is now a restaurant, *Auberge Nicolas Flamel*.

Musée des Arts et Métiers

60 rue de Réaumur, 3ᵉ • Tues–Sun 10am–6pm, Thurs till 9.30pm • €6.50 • ☎ 01 53 01 82 00, ⓦ arts-et-metiers.net • Ⓜ Arts-et-Métiers

The **Musée des Arts et Métiers** is a fascinating museum of technological innovation. It's part of the Conservatoire des Arts et Métiers and incorporates the former Benedictine priory of St-Martin-des-Champs, its original chapel dating from the fourth century. The most important exhibit is **Foucault's pendulum**, which the scientist used to demonstrate the rotation of the earth in 1851, a sensational event held at the Panthéon and attended by a huge crowd eager to "see the earth go round". The orb itself, a hollow brass sphere, is under glass in the chapel, and there's a working model set up nearby.

Other exhibits include the laboratory of Lavoisier, the French chemist who first showed that water is a combination of oxygen and hydrogen, and, hanging as if in mid-flight above the grand staircase, the elegant "Avion 3", a flying machine complete with feathered propellers, which was donated to the Conservatoire after several ill-fated attempts to fly it.

La Gaîté Lyrique

3bis rue Papin, 3ᵉ • Tues–Sat 2–8pm, Sun noon–6pm • ☎ 01 53 01 51 51, ⓦ gaite-lyrique.net • Ⓜ Réaumur-Sébastopol/Arts-et-Métiers

The **Gaîté Lyrique** is a centre for digital arts and electronic music, opened in 2011. This venerable Italian-style theatre, built in 1862, was once renowned as a venue for operettas under such illustrious directors as Jacques Offenbach, and hosted the Ballets Russes in the 1920s. The facade, entrance hall and splendid first-floor marble foyer (a wonderful setting for the café) have been restored, and the interior has been opened up to accommodate a state-of-the-art concert hall, exhibition spaces and artists' studios. The busy programme of events includes regular concerts, exhibitions, film, dance and theatre performances, and art installations. There's also a free video-games room.

Quartier St-Paul

Ⓜ St-Paul/Sully-Morland/Pont Marie

The southern part of the Marais, the **Quartier St-Paul**, between the rue de Rivoli, rue de St-Antoine and the Seine, is less buzzy than the rest of the district, its quiet, atmospheric streets lined with attractive old houses. The chief sights are the moving **Mémorial de la Shoah**, with its museum documenting the fate of French Jews in World War II; the **Maison Européenne de la Photographie**, which hosts exhibitions by contemporary photographers; and the **Pavillon de l'Arsenal**, a showcase for the city's current architectural projects. The area is also a good hunting ground for antiques, concentrated mostly in the **Village St-Paul** and rue St-Paul.

St-Gervais-St-Protais

Place St-Gervais, 4ᵉ • Ⓜ Hôtel-de-Ville

There's been a church on the site of **St-Gervais-St-Protais** since the sixth century; the current building was started in 1494, though not completed until the seventeenth century, which explains the mismatched late Gothic interior and Classical exterior. There's some lovely stained glass inside, sixteenth-century carved misericords and a seventeenth-century organ; it's one of Paris's oldest and has been played by eight generations of the Couperin family, including the famous François Couperin. The third chapel down on the right commemorates the 88 victims of a German shell that hit the church on Good Friday 1918 and caused part of the nave to collapse.

Exiting the church round the altar at the back, you enter cobbled **rue des Barres**, a picturesque little street, filled with the scent of roses from nearby gardens in summer, and a nice setting for the outdoor terrace of *L'Ebouillanté* café (see p.280).

Mémorial de la Shoah

17 rue Geoffroy l'Asnier, 4ᵉ • Daily except Sat 10am–6pm, Thurs till 10pm • Free • ☎ 01 42 77 44 72, ⓦ memorialdelashoah.org • Ⓜ St-Paul/Pont-Marie

The grim fate of French Jews in World War II is commemorated at the **Mémorial de la Shoah**, within the Centre de Documentation Juive Contemporaine, access to which usually involves queuing, as visitors and bags are scanned at the entrance. President Chirac opened a new museum here in 2005 and, alongside the sombre **Mémorial du Martyr Juif Inconnu** (Memorial to the Unknown Jewish Martyr), unveiled a Wall of Names; ten researchers spent two and a half years trawling Gestapo documents and interviewing French families to compile the list of the 76,000 Jews – around a quarter of the wartime population – sent to death camps from 1942 to 1944. In 2006, the **Mur des Justes** was added, a wall listing the names of French people who aided Jews at this time.

Chirac, in 1995, was the first French president to acknowledge that France was involved in systematically persecuting Jews during World War II. In most instances, it was the French police, not the Nazi occupiers, who rounded up the Jews for deportation. The most notorious case was in July 1942, when 13,152 Jews (including more than 4000 children) were rounded up in the Vel d'Hiv bicycle stadium in Paris and sent to death camps.

The museum

The Vel d'Hiv incident, along with much else, is documented in the excellent **museum**, with plenty of information in English. The main focus is events in France leading up to and during World War II, but there is also lots of background on the history of Jews in France and in Europe as a whole. Individual stories are illustrated with photos,

ID cards, letters and other documents. You learn about model citizens such as the Javel family, who were all deported and died in the camps, their long-established residence in France and distinguished record of military service counting for naught in the relentless Nazi drive to exterminate all Jews. Others, such as the Lifchitz family, who fled pogroms in Russia and settled in France in 1909, managed to survive the war – in this case by going into hiding and obtaining false ID as Orthodox Christians. The collection also features drawings and letters from Drancy, the holding station outside Paris, from which French Jews were sent on to camps in Germany. The museum ends with the **Mémorial des Enfants**, an overwhelming collection of photos, almost unbearable to look at, of 2500 French children, each image marked with the date of their birth and the date of their deportation.

Maison Européenne de la Photographie

4 rue de Fourcy, 4ᵉ • Wed–Sun 11am–7.45pm • €8, free Wed after 5pm • ☎ 01 44 78 75 00, ⓦ mep-fr.org • Ⓜ St-Paul/Pont-Marie

Between rues Fourcy and François-Miron, a gorgeous Marais mansion, the early eighteenth-century Hôtel Hénault de Cantobre, houses the **Maison Européenne de la Photographie**, dedicated to the art of contemporary photography. Temporary shows combine with a revolving exhibition of the permanent collection; young photographers and photojournalists get a look-in, as well as artists using photography in multimedia creations or installation art. There's also a library, *vidéothèque* and stylish café.

Village St-Paul and around

Ⓜ St-Paul/Pont-Marie

East of the Maison Européenne de la Photographie is **Village St-Paul**, a network of courtyards and streets housing around a hundred antique, interior-design and art shops. This part of the Marais suffered a postwar hatchet job, and, although seventeenth- and eighteenth-century magnificence is still in evidence (there's even a stretch of the city's defensive wall dating from the early thirteenth century in the *lycée* playground on rue des Jardins St-Paul), it lacks the architectural cohesion of the Marais to the north. The fifteenth-century **Hôtel de Sens**, on the rue du Figuier, looks bizarre in its isolation. The public library it now houses, the **Bibliothèque Forney** (see p.344), filled with volumes on fine and applied arts, provides a good excuse to explore this outstanding medieval building.

Musée de la Magie

11 rue St-Paul, 4ᵉ • Wed, Sat & Sun 2–7pm; live magic show every 30min 2.30–6pm • €12, children €9 • ☎ 01 42 72 13 26, ⓦ museedelamagie.com • Ⓜ St-Paul/Sully-Morland

Set amid the antique shops on rue St-Paul is the **Musée de la Magie**, a delightful museum of magic and illusion. Automata, distorting mirrors and optical illusions, objects that float on thin air, a box for sawing people in half – they're all on view, with examples from the eighteenth and nineteenth centuries, as well as contemporary magicians' tools and hands-on exhibits for children. Most fun is a live magician's demonstration. The museum shop sells books on conjuring, plus magic cards, wands, boxes, scarves and the like. School groups tend to visit on Wednesdays, so it's better to visit at weekends.

Pavillon de l'Arsenal

21 bd Morland, 4ᵉ • Tues–Sat 10.30am–6.30pm, Sun 11am–7pm • Free • ☎ 01 42 76 33 97, ⓦ pavillon-arsenal.com • Ⓜ Sully-Morland

The **Pavillon de l'Arsenal** is an exhibition centre that presents the capital's current **architectural projects** to the public. There's also a permanent exhibition on Paris's architectural development, centring on a huge interactive screen on the floor showing Google Earth images of Paris; superimposed on it are all the major construction projects planned over the next twenty years, so you can bring up a projected image of what, for example, the Les Halles district will look like when its makeover is complete.

Bastille and around

A symbol of revolution since the toppling of the Bastille prison in 1789, the Bastille quarter used to belong in spirit and style to the working-class districts of eastern Paris. After the construction of the opera house in the 1980s, however, it became a magnet for artists, fashion folk and young people, who brought with them over the years stylish shops and an energetic nightlife. Much of the action takes place around rue Amelot, rue de Charonne and rue de Lappe, where cocktail lounges and theme bars have edged out the old tool shops, cobblers and ironmongers. However, some of the working-class flavour lingers on, especially along rue de la Roquette and in the furniture workshops off rue du Faubourg-St-Antoine, testimony to a long tradition of cabinet making and woodworking in the district.

South of Bastille, the relatively unsung **twelfth arrondissement** offers an authentic slice of Paris, with its neighbourhood shops and bars, and traditional markets, such as the lively Marché d'Aligre. Among the area's attractions are the **Promenade Plantée**, an ex-railway line turned into an elevated walkway running from Bastille to the green expanse of the **Bois de Vincennes**, and **Bercy Village**'s attractive cafés and shops set in old wine warehouses.

Place de la Bastille

Ⓜ Bastille

Place de la Bastille, a vast, traffic-choked square, is indissolubly linked with the events of July 14, 1789, when the Bastille prison fortress was stormed, triggering the **French Revolution** and the end of feudalism in Europe. Bastille Day (July 14) is celebrated throughout France and the square is the scene of dancing and partying on the evening of July 13. The prison itself no longer stands – its only visible remains have been transported to square Henri-Galli at the end of boulevard Henri-IV. A Société Générale bank is situated on the site of the prison and the place de la Bastille is where the fortress's ramparts would have been.

Opéra Bastille

Place de la Bastille, 11ᵉ • ☎ 08 92 89 90 90 (from within France), ☎ 01 71 25 24 23 (from abroad), ⓦ operadeparis.fr • Ⓜ Bastille

The Bicentennial of the French Revolution in 1989 was marked by the inauguration of a new opera house on place de la Bastille, the **Opéra Bastille**, one of François Mitterrand's pet projects. It fills almost the entire block between rues de Lyon, Charenton and Moreau. One critic described it as a "hippopotamus in a bathtub", and you can see his point. The architect, Uruguayan Carlos Ott, was concerned that his design should not bring an overbearing monumentalism to place de la Bastille. The different depths and layers of the semicircular facade do give a certain sense of the building stepping back, but self-effacing it is not. With time, use and familiarity, Parisians became reconciled to it, and today people happily sit on its steps, wander into its shops and libraries, and camp out all night for the free performance on July 14.

Port de l'Arsenal

Ⓜ Bastille

Just south of the place de la Bastille is the **Port de l'Arsenal** marina, occupying part of what was once the moat around the Bastille. The Canal St-Martin starts here, flowing underneath the square and emerging much further north, just past place de la République, a route plied by canal pleasure-boats run by Canauxrama (see p.28). Some two hundred boats are moored up in the marina, and the landscaped banks, with children's playgrounds, make it quite a pleasant spot for a wander.

Maison Rouge

10 bd de la Bastille, 11ᵉ • Wed & Fri–Sun 11am–7pm, Thurs 11am–9pm • €9 • ☎ 01 40 01 08 81, ⓦ lamaisonrouge.org • Ⓜ Bastille/Quai de la Rapée

One of the former industrial spaces bordering the port de l'Arsenal has been converted into a light and spacious contemporary art gallery, called the **Maison Rouge – Fondation Antoine de Galbert**. Founded in 2004 by collector Antoine de Galbert, the Maison Rouge, which takes its name from the bright-red pavilion at the centre of the building, has become a major player on the contemporary art scene, hosting quality exhibitions, either devoted to an individual artist or a private collection. The presence of a branch of *Rose Bakery* here also makes it a nice place for a bite to eat. The whole place closes between exhibitions.

East of place de la Bastille

Northeast of place de la Bastille, off rue de la Roquette, narrow, cobbled **rue de Lappe** is a lively place at night, crammed with bars drawing a largely teenage and out-of-town

7

BARS
Le Lèche-Vin 2
Moonshiner 1

CLUBS
Badaboum 5

LIVE MUSIC
L'Atelier Charonne 6
Café de la Danse 3
Café de la Plage 4
Instants Chavirés 7

ACCOMMODATION
Auberge Flora 1
Hôtel Marais Bastille 2
Maurice Ravel 3

11ᵉ

BASTILLE AND EAST

crowd. At no. 32, *Balajo* is one remnant of a very Parisian tradition: the *bals musettes*, or music halls of 1930s *gai Paris*, established by the area's large Auvergnat population and frequented between the wars by such luminaries as Edith Piaf, Jean Gabin and Rita Hayworth. It was founded by one Jo de France, who introduced glitter and spectacle into what were then seedy gangster dives, enticing Parisians from the other side of the city to drink absinthe and savour the rue de Lappe lowlife. Parisians are still drawn here and to the bars on neighbouring streets, such as **rue Daval** to the north.

Off rue Daval, on the left as you walk up from rue de Lappe, is charming little pedestrianized **cour Damoye**, a narrow cobbled street formerly lined with furniture workshops and now mostly inhabited by architects' studios, design shops and the fragrant Brûlerie Daval coffee merchant. Other streets worth exploring are the nearby section of **rue de Charonne**, home to fashion boutiques and wacky interior designers, and **rue Keller**, clustered with alternative, hippie outfits, indie record stores and young fashion designers.

7 Ste-Marguerite

36 rue St-Bernard, 11ᵉ • Mon–Sat 8am–noon & 3–7.30pm, Sun 8.30am–noon & 5–7.30pm • Free • ⓂCharonne

South of rue de Charonne, between rue St-Bernard and impasse Charrière, stands the rustic-looking church of **Ste-Marguerite**, with a garden dedicated to the memory of Raoul Nordling, the Swedish consul who persuaded the retreating Germans not to blow up Paris in 1944. The church itself was built in 1627 to accommodate the growing local population, which was about 40,000 in 1710 and 100,000 in 1900. The sculptures on the transept pediments were carved by its first full-blown parish priest. The inside of the church is wide-bodied, low and quiet, with a distinctly rural feel. The stained-glass windows record a very local history: the visit in 1802 of Pope Pius VII, who was in Paris for Napoleon's coronation; the miraculous cure of a Madame Delafosse in the rue de Charonne in 1725; the fatal wounding of Monseigneur Affre, the archbishop of Paris, in the course of a street battle in the faubourg in 1848; the murder of sixteen Carmelite nuns at the Barrière du Trône in 1794; and the *quartier*'s dead of World War I. The church was once surrounded by a cemetery, where many victims of the Revolutionary Terror were buried, though only a small portion now survives.

Rue de la Roquette

ⓂBastille/Voltaire

Running parallel to rue de Charonne is buzzy **rue de la Roquette**, home to cheap and cheerful shops, Turkish restaurants and local bars. Towards its eastern end is **square de**

THE COLONNE DE JUILLET

A gleaming gold statue, a winged figure of Liberty, stands atop the bronze **Colonne de Juillet** at the centre of place de la Bastille. The plinth on which it stands was once intended to hold quite a different monument – **Napoleon** had wanted a giant elephant fountain to stand here, with a spiral staircase inside one leg and viewing platform on top. The project never came to fruition, but the full-scale model that was made became a curiosity in its own right and stood for a while near the Gare de Vincennes (Gavroche in Victor Hugo's *Les Misérables* sought shelter in it). After 35 years it was sold for 3833 francs. The same architect (Jean-Antoine Alavoine) who had worked on the elephant built the present column, which was erected to commemorate the **July Revolution of 1830**, replacing the autocratic Charles X with the "Citizen King" Louis-Philippe. When Louis-Philippe fled in the more significant 1848 Revolution, his throne was burnt beside the column and a new inscription added. Four months later, the workers again took to the streets. All of eastern Paris was barricaded, with the fiercest fighting on rue du Faubourg-St-Antoine, until the rebellion was quelled with the usual massacres and deportation of survivors. The square is still an important rallying point for political protest.

la Roquette, the site of an old prison, where four thousand members of the Resistance were incarcerated in 1944. The low, forbidding gateway on rue de la Roquette has been preserved in their memory.

Faubourg-St-Antoine
Ⓜ Bastille/Ledru-Rollin/Faidherbe Chaligny

After Louis XI licensed the establishment of craftsmen in the fifteenth century, the **rue du Faubourg-St-Antoine**, running east from place de la Bastille, became the principal working-class *quartier* of Paris, cradle of revolutions and mother of street-fighters. From its beginnings, the principal trade associated with it has been **furniture making**, and this was where the classic styles of French furniture – Louis XIV, Louis XV, Second Empire – were developed. There are still quite a few furniture shops on the street, and a number of workshops, as well as related trades such as inlayers, stainers and polishers, still inhabit the maze of interconnecting yards and *passages* that run off the faubourg, especially at the western end. One of the most attractive courtyards is at no. 56, the cour du Bel Air, with its lemon trees and ivy- and rose-covered buildings.

7

Place de la Nation
Ⓜ Nation

Rue du Faubourg-St-Antoine leads eastwards to **place de la Nation**. The *place* is adorned with the *Triumph of the Republic*, a monumental bronze group topped with a stately female figure personifying the Republic. To the east, framing the avenue du Trône, are two tall Doric columns, surmounted by statues of medieval monarchs, looking very small and insignificant. During the Revolution, when the old name of place du Trône became place du Trône-Renversé ("the overturned throne"), more people were guillotined here than on the more notorious execution site of place de la Concorde.

Marché d'Aligre
Ⓜ Ledru-Rollin

South of rue du Faubourg-St-Antoine is the **Marché d'Aligre**, a lively, raucous market, held every morning except Monday, and particularly animated on Saturdays and Sundays. The square itself is given over to clothes and bric-a-brac stalls, selling anything from old gramophone players to odd bits of crockery. There's also a covered food market with traditional fromageries and charcuteries, plus more unusual stalls such as Sur les Quais, selling numerous varieties of olive oil. It's along the adjoining **rue d'Aligre**, however, where the market really comes to life, with the vendors, many of Algerian origin, doing a frenetic trade in fruit and veg. As the market winds down, you could follow the locals to the old-fashioned *Le Baron Rouge* wine bar (see p.281) for a glass of wine and some *saucisson*, or drink in the North African atmosphere at the *Ruche à Miel* café (see p.281) at 19 rue d'Aligre and order some mint tea with sticky cakes.

The Promenade Plantée and around
Ⓜ Bastille/Ledru-Rollin

The **Promenade Plantée**, also known as the Coulée Verte, is an excellent way to see a little-visited part of the city – and from an unusual angle. This disused railway viaduct, part of the old Paris–Cherbourg line, has been ingeniously converted into an **elevated walkway**, similar to New York's High Line, and planted with a profusion of trees and flowers – cherry trees, maples, limes, roses and lavender.

The walkway starts near the beginning of **avenue Daumesnil**, just south of the Bastille opera house, and is reached via a flight of stone steps – or lifts (though these are frequently out of order) – with a number of similar access points further along. It takes you to the Parc de Reuilly, then descends to ground level and continues as far as the *périphérique*, from where you can walk to the Bois de Vincennes. The whole walk is around 4.5km long, but if you don't feel like doing the entire thing you could just walk the first part, along the viaduct – a twenty-minute stroll – which also happens to be the most attractive stretch, running past venerable old mansion blocks and giving you a bird's-eye view of the street below. Small architectural details such as decorative mouldings and elaborate wrought-iron balconies (not to mention elegant interiors) that you wouldn't normally notice at street level come to light – the oddest sight is the series of caryatids adorning the police station at the end of avenue Daumesnil.

Viaduc des Arts
Ⓜ Bastille/Gare de Lyon/Ledru-Rollin

Underneath the Promenade Plantée, the red-brick arches of the viaduct itself have been converted into attractive spaces for artisans' studios and craft shops, collectively known as the **Viaduc des Arts**. The workshops house a wealth of creativity: furniture and tapestry restorers, interior designers, cabinet-makers, violin- and flute-makers, embroiderers, and fashion and jewellery designers.

Jardin de Reuilly
Ⓜ Montgallet/Dugommier

The Viaduc des Arts ends around halfway down avenue Daumesnil, but the Promenade Plantée continues, taking you to the **Jardin de Reuilly**, an old freight station, now an inviting, circular expanse of lawn, popular with picnickers on sunny days, and bordered by terraces and arbours. The open-air café here makes a good refreshment stop if you're walking the length of the *promenade*. You can also choose to bypass the park altogether by taking the gracefully arching wooden footbridge that spans it.

Allée Vivaldi to the boulevard périphérique

Towards the eastern end of the Promenade Plantée walkway is the nondescript **allée Vivaldi**, lined with modern blocks. Next, you go through a tunnel to emerge in the old railway cutting, a delightful stretch that meanders through a canopy of trees and flowers below street level. At this point the path divides into two – one for pedestrians, the other for cyclists – landscaped all along, taking you through a series of ivy-draped ex-railway tunnels and shadowing the rue du Sahel for most of the way. The walk ends at the *boulevard périphérique*. From here you're not far from the Porte Dorée métro station and the Porte Dorée entrance to the **Bois de Vincennes**. A pathway to the right takes you behind a sports stadium (with the *périphérique* on your left) before turning into rue Edouard Lartet, then rue du Général Archinard. At the end of this turn left into avenue du Général Messimy, which leads into the main avenue Daumesnil; the métro station is to the right and entrance to the *bois* to the left.

Bercy
Ⓜ Bercy

The former warehouse district of **Bercy**, along the Seine east of the Gare de Lyon, has been transformed recently by a series of ambitious and ultramodern developments designed to complement the grand-scale "Paris Rive Gauche" project (see p.178) on the opposite bank.

Ministère des Finances
139 rue de Bercy, 12ᵉ • Ⓜ Bercy

As you emerge from Bercy métro station, the first thing you notice is the imposing bulk of the **Ministère des Finances**, constructed in 1990 to house the treasury staff after they had finally agreed to move out of the Richelieu wing of the Louvre. Housing some 4700 employees, it stretches like a giant loading bridge from above the river (where higher bureaucrats and ministers arrive by boat) to rue de Bercy, a distance of around 400m.

Parc de Bercy

Maison du Jardinage April–Sept Tues–Fri 1.30–5.30pm, Sat & Sun 1.30–6.30pm; Oct–March Tues–Sat 1.30–5pm • Free • Ⓜ Bercy

Southeast of the Ministère des Finances squats the charmless **Bercy Arena**. Built in 1983, its concrete bunker frame clad with grass covers a vast space used for sporting and cultural events (see p.344). Beyond it, the area that used to house the old Bercy warehouses, where for centuries the capital's wine supplies were unloaded from river barges, is now the extensive **Parc de Bercy**. Here, the French formal garden has been given a modern twist with geometric lines and grid-like flowerbeds, but it also cleverly incorporates elements of the old warehouse site such as disused railway tracks and cobbled lanes. The western section of the park is a fairly unexciting expanse of grass with a huge stepped fountain

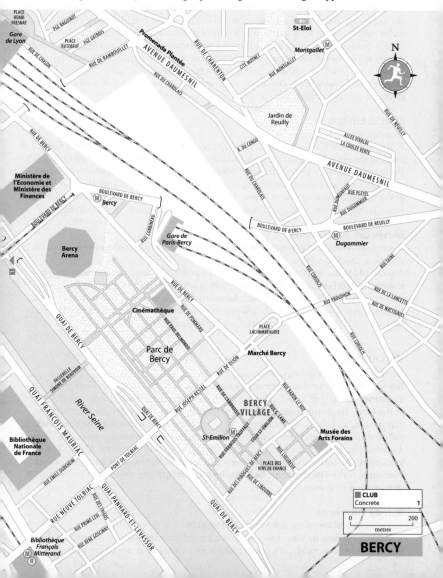

(popular with children) set into one of the grassy banks, but the area east is attractively landscaped with arbours, rose gardens, lily ponds and an orangerie. There's also a **Maison du Jardinage**, a garden exhibition centre, where you can consult gardening books and magazines and visit the adjoining greenhouse and vegetable garden.

Cinémathèque

51 rue de Bercy, 12ᵉ • Museum Mon, Wed–Sat noon–7pm, Sun 10am–8pm • €5, free Sun 10am–1pm • ☎ 01 71 19 33 33, ⓦ cinematheque.fr • Ⓜ Bercy

Of the new buildings surrounding the Parc du Bercy, the most striking, on the north side, is the **Cinémathèque**. Designed by Guggenheim architect Frank Gehry, it's constructed from zinc, glass and limestone and resembles a falling pack of cards – according to Gehry, the inspiration was Matisse's collages, created "with a simple pair of scissors". Its huge archive of films dates back to the earliest days of cinema, and regular retrospectives of French and foreign films are screened in its four cinemas. It also has an engaging **museum**, tracing the history of cinema, with lots of early cinematic equipment, magic lanterns, silent-film clips and costumes including outfits from Eisenstein's *Ivan the Terrible*. On the upper floor, the **Galerie des Donateurs** stages exhibitions on the work of various film directors such as François Truffaut, or on other cinema-related themes.

Cour St-Emilion

Ⓜ Cour-St-Emilion

A little east of the Cinémathèque, arched footbridges take you over the busy rue Kessel into the eastern extension of the park and the adjoining **Bercy Village**, the hub of which is the **Cour St-Emilion**, a pedestrianized, cobbled street lined with former wine warehouses that have been stylishly converted into shops, restaurants and wine bars. These are popular places to come before or after a film at the giant Bercy multiplex at the eastern end of the street, particularly on Sundays when shops in most other areas of Paris are closed.

Musée des Arts Forains

53 av des Terroirs-de-France, 12ᵉ • Daily tours (1hr 30min) to be booked in advance by phone or online • €16, children €8 • ☎ 01 43 40 16 15, ⓦ arts-forains.com • Ⓜ Cour-St-Emilion

A set of old stone wine warehouses houses the privately owned funfair museum, the **Musée des Arts Forains**, with its collection of nineteenth- and early twentieth-century funfair rides (which you can try out), fairground music and Venetian carnival rooms. It's only open to groups, though individuals can join a tour if they book in advance; tours are in French, but you can ask for a leaflet in English.

Vincennes

Ⓜ Porte Dorée/Porte de Charenton/Château-de-Vincennes

Beyond the 12ᵉ arrondissement, across the *boulevard périphérique*, lies the **Bois de Vincennes**, the largest green space the city has to offer aside from the Bois de Boulogne in the west. The main draws are the **Parc Floral**, an attractive park with an adventure playground, and the newly reopened **zoo**. To the east the **Cartoucherie de Vincennes**, an old munitions factory, is home to four theatre companies, including the radical Théâtre du Soleil (see p.314), while bordering the Bois to the north stands the **Château de Vincennes**, the country's only surviving medieval royal residence. West of the Bois de Vincennes is the **Cité Nationale de l'Histoire de l'Immigration**, devoted to the history of immigration in France.

Bois de Vincennes

Ⓜ Porte Dorée/Porte de Charenton/Château-de-Vincennes; buses #46 and #86

The extensive **Bois de Vincennes** was once a royal hunting ground roamed by deer; nowadays, unfortunately, it's crisscrossed with roads, but it does have some pleasant corners, including the Parc Floral and the two lakes. The sights are quite a long distance from each other, so you may want to target one or two, or you could pick up a Vélib' bike (see p.30) from near the entrance to the Parc Floral or near Lac Daumesnil.

Parc Floral

Bois de Vincennes • Daily 9.30am–8pm, winter till dusk • Free except June–Sept Wed, Sat & Sun, when entry is €5.50 • ☎ 01 49 57 24 84, ⓦ parcfloraldeparis.com • Ⓜ Château-de-Vincennes, then bus #112 or a short walk

If you've only got a limited amount of time in the Bois de Vincennes, make for the **Parc Floral**, just behind the Château de Vincennes. This is one of the best gardens in Paris – flowers are always in bloom in the Jardin des Quatre Saisons, and you can picnic beneath pines, then wander through camellias, rhododendrons, cacti, ferns, irises and bonsai trees. Between April and September there are art and horticultural exhibitions in several pavilions, free jazz and classical concerts, and numerous activities for children including a mini-golf course studded with mini Parisian monuments and an adventure playground (see p.349 for more details).

The lakes and around

For a lazy afternoon in the park, you could go boating on the **Lac Daumesnil**, near the Porte Dorée entrance, or feed the ducks on the **Lac des Minimes** (bus #112 from Vincennes métro), on the other side of the wood.

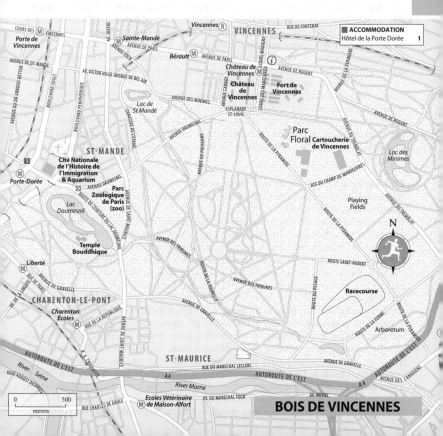

BOIS DE VINCENNES

Parc Zoologique de Paris

Junction of av Daumesnil and route de la Ceinture du Lac, 12ᵉ • Mid-March to mid-Oct Mon–Fri 10am–6pm, Sat, Sun & hols 9.30am–7.30pm; mid-Oct to mid-March daily 10am–5pm • €22, 3–11-year-olds €14, 12–25-year-olds €16.50 ☎ 08 11 22 41 22, Ⓦ parczoologiquedeparis.fr • Ⓜ Porte Dorée

North of the Lac Daumesnil lies the **Parc Zoologique de Paris**, the city's main **zoo**, reopened in 2014 after a six-year closure. Its landmark Grand Rocher, an extraordinary 65m-high fake boulder, built in 1934 when the zoo first opened, is still here, but just about everything else has been completely rebuilt. The zoo has tried to improve conditions for its one thousand-odd animals (representing 180 species) by re-creating as far as possible their natural habitats. Animals are grouped by region rather than by type: Patagonia, Sahel-Sudan, Europe, Guyana and Madagascar. As well as the more usual lions and zebras, there are less well known and endangered species such as manatees, wolverines, anteaters and white rhino. Highlights include the giant tropical hothouse harbouring tortoises, iguanas, caimans and other reptiles; and the giraffe house, where you get a great view of the leggy beasts from the glass viewing balcony. Plenty of information is provided on the animals and their habitats in French only, though you can buy an English-language leaflet for €3 from the ticket office. There are picnic areas, two restaurants and plenty of snack stands.

Château de Vincennes

Donjon Daily: mid-May to mid-Sept 10am–6pm; rest of year 10am–5pm • **Sainte-Chapelle** Daily: mid-May to mid-Sept 10.30am–1pm & 2–5.15pm; rest of year 10.30am–1pm & 2–6.15pm • €8.50 • ☎ 01 48 08 31 20, Ⓦ chateau-vincennes.fr • Ⓜ Château-de-Vincennes

On the northern edge of the Bois de Vincennes stands the **Château de Vincennes**, enclosed by an impressive defensive wall and surrounded by a (now empty) moat. France's only surviving medieval royal residence was built by Charles V, and subsequently turned into a state prison, porcelain factory, weapons dump and military training school. It presents a rather austere aspect on first sight, but is worth visiting for its beautiful Flamboyant Gothic **Sainte-Chapelle**, completed in the mid-sixteenth century and decorated with superb Renaissance stained-glass windows. Nearby, in the impressive fourteenth-century **donjon** (keep), you can see some fine vaulted ceilings and Charles V's bedchamber, as well as graffiti left by prisoners, whose number included the Marquis de Sade. The château fell into the hands of the English in the fifteenth century and it was in Charles V's bedchamber that Henry V of England died of dysentery.

Cité Nationale de l'Histoire de l'Immigration

293 av Daumesnil, 12ᵉ • Tues–Fri 10am–5.30pm, Sat & Sun 10am–7pm • €4.50–6; aquarium €5–7, children €3.50–5 • ☎ 01 53 59 58 60, Ⓦ histoire-immigration.fr • Ⓜ Porte Dorée

Just outside the Bois de Vincennes, across the way from the Porte Dorée entrance, a huge Art Deco building, the Palais de la Porte Dorée, houses the **Cité Nationale de l'Histoire de l'Immigration**, which examines the history of immigration to France over the last two centuries (around fifteen million French citizens have foreign roots) through photos, artwork, multimedia displays and audio installations. The museum is located in a building erected for the 1931 Colonial Exhibition and sports a vast, somewhat dubious bas-relief illustrating the former French colonies. Artworks themed around immigrants' struggles to integrate into French society and images of vehicles loaded with possessions arriving at the border are among the thought-provoking exhibits. Perhaps the most poignant items on display, though, are the suitcases brought over by immigrants, containing photos of loved ones, religious texts and teddy bears. There are also regular temporary exhibitions, such as the recent one on the contribution made to French fashion by immigrant designers and artisans. On the lower ground floor is an **aquarium** with a collection of tropical fish and a crocodile pit, left over from the *palais'* previous incarnation as the Musée des Arts Africains et Océaniens, whose exhibits have been transferred to the Musée du Quai Branly.

The Quartier Latin

The traditional heartland of the Quartier Latin lies between the river and the Montagne Ste-Geneviève, a hill once crowded with medieval colleges and now proudly crowned by the giant dome of the Panthéon. In medieval times, the name "Latin quarter" was probably a simple description, as this was the area whose inhabitants – clergymen and university scholars for the most part – ordinarily spoke Latin. It's still a scholarly area, home to the famous Sorbonne and Jussieu campuses, plus two of France's most elite lycées and a cluster of stellar academic institutes. Few students can afford the rents these days, but they still maintain the quarter's traditions in the cheaper bars, cafés and *bistrots*, decamping to the Luxembourg gardens, over in the 6e arrondissement (see p.140), on sunny days.

RIVE GAUCHE

In French, **rive gauche** means much more than just the "left bank" of the Seine. Technically, all Paris south of the river is the Left Bank (imagine you're looking downstream), but to Parisian ears the name conjures up the cerebral, creative, sometimes anarchic spirit that once flourished in the two central arrondissements, the 5ᵉ and 6ᵉ, in vigorous opposition – supposedly – to the more conformist, commercial and conservative *rive droite*. In the **Quartier Latin**, around the 5ᵉ, a distinctively alternative ambience has long been sustained by the powerful and independent-minded university, while for much of the twentieth century any painter, writer or musician with good bohemian credentials would have lived or worked in or around **St-Germain** and the 6ᵉ arrondissement. Between the wars you could find the painters Picasso and Modigliani in the cafés of **Montparnasse**, hobnobbing with writers such as Guillaume Apollinaire, André Breton, Jean Cocteau and Anaïs Nin, and expat wannabes like Henry Miller and Ernest Hemingway. After World War II the glitterati moved on to the cafés and jazz clubs of St-Germain, which became second homes to writers and musicians such as Jacques Prévert, Boris Vian, Sidney Bechet and Juliette Gréco – and, most famously, to the existentialists Jean-Paul Sartre and Simone de Beauvoir.

But what really defined the Rive Gauche's reputation for turbulence and innovation were *les événements*, the political "events" of **May 1968** (see box, p.124). Escalating from leftist student demonstrations to factory occupations and massive national strikes, they culminated in the near-overthrow of De Gaulle's presidency. Since that infamous summer, however, conservatives have certainly had their vengeance on the spirit of the Left Bank. The streets that saw revolution now house expensive apartments, art galleries and high-end fashion boutiques, while the cafés once frequented by penniless intellectuals and struggling artists are filled with designers, media and political magnates, and scores of well-heeled foreign residents.

8

These days, the term Quartier Latin is often used, as here, as shorthand for the entire 5ᵉ arrondissement. It's one of the city's more palpably ancient districts, retaining some of the medieval lanes, venerable churches and hidden corners that, elsewhere in Paris, were so often "improved" in later centuries. The romantically antiquated thoroughfare of the **rue Mouffetard** still snakes its way south to the boundary of the 13ᵉ arrondissement, while Roman and sixteenth-century buildings house the **Musée National du Moyen Age** – a medieval museum worth visiting for the sublime tapestry series, *The Lady and the Unicorn*, alone. The churches of St-Séverin and St-Etienne-du-Mont are among the most atmospheric in the city, too. The giant domed **Panthéon**, meanwhile, provides a touch of splendour atop the Left Bank's highest point. Out towards the eastern flank of the 5ᵉ, beside the Seine, the theme is more Arabic than Latin, what with the brilliantly designed **Institut du Monde Arabe** and **Paris mosque**. Nearby, the verdant **Jardin des Plantes** stretches lazily down to the river, a lovely swathe of lawns and flowerbeds with splendid hothouses and a zoo.

Place St-Michel and the riverside

Ⓜ St-Michel

The pivotal point of the Quartier Latin is **place St-Michel**, where the tree-lined boulevard St-Michel or "boul' Mich" begins. The once-famous student chic has these days given way to commercialization, but the cafés around the square are still jammed with students and backpackers. A favourite meeting place is by the fountain, which spills down magnificently from a statue of the archangel Michael stamping on the devil. Just east of the square, rue de la Huchette and the surrounding huddle of streets – notably the tight-squeezed rue du Chat-qui-Pêche – are rare vestiges of the medieval city's pinched footprint. Sadly, the ubiquitous kebab joints and Greek tavernas rather strip the zone of its atmosphere. There's also a single relic of the era when rue de la Huchette was a hub for postwar Beat poets and Absurdists, too: the pocket-sized **Théâtre de la Huchette**, at no. 23 (Ⓦ theatrehuchette.com). After nearly sixty years, it's still showing two Ionesco plays nightly – well worth a trip if your French is up to it.

At the end of rue de la Huchette, **rue St-Jacques** follows the line of Roman Paris's main thoroughfare, though its name comes from the celebrated pilgrimage to the shrine of Santiago (St James/St-Jacques) de Compostela. The pilgrimage began at Paris's church of St-Jacques (the tower of which still remains; see p.92), just across the river, and for countless medieval pilgrims this gentle slope was the first taste of what lay ahead.

St-Séverin

1 rue des Prêtres St-Séverin, 5ᵉ • Mon–Sat 11am–7.30pm, Sun 9am–8.30pm • Ⓜ St-Michel/Cluny-La Sorbonne

The mainly fifteenth-century church of **St-Séverin** is one of the city's more intense churches, its interior seemingly focused on the single, twisting, central pillar of the Flamboyant choir. The effect is heightened by deeply coloured stained glass designed by the modern French painter Jean Bazaine. The flame-like carving that gave the *flamboyant* ("flaming") style its name flickers in the window arch above the entrance while, inside, the first three pillars of the nave betray the earlier, thirteenth-century origins of the church. Outside, on the south side of the building, you can see the remains of what looks like a cloister enclosing a modest courtyard garden on two sides; this was in fact a **charnel house** for the mortal remains of fifteenth-century parishioners. Today, it's the last surviving one anywhere in the city.

One block to the south of the church, **rue de la Parcheminerie** is where medieval scribes and parchment sellers used to congregate. It's worth cricking your neck to look at the decorations on the facades, including that of no. 29, where you'll find the Canadian-run Abbey Bookshop.

8

St-Julien-le-Pauvre

1 rue St-Julien-le-Pauvre, 5ᵉ • Daily 9.30am–1pm & 3–6pm • Ⓜ St-Michel/Maubert-Mutualité

The much-mutilated church of **St-Julien-le-Pauvre** is almost exactly the same age as Notre-Dame. It used to be the venue for university assemblies until rumbustious students tore it apart in 1524. For the last hundred years it has belonged to an Arabic-speaking Greek Catholic sect, the Melchites, hence the unexpected iconostasis screening the sanctuary, and the liturgy of St John Chrysostom sung in Greek and Arabic every Sunday at 11am. It's also a popular venue for classical music concerts (see p.319).

Outside, look for a hefty slab of brownish stone by the well, to the right of the entrance; it is all that remains of the paving of the Roman thoroughfare now replaced by rue St-Jacques. The adjacent pocket of worn grass that is **square Viviani** provides a perfect view of Notre-Dame. The three-quarters-dead tree propped on a couple of concrete pillars is reputed to be Paris's oldest, a false acacia planted in 1601.

Shakespeare and Company

37 rue de la Bûcherie, 5ᵉ • Daily 10am–11pm • ☎ 01 43 25 40 93, ⓦ shakespeareandcompany.com • Ⓜ St-Michel

A few steps from square Viviani is the home of the American-run English-language bookshop **Shakespeare and Company**. The original Shakespeare and Company, owned by the American Sylvia Beach, long-suffering publisher of James Joyce's *Ulysses*, was on rue de l'Odéon, over in St-Germain, but this "new" incarnation has played host to plenty of literati since it opened in 1951. In 1957, when Allen Ginsberg, William Burroughs and Gregory Corso were living in the so-called Beat Hotel, over on rue Gît-le-Cœur, they'd read their poems on the street outside the store. It still has a lively roster of literary events and has just opened a café in an adjacent building. The shop is staffed by "tumbleweeds": young would-be Hemingways who sleep upstairs, borrow freely from the library and pay their rent by manning the tills. More books, postcards and prints are on sale from the **bouquinistes**, who display their wares in green padlocked boxes hooked onto the parapet of the riverside *quais*.

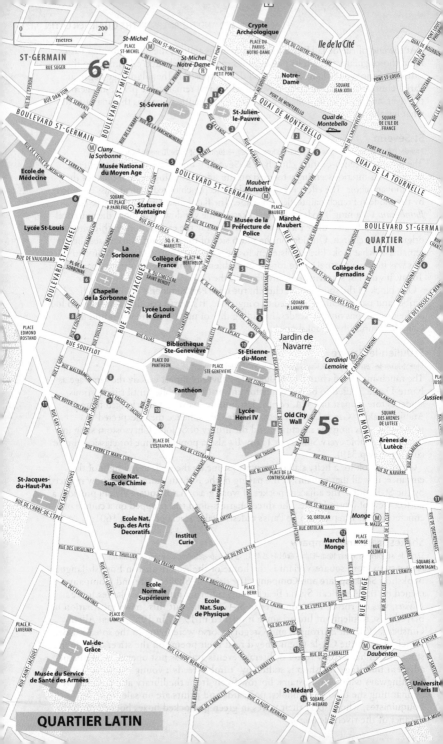

QUARTIER LATIN

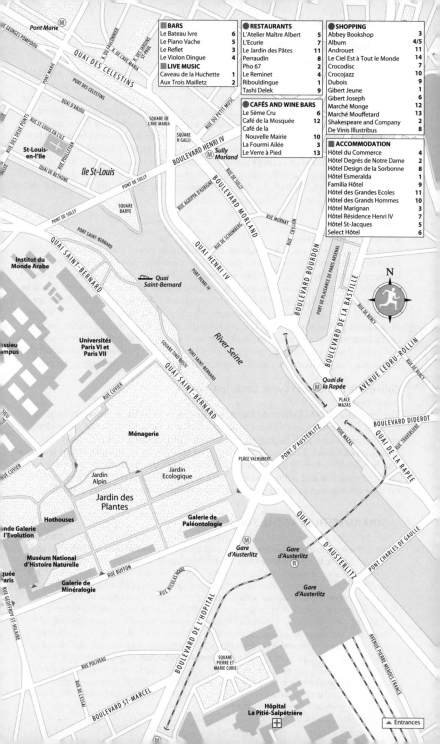

The University quarter

Ⓜ Cluny-La Sorbonne/RER Luxembourg

Rue des Ecoles – the appropriately named "street of the schools" – marks the beginning of the student quarter. It's here you'll find a bronze statue of the great Renaissance essayist, **Michel de Montaigne**, his toe rubbed shiny by generations of students seeking good luck in their exams. Above stretch the slopes of the Montagne Ste-Geneviève, clustered with the modern heirs of the colleges that once attracted the finest scholars from all over medieval Europe. Paris doesn't have quite the same world-beating status now, but the Lycée Louis-le-Grand attracts the cream of France's schoolchildren, the Sorbonne remains one of France's top universities for the arts, and the Collège de France is the leading research institution for the humanities. For visitors, the chief draw of this area is the **Musée National du Moyen Age**, an astoundingly rich storehouse of medieval art, set in an early Renaissance palace.

The Sorbonne

Ⓜ Cluny-La Sorbonne/RER Luxembourg

From rue des Ecoles, rue Champollion, with its huddle of arty cinemas, leads to the **place de la Sorbonne**. It's a peaceful place to sit, in a café or just under the lime trees, listening to the play of the fountains and watching students toting their books about. Overshadowing the graceful ensemble is the **Chapelle Ste-Ursule**, built in the 1640s by the great Cardinal Richelieu, whose tomb it contains. It helped establish a trend for Roman Counter-Reformation-style domes, which mushroomed over the city's skyline in the latter part of the century. It is certainly the most architecturally distinctive part of the **Sorbonne**, as the university buildings were entirely (and unfortunately) rebuilt in the 1880s. Sadly, you can't get inside, or even look into the Sorbonne's main **courtyard**, unless you can produce some kind of student ID and bluff convincingly in French.

Collège de France and Lycée Louis-le-Grand

Ⓜ Maubert-Mutualité

The foundation of the **Collège de France** was first mooted by the Renaissance king François I, in order to establish the study of Greek and Hebrew in France. Its modern incarnation, as a research institution, has attracted intellectual giants such as Michel Foucault and Claude Lévi-Strauss. Behind it, on rue St-Jacques, the **Lycée Louis-le-Grand** numbers Molière, Robespierre, Sartre and Victor Hugo among its former pupils. It's a portal to academic and political success, hothousing some of France's brightest students for their entry exams to the *grandes écoles*, France's elite colleges of higher education.

SOIXANTE-HUIT AT THE SORBONNE

The Sorbonne is much more to Parisians than just a world-famous educational institution. It's a living memorial to one of the defining events of the postwar era. On **May 3, 1968**, a riot broke out here after police violently intervened to break up a political meeting. The Sorbonne wasn't actually the first to flare up – the lead was taken by the campus in suburban Nanterre – but it was the university's central, historical location that caught the nation's attention. To send police into the Sorbonne was a flagrant contravention of centuries of tradition separating the university and civic authorities. To see students fighting police down on the boulevard St-Michel – as millions did, on national television – aroused powerful national memories of revolution, and the unions came out on strike in sympathy. The Sorbonne's faculty buildings were occupied by a potent mix of left-wing radicals, poseurs and intellectuals, and the college briefly became the flashpoint of France's **student-led rebellion** against institutional stagnation, housing a vibrant, anarchic commune before finally being stormed by the police on June 16. The shake-up in the higher education system that followed transformed the Sorbonne into the more prosaic Paris IV (though the old name is still used unofficially), largely attended by arts and social science students.

Musée de la Préfecture de Police

4 rue de la Montagne-Ste-Geneviève, 5e • Mon–Fri 9.30am–5pm, third Sat of the month 10.30am–5.30pm • Free • ☎ 01 44 41 52 50 •
Ⓜ Maubert-Mutualité

The **Musée de la Préfecture de Police** offers its few visitors a dusty collection of
uniforms, arms and documents, thus stitching together a history of the Paris police
force. It's dry stuff, for the most part, but the murder weapons used by legendary
criminals may titillate, and voluntarily walking into a working Paris police station –
even one as brutally ugly as this – has its own frisson. To the north, **place Maubert**
provides a spot of colour on an otherwise lifeless stretch of the broad boulevard
St-Germain, with its busy food market (Tues, Thurs and Sat mornings) and associated
cluster of food and wine shops.

Collège des Bernardins

20 rue de Poissy, 5e • Mon–Sat 10am–6pm, Sun 2–6pm • Free • English guided tours Mon, Wed & Fri • ☎ 01 53 10 74 40,
Ⓦ collegedesbernardins.fr • Ⓜ Cardinal-Lemoine

In 1300, at the height of Paris's medieval Renaissance, there were some three thousand
students living in colleges dotted all over the Left Bank. One of the few remaining
vestiges of this period is the beautifully restored **Collège des Bernardins**, founded by the
English monk Etienne de Lexington in 1247. It provided lodgings for Cistercian monks
from all over Europe until it was confiscated during the Revolution. The building was
subsequently put to a variety of uses, including as a police barracks and fire station.
Purchased and restored by the Diocese of Paris in 2001–8, it has returned to its teaching
tradition and is now a theological conference and research centre. Visitors can enter for
free the impressively long Gothic vaulted nave (the former monks' refectory), as well as
the lofty sacristy, which once adjoined the long-demolished church and now hosts
contemporary art installations. The rest of the building, including its vaulted cellars and
upper floor, can be visited as part of a guided tour (phone to book).

Musée National du Moyen Age

6 place Paul Painlevé, 5e • Daily except Tues 9.15am–5.45pm • €8–9, under-18s and EU citizens under 26 free, free to all first Sun of the month •
Free audioguide in English (bring ID) • For concert tickets call ☎ 01 53 73 78 16, or book online Ⓦ musee-moyenage.fr • Ⓜ Cluny-La Sorbonne

The best-preserved Roman remains in all Paris, the third-century **baths**, front onto the
busy boulevard St-Michel, and behind, on rue du Sommerard, stands the sixteenth-
century **Hôtel de Cluny**. It's a beautiful Renaissance mansion, as befits the Paris
pied-à-terre of the abbots of Burgundy's powerful Cluny monastery, and provides a fine
setting for the **Musée National du Moyen Age**. This treasure house of medieval art owns
one of the great masterpieces of European art: the tapestry series *La Dame à la licorne*
("The Lady and the Unicorn"). It also puts on an excellent programme of medieval
music **concerts**; look out especially for the regular "concerts-rencontres", held on
Monday lunchtimes (12.30pm) and Sunday afternoons (4pm), with tickets at just €6.
There's no charge to enter the gorgeous courtyard or the grounds running along
boulevard St-Germain, where you'll find lawns, benches and a children's playground.

Ground floor

Seemingly the backdrop to the artefacts on display, the **tapestries** that hang in most rooms
are in fact the highlight of the collection. In room 2, there's an exquisite Resurrection
scene, while gloriously naturalistic scenes of manorial life are hung in room 3. Room 5
holds attractively naive wood and alabaster **altarpiece plaques** found in homes and
churches all over Europe. In room 6 there are some wonderful backlit fragments of **stained
glass** from the Sainte-Chapelle. It's fascinating to see the artistry so close up, and to feel the
storytelling urge behind scenes such as one of Samson having his eyes gouged out.

Down the steps, in the modern structure built around the old baths, you'll find the
melancholy row of 21 thirteenth-century heads of the **Kings of Judah**. Lopped off the
west front of Notre-Dame during the Revolution, they were only discovered in a 1977

8

excavation. Arching over the frigidarium, the cold room of the **Gallo-Roman baths**, the magnificent brick-and-stone vaults are preserved intact. They shelter some beautifully carved pieces of first- and second-century columns, notably the so-called *Seine Boatmen's Pillar*, inscribed with the legend "Boatmen of the city of the Parisii", and the *Pillar of St-Landry*, which has gods and musicians animating three of its faces.

The Lady and the Unicorn

Undisputed star of the collection is the truly exquisite **Lady and the Unicorn tapestry series**, displayed in a specially darkened, chapel-like chamber on the first floor. Dating from the late fifteenth century, the highly allegorical tapestries were probably made in Brussels for the Le Viste family, merchants from Lyon, perhaps to celebrate the family acquiring its own coat of arms – three crescents on a diagonal blue stripe, as shown on the flags floating in various scenes. Each tapestry centres on a richly dressed woman, a lion, a unicorn and a monkey, set against a deep red millefleurs or "thousand-flower" background. Scholarly debate rages over the meaning of the tapestries but, at one level, they are clearly allegories of the five senses: the woman takes a sweetmeat from a goblet (taste); plays the organ (hearing); strings together a necklace of carnations (smell); holds a mirror up to the unicorn (sight); and holds the unicorn's horn (touch). The final panel, entitled *A Mon Seul Désir* ("To My Only Desire") and depicting the woman putting away (or picking up) her necklace, remains ambiguous. Some authorities think it represents the dangerous passions engendered by sensuality – the open tent behind is certainly suggestive – others that it shows the sixth "moral sense" that guards against such sinfulness.

The first floor

The rest of the first floor is an amazing ragbag of carved choir stalls, altarpieces, ivories, stained glass, illuminated Books of Hours, games, brassware and all manner of precious *objets d'art*, including the stunning **Golden Rose of Basel**, a papal gift dating from 1330. In the main Hôtel de Cluny section, the bright tapestries, beams and carved fireplaces make it possible to forget you're in a museum. The *hôtel's* original Flamboyant **chapel**, for instance, preserves its remarkable vault splaying out from a central pillar.

The Panthéon

Place du Panthéon, 5ᵉ • Daily 10am–6.30pm, Oct–March till 6pm; last entry 45min before closing • €8.50 • ☎ 01 44 32 18 00, ⓦ pantheon.monuments-nationaux.fr • Ⓜ Cardinal-Lemoine/RER Luxembourg

The towering hulk of the **Panthéon** squats atop the Montagne Ste-Geneviève under its vast dome. It was originally built as a church by Louis XV, on the site of the ruined Ste-Geneviève abbey, to thank the saint for curing him of illness and to emphasize the unity of the church and state, troubled at the time by growing divisions between Jesuits and Jansenists. Not only had the original abbey church entombed Geneviève, Paris's patron saint, but it had been founded by Clovis, France's first Christian king. The building was only completed in 1789, whereupon the revolutionary state promptly turned it into a secular mausoleum, adding the words *Aux grands hommes la patrie reconnaissante* ("The nation honours its great men") underneath the pediment of the giant portico. The remains of French heroes such as Voltaire, Rousseau, Hugo and Zola are now entombed in the vast crypt below. Of the 77 interred only four are women: Marie Curie (1995); the wife of chemist Marcellin Berthelot (who was allowed in on sentimental grounds rather than on her own merits); and Germaine Tillion and Geneviève de Gaulle-Anthonioz (2014), both Resistance fighters who were captured and sent to Ravensbrück concentration camp during the war. Other recent arrivals include Alexandre Dumas (2002), who arrived in a coffin covered with a cloth embroidered with the phrase "All for one, one for all", from his novel *The Three Musketeers*. There's also a plaque to Saint-Exupéry, author of the much-loved *Le Petit Prince*. He'd have a full-scale monument, but because his plane was lost at sea he fell foul of the rule that without a body part to inter, you cannot be *panthéonizé*.

The interior and dome

The Panthéon's **interior** is bleak and chilly, and its muscular frescoes and sculptures do little to lift the spirits. The **dome**, however, is pretty impressive – it was from here, in 1851, that French physicist Léon Foucault suspended a pendulum to demonstrate vividly the rotation of the earth. While the pendulum appeared to rotate over a 24-hour period, it was in fact the earth beneath it turning. The demonstration wowed the scientific establishment and the public alike, with huge crowds turning up to watch the ground move beneath their feet. Unfortunately, the working model of the pendulum that usually hangs from the dome has been removed while the building undergoes lengthy restoration work. You can view another working model, as well as the original, at the Musée des Arts et Métiers (see p.105). Guided tours up onto the balcony running around the dome are also suspended for the time being.

St-Etienne-du-Mont

Place Ste-Geneviève, 5ᵉ • Sept–June Tues–Sat 8.45am–noon & 2–7.45pm, Sun 8.45am–12.15pm & 2.30–7.45pm; July & Aug Tues–Sun 10am–noon & 4–7.15pm • ⓦ saintetiennedumont.fr • ⓜ Cardinal-Lemoine /RER Luxembourg

Sloping downhill from the main portico of the Panthéon, broad rue Soufflot entices you west towards the Luxembourg gardens. On the east side of the Panthéon, however, peeping over the walls of the Lycée Henri IV, look out for the lone Gothic tower that is all that remains of the earlier church of Ste-Geneviève. The saint's remains, and those of two seventeenth-century literary greats who didn't make the Panthéon, Pascal and Racine, lie close at hand in the church of **St-Etienne-du-Mont**. The church's facade is a splendidly mad seventeenth-century dog's dinner, its three levels stacking Gothic atop Renaissance atop neo-Grecian. The interior is no less startling, the transition from Flamboyant Gothic choir to sixteenth-century nave smoothed by a strange high-level catwalk which springs from pillar to pillar before transforming itself into a rood screen which arches across the width of the nave. This last feature is highly unusual in itself, as most French rood screens were destroyed by Protestant iconoclasts, reformers or revolutionaries. Exceptionally tall windows flood the church with light, while an elaborately carved organ-loft crams itself into the west end of the nave. In the fifth chapel along, on the south side of the nave, there's a finely sculpted, sixteenth-century Entombment scene – done life-size, as was long the custom in France.

North of the church, the villagey **rue de la Montagne-Ste-Geneviève** descends towards place Maubert (see p.125), passing the pleasant cafés and restaurants around rue de l'Ecole-Polytechnique.

Val-de-Grâce

1 place Alphonse Laveran, 5ᵉ • Tues–Thurs, Sat & Sun noon–6pm; closed Aug • €5 • ⓜ Censier-Daubenton/RER Luxembourg

The southern half of the student quarter is lorded over by the elite, scientific Curie Institute and the **Ecole Normale Supérieure**, on rue d'Ulm, which grooms its *normaliens* for the top arts jobs in the country. It's a closed world to outsiders, however, and the only sight as such is the magnificent church of **Val-de-Grâce**, set just back from rue St-Jacques. Built by Anne of Austria as an act of pious gratitude following the birth of her first son in 1638, it's a suitably awesome monument to the young prince who went on to reign as Louis XIV.

You can only enter Val-de-Grâce via the **Musée du Service de Santé des Armées**, a thorough history of military medicine that probably isn't for non-French-speakers – though the mock-ups of field hospitals, prosthetic limbs and reconstructive plastic surgery exert a gruesome fascination. The church, properly known as the **Chapelle St-Louis**, is reached via a curved iron grille behind which the Benedictine nuns once attended Mass. Inside, Roman Baroque extravagance is tempered by cool French Classicism. In the dome, Pierre Mignard's trompe l'oeil fresco of Paradise depicts Anne of Austria offering a model of the church up to the Virgin.

8

If you're quailing before all this piety, bear in mind that it's only a short step from here to the big, brash cafés of Montparnasse (see p.165).

The Mouffetard quarter

Ⓜ Monge/Censier-Daubenton

Medieval travellers heading south would leave Paris along the narrow, ancient incline of **rue Descartes** and its continuation, **rue Mouffetard**, following the line of the old Roman road to Italy. The quarter still feels something like a border town, its cheap restaurants and watering holes drawing students and tourists alike.

Place de la Contrescarpe

Ⓜ Monge

Just south of the church of St-Etienne-du-Mont, you pass the medieval city limits – a giant stump of Philippe-Auguste's early thirteenth-century **city wall** still protrudes into rue Clovis, a few steps short of rue Cardinal-Lemoine. Rue Descartes climbs briefly from here, past a landmark blue **mural** of a tree by the Belgian artist Pierre Alechinsky, before suddenly arriving at the pleasingly run-down oasis of **place de la Contrescarpe**. The little square has been a dubious watering hole for centuries: the medieval poet-outlaw François Villon drank at taverns here, as did the scurrilous sixteenth-century writer François Rabelais; and the modern-day *Café Delmas*, on the square's sunny side, was once the run-down café *La Chope*, as described by Ernest Hemingway in *A Moveable Feast*. He lived just round the corner on the fourth floor of 74 rue Cardinal-Lemoine, in a miserable flat paid for by his wife's trust fund. Just east of the square, the curved frontage of a municipal crèche on rue Lacépède was inspired by the shape of a pregnant belly.

Rue Mouffetard

Ⓜ Monge

"La Mouffe", as the **rue Mouffetard** is known to locals, was for generations one of the great **market streets** of Paris. Some traces of the past can be found on the old shop fronts overlooking place de la Contrescarpe, most obviously the two cows adorning a former butcher's at no. 6, and no. 12's hand-painted sign depicting a black man in striped trousers waiting on his mistress, with the unconvincing legend, "Au Nègre Joyeux". These days, the top half of rue Mouffetard is given over to tacky eating places, especially around rue du Pot de Fer – which George Orwell described as a "ravine of tall, leprous houses" given over to cheap drunkenness; things haven't changed much since. Mouffetard's market traditions still cling on at the southern end, however, where you'll find fruit and vegetable stalls in the mornings, excellent shops selling fine cheeses and wines, and a couple of old-fashioned market cafés, notably *Le Verre à Pied* (see p.283). There are more old shop signs, too: at no. 69 there's a fine carved oak tree, while no. 122, labelled "*La Bonne Source*" (the Good Spring), seems to advertise the fresh water or perhaps produce once available there.

St-Médard and around

141 rue Mouffetard, 5ᵉ • Mon 5–7pm, Tues–Sat 8am–12.30pm & 2.30–7.30pm, Sun 8.30am–12.30pm & 4–8.30pm • Ⓦ saintmedard.org • Ⓜ Censier-Daubenton

Opposite the beautiful painted facade at no. 134 rue Mouffetard sits **St-Médard**. It's easy to imagine that it was once a country parish church, and only brought within the city walls during the reign of Louis XV. The church twice achieved notoriety: in 1561, when it was sacked by Protestant rioters in the so-called Tumult of St-Médard, and again in 1727, when fanatical supporters of François de Paris – a leading light in the reforming Jansenist movement, which had been condemned by pope and king alike but drew massive popular support in Paris – gathered at his fresh grave. Rumours of miracles led

crowds of "*convulsionnaires*" into collective hysteria, rolling on the ground around their saint's tomb, eating the earth and even wounding or crucifying themselves. These excesses helped split the Jansenist movement, and led the authorities to post armed guards at the church gates in 1732, beside a sign reading "*De par le roi, défense à Dieu/De faire miracle en ce lieu*" (By order of the king, God is forbidden to work miracles in this place). The church today preserves its simple, narrow Gothic nave and more elaborate late sixteenth-century choir. A fine Zurbarán painting of *The Promenade of St Joseph and the Child Jesus* lurks in the right transept, while the outstanding organ loft is topped by statues carved by the great Renaissance sculptor Germain Pilon in the 1640s.

Below St-Médard lay the marshy ground of the now-covered **River Bièvre** (see p.175) where tanners and dyers worked in the Middle Ages – which may explain the origin of the name Mouffetard, from a slang term for "stinking". Today, avenue des Gobelins leads into the 13e arrondissement, passing the Gobelins tapestry workshops (see p.175) on the way up to busy place d'Italie.

Jardin des Plantes and around

Jardin des Plantes • Daily: April–Aug 7.30am–8pm; Sept–March 8am–dusk • Free • ⓦ jardindesplantes.net • Ⓜ Gare d'Austerlitz/Jussieu/Monge

The **Jardin des Plantes**, which stretches east all the way to the Seine, is one of Paris's loveliest green spaces, an oasis of shady woods, lawns, meticulously tended flowerbeds, hothouses and even a zoo. It's more than just a place for jogging, strolling and lolling, however. Founded as a medicinal herb garden in 1626, it has long retained a scientific role. Its great eighteenth-century director, the Comte de Buffon, is rightly regarded as the father of natural history, while Henri Becquerel stumbled upon radioactivity in the physics labs overlooking the gardens, in 1896, and the Curies cooked up radium here two years later. The gardens still house a suite of natural history museums.

The gardens

There are **entrances** to the Jardin des Plantes on all sides except around the northern corner. The southwesternmost entrance, on the corner of rues Buffon and Geoffroy St-Hilaire, takes you past a sophora tree planted by Buffon in 1747 and straight to the **roseraie**, which contains more than three hundred varieties of rose and is at its glorious best in June. If you enter by the rue Cuvier/rue Lacépède gate, at the northwest corner, and climb the little mazy hillock on the right up to an elegant gazebo (it actually predates the Revolution, making it the oldest ironwork structure in Paris), you can then descend along shaded, winding paths, past a stately cedar of Lebanon planted in 1734, to the central area of lawns and flowerbeds. If you're here in spring, don't miss the flowering of the two Japanese cherries – one white, one pink – two-thirds of the way down.

The hothouses

Jardin des Plantes • Daily except Tues: April–Sept 10am–6pm; Oct–March 10am–5pm • €6 • Ⓜ Jussieu

The *serres*, or **hothouses**, are one of the glories of the Jardin des Plantes. You enter via the Art Deco *serre tropicale*, with its graceful, vegetal-themed facade. It's hot, humid and splendidly lush, and there's a three-storey grotto that you can climb as far as the canopy level, and a section, on the sunny side, of desert plants. From here you pass into the elegant twin hothouses, revolutionary structures when they were built in the 1830s. The first houses an amazing diversity of plants from Nouvelle Calédonie, in the Pacific; the second is a kind of living exhibition on the evolution of plant life.

Jardin Alpin and Jardin Ecologique

Jardin des Plantes • **Jardin Alpin** April–Oct Mon–Fri 8am–4pm, Sat & Sun 1.30–6pm • Mon–Fri free; Sat, Sun & hols €2 • **Jardin Ecologique** Occasional guided tours only, call ☏ 01 40 79 56 01 • Ⓜ Jussieu/Gare d'Austerlitz

The north side of the Jardin des Plantes' central lawns is given over to the **Jardin Alpin**, a sheltered, sunken space filled with mountain plants from all over the world – and a favourite spot among Parisians. You can stroll freely here, but you'll probably have to just peer through the fence at the **Jardin Ecologique**, a hidden gem that was an arboretum before being closed off for forty years. It now shelters the natural flora of the Parisian basin, somehow cramming in miniature wildflower meadows, the typical mixed oak-and-hornbeam woodland of the region and even a small stream. It attracts bees, butterflies and, so far, more than 35 species of bird – including a kingfisher.

The ménagerie

Jardin des Plantes • April–Sept Mon–Sat 9am–6pm, Sun 9am–6.30pm; Oct–March daily 9am–5pm • €9, under-26s €7, under-4s free • ☎ 01 40 79 37 94 • Ⓜ Jussieu/Gare d'Austerlitz

The small **ménagerie** in the Jardin des Plantes near rue Cuvier was founded just after the Revolution; it is France's oldest zoo – and feels like it. The old-fashioned iron cage housing the Chinese panthers and the glazed-in primate house are not exactly uplifting, even if they are historic Art Deco structures. Thankfully, most of the rest of the zoo is pleasantly park-like and given over to deer, antelope, goats, flamingos and other marvellous beasts that seem happy enough in their outdoor enclosures.

Muséum National d'Histoire Naturelle

Jardin des Plantes • ☎ 01 40 79 54 79, Ⓦ mnhn.fr/fr • Ⓜ Jussieu/Gare d'Austerlitz

The southern edge of the Jardin des Plantes is lined with the grand neoclassical buildings of the **Muséum National d'Histoire Naturelle**. The first, the **Galerie de Minéralogie et de Géologie** (daily except Tues 10am–5pm; €6), is undergoing lengthy restoration, though recently reopened one of its rooms for an exhibition (ongoing till 2018) entitled "Trésors de la Terre", drawing on its splendid collection of giant rock crystals, meteorites and precious gems.

8

Galeries d'Anatomie Comparée et de Paléontologie

Mon & Wed–Fri 10am–5pm, Sat & Sun 10am–6pm • €7

At the eastern end of the garden, towards the river, the **Galeries d'Anatomie Comparée et de Paléontologie** isn't as dull as it might sound. On the ground floor of the vast, vaulted hall, serried thousands of **animal skeletons** seemingly evolve in well-marshalled order. Among them is the skeleton of the rhino that was shipped to Versailles in 1770, and that of Rock-Sand, the horse that won the triple crown in 1903. On the first floor, dinosaurs (some plastercast, some real) are arranged by era. Don't miss – well, you can't miss – the mammoth, the diplodocus and the magisterial megatherium, the giant ancestor of the crocodile.

Grande Galerie de l'Evolution

Daily except Tues 10am–6pm • €9

The splendidly restored **Grande Galerie de l'Evolution** stands beside the Jardin des Plantes' southwestern entrance. It tells the story of evolution using **stuffed animals**, rescued from the dusty old zoology museum, and given new life with clever lighting and ambient sounds, with wooden lecture boards in English. On the lower level, submarine light suffuses the space where the murkiest deep-ocean creatures are displayed. Above, glass lifts rise silently from the savannah, where a closely packed line of huge African animals look as if they're stepping onto Noah's ark. It's great fun for children, and there's a small interactive centre for kids on the first floor (see p.355).

Mosquée de Paris

2bis place du Puits de l'Ermite, 5ᵉ • Daily except Fri & Muslim holidays 9am–noon & 2–6pm • €3 • ☎ 01 45 35 97 33, Ⓦ mosqueedeparis.net • Ⓜ Jussieu

Just over the road from the main entrance to the Muséum National d'Histoire Naturelle, the main **Mosquée de Paris** (Paris Mosque) stands behind its crenellated walls, with its gate on the western side. Built by Moroccan craftsmen in the early 1920s, in a style influenced by Moorish Spain, it feels oddly repro in style, though the artisanship of tiles and woodcarvings is very fine, and the cloistered gardens are deliciously peaceful. You can stroll freely, but non-Muslims are asked not to enter the prayer room. Towards the back of the building, on the rue Geoffroy St-Hilaire side, lies a simple monument to the Algerian scholar and national hero Abd el-Kader, who led the resistance against French invasion before finally being forced to surrender in 1847. The gate on the southeast corner of the mosque complex, on rue Daubenton, leads into a lovely courtyard **tearoom** (see p.283), and an atmospheric **hammam** (see p.343). Atmosphere and charm also linger about the leafy **place Monge**, a few blocks west, with its busy market (Wed, Fri & Sun mornings), selling exquisite cheeses and other fine regional produce.

Arènes de Lutèce

Entrances in rue de Navarre, rue des Arènes and through a passage on rue Monge • ⓜ Jussieu

The surprisingly large – and remarkably well hidden – open space of the **Arènes de Lutèce** lies a few steps to the north of the Paris mosque. A few ghostly rows of stone seats are all that's left of the Roman amphitheatre that once amused ten thousand here; the entertainment is now provided by the old men playing boules in the sand below. Benches, gardens and a kids' playground stand behind.

Institut du Monde Arabe

1 rue des Fossés-St-Bernard, 5ᵉ • **Institut** Daily except Mon • Free • **Museum** Tues, Wed & Fri 10am–6pm, Thurs 10am–9.30pm, Sat & Sun till 7pm • €8 • ☏ 01 40 51 38 38, ⓦ imarabe.org • ⓜ Jussieu/Cardinal-Lemoine

North of the Jardin des Plantes stands the loathed **Jussieu campus**, an uncompromising structure constructed around the brutal skyscraper of the Tour Zamansky. Built to house the baby-boomers coming of university age in the late 1960s – and, they say, to thwart any unseemly outbreaks of student rebellion with its single entrance **gate** – its population has since outgrown it and partly decamped upstream to a new site (see p.178).

The campus also hides a vastly more successful piece of modern metal-and-glass architecture. Created by the Mitterrand government in collaboration with the Arab League, the **Institut du Monde Arabe** is a stunning and radical piece of architectural engineering, designed by a team including Jean Nouvel, who subsequently built the Musée du Quai Branly and the Philharmonie, the city's new concert hall. Its broad southern facade comprises thousands of tiny light-sensitive shutters that were designed to modulate the light levels inside while also mimicking a *moucharabiyah*, the traditional Arab latticework balcony. Unfortunately, the computer system operating the little steel diaphragms has a habit of crashing, so it's rarely in operation. On the riverfront side of the building, a boldly curving curtain wall of glass seems to symbolize the transition from the glass box behind to the flowing water at its feet. To the north, the **Pont de Sully** cuts across to the tip of the Ile-St-Louis, providing a fine view downstream towards Notre-Dame.

Inside the institute

Exhibitions, films and concerts by leading artists from the Arab world pull in the Parisian intelligentsia, while a thoughtful **museum** traces five themes – Arabs, the sacred, cities, beauty and daily life – using its collection of exquisite ceramics, metalwork and textiles, some going back as far as prehistoric times (the oldest exhibit, a statuette of an earth goddess from Jordan, dates from the seventh century BC). Scholars have use of a library and multimedia centre, and there's a specialist bookshop with an excellent selection of Arab music. Up on the ninth floor, the terrace offers some of the best **views** in the city, looking downriver towards the apse of Notre-Dame. At the adjacent **café-restaurant** *Le Moucharabié* you can drink mint tea and eat sweet cakes, but to eat and enjoy the view at the same time you'll have to sit down at the more formal (and more expensive) Lebanese restaurant, *Le Ziryab* (☏ 01 55 42 55 42).

TOY BOATS IN THE JARDIN DU LUXEMBOURG

St-Germain

Encompassing the 6^e arrondissement and the eastern fringe of the 7^e, St-Germain has all the sophistication of the Right Bank, but has a certain easy-going chic that makes it uniquely appealing. The *quartier* has moved ever further upmarket since the postwar era, when it was the natural home of arty mould-breakers and trendsetters, but it still clings to its offbeat charm. Among the designer boutiques and fashionable *bistrots*, you can still find the cafés that made the quarter famous, and left-wing media types and intellectuals still rub shoulders along with crowds of well-dressed Parisians and international visitors. The quarter also preserves its two landmark attractions: the lovely Jardin du Luxembourg and the Musée d'Orsay.

9

Historically, St-Germain has stood outside the city proper for most of its life. From the sixth century onwards, its fields and riverine meadows fell under the sway of the giant Benedictine abbey of St-Germain-des-Prés. Marie de Médicis built the Palais du Luxembourg in the early seventeenth century, but the area only became urbanized a hundred years later, as aristocrats migrated across the Seine from the Marais in search of spacious plots of land for their mansions. The Faubourg St-Germain thus became one of Europe's most fashionable districts.

The now-celebrated **boulevard St-Germain** was driven right through the heart of the quarter by Baron Haussmann in the mid-nineteenth century, but it became famous in its own right after the war, when the cafés **Flore** and **Les Deux Magots** attracted the resurgent Parisian avant-garde – Sartre debated existentialism with de Beauvoir and Boris Vian sang in smoky cellar jazz bars. As Guy Béart and, later, Juliette Gréco sang, "*Il n y a plus d'après à Saint-Germain-des-Prés*" – there's no tomorrow in St-Germain.

Of course, there was – even if an older Juliette Gréco tried to fight it with her movement "SOS St-Germain" in the late 1990s. The glitterati may still prefer the Left Bank – in addition to Gréco, **Serge Gainsbourg** lived here until his death in 1991 – but high-rolling publishers, designers and politicians have long since shouldered out boho intellectuals and musicians. **Fashion**, now, is king; the streets around the carrefour de la Croix Rouge and place St-Sulpice, in particular, swarm with internationally known clothing boutiques, while a little further west the historic Bon Marché department store stocks an ever-classier range. Towards the river, antique shops and **art dealers** dominate, with one pricey cluster around rue Jacob and rue Bonaparte, and another in the carré Rive Gauche, the three blocks south of quai Voltaire. After shopping, eating and drinking are the main attractions, though, once again, the scene is distinctly chichi these days. Well-heeled foodies now flock to the gastronomic **restaurants** of celebrity chefs like Hélène Darroze and Joël Robuchon, and foreign visitors fill the *bistrots* around Mabillon.

There are excellent markets and cafés to take in as you shop or stroll, as well as some fine buildings – from the domed **Institut de France**, by the river, to the churches of St-Germain-des-Prés and majestic **St-Sulpice**. Two small museums, the **Musée Maillol** and **Musée Delacroix**, make intimate antidotes to the grand Right Bank institutions, while the exhibitions at the **Musée du Luxembourg** are regularly among the city's most exciting. And of course there's the **Musée d'Orsay**, at the western edge of the quarter, loved as much for its stunning railway-station setting as its Impressionist collection. Meanwhile, in the southeastern corner of the quarter, hard against the Quartier Latin, the romantic **Jardin du Luxembourg** is one of the largest green spaces in the city – and surely the loveliest.

The riverside quarter

The **riverside** slice of St-Germain – north of the bustling, restaurant-lined rue St-André-des-Arts – feels both secretive and aristocratic, its fine seventeenth- and eighteenth-century mansions concealing private gardens and courtyards behind massive *portes cochères* gates. The area is also strewn with artistic and philosophical memories. Picasso painted *Guernica* in rue des Grands-Augustins. In rue Mazarine, Molière opened his first theatre, and Champollion finally deciphered Egyptian hieroglyphics in his attic rooms. In rue Visconti, Racine died, Delacroix painted and Balzac's printing business went bust. In the parallel rue des Beaux-Arts, the Romantic poet Gérard de Nerval went walking with a lobster on a lead and a disgraced Oscar Wilde died "fighting a duel" with his hotel room's wallpaper – "One or the other of us has to go," he remarked. You can still stay in the hotel, now named simply *L'Hôtel* (see p.262), or call in for a drink at its fashionable bar.

Pont des Arts

Ⓜ St-Germain-des-Prés/Louvre-Rivoli

The pedestrian **Pont des Arts** became as famous recently for its controversial "love locks" as for its classic river views. In 2015, its fragile metal grilles were removed and replaced with glass panels in order to prevent couples from attaching locks, which had become as much a safety risk as an eyesore. The tradition of attaching a **padlock** to the bridge and throwing the key into the Seine to express undying love started in 2008; by 2014 the bridge was so weighed down with locks that a section of the railings collapsed (luckily falling inwards and not onto passing boats below). The authorities decided to step in and removed all the locks (around a million of them), promising they would come up with new initiatives to enable couples to express their love. Even if the bridge has lost a little of its charm, at least the views – upstream to the Ile de la Cité and across to the Louvre, screened behind its elegant double row of gentle white poplars and muscular plane trees – remain as beguiling as ever.

Institut de France

23 quai de Conti, 6ᵉ • Bibliothèque Mazarine Mon–Fri 10am–6pm • Free • ☎ 01 44 41 44 41, ⓦ institut-du-france.fr • Ⓜ Mabillon/Pont-Neuf

The Pont des Arts owes its name not to the artists who have long sold their work here but to the institute that sits under the elegant dome on the St-Germain side. This is the **Collège des Quatre-Nations**, seat of the **Institut de France**. Of the Institut's five academies of arts and sciences, the most famous is the **Académie Française**, an august body of writers and scholars whose mission is to award literary prizes and defend the integrity of the French language against Anglo-Saxon invasion. The chosen few are known as *Immortels* – though ironically, by the time they have accumulated enough prestige to be elected, most are not long for this world. That said, the list has evolved in recent years: among the forty-strong group at the time of writing, five were women.

You need an invitation to attend one of the Institut's lectures, but if you ask politely at the gate and present ID and a couple of passport-sized photos for registration, you will be given a pass for the exquisite **Bibliothèque Mazarine**, where scholars of religious history sit in hushed contemplation of some of the 200,000 sixteenth- and seventeenth-century volumes, surrounded by *rocaille* chandeliers, marble busts and Corinthian columns.

Monnaie de Paris

11 quai de Conti, 6ᵉ • ☎ 01 40 46 56 66, ⓦ monnaiedeparis.fr • Ⓜ Pont-Neuf/St-Michel

Next door to the Institut de France extends the **Monnaie de Paris**, the French Mint, housed in an imposing eighteenth-century palace complex, the Hôtel des Monnaies, with one of the largest façades fronting the Seine. Traditionally, the Monnaie's museum of coinage was the only part of this grand Neoclassical building that was open to visitors, but after major renovation work (due for completion in 2017), the entire site, including three interior courtyards and a newly landscaped garden, will be open to the public. An exhibition space has already opened and Guy Savoy's Michelin-starred restaurant recently transferred here; diners can enjoy superb views of the river and the Louvre from the eleven huge windows. Savoy is also opening a more affordable brasserie, the *MetaLcafé*, sometime in 2016. Also planned are shops, cultural events and a chance to see metal being worked in the ateliers; collector coins and medals are made in the workshops here, while everyday euros are minted at the sister site in the Gironde.

Ecole Nationale Supérieure des Beaux-Arts (ENSBA)

14 rue Bonaparte, 6ᵉ • Mon–Fri 9.30am–6pm, exhibitions usually Mon–Fri 1–6pm • Admission for exhibitions varies • ☎ 01 47 03 50 00, ⓦ beauxartsparis.com • Ⓜ St-Germain-des-Prés.

To the west of the Institut de France lies the **Ecole Nationale Supérieure des Beaux-Arts (ENSBA)**, the School of Fine Art, whose glory days gave its name to an entire epoch. It's worth poking your nose into the courtyard. The elaborate, three-storey façade of the chapel on the right actually came from the sixteenth-century château d'Anet, which was built by Henri II for his lover, Diane de Poitiers – you can see their intertwined initials above the doors. On the left is what the French call a *mur renard* – a false or "fox" façade, built to mask a neighbour's blank gable end. But the

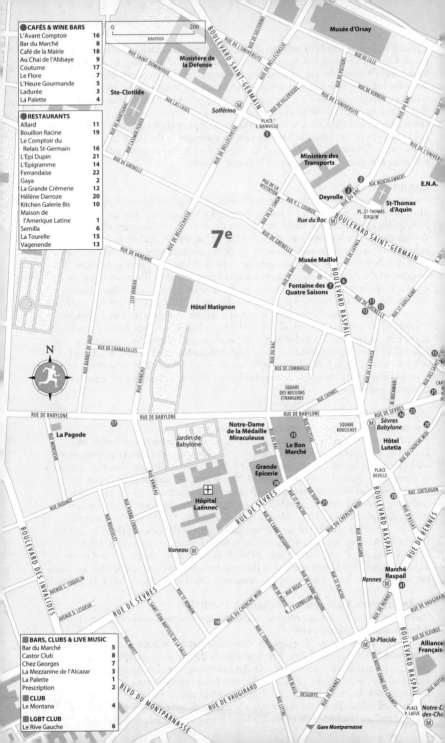

CAFÉS & WINE BARS
L'Avant Comptoir	16
Bar du Marché	8
Café de la Mairie	18
Au Chai de l'Abbaye	9
Coutume	17
Le Flore	7
L'Heure Gourmande	5
Ladurée	3
La Palette	4

RESTAURANTS
Allard	11
Bouillon Racine	19
Le Comptoir du Relais St-Germain	16
L'Epi Dupin	21
L'Epigramme	14
Ferrandaise	22
Gaya	2
La Grande Crèmerie	12
Hélène Darroze	20
Kitchen Galerie Bis	10
Maison de l'Amerique Latine	1
Semilla	6
La Tourelle	15
Vagenende	13

BARS, CLUBS & LIVE MUSIC
Bar du Marché	5
Castor Club	8
Chez Georges	7
La Mezzanine de l'Alcazar	3
La Palette	1
Prescription	2

CLUB
Le Montana	4

LGBT CLUB
Le Rive Gauche	6

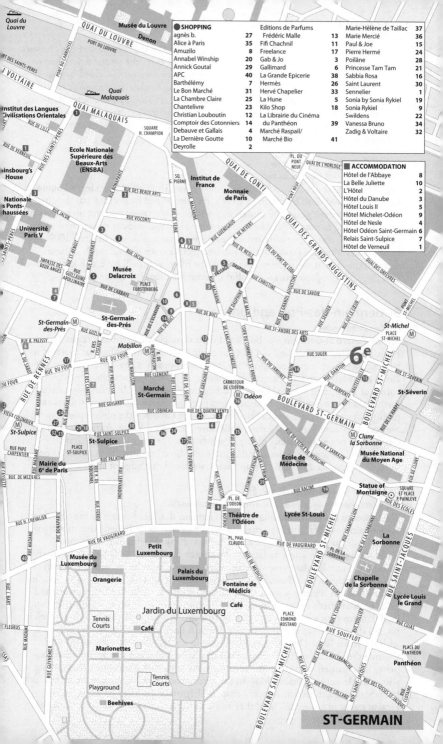

SHOPPING

agnès b.	27
Alice à Paris	35
Amuzilo	8
Annabel Winship	20
Annick Goutal	29
APC	40
Barthélémy	7
Le Bon Marché	31
La Chambre Claire	25
Chantelivre	23
Christian Louboutin	12
Comptoir des Cotonniers	14
Debauve et Gallais	4
La Dernière Goutte	10
Deyrolle	2
Editions de Parfums Frédéric Malle	13
Fifi Chachnil	11
Freelance	17
Gab & Jo	3
Gallimard	6
La Grande Epicerie	38
Hermès	26
Hervé Chapelier	33
Kilo Shop	18
La Librairie du Cinéma du Panthéon	39
Marché Raspail/ Marché Bio	41
Marie-Hélène de Taillac	37
Marie Mercié	36
Paul & Joe	15
Pierre Hermé	24
Poilâne	28
Princesse Tam Tam	21
Sabbia Rosa	16
Saint Laurent	30
Sennelier	1
Sonia by Sonia Rykiel	19
Sonia Rykiel	9
Swildens	22
Vanessa Bruno	34
Zadig & Voltaire	32

ACCOMMODATION

Hôtel de l'Abbaye	8
La Belle Juliette	10
L'Hôtel	2
Hôtel du Danube	3
Hôtel Louis II	5
Hôtel Michelet-Odéon	9
Hôtel de Nesle	4
Hôtel Odéon Saint-Germain	6
Relais Saint-Sulpice	7
Hôtel de Verneuil	1

ST-GERMAIN

9

centrepiece is the grand Italianate building at the end of the courtyard, Félix Duban's **Palais des Etudes**, which dates to the 1830s. You can enter the serene covered court, with its polychrome decoration and immense conservatory roof – added by the architect in 1863. You're not supposed to explore any further, so you won't see the gardens, Duban's Cour du Mûrier – a lovely cloister set around a mulberry tree – or the remnants of the sixteenth-century Hôtel de Chimay. Regular exhibitions, however, are held, displaying work from its collections and past and current students; the entrance is on quai Malaquais.

Serge Gainsbourg's House

5bis rue de Verneuil, 6ᵉ • ⓂSt-Germain-des-Prés

West of the Ecole des Beaux-Arts is the house where iconoclastic pop legend **Serge Gainsbourg** lived until his death in 1991 – it's now owned by his film-star daughter Charlotte. Over the years, the garden wall was steadily covered by layer upon layer of graffiti quoting famous lyrics like "God smokes Havanas" and aerosol-sprayed versions of *Gainsbarre*'s distinctive silhouette. Ever since a catastrophic day in April 2000, however, the **Mur de Gainsbourg** has received regular coats of whitewash. It hasn't deterred the fans in the slightest, but to get the full effect you'll have to hope you don't visit just after the decorators – the official decorators, that is – have visited.

St-Germain-des-Prés and Odéon

ⓂSt-Germain-des-Prés/Odéon

The **boulevard St-Germain** was bulldozed right through the Left Bank under Baron Haussmann (see p.370), and is a fairly undistinguished thoroughfare for much of its length. One short stretch around **place St-Germain-des-Prés**, however, makes up one of Paris's most celebrated micro-neighbourhoods. The **Deux Magots** café stands on one corner of the square, while the equally celebrated **Flore** (see p.285) lies a few steps further along the boulevard. Both are chiefly renowned for the postwar writers and philosophers who drank and debated there – most famously the philosopher-novelist Simone de Beauvoir and her existentialist lover, Jean-Paul Sartre. Although both cafés charge high prices and attract plenty of tourists, they're still genuine St-Germain institutions – albeit patronized by designers and directors rather than writers these days. The cognoscenti judge *Flore* to have maintained that edge of authenticity.

Church of St-Germain-des-Prés

Place St-Germain-des-Prés, 6ᵉ • Daily 8am–7.45pm • Free • ⓂSt-Germain-des-Prés

The powerful tower dominating place St-Germain-des-Prés belongs to the church of **St-Germain-des-Prés**, and is all that remains of an enormous Benedictine monastery whose lands once stretched right across the Left Bank. Having survived a post-Revolution stint as a saltpetre factory, the church itself is one of Paris's oldest surviving buildings, a rare Romanesque structure that dates back to the late tenth and early eleventh centuries. The choir, however, was rebuilt in the fashionable Gothic style in the mid-twelfth century – work that's just about visible under the heavy greens and golds of nineteenth-century paintwork. The marble columns of its middle triforium level date from an even earlier church on this site, erected in the sixth century, which housed the remains of the Merovingian kings. A later tomb, a simple slab engraved with the name René Descartes, can be found in the last chapel on the south side. Outside the church, on the corner of rue de l'Abbaye and rue Bonaparte, there's a pretty little garden with some strange fragments of Gothic stonework. These, along with a single stained-glass window in the apse of the main church, are the melancholy last remains of a thirteenth-century chapel. They make a perfect backdrop to the Picasso statue of a woman's head that also stands here, dedicated to the memory of the poet Apollinaire.

Musée Delacroix

6 rue de Furstenberg, 6ᵉ • Daily except Tues 9.30am–5pm • €6; free for under-18s and EU citizens under 26, and to all first Sun of month •
☎ 01 44 41 86 50, ⓦ musee-delacroix.fr • Ⓜ Mabillon/St-Germain-des-Prés

Hidden away round the back of St-Germain-des-Prés, **place de Furstenberg** is one of Paris's most lovable squares, huddling round its quartet of Paulownia trees and candelabra-like street lamp. Tucked into its northwest corner is the **Musée Delacroix**, a charming miniature museum displaying sketches by the artist and various personal effects. Delacroix lived and worked in the house here from 1857 until his death in 1863, watched over by Jenny Le Guillou, who'd been his servant since 1835. You can visit the bedroom where he died, now graced by Jenny's portrait, while the little sitting room houses the museum's only really important work, the intense *Madeleine au désert* (1845). Delacroix had his studio built outside, its large window overlooking a hidden garden. Today, watercolours and a few more substantial works are hung here, alongside temporary exhibitions, but for Delacroix's major work you'll have to visit the Louvre and Musée d'Orsay, or head over to the murals at nearby St-Sulpice (see p.140).

Rue de Buci

Ⓜ Mabillon/Odéon

Rue de Buci was once a proper street market, and still preserves a brash and faintly chaotic air. That said, the morning-only greengrocers' stalls are known locally as jewellery shops – for their prices rather than the colour of the fruit. The oyster-seller works for the *Atlas* brasserie, and even the *Bar du Marché* (see p.284) has given in to a fashionable clientele, its waiters wearing natty cloth caps and overalls. The entire street is now ringed by delis, sandwich shops and restaurants – as well as some of the livelier bars on the Left Bank, such as *Les Étages St-Germain* (see p.298).

Cour du Commerce St-André

Ⓜ Odéon

A few steps east of the main rue de Buci crossroads on rue de Seine, the little covered *passage* of the **cour du Commerce St-André** cuts through enticingly from rue St-André-des-Arts to the boulevard St-Germain. Marat had a printing press here, and Dr Guillotin honed his fabled scientific execution device by practising on sheep's heads. Backing onto the street is *Le Procope* – Paris's first coffee house, which opened its doors in 1686. It was the favourite watering hole and talking shop of Voltaire and Rousseau, among others, and the Enlightenment's great project, the *Encyclopédie*, was dreamed up here in a fug of caffeine. The café is still open for business, but sadly commercialized; you'll find laminated menus there now, not philosophers. A couple of smaller courtyards open off the alleyway, revealing another stretch of Philippe-Auguste's twelfth-century city wall.

Marché St-Germain

Ⓜ Mabillon

The **Marché St-Germain** is a 1990s reconstruction of a covered market that was one of the few architectural legacies left to the city by Napoleon. The site is more ancient still, having been the venue for the raucous St-Germain fair, held at the gates of the abbey in medieval times. Sadly, market stalls have been replaced by boutique shops and a swimming pool and gym complex. The area around the Marché, on rues Princesse, Lobineau, Guisarde and des Canettes, is known collectively as *rue de la soif*, or the "street of thirst", and it heaves with diners and drinkers of an evening. There are plenty of passable (and very popular) "pubs", but few really good addresses – though the wine bar *Chez Georges* (see p.299) is a classic.

The Odéon quarter

Ⓜ Odéon

The broad **Odéon** stretch of the boulevard St-Germain is best known for its cinemas. At this eastern edge of St-Germain you feel the gravitational pull of the university; indeed,

9

this area is sometimes considered to be part of the Quartier Latin. The ethnic restaurants of **rue Monsieur le Prince** cater for student budgets while, around the **Ecole de Médecine**, university bookshops display skeletons and instruments of medical torture. The defining landmark of the area, however, is the restored **Théâtre de l'Odéon**, its proud Doric facade fronting a handsome semicircular plaza. This was one of the learned King Louis XVI's last projects before the Revolution, and had a then-unheard-of capacity of 1900.

St-Sulpice
Ⓜ St-Sulpice

The fact that the actress Catherine Deneuve has an apartment on **place St-Sulpice** is a good clue to its character. This is a classy yet still faintly arty corner of the city. On the sunny north side of the square, the outside tables at the *Café de la Mairie* (see p.284) hum with chatter on fine days – it's one of the city's finest outdoor *terrasses* – facing the original boutique of **Yves Saint Laurent Rive Gauche**. Architecturally the square is enchanting, with its lion fountain and chestnut trees overlooked by the church's not-quite-twin towers: the south tower has long waited in sculptural limbo – you can see uncut masonry blocks at the top, still awaiting the sculptor's chisel.

Church of St-Sulpice
Place St-Sulpice, 6ᵉ • Daily 7.30am–7.30pm • Free • Ⓦ pss75.fr/saint-sulpice-paris • Ⓜ St-Sulpice

The church of St-Sulpice is a muscular Classical edifice erected either side of 1700. For decades, the gloomy **interior** was best known for three **Delacroix murals**, found in the first chapel on the right, and a huge, 101-stop, five-manual, part-eighteenth-century **organ**, which is thought to be among the finest in the world and is used at frequent recitals. Since the publication of *The Da Vinci Code*, however, the chief sight is the remains of the **solar observatory**. A lens in the south transept window, long since removed, once focused the sun's rays on a narrow brass strip, or meridiana, which still runs right across the floor of the nave and up a stone pillar on the north side. At its winter low, the sun would exactly crown the obelisk at noon; at its summer height, it would burn down on the start of the brass line. As a printed notice points out, the device is an "instrument of astronomy" designed in 1727 by an English clock-maker called Henry Sully. The original project was liturgical: to establish the exact time of noon and determine the proper dates for the church's moveable feasts. The instrument as it survives now, however, is the remnant of a 1740s scientific attempt to measure the exact time of the winter and summer solstices. Either way, as the sign tartly observes, "no mystical notion can be derived" from it. And the brass strip does not follow any "Rose Line", nor even the Paris meridian – though it runs close by.

Jardin du Luxembourg
Roughly dawn–dusk • Ⓜ Odéon/RER Luxembourg

Hemingway liked to claim he fed himself in Paris by shooting pigeons in the **Jardin du Luxembourg**. These lovely gardens belong to the **Palais du Luxembourg**, which now houses the French Senate, but was originally built for Marie de Médicis, Henri IV's widow. They are the Left Bank's heart, and quite possibly its lungs as well. They get fantastically crowded on summer days, especially the shady **Fontaine de Médicis** in the northeast corner and the tail of the gardens that points south towards the Paris observatory – the latter being the only place where you're allowed to sit out on the **lawns**. Everywhere else you'll have to settle yourself on the heavy, sage-green metal chairs, which are liberally distributed around the gravel paths. Alternatively, there's a pleasant, tree-shaded (and not exorbitantly priced) **café** a few steps east of the central pond and another on the western side near the playgrounds.

9

Exploring the gardens

Children rent toy yachts to sail on the octagonal pond, the **Grand Bassin**, but the western side of the gardens, beside the **tennis courts** (see p.345), is the more active area: there are pony rides, a marionette show (see p.350) and playgrounds for children, plus the inevitable sandy area for boules. **Sculptures** are scattered around the park, including an 1890 monument to the painter Delacroix by Jules Dalou and a suitably bizarre homage to the Surrealist poet Paul Eluard by the sculptor Ossip Zadkine (see p.165). In the quieter, wooded, western section of the park you can also find one of Paris's miniature versions of the Statue of Liberty, just bigger than human size, and a cluster of well-tended beehives. The southwest corner ends in a fabulous miniature orchard of elaborately espaliered pear trees whose fruit graces the tables of senators or, if surplus to requirements, are given to organizations for the homeless.

The north–south spine of the gardens extends down into a tail pointing towards the Paris observatory, following the line of the old Paris meridian (see p.168). At the extreme southern end of the gardens, the circular **Fontaine de l'Observatoire** symbolizes Paris's historic self-conception as the very navel of the world, with Jean-Baptiste Carpeaux's fine sculptures of the four continents supporting a mighty iron globe.

Orangerie

Jardin du Luxembourg • Exposition d'Automne hours and prices vary, see Ⓦ senat.fr/evenements • Ⓜ St-Sulpice/RER Luxembourg

For two or three weeks in late September, the half-glazed **Orangerie** is the venue for the annual **Exposition d'Automne**, which shows off the garden's finest fruits and floral decorations. It's closed for the rest of the winter, sheltering scores of exotic trees – palms, bitter oranges, oleanders and pomegranates, some of them more than two hundred years old. All are wheeled back outside, in their giant wooden containers, every spring.

Musée du Luxembourg

19 rue de Vaugirard, 6ᵉ, Jardin du Luxembourg • Hours and prices vary • ☎ 01 40 13 62 00, Ⓦ museeduluxembourg.fr • Ⓜ St-Sulpice/ RER Luxembourg

Immediately behind the Orangerie, but with its entrance on rue de Vaugirard – Paris's longest street – stands the **Musée du Luxembourg**. Some of Paris's biggest and most exciting art exhibitions are held here, often causing long queues to form alongside the giant railings of the Jardin du Luxembourg. Recent successes have included the Tudors and an exhibition featuring Manet, Renoir and Monet.

The western fringe of St-Germain

The broad, ugly gash of rue de Rennes signals the western boundary of the core St-Germain neighbourhood, but the 6ᵉ arrondissement continues officially as far west as rue des Sts-Pères – and, in feel, this quarter extends well into the 7ᵉ arrondissement, or at least as far as rue du Bac. The whole area, certainly, is stuffed to bursting with chichi shops, and it's here that you'll find the landmark Left Bank department store, Le Bon Marché. On Sunday mornings, meanwhile, the celebrated Raspail organic food market, or **Marché Bio** (see p.340), lines the boulevard Raspail between the Sèvres-Babylone and Rennes métro stations.

Around the carrefour de la Croix Rouge

Ⓜ St-Sulpice/Sèvres-Babylone

You might not find the most exclusive Right Bank designers or the more alternative-minded Marais boutiques here, but rues Bonaparte, Madame, de Sèvres, de Grenelle, du Vieux-Colombier, du Dragon, du Four and des Sts-Pères are lined with the big names in Parisian clothes and accessories, from Agnès b. to Zadig et Voltaire. It's hard to imagine now, but smack in the middle of all this, at the **carrefour de la Croix Rouge**, there was a major barricade in 1871, during the Paris Commune (see box, p.186). These days you're more likely to be suffering from till-shock than shell-shock, though César's 4m statue of a **Centaure**, cast in homage to Picasso in 1983, is distinctly alarming. It surveys the crossroads with ferocity, and two sets of genitals.

Le Bon Marché

24 rue de Sèvres, 6ᵉ • Mon–Wed & Sat 10am–8pm, Thurs & Fri 10am–9pm • Ⓦ lebonmarche.com and Ⓦ lagrandeepicerie.com • Ⓜ Sèvres-Babylone

Just across the boundary with the 7ᵉ arrondissement, at the far side of the green square Boucicaut, stands the grand department store, **Le Bon Marché** (see p.324). One of the great institutions of the nineteenth century (and the setting for Zola's novel *Au Bonheur des Dames*), its name means "inexpensive", but these days it's one of Paris's most upmarket shopping spaces. A 1920s annexe on the west side of rue du Bac now houses the luxurious **Grande Epicerie**, or "big grocer's".

Notre-Dame de la Médaille Miraculeuse

140 rue du Bac, 7ᵉ • Daily 7.45am–1 & 2.30–7pm • Free • Ⓦ chapellenotredamedelamedaillemiraculeuse.com • Ⓜ Sèvres-Babylone

If you stand outside Le Bon Marché, especially on a Sunday, you'll notice that a surprisingly large proportion of people among the crowds isn't here for the shopping. The reason lies down an alley hidden behind 140 rue du Bac, just north of the aerial bridge joining the two wings of the department store. Tucked away at its end is a little chapel with the unwieldy name of **Notre-Dame de la Médaille Miraculeuse**. It was here, in 1830, that a 24-year-old nun called Catherine Laboure had visions of the Virgin Mary dressed in silk, with her feet resting on a globe. A voice told Catherine to "have a medal struck like this – those who wear it will receive great graces". The nuns duly obeyed, and have been quite literally coining it ever since. You can buy a souvenir medal and visit the chapel, which was rebuilt to accommodate huge pilgrim congregations in 1930.

Hôtel Lutetia

45 bd Raspail, 6ᵉ • Ⓦ lutetia-paris.com • Ⓜ Sèvres-Babylone

Facing the Bon Marché department store across square Boucicaut is the monumental **Hôtel Lutetia**, one of the finer Art Deco buildings in the city. It closed in 2014 for a major refit of its interior, including its glorious Art Deco brasserie and bar. At the outbreak of World War II, scores of artists fled here, seeking sanctuary of a kind. Among them was James Joyce – peeved, it's said, that the growing conflict of war had overshadowed the publication of his novel, *Finnegans Wake*.

Musée Maillol and around

61 rue de Grenelle, 7ᵉ • ☎ 01 42 22 59 58, Ⓦ museemaillol.com • Ⓜ Rue du Bac

The **Musée Maillol**, dedicated to post-Impressionist sculptor Aristide Maillol, closed in 2015 after the company owning it went bankrupt, and seems unlikely to reopen any time soon. Meanwhile, admirers of the sculptor's buxom nudes can see copies of them in the Louvre's Jardin du Carrousel.

A few steps east of the museum stands the **Fontaine des Quatre-Saisons**, less a fountain than a piece of early eighteenth-century architectural theatre. At the centre of the curved stone arcade sits the City of Paris herself, flanked by two sinuous figures representing the rivers Seine and Marne.

Deyrolle

46 rue du Bac, 7ᵉ • Mon 10am–1pm & 2–7pm, Tues–Sat 10am–7pm • Free • ☎ 01 42 22 30 07, Ⓦ deyrolle.com • Ⓜ Rue du Bac

You might not normally go out of your way to visit a **taxidermist's**, but **Deyrolle** should be an exception. The fancy garden tool shop below is a mere front for the real business upstairs, in a room perfumed with the sharp, coal-tar smell of taxidermy. Giant,

9

antique wooden display cases are stuffed with pinned butterflies and shards of prehistoric trilobites, while above and all around them are scores of stuffed rabbits, ducks, sheep, boar, bears and even big cats. Astonishingly, this isn't a museum: the entire stock (apart from a billy goat and a donkey) was replaced from scratch after a disastrous fire in 2008, and all the pieces on view are for sale. A lion could be yours for around €10,000, or you can pick up a fossil for a couple of euros. Children, in particular, tend to be fascinated by the place.

Musée d'Orsay

62 rue de Lille, 7ᵉ, entrance at 1 rue de la Légion d'Honneur • Tues, Wed & Fri–Sun 9.30am–6pm, Thurs 9.30am–9.45pm • €11; free to under-18s, to under-26s from the EU, and to all on first Sun of the month; €8.50 to non-EU citizens aged 18–26, to all after 4.30pm on Tues, Wed & Fri–Sun, after 6pm on Thurs; a combined ticket with the Musée de l'Orangerie costs €16 (valid for up to three months) and a combined ticket with the Musée Rodin €15, valid on the same day only (if you keep your ticket you can also get reductions on admission to the Opéra Garnier and the Musée Moreau); worth booking tickets in advance to avoid long queues • ☎ 01 40 49 48 14, Ⓦ musee-orsay.fr • Ⓜ Solférino/RER Musée-d'Orsay

As it comes into the 7ᵉ arrondissement, boulevard St-Germain swings up towards the river, disgorging its traffic across the Pont de la Concorde onto the Right Bank. On the east side of this wedge of the city are the expensive art and antiques shops of the **carré Rive Gauche**, between rue de l'Université and the quai Voltaire. To the west, facing the Tuileries gardens across the river, is the **Musée d'Orsay**. The museum's collection of the electrifying works of the **Impressionists** and Post-Impressionists has made it one of Paris's most-visited attractions. There's more to it than just Monet and Renoir, however. The collection covers the artistically revolutionary era between 1848 and 1914 – between the end of the Louvre's Classical traditions and the start of the modern era, as represented in the Pompidou Centre. The museum came out of a bold **revamp** in 2011: the cramped attic rooms at the top, displaying the Impressionist paintings, were remodelled, creating more open space and better presentation of the paintings, lighting was much improved, and the stark white walls were painted a riot of different colours – red, purple, green and grey.

Though the museum covers a lot, it's easy to confine your visit to a specific **section**, each of which has a very distinctive atmosphere. Chronologically, the collection begins on the ground floor, under the huge vault of steel and glass, and continues up on the fifth floor with the Impressionists, accessed via the Pavillon Amont, the station's former engine room, devoted to decorative arts. It then continues through to the Post-Impressionists, displayed on the terraces and galleries of the middle level (floor 2), overlooking the main "nave" chamber.

The building

The building itself was inaugurated as a **railway station** for the 1900 World Fair. It spans the worlds of nineteenth-century Classicism and industrial modernity brilliantly, its elegant, formal stone facade cunningly disguising the steel-and-glass construction of the railway arch within. It continued to serve the stations of southwest France until 1939, but its platforms became too short for postwar trains and it fell into disuse.

De Gaulle made it the backdrop for the announcement of his *coup d'état* of May 19, 1958, but such was the site's degradation by the 1960s that Orson Welles thought it

---

REFUELLING AT THE MUSÉE D'ORSAY

The Musée d'Orsay has two fine places to take stock: a resplendent **restaurant** on the middle level, gilded in stunning period style, and a stylish **café** on level 5, designed by the Brazilian Campana brothers, inspired by the dreamlike works of Art Nouveau artist Emile Gallé; it also has a **summer terrace** and a wonderful view of Montmartre through the giant railway clock. For drinks and snacks there's the small *Café de l'Ours*, on the ground floor.

the perfect location for his film of Kafka's nightmarish *The Trial*. Despite this illustrious history, the station was only saved from destruction by the backlash of public opinion that followed the demolition of Les Halles. The job of redesigning the interior as a museum was given, in 1986, to the fashionable Milanese architect Gae Aulenti.

Ground-floor paintings
On the south side of the ground-floor level, towards rue de Lille, one set of rooms is dedicated to **Chassériau**, **Gérôme**, **Ingres**, **Delacroix** – the bulk of whose work is in the Louvre – and the serious-minded artworks of the "academic" painters, acceptable to the mid-nineteenth-century salons. The influential **Barbizon School** and the **Realists** are also represented with canvases by Daumier, Corot and Millet. These were some of the first to break with the established norms of moralism and idealization of the past. The soft-toned landscapes by Millet and Corot, and quickly executed scenes by Daubigny, such as his *La Neige*, were influential on later, avowed Impressionists. There are also some early Degas, portraying intimate scenes, such as *La Femme dans le bain s'épongeant sa jambe* ("Woman washing her leg in the bath"), and some iconic caricatures by **Toulouse-Lautrec**, including the splendidly smoky *Danse Mauresque*, which depicts the celebrated cancan dancer, La Goulue, entertaining an audience of lowlifes including an obese, washed-up Oscar Wilde.

The adjacent Galerie Symboliste displays the relatively wacky works of Gustave Moreau and Odilon Redon, and a superb collection of paintings by Vuillard, Maurice Denis and Bonnard, painters who began their careers as part of an Art Nouveau group known as the **Nabis**; strong Japanese influences can be seen in Vuillard's decorative screen, *Jardins publics*, and Bonnard's *Femmes au jardin*.

On the Seine side are rooms dedicated to early Impressionist landscapes by **Monet** and **Cézanne**, and a room of Orientalist works. A display of early photographs, mostly of female nude models, leads up to Courbet's *L'Origine du monde*, which still has the power to shock even contemporary audiences – many of whom simply pretend it's not hanging there. The explicit nude female torso was acquired from psychoanalyst Jacques Lacan, who concealed it behind a decorative panel in his offices.

Upper level: Impressionism
To continue chronologically, proceed via the Pavillon Amont straight to level 5, where you'll find the **Impressionists' gallery**. It is here that the results of the museum's recent revamp are most tangible. In a series of large, warmly lit rooms, well-spaced paintings hang against walls of charcoal grey. The result is stunning: the vibrant colours and vigorous brushstrokes of even the almost-too-familiar Monets and Renoirs strike you afresh and seem to almost jump off the walls. The first painting to greet you,

---

THE SHOCKING SALON OF 1863
Manet's painting *Le Déjeuner sur l'herbe*, or *The Picnic*, which hangs in the Musée d'Orsay, caused outrage at the **1863 Salon des Refusés**. This was a deliberately confrontational show of works (a "salon") that had been rejected by the judges of the official Salon of 1863. It has often been said to mark the beginning of the **Impressionist** movement. The problem with Manet's picnic scene wasn't so much the nakedness of its female figure, as female nudity was absolutely standard in French Classical art (just look at the extremely erotic canvases hung on the ground floor, by the likes of Bouguereau and Chabanel). It was rather the fact that Manet had juxtaposed her with male figures in modern dress, making her look not like an idealized representation of womanhood so much as a common harlot. Manet had shifted his interest away from the ideal and towards the everyday, and this was regarded as amoral at best. Manet's provocative *Olympia*, with its brash and sensual surfaces, appeared at the same salon. No less shocking, it portrayed Olympia as a high-class whore who returns the stares of her audience with a look of insolent defiance.

9

magnificent in its isolation, is Manet's scandalous *Déjeuner sur l'herbe*, the work held to have announced the arrival of Impressionism (see box, p.145). Thereafter follows masterpiece after masterpiece: Degas' *Dans un café (L'Absinthe)*, Renoir's *Bal du Moulin de la Galette*, Cézanne's *Joueurs de cartes* and Monet's *Femme à l'ombrelle* and *Coquelicots* ("Poppies"), the last given a whole wall to itself.

A host of small-scale landscapes and outdoor scenes by Renoir, Sisley, Pissarro and Monet are owed to the novel practice of setting up easels in the open – often as not, on the banks of the Seine. Less typical works include Degas' ballet dancers, which demonstrate his principal interest in movement and line as opposed to the more common Impressionist concern with light. Monet's obsessive Rouen cathedral series, each painted in different light conditions, fills one wall, while one room is dominated by the pink and green tones of Renoir's fleshy nudes – an obsession quite as intense as Monet's with cathedrals – along with his joyous pairing *Danse à la ville/Danse à la campagne*. Berthe Morisot, the first woman to join the early Impressionists, is represented by her famous *Le Berceau*, among others.

Middle level

On the rue de Lille side of the **middle level**, the flow of the painting section continues with the various offspring of Impressionism. In works such as **Van Gogh**'s *La Nuit étoilée*, with its fervid colours and disturbing rhythms, and **Gauguin**'s ambivalent Tahitian paintings there's an edgier, more modern feel, with a much greater emphasis on psychology. More decorative effects are attempted by **Pointillists** such as Seurat (the famous *Cirque*) and Signac. On the Seine side, you can see a less familiar side of late nineteenth-century painting, with epic, naturalist works such as Detaille's stirring *Le Rêve* (1888) and Cormon's *Caën* (1880).

On the **sculpture terraces**, amid works by Maillol, Bourdelle and others, it is pieces by **Rodin** that stand out. Rodin's *Ugolin* is even grimmer than Carpeaux's, immediately below, while his *Fugit amor*, a response to his pupil and lover Camille Claudel's *L'Age mûr*, is a powerful image of the end of their liaison. If you still have some energy left, it's well worth seeking out the half-dozen rooms dedicated to **Art Nouveau** furniture and objets d'art by designers such as Hector Guimard, Victor Horta and Emile Gallé.

The Pavillon Amont

More superb **Art Nouveau** furniture and objets, together with paintings from the same period by Vuillard, Bonnard and Maurice Denis, are displayed on levels two, three and four of the Pavillon Amont. Art Deco pieces by non-French artists, notably from the Vienna and Glasgow schools, are also represented. The ground floor is hung with Courbet's impressive large-format paintings, including *A Burial at Ornans*, a stark depiction of a family funeral; these large-format works were groundbreaking in their day for depicting everyday scenes on a scale usually reserved for "noble" subjects, such as historic or mythical scenes.

THE EIFFEL TOWER

The Eiffel Tower quarter

Standing sentinel over a great bend in the Seine as it flows southwest out of Paris is the monumental flagpole that is the Eiffel Tower. It surveys the most relentlessly splendid of all Paris's districts, embracing the palatial heights of the Trocadéro, on the Right Bank, and the wealthy, western swathe of the 7ᵉ (septième) arrondissement, on the Left. These are street vistas planned for sheer magnificence: as you look out across the river from the terrace of the Palais de Chaillot to the Eiffel Tower and the huge Ecole Militaire, or let your gaze run from the ornate Pont Alexandre III past the parliament building to the vast Hôtel des Invalides, you are experiencing city design on a truly monumental scale.

MODERN ARCHITECTURE IN THE SEPTIÈME

The septième is renowned for its grand state monuments and extravagant aristocratic mansions, which mostly date from the seventeenth and eighteenth centuries, but you can also seek out a trio of the city's most exciting **Art Nouveau** apartment buildings, the work of Jules Lavirotte at the turn of the nineteenth century. From the **contemporary era**, the Musée du Quai Branly is the most trumpeted representative, but hidden away nearby is a fascinating example of the postmodernist architecture of Christian de Portzamparc.

29 avenue Rapp (RER Pont de l'Alma). Art Nouveau to the extreme, with colourful, glazed ceramic tiles and an extravagant doorway representing an inverted phallus inside a vulval arch. Designed by Jules Lavirotte in 1901.
3 square Rapp Off avenue Rapp (RER Pont de l'Alma). More of Lavirotte's extravagant Art Nouveau work, dating from 1900. There's also a fine trellis trompe l'oeil alongside.
12 rue Sédillot (RER Pont de l'Alma). From the studio of Lavirotte in 1899, featuring Art Nouveau and Art Deco elements, with superb dormers and wrought-iron balconies.
Conservatoire de Musique Erik Satie 7 rue Jean-Nicot (Ⓜ Invalides). Architect Christian de Portzamparc plays with a half-peeled tube of a tower in this building dating from 1988.

The quarter is home chiefly to diplomats, government officials and aristocrats, both old-school and new. It's here that the Prime Minister has his well-guarded official residence, the **Hôtel Matignon**, with its giant garden stretching south as far as rue de Babylone. Unsurprisingly, it's pretty dead in terms of shops and restaurants, but it is studded with some compelling **museums**, from the stunningly designed new one devoted to "primitive" art at **quai Branly**, down to another dedicated to Paris's sewer system – found, appropriately enough, down in the **sewers**. In the heart of the septième, the imposing **Hôtel des Invalides** houses the French army's vast **war museum**, centred on the tomb of the still-idolized little general, Napoleon. The **Musée Rodin**, nearby, shows off the sculptor's works in the intimate surroundings of a handsome private *hôtel*, or mansion house. Just across the river, in the **Trocadéro** quarter of the 16ᵉ arrondissement, you'll find a pocket of fine museums specializing in Asian Buddhist art, fashion and architecture, along with two of the most exciting art museums in the city: the **Palais de Tokyo**'s galleries of Parisian modern art and contemporary French artworks.

For all the pomp, there are some appealing little neighbourhoods, notably in the wedge of homely streets centred on the **rue Cler** market and in the arrondissement's eastern fringe, towards the 6ᵉ. Note, however, that this easternmost end of the 7ᵉ – including the Musée d'Orsay and the shopping area around rue du Bac and the Sèvres-Babylone métro – belongs more in feel to the St-Germain quarter (see pp.133–146).

The Eiffel Tower and around

Daily: mid-June to Aug 9am–12.45am; Sept to mid-June 9.30am–11.45pm; upward-bound lifts stop 45min before closing time, Sept to mid-June access to stairs closes 6pm; ticket sales for the top end at 10.30pm (or 11pm from mid-June to Aug) • Tickets €15.50 (for the top), €9 (second level); you can climb the stairs (not as gruelling as it might sound if you're reasonably fit) as far as the second level for €5 and buy a "supplément ascenseur" ticket to the top for a further €6; save queueing time by buying tickets online (well in advance), or, to beat the worst of the queues, turn up on the day early in the morning (around 1–2hr before the tower opens for the lift, around 20min in advance for the stairs) • ☎ 08 92 70 12 39, ⓦ tour-eiffel.fr • RER Champ de Mars-Tour Eiffel

Despite being one of the most familiar landmarks in the world, the **Eiffel Tower** – the quintessential symbol of Paris – has lost none of its power to dazzle, both from a distance and up close. The city looks surreally microscopic from the top and the **views** are arguably better from the second level, especially on hazier days. But there's something irresistible about taking the lift all the way up. At the very top, you can peer through a window into Eiffel's airy little show-off study, while at the second level is the gastronomic restaurant, *Jules Verne* (see p.289). Many visitors overlook the first level, but it was recently renovated and made more inviting, with part of the floor being replaced with **glass**, affording dizzying views of the ground (and long queues) below. Also upping its appeal is its transformation in summer (mid-June to Sept) into a sun terrace, complete with sun loungers and a café selling ice cream. There's also a shop and restaurant (*58 Tour Eiffel*).

Outside daylight hours, sodium **lights** illuminate the main structure, while twin xenon arc-lamps, added for the millennium celebrations, have turned the tower into an oversized urban lighthouse. There's also a third lighting system: for the first ten minutes of every hour thousands of lamps scramble about the structure, defining the famous silhouette in luminescent champagne.

10

Brief history

It's hard to believe that this brilliant feat of industrial engineering was designed to be a **temporary structure** for a fair. Late nineteenth-century Europe had a taste for giant-scale, colonialist–capitalist extravaganzas, but Paris's 1889 **Exposition Universelle** was particularly ambitious: at 300m, its tower was the tallest building ever yet built. Outraged critics protested against this "grimy factory chimney". "Is Paris", they asked, "going to be associated with the grotesque, mercantile imaginings of a constructor of machines?" Eiffel believed it was a piece of perfectly utilitarian architecture. "The basic lines of a structure must correspond precisely to its specified use," he said. "To a certain extent the tower was formed by the wind itself."

Curiously, this most celebrated of landmarks was only saved from demolition by the sudden need for "wireless telegraphy" aerials in the first decade of the twentieth century, and nowadays the original crown is masked by an efflorescence of antennae. The tower's colour scheme has changed too: the early coats of deep red then canary-yellow paint have been covered with a sober, dusty brown since the late 1960s. The only structural maintenance it has ever needed was carried out in the 1980s, when one thousand tonnes of metal were removed to make the tower ten percent lighter, and the frame was readjusted to remove a slight warp.

The Champ de Mars

Parading back from the Eiffel Tower, the **Champ de Mars** has been an open field ever since it was used as a mustering ground for royal troops – hence the name "Martial Field". After 1789 it became the venue for the great revolutionary fairs, including Robespierre's vast "Fête of the Supreme Being" in 1794, while the Second Empire turned it into a giant industrial exhibition area, which explains the location of the Eiffel Tower. It's now a popular place for sunbathing on hot days. At the far southern end lie the eighteenth-century buildings of the **Ecole Militaire**, originally founded in 1751 by Louis XV for the training of aristocratic army officers – including the "little corporal", Napoleon Bonaparte.

The UNESCO building

7 place de Fontenoy, 7ᵉ • Book guided tours well in advance on @ visits@unesco.org, ☎ 01 45, 68 10 00; ID required for visit • Ⓜ Ecole-Militaire

The *quartier* surrounding the Ecole Militaire is expensive, elegant and classic, and the Y-shaped **UNESCO building** is the controversial exception. Built in reinforced concrete in 1958 by, appropriately, an international team, it houses artworks by Giacometti, Calder, Le Corbusier, Miró and Picasso, as well as the so-called "Nagasaki angel" – a rare survivor of the atomic atrocities of August 1945. You can join a **guided tour** of the building if you book in advance. Alternatively, come for one of the regular exhibitions or evening concerts, which range from "Colours and Impressions of Albania" to Tchaikovsky dances.

Behind UNESCO, the avenue de Saxe continues the grand line southeast towards the giant Necker hospital, passing through the **place de Breteuil**, a huge roundabout – even by Parisian standards – centred on a **monument to Louis Pasteur**, the much-loved inventor of pasteurization. His role as a hero who saved millions of lives is represented by the Grim Reaper cowering beneath him, while healthy lambs and children gambol all around.

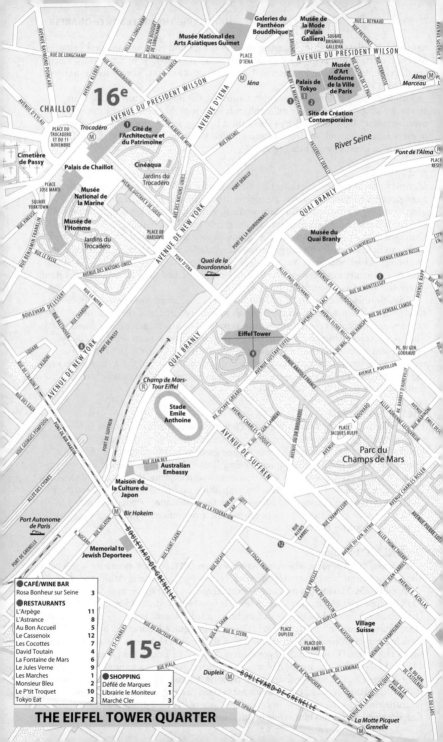

16e

CHAILLOT

AVENUE DU PRESIDENT WILSON

Musée National des
Arts Asiatiques Guimet

Galeries du
Panthéon
Bouddhique

Musée de
la Mode
(Palais
Galliera)

RUE L. REYNAUD

AVENUE DU PRESIDENT WILSON

PLACE
D'IENA

Iéna Ⓜ

Palais de
Tokyo
❶
❷

Musée
d'Art
Moderne
de la Ville
de Paris

Alma Ⓜ
Marceau

Trocadéro Ⓜ

❶ Cité de
l'Architecture
et du Patrimoine

Site de Création
Contemporaine

River Seine

Pont de l'Alma Ⓡ

Cimetière
de Passy

Palais de Chaillot

PLACE
JOSE MARTI

SQUARE
YORKTOWN

Cinéaqua

Jardins du
Trocadéro

QUAI BRANLY

Musée National de
la Marine

Musée du
Quai Branly

Musée de
l'Homme

PLACE DE
VARSOVIE

Jardins du
Trocadéro

AVENUE DE NEW YORK

Quai de la
Bourdonnais

BOULEVARD DELESSERT

Eiffel Tower

Parc du
Champs de Mars

AVENUE DE NEW YORK

QUAI BRANLY

Champ de Mars-
Tour Eiffel Ⓡ

Stade
Emile
Anthoine

AVENUE DE SUFFREN

Australian
Embassy

Maison de
la Culture du
Japon

Bir Hakeim Ⓜ

Port Autonome
de Paris

Memorial to
Jewish Deportees

Village
Suisse

PLACE
DUPLEIX

PLACE DU
CARD AMETTE

15e

Dupleix Ⓜ

BOULEVARD DE GRENELLE

La Motte Picquet
Grenelle Ⓜ

● CAFÉ/WINE BAR	
Rosa Bonheur sur Seine	3

● RESTAURANTS	
L'Arpège	11
L'Astrance	8
Au Bon Accueil	5
Le Cassenoix	12
Les Cocottes	7
David Toutain	4
La Fontaine de Mars	6
Le Jules Verne	9
Les Marches	1
Monsieur Bleu	2
Le P'tit Troquet	10
Tokyo Eat	2

● SHOPPING	
Défilé de Marques	2
Librairie le Moniteur	1
Marché Cler	3

THE EIFFEL TOWER QUARTER

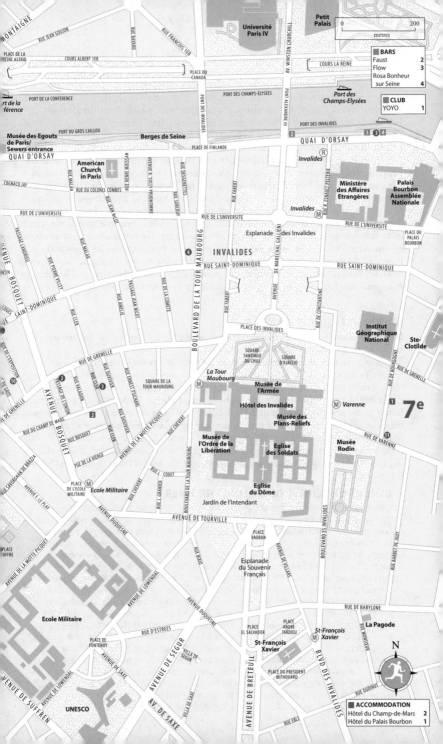

Musée du Quai Branly

37 quai Branly, 7ᵉ • Tues, Wed & Sun 11am–7pm, Thurs–Sat 11am–9pm • €9 • ☎ 01 56 61 70 00, ⓦ quaibranly.fr • Ⓜ léna/RER Pont de l'Alma

A short distance upstream of the Eiffel Tower, the brash **Musée du Quai Branly** cuts a postmodern swathe along the riverbank. It's well worth visiting for Jean Nouvel's exciting architectural design alone, which plays with the divide between structure and outside world. Fronting the riverbank is a tall glass wall, which turns the glorious, half-wild garden into a half-indoor space. Elsewhere, there's a huge, living "green wall". The building itself curls on stilts, its brightly coloured panels revealing sudden cavities or box-like swellings that pop outwards from the skin of the structure.

Parisians have taken to Nouvel's design, but the museum is more controversial. It was the pet project of former president Jacques Chirac, who has a passion for non-Western art, or what was once called "Arts Premiers" – "**Primitive Art**". Inside the museum, folk artefacts (from every part of the world except Europe and North America) are arranged by their place of origin. As if to emphasize some sort of ethnic spookiness, you follow a trail in semi-darkness on blood-red flooring between curving "mud" walls in brown leather, while screens show film footage collected in the field by anthropologists. The actual artefacts, or artworks, are stunning. Even if their original contexts aren't always made clear, it's hard not to be moved by the potency and craftsmanship of – to pick a few examples – Papua New Guinean full-body masks, Aboriginal Australian dot-paintings, exquisite Indonesian gold jewellery, or man-sized wooden statues of the spirits of god-kings from Abomey, in West Africa.

Musée des Egouts de Paris

Quai d'Orsay, 7ᵉ • Entrance on northeast side of place de la Résistance • Sat–Wed: May–Sept 11am–6pm; Oct–April 11am–5pm • €4.40 • ☎ 01 53 68 27 81 • Ⓜ Alma-Marceau/RER Pont de l'Alma

The chief attraction of the **Musée des Egouts de Paris**, or **Sewers Museum**, is that it's actually in the sewers. The main part of the visit runs along a gantry walk poised alarmingly above a main sewer. It's dark, damp and noisy with gushing water, but not as smelly as you might fear. A good companion guide might be Victor Hugo's *Les Misérables*: he turns the history of the sewer system – "a dread sink-hole which bears the traces of the revolutions of the globe as of the revolutions of man, and where are to be found vestiges of all cataclysms from the shells of the Deluge to the rag of Marat" – into a magnificent lecture.

The museum is more than half a publicity exercise by the sewage board. Bilingual displays of photographs, engravings, dredging tools, lamps and other flotsam and jetsam

---

BERGES DE SEINE: RECLAIMING THE RIVER

One of the most scenic stretches of the river, between the Musée du Quai Branly and Musée d'Orsay, was recently **opened up to pedestrians**. What was once a noisy traffic-choked road is now an attractive **promenade** (ⓦ lesberges.paris.fr), particularly lively on weekends in the warmer months, where you can eat out on a sunny terrace, listen to occasional concerts, play a game of chess over a cup of coffee or simply relax in a deckchair and enjoy some of the best **views** the city has to offer. One of the features of the design is that in the event of a flood warning everything can be dismantled within 24 hours, even the grand set of steps (known as the *emmarchement*) giving access to the *quai* from the Musée d'Orsay. The promenade also has an athletics track, a fitness course (check out the daily programme of free exercise classes) and a "zen" space where you might be offered a massage or join a t'ai chi class. Children (and grown-ups) can draw on a huge slate wall with chunky chalks, there's a kids' climbing wall, and Velib' bikes for all ages. If you fancy staking out a piece of the Seine all for yourself, you can book for free one of four grey cabins, called **Zzzzs**, available for ninety-minute slots. Near the Pont de l'Alma are five small floating gardens, each on a different theme: one is an "orchard" planted with apple trees, for example, another is planted with meadow grasses. Picnic tables and benches are dotted all along the promenade, while riverside restaurant-bars such as *Faust, Flow* and *Rosa Bonheur* (see p.299) – the last on a floating barge – offer a good selection of food and drink. The Berges has proved so successful that there are now plans to create something similar on the Right Bank.

turn the history of the city's water supply and waste management into a fascinating topic, revealing how the natural water cycle was disrupted by the city's dense population, then slowly controlled by increasingly good management. What it doesn't say is that the work isn't quite finished. Almost all the effluent from the sewers goes to the Achèves treatment plant, northwest of Paris, but several times a year parts of the system get overloaded with rainwater, and excess – waste and all – has to be emptied straight into the Seine.

The Invalides quarter

10

Ⓜ/RER Invalides/La Tour-Maubourg

The broad green **Esplanade des Invalides** runs down from the Pont Alexandre III towards the resplendently gilded dome of the **Hôtel des Invalides**, home to the **Musée de l'Armee** and Napoleon's tomb. Despite its palatial appearance, it was actually built for wounded soldiers in the reign of Louis XIV – whose foreign wars gave the building a constant supply of residents and whose equestrian statue lords it over a massive central arch. Architecturally, the building evokes a kind of barracks version of the awesome spirit of Versailles, stripped of finer flourishes – other than the gilded dome – but crushingly grand nonetheless. Even the cobbles on the esplanade seem made for giants' feet. You'll find muscularity of a more stirring kind in the **Musée Rodin**, which brings the sculptor's greatest works under the roof of a fine Parisian mansion.

Musée de l'Armée

51 bd de La Tour-Maubourg, 7ᵉ • Daily: April–Oct 10am–6pm; Nov–March 10am–5pm; closed first Mon of each month, except July–Sept • €9.50; ticket also valid for Napoleon's tomb (see p.154) • ☎ 01 44 42 38 77, Ⓦ musee-armee.fr • Ⓜ La Tour-Maubourg/Varenne

Les Invalides today houses the vast **Musée de l'Armée**, the national war museum. The moat around the whole Invalides complex means you can only approach from the north or south ends of the building; the ticket office is in the southwest wing, where it faces in towards the Eglise du Dôme.

Antique arms to Napoléon III

The northern half of the museum, on either side of the front court, is a relatively traditional display of uniforms and weaponry. In the **west wing**, the lofty old refectory and arsenal have been filled with a staggering array of **medieval** and **Renaissance** weaponry and armour, including the extraordinary mail made for François I, a big man for his time, and a chamber of beautifully worked Oriental arms and armour. The east wing, covering 1643 to 1871, is relatively dreary, apart from the glossy Ingres portrait of **Napoleon** on his throne and the room devoted to the little emperor's personal effects – notably his campaign bed and trademark hat and coat. The collection of super-scale models of French ports and fortified cities in the **Musée des Plans-Reliefs**, on the top floor, is surprisingly engaging, however. Essentially giant three-dimensional maps, they were created to plan defences and plot artillery positions from the late seventeenth century. With the eerie green glow of their landscapes only just illuminating the long, tunnel-like attic, the effect is rather chilling. All that's missing is a few miniature armies.

The World Wars

The "modern" section of the museum pushes the ultra-traditionalist view of modern French history: that, after a seventy-year struggle with the German aggressor, *la Patrie* finally emerged victorious. The area covering 1871 to **World War I** focuses more on maps, uniforms and strategy. The horrors – ten million dead soldiers, 1.37 million of them French – are only really represented by the gas shells, machine guns and grenades that killed them. The section on **World War II** is much more excitingly presented. War, resistance and liberation are reconstructed using clever memorabilia and gripping film reels (most of which have an English-language option). You leave shocked, stirred, and with the distinct impression that Général de Gaulle was personally responsible for the

---

BONAPARTE'S BONES

In 2002 a French historian asked for **Napoleon's ashes** to be exhumed for DNA testing, claiming that the remains had been swapped for those of his *maître d'hôtel* on St Helena, one Jean-Baptiste Cipriani. Apparently, a witness at the original 1821 burial observed that the great man's teeth were "most villainous", whereas at the exhumation it was reported that they were "exceptionally white". There was some reason for suspicion, as the last round of tests – on a lock of the emperor's hair – suggested he had died of **arsenic poisoning**, not cancer, as the British claimed. Some said the traces were caused by the green – and therefore arsenic-laced – pigment in the imperial wallpaper, others that he was murdered by his captors. In 2008, however, the latter conspiracy theory was rebutted. Italian researchers found hairs from Napoleon's boyhood home and compared them with others taken on Elba and on St Helena. The arsenic levels were found to be consistently high, not just in the final sample; the British, it seems, were not as perfidious as all that.

10

---

liberation of France – an impression that's reinforced by the hagiographic **Historial de Gaulle** in the basement, an exhibition celebrating the man and his myth using ultra-high-tech audiovisuals and interactive screens.

Eglise des Soldats
Hôtel des Invalides • Daily 9.30am–5.30pm • Free • Ⓜ La Tour-Maubourg/Varenne

At the core of the Invalides complex is a double church, built by Jules Hardouin-Mansart in the 1670s. The giant Eglise du Dôme, to the south, was formerly the Eglise Royale, intended for the private worship of Louis XIV and the royal family, while the relatively spartan northern section is known as the **Eglise des Soldats** (or **Eglise St-Louis**). A glass wall divides the two churches, a design innovation which would have allowed worshippers to share the same high altar without the risk of coming into social contact. The door to the Soldiers' Church (no ticket required) is in the main northern courtyard of Les Invalides. Inside it's bright and airy, the high walls lined with almost a hundred banners captured by the French army over the centuries. The collection once numbered three thousand trophies at its peak, but was largely destroyed in 1817 by a governor of Les Invalides too proud to see them fall back into the hands of Napoleon's triumphant enemies. A commemorative Mass is still said here on May 5, the anniversary of the emperor's death.

Eglise du Dôme
Hôtel des Invalides • Daily: April, May & Sept 10am–6pm; July & Aug 10am–7pm; Oct–March 10am–5pm • €9.50; ticket also valid for the Musée de l'Armée (see p.153) • Ⓜ La Tour-Maubourg/Varenne

The **Eglise du Dôme** has a separate entrance on the south side of the complex. Unlike its northern twin, the Soldiers' Church, it's awesomely grand. **Napoleon's tomb**, a mighty sarcophagus of deep red quartzite, is itself entombed in a giant circular pit, overlooked by guardian statues that represent his military victories. Friezes on the surrounding gallery parade the emperor's civic triumphs, along with quotations of gigantic (and occasionally accurate) conceit such as "Wherever the shadow of my rule has fallen, it has left lasting traces of its value". Napoleon's shadow still fell heavily on Paris on December 14, 1840, the day on which his ashes, freshly returned from St Helena, were carried through the streets from the newly completed Arc de Triomphe to Invalides. Even though Louis-Philippe, a Bourbon, was on the throne, and Napoleon's nephew, Louis-Napoléon, had been imprisoned for attempting a coup four months earlier, the Bonapartists came out in force – half a million of them – to watch the emperor's last journey.

More affecting than Napoleon's tomb is the simple memorial to **Maréchal Foch**, commander-in-chief of the allied forces at the end of World War I, which stands in the side chapel by the stairs leading down to the crypt. The marshal's effigy is borne by a phalanx of bronze infantrymen displaying a soldierly grief, the whole chamber flooded by blue light from the stained-glass windows.

Musée Rodin

77 rue de Varenne, 7ᵉ • Tues–Sun 10am–5.45pm • €10 • ☎ 01 44 18 61 10, ⓦ musee-rodin.fr • Ⓜ Varenne

The recently refurbished **Musée Rodin** has surely the loveliest setting of all Paris's museums: a superb, generously gardened eighteenth-century mansion which the sculptor leased from the state in return for the gift of all his work upon his death. Bronze versions of major projects like *The Burghers of Calais*, *The Thinker* and *The Gate of Hell* are set among the grounds – the last forming the centrepiece of the ornamental pond. There's a pleasant outdoor café at the back and a collection of roses at the front.

Inside, the passionate intensity of the sculptures contrasts with the graceful wooden panelling and chandeliers, while the many tarnished mirrors make the perfect foil for Rodin's theory of profiles, in which each sculpture is formed from a collection of views from different standpoints. The museum is usually crowded with visitors eager to see much-loved works like **The Kiss**, which actually portrays Paolo and Francesca da Rimini, from Dante's *Divine Comedy*, in the moment before they were discovered and murdered by Francesca's husband. Contemporaries were scandalized by Francesca's distinctly active engagement; art critics today like to think of it as the last masterwork of figurative sculpture before the whole art form was reinvented – largely by Rodin himself. Paris's *Kiss* is one of only four marble versions of the work. Don't miss Paolo's ecstatically scrunched-up toes.

It's worth lingering over the museum's vibrant, impressionistic clay works, small studies that Rodin took from life. In fact, most of the works here are in clay or plaster, as these are considered to be Rodin's finest achievements – after completing his apprenticeship, he rarely picked up a chisel, in line with the common nineteenth-century practice of delegating the task of working up stone and bronze versions to assistants. Some space is devoted to **Camille Claudel**, Rodin's pupil, model and lover. Among her works is *The Age of Maturity*, symbolizing her ultimate rejection by Rodin, and a bust of the artist himself.

La Pagode

57bis rue de Babylone, 7ᵉ • ☎ 01 46 34 82 54, ⓦ etoile-cinemas.com • Ⓜ St-François-Xavier

The Chinese-style roofs of **La Pagode**, overlooking the corner of rue Monsieur, were built as a fashionable toy for the wife of a director of the Bon Marché department store, and later turned into a historic cinema – in 1959 it premiered Cocteau's *Le Testament d'Orphée*, and, a year later, was one of the cinemas to first screen the movies of the Nouvelle Vague. Following a superb renovation, it is now once again one of the most enjoyable art-house cinemas in the city, with its Art Deco-meets-Oriental decor and delightful garden.

Pont Alexandre III

Ⓜ /RER Invalides

North of the Invalides complex, the eastern end of the quai d'Orsay opens out into a grand esplanade. Parading across the river towards the giant conservatories of the Grand and Petit Palais is the **Pont Alexandre III**. The vista here was so cherished that when this bridge was built it was set as low as possible above the water so as not to get in the way of the view. That said, it's surely the most extravagant bridge in the city, its single-span metal arch stretching 109m across the river. It was unveiled in 1900, just in time for the Exposition Universelle, its name and elaborate decoration symbolizing Franco–Russian friendship – an ever more important alliance in the face of fast-growing German power. The nymph stretching out downstream represents the Seine, matched by St Petersburg's River Neva facing upstream.

Quai d'Orsay

Ⓜ Alma-Marceau/Pont de l'Alma

To the west of the Pont Alexandre III, the pale neo-Gothic tower and copper spire of the **American Church** stand out on the **quai d'Orsay**. Together with the American College nearby at 31 avenue Bosquet, it plays a key role in the busy life of Paris's large expat American community. News stories on French foreign policy use "the quai d'Orsay" to refer to the Ministère des Affaires Etrangères (Ministry of Foreign Affairs), which sits next to the Esplanade des Invalides and the Palais Bourbon, home of the **Assemblée Nationale**. Napoleon, never a great one for democracy, had the riverfront facade of the Palais Bourbon done to match the pseudo-Greek of the Madeleine. The result is an entrance that sheds little light on what's happening within.

Rue Cler

Ⓜ La Tour-Maubourg/Ecole-Militaire

10

An attractive, villagey wedge of early nineteenth-century streets huddles between avenue Bosquet and the Invalides, contrasting starkly with the grand austerity of much of the rest of the septième. At its heart is the market street **rue Cler**. It's a well-to-do affair – as much permanent delicatessens as fruit stalls on barrows – and the cross-streets, rue de Grenelle and rue St-Dominique, are full of classy boutiques, posh *bistrots* and little hotels.

The Trocadéro and Palais de Chaillot

Ⓜ Trocadéro

On the western side of the Eiffel Tower area, the **Trocadéro quarter** lies on the elevated northern bank of the Seine. The river forms little barrier to a visit, however, as there's a picturesque above-ground métro line (line 6, which crosses the river on the Pont de Bir-Hakeim, offering excellent views of the Eiffel Tower). The *quartier* is also connected to the septième by three fine bridges: the businesslike Pont de l'Alma, the graceful Passerelle Debilly and the handsome Pont d'Iéna, which thrusts north as if from under the very legs of the Tower into the embrace of the breathtakingly ugly **Palais de Chaillot**.

Palais de Chaillot

1 place du Trocadéro et du 11 novembre, 16ᵉ • Ⓜ Trocadéro

The **Palais de Chaillot** stands on a site favoured by imperialist-minded rulers ever since Catherine de Médicis constructed one of her playpens here in the early sixteenth century. Napoleon planned (but never built) a palace here for his short-lived son, and, in 1878, an Oriental-style confection was erected (but soon after demolished). The current Modernist–Neoclassical monster went up in 1937 as part of the globalist-minded Exposition Universelle. Adorned as it is with heroic statues and symmetrical acres of marble paving, it would look less out of place in Fascist Rome than here, though the two curving wings do neatly embrace the shadow of the Eiffel Tower.

The *palais* houses several museums, including the **Musée de l'Homme**, which charts human evolution and is due to reopen at the end of 2015 after major renovation work. Beneath the central terrace lies the **Théâtre National de Chaillot**, which stages diverse and usually radical productions; enter via the northern wing.

Musée National de la Marine

Palais de Chaillot • Mon–Fri 11am–6pm, Sat & Sun 11am–7pm • €8.50 • ☎ 01 53 65 69 69, Ⓦ musee-marine.fr • Ⓜ Trocadéro

The southern wing of the Palais de Chaillot houses the rather specialized **Musée National de la Marine**, which traces French naval history using model ships. It's also home to the original Jules Verne trophy, awarded for nonstop round-the-world sailing – a hull-shaped streak of glass invisibly suspended by magnets within its cabinet.

Cité de l'Architecture et du Patrimoine

Palais de Chaillot • Mon, Wed & Fri–Sun 11am–7pm, Thurs 11am–9pm • €8 • ☎ 01 58 51 52 00, Ⓦ citechaillot.fr • Ⓜ Trocadéro

The splendid **Cité de l'Architecture et du Patrimoine**, a combined institute, library and **museum of architecture**, occupies the northern wing of the Palais de Chaillot. The bedrock of the museum, the long and lofty **Galerie des Moulages**, on the ground floor, displays giant plaster casts of sections of great French buildings. There are entire portals from Romanesque cathedrals, Gothic windows, Renaissance tombs and exact reproductions of the finest statuary in France. The casts date from an earlier, nineteenth-century museum, and to see French architecture laid out as a kind of grand historical panorama is as eye-opening now as it was for the original curiosity-seekers.

On the second floor, the **Galerie d'Architecture Moderne et Contemporaine** showcases the nineteenth and twentieth centuries with some stunning, original architectural models, and a full-size – and distinctly poky – reconstruction of an "E2 superior" apartment from Le Corbusier's Cité Radieuse, which you can actually walk around in. This gallery offers a fascinating lesson in the evolution of modern design, but more wondrous is the **Galerie des Peintures Murales et des Vitraux**, which occupies the central pavilion on the second and third floors. In the same spirit as the *moulages* gallery, it displays life-size copies of French wall paintings, frescoes and stained glass. Its stunning centrepiece is the lofty, Byzantine-style cupola from Cahors cathedral, but it's well worth penetrating deeper into the maze-like sequence of rooms as far as the claustrophobic reconstruction of the Romanesque crypt of the church of Tavant, in the Loire region, and heading up to the third floor for the terrifying sequence of medieval Passions and Last Judgements. The **library** on the first floor is also well worth visiting for its copy of a Romanesque vault mural from the church of St-Savin-sur-Gartempe, and the **temporary exhibitions** are generally excellent.

Cinéaqua

2 av des Nations Unies • Daily 10am–7pm • ☎ 01 40 69 23 23, ⓦ cineaqua.com • €20.50, children aged 3–12 €13, aged 13–17 €16; it's best to book online to avoid queues • Ⓜ Trocadéro/Iéna

Paris's aquarium, the **Cinéaqua**, accessed from a ramp on the riverfront side of the Palais de Chaillot, features hundreds of tropical fish, including sharks, as well as the more humble specimens found in the River Seine. Children will particularly enjoy the *bassin des caresses*, where you can feed and touch tame koi carp, and there's special weekend entertainment, such as mermaid and pirate shows. The aquarium's cinemas regularly show animations and films about sea creatures.

Musée National des Arts Asiatiques Guimet

6 place d'Iéna, 16ᵉ • Daily except Tues 10am–6pm • €7.50 • ☎ 01 56 52 53 00, ⓦ guimet.fr • Ⓜ Iéna

The **Musée National des Arts Asiatiques Guimet** winds round four floors groaning under the weight of statues of Buddhas and gods, some fierce, some meditative, all of them dramatically displayed alongside ceramics, paintings and other objets d'art. Each room is devoted to a different country of origin, stretching from the Greek-influenced Buddhist statues of the **Gandhara civilization**, on the first floor, to fierce demons from Nepal and pot-bellied Chinese Buddhas. The highlight, however, is the breathtaking roofed-in **courtyard**: it's a perfectly airy space in which to show off the museum's world-renowned collection of **Khmer sculpture** – from the civilization that produced Cambodia's Angkor Wat. On the third floor is a rotunda used by the collection's founder, **Emile Guimet**, for the first Buddhist ceremony ever held in France. A great collector and patron of the arts, Guimet espoused the Christian-socialist-egalitarian theories proposed by Fournier, Saint-Simon and, in Britain, Robert Owen.

Galeries du Panthéon Bouddhique

19 av d'Iéna, 16ᵉ • Daily except Tues 10am–5.45pm • Free • ☎ 01 40 73 88 00, ⓦ guimet.fr • Ⓜ Iéna

Emile Guimet's original collection, which he brought back from his travels in Asia in 1876, is exhibited near the Musée Guimet in the **Galeries du Panthéon Bouddhique**. While far smaller, in some ways it's a more satisfying affair than the larger museum, as the gilded ranks of Buddhas are presented with a Buddhist's eye rather than an art collector's. At the back is a small Japanese garden with bamboo, pussy willow and watery reflections.

Palais Galliera Musée de la Mode

10 av Pierre 1er de Serbie, 16ᵉ • Tues–Sun 10am–6pm, Thurs till 9pm • Admission varies • ☎ 01 56 52 86 00, ⓦ palaisgalliera.paris.fr • Ⓜ Iéna/Alma-Marceau

The rather exquisite and bizarrely Italianate bijoux box of the recently renovated Palais Galliera was built in the 1880s by the Duchesse de Galliera to house her private art collection. It now belongs to the city, and is the home of the **Musée de la Mode**. The museum's unrivalled collection of historic and modern clothes and fashion accessories is exhibited in two or three shows a year, with themes such as "Creating the Myth of Marlene Dietrich" or focusing on single designers such as Jeanne Lanvin or Azzedine Alaïa. During changeovers the museum is closed.

The Palais de Tokyo

13 av du Président-Wilson, 16ᵉ • Ⓜ Iéna/Alma-Marceau

The **Palais de Tokyo** houses two galleries of modern art, both of which are among the most rewarding in Paris, though they see fewer visitors than the Pompidou Centre. The entrance to the palace is on its north side, but most people arrive across the Seine via the pedestrian **Passerelle Debilly**. Rather surprisingly, given its modern looks, this bridge is a contemporary of its near neighbour, the profoundly more ornate Pont Alexandre III – both were opened in 1900, in time for the Exposition Universelle. The Palais de Tokyo dates from a later exhibition, the tension-filled 1937 World Fair, at which the German and Russian pavilions faced each other across the Seine in an architectural standoff. **Antoine Bourdelle**'s bronze statue of "Eternal France", which surveys the central terrace of the Tokyo building, is a living reminder of the fervid nationalism of those times. The palace was always intended to be a gallery of **modern art**, however, and most of its decoration takes a more consciously artistic theme; Alfred Auguste Janniot's vast Art Deco bas-reliefs, which frame the central staircase, represent the nine muses. The colonnaded building itself is simple and beautiful. It's also a perfect suntrap, and much favoured by skateboarders and graffiti artists.

On Wednesday and Saturday mornings a bustling **market** takes over avenue du Président-Wilson, from Iéna métro station down to the palace.

Musée d'Art Moderne de la Ville de Paris

Palais de Tokyo • Tues–Sun 10am–6pm • Free; charges for temporary exhibitions • ☎ 01 53 67 40 00, ⓦ mam.paris.fr • Ⓜ Iéna/Alma-Marceau

The east wing of the Palais de Tokyo houses the **Musée d'Art Moderne de la Ville de Paris**. The collection can't rival the Pompidou Centre's, but it's free, relatively uncrowded and the environment is far more contemplative – and architecturally more fitting when it comes to works by early twentieth-century artists. The ground floor, by the entrance, is given over to temporary exhibitions.

The Dufy and Matisse murals

The gallery received unwelcome publicity in May 2010 when a lone thief made off with half a dozen priceless canvases by Picasso, Matisse, Modigliani and others, but it still has its two marvellous (and entirely untransportable) centrepieces. Just above the main stairs leading down to the permanent collections, a vast, curving chamber provides wall-space for Raoul Dufy's mural *La Fée Électricité* ("The Electricity Fairy"). Originally designed for the Electricity Pavilion in the 1937 Exposition Universelle, its 250 vivid, cartoon-like panels tell the story of electricity from the earliest experimenters to the triumph of industrialization that was the power station. Facing the stairs as you descend, the chapel-like **salle Matisse** is devoted to Matisse's balletic and heart-lifting *La Danse de Paris*, beginning with an incomplete early version and progressing through to the finished work, displayed high on the wall. Daniel Buren's *Mur de Peintures* (1995–2006), in his trademark stripes, is displayed in the same room.

The permanent collection

The main permanent collection is chronologically themed, starting with Fauvism and Cubism, and progressing through to Dada and the Ecole de Paris, and beyond. Most artists working in France – Braque, Chagall, Delaunay, Derain, Duchamp, Dufy, Klein, Léger, Modigliani, Picasso and many others – are represented, and there is a strong Parisian theme to many of the works. The collection is kept up to the minute by an active buying policy, and some bold acquisitions of sculpture, painting and video by contemporary artists are displayed in the final suite of rooms. Look out in particular for the intimate scrapbook works of Annette Messager, Jean-Marc Bustamante's chilly photography, Christian Boltanski's sinister photographs and harrowing installations of old clothing and phone books, and, towards the end, Philippe Parreno's mesmerizing video works.

10

Palais de Tokyo Site de Création Contemporaine

Palais de Tokyo • Daily except Tues noon–midnight • €10, under-18s free • ☎ 01 47 23 54 01, ⓦ palaisdetokyo.com • Ⓜ Iéna/Alma-Marceau

Set in the western wing of the Palais de Tokyo, the **Palais de Tokyo Site de Création Contemporaine** was opened in 2002 and quickly established a reputation for exciting avant-garde exhibitions. A major revamp completed in 2012 made it one of Europe's largest and most ambitious contemporary art spaces. The original architects of the museum, Lacaton and Vassal, added two new floors – in the cavernous and rather eerie basement, which was sealed up after World War II and abandoned – to the existing two, tripling the exhibition space, demolishing partitions and mezzanines and introducing natural light. As with the rest of the building, however, the new spaces remain deliberately semi-derelict, with industrial-looking concrete walls and exposed piping creating a sense of "work in progress". The museum has no permanent exhibits, but instead mounts large-scale exhibitions involving multiple curators. Prominence is given to French artists, but many international artists are also represented, ranging from the well established, such as Julio Le Parc, to emerging young artists such as Hicham Berrada. The museum has two restaurants: trendy *Tokyo Eat* (see p.288) and classy *Monsieur Bleu* (see p.288), overlooking the Seine, as well as a café, *Le Smack*. There's also a well-stocked bookshop on the ground floor.

Place de l'Alma and around

Ⓜ Alma-Marceau

A few steps upstream of the Palais de Tokyo, on **place de l'Alma**, stands a full-scale, golden replica of the flame from the Statue of Liberty. It was given to France in 1987 as a symbol of Franco-American relations but is now an unofficial memorial to **Princess Diana**, whose Mercedes crashed in the underpass beneath. The authorities clean up the site regularly, but you'll often find bunches of withered flowers and graffiti messages left as tributes.

Pont de l'Alma

Ⓜ Alma-Marceau

The **Pont de l'Alma**, which crosses the Seine towards the sewers, is a rather brutal 1970s steel-and-concrete affair. It's worth taking a peek at its celebrated **zouave** statue, however, which hides away by the waterline, on the upstream side. The name comes from the North African soldiers who fought in the French army during the Crimean War, and it was one of four military statues that adorned the previous Alma bridge. It has long served as Parisians' yardstick for describing the Seine's flooding. In 1910, for instance, the water came up to the zouave's shoulders. On the new bridge, he actually stands slightly higher than he used to, so even a knee-high flood is a fairly serious event.

MUSÉE BOURDELLE

Montparnasse and southern Paris

The swathe of cafés, brasseries and cinemas that runs through the heart of modern Montparnasse has long been a honeypot for pleasure-seekers, as well as a kind of border town dividing well-heeled St-Germain from the amorphous populations of the three arrondissements of southern Paris, the 13e, 14e and 15e. Overscale developments from the 1950s to the present day have scarred parts of this southern side of the city, but there are three great parks – André-Citroën (with its very own tethered balloon), Georges-Brassens and Montsouris – and some enticing pockets of Paris that have been allowed to evolve in a happily patchy way. Lively areas such as Pernety and Plaisance in the 14e, the quartier du Commerce in the 15e and the Butte-aux-Cailles in the 13^e are pleasant places to explore.

Montparnasse and the 14ᵉ

The story goes that, before it was levelled in the early eighteenth century, students used to drink and declaim poetry from the top of a pile of spoil deposited from the Denfert-Rochereau quarries, calling the mound "Mount Parnassus" after the legendary home of the muses of poetry and song, and of drunken Bacchus. This may or may not be how the area got its name, but the reputation of **Montparnasse** for carousing persists to this day, though its status as a nightspot really stems from the construction of the Mur des Fermiers Généraux in 1784, or "Customs Wall", which split the high-taxed city from the poorer, less-regulated township areas beyond. In the nineteenth century, bohemians, left-leaning intellectuals and poets such as Verlaine and Baudelaire abandoned the city centre for Montparnasse, drawn by the inexpensive cafés and nightlife. The quarter's lasting fame, however, rests on its role as the **birthplace of Modernism**, following the artistic exodus from Montmartre. In the *années folles*, or "Mad Years" following World War I, artists such as Picasso, Matisse, Brancusi, Kandinsky, Modigliani, Giacometti and Chagall were all habitués of the celebrated cafés around **place Vavin**. They were soon joined by a self-professed "lost generation" of bohemia-hunting and Prohibition-fleeing Americans – Hemingway, Pound, Man Ray and Dos Passos among them. Many were buried in **Montparnasse cemetery**, and still more bones lie nearby in the grim **catacombs**.

The area immediately around Montparnasse's Modernist railway station is dominated by the gigantic **Tour Montparnasse**, which you can ascend for a superb view of the city. North of Montparnasse station are two little-visited but beguiling **artists' museums**, recalling the area's artistic heyday, while the nearby **Fondation Cartier** showcases contemporary art and architecture. South of the station, the **14ᵉ** is one of the most characterful of the outer arrondissements. The old-fashioned networks of streets still exist in the **Pernety** and **Plaisance** *quartiers*, where many artists chose to live in the affordable *villas* (similar to mews) built in the 1920s and 1930s. Down in the southeast corner of the arrondissement you'll find plenty of green space in the **Parc Montsouris** and the giant student campus of the **Cité Universitaire**.

11

Tour Montparnasse

33 av du Maine, 15ᵉ • Rooftop platform daily: April–Sept 9.30am–11.30pm; Oct–March 9.30am–10.30pm, Fri & Sat till 11pm • €15 • ☎ 01 45 38 52 56, ⓦ tourmontparnasse56.com • Ⓜ Montparnasse-Bienvenüe

Montparnasse station's arch gives onto a broad concrete esplanade surrounded by traffic, the prospect of the city blocked by the brown glass blade of the **Tour Montparnasse**. At the time of its deeply controversial construction, this was one of Paris's first skyscrapers, defying the problem of the city's quarried-out limestone bedrock with 56 massive piles driven into a chalk layer over 40m below ground. Few Parisians have a good word to say for such a monolithic landmark, but the **view** from the open, often windy **rooftop platform** is arguably better than the one from the Eiffel Tower – it has the Eiffel Tower in it, after all, plus there are no queues. Nervous view-seekers can settle for the 56th-floor café and gallery room. Sunset is the best time to visit.

Jardin Atlantique

Behind Montparnasse train station; access is via lifts on rue du Commandant Mouchotte and bd Vaugirard, or by the stairs alongside platform #1 • Daily 9am–dusk • Free • Ⓜ Montparnasse-Bienvenüe

Montparnasse was once the great arrival and departure point for boat travellers across the Atlantic and Bretons seeking work in the capital. Brittany's influence is still evident in the abundance of crêperies near the station, such as *Crêperie Josselin* (see p.289), but the connection is also evoked by the **Jardin Atlantique**, a public park suspended above the tracks behind the station. Completed in 1994, between cliff-like glass walls of high-rise blocks, it's a remarkable piece of engineering – and imagination. Well-hidden ventilation holes reveal sudden glimpses of TGV roofs and rail sleepers, while the

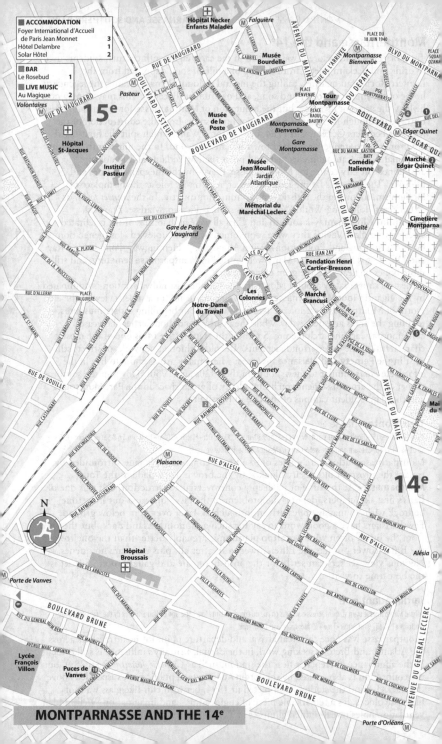

MONTPARNASSE AND THE 14e

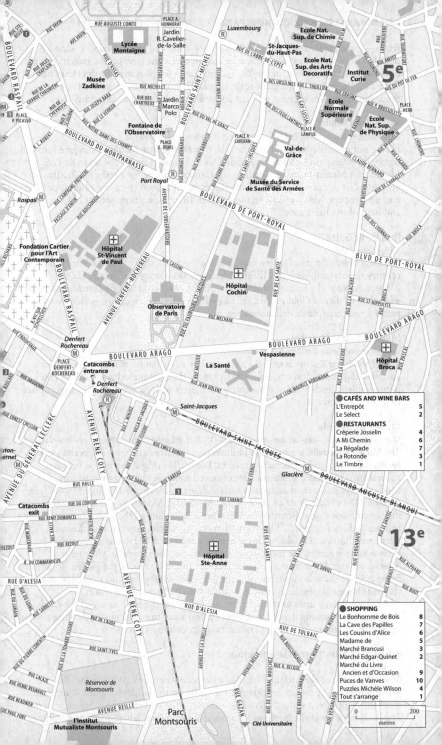

RUE AUGUSTE COMTE
PLACE A. HONNORAT
Luxembourg

Lycée Montaigne
Jardin R. Cavelier-de-la-Salle

Ecole Nat. Sup. de Chimie
St-Jacques-du-Haut-Pas
Ecole Nat. Sup. des Arts Decoratifs
Institut Curie

5e

Musée Zadkine

Jardin Marco Polo

Ecole Normale Supérieure
Ecole Nat. Sup. de Physique

Fontaine de l'Observatoire

Val-de-Grâce

BOULEVARD DU MONTPARNASSE

Port Royal

Musée du Service de Santé des Armées

Raspail

BOULEVARD DE PORT-ROYAL

Fondation Cartier pour l'Art Contemporain

Hôpital St-Vincent de Paul

BLVD DE PORT-ROYAL

Hôpital Cochin

Observatoire de Paris

Denfert Rochereau

BOULEVARD ARAGO

BOULEVARD ARAGO

Vespasienne

Hôpital Broca

PLACE DENFERT-ROCHEREAU

Catacombs entrance

Denfert Rochereau

La Santé

Saint-Jacques

BOULEVARD SAINT JACQUES

Catacombs exit

Glacière

BOULEVARD AUGUSTE-BLANQUI

13e

Hôpital Ste-Anne

RUE D'ALESIA

Réservoir de Montsouris

l'Institut Mutualiste Montsouris

AVENUE REILLE

Parc Montsouris

Cité Universitaire

● CAFÉS AND WINE BARS
L'Entrepôt   5
Le Select   2
● RESTAURANTS
Crêperie Josselin   4
A Mi Chemin   6
La Régalade   7
La Rotonde   3
Le Timbre   1

● SHOPPING
Le Bonhomme de Bois   8
La Cave des Papilles   7
Les Cousins d'Alice   6
Madame de   5
Marché Brancusi   3
Marché Edgar-Quinet   2
Marché du Livre
 Ancien et d'Occasion   9
Puces de Vanves   10
Puzzles Michèle Wilson   4
Tout s'arrange   1

0   200
metres

lawns – some planted with long coastal grasses – rise and fall in symbolic waves. A double line of trees runs south from the station end – the trees on the eastern side are of American origin, those on the West, European – to the central **Ile des Hespérides** fountain. The fountain is a giant-scale, disguised weather station, with a large thermometer and rain gauge, and is a favourite spot for children on sunny days.

Musée Jean Moulin

Jardin Atlantique • Tues–Sun 10am–6pm • Free • ☎ 01 40 64 39 44 • Ⓜ Montparnasse-Bienvenüe

Facing out onto the Jardin Atlantique, the tiny **Musée Jean Moulin** (or to give it its full name, the Musée du Général Leclerc de Hauteclocque et de la Libération de Paris – Musée Jean Moulin) may be worth a stop if you're waiting for a train to Chartres. It gives a rather dry potted history of the Resistance illustrated by a few photos, posters and newspapers, with a special section on Jean Moulin, wartime prefect of Chartres and hero of the Resistance.

11 Rue de la Gaîté

Ⓜ Edgar-Quinet/Gaîté

Rue de la Gaîté, the street where Trotsky once lived, is a slice of turn-of-the-twentieth-century theatreland, with the Théâtre Montparnasse facing the Théâtre Gaîté-Montparnasse at the bottom of the street. At the northern end, the **Comédie Italienne** advertises its diet of Goldoni and the like with a wonderfully camp, golden exterior painted with commedia dell'arte scenes.

Marché Edgar Quinet

Wed & Sat mornings, Sun roughly 10am–dusk • Ⓜ Edgar-Quinet

Boulevard Edgar-Quinet is entirely consumed by a lively food **market** on Wednesday and Saturday mornings, while on Sundays more than a hundred craftworkers take over; photographers jostle with potters, clothes designers with painters, and it's a great place to browse away the day.

Musée Bourdelle

18 rue Antoine Bourdelle, 15ᵉ • Tues–Sun 10am–6pm • Free • ☎ 01 49 54 73 73, Ⓦ bourdelle.paris.fr • Ⓜ Montparnasse-Bienvenüe/Falguière

The **Musée Bourdelle** is a museum built around the artist's former studio and garden. As Rodin's pupil and Giacometti's teacher, Bourdelle bridged the period between naturalism and a more geometrically conceived style; he was arguably the first Modernist. Monumental sculptures such as *Hercules the Archer* (1910) and *The Dying Centaur* (1914) take pride of place in the chapel-like, Modernist grand hall; asked why the centaur was dying, Bourdelle replied that he dies, like all the gods, "because no one believes in him any more". Elsewhere, there's a wonderful series of tumultuous Beethoven busts and masks, sculpted between 1887 and 1929, and a basement extension with studies for the sculptor's great works, the muscular *Monument à Mickiewicz* and *Monument au Général Alvear*. On the far side of the garden Bourdelle's living quarters have been preserved, complete with shabby bed and stove, and you can also visit his atmospheric old **studio**, littered with half-completed works.

Just around the corner to the right, on rue Falguière, the bold facade of the Ile-de-France urban planning department veers up and away from the line of the street in the smoothest of curves, like the hull of a fantasy spaceship.

Boulevard Montparnasse and around

Ⓜ Vavin

Most of the life of the Montparnasse *quartier* is concentrated on **boulevard du Montparnasse**. The numerous **cinemas** here – six on the boulevard alone – are almost all of the multiscreen variety, specializing in mass-market French and American films. The liveliest point of the boulevard is around Vavin métro, where you'll find Rodin's

MONTPARNASSE ARCHITECTURE

Dominated as it is by the skyscraping blade of its tower, the busy boulevards, and the large-scale developments around the station, Montparnasse can feel a little inhuman and over-modernized. Wandering down the backstreets, however, you can find some kindlier examples of **architecture**, ranging from the playful lines of early **Art Deco** to the diaphanous **contemporary** glasswork of Jean Nouvel's Fondation Cartier.

26 rue Vavin 6ᵉ; Ⓜ Vavin. Decked in white and blue tiles, the terraced balconies of this apartment block are stepped back, allowing gardens to flourish in the light. Built by Henri Sauvage in 1912.

Rue Schoelcher and rue Froidevaux 14ᵉ; Ⓜ Raspail/Denfert-Rochereau. A parade of varied nineteenth- and early twentieth-century styles. Check out 5 rue Schoelcher, especially, for its beautiful Art Deco balconies and windows, dating from 1911 (Picasso had his studio at 5bis for a short time in 1916). The artists' studios at 11 rue Schoelcher are just sixteen years younger, but the transformation to modernity is complete. Also worth seeing are nos. 11 and 23 rue Froidevaux, the latter being a 1929 block of artists' studios, with huge windows for northern light and fabulous ceramic mosaics.

266 bd Raspail 14ᵉ; Ⓜ Raspail/Denfert-Rochereau. A recently completed private architecture and interior design academy with a marked Beaubourg influence, notably the external stairs and blue pipe columns in front. The original Ecole Spéciale d'Architecture building nearby, at no. 254, dates from 1904.

31 rue Campagne-Première 14ᵉ; Ⓜ Raspail. Myriad shell-like, earthenware tiles by Alexandre Bigot encrust the concrete structure of André Arfvidson's desirable 1912 *appartements*, with their huge, iron-framed studio windows. Man Ray had a studio here in the early 1920s.

Fondation Cartier pour l'Art Contemporain 261 bd Raspail, 14ᵉ; Ⓜ Raspail. One of Jean Nouvel's most successful, airy, postmodern steel-and-glass structures. See p.166.

Passage d'Enfer 14ᵉ; Ⓜ Raspail. Parallel to rue Campagne-Première, this narrow cobblestone street – whose name translates as "Hell Alley" – was once a Cité Ouvrière, or cul-de-sac of nineteenth-century workers' housing. The unusually small, terraced buildings are now extremely covetable.

11

Balzac ruminating over the crossroads, and a cluster of celebrated **cafés**: the *Select*, *Coupole*, *Dôme* and *Rotonde*. Their heyday was in the 1910s and 1920s, when artists and poets such as Apollinaire, Chagall, Léger, Modigliani, Picasso and Zadkine rubbed shoulders with exiled revolutionaries, including Lenin and Trotsky, paying a few centimes to occupy tables for hours on end. Even by the 1930s, the fashionable intelligentsia were moving on to St-Germain, but the brasseries remain proudly Parisian classics – if no longer bohemian haunts – and this stretch of the boulevard still stays up late.

All the cafés except the *Select* have moved steadily upmarket, and the swankiest by far is the **Closerie des Lilas**, with its fabled (and now sadly glazed-in) *terrasse* on the corner of the tree-lined avenue de l'Observatoire. In the days when it was a cheap café, Hemingway wrote most of *The Sun Also Rises* here. The café's most stirring historical association, however, is with Napoleon's Marshal Ney, the "bravest of the brave", as his master called him. His sword-wielding statue – admired by everyone from Auguste Rodin to George Orwell, as well as Hemingway – now marks the spot on the pavement where he died at the hands of a royalist firing squad.

Musée Zadkine

100bis rue d'Assas, 14ᵉ • Tues–Sun 10am–6pm • Free; audioguide €5 • ☎ 01 55 42 77 20, ⓦ zadkine.paris.fr • Ⓜ Vavin/RER Port-Royal

The minuscule, delightful **Musée Zadkine**, recently renovated to let in more light, occupies the Russian-born **sculptor Ossip Zadkine**'s studio-house, where he lived and worked from 1928 until his death in 1967. In the garden, enclosed by ivy-covered studios and dwarfed by tall buildings, angular Cubist bronzes such as his compelling *Orphée* seem to struggle for light. Inside is a collection of his gentler wooden torsos, along with smaller-scale bronze and stone works, notably *Femme à l'éventail*. Studies for *La Ville détruite*, whose twisted, agonized torso was intended to express the horror of aerial bombing, can be seen inside and in the garden.

Fondation Cartier pour l'Art Contemporain

261 bd Raspail, 14ᵉ • Tues 11am–10pm, Wed–Sun 11am–8pm • €10.50 • ☎ 01 42 18 56 50, ⓦ fondation.cartier.com • Ⓜ Raspail

The **Fondation Cartier pour l'Art Contemporain** occupies one of the finest contemporary buildings in Paris, a stunning glass-and-steel construction designed in 1994 by Jean Nouvel, architect of the Institut du Monde Arabe (see p.132). A glass wall follows the line of the street like a false start to the building proper, leaving space for the Tree of Liberty, planted by Chateaubriand during the Revolution, to grow in the garden behind. The glass of the building itself cleverly suggests a kind of fade-out into the air. Inside, all kinds of contemporary art – installations, videos, multimedia, graffiti – often by foreign artists little known in France, are shown in temporary exhibitions that use the light and generous spaces to maximum advantage.

Montparnasse cemetery

3 bd Edgar-Quinet, 14ᵉ • March 16–Nov 5: Mon–Fri 8am–6pm, Sat 8.30am–6pm, Sun 9am–6pm; Nov 6–March: 15 Mon–Fri 8am–5.30pm, Sat 8.30am–5.30pm, Sun 9am–5.30pm • Free • ☎ 01 44 10 86 50 • Ⓜ Raspail/Gaîté/Edgar-Quinet

Montparnasse cemetery suffers by being second in size to Père-Lachaise (see p.210), and a long way behind it in celebrity. It's an impressive space, nonetheless, sheltering in the lee of the Tour Montparnasse behind high walls. In the southwest corner, the old, sail-less windmill was once one of the taverns whose literary-minded customers are said to have given the Montparnasse district its name.

To track down the cemetery's illustrious residents, pick up a leaflet and map from the guardhouse by each entrance. The joint grave of Jean-Paul Sartre and Simone de Beauvoir lies immediately right of the entrance on boulevard Edgar-Quinet – Sartre lived out the last few decades of his life just a few metres away on boulevard Raspail. Down avenue de l'Ouest, which follows the inside western wall of the cemetery, you'll find the tombs of Baudelaire (who has a more impressive cenotaph by rue Emile-Richard, on the cemetery's avenue Transversale), the sculptor Zadkine and the Fascist Pierre Laval, who was executed for treason. As an antidote, you can pay homage to Proudhon, the anarchist who coined the phrase "Property is theft!"; he lies in Division 2, by the central roundabout, near the great photographer of Paris, Brassaï. In the adjacent Division 1, the tomb of singer Serge Gainsbourg is regularly festooned with métro tickets – the "lilacs" of his ticket-punching song *Le Poinçonneur des lilas* – and packets of Gitanes cigarettes.

Monuments and sculptures

Grave-hunting aside, it's worth seeking out some of the cemetery's finer **monuments**. Horace Daillion's 1889 winged bronze, *Le Génie du sommeil éternel*, dominates the central roundabout, but far more moving is the tragic sculptural scene *La Séparation du couple*, which stands a short distance below the windmill (in Division 4, beside the allée des Sergeants de la Rochelle). A giant bird created by the sculptor Niki de Saint Phalle in mirrored mosaic hovers in the northeast corner of Division 18, next to the avenue de l'Est; the title reads "To my friend Jean-Jacques: a bird which has flown too soon". The most poignant monument of all is found in the eastern angle of the cemetery, on the other side of rue Emile-Richard; in the far northern corner of this section is a tomb crowned with a version of Brancusi's sculpture *The Kiss*. Seekers of the bizarre should make for the inside wall of this part of the cemetery, along avenue du Boulevard (parallel to boulevard Raspail), where you can see the inventor of a safe gas lamp, Charles Pigeon, in bed next to his sleeping wife, reading a book by the light of his invention.

FROM TOP MUSÉE BOURDELLE (P.164); PARC ANDRÉ-CITROËN (P.171) >

The catacombs

1 av du Colonel Henri Rol-Tanguy, 14e, on place Denfert-Rochereau • Tues–Sun 10am–8pm, last entry at 7pm • €10; book online to avoid long queues • ☎ 01 43 22 47 63, ⓦ catacombes.paris.fr • Ⓜ Denfert-Rochereau

Unlike in the nearby Montparnasse cemetery, you won't find any celebrity dead in the **catacombs**, just row on row of anonymous human bones. The entrance is on the square that Parisians have long known as place d'Enfer, or "Hell Square", though the name may derive from nothing more sinister than the Latin Via Inferiora ("The Low Road"). The huge lion in the middle of the square was designed by Bartholdi, better known for the Statue of Liberty. Underneath lies an underground warren of tunnels, originally part of the gigantic quarry network underlying Paris (see box, p.170). From 1785, a use was found for all that empty space, when it was realized that the city's overflowing graveyards and charnel houses were poisoning the water supplies and sparking epidemics. For the next eighty years, the stony corridors were gradually filled with skeletal remains, and it's estimated that the remains of six million Parisians are interred here – more than double the population of the modern city, not counting the suburbs.

The underground passages

There's one claustrophobic passageway to follow. The first turning takes you into the **Galerie de Port-Mahon**, a chamber dominated by a bas-relief of a fortress in Menorca, where its sculptor was once imprisoned. Beyond, passing a door inscribed *Arrête! C'est ici l'empire de la mort* ("Stop! This is Death's empire"), the catacombs proper begin. Passages are lined with long thigh bones stacked end-on, forming a wall to keep in the smaller ones heaped higgledy-piggledy behind. These macabre walls are inset with skulls and plaques carrying light-hearted quotations such as "Happy is he who always has the hour of his death in front of his eyes, and readies himself every day to die". Older children often love the whole experience, though there are a good couple of kilometres to walk, and if you're unlucky, you might find yourself in a bottlenecked queue of shrieking teenagers. It's fairly cold (a constant 14°) and a touch squidgy underfoot, so flip-flops and a T-shirt aren't the best attire for a visit. Only two hundred people at a time are allowed in, so be prepared to queue or book tickets in advance.

Back up at street level, the area just west of Denfert-Rochereau is worth exploring. **Rue Daguerre** is one of Paris's more appealing market streets, almost like a provincial high street, and there's some interesting architecture (see box, p.165) around the cemetery.

Observatoire de Paris and around

Av de l'Observatoire, 14e • Ⓜ Denfert-Rochereau/RER Port Royal

About 500m northeast of the catacombs is the classical **Observatoire de Paris** which sat precisely on 0° longitude from the 1660s, when it was constructed, until 1914, when France finally gave in and agreed to recognize the Greenwich Meridian as the standard. The Observatoire itself is rarely open to visitors, but you can check out a couple of commemorative bronze medallions set in the pavement on either side of the front gate. Similar discs run right through the city, marking the old meridian, now named the **Arago line** after the early nineteenth-century astronomer. The building itself was the work of Claude Perrault, brother of the more famous Charles, the original author of *Sleeping Beauty*. It's a graceful structure, and the telescope cupola perched on the east tower adds an exotic touch.

On the other side of the boulevard de Port-Royal, the green avenue de l'Observatoire stretches due north into the Jardin du Luxembourg (see p.140). Curiosity-seekers might want to stroll down to boulevard Arago where, beside the high wall of the Santé prison, a few steps west of rue de la Santé, stands Paris's last remaining **Vespasienne**: Paris's last open-air, public urinal. It still works – and still stinks.

Fondation Henri Cartier-Bresson

2 impasse Lebouis, 14ᵉ • Tues, Thurs, Fri & Sun 1–6.30pm, Wed 1–8.30pm, Sat 11am–6.45pm; closed around Easter and during Aug • €6 • ☎ 01 56 80 27 00, ⓦ henricartierbresson.org • Ⓜ Gaîté

The slender steel-and-glass **Fondation Henri Cartier-Bresson** houses the archive of the father of photojournalism and arch-documenter of Paris, who died shortly after its opening in August 2004. Fascinating, often intimate shows of the work of Cartier-Bresson and his contemporaries alternate with exhibitions promoting younger photographers, including the winner of the foundation's annual prize.

Notre-Dame du Travail

36 rue Guilleminot, 14ᵉ • Mon–Fri 7.30am–7.45pm, Sat 9am–7.30pm, Sun 8.30am–7.30pm • Free • ⓦ notredamedutravail.net • Ⓜ Gaîté

The name of this distinctly odd church – **Notre-Dame du Travail**, or "Our Lady of Work" – reflects the artisanal and industrial jobs of the men it was built for: the workers who constructed the 1899 Exposition Universelle, including the Eiffel Tower. Its construction is deliberately factory-like too: some of its stone came from the Cloth Pavilion, when it was dismantled after the Exhibition closed, while the exposed metal columns of the interior came from the Palace of Industry. Architecturally, it's a fascinating industrial take on Gothic, and was way ahead of its time.

11

Les Colonnes and around

Ⓜ Gaîté

Immediately north of the church of Notre-Dame du Travail stand the two great wings – one oval, the other squared off – of Ricardo Bofill's postmodern housing development, **Les Colonnes**. Beyond again, circular **place de Catalogne** is filled with a giant, flat disc of a fountain designed by the Israeli artist Shamaï Haber. Looking northwest, **place des 5 Martyrs du Lycée Buffon** offers a little-known but lovely view down the horse-chestnut-lined slope of boulevard Pasteur towards the Eiffel Tower, apparently floating over the city below.

Pernety

Ⓜ Pernety/Plaisance

The southwestern swathe of the 14ᵉ arrondissement is deeply residential, often village-like in atmosphere, especially around **Pernety** métro station. Wandering around Cité Bauer, rue des Thermopyles and rue Didot reveals adorable houses, secluded courtyards and quiet mews, and on the corner of rue du Moulin Vert and rue Hippolyte-Maindron you'll find **Giacometti**'s ramshackle old studio and home. Cinema has one of its best Parisian venues, meanwhile, at **L'Entrepôt**, 7–9 rue Francis-de-Pressensé (see p.309), with spaces for talks, meals and drinks, an excellent live music programme and even a garden.

Puces de Vanves

Sat & Sun 7am–1pm • ⓦ pucesdevanves.typepad.com • Ⓜ Porte de Vanves

At the weekend it's worth heading out to the southern edge of the 14ᵉ arrondissement for one of the city's best **flea markets**, known as the **Puces de Vanves** (see p.339). Starting at daybreak, it spreads along the pavements of avenues Marc Sangnier and Georges Lafenestre (where some stalls open in the afternoon as well), petering out at its western end in place de la Porte-de-Vanves, where the city fortifications stood until the 1920s. It's smaller and less formal than the St-Ouen Clignancourt market (see p.223), with more bric-a-brac and fewer out-and-out antiques.

Parc Montsouris and around

RER/Tramway Cité-Universitaire

With its undulating contours, waterfall cascading into a lake and RER tracks cutting right through the middle, **Parc Montsouris** (daily 9am–dusk) is one of Paris's more

11

UNDERGROUND PARIS

In September 2004, while on a training exercise in a group of **tunnels** underneath the Palais de Chaillot, the Parisian police stumbled upon a clandestine underground cell. Nothing to do with terrorism, this one, but an actual **subterranean chamber**, 400 square metres in size, which had been fitted out as a cinema by a dedicated club of *film noir* lovers. As the story hit the press, a band of troglodytes emerged blinking into the full beam of the media spotlight. Since the 1980s, it turned out, hundreds of these *"cataphiles"* had been holding anything from underground parties and art exhibitions to festivals and, it was rumoured, orgies. Experienced tunnel-goers talked of elaborate murals and a huge, pillared party room known as "La Plage", overlooked by a graffiti version of Hokusai's *The Wave*.

In fact, the tunnels underneath Chaillot form only a small part of a vast network that dates back to the **medieval era**, when the stone for building Paris was quarried out from its most obvious source, immediately underfoot. Today, more than 300km of underground galleries lie beneath the city, especially on the Left Bank's 5ᵉ, 6ᵉ, 14ᵉ and 15ᵉ arrondissements, where the Grand Réseau Sud runs for more than 100km. Another separate network lurks beneath the 13ᵉ arrondissement, while in the 16ᵉ, it's said that the rock is like Gruyère cheese – full of holes. In 1774, after a cave-in swallowed up whole buildings in what is now avenue Denfert-Rochereau, a **royal commission** was set up to map the old quarries and shore up the most precarious foundations. Great galleries were cut along the lines of the roads and the material used to infill the worst voids. Today, some of these underground "streets" still exist, while those above have disappeared. Some attribute modern Paris's relative lack of skyscrapers to doubts about the quality of the city's foundations.

In the nineteenth century, many tunnels were used for mushroom cultivation (the everyday supermarket variety is still known in France as the *champignon de Paris*), others for growing endives or brewing, while Carthusian monks even practised distillation under the modern-day Jardin du Luxembourg. The most creative scheme, however, involved the hygienic storage of human remains. From the 1780s, the contents of Paris's overcrowded cemeteries were slowly transferred underground. In Montparnasse, one bone-lined section of the **catacombs** can still be visited (see p.168) but, otherwise, "penetrating into or circulating within" the network has been illegal since 1955. You can get down into the métro, of course, and at the Musée des Egouts de Paris (see p.152) you can descend into a part of the city's 2300km of sewers. But it would be foolish to try anything more adventurous; in 1993, one *cataphile* apparently disappeared into the labyrinth, never to return.

eccentric parks, but also one of the more charming. Surprising features include a meteorological office, a marker of the old meridian line, near boulevard Jourdan, and, by the southwest entrance, a kiosk run by the French Astronomy Association. The surrounding area offers plentiful artistic and historic associations. Le Corbusier's first building in Paris was the **Studio Ozenfant**, at 53 avenue Reille – designed for his co-founder of the Purist movement, Amédée Ozenfant. The handsome, 1920s private mews of **Villa Seurat**, off rue de la Tombe-Issoire, was home to the artists Dalí, Chaïm Soutine, André Derain and Jean Lurçat, along with expat writers Henry Miller and Lawrence Durrell – it was here that Miller wrote his notorious *Tropic of Cancer*.

Cité Universitaire
17 bd Jourdan, 14ᵉ • ⓦ ciup.fr • RER/Tramway Cité-Universitaire

Several thousand students from more than a hundred different countries occupy the **Cité Universitaire**, whose buildings follow a kitsch international theme. The central Maison Internationale resembles a traditional French château, while the red brick of the Collège Franco-Britannique all too accurately recalls Britain's institutional buildings. Two of the most remarkable buildings, however, were designed by Le Corbusier: the graceful suspended shoebox of the Pavillon de la Suisse (1931–33) is one of his major works, and still has original mural paintings inside; the more brutal Pavillon du Brésil (1957–59) recalls his famous Cité Radieuse in Marseille. As you'd expect, there's an active programme of film, theatre and other events.

The 15ᵉ

Though it's the largest and most populous of them all, the **quinzième (15ᵉ) arrondissement** falls off the agenda for most visitors as it lacks even a single important building or monument. Its most distinctive features, in fact, are an odd island walkway in the middle of the Seine, the **Allée des Cygnes**, and a bristle of miniature skyscrapers on the riverbank, the shabby remainder of a 1960s and 1970s development known as the Front de Seine. There's little reason to penetrate this latter maze unless you're a particular fan of postwar architecture, or perhaps raised pedestrian walkways; even the distinctively slender, Skylon-like white tower turns out to be nothing more interesting than a central-heating chimney. The 15ᵉ does, however, have a delightfully provincial high street, the rue du Commerce, and two lovely and distinctly offbeat parks in its southern corners, the **Parc André-Citroën** and the **Parc Georges-Brassens**.

Around the Pont de Bir-Hakeim

Ⓜ Bir-Hakeim

As you head south from the Eiffel Tower, the first landmark you come to on the city's southwestern **riverbank** front is the glass **Maison de la Culture du Japon à Paris** (ⓦmcjp.asso.fr), which puts on excellent Japanese theatre, dance, music and cinema. Immediately south, you can watch the métro trains trundling across to Passy on the top level of the two-decker **Pont de Bir-Hakeim**, a lovable structure dating from 1902. Up on the adjacent raised walkway, at the start of boulevard de Grenelle, a bronze sculptural group stands in memorial to the notorious **rafle du Vel d'Hiv**, the mass arrest of 13,152 Parisian Jews in July 1942. Nine thousand people, including four thousand children, were interned for a week at the cycle track that once stood here, before being carted off to the death camps. Only thirty adults survived.

Allée des Cygnes

Ⓜ Bir-Hakeim

One of Paris's most curious walks leads down from the very middle of the Pont de Bir-Hakeim, along the **Allée des Cygnes**, a narrow, midstream island built up on raised concrete embankments. It's a strange place – one of Samuel Beckett's favourites – with just birds, trees and a path to walk along, and, at its furthest point downstream, a smaller-scale version of the **Statue of Liberty**, or *Liberty Lighting the World*, to give it its full title. This was one of the four preliminary models constructed between 1874 and 1884 by sculptor Auguste Bartholdi, with the help of Gustave Eiffel, before the finished article was presented to New York.

Parc André-Citroën

2 rue Cauchy, 15ᵉ • Daily 9am–dusk • Ⓜ Javel-André-Citroën/Balard

The **Parc André-Citroën**, on the banks of the Seine between Pont du Garigliano and Pont Mirabeau, is not a park for traditionalists. The central grassy area is straightforward enough, but around it you'll find futuristic terraces and concrete-walled gardens with abstract themes. It's as much a sight to visit in its own right as a place to lounge around or throw a frisbee.

At the top end, away from the river, are two large glass **hothouses**, one housing mimosa, fish-tailed palms and all manner of sweet-smelling shrubbery, the other used for temporary exhibitions. On hot days, however, the most tempting feature is the large platform between them, which sprouts a capricious set of automated **fountain** jets, luring children, and occasionally adults, to dodge the sudden spurts of water. On either side of the greenhouses, the White and Black gardens are for plants that show off the two extreme colours, but the most exciting themed gardens lie along the northern side of the park, where high walls surround the **Serial Gardens**. Here, the Green Garden is dedicated to sound, with bubbling water and *Miscanthus sinensis* grasses rustling dryly in the wind; the Blue Garden is for scent, planted with wisteria and strong-smelling

11

THE 15e

16e

RUE DE L'ASSOMPTION
RUE RAYNOUARD
Avenue du Président Kennedy
Port Autonome de Paris
Bir Hakeim

AVENUE DU RECTEUR POINCARÉ
RUE DE L'ASSOMPTION
RUE RAYNOUARD
Avenue du Président Kennedy
AVENUE DU PRÉSIDENT KENNEDY
PONT DE PASSY
PORT DE PASSY
RUE NOLARD
RUE NELATON

AVENUE LÉOPOLD II
RUE JEAN DE LA FONTAINE
RUE DE BOULAINVILLIERS
Maison de Radio-France
VOIE GEORGES POMPIDOU
Île aux Cygnes
ALLÉE DES CYGNES
RUE DU DOCTEUR FINLAY

AVENUE THÉOPHILE GAUTIER
RUE GROS
PONT DE GRENELLE
PORT DE GRENELLE
QUAI DE GRENELLE
SQUARE BELA BARTOK
PLACE DE BRAZZAVILLE
RUE SEXTIUS MICHEL
RUE ST-CHARLES

AVENUE PERRICHONT
RUE FÉLICIEN DAVID
RUE DEGAS
Statue de la Liberté
RUE DU THÉÂTRE
RUE EMERIAU
PLACE ST-CHARLES
RUE ROUELLE
G. CITERNE

AVENUE DE VERSAILLES
QUAI LOUIS-BLÉRIOT
River Seine
PONT DE GRENELLE
PLACE FERNAND FOREST
RUE G.DE L'ESS
RUE LINOIS
SQUARE HÉRICART
RUE HÉRICART
RUE ST-CHARLES
RUE GINOUX
RUE DE LOURM

Mirabeau
QUAI LOUIS-BLÉRIOT
RUE DE L'INGÉNIEUR R. KELLER
RUE ROBERT DE CAILLAVET
BEAUGRENELLE
RUE ST-CHARLES

RUE MIRABEAU
RUE WILHEM
PONT MIRABEAU
QUAI ANDRÉ-CITROËN
Javel
Javel-André Citroën
AVENUE EMILE ZOLA
PLACE CHARLES MICHELS
Charles Michels
RUE DES ENTREPRENEURS

AVENUE DE VERSAILLES
QUAI LOUIS-BLÉRIOT
RUE AUGUSTE VITU
RUE DU CAPITAINE MÉNARD
Imprimerie Nationale
RUE GUTENBERG
RUE ST-CHARLES
RUE DE L'ÉGLISE
RUE DE JAVEL
RUE DE LOURMEL
RUE DE LA ROTISS
RUE DE JAVEL

RUE BALARD
RUE SÉBASTIEN MERCIER
RUE DES BERGERS
RUE ST-LUC
RUE DE L'ÉGLISE

Parc André-Citroën
RUE CAUCHY
RUE DES CÉVENNES
RUE GUTENBERG
RUE ST-CHARLES
RUE DE LA CONVENTION
RUE OSCAR ROTY
RUE DE JAVEL

RUE CAUCHY
RUE GUTENBERG
RUE ST-CHARLES
RUE LACORDAIRE
Hôpital Boucicaut
R. HENRI BOCQU
AVENUE FÉLIX FAURE

Cimetière de Grenelle
RUE ST-CHARLES
RUE DES CÉVENNES
Boucicaut

Fountains
RUE BALARD
RUE ST-CHARLES
RUE VARET
RUE DE LOURMEL
R. TISSERAND
RUE DE BELLO
RUE DURANTON

Pont du Garigliano
RUE LEBLANC
RUE JEAN MARIDOR
RUE DE LA CR

RUE LEBLANC
RUE DE LOURMEL
AVENUE FÉLIX FAURE
Lourmel
Cimetière de Vaugirard
RUE DE LA CROIX NIVERT

BOULEVARD VICTOR
RUE LECOURBE
RUE VASCO DE GAMA
RUE DESNOUETTES
RUE DE CADIX

Balard
Notre Dame de Nazareth
PORTE DE VERSAILLES
RUE DU HAMEAU

Armée de l'Air (Etat Major)
RUE DE LA PORTE D'ISSY
Paris Expo
Palais des Sports

herbs; the Orange Garden, for touch, is highly textured; and there are Red, Silver and Gold gardens too. At the foot of this section, towards the river, is the Garden in Movement, whose semi-wild, constantly changing plants are broken up by miniature greenhouses, and a long stone staircase flowing with water. The park's southern end was recently extended and includes a new playground for children and a picnic area.

The Ballon de Paris tethered balloon

Parc André-Citroën • Daily 9am to 30min before the park closes at dusk; call for weather conditions on the day • €12, children 3–11 €6 • ⓣ 01 44 26 20 00, ⓦ ballondeparis.com

Perhaps the best feature in the Parc André-Citroën is the **tethered balloon**, which rises and sinks regularly on calm days, taking small groups 150m above the ground – higher than the second level of the Eiffel Tower – for great views of the city. In the fifteen years since it was installed, it has become one of the chief landmarks of the 15ᵉ, but in 2008 it took on a new complexion – quite literally: the balloon now changes colour to reflect levels of air pollution. A strip of LEDs on the south side indicates the air quality near traffic – from green (good) via orange (don't panic) to red (gas masks on). At night, the whole thing lights up – rather charmingly – to reflect the ambient air quality across the entire city.

The quartier du Commerce

Ⓜ Av Emile Zola/Commerce

The best way to get the flavour of the **quartier du Commerce** is to start walking down **avenue de la Motte-Picquet**, where the Champ de Mars meets the Ecole Militaire. At the corner, the brasseries throng with officers from the Ecole, and the hundred-odd antique shops in the 1960s-built **Village Suisse** (all Thurs–Mon; ⓦ villagesuisse.com) display everything from crystal chandeliers to gilt-framed oils. At the **boulevard de Grenelle**, where the métro trundles above the street on iron piers, things relax a little. **Rue du Commerce**, which stretches to the south, preserves a distinctive and very pleasant village atmosphere, its prettily shuttered houses lined with small shops and cafés. This upscale respectability would have been a surprise to the working-class diners who once filled the three storeys of *Le Café du Commerce* (see p.290), or to George Orwell, who worked on the street as a dishwasher, a gritty experience described in his *Down and Out in Paris and London*. Towards the street's southern end, place du Commerce is distinguished by its bandstand, while, just beyond, the nineteenth-century church of **St-Jean Baptiste de Grenelle** frames the end of the road handsomely.

Parc Georges-Brassens

Entrance on rue des Morillons, 15ᵉ • Daily dawn–dusk • Ⓜ Convention/Porte de Vanves

The main entrance of the **Parc Georges-Brassens** is flanked by two bronze bulls. The old Vaugirard abattoir was transformed into this park in the 1980s, and named after the legendary postwar poet-singer-satirist, who lived nearby at 42 villa Santos-Dumont. The abattoir's original clock tower remains, surrounded by a pond, and the park is a delight, especially for children; attractions include puppets, rocks and merry-go-rounds for the kids, a mountain stream with pine and birch trees, beehives and a tiny terraced vineyard, a climbing wall and a garden of scented herbs and shrubs designed principally for the blind (best in late spring). The corrugated pyramid with a helter-skelter-like spiral is a theatre, the Théâtre Silvia Montfort.

On Saturdays and Sundays, take a look in the sheds of the old horse market between the park and **rue Brancion**, to the east, where dozens of **book dealers** set out their stock. On the west side of the park, in a secluded garden in passage Dantzig, off rue Dantzig, stands an odd polygonal building known as **La Ruche**, or The Beehive, after its honeycomb-like cells radiating from the central staircase. It started life as an Eiffel-designed pavilion for the 1900 World Fair, showcasing fine wines, after which it was resurrected here as a studio space, becoming home to Fernand Léger, Modigliani (briefly), Chagall, Soutine, Ossip Zadkine and many other artists, mainly Jewish refugees from pogroms in Poland and Russia. It's still something of a Tower of Babel, with Irish, American, Italian and Japanese artists now in residence.

The 13ᵉ

The **treizième arrondissement (13ᵉ)**, in the southeastern corner of Paris, has two faces. North of the mega-roundabout of **place d'Italie**, the genteel neighbourhood around the ancient **Gobelins** tapestry works seems to look towards the adjacent Quartier Latin. The southern swathe of the arrondissement, by contrast, has more in common with the suburbs, as it was almost completely cleared in the 1960s, and filled in by tower blocks. There's little here for the visitor except in **Chinatown**, with its many Asian restaurants, and on the minor hillock of the **Butte-aux-Cailles**, which is like a budget Montmartre, its pretty, gentrified old streets alive with restaurants and bohemian bars. Since the 1990s, the planners have been at work again along the eastern edge of the 13ᵉ, beside the Seine. The old quays, mills and warehouses have been transformed into an upscale new *quartier* called **Paris Rive Gauche**, centred on the flagship **Bibliothèque Nationale**.

11

Place d'Italie

Ⓜ Place d'Italie

One of those Parisian roundabouts that takes half an hour to cross, **Place d'Italie** is the central junction of the 13ᵉ. On its north side is the *mairie* of the arrondissement, while to the south is Kenzo Tange's huge **Grand Ecran Italie** building. Its curving glass facade cleverly advertised the giant film screen within – the two were roughly the same size – until the cinema was shut in 2006. Outraged cinephiles are still battling the council to reopen a cinema on the site in the face of encroaching shops. There is some consolation, however: just up the road, at 73 avenue des Gobelins, the Jérôme Seydoux-Pathé cinema research foundation now occupies the old Cinéma Rodin (see box, p.309).

Gobelins workshops

42 av des Gobelins, 13ᵉ • Exhibition gallery Tues–Sun 11am–6pm; guided tours (1hr 30min; French only) Tues–Thurs 1pm • €6 for exhibition gallery, or free on last Sun of month; guided tours €12.50 – there are usually tickets for the tour available on the day if you turn up when the workshops open at 11am, or you can book in advance through Fnac (see p.332) • ☎ 01 44 08 53 49, ⓦ mobiliernational .culture.gouv.fr • Ⓜ Gobelins

The **Gobelins workshops** are where the highest-quality **tapestries** have been created for some four hundred years. On the guided tour, you can watch tapestries being made by painfully slow, traditional methods; each weaver completes between one and four square metres a year. The designs are now exactingly specified by contemporary artists, and almost all of the dozen or so works completed each year are destined for French government offices.

Along the vanished River Bièvre

The site of the Gobelins tapestry works owes everything to the hidden presence of the Bièvre. Once a virtual sewer for tanners and dye-makers, the river was finally covered over in 1910, although its course is still marked by the curves of rues Berbier-du-Mets and Croulebarbe, and by the row of poplars in the green space of the **square René-le-Gall** – a former island once known as the Ile aux Singes for the jugglers' monkeys that lived there. Just off rue Geffroy, which itself turns off rue Berbier-du-Mets, stands the surprising, fairy-tale rump of the **Château de la Reine Blanche**, which once guarded the main medieval route into Paris from the south – along what is now avenue des Gobelins. The turreted wing (now luxury apartments) was built in the 1520s and 1530s by the aristocratic Gobelins family, but it occupied the site of a much older château torn down after a tragic party in 1393 in which the young Charles VI of

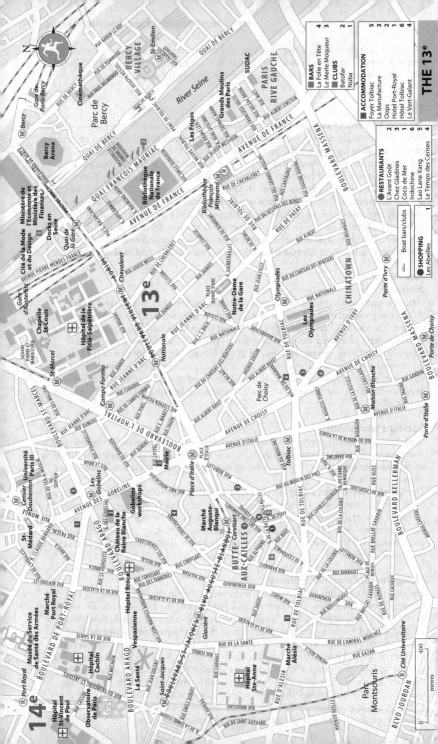

France nearly died. Charles and five friends had disguised themselves as tarred-and-feathered savages but one of them brushed against a candle flame; the king was the only survivor of the ensuing conflagration, and never recovered his sanity.

Hôpital de la Pitié-Salpêtrière

47–83 bd de l'Hôpital, 13e • Chapelle St-Louis 8.30am–5.30pm • Free • Ⓜ St-Marcel/RER Austerlitz

East of the Gobelins tapestry workshops, towards the Gare d'Austerlitz, the ornate boulevards St-Marcel and Vincent-Auriol are dominated by the immense **Hôpital de la Pitié-Salpêtrière**, built under Louis XIV to house the sick, the disabled and the poor, to jail prostitutes and generally to dispose of the dispossessed. The imprisoned women were released by a revolutionary mob who broke in by force in September 1792. It later became a psychiatric hospital – Jean Charcot staged his theatrical demonstrations of hysteria and hypnosis here, with Freud as one of his fascinated witnesses. Today, it's a leading teaching hospital, but the **Chapelle St-Louis**, at the northern side of the complex, is open to visitors. It's a bleakly beautiful Baroque structure under a modest dome, a fairly typical work by Libéral Bruant, the architect of Les Invalides. It comes to life during the Festival d'Automne (see p.322), when it's used for art installations, attracting artists of the calibre of Bill Viola, Jenny Holzer and Tadashi Kawamata.

11

Butte-aux-Cailles

Ⓜ Corvisart/Place d'Italie

Between boulevard Auguste-Blanqui and rue Bobillot is the **Butte-aux-Cailles**, whose name can be translated picturesquely as the hill (*butte*) of the quails (*cailles*). It's a pleasantly animated miniature quarter, the main sloping rue de la Butte-aux-Cailles cobbled and furnished with attractive lampposts, as well as one of the classic, green Art Nouveau drinking fountains (see box, p.8). Alongside the old left-wing establishments – the bar *La Folie en Tête* at no. 33 and the restaurant *Le Temps des Cerises* at nos. 18–20 (see p.290) – are plenty of relaxed places to eat and drink till the small hours, making this an attractive area for low-key nightlife. If you're coming from métro Corvisart, cross the road and head straight through the passageway in the large apartment building opposite, then climb the steps that lead up through the small Brassaï gardens to rue des Cinq Diamants. Alternatively, it's a short walk up rue Bobillot from place d'Italie.

Chinatown

Ⓜ Olympiades

The area between rue de Tolbiac, avenue de Choisy and boulevard Masséna is what is known as the **Chinatown** (or the *quartier Chinois*) of Paris, despite the fact that it was founded by Vietnamese refugees in the late 1970s, and is now home to several other East Asian communities. Avenues de Choisy and d'Ivry are full of Vietnamese, Thai, Cambodian, Laotian and indeed Chinese restaurants and food shops. On avenue d'Ivry, you'll find the huge Tang Frères **Chinese supermarket**, a former railway warehouse now stocked with an incredible variety of Asian goods. The chief landmark of Chinatown, however, is **Les Olympiades**, a set of giant tower blocks, each named after a city that has hosted the games, with a mall below and a pedestrian area strangely suspended above. One escalator leads up from 66 avenue d'Ivry; alongside this escalator, an easily missable slip road, rue du Disque, leads down to an underground car park; and part of the way down this access road lurks a tiny **Buddhist temple** and community centre: the Association des Résidents en France d'Origine Indochinoise. It's advertised by a pair of red Chinese lanterns dimly visible in the gloom. Another Buddhist temple, belonging to a community organization for the Téochew people, the Amicale des Téochew en France, can be reached by heading up the escalator at 66 avenue d'Ivry to the "Stadium" sports centre; from here head for the Tour Anvers tower block – the temple is tucked away behind, on the right. Ceremonies with traditional chants take place every day at around 10am and 3pm.

Paris Rive Gauche

Ⓜ Quai de la Gare/Bibliothèque François Mitterrand

Stretching from the Gare d'Austerlitz right down to the *boulevard périphérique*, the once-isolated, desolate, industrial strip between rail tracks and river is being transformed into the swanky new **Paris Rive Gauche** district. The railway lines are slowly being roofed over; the old docks have become "**Docks en Seine**", incorporating a fashion institute; the Austerlitz station is undergoing a major makeover (it's being connected to a new TGV line to Bordeaux); and a fine pedestrian footbridge, the **Passerelle Simone de Beauvoir** crosses the Seine in a futuristic double-ribbon strip. Tethered beside the **Bibliothèque Nationale**, the flagship of the quarter, is a floating swimming pool, the **Piscine Josephine Baker** (see p.346), and two unusual **barges** have also made the area a nightlife attraction in its own right, notably the ex-lighthouse boat, *Batofar* (see p.302).

In the south of the quarter, the massive **Grands Moulins de Paris** and Halle aux Farines have been ambitiously rebuilt for the Université Denis Diderot, aka "Paris 7", an annexe of the Jussieu site (see p.132), while, just short of the *périphérique*, another early twentieth-century industrial-era site, the handsomely arched **SUDAC** compressed-air building, is now the home of a new school of architecture. If in the area, serious **Le Corbusier** fans might want to slog across to rue Cantagrel, where the architect's colourful Cité de Refuge (1933), or Salvation Army building, stands at no. 12.

Bibliothèque Nationale François Mitterrand

Quai François-Mauriac, 13e • **Exhibitions** Tues–Sat 10am–7pm, Sun 1–7pm • €9 • **Public reading rooms** Tues–Sat 10am–8pm, Sun 1–7pm • €3.50 for a day-pass, bring ID • ☎ 01 53 79 59 59, Ⓦ bnf.fr • Ⓜ Quai de la Gare/Bibliothèque François Mitterrand

The architectural star of the **Paris Rive Gauche** development, which Mitterrand managed to inaugurate, though not open, just before his death in 1996, is the **Bibliothèque Nationale François Mitterrand**. There are regular exhibitions – typically serious, arty and high quality – and the **reading rooms** on the "haut-jardin" level, along with their unrivalled collection of foreign newspapers, are open to everyone over 16. The garden level, below, is reserved for accredited researchers only, while the garden itself is out of bounds.

The four enormous L-shaped towers at the corners of the site were intended to look like open books, but attracted widespread derision after shutters had to be added behind the glazing in order to protect the collections from sunlight. Once you mount the dramatic wooden steps surrounding the library, however, the perspective changes utterly. From here you look down into a huge sunken pine wood, with glass walls that filter light into the floors below your feet; it's like standing at the edge of a secret ravine. The concept is startlingly original, and almost fulfils architect Dominique Perrault's intention to combine "rigour and emotion", to "generate a sense of dignity, a well-tempered soul for the buildings of the French Republic". Cynics might feel that the steel stays added to stop the trees blowing over are rather less than dignified.

Les Frigos and the private galleries

On the south side of rue de Tolbiac, opposite the library, the giant, decaying cold-storage warehouse of **Les Frigos** (Ⓦles-frigos.com; Ⓜ Quai de la Gare/Bibliothèque François Mitterrand) has been occupied by artists and musicians since the 1980s when it was an infamous squat. It's now officially sanctioned, and holds open-door exhibitions once or twice a year. There's often a gig or an event going on in the space known as **Les Voûtes** ("The Vaults"; Ⓦlesvoutes.org), plus a couple of galleries, and you can visit the bar/restaurant – though it's officially only for the artists. Just west of the library, near métro Chevaleret, a few small but cutting-edge **art galleries** are now well settled on **rue Louise Weiss** and round the corner on rue du Chevaleret. You can also take a tour of the private and up-to-the-moment **Rosenblum Collection** of art at 183 rue du Chevaleret, 13e (tours Sat 10am & 3pm; €10, online booking only; Ⓦrosenblumcollection.fr; ⓂChevaleret).

Docks en Seine

34 quai d'Austerlitz, 13ᵉ • Daily 10am–midnight • ☎ 01 76 77 25 30, ⓦ citemodedesign.fr • Ⓜ Austerlitz/Quai de la Gare

The most recent Paris Rive Gauche development, the **Docks en Seine** complex on the quai d'Austerlitz, lies upstream of the Pont de Bercy. The ugly concrete warehouses that once belonged to Paris's central port have been rebuilt as the **Cité de la Mode et du Design**, a fashion institute, whose intrusive design of twisting, lime-green tubes, by Dominique Jacob and Brendan MacFarlane, is supposed to recall the sinuous shape of the river. The complex houses a new fashion school, the **Institut Français de la Mode** (ⓦ ifm-paris.com), a museum, a number of shops and a rooftop restaurant. It also hosts occasional exhibitions, but perhaps its biggest draw is its two clubs, rooftop *Nüba* (see p.304), and riverside *Wanderlust*, which have become firm fixtures on the city's nightlife scene. You can stroll along the riverbank here along a new pedestrian promenade, perhaps admiring the giant Bercy development across the river (see p.114). If you start to tire of postindustrial mega-design you could walk just a little further north, beyond the Gare d'Austerlitz, to the refreshingly historic green space of the Jardin des Plantes (see p.130).

11

Art Ludique-Le Musée

34 quai d'Austerlitz, Docks en Seine, 13ᵉ • Mon & Thurs 11am–7pm, Wed & Fri 11am–10pm, Sat & Sun 10am–8pm • ☎ 01 45 70 09 49, ⓦ artludique.com • €16.50, children €4–12 11 • Ⓜ Austerlitz/Quai de la Gare

Art Ludique-Le Musée is a new museum entirely dedicated to the art of animation, manga, comics and video games. Its permanent collection, which looks at the first creators of comics as well as contemporary artists, is interesting enough, but the main attraction is its hugely popular exhibitions (book online to avoid queuing), which have recently focused on Aardman Animations and the Studio Ghibli.

Montmartre and northern Paris

Stacked on its hilltop in the northern 18e arrondissement of Paris, Montmartre sets itself apart from the city at its feet. Its chief landmark, visible from all over the city, is the church of Sacré-Coeur, crowning the Butte as if an over-enthusiastic pâtissier had run riot with an icing gun. The slopes below, around Abbesses métro, preserve something of the spirit of the village that once basked here, but unlike most villages Montmartre has a diverse population, by turns lefty, trendy and sleazy. Between Montmartre and the Grands Boulevards, which define the edge of the city centre proper, stretch the 9e and 10e arrondissements, whose nineteenth-century architecture and lack of green space make them look quite similar. Yet where the 9e arrondissement is largely genteel, the 10e is more rough-edged – though fast becoming one of the city's most vibrant areas, as young, hip Parisians move in, attracted by the low rents.

The 9ᵉ arrondissement has two beguiling museums devoted to its nineteenth-century artistic heyday, the **Musée Moreau** and **Musée de la Vie Romantique**, and the northern fringe of the arrondissement, around Pigalle, just below the Butte Montmartre, is famous for its cabarets and sex shows. The main interest of the 10ᵉ lies in its burgeoning culinary scene; young, dynamic chefs are opening up small, so-called "neobistros" (see p.269), making this one of the best places in Paris to eat. Another good area for eating is bourgeois **Batignolles**, just west of Montmartre.

Montmartre
Ⓜ Abbesses/Anvers/Lamarck-Caulaincourt

In spite of being one of the city's chief tourist attractions, **Montmartre** retains a surprising whiff of its rural origins. It's an unusually proud and tight-knit neighbourhood, and there are few cars. Incorporated into the city only in the mid-nineteenth century, its heyday was from the last years of the nineteenth century to World War I, when its rustic charms and low rents attracted crowds of artists. Since then, the *quartier*'s physical appearance has changed little, thanks largely to the warren of **plaster-of-Paris quarries** that perforate its bowels and render the ground too unstable for new building. Tiny squares still give way to sudden vistas south over the rooftops of central Paris, and the occasional studio window is a tangible reminder of its illustrious artistic past.

In the second half of the twentieth century, the Butte, along with Pigalle at its foot (see p.188), slumped into a sleazy half-life of porn shows and semi-genteel poverty, but both neighbourhoods have undergone radical gentrification in recent years. Fashionable nightspots have displaced the sex shows, and the young and moneyed have largely replaced artists and prostitutes. The heart of the action is around **Abbesses** métro, extending right down to Pigalle, with **rue des Martyrs** as the chief artery of cool. It's a lively area on Sundays but relatively dead on a Monday.

Most visitors make straight for the landmark church of **Sacré-Coeur** via the steps or **funicular** railway (covered by ordinary métro tickets) immediately below. But for a less touristy approach, head up via place des Abbesses, around which you'll find a host of bijou bars and cafés.

Abbesses
Ⓜ Abbesses

You could almost be persuaded that pretty, tree-shaded **place des Abbesses** was a village square – if it weren't for its centrepiece, one of Guimard's rare, canopied Art Nouveau métro entrances; there are only two others in the city (see box, p.184). The métro canopy isn't in fact an authentic Abbesses sight, as it was transferred from the Hôtel de Ville, complete with its glass porch, tendril-like railings and lascivious-looking

---

MONTMARTROBUS

The diminutive size of the **Montmartrobus** (which looks like a miniature version of a regular Paris bus) is designed to help it negotiate the twisting streets of the Butte, but its eccentric shape and determinedly ecological electric engine also make it fit right in with the *quartier*'s spirit. If you don't want to walk, taking this bus is probably the best way of doing a Montmartre tour, and **normal métro/bus tickets** are valid. Starting at place Pigalle, the route heads up rue des Martyrs and west along rue des Abbesses and rue Durantin, then follows the curve of rue Lepic to rue des Saules and rue Caulaincourt, before jinking up to Jules-Joffrin métro. On the return leg it heads down rues Ramey, Custine and Lamarck, curling round the foot of Sacré-Coeur and the *funiculaire* and heading back up to place du Tertre. It then winds back towards place des Abbesses via rues Cortot, Girardon and Gabrielle, before finally running down rues Chappe, Yvonne Le Tac and Houdon, back to place Pigalle.

MONTMARTRE AND THE 9e

● SHOPPING
Antoine et Lili	8
APC Surplus	3
Belle de Jour	
Chezel	11
Comptoir	
des Cotonniers	5
La Fausse Boutique	10
Gontran Cherrier	
Le Grenier à Pain	4
Marché Dejean	
Mesdemoiselles	
Madeleines	13
L'Oeuf	14
Popelini	15
Les P'tits Bo'Bo	
Sébastien Gaudard	16
Spree	6
Tati	9

■ LIVE MUSIC
Autour de Midi… et Minuit	5
Casino de Paris	15
La Cigale	9
Le Divan du Monde	8
Au Lapin Agile	1
Les Trois Baudets	7

■ BARS
Au Clair de la Lune	2
Le Carmen	12
Chez Camille	4
Le Fantôme	16
La Fourmi	10
Glass	13
Au Rendez-Vous des Amis	3
Le Sans Souci	14

● CLUBS
La Machine du Moulin Rouge	6
Le Rouge	1

■ ACCOMMODATION
Hôtel Amour	8
Hôtel des Arts	3
Hôtel Bonséjour	
Montmartre	4
BVJ Opéra	10
Ermitage Hôtel	1
Hôtel Langlois	12
Lorette Opéra	9
Palm Opéra	11
Hôtel Particulier	
Montmartre	2
Perfect Hotel	7
Regent Hostel	6
Le Village Hostel	5

● CAFÉS AND WINE BARS
Café des Deux Moulins	8
La Guêpe	9
Le Progrès	12
Le Refuge	1
Relais de la Butte	5
Le Village	7

● RESTAURANTS
Le Coq Rico	3
Cul de Poule	13
Le Grand 8	6
Le Mono	4
Le Moulin de la Galette	2
Refuge des Fondus	10
Le Relais Gascon	11
Les Rillettes	14

▲ Entrances

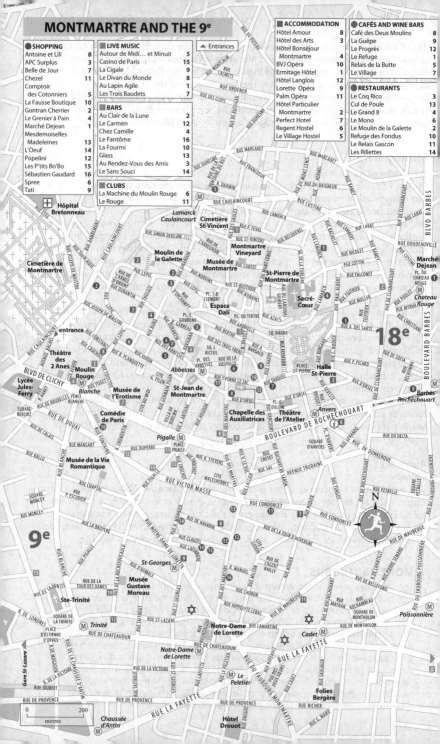

lanterns – but it looks perfectly at home here in the square. At the north end of the square, "Le mur des je t'aime" is a tiled wall inscribed with the words for "I love you", handwritten in eighty languages; it is something of a rendezvous for courting couples. For aimless wandering and café life, the area around Abbesses is particularly satisfying, and the unusual number of high-quality, artisan boulangeries is proof that the quarter has held on to its residential roots – you'll find three on rue des Abbesses alone.

St-Jean de Montmartre

Place des Abbesses, 18ᵉ • Daily 9am–7pm • Free • Ⓜ Abbesses

On the downhill side of place des Abbesses, the red-brick church of **St-Jean de Montmartre** is well worth peeping inside for its radical construction, dating from the early 1900s. The incredibly slender pillars and broad vaulting were only made possible by the experimental use of reinforced concrete, a material that was, as the church's architect Anatole de Baudot claimed, both the bones and the skin.

Chapelle des Auxiliatrices and around

11 rue Yvonne-Le-Tac, 18ᵉ • Fri 3–6pm • Free • Ⓜ Abbesses

East of place des Abbesses, the **Chapelle des Auxiliatrices** is where Ignatius Loyola founded the **Jesuit** order in 1534. This is also supposed to be the spot where **St Denis**, the first Bishop of Paris, was decapitated by the Romans, shortly before he carried his own head to St-Denis (see p.226). One block south, rue d'Orsel makes the transition from chichi Montmartre to cheap Barbès, with trendy clothes shops at its top end, near Abbesses, and cheap fabric shops at the bottom. Towards its western end is the picturesque **place Charles Dullin**, centred on the small Théâtre de l'Atelier, where the great mime Jean-Louis Barrault – the inimitable Baptiste in *Les Enfants du Paradis* – made his debut.

Butte Montmartre

At 130m, the "Mound", or **Butte Montmartre**, is the highest point in Paris. The various theories as to the origin of its name all have a Roman connection: it could be a corruption of *Mons Martyrum* – "the Martyrs' hill", the martyrs being St Denis and his companions; on the other hand, it might have been named *Mons Mercurii*, in honour of a Roman shrine to Mercury; or possibly *Mons Martis*, after a shrine to Mars.

If you're in any doubt about finding your way **up the Butte**, just keep heading uphill – the area is so charming that there's no such thing as a wrong turn. One of the quietest and most attractive paths begins at place des Abbesses, climbing **rue de la Vieuville** and the stairs in rue Drevet to the minuscule **place du Calvaire**, which has a lovely view back over the city.

Bateau-Lavoir

Place Emile-Goudeau, 18ᵉ • Ⓜ Abbesses

With its graceful Wallace fountain (see box, p.8), its steps and its view, the tiny place Emile-Goudeau is one of the more adorable squares in Paris. It's also overlooked by a building that encapsulates Montmartre's rich artistic history: a former piano factory known as the **Bateau-Lavoir**. In 1904 Picasso took up a studio here, and he stayed for the best part of a decade, painting *Les Demoiselles d'Avignon* and sharing loves, quarrels and opium trips with Braque, Juan Gris, Modigliani, Max Jacob, Apollinaire and others, both famous and obscure. It was on the place Emile-Goudeau that he had his first encounter with the beautiful Fernande Olivier, thrusting a kitten into her hand as she passed by. "I laughed," she said, "and he took me to see his studio." Fernande became his model and lover. Although the original building burnt down some years ago, the modern reconstruction still provides studio space for artists, and you wouldn't notice any change on the square itself.

12

THE MÉTRO: AN OVERVIEW OF THE UNDERGROUND

When you descend into the **métro** network, Paris's true ethnic and social mix is revealed. The city centre may be flush with the white and wealthy, but the *franciliens* who live beyond the *périphérique* ring road – women in Islamic veils, streetwise kids from the housing projects, working men in overalls – mostly travel to and from work underground. And every new immigrant group sends a wave of buskers down the tunnels. The métro also has its own **culture**. When it gets crowded everyone knows not to use the *strapontins*, the folding seats by the doors, and it's understood that only someone really pushy walks up or down an escalator. There's a certain style about the way Parisians travel, too, notably the casual upward flick of the wrist that turns the door handle just before the train stops moving.

Internationally, however, the métro is best known for its beautiful Art Nouveau signs and entrances, designed by **Hector Guimard** in 1900. (As usual when confronted with cutting-edge design, Parisians were initially less than impressed, comparing Guimard's sinewy green railings and lantern holders to threatening tentacles.) The last three complete Guimard stations, with their glazed roofs intact, can be found at **Abbesses**, below Montmartre; at the **Porte Dauphine**, on the edge of the Bois de Boulogne; and at **Châtelet**'s place St-Opportune entrance. Not far away from the last, at the Palais-Royal-Musée-du-Louvre métro entrance on place Colette, you can see a different take on Guimard's design: arching over the entrance are two colourful "crowns" made of glass and aluminium designed by artist Jean-Michel Othoniel and known as the "Kiosque des Noctambules". Some stations have distinct characters below ground, too: check out the funky multicoloured lamps at Bonnes Nouvelles station; the hanging globe lights at Cité; the museum cabinets and jewelled entrance at Palais-Royal-Musée-du-Louvre; the sci-fi copper-submarine styling of Arts-et-Métiers; Varennes' massive Rodin sculptures; St-Germain-des-Prés' sleek comic-book projections; the historic cartoons at Bastille; and the one-letter-per-tile decor of Concorde – which spells out the Revolutionary Declaration of the Rights of Man.

Technologically, the métro is one of the finest underground systems in the world, though its famous rubber tyres are actually restricted to lines 1, 4, 6, 11 and 14. Lines 1 and 14 have the latest in air-conditioned, articulated, driverless trains (sitting right in the front carriage offers exciting views down the tunnels). There are more elevated métro pastimes than playing train drivers, too. The writer Jacques Jouet and the avant-garde literary group, Oulipo, invented a system for composing **métro poems**; you have to write a line every time the train is still, and think up the next while the train is moving. For tourists, the best things about the métro are its reliability – except when there's a strike – and its cost: roughly two-thirds of the ticket price is subsidized by the French taxpayer.

Moulin de la Galette
Rue Lepic, 18ᵉ • Ⓜ Abbesses

Perhaps the most historic route up the Butte is via rue Lepic, which owes its winding contours to the requirements of the slow wagons that carried plaster of Paris down from the quarries. The street begins at the seedy place Blanche (near Moulin Rouge métro), which is occupied by a resolutely ordinary food market at its lower end. Above rue des Abbesses, however, it becomes progressively more elegant. Just short of the top, the **Moulin de la Galette** windmill looks down from atop its modest patch of green – the last remnant of Montmartre's *maquis*, the scrub that once covered the Butte. The abandoned dances here were immortalized by Renoir in his *Bal du Moulin de la Galette*, now hanging in the Musée d'Orsay. Today, the windmill is one of just two survivors of the many that once spun atop Montmartre. The other, the Moulin Radet, stands at its feet, above the confusingly named *Moulin de la Galette* restaurant (see p.291). If you're approaching from place des Abbesses, you can cut straight up to the windmills via rue Durantin and rue Tholozé.

Place Marcel Aymé to place Dalida

Towards the top of rue Lepic, rue Girardon climbs up to **place Marcel Aymé**, a peaceful square with a lovably eccentric statue that celebrates Aymé's best-loved short story: *Le Passe-Muraille* or *The Man Who Could Walk Through Walls*. A few steps higher up, square Suzanne-Buisson provides another quiet haven, with a sunken boules pitch and fountains overlooked by a statue of St Denis clutching his head to his breast. Above that again, **place Dalida** offers fine views of Sacré-Coeur; it has as its centrepiece a distinctly busty bust of the singer and gay icon Dalida. Her statue is overlooked by the elegant Château des Brouillards, or "Fog House", where Renoir once lived. It gets its romantic name not from the fact that Renoir used to sit on the steps smoking, but from the clouds that used to gather around the top of the Butte.

Avenue Junot

From place Marcel Aymé, the gorgeously exclusive avenue Junot sweeps west, giving onto still more exclusive enclaves. Beside no. 11 is a desirable nest of houses and gardens, the **Hameau des Artistes** – its digicoded gate usually firmly shut against the hoi polloi. Behind the (closed) gate of the next private lane, the **passage Lepic–Junot**, lies the weighty "witch's stone" that gives it its local name: the passage de la Sorcière. The secluded cul-de-sac **Villa Léandre**, with its lovingly tended plants and village-like feel, is just round to the left. Don't miss the house of Dadaist poet Tristan Tzara at 15 avenue Junot; built by Adolf Loos in 1926, it's a Cubist masterpiece.

Espace Dalí

9–11 rue Poulbot, 18ᵉ • Daily 10am–6pm, July & Aug till 8pm • €11.50 • ☎ 01 42 64 40 10, ⓦ daliparis.com • Ⓜ Abbesses

Rue Poulbot, at the beginning of rue des Norvins, leads round to the underground **Espace Dalí**. It mostly shows reproduced engravings and wacky sculptures signed off by the artist. There's a certain interest in seeing this, less familiar side of his work, but it's really more of a giant souvenir shop than a museum, and lives up to the anagram that André Breton made of Dalí's name: Avida Dollars.

Place du Tertre

Ⓜ Abbesses/Lamarck-Caulaincourt

If you want to preserve romantic memories of the Butte Montmartre, stop short of the top. What was once a pretty, tree-shaded square at Montmartre's crown, **place du Tertre**, has completely fallen victim to its own fame. Today, it's jammed with tour groups, souvenir stalls and street artists knocking up lurid oils of Paris landmarks from memory or offering to paint your portrait. Even the famous trees are mostly modern replacements for the ones planted here in the seventeenth century.

St-Pierre de Montmartre

2 rue du Mont-Cenis, 18e • Daily 8.30am–7.30pm • Free • ⓦ saintpierredemontmartre.net • Ⓜ Abbesses/Lamarck-Caulaincourt

The **church of St-Pierre de Montmartre**, between place du Tertre and the Sacré-Coeur, offers sanctuary from the tourist bustle. It once served a Benedictine convent that occupied the Butte Montmartre from the twelfth century onwards, and now rivals St-Germain-des-Prés for the title of oldest church in Paris. Though much altered, with modern stained glass by Max Ingrand throughout, it still retains its Romanesque and early Gothic structures. More ancient still are four columns inside the church, two by the west door and two in the choir; they probably date from a Roman shrine that stood on the hill, though their capitals were carved in Merovingian times.

Sacré-Coeur

Church Daily 6am–10.30pm • Free **Tower access** Daily: May–Sept 8.30am–8pm; Oct–April 9am–5pm • €6 • ⓦ sacre-coeur-montmartre .com • Ⓜ Abbesses/Anvers

Parisian poet Jacques Roubaud compared the **Sacré-Coeur** to a big baby's bottle for the angels to suck. Certainly, it's a sickly sweet confection of French and Byzantine architecture, yet its pimpled tower and white ice-cream dome has become an essential part of the Paris skyline. The site has been sacred since the Romans venerated Mars and Mercury here, but today's temple dates from the 1870s, after the Catholic Church

THE PARIS COMMUNE

In March 1871, **Montmartre** saw the first sparks fly in what would become the great conflagration of the **Paris Commune**. After Napoléon III's disastrous campaign against the Prussians in the summer of 1870, and the declaration of the Third Republic in September of the same year, Paris finally fell to the Prussian army on January 28, 1871, after a four-month siege. Peace terms were agreed by the end of February, and the Prussians withdrew, leaving the new Republic in the hands of a shaky conservative administration. Paris's situation was least secure of all, as the city's workers – and their armed representatives in the National Guard – had been disenfranchised by the February settlement, and were not inclined to respect it. The new Prime Minister, **Adolphe Thiers**, dispatched a body of regular troops under General Lecomte to take possession of 170 guns which the National Guard controlled on the high ground of the Butte Montmartre. Although the troops seized the guns easily in the darkness before dawn, they had failed to bring any horses to tow them away. That gave the revolutionary Louise Michel time to raise the alarm.

An angry crowd of workers and National Guard members quickly gathered. They persuaded the troops to take no action and arrested General Lecomte, along with another general, Clément Thomas, who was notorious for the part he had played in the brutal repression of the 1848 republican uprising. The two generals were shot and mutilated in the garden of no. 36 rue du Chevalier-de-la-Barre, behind the Sacré-Coeur. Across the city, soldiers and National Guard members joined the rebellion, and, by the following morning, a panicking government had decamped to Versailles, leaving the Hôtel de Ville and the whole of the city in the hands of the National Guard. The rebels quickly proclaimed a **revolutionary Commune**, decreeing the separation of church and state, the enfranchisement of women and numerous measures to protect workers' rights.

By the beginning of April, the Communards were under attack from Thiers' army, its numbers newly swelled by prisoners of war helpfully released by the Prussians. Isolated and ill equipped, the Communards didn't stand a chance. In the notorious **semaine sanglante**, of May 21–28, around 25,000 of their number died – no one knows the exact figure – with some 10,000 executed or deported. The cost to Paris was also severe; the Hôtel de Ville and Tuileries palace (see box, p.70) were reduced to smouldering ashes. Today the Communards are commemorated in Père-Lachaise cemetery (see p.210), and in the enduringly martial spirit of the French Left; since 1871, not to be revolutionary has somehow seemed a betrayal of the dead.

raised a public subscription to atone for the "crimes" of the Commune (see box above). The thwarted opposition, which included Clemenceau, eventually got its revenge by naming the space at the foot of the monumental staircase **square Willette**, after the local artist who turned out on inauguration day to shout "Long live the devil!"

The interior is gloomily neo-Byzantine, and apart from its carillon of bells – the largest bell in France, at nineteen tonnes, swings here – and its collection of holy relics from all over France, the only exciting thing about the Sacré-Coeur is the **view from the top**. The gateway to the stairs – with 300 steps, it's a steep and claustrophobic climb – is under the church's west flank; you'll need change for the automatic ticket machine by the turnstile. Once at the top, you're almost as high as the Eiffel Tower, and you can see the layout of the whole city – a wide, flat basin ringed by low hills, with stands of high-rise blocks in the corners.

Montmartre vineyard

Rue des Saules, 18e • ⓦ fetedesvendangesdemontmartre.com • Ⓜ Lamarck-Caulaincourt

Rue des Saules tips steeply down the northern slopes of the Butte past the terraces of the tiny **Montmartre vineyard**, whose annual harvest yields an extraordinary 1500-odd bottles of wine. Sadly, the actual pressing is no longer down on place du Tertre, as it was in the 1940s; it's now done in a basement of the arrondissement's own town hall. The result is pretty rough, yet few wine buffs would be hard-hearted enough to resist having at least one bottle in the cellar. A raucously celebrated festival marks the *vendange*, or wine harvest, on the first or second weekend of October. It's a celebration of Montmartre's left-wing spirit, and now includes the riotously romantic Cérémonie des Non-Demandés en Mariage, at which ardently secular, republican couples publicly state that they "have the honour not to ask your hand in marriage" – as the singer Georges Brassens famously put it.

The picturesque house standing opposite the lowest corner of the vineyard is the cabaret club **Au Lapin Agile**, made famous by the Montmartre artists who drank there in the 1900s – among them Picasso, whose $50 million self-portrait as a harlequin is set inside. The "nimble rabbit" is alive today and still serves up classic French *chanson* (see p.307).

Musée de Montmartre

12 rue Cortot, 18ᵉ • Daily: May–Aug 10am–7pm; Sept–April 10am–6pm; café Wed–Sun 11.30am–5.30pm • €9.50 • ☎ 01 49 25 89 37, Ⓦ museedemontmartre.fr • Ⓜ Lamarck-Caulaincourt

The recently expanded **Musée de Montmartre** occupies two fine old buildings. The elegant Maison du Bel Air, which houses the **permanent collection**, is particularly rich in artistic associations: it was home, at various times, to Auguste Renoir, Raoul Dufy, Suzanne Valadon and Maurice Utrillo. Its low-key exhibits attempt to re-create the atmosphere of Montmartre's heyday via a selection of Toulouse-Lautrec posters, mock-ups of period rooms and painted impressions of how the Butte once looked. Generally more engaging are the **temporary exhibitions** on themes such as the *Chat Noir* cabaret, held in the newly renovated Hôtel Demarne. This also gives access to Suzanne Valadon's studio-apartment, restored and opened for the first time to the public in 2014. The artist lived here with her troubled son Maurice Utrillo and partner André Utter from 1912 to 1926, their turbulent life and frequent rows earning them the nickname the "trio infernal". The apartment's cramped living quarters contrast with the spacious, light-filled studio, convincingly re-created from old photos. The bold, confident lines of the drawings on display reveal Valadon's strong character; she was the first woman to exhibit at the Société Nationale des Beaux Arts. The museum's three small gardens have been charmingly renovated too (you get a fine view from the back garden over the hilly northern reaches of the city and the vineyard) and there's also a café – the *Renoir* – in the grounds.

The street outside the museum is overlooked by a lighthouse-like white **water-tower**, which is one of the landmarks of the city's skyline. Nearby, the composer Berlioz lived with his English wife in the corner house on the steps of rue du Mont-Cenis, from where there's a breathtaking view northwards to the Stade de France, along the canyon of the steps. This is perfect, sepia-tinged, romantic Montmartre – a double handrail runs down the centre, with the lampposts between – and the streets below are among the quietest and least touristy in the neighbourhood.

The eastern slopes of the Butte

Ⓜ Abbesses/Château-Rouge

To the south and east of the Sacré-Coeur, the **slopes of the Butte** drop steeply down towards boulevard Barbès and the Goutte d'Or quarter. Directly below are the gardens of square Willette, milling with tourists. To avoid the crowds, make for the quiet gardens to the north of the Sacré-Coeur, the **Parc de la Turlure**, and descend via rue Chevalier de la Barre, a pretty little road whose steep stairs, towards the top, are adorned with an art installation made up of LED lights. Alternatively, make your way down the steps of rue Utrillo, passing the pleasant café, *L'Eté en Pente Douce*, which has outdoor tables.

From here, more steps lead down along the edge of the gardens to rue Ronsard; at the end of rue Ronsard, in Square Louise Michel, you can see the (sealed) entrances to the quarries where the original plaster of Paris was extracted.

Halle St-Pierre

2 rue Ronsard, 18ᵉ • Mon–Fri 10am–6pm, Sat 10am–7pm, Sun 11am–6pm • €8 • ⓦ hallesaintpierre.org • Ⓜ Anvers

Once a workaday market building, the pavilion-like **Halle St-Pierre** is now an exhibition space dedicated to Art Brut, or works by artists – often autodidacts – that mainstream galleries won't touch, and the biannual exhibitions are often visionary and inspiring. The Halle is energetically run by a charitable association, with evening concerts, kids' workshops, book readings and a café with good cakes and teas. All around the Halle are bustling shops selling cheap fabrics by the metre. From here it's a short walk to the busy, multiethnic crossroads around Barbès-Rochechouart métro station. Contraband cigarettes are sold under the iron viaduct here, among other scams, while the streets around are lined with takeaway couscous joints.

Montmartre cemetery

Entrance on av Rachel, 18ᵉ, underneath the bridge section of rue Caulaincourt • March 16–Nov 5 Mon–Fri 8am–6pm, Sat 8.30am–6pm, Sun 9am–6pm; Nov 6–March 15 closes 5.30pm • Free • Ⓜ Blanche/Place de Clichy

West of the Butte, near the beginning of rue Caulaincourt in place Clichy, lies the **Montmartre cemetery**. Tucked down below street level in the hollow of an old quarry, it's a tangle of trees and funerary stone, more intimate and less melancholy than Père-Lachaise or Montparnasse. A few metres inside the gates, watch out for the antique cast-iron poor-box (marked "Tronc pour les Pauvres").

The illustrious dead at rest here include Stendhal, Berlioz, Degas, Feydeau, Offenbach, Nijinsky and François Truffaut, as well as La Goulue, the dancer at the *Moulin Rouge* immortalized by Toulouse-Lautrec. Emile Zola's grave stands beside the roundabout, near the entrance, though his actual remains have been transferred to the Panthéon (see p.126). In division 15, left of the entrance, lies Alphonsine Plessis, the real-life model for the consumptive courtesan Marguerite, the "Dame aux Camélias" of Alexander Dumas' novel and, later, the original "Traviata". Liszt, who became her lover after Dumas, called her "the most absolute incarnation of Woman who has ever existed". Dumas himself lies on the other side of the cemetery, in division 21. Nearby, in division 22, beside avenue Samson, Vaslav Nijinsky's tomb is adorned with a bronze statue of the dancer in his famous role as the Harlequin in Diaghilev's production of *Carnaval*. Tucked away behind him, the tomb of the 1830s ballerina Marie Taglioni is usually strewn with rotting ballet shoes, left there by dancers from the Paris ballet in honour of the first woman to dance on pointe. A large Jewish section lies by the east wall.

The 9ᵉ

Ⓜ St-Georges/Blanche/Ste-Trinité/Notre-Dame de Lorette

Immediately south of Montmartre, the **9ᵉ** (neuvième) arrondissement isn't much visited by tourists. Yet lurking inside the limits of the broad east–west boulevards that frame it is a handsome, distinctly urban residential district with a powerful nineteenth-century atmosphere, especially around place St-Georges. The once-seedy northern fringe has now been rebranded as the trendy **SoPi**, or "South of Pigalle" district; it still has its gritty elements, though bohemian shops, restaurants and bars have moved in, especially in the streets around rue des Martyrs. The wealthier, more commercial, southernmost strip of the arrondissement, next to the Opéra and Grands Boulevards, is covered in Chapter 4.

Blanche and Pigalle

From place de Clichy in the west to Barbès-Rochechouart métro in the east, the hill of Montmartre is underlined by the sleazy **boulevards de Clichy** and **de Rochechouart**. The pedestrianized centre of the boulevards was occupied by dodgem cars and other tacky sideshows for most of the twentieth century, but Montmartre's upward mobility is now

dragging its shabby hem along with it. The traffic-choked roads have been "civilized", as the Paris planners put it, with bus and cycle lanes, and lots more greenery. It remains to be seen whether or not they will be recolonized by the sophisticated strollers, or *flâneurs*, who defined them in the late nineteenth century. At the eastern **Barbès** end, where the métro clatters by on iron trestles, the crowds teem round the Tati department store, the cheapest in the city, while the pavements are thick with Arab and African street vendors hawking watches, trinkets and textiles.

At the **place de Clichy** end, tour buses from all over Europe feed their contents into massive hotels. In the middle, between **place Blanche** and **place Pigalle**, sex shows, sex shops and prostitutes – male and female – vie for the custom of *solitaires* and couples alike. In the adjacent streets, however, the character of the area is changing; the exploitative "hostess" clubs are closing and being replaced by trendy cocktail bars, *bistrots* and organic grocers. Rues de Douai, Victor-Massé and Houdon sport a large number of electric guitar and hi-fi shops, while **rue des Martyrs** is one of Paris's most enjoyable gastro-streets, lined with fancy food and flower shops as it descends southwards from the Butte.

Musée de l'Erotisme

72 bd de Clichy, 18e • Daily 10am–2am • €10 • ⓦ musee-erotisme.com • Ⓜ Blanche

Perfectly placed among all the sex shops and shows of Pigalle is the **Musée de l'Erotisme**. It's more sincere than smutty: the ground floor and first floor are awash with phalluses, fertility symbols and intertwined figurines from all over Asia, Africa and pre-Columbian Latin America, while the European pieces tend to the satirical, with lots of naughty nuns and priests caught in compromising situations. There's also plentiful cabaret memorabilia, screens showing vintage pornography and displays relating to Paris's historic *maisons closes*, or brothels. The upper floors are devoted to generally excellent temporary exhibitions on themes such as Japanese erotica. A few steps west, the photogenic **Moulin Rouge** still thrives on place Blanche. Once Toulouse-Lautrec's inspiration, it's now a shadow of its former self (see box below).

Avenue Frochot

Ⓜ Blanche

One of the city's most elegant *villas* (private streets), **avenue Frochot**, leads off place Pigalle. Ordinary mortals are kept out by a digicoded gate, so you'll never get to see

---

PARIS CABARETS

For many foreigners, entertainment in Paris is still synonymous with cabaret, especially that mythical name, Pigalle's **Moulin Rouge**, at 82 bd de Clichy (☎01 53 09 82 82, ⓦmoulinrouge.fr). Unlike the **Folies Bergère**, further south at 32 rue Richer (☎08 92 68 16 50, ⓦfoliesbergere.com), which has gone for a mixed programme of music and magic shows, the *Moulin Rouge* still trades on its bare-breasted, cancanning "Doriss Girls". The show is as glitzy and kitsch as you'd expect, full of high-tech special effects and nodding feathers, and audiences are mainly made up of package tourists whose deal includes a ticket (otherwise around €100, or from €180 with dinner). For similar alternatives, try the **Lido** (116bis av des Champs-Elysées, 8e; ☎01 40 76 56 10, ⓦlido.fr), best known for its "Bluebell Girls" – and, these days, its "Lido Boys" too – and its high-tech, Vegas-style shows. At the **Crazy Horse** (12 av George V, 8e; ☎01 47 23 32 32, ⓦlecrazyhorseparis .com), performances are relatively arty – and nude.

The crowds are thinner at the pair of tiny **transvestite cabarets** on rue des Martyrs, just up from Pigalle métro. At its best, *Chez Michou*, at no. 80 (☎01 46 06 16 04, ⓦmichou.com), is like a scene from an Almodóvar film, with singing transvestites masquerading as various female celebrities, but you'll need to know French pop culture to get much out of it. *Chez Madame Arthur*, at no. 75bis (☎01 42 54 15 92), is similar. Both can be outrageously camp good fun, or rather desperate on a quiet night, and your bill is likely to be larger than you might expect; dinner menus (not obligatory) start at around €100.

Jean Renoir's house at no. 7. Still, the facade of the house beside the gate at the south end is worth a look: it's a giant, Art Deco, stained-glass take on Hokusai's famous print of Mount Fuji being engulfed by a tidal wave. It owes its existence to a cabaret that stood here in the 1920s, *Le Shangaï*, and looks particularly splendid at dusk, when it's lit from behind.

Place St-Georges

Ⓜ St-Georges

The handsome centrepiece of the 9e is the circular **place St-Georges**. The central fountain – still with its horse trough – is topped by a bust of Paul Gavarni, a nineteenth-century cartoonist who made a speciality of lampooning the mistresses who were *de rigueur* for bourgeois males of the time. This was the mistresses' quarter – they were known as *lorettes*, after the nearby church of **Notre-Dame de Lorette**, built in the 1820s in the Neoclassical style. On the east side of place St-Georges, the **Hôtel de la Païva** was built in the 1840s in an extravagant French Renaissance style for Thérèse Lachman, a famous Second Empire courtesan who married a marquis. On the west side, the **Hôtel Thiers** was destroyed by the Communards in 1871 but quickly rebuilt; it now houses the Dosne-Thiers foundation, with a huge library specializing in nineteenth-century French history (Ⓦ institut-de-france.fr).

Nouvelle Athènes

Ⓜ St-Georges

The heart of the 9e arrondissement was first developed in the early nineteenth century as a fashionable suburb. It was soon dubbed **Nouvelle Athènes**, or New Athens, after the Romantic artists and writers who came to live here made it the centre of a minor artistic boom. **Place Toudouze** and rues **Clauzel**, **Milton** and **Rodier** are worth wandering along for their elegantly ornamented facades. A short distance southwest of St-Georges, a passageway off rue Taitbout leads through to the serene **square d'Orléans**, an 1829 development which aped Regency London and attracted Chopin, Alexandre Dumas *fils* and George Sand as early residents. Some of the fine townhouses of the original Nouvelle Athènes scheme can still be spotted just to the west, along **rue de la Tour des Dames**.

12

La Sainte-Trinité

Ⓜ Trinité d'Estienne d'Orves

As it cuts its bustling way towards the relatively down-at-heel commuter hub of the Gare St-Lazare, **rue St-Lazare** passes the bulbous church of **La Sainte-Trinité**. Its single, over-size French Renaissance-style tower is its most exciting feature. Inside, the vast space under the barrel vault feels cold and sterile – hard to imagine that the deeply spiritual composer Olivier Messiaen was organist here for the best part of half a century.

Musée de la Vie Romantique

16 rue Chaptal, 9e • Tues–Sun 10am–6pm; café March–Oct 10am–5.30pm • Entry price varies during exhibitions, otherwise free • ☎ 01 55 31 95 67 • Ⓜ St-Georges/Blanche/Pigalle

To get the full flavour of the neuvième's nineteenth-century heyday, make for the **Musée de la Vie Romantique** in the house of the painter Ary Scheffer. He was art tutor to Louis-Philippe's children (and upstairs are a number of his hideously sentimental aristocratic portraits) but he is more renowned today for his friendships with the writer George Sand and her lover, Frédéric Chopin, who used to give private, improvised concerts here. The shuttered building, standing at the end of a private alley, is a delightful surprise, with its tree-shaded, courtyard rose garden where you can take tea on sunny days. The interior preserves the rich colours of a typical bourgeois home of the nineteenth century. The ground floor displays fine furnishings and *objets* once owned by George Sand – whom you might think of as France's George Eliot, though she was still more unconventional, what with her cross-dressing and serial taking of lovers. There are family portraits, jewels, locks of hair and a cast of Chopin's exquisite left hand.

Musée Gustave Moreau

Rue de la Rochefoucauld, 9ᵉ • Mon, Wed, Thurs 10am–12.45pm & 2–5.15pm, Fri–Sun 10am–5.15pm • €6 • ☎ 01 48 74 38 50, ⓦ musee-moreau.fr • Ⓜ St-Georges/Blanche/Pigalle

The design of the eccentric little **Musée Gustave Moreau** was conceived by the artist himself, to be carved out of the house he shared with his parents for many years, and you can visit their tiny, stuffy apartment rooms, crammed with furniture and trinkets and paintings given to Moreau by his friends Degas, Chassériau and Fromentin. His fantastical Symbolist paintings get a lot more room – two huge, studio-like spaces connected by a beautiful spiral staircase, as well as the ground floor, recently renovated and restored to its original decor – but the effect is no less cluttered. Moreau's canvases hang cheek-by-jowl, every surface crawling with figures and decorative swirls – literally crawling in the case of *The Daughters of Thespius* – or alive with deep colours and provocative symbolism, as in *Jupiter and Semele*, the museum's *pièce de résistance*. For all the rampantly decadent symbolism, some viewers haven't been quite convinced that he wasn't more than an oddball pedant. Degas, for one, commented that Moreau was "a hermit who knows the train timetable".

The 10ᵉ

12

Ⓜ Poissonnière/Gare du Nord/Gare de l'Est/Château d'Eau

The rue du Faubourg-Poissonnière (so called because it used to be the route along which fish – poisson – was brought into the city from the coast) separates the 9ᵉ from its grittier twin, the **10ᵉ (dixième) arrondissement**. At its upper end the **northern stations** dominate, while to the south lies the fast-changing quarter of the **faubourgs St-Denis** and **St-Martin**, traditionally working-class, but increasingly popular with young Parisian bobos, priced out of the more affluent areas of the city. In the far north, just inside the 18ᵉ, east of Montmartre, lies the African quarter of the **Goutte d'Or**. The prettier end of the arrondissement is to the east, on the far side of the Canal St-Martin (see p.197).

The northern stations

Ⓜ Gare du Nord/Gare de l'Est

The life of the 10ᵉ is coloured by the presence of the big **northern stations**. Most travellers scarcely give them a glance, intent on hurrying off to more salubrious parts of the city, but the station buildings are in fact very beautiful, closer to Classical orangeries in style than icons of the industrial age. The **Gare du Nord** (serving all places north, including the high-speed train lines to Germany and London) was built by the architect Hittorff in the early 1860s, and is aggressively dominated by its three giant arches, crowned by eight statues representing the original terminus towns, from Amsterdam and Berlin to Vienna and Warsaw. Facing the boulevard de Strasbourg, the slightly earlier **Gare de l'Est** (serving northeastern and eastern France, and Eastern Europe) is more delicate, though when its central arch was open to the elements, as it was when originally built, the steam and smoke billowing out would have had a powerful effect.

The area around the stations is mostly unappealing. Beside the Gare de l'Est, however, a high wall encloses the gardens of **square Villemin** (entrance on rue des Récollets and avenue de Verdun), which provides a welcome green haven. The garden once belonged to a convent, the **Couvent des Récollets**, one much-restored, seventeenth-century wing of which still stands on rue du Faubourg-St-Martin. Further east again, the **Canal St-Martin** (see p.197) is an even more tranquil place to escape the city hustle. Just south of the Gare de l'Est, the **church of St-Laurent** has a handsome choir dating from the fifteenth century. Thanks to Haussmann, who thought its original facade irritatingly off-centre, the church's Gothic-looking west front actually dates from the same era as the Gare du Nord.

The faubourgs

The southern end of the 10e arrondissement is its liveliest; it's a gritty, vibrant quarter home to Indian, black African and Near Eastern communities as well as a growing number of young, trendy Parisians, bringing in their wake a slew of

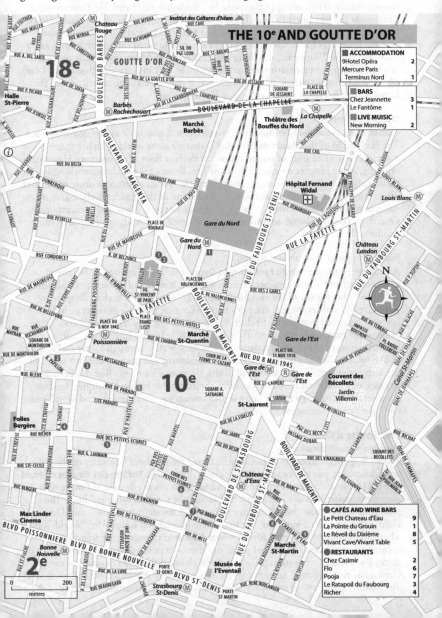

THE 10e AND GOUTTE D'OR

ACCOMMODATION
9Hotel Opéra	2
Mercure Paris	
Terminus Nord	1

BARS
Chez Jeannette	3
Le Fantôme	1

LIVE MUISIC
New Morning	2

CAFÉS AND WINE BARS
Le Petit Chateau d'Eau	9
La Pointe du Grouin	1
Le Réveil du Dixième	8
Vivant Cave/Vivant Table	5

RESTAURANTS
Chez Casimir	2
Flo	6
Pooja	7
Le Ratapoil du Faubourg	3
Richer	4

cutting-edge *bistrots*, chic boutiques, delis and cocktail bars. The two main thoroughfares, the rue du Faubourg-St-Denis and rue du Faubourg-St-Martin, bear the names of the faubourgs, or suburbs, that once stood just outside the town walls. For once, you can still get a vivid sense of the old city limits, as two triumphal arches stand marooned by traffic at either end of the boulevard St-Denis. The Porte St-Denis was erected in 1672 to celebrate Louis XIV's victories on the Rhine – below the giant letters spelling out Ludovico Magno, or "Louis the Great", are the bas-reliefs *The Crossing of the Rhine* (on the south side) and *The Capture of Maastricht* (on the north). With France's northern frontier secured, Louis ordered Charles V's city walls to be demolished and replaced by leafy promenades; they became known as the boulevards after the Germanic word for an earth rampart, a bulwark. Some 200m east, the more graceful Porte St-Martin was built two years after its sibling, in celebration of further victories in Limburg and Besançon. Louis planned a veritable parade of these arches, but the military misadventures of the latter part of his reign were hardly worth celebrating.

Musée de l'Eventail

2 bd de Strasbourg, 10ᵉ · Mon–Wed 2–6pm; closed Aug · €6.50 · ☏ 01 42 08 90 20, ⓦ annehoguet.fr/musee · Ⓜ Strasbourg-St-Denis

The fascination of the **Musée de l'Eventail** is that it's more working atelier than museum. In a small suite of period rooms on the first floor of an ordinary Haussmann building, Anne Hoguet continues the family tradition of fan-making, working almost exclusively on commission for customers from the worlds of haute couture or theatre. There is always an exhibition drawing on a selection of the museum's thousand-strong collection of fans, both historic – some date back to the 1720s – and contemporary. Of course, you can always commission a fan yourself, and ready-made models can be had for as little as €10.

Rue du Faubourg-St-Denis and around

At its lower end, the **rue du Faubourg-St-Denis** is full of charcuteries, butchers, greengrocers and ethnic delicatessens, as well as a number of restaurants, including the historic **brasseries** *Julien* and *Flo* (see p.292). The latter is tucked away in an attractive old stableyard, the cour des Petites-Ecuries, one of a number of hidden lanes and covered *passages* that riddle this corner of the city. The best known is the glazed-over **passage Brady**, the hub of Paris's "Little India", lined with Indian barbers', grocers' shops and restaurants. The *passage* runs through to **rue du Faubourg-St-Martin**, crossing the busy boulevard de Strasbourg and coming out just south of the impressive neo-Gothic **town hall** of the 10ᵉ arrondissement. Rue des Petites-Ecuries, one block north, has a real buzz about it, with its hip boutiques, foodie shops and cutting-edge *bistrots*, and is also known for the large jazz and world music club, the *New Morning* (see p.307).

The Goutte d'Or
Ⓜ Barbès-Rochechouart/Château-Rouge

The wide, grotty boulevard de la Chapelle forms the northern boundary of the 10ᵉ arrondissement, its only beacon the gloriously dilapidated **Théâtre des Bouffes du Nord** (see p.314). Immediately north of the *boulevard*, the poetically named **Goutte d'Or** *quartier* stretches between boulevard Barbès and the Gare du Nord rail lines. The setting for Zola's classic novel of gritty realism, *L'Assommoir*, its name – the "Drop of Gold" – comes from a vineyard that stood here in medieval times. After World War I, when large numbers of North Africans were imported to restock the trenches, it became an immigrant ghetto. For years, the streets languished in a lamentable state of decay, but a major renovation programme has changed the area's character – rue des Gardes has even become "fashion street", lined with city-subsidized design boutiques. The *quartier* has changed ethnically, too, and is now predominantly the home of West

African and Congolese people, rather than North Africans, along with South Asian, Haitian, Kurdish and other communities.

Marché Dejean and around

Ⓜ Château-Rouge

On the rue de la Goutte d'Or you could seek out one of the city's **Wallace fountains** (see box, p.8), on the corner with the rue de Chartres, but the main sight is a few steps north on rue Dejean, where the **Marché Dejean** (daily except Sun afternoon and Mon) thrums with shoppers, including lots of women in brightly coloured West African dress. You can pick up imported African beers and drinks; if you're self-catering you may want to try vegetables such as plantain, yam and taro root. Another more general market takes place in the mornings twice weekly (Wed and Sat) underneath the métro viaduct on the **boulevard de la Chapelle**.

Institut des Cultures d'Islam

56 rue Stephenson, 18ᵉ • ☎ 01 53 09 99 84, ⓦ institut-cultures-islam.org • Tues–Thurs, Sat & Sun 10am–9pm, Fri 4–9pm • Ⓜ La Chapelle/Marx Dormoy

Opened in 2013, an annexe to the smaller, original site on rue Léon, the **Institut des Cultures d'Islam** stages exhibitions of contemporary art from the Islamic world. These are usually fascinating and thought-provoking, with recent exhibitions including Syrian artists responding to the current war and chaos in their country, and women artists depicting domestic life in the Middle East and Iran. On the first floor is a prayer room, while the lower floor has a hammam.

Batignolles

Ⓜ Place de Clichy/Brochant

West of Montmartre cemetery, in a district bounded by the St-Lazare train lines, marshalling yards and avenue de Clichy, lies **Batignolles** "village", which is sufficiently conscious of its uniqueness to have formed an association for the preservation of its *caractère villageois*. Its heart is the attractive **place du Dr Félix Lobligeois**, framing the elegant Neoclassical church of **Ste-Marie-des-Batignolles** – worth a peek inside if only for the extraordinary trompe l'oeil Assumption behind the altar, in which Mary apparently rockets up through the ceiling. On the corners of the *place*, a handful of modern bars and restaurants attract the neighbourhood's young, bourgeois parents, while, behind, the green **square des Batignolles** is filled with pushchairs and handsome old plane trees.

The poet Verlaine was brought up on the **rue des Batignolles**, which runs southeast past the *mairie* of the 17ᵉ arrondissement to the junction with **rue des Dames**. This narrow but lively thoroughfare winds its way east from the flamboyant food and clothes market of the **rue de Lévis** (daily except Mon), beside the Villiers métro stop, to the avenue de Clichy. Just below lies the traffic- and neon-filled roundabout of the **place de Clichy**, dominated by its Pathé cinema and classic old brasserie, *Wepler* (see p.293). Northeast of Ste-Marie-des-Batignolles, the long **rue des Moines** runs past a bustling and covered market, the **Marché des Batignolles**, into an increasingly working-class area.

In the northwest lies the **Parc Clichy-Batignolles**, an ecologically designed public park created on land recovered from the railway. The park is at the centre of a major new redevelopment, the **Clichy-Batignolles** quarter, covering some 124 acres, much of which is scheduled for completion in 2017. As well as the usual apartment blocks, shops and offices, the quarter will house in one huge building the new Palais de Justice and Préfecture de Police, due to move out of their central premises on the Ile de la Cité. Designed by Renzo Piano and set to reach 160m, the **Cité Judiciaire** will be the second-highest building in Paris after the Montparnasse tower.

12

Cimetière des Chiens

4 Pont de Clichy, Asnières-sur-Seine • Tues–Sun: mid-March to mid-Oct 10am–6pm; mid-Oct to mid-March 10am–4.30pm • €3.50 •
☎ 01 40 86 21 11, ⓦ asnieres-sur-seine.fr • Ⓜ Mairie-de-Clichy; it's a 15min walk north from the métro along rue Martre, then left at the
far end of the Pont de Clichy

At the frontier of the 17ᵉ, lies the little-visited **Cimetière des Batignolles**, with the graves
of André Breton, Verlaine and Blaise Cendrars (Ⓜ Porte-de-Clichy). More curious is the
Cimetière des Chiens, a **pet cemetery** hidden away on a former islet that is now attached
to the north bank of the Seine at Asnières – it's outside the city proper but accessible on
métro line 13. Most of the cemetery's tiny graves, some going back as far as 1900,
belong to beloved pets, and come adorned with photos, plastic flowers and visiting cats
from the adjacent sanctuary. The inscriptions are telling: "26 years of complicity and
shared tenderness"; "Cheated by people; by my dog – NEVER". Some of the more
exotic tombs are dedicated to the 1920 Grand National winner; a St Bernard named
Barry who saved the lives of many snow-disoriented travellers over forty years of service;
and that Hollywood megastar of the 1920s – the German shepherd Rin Tin Tin.

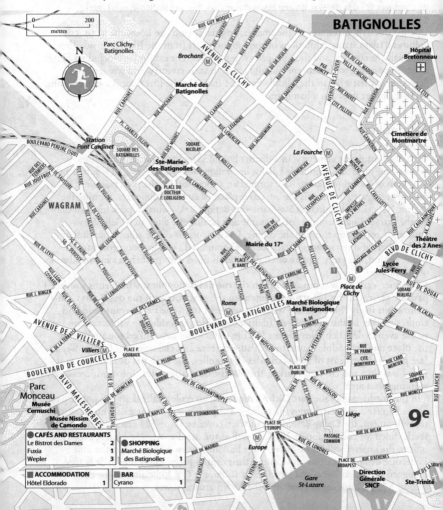

Canal St-Martin and La Villette

La Villette and the Canal St-Martin, in the northeast of the city, were for generations the centre of a densely populated working-class district whose main sources of employment were the La Villette abattoirs and meat market. These have long gone, replaced by the Parc de La Villette, a postmodern park of science, art and music. La Villette stands at the junction of the Ourcq and St-Denis canals. The first was built by Napoleon to bring fresh water into the city; the second is an extension of the Canal St-Martin, built in 1825 as a shortcut to the great western loop of the Seine around Paris. The canals have undergone extensive renovation over the last few decades, and derelict sections of the *quais* have been made more appealing to cyclists, rollerbladers and pedestrians. A major new arts centre, Le 104, has also helped to regenerate the area.

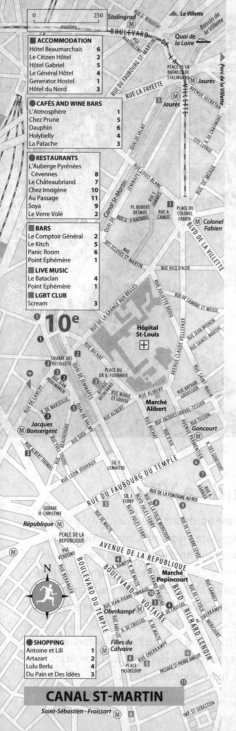

CANAL ST-MARTIN

Canal St-Martin and around

Ⓜ Jacques-Bonsergent

The **Canal St-Martin** runs underground at the Bastille, emerging after 2.5km near the **place de la République**, and continuing north up to the **place de la Bataille de Stalingrad**. The northern reaches of the exposed canal still have a slightly industrial feel, but the southern part, along the **quai de Jemmapes** and **quai de Valmy**, has a great deal of charm, with plane trees lining the cobbled *quais*, and elegant, high-arched iron footbridges punctuating the spaces between the locks, from where you can still watch the odd barge slowly rising or sinking to the next level. Lining this stretch are cool cafés, such as *Chez Prune* (see p.293), and stylish boutiques, the most eye-catching of which is Antoine et Lili (see p.327), with its candy-coloured frontages.

Inevitably, having acquired a certain cachet, the district has attracted property developers, and bland apartment blocks have elbowed in among the traditional, mid-nineteenth-century residences. One of the older buildings, at 102 quai de Jemmapes, is the **Hôtel du Nord**, so named because the barges that once plied the canal came from the north. Made famous by Marcel Carné's film of the same name, starring Arletty and Jean Gabin, it now thrives as a bar-restaurant. Sunday is one of the best days to come for a wander, as the *quais* are closed to traffic and given over to rollerbladers and cyclists. It's especially lively in summer when people hang out along the canal's edge and on the café terraces. Another leisurely way to enjoy the canal is to take a boat trip (see p.28).

Place de la République

Ⓜ République

Just west of the canal, bordering the Marais, lies the **place de la République** (or Répu, as it's affectionately known by locals), one of the city's largest squares, at the centre of which stands an enormous bronze statue of **Marianne**, the female symbol of the Republic, holding an olive branch in one hand, and a tablet inscribed with the words "Droits de l'Homme" in the other. The statue still bears graffiti from the huge crowd that packed the square in January 2015 to protest against the *Charlie Hebdo* massacres; by long-standing tradition, rallies and demonstrations often end at the place de la République. In an attempt to make the square more attractive and pedestrian-friendly it was recently repaved, more trees were planted, and fountains and benches installed (though it's hard to forget that it's still basically a giant, noisy roundabout). In the summer an open-air "games kiosk", l'R de jeux (mid-June to mid-Sept Tues–Sun 2–8pm), sets up on the eastern side of the square; it has some six hundred toys and games for both adults and children, including construction games, scooters, Monopoly and other board games, any of which you can borrow for free (bring ID).

Boulevard Richard-Lenoir
Ⓜ Oberkampf/Breguet-Sabin/Richard-Lenoir

The wide *boulevard* built over the covered section of the canal, **boulevard Richard-Lenoir**, is attractively landscaped all down its centre, dotted with arched footbridges reminding you of the water flowing underground. It's well worth a wander on Thursday and Sunday mornings in particular, when a big, traditional **food market**, known for its choice range of regional produce, sets up on the lower stretch near the place de la Bastille.

Hôpital St-Louis and around
Ⓜ Jacques-Bonsergent/Goncourt

Some of the side streets off the canal are worth exploring, such as **rue des Vinaigriers**, a little south of the **square Villemin gardens**, where a Second Empire shop front bears fluted wooden pilasters crowned with capitals of grapes and a gilded Bacchus. At no. 35, Poursin has been making brass buckles and harnesses for horses since 1830 and preserves its old wooden interior.

Just across the canal from rue des Vinaigriers lies the splendid, early seventeenth-century **Hôpital St-Louis** (Mon–Fri 9am–5pm), built in the same style as the elegant place des Vosges in the Marais. Although it still functions as a hospital, you can walk into its quiet central courtyard and admire the fine brick-and-stone facades and steep-pitched roofs that once sheltered Paris's plague victims – the original purpose for which it was built.

Le Comptoir Général
80 quai de Jemmapes, 10ᵉ ☎ 01 44 88 24 48, ⓦ lecomptoirgeneral.com • Daily 11am–2am • Free, but donation requested • Ⓜ République/Goncourt

Tucked away off the canal, **Le Comptoir Général** is a vast, rambling space housing a "ghetto museum", an ongoing art and social project that uses found objects, ephemera and vintage domestic bits and bobs to celebrate the creativity of different African countries in all its forms. Little themed areas include a reconstructed photographic studio, a travel agent and a record shop/radio station/dancefloor, all packed with quirky

---

THE MONTFAUCON GALLOWS

Long ago, **rue de la Grange-aux-Belles**, on the north side of the Hôpital St-Louis, was a dusty track leading uphill, past fields, en route to Germany. Where no. 53 now stands, a path led to the top of a small hillock. Here, in 1325, on the king's orders, an enormous **gallows** was built, consisting of a plinth 6m high, on which stood sixteen stone pillars each 10m high. These were joined by chains, from which executed malefactors were hanged in clusters. They were left there until they disintegrated, by way of example, and they stank so badly that when the wind blew from the northeast they reached the nostrils of the still far-off city. The practice continued until the seventeenth century. Bones and other remains from the pit into which they were thrown were found during the building of a garage in 1954.

13

interest and with many items available to buy. There's also a wild garden, secondhand books to browse or buy, an African thrift store, a coffee bar and simple world food served at lunchtime, often with live Malian kora music. At night, the whole place transforms into a bar (see p.301).

Rotonde de la Villette and around

Ⓜ Stalingrad/Jaurès

The Canal St-Martin goes underground at the busy **place de la Bataille de Stalingrad**, dominated by the Neoclassical **Rotonde de la Villette**, a handsome stone rotunda fronted with a portico, inspired by Palladio's Villa La Rotonda in Vicenza. This was one of the toll houses designed by the architect Ledoux as part of Louis XVI's scheme to tax all goods entering the city. At that time, every road out of Paris had a customs post, or *barrière*, linked by a 6m-high wall, known as "Le Mur des Fermiers-Généraux" – a major irritant in the run-up to the Revolution. Cleaned and restored, the *rotonde* is used for occasional exhibitions and has a restaurant. Backing the toll house is an elegant aerial stretch of métro, supported by Neoclassical iron-and-stone pillars. The area has a dodgy reputation at night, as it's a known haunt of drug dealers.

Bassin de la Villette

Ⓜ Stalingrad/Riquet/Laumière

13

Beyond the Rotonde de la Villette the canal widens out into the **Bassin de la Villette**, built in 1808. The recobbled docks area bears few traces of its days as France's premier port, its dockside buildings now offering **canal boat trips** (see p.28) and housing a multiplex cinema, the **MK2** (see p.310), which has screens on both banks, linked by shuttle boat. On Sundays and public holidays people stroll along the *quais*, jog, cycle, play boules, fish or take a rowing boat out in the dock; in August, as part of the **Paris Plage** scheme (see p.322), you can rent canoes and pedaloes. Continuing regeneration has seen the arrival of new bars, restaurants and the *St Christopher's* hostel (see p.267), housed in a converted boat hangar.

At rue de Crimée a hydraulic lift bridge with huge pulleys (rather fun to watch in action) marks the end of the dock and the beginning of the **Canal de l'Ourcq**, built in 1802 to bring drinking water to Parisians and to link two branches of the Seine. If you keep to the south bank on quai de la Marne, you can cross directly into the Parc de la Villette.

Le Centquatre/Le 104

104 rue d'Aubervilliers, 19ᵉ • Centre Tues–Fri 11am–7pm, Sat & Sun noon–7pm; La Maison des Petits Tues–Fri 3–6pm, Sat & Sun 2–7pm • Free entry to the main hall, artists' ateliers & Maison des Petits • ☎ 01 53 35 50 00, ⓦ 104.fr • Ⓜ Riquet

West of the Bassin de la Villette, in one of the poorest parts of the 19ᵉ, is the **Le Centquatre/Le 104**, a huge arts centre. A former grand nineteenth-century funeral parlour, it has two performance spaces and numerous artists' studios, which regularly open their doors to the public. Its main performance space, the central *nef curial*, is an impressive hall, with a high glass roof, grey-painted ironwork and exposed brick walls. After an uncertain start in 2008, the centre finally seems to have found its feet, and puts on a varied programme of contemporary art exhibitions, music, dance and theatre, with an emphasis on the experimental and cutting edge. The complex also houses a good bookshop, café, restaurant and **La Maison des Petits**, a supervised play area for 0- to 5-year-olds with plenty of activities such as painting and crafts. Numbers are limited to thirty at a time, so there can be a wait to get in.

Parc de la Villette

ⓦ villette.com • Ⓜ Porte de la Villette/Porte de Pantin

All the meat for Paris used to come from the slaughterhouses in **La Villette**, an old village that was annexed to the city in the mid-nineteenth century. Slaughtering and butchering, and industries based on the meat markets' by-products, provided plenty of jobs for its dense population, whose recreation time was spent betting on cockfights, skating or swimming, and eating in the numerous local restaurants famed for their fresh meat. In the 1960s, vast sums of money were spent building a huge new abattoir, yet just as it neared completion, the emergence of new refrigeration techniques rendered the centralized meat industry redundant. The only solution was to switch course entirely; millions continued to be poured into La Villette in the 1980s, with the revised aim of creating a mind-blowing **music, art and science complex**.

The end result, the **Parc de la Villette**, which opened in 1986, is enormous in scope and volume. There's so much going on here, most of it stimulating and entertaining (see box, p.203), but it's all so disparate and disconnected, with such a clash of styles, that it can feel more overwhelming than inspiring. According to the park's creators, this is all intentional, and philosophically justified. It was conceived by Bernard Tschumi as a futuristic "activity" park that would dispel the eighteenth- and nineteenth-century notion of parks and gardens as places of gentle and well-ordered relaxation. Instead of unity, meaning and purpose we're offered a deconstructed landscape: the whole is broken down into its parts. Certainly there's something vaguely disconcerting about the setting. The 900m-long straight **walkway**, with its wavy shelter and complicated metal bridge across the Canal de

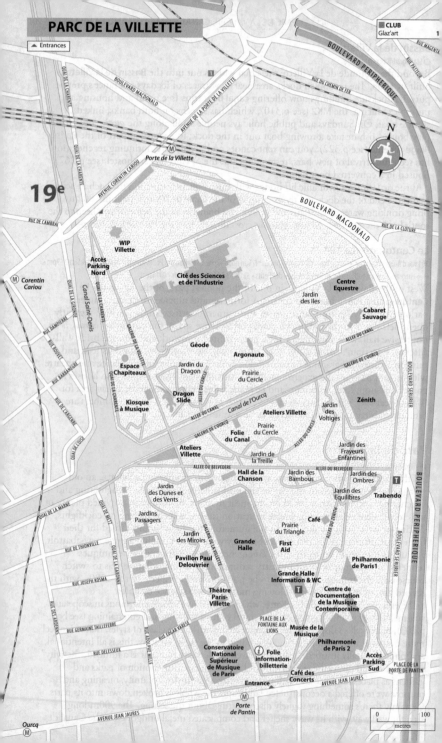

l'Ourcq, seems to insist that you cover the park from end to end, and there's something too dogmatic about the arrangement of the bright red **follies**, like chopped-off cranes, each slightly different but all spaced exactly 120m apart. Some areas of the park grounds have come to feel rather neglected, with parts of it cordoned off for "repairs". Usually, the liveliest area is the **southern section**, near Porte de Pantin and around the Grande Halle.

Key attractions include the **Cité des Sciences et de l'Industrie**, a huge science museum with a special section for children, an Imax cinema and a decommissioned naval submarine; and the **Philharmonie de Paris**, comprising the city's brand-new concert hall and the old Cité de la Musique with its superb **museum of music**. In addition, as well as large expanses of lawn, the park has twelve themed **gardens**, including the Garden of Mirrors, of Shadows and of Dunes, all linked by a walkway called the Promenade des Jardins.

Cité des Sciences et de l'Industrie

Tues–Sat 10am–6pm, Sun 10am–7pm • Free entry to interior; €9 includes admission to Explora (valid all day, but for four entries only), plus certain temporary exhibitions and the Louis-Lumière 3D Cinema, subject to availability • ☎ 01 40 05 70 00, ⓦ cite-sciences.fr • Ⓜ Porte de la Villette

The park's dominant building is the enormous **Cité des Sciences et de l'Industrie**, an abandoned abattoir redesigned by architect Adrien Fainsilber and transformed into a high-tech science museum. Four times the size of the Pompidou Centre, from the outside it appears fortress-like, despite the transparency of its giant glass walls beneath a dark-blue lattice of steel, reinforced by walkways that accelerate out towards the Géode (see p.204) across a moat that is level with the underground floors. Once you're inside, however, the solidity of first impressions is totally reversed by the three themes of water (around the building), vegetation (in the greenhouses) and light – which floods the building from vast skylights and through the glass facade. As well as the permanent exhibition, Explora, the complex includes the brilliant **Cité des Enfants**, specifically designed for children (see p.354). There's a café on the ground floor and a more formal restaurant downstairs, next to a small aquarium. Although it is undoubtedly impressive inside, with its huge central space open to the full 40m height of the roof, the building is starting to look rather worn and shabby in places.

Explora

Cité des Sciences • Tues–Sat 10am–6pm, Sun 10am–7pm • Included in €9 Cité des Sciences ticket

The **Explora** exhibition space is set across the top two floors of the Cité des Sciences (pick up a plan in English from the welcome desk on level 0) and includes both

---

PARC DE LA VILLETTE ENTERTAINMENT

The park has a number of distinguished music, arts and theatre venues and festivals.

Cabaret Sauvage ⓦ cabaretsauvage.com. Live world-music performances.

Espace Chapiteaux ⓦ lavillette.com. Avant-garde circus venue.

Festival de Cinéma en Plein Air ⓦ lavillette.com. On summer nights join the crowds lounging on the acres of grass known as "prairies" for an open-air film screening. See p.322.

Grande Halle ⓦ lavillette.com. The elegant old iron-framed beef market hall hosts art exhibitions and experimental theatre and dance performances.

Hall de la Chanson ⓦ lehall.com. Variety shows, held in the old meat market's canteen.

Jazz à la Villette ⓦ jazzalavillette.com. La Villette's popular jazz festival takes place in September. See p.322.

Philharmonie de Paris ⓦ philharmoniedeparis.fr. The city's new premier classical music venue. See p.204.

Théâtre Paris-Villette ⓦ theatre-paris-villette.fr. A theatre that encourages young talent and puts on mostly contemporary works for children.

Trabendo ⓦ letrabendo.net. A live music venue for jazz and rock.

Zénith ⓦ zenith-paris.com. Rock and pop concerts are staged at this 6000-seat concert hall.

13

temporary shows and a permanent exhibition divided into twenty units, many accompanied by English translations. These cover a variety of subjects, among them water, the universe, automobiles, aeronautics, energy, images, genes, sound, mathematics, light and matter, and there's also a section on current scientific developments. As the name suggests, the emphasis is on exploring, by means of interactive computers, multimedia displays, videos, holograms and games.

On **level 1**, a classic example of chaos theory introduces the **maths section**; La Fontaine Turbulente is a wheel of glasses rotating below a stream of water in which the switch between clockwise and anticlockwise motion is unpredictable beyond two minutes. In **Les Sons** (sounds), you can sit in a cubicle and feel your body tingle with physical sensations as a rainstorm crashes around you, while videos in **L'homme et les gènes** trace the development of an embryo from fertilization to birth and in **Images** you can use computer simulation to manipulate the *Mona Lisa*'s smile. On **level 2**, the **Jeux de Lumière** offers experiments to do with colour, optical illusions, refraction and the like. You can have your head spun further by a session in the **planetarium** (around six shows daily; €3 supplement).

Back on the ground floor, the **Cinéma Louis-Lumière** shows short stereoscopic (3D) films every thirty minutes or so, for which you'll have to queue.

The Géode

Géode Tues–Sun 10.30am–8.30pm; hourly shows • €12 • ☎ 01 40 05 79 99, ⊕ lageode.fr • **Argonaute** Tues–Sat 10am–5.30pm, Sun till 6.30pm • €3

In front of the Cité des Sciences et de l'Industrie complex floats the **Géode**, a bubble of reflecting steel dropped from an intergalactic boules game into a pool of water that ripples with the mirrored image of the Cité. Inside, the sphere holds a screen for Imax and 3D documentary films on subjects such as the deep sea and the Grand Canyon. Next to the Géode, you can clamber around a real 1957 French military submarine, the **Argonaute**, and view the park through its periscope.

Philharmonie de Paris

221 av Jean-Jaurès, 19ᵉ • ☎ 01 44 84 44 84, ⊕ philharmoniedeparis.fr • ⓜ Porte de Pantin

The latest addition to La Villette's collection of futuristic architecture is the **Philharmonie de Paris** concert hall, opened in 2015. Designed by Jean Nouvel (whose other buildings include the Institut du Monde Arabe and Musée du Quai Branly), it's a huge, angular, metal-clad structure. A ramp, giving access to the panoramic rooftop, zigzags its way up the facade, covered in a pattern of Escher-like, interlocking, bird-shaped aluminium tiles. If the exterior is all jagged and spiky Stravinsky, inside is smooth, seductive Mozart, with soothing cream and ochre colours, rounded balconies and comfy seats. With its state-of the-art acoustics and modular seating and stage, it feels a worthy new venue for grand-scale symphonic concerts.

Concerts (⊕ philharmoniedeparis.fr) are also held at the smaller hall in the nearby Cité de la Musique, now renamed **Philharmonie 2**. There's a fabulous music museum here too (see below) and a stylish café, the *Café des Concerts*. The building, designed by Christian de Portzamparc in 1995, feels less intimidating than its new twin and conceals a sensual interior; a glass-roofed arcade spirals round the auditorium, the combination of pale blue walls, a subtly sloping floor and the height to the ceiling creating a sense of calm.

To the west, on the other side of the park's main entrance, lies the **Conservatoire National Supérieur de Musique et de Danse de Paris** (also designed by Portzamparc), where regular free recitals and performances are given by the students (see p.318).

Musée de la Musique

Philharmonie 2 • Tues–Sat noon–6pm, Sun 10am–6pm • €7, under-26s free • ⓜ Porte de Pantin

The **Musée de la Musique** presents the history of mainly Western music from the end of the Renaissance to the present day, both visually, exhibiting some one thousand instruments and artefacts, and aurally, via excellent audioguides (available in English, with special ones for children; free), which narrate the history of the instruments, accompanied by extracts of music. It's a truly transporting experience to gaze, for example, at the grouping of harps, made in Paris between 1760 and 1900, and hear an excerpt of music as heavenly as the instruments you're looking at. Other exquisite items include jewel-inlaid crystal flutes, ornately carved theorbos and viola da gambas, a piano that belonged to Chopin and guitars once played by Jacques Brel and Django Reinhardt. Interactive displays can tell you about such subjects as the history of musical notation or the importance of Nuremberg in the manufacture of musical instruments. There's also a small display of instruments from around the world, including Arab ouds and Persian *kamanchehs*. You can hear **live music** too; every afternoon a different instrument is played in the museum, with the chance to meet and talk to the musician.

ARRIVAL AND INFORMATION   PARC DE LA VILLETTE

Access points The Parc de la Villette is accessible from Ⓜ Porte de la Villette at the northern end by av Corentin-Cariou and the Cité des Sciences et de l'Industrie; from the Canal de l'Ourcq's quai de la Marne to the west; or from Ⓜ Porte de Pantin on av Jean-Jaurès at the southern entrance by the Philharmonie 2.

Information There's an information centre at the southern entrance, which will help you get your bearings, and plenty of restaurants and cafés.

PÈRE-LACHAISE CEMETERY

Belleville and Ménilmontant

The old working-class quarters of Belleville and Ménilmontant in the east of Paris are some of the most cosmopolitan in the city, home to North Africans, Malians, Turks, Chinese and inhabitants of the former Yugoslavia. The area is also favoured by students and artists, who have done a great deal to create a thriving alternative scene and some of the city's best nightlife. Probably the main reason visitors come to this part of town, though, is to seek out the graves of various famous people – from Modigliani to Jim Morrison – at Père-Lachaise cemetery. A couple of parks, the Buttes-Chaumont and the modern Parc de Belleville, also make for rewarding visits, not least for their fine views over the city, and there are some worthy destinations for contemporary art fans, too.

Belleville and **Ménilmontant** were once villages outside Paris, whose populations were swelled during the Industrial Revolution in the mid-nineteenth century with the arrival of migrants from the countryside. These new arrivals supplied the people-power for the many insurrections in the nineteenth century, including the short-lived Commune of 1871 (see p.186), with the centre and west of Paris battling to preserve the status quo against the oppressed, radical east. Indeed, for much of the nineteenth century, the establishment feared nothing more than the "descente de Belleville" – the descent of the mob from the heights of Belleville. It was in order to contain this threat and be able to swiftly dispatch troops to the eastern districts that so much of the Canal St-Martin (see p.197), a natural line of defence, was covered over by Baron Haussmann in 1860.

14

Today, only a few reminders of these turbulent times survive, such as the Mur des Fédérés in **Père-Lachaise cemetery** recording the deaths of 147 Communards, and a few streets bearing the names of popular leaders. Some of the old working-class character of the district lives on: narrow streets and artisans' houses survive in places. Much of the area, however, has undergone **redevelopment** over the last few decades. Crumbling, dank and insanitary houses were replaced by shelving-unit apartment blocks in the 1960s and 1970s, giving way in recent years to more imaginative and attractive constructions.

Belleville

Ⓜ Belleville/Pyrénées/Jourdain/Télégraphe

The old village of **Belleville**, only incorporated into the city in 1860, is strung out along the western slopes of a ridge that rises steadily from the Seine at Bercy to an altitude of 128m near the place des Fêtes, the highest point in Paris after Montmartre. "Belle" is not the first adjective that springs to mind when describing Belleville, with its many bland apartment blocks, but there are pockets of charm, especially around the attractive **Parc des Buttes-Chaumont** and **Parc de Belleville**. It's home to what is probably one of the most diverse populations in the city: a mix of traditional working class, various ethnic communities and a good number of students and artists, drawn to the area by the availability of affordable and large spaces, ideal for ateliers. The best opportunity to view local artists' work is during the **Journées portes ouvertes ateliers d'artistes de Belleville** at the end of May (for dates see ⓦateliers-artistes-belleville.fr), when around 250 artists living or working in Belleville open their doors to the public. There's plenty of **street art** too; the best examples can be found on **rue Dénoyez**, off the lower end of rue de Belleville, whose 30m-long wall, dubbed a "mur d'expression", is completely covered with graffiti, renewed almost daily.

Rue de Belleville and around

Ⓜ Jourdain/Belleville/Pyrénées/Télégraphe

Belleville's main artery is **rue de Belleville**. Its lower, western end is liveliest, with numerous Chinese restaurants and *traiteurs* doing a brisk trade, while adjoining **boulevard de Belleville** is home to Algerian pastry shops, grocers and *shisha* cafés. The boulevard is lined with dramatic new architecture, employing jutting triangles, curves and the occasional reference to the roof lines of nineteenth-century Parisian blocks. Things are particularly vibrant on Tuesday and Friday mornings when the **market** sets up, stretching the whole length of the boulevard. Kosher food shops and cafés, belonging to Sephardic Jews from Tunisia, are also in evidence here and on **rue Ramponeau**, running parallel to the rue de Belleville. It was at the junction of rue Ramponeau and rue de Tourtille that the final remaining barricade of the Commune was defended single-handedly for fifteen minutes by the last fighting Communard in 1871.

The upper stretch of rue de Belleville is not as distinctive as its lower end and, with its boulangeries and charcuteries, could be the busy main street of any French provincial

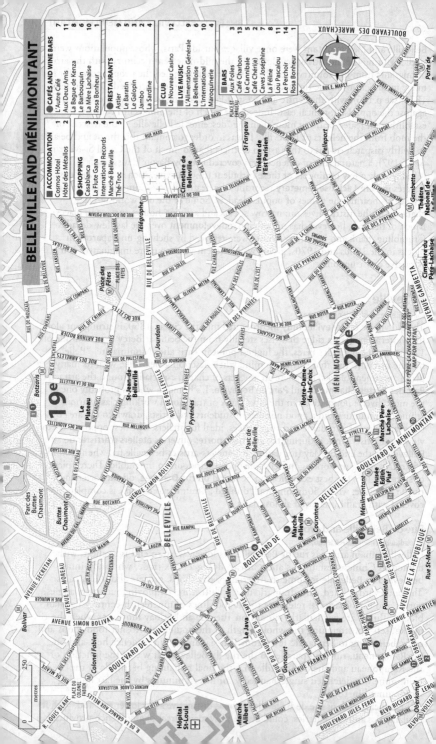

BELLEVILLE AND MÉNILMONTANT

CLAUDE CHAPPE AND THE RUE DU TÉLÉGRAPHE

The rue du Télégraphe, running south off the eastern end of rue de Belleville alongside the Cimetière de Belleville, is named in memory of Claude Chappe's invention of the **optical telegraph**. Chappe first tested his device here in September 1792, in a corner of the cemetery. When word of his activities got out, he was nearly lynched by a mob that assumed he was trying to signal to the king, who was at that time imprisoned in the Temple (see box, p.104). Eventually, two lines were set up, from Belleville to Strasbourg and the east, and from Montmartre to Lille and the north. By 1840, it was possible to send a message to Calais in three minutes, via 27 relays, and to Strasbourg in seven minutes, using 46 relays. Chappe himself did not live to see the fruits of his invention; his patent was contested in 1805 and, distraught, he threw himself into a sewer (his grave is in nearby Père-Lachaise).

14

town. On the wall of no. 72, a plaque commemorates the birth of the legendary chanteuse **Edith Piaf**; the story goes that she was born under a street lamp just here. One of Piaf's favourite hangouts is back down at rue de Belleville's lower end, at 105 rue du Faubourg-du-Temple, the street's busy lower extension: *La Java* (⊕la-java.fr), a former *bal musette* venue, still a fixture of Paris nightlife, whose original dancehall interior survives intact.

Parc de Belleville and around
Daily 8/9am till dusk • Free • ⓂPyrénées/Couronnes

A turn off rue de Belleville onto the cobbled **rue Piat** will take you past the beautiful wrought-iron gate that used to mark the entrance to the Villa Ottoz (a little street of houses, long demolished) to the **Parc de Belleville**, created in the mid-1990s. From the terrace at the junction with rue des Envierges, there's a fantastic view across the city, especially at sunset. At your feet, the small park descends in a further series of terraces and waterfalls.

A path crosses the top of the Parc de Belleville past a minuscule vineyard and turns into steps that drop down to **rue des Couronnes** (which leads back to boulevard de Belleville). Some of the adjacent streets are worth a wander for a feel of the changing times – rue de la Mare, rue des Envierges, rue des Cascades – with two or three beautiful old houses in overgrown gardens, alongside new housing that follows the height and curves of the streets and *passages* between them.

Parc des Buttes-Chaumont
Daily: May & mid-Aug to Sept 7am–9.15pm; June to mid-Aug 7am–10.15pm; Oct–April 7am–8.15pm • Free • ⓂButtes-Chaumont/Botzaris

The delightful, hilly **Parc des Buttes-Chaumont**, north of the Belleville heights, was constructed under Haussmann in the 1860s to camouflage what until then had been a desolate warren of disused quarries, rubbish dumps and shacks. Out of this unlikely setting, a park was created – there's a grotto with a cascade and artificial stalactites, and a picturesque lake from which a huge rock rises up, topped with a delicate Corinthian temple. You can cross the lake via a suspension bridge, or take the shorter **Pont des Suicides**. This, according to Louis Aragon, the literary grand old man of the French Communist Party, "before metal grilles were erected along its sides, claimed victims even from passers-by who had had no intention whatsoever of killing themselves but were suddenly tempted by the abyss" (*Le Paysan de Paris*). You can go boating on the lake, and, unusually for Paris, you're not cautioned off the grass.

There are some rather desirable **residences** around the park, especially to the east, between rue de Crimée and place de Rhin-et-Danube; little cobbled *villas* (mews) lined with ivy-strewn houses, their gardens full of roses and lilac trees, can be found here, off rue Miguel-Hidalgo, rue du Général-Brunet, rue de la Liberté, rue de l'Egalité and rue de Mouzaïa.

Le Plateau

33 rue des Alouettes, 19ᵉ • Wed–Sun 2–7pm • Free • ⓦ fracidf-leplateau.com • Ⓜ Jourdain

One block south of the Parc des Buttes-Chaumont is a small contemporary arts centre, **Le Plateau**, set up following a vigorous campaign by local residents who successfully acquired the space after fighting off property developers. Exhibitions tend to focus on experimental, cutting-edge French and international artists.

14 Ménilmontant

Ⓜ Ménilmontant

Like Belleville, much of **Ménilmontant** aligns itself along one straight, steep street, the **rue de Ménilmontant** and its lower extension, rue Oberkampf. Although run-down in parts, its popularity with artists and young professionals, or bobos (*bourgeois-bohémiens*), has helped to revitalize the area. Alternative shops and cool bars and restaurants have elbowed in among the grocers and cheap hardware stores, especially along **rue Oberkampf** and its parallel street **rue Jean-Pierre-Timbaud**, the city's most vibrant nightlife hub (see p.300). The upper, eastern reaches of rue de Ménilmontant, above rue Sorbier, are quieter, and looking back you find yourself dead in line with the rooftop of the Pompidou Centre, a measure of how high you are above the rest of the city.

Musée Edith Piaf

5 rue Crespin-du-Gast, 11ᵉ • Mon–Wed 1–6pm; closed Sept • Donation • Admission by appointment only on ☎ 01 43 55 52 72 • Ⓜ Ménilmontant/St-Maur

Sitting very close to the Ménilmontant métro is the **Musée Edith Piaf**. Piaf was not an acquisitive person; the few clothes (yes, including a little black dress), letters, toys, paintings and photographs that she left are almost all here, along with every one of her recordings. The venue is a small flat lived in by her devoted admirer Bernard Marchois, who will show you around and gladly answer any questions (in French).

Père-Lachaise cemetery

Main entrance on bd de Ménilmontant • Mon–Fri 8am–5.30pm, Sat 8.30am–5.30pm, Sun 9am–5.30pm • Free • ⓦ pere-lachaise.com • Ⓜ Père-Lachaise/Philippe-Auguste

Final resting place of a host of French notables, as well as some illustrious foreigners, **Père-Lachaise** is one of the world's largest and most famous cemeteries. Sited on a hill commanding grand views of Paris, it's a bit like a miniature town, with its grid-like layout, cast-iron signposts and neat cobbled lanes – a veritable "city of the dead". It's surely also one of the world's most atmospheric cemeteries, an eerily beautiful haven, with terraced slopes and magnificent old trees (around six thousand of them) spreading their branches over the moss-grown tombs as though shading them from the outside world.

Finding individual graves can be a tricky business. Our **map** (see opposite) and the free plans given out at the conservation office near the main entrance will point you in the right direction, though it's worth buying a slightly more detailed one from one of the newsagents or florists near the **main entrance**, as it's easy to get lost.

Père-Lachaise was opened in 1804 and turned out to be an incredibly successful piece of land speculation. Nicolas Frochot, the urban planner who bought the land, persuaded the civil authorities to have **Molière**, **La Fontaine**, **Abélard** (see box, p.47) and **Héloïse** reburied in his new cemetery, and it began to acquire cachet, but it really took off when Balzac set the final scene of his 1835 novel *Le Père Goriot* here. Ironically, Frochot even sold a plot to the original owner for considerably more than the price he had paid for the entire site. Even today, rates are extremely high.

Chopin, Jim Morrison and Oscar Wilde

Among the most visited graves is that of **Chopin** (Division 11), who has a willowy muse mourning his loss and is often attended by groups of Poles laying wreaths and flowers in the red and white colours of the Polish flag.

Swarms also flock to the grave of ex-Doors lead singer **Jim Morrison** (Division 6), who died in Paris in 1971 at the age of 27. Once graffiti-covered and wreathed in marijuana fumes, it has been cleaned up and now has a metal barrier around it, though this hasn't stopped fans scribbling messages in praise of love and drugs on other graves, and trees, nearby. In fact things got so bad some years ago that relatives of undistinguished Frenchmen interred nearby signed a petition asking for the singer's

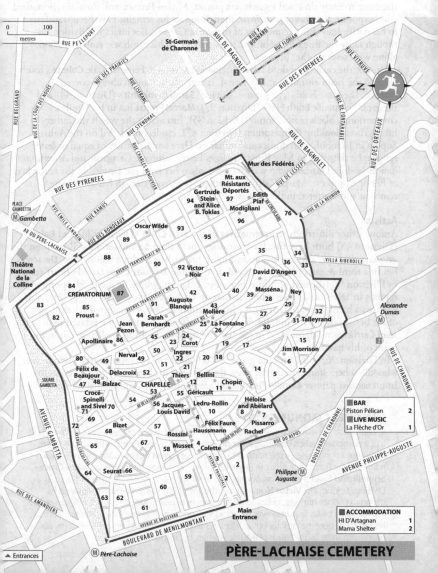

PÈRE-LACHAISE CEMETERY

body to be exhumed and sent home, but the grave, unlike many here, is on a perpetual lease, so the Lizard King is here to stay.

Another tomb that attracts many visitors is **Oscar Wilde**'s (Division 89), topped with a sculpture by Jacob Epstein of a Pharaonic winged messenger (sadly missing its once prominent member, which was last seen being used as a paperweight by the director of the cemetery). The inscription behind is a grim verse from *The Ballad of Reading Gaol*.

Writers and musicians

Many other **musicians** repose near Chopin, among them Bellini, Cherubini, the violinist Kreutzer, whose commemorative column leans precariously to one side, and the more recently deceased French jazz pianist, Michel Petrucciani. Rossini is honoured with a spot on the *avenue principale*, though in fact his remains have been transferred to his native Italy. Bizet, composer of the opera *Carmen*, lies intact in Division 68, though sadly the fine bronze bust that used to adorn his tomb was stolen in 2006, along with several other bronzes.

Most of the celebrated dead have unremarkable tombs. Femme fatale **Colette**'s tomb, close to the main entrance in Division 4, is very plain, though always covered in flowers. The same holds true for the "Divine" **Sarah Bernhardt**'s (Division 44) and the great chanteuse **Edith Piaf**'s (Division 97). **Marcel Proust** lies in his family's conventional, black marble tomb (Division 85). Just across the way is the rather incongruous-looking **Crematorium** (Division 87), crudely modelled on the Aghia Sophia in Istanbul, with domes and minarets. Here among others of equal or lesser renown lie the ashes of Max Ernst, Georges Perec, Stéphane Grappelli and American dancer Isadora Duncan, who was strangled when her scarf got tangled in the rear wheel of her open-top car. Maria Callas has a plaque here, too, though her ashes were removed and scattered in the Aegean.

Artists

Among other illustrious representatives of the arts, **Corot** (Division 24) and **Balzac** (Division 48) both have fine busts, as does poet **Alfred de Musset**, near Rossini on the *avenue principale*, and buried, according to his wishes, under a willow tree. **Delacroix** lies in a sombre sarcophagus in Division 49, while **Jacques-Louis David**'s heart rests in Division 56 (the rest of him is buried in Belgium, where he died). His pupil **Ingres** reposes in Division 23. **Géricault** reclines on cushions of stone (Division 12), paint palette in hand, his face taut with concentration; below is a sculpted relief of part of his best-known painting *The Raft of the Medusa*. Close by is the relaxed figure of **Jean Carriès**, a model-maker, in felt hat and overalls, holding a self-portrait in the palm of his hand.

In Division 96, you'll find the grave of **Modigliani** and his lover Jeanne Herbuterne, who killed herself in crazed grief a few days after he died in agony from meningitis. Impressionist painter **Camille Pissarro** lies among the sober, unadorned tombs of the

---

IMMODEST MONUMENTS

In contrast to the many modest monuments marking the tombs of the famous, in Division 48 a now-forgotten French diplomat, **Félix de Beaujour**, is marked with an enormous tower, rather like a lighthouse. To the north in Division 86, one **Jean Pezon**, a lion-tamer, is shown riding the pet lion that ate him. In Division 71, two men lie together hand in hand – **Croce-Spinelli and Sivel**, a pair of balloonists who went so high they died from lack of oxygen. In Division 92, journalist **Victor Noir** – shot at the age of 22 in 1870 by Prince Napoléon for daring to criticize him – is portrayed at the moment of death, flat on his back, fully clothed, his top hat fallen by his feet. However, it's not as a magnet for anti-censorship campaigners that his tomb has become famous, but as a lucky charm – a prominent part of his anatomy has been worn shiny by the touch of infertile women, hoping for a cure.

Jewish plot near the main entrance, as does the beautiful nineteenth-century actress **Rachel**, known for one of the briefest love-letter exchanges in history; after seeing her on stage, Prince de Joinville sent her his card with the note "Où? Quand? Combien?", to which Rachel scribbled back, "Chez toi. Ce soir. Pour rien."

Politicians

Notable politicians include **Félix Faure** (on the *avenue principale*, Division 4), French president, who died in the arms of his mistress in the Elysée palace in 1899; draped in a French flag, his head to one side, he cuts rather a romantic figure. **Auguste Blanqui**, after whom so many French streets are named, lies in Division 91. Described by Karl Marx as the nineteenth century's greatest revolutionary, he served his time in jail – 33 years in all – for political activities that spanned the 1830 Revolution to the Paris Commune. Karl's daughter, **Laura Marx**, and her husband **Paul Lafargue**, who committed suicide together in 1911, lie south from Blanqui's grave, in Division 76.

War memorials and the Mur des Fédérés

Monuments to collective, violent deaths have the power to change a sunny outing to Père-Lachaise into a much more sombre experience. In Division 97, in what's become known as the "coin des martyrs", you'll find memorials to the victims of the Nazi concentration camps, to executed Resistance fighters and to those unaccounted for in the genocide of World War II. The sculptures are relentless in their images of inhumanity, of people forced to collaborate in their own degradation and death.

Marking one of the bloodiest episodes in French history is the **Mur des Fédérés** (Division 76), the wall where the last troops of the Paris Commune were lined up and shot in the final days of the battle in 1871. A total of 147 men were killed, after a frenetic chase through the tombstones, and the remains of around a thousand other Communards were brought here and thrown into a grave-pit. The wall soon became a place of pilgrimage for the Left, and remains so today. The man who ordered the execution, Adolphe Thiers, lies in the centre of the cemetery in Division 55.

Charonne and around

Ⓜ Porte de Bagnolet/Gambetta

Charonne, just south of Père-Lachaise cemetery, retains its village-like atmosphere, with a perfect little Romanesque church and the cobbled street of rue St-Blaise. **St-Germain-de-Charonne**, in place St-Blaise, has changed little, and its Romanesque belfry not at all, since the thirteenth century. It's one of a handful of Paris churches to have its own graveyard; several hundred Communards were buried here after being accidentally disinterred during the construction of a reservoir in 1897. Elsewhere in Paris, charnel houses were the norm, with the bones emptied into the catacombs as more space was required. It was not until the nineteenth century that public cemeteries appeared on the scene, the most famous being Père-Lachaise.

Opposite the church of St-Germain-de-Charonne, the old cobbled village high street, **rue St-Blaise**, pedestrianized to place des Grès, was once one of the most picturesque in Paris, and still has a measure of charm, with its wooden shuttered houses, cafés and artists' *ateliers*.

Bagnolet

From the top of rue St-Blaise, on rue de Bagnolet, heading southwest will lead you into the heart of the cool, diverse and steadily gentrifying **Bagnolet** district, a former suburb that was incorporated into the city in 1860. A great place for an evening drink, Bagnolet has a collection of bohemian bars, the grungy, electro-chic club *La Flèche d'Or* (see p.305) and one of the city's most hyped concept hotels, the Philippe Starck-designed *Mama Shelter* (see p.265).

FONDATION LOUIS VUITTON

Auteuil and Passy

The affluent districts of Auteuil and Passy, once villages on the outskirts of Paris, were only incorporated into the city in 1860. They soon became the capital's most desirable neighbourhoods, where well-to-do Parisians commissioned new houses. Hector Guimard, designer of the swirly green Art Nouveau métro stations, worked here, and there are also rare Parisian works by interwar architects Le Corbusier and Mallet-Stevens. The area has an almost provincial air, with its tight knot of streets and charming villas – leafy lanes of attractive old houses, fronted with English-style gardens, full of roses, ivy and wisteria. Flowers, especially waterlilies, feature abundantly in the shimmering Monet canvases displayed in the Musée Marmottan, while contemporary art takes centre stage in the spectacular new Fondation Louis Vuitton in the Bois de Boulogne, Paris's second-largest park after the Bois de Vincennes.

Auteuil

Ⓜ Eglise d'Auteuil

The **Auteuil** district is now completely integrated into the city, but there's still a villagey feel about its streets, and it holds some delightful little *villas* as well as fine specimens of early twentieth-century architecture. The ideal place to start an exploration is the **Eglise d'Auteuil** métro station, close to several of Hector Guimard's **Art Nouveau** buildings.

Rue Boileau to the avenue de Versailles

The house at no. 34 **rue Boileau** was one of Guimard's first commissions, in 1891. To reach it from the Eglise d'Auteuil métro, head west along rue d'Auteuil for 200m, then turn left (south) into Boileau. A high fence and wisteria obscure much of the view, but you can see some decorative tile-work under the eaves and around the doors and windows. Further down the street, just before you reach boulevard Exelmans, the Vietnamese embassy at no. 62 successfully combines 1970s Western architecture with the traditional Vietnamese elements of a pagoda roof and earthenware tiles. Continue south for 0.5km along rue Boileau beyond boulevard Exelmans, turn right onto rue Parent de Rosan and you'll find a series of enchanting *villas* off to the right, backing onto the Auteuil cemetery.

Rue Boileau terminates on avenue de Versailles, where you can turn left and head back to the métro via the Guimard apartment block at no. 142 (1905), with its characteristic Art Nouveau flower motifs and sinuous, curling lines. It's just by the Exelmans crossroads (on bus route #72). You can then cut across the **Jardin de Ste-Périne**, once the rural residence of the monks of Ste-Geneviève's abbey, established in 1109, to get back to the métro. Enter the garden opposite 135 avenue de Versailles, or alongside the hospital on rue Mirabeau, just north of the rue Chardon-Lagache junction.

Rue de la Fontaine and around

The old village high street, **rue d'Auteuil**, runs west to **place Lorrain**, which hosts a Saturday market. From here **rue de la Fontaine** runs northeast to the Radio-France building, with Guimard buildings at nos. 14, 17, 19, 21 and 60. No. 14 is the most famous: the "Castel Béranger" (1898), with exuberant Art Nouveau decoration in the bay windows, the roof line and the chimney. At no. 65 there's a huge block of artists' studios by Henri Sauvage (1926) with a fascinating colour scheme, bearing signs of a Cubist influence. Alternatively, head up **rue du Dr-Blanche** for the cool, rectilinear lines of Cubist architects Le Corbusier and Mallet-Stevens (see p.217).

Musée de Radio-France

116 av du Président Kennedy, 16ᵉ • ☎ 01 56 40 15 16, ⓦ radiofrance.fr • Ⓜ Ranelagh /RER Av-du-Prés-Kennedy–Maison-de-Radio-France

The **Maison de Radio-France**, the national radio headquarters, puts on free concerts in its two auditoriums (see p.318), and has a museum, the **Musée de Radio-France**, which illustrates the history of broadcasting, though it has been undergoing renovation, scheduled to reopen in 2017.

> ### AUTEUIL BUS ROUTES
>
> Handy **bus routes** for exploring Auteuil are the #52 and the #72. The #52 runs between Ⓜ Opéra in the centre and Ⓜ Boulogne-Pont-de-St-Cloud near the Parc des Princes, stopping at rue Poisson en route, while the #72's route extends between Ⓜ Hôtel-de-Ville in the Marais and Ⓜ Boulogne-Pont-de-St-Cloud, stopping en route by the Exelmans crossroads near some of Guimard's buildings on avenue de Versailles.

15

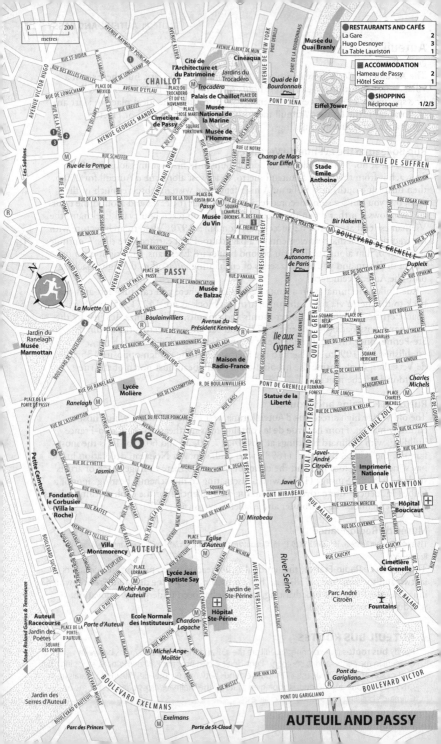

Villa La Roche

8–10 square du Dr-Blanche, 16ᵉ • Mon 1.30–6pm, Tues–Sat 10am–6pm; closed Aug • €8 • ☎ 01 42 88 75 72, ⓦ fondationlecorbusier.fr •
Ⓜ Jasmin; #52 bus

North of place Lorrain, in a cul-de-sac off rue du Dr-Blanche, are **Le Corbusier**'s first private
houses (1923), the Villa Jeanneret and the Villa La Roche, now in the care of the Fondation
Le Corbusier. You can visit **Villa La Roche**, which was built in strictly Cubist style; it is very
plain with strip windows, the only extravagance a curved frontage. The interior, meanwhile,
is sparsely furnished, but originally the walls were hung with the outstanding collection of
modern art built up by the financier Raoul Albert La Roche, for whom the *villa* was built.
The walls are painted in soothing greys, creams and blues, colours that Le Corbusier was
fond of using in his easel painting. The two houses look commonplace enough now from
the outside, but were a great contrast with anything that had gone before, and once you're
inside La Roche, the spatial play still seems ground-breaking.

Rue Mallet-Stevens

Ⓜ Jasmin

Heading north along rue du Dr-Blanche and off to the right, you'll come to the tiny
rue Mallet-Stevens, built by the architect of the same name in Cubist style. The original
proportions of the houses were altered by the addition of three storeys in the 1960s,
but you can still see the architectural intention of sculpting the entire street space as a
cohesive unit. Continue to the end of rue du Dr-Blanche, turn left and then right onto
boulevard de Beauséjour; a shortcut immediately opposite rue du Ranelagh across the
disused Petite Ceinture rail line (see box, p.218) takes you to shady avenue Raphaël,
which runs alongside the pretty **Jardin du Ranelagh** (featuring a rather engaging sculpture
of the fabulist La Fontaine with an eagle and fox) and on to the Musée Marmottan.

Musée Marmottan

2 rue Louis-Boilly, 16ᵉ • Tues–Sun 10am–6pm, Thurs till 9pm • €11 • ☎ 01 44 96 50 33, ⓦ marmottan.fr • Ⓜ La Muette

The **Musée Marmottan** is best known for its excellent collection of **Monet paintings**,
bequeathed by the artist's son. Among them is *Impression, soleil levant*, a canvas from 1872
of a misty Le Havre morning, whose title the critics usurped to give the Impressionist
movement its name. There's also a dazzling selection of canvases from Monet's last years at
Giverny, showing the increasingly abstract quality of his later work, including several
Nymphéas (Water lilies), *Le Pont japonais*, *L'Allée des rosiers* and *Le Saule pleureur*, where
rich colours are laid on in thick, excited whorls and lines. The collection also features some
of Monet's contemporaries – Manet, Renoir and **Berthe Morisot**. Morisot, who lived most
of her life in Passy, is particularly well represented, with two rooms devoted to her work,
characterized by vigorous, almost aggressive, brushwork, seen to best effect in paintings
such as *Branches d'oranger* (1889) and *Dans le Jardin à Bougival* (1884).

In addition, the museum has a small and beautiful collection of thirteenth- to
sixteenth-century **manuscript illuminations** – look out for the decorated capital "R"
framing an exquisitely drawn portrait of St Catherine of Alexandria.

West of Auteuil

Attractive gardens west of Auteuil include the **Jardin des Serres d'Auteuil**, the municipal
greenhouses and gardens that supply Paris with its plants and flowers, as well as the
beautiful **Jardins Albert Kahn**, with pretty French and Japanese gardens and an
intriguing museum of early colour photos from around the world.

Jardin des Poètes and Jardin des Serres d'Auteuil

Jardin des Poètes Av du Général Sarrail • Daily 9am–6pm • Free Jardin des Serres d'Auteuil 3 av de la Porte d'Auteuil • Daily
10am–6pm, closes 5pm in winter • Free • Ⓜ Porte d'Auteuil

West of place de la Porte d'Auteuil lie two gardens: the **Jardin des Poètes**, with its

15

THE PETITE CEINTURE

The **Petite Ceinture** ("Little Belt"), a disused railway line, nearly 20 miles long, that circles the city, was built in the 1850s. Closed in the 1970s and abandoned to nature (and graffiti artists), the line has become overgrown with wild flowers and grasses, and provides a much-needed refuge for birds and butterflies. Seeing the potential of this "green corridor", the city council has opened up one or two stretches to the public and turned them into *sentiers natures*, or **nature trails**. The stretch in the 16ᵉ is just over 1km long and extends from boulevard Montmorency (the entrance is opposite no. 37; ⓂPorte d'Auteuil) to La Muette métro station (entrance opposite 27 bd de Beauséjour). Open in the daytime only, the path makes a nice getaway from the city, with an appealingly abandoned, rather secretive air. It meanders through trees and bushes, with grand apartment blocks just visible to either side. Another section that has been opened up recently lies in the 15ᵉ, between place Balard and rue Olivier de Serres, a stretch of 1.3km linking the Parc André-Citroën and Parc Georges-Brassens. Whether the rest of the railway line can be preserved as a green corridor looks rather precarious in the face of housing shortages and other urban demands. See ⓦparis.fr for more details.

entrance on avenue du Général Sarrail, and the adjoining **Jardin des Serres d'Auteuil**, entered either at 3 avenue de la Porte d'Auteuil or via the Jardin des Poètes. You can't escape the traffic noise completely, but the Jardin des Poètes is extremely tranquil and very informal. Famous French poets are remembered by verses (mostly of a pastoral nature) engraved on small stones surrounded by little flowerbeds, and a statue of Victor Hugo by **Rodin** stands in the centre. Approaching the Auteuil garden and the greenhouses (*serres*) from the Jardin des Poètes, you pass delightful potting sheds with rickety wooden blinds. Then you're into a formal garden, beautifully laid out around the big old-fashioned metal-frame greenhouses. Among them is a **palm house** containing two hundred tropical species and a greenhouse devoted entirely to flora rarely seen outside their native New Caledonia. Sadly, some of these greenhouses may be extinct soon if the French Tennis Federation gets its way; it is seeking to extend the neighbouring Roland Garros stadium into the gardens to create more tennis courts.

Stade Roland Garros and the Musée de la Fédération Française de Tennis

2 av Gordon Bennett, 16ᵉ • **Museum** Wed, Fri, Sat & Sun 10am–6pm • €8 • ☎ 01 47 43 48 48, ⓦ fft.fr/roland-garros/musee /le-musee-de-la-fft • ⓂPorte d'Auteuil

The **Stade Roland Garros**, beyond the Jardin des Serres d'Auteuil, is the venue for the French Open tennis championships (see p.321). Within it, the **Musée de la Fédération Française de Tennis** fills you in on the history of the game and its development from *jeu de paume*, or "real tennis"; Paris boasted over a hundred real tennis courts under Henri IV, while students in Orléans in 1656 spent so much time hitting a ball around that the only way to get them back to their studies was to close the courts down. Much of the museum is given over to photos and footage of mainly French tennis stars, such as René Lacoste and Yannick Noah. A multimedia centre shows archive films dating from 1897 to the present day.

Jardins et Musée Albert Kahn

10–14 rue du Port, Boulogne-Billancourt • Tues–Sun 11am–7pm, Oct–April till 6pm • €4 • ☎ 01 55 19 28 00, ⓦ albert-kahn.hauts-de -seine.net • ⓂBoulogne-Pont-de-St-Cloud/Marcel-Sembat

The **Jardins et Musée Albert Kahn**, in the suburb of Boulogne-Billancourt, consist of a very pretty garden and a small **museum** dedicated to temporary exhibitions of "*Les Archives de la Planète*" – photographs, many in colour, and films collected by banker and philanthropist Albert Kahn between 1909 and 1931. Kahn wanted to record human activities and ways of life that he knew would soon disappear forever. His aim in the design of the garden was to combine English, French, Japanese and other styles to demonstrate the possibility of a harmonious, peaceful world. It's an enchanting place, with rhododendrons and camellias under blue cedars, a rose garden, an espaliered orchard, a forest of Moroccan pines, streams with Japanese bridges beside pagoda teahouses, Buddhas and pyramids of pebbles. The gardens are currently being restored, though remain open, and a new building is being erected to house Kahn's photographs; there will also be a shop, restaurant and *salon de thé* when work is complete in 2017.

Passy

Northeast of Auteuil, the area around the old village of **Passy** offers scope for a good meandering walk. From **La Muette** métro, head east along the old high street, **rue de Passy**, past an eye-catching parade of boutiques, until you reach **place de Passy** and the crowded but leisurely café terrace of *Le Paris Passy*. From the *place*, stroll southeast along cobbled, pedestrianized **rue de l'Annonciation**, a pleasant blend of down-to-earth and genteel well-heeled that gives more of the flavour of old Passy. You may no longer be able to have your Bechstein repaired here or your furniture lacquered, but the food shops that now dominate the street have delectable displays guaranteed to make your mouth water.

15

Maison de Balzac

47 rue Raynouard, 16ᵉ • Tues–Sun 10am–6pm • Free • ☎ 01 55 74 41 80 • Ⓜ Passy /RER Av-du-Prés-Kennedy–Maison-de-Radio-France

The **Maison de Balzac** is a delightful little house with pale-green shutters and a decorative iron entrance porch, tucked down some steps in a tree-filled garden. Balzac moved to this secluded spot in 1840 in the hope of evading his creditors. He lived under a pseudonym, and visitors had to give a special password before being admitted. Should any unwelcome callers manage to get past the door, Balzac would escape via a back door and go to the river via a network of underground cellars. Well-known works he wrote here include *La Cousine Bette* and *Le Cousin Pons*.

The museum preserves his study, writing desk and monogrammed cafetiere (his writing stints could extend up to eighteen hours a day for weeks on end). One room is devoted to the development of ideas for a monument to Balzac, resulting in the famously blobby **Rodin** sculpture of the writer (installed on boulevard du Montparnasse), cartoon caricatures of which are on display. Other exhibits include letters to Mme Hanska, whom he eventually married after an eighteen-year courtship, and a complex family tree of around a thousand of the four thousand-plus characters that feature in his *Comédie Humaine*. Outside, the shady, serene, rose-filled **garden** is a pleasant place to dally on wrought-iron seats amid busts of Balzac.

Rue Berton and around

Ⓜ Passy/La Muette

Reached via steps that drop from rue Raynouard behind the Maison de Balzac, **rue Berton** is a cobbled path with gas lights still in place, blocked off by the heavy security of the **Turkish embassy**. The building is an early twentieth-century reconstruction of the seventeenth-century château that stood on this site, the **Hôtel de Lamballe**, once home to Marie-Antoinette's friend, the Princesse de Lamballe, who met a grisly fate at the hands of revolutionaries in 1792. Later, it became a private asylum where the pioneering Dr Blanche treated patients with nervous disorders. The poet Gérard de Nerval was admitted in 1854, driven insane partly by the task of translating Goethe's *Faust* into French. And in 1892, Guy de Maupassant, suffering serious mental illness brought on by syphilis, was committed; he died here a year later. Get a better view of the building from **rue d'Ankara**, reached by heading down avenue de Lamballe, then left into avenue du Général-Mangin.

Rue des Eaux and the Musée du Vin

Museum 5 square Charles Dickens, 16ᵉ • Tues–Sat 10am–6pm • €10, glass of wine €5 • ☎ 01 45 25 63 26, Ⓦ museeduvinparis.com • Ⓜ Passy

From rue d'Ankara, head northeast along avenue Marcel-Proust, turn right and then left onto rue Charles-Dickens and follow it until it hits rue des Eaux, where fashionable

Parisians came in the eighteenth century for the therapeutic benefits of the once-famous, iron-rich Passy waters. Today, the street is enclosed by a canyon of moneyed apartments that dwarf the eighteenth-century houses of **square Charles Dickens**. One of these houses, burrowing back into the cellars of a vanished fourteenth-century monastery that produced wine until the Revolution, holds the **Musée du Vin**, an exhibition of viticultural bits and bobs about as exciting as flat champagne, though the cellar bar is an atmospheric place for a glass of wine or lunch.

Bois de Boulogne

Ⓜ Porte Maillot/Porte Dauphine/bus #244

Designed by Baron Haussmann, the **Bois de Boulogne** was supposedly modelled on London's Hyde Park – though it's a very French interpretation. The *bois*, or "wood", of the name is somewhat deceptive, though the extensive parklands do contain remnants of the once-great Forêt de Rouvray. The Bois was the playground of the wealthy, especially in the nineteenth century, but today the area is a favoured haunt for prostitutes and kerb-crawlers who, despite an obvious police presence and night-time road closures, still do business along its periphery. A certain amount of crime accompanies the sex trade; this is no place for a midnight walk.

By day, however, the Bois de Boulogne is delightful. Entry to the park as a whole is free, but several attractions within it charge entry fees or open for limited times: the new **Fondation Louis Vuitton** contemporary art space; the **Jardin d'Acclimatation**, aimed at children (see p.349); the beautiful floral displays of the **Parc de Bagatelle**; and the

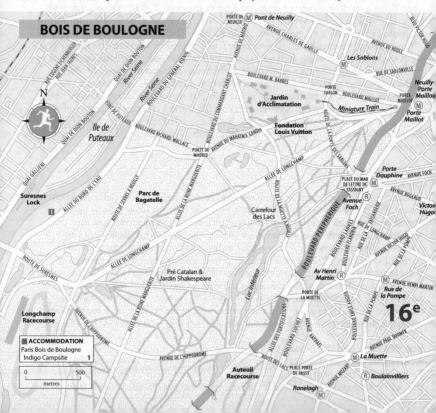

racecourses at Longchamp and Auteuil. There are 14km of **cycling** routes and **boating** on the Lac Inférieur, while the best, and wildest, part for **walking** is towards the southwest corner.

Fondation Louis Vuitton

8 av du Mahatma-Gandhi, Bois de Boulogne, 16ᵉ • Mon, Wed & Thurs 11am–8pm, Fri 11am–11pm, Sat & Sun 10am–8pm • €14, under-18s €5 (ticket includes entry to the adjoining Jardin d'Acclimatation) • ☎ 01 40 69 96 00, ⓦ fondationlouisvuitton.fr • ⓜ Les Sablons; rather than walk from the métro (10–15min) you could take the shuttle minibus (every 10–15min during museum opening hours; 5–10min; €1) from av de Friedland, just off place Charles de Gaulle (aka place de l'Etoile)

Rising amid the trees and greenery of the Bois de Boulogne is the dramatic, Frank Gehry-designed contemporary art centre, the **Fondation Louis Vuitton**, opened in 2014. It houses the collection of France's richest man, Bernard Arnault, head of the luxury goods empire LVMH. From the moment you approach the main entrance, above which gleams a conspicuous silver LV monogram, you get the impression of an extravagant building conceived with no expense spared. The huge, abstract structure, dubbed the "cloud of glass", consists of twelve glass "sails", made up of 3600 panels, and sits surrounded by a moat of water. Evoking a ship buffeted by the wind (or possibly a giant insect), the glass sails jut out at odd angles, revealing here and there the dazzling-white inner walls.

Exploring the **interior** is fun; escalators take you down to the moat level (or "grotto") with its striking Olafur Eliasson installation of coloured glass, mirror and sound, while stairways spiral up to several roof terraces revealing unexpected vistas of the Eiffel Tower and La Défense. There are eleven galleries, some vast, some intimate, an auditorium (used for music recitals), a restaurant and a shop. The building has an unfinished feel in places and there's a lot of empty space, something which Gehry says is deliberate, seeing it as a work in progress, with opportunities for artists to interact with the space and install artworks. The **exhibitions** held here so far augur well for the future quality of the offerings. The acclaimed exhibition in 2015, *Les Clefs d'une Passion*, for example, brought together masterpieces such as Matisse's *La Danse* and Munch's *The Scream*, both rarely loaned. The Fondation's **permanent collection**, shown in changing themed exhibitions, includes choice works by Rothko, Jeff Koons, Takashi Murakami, Richard Serra and Jean-Michel Basquiat.

Parc de Bagatelle

Bois de Boulogne • Daily: May–Sept 9.30am–8pm; Oct–April 9.30am–5.30pm • €6, free Nov–April • ⓜ Porte Maillot, then bus #244, which takes you to the entrance on allée de Longchamp; there's also an entrance on rte de Sèvres à Neuilly

The **Parc de Bagatelle** comprises garden styles ranging from French and English to Japanese. Its most famous feature, the stunning **rose garden** of the charming Château de Bagatelle, was designed and built in just over sixty days in 1775 as a wager between Comte d'Artois and his sister-in-law Marie-Antoinette, who said it could not be achieved in less than three months. The best time for the roses is June, while other parts of the garden see beautiful displays of tulips, hyacinths and daffodils in early April, irises in May and water lilies in early August. The park's attractive orangerie is the setting for candlelit recitals of Chopin's music during the Festival de Chopin in late June (see p.321).

Jardin Shakespeare

Bois de Boulogne • Daily 2–4pm • Free • ⓜ Porte Maillot

In the middle of the Bois de Boulogne, the Pré Catalan park is famous for its huge two-hundred-year-old copper beech tree and the prestigious *Pré Catalan* restaurant. Also here is the **Jardin Shakespeare**, where you can study the herbs, trees and flowers referred to in the Bard's plays; in summer, open-air Shakespearean works, French classics and plays for children are staged here.

15

VERSAILLES

The suburbs

To talk of "the suburbs", in French, doesn't at all have the same connotations as it does in English. In the imagination of those safely ensconced intra-muros, or within the historic centre defined by the old city walls, the banlieue is no sleepily conservative ring of dormitory towns, but a dangerous belt populated by thugs, rioters and gangs. It's true that politically, ethnically and economically, the outskirts of Paris are almost the reverse of the centre. The architecture of the banlieue is utterly different too, characterized by cités (high-rise housing estates) and industrial estates, with few historic vestiges – and little, at first glance, to attract visitors. The suburbs do have a handful of important sights, however, from opulent palaces to flea markets to gleaming skyscrapers.

Most easily accessible is the **St-Ouen market**, a treasure-trove of antiques and curios that sprawls just outside the official city limits north of Montmartre. North of here stands the proud basilica of **St-Denis**, which was the birthplace of the Gothic style and the burial place of almost all the French kings. To the west, meanwhile, the great suburban landmark is the **Grande Arche**, the huge centrepiece of Paris's modern business district, **La Défense**. Perhaps the most visited out-of-town destination, however, is **Versailles**, an overwhelming monument to the reigns of Louis XIV, who built it, and Louis XVI, whose furniture now fills it; the palace sits in its own vast landscaped park on the very edge of the Paris conurbation, southwest of the city. An elegant and far less visited alternative is the château of **Malmaison**, a little way north, which preserves the exquisite Empire furnishings of Napoleon's wife, Joséphine, along with her delightful gardens. Other than these, whether the various suburban museums deserve your attention will depend on your degree of interest in the subjects they cover: air and space travel or contemporary art at **Le Bourget**; modern art in Vitry-sur-Seine's **Mac/Val**; and the specialist collection of china at **Sèvres**.

Paris has traditionally kept its suburbs at arm's length, keeping its eyes shut and holding its nose, but in 2009, Nicolas Sarkozy revealed ambitious – or hubristic, depending on your point of view – plans for his presidential legacy. Paris would be transformed into an ecofriendly metropolis dubbed "**Le Grand Paris**" (see box, p.377), with easy transport connections between the suburbs and the centre. Since then, of course, there's been a change of government and an economic crisis. President Hollande didn't throw out the idea altogether, though, and came up with a rebranded, watered-down concept for a "nouveau Grand Paris". Today, while those transport links with central Paris are being improved, and areas like **Pantin** on the northeast edge of the city by the Canal Ourcq are drawing interest from digital and creative businesses, gentrification is a slow – and, as always with urban gentrification, a not uncontroversial – process.

All of the sights listed in this chapter are accessible by RER, métro and bus. Sights further afield, for which you'll need to take a train or have access to a car, are covered in Chapter 17.

St-Ouen flea market

Sat–Mon; different markets keep slightly different hours, but as a rule Sat & Sun 10am–5.30pm, Mon 11am–5pm • ⓦ marcheauxpuces -saintouen.com • ⓜ Porte de Clignancourt, from where it's a 5min walk up the busy av de la Porte-de-Clignancourt, passing under the *périphérique*, or ⓜ Garibaldi, from where you approach the market from the north, along rue Kléber, rue Edgar-Quinet and rue des Rosiers

The vast **St-Ouen market**, sometimes called the Clignancourt market, is located just outside the northern edge of the 18ᵉ arrondissement, in the suburb of St-Ouen. Its popular name of **les puces de St-Ouen**, or the "St-Ouen flea market", dates from the days when secondhand mattresses, clothes and other infested junk was sold here in a free-for-all zone outside the city walls. Nowadays, however, it's predominantly a proper – and generally expensive – **antiques** market, selling mainly furniture, but abounding in all sorts of fashionable junk like old zinc café counters, telephones, traffic lights, posters, vintage record players, jukeboxes and so on. Note that it's quieter on wet days and Mondays.

When walking from the Porte de Clignancourt métro, bear in mind that **rue Jean-Henri-Fabre**, shaded by the flyover, is the market's unofficial fringe area, lined with stalls flogging leather jackets, rip-off DVDs and African souvenirs. Watch your belongings, and don't fall for the guys pulling the three-card monte or cup-and-hidden-ball scams. For a quieter and scarcely slower approach, use Garibaldi station.

The markets

The official complex is a huge, sprawling area, with fourteen separate markets, covered and open air, and some two thousand shops. While you may not find any breathtaking bargains, prices aren't too bad for the smaller items, and the atmosphere provides plenty to enjoy. If time is short, focus on the following four: Marché **Vernaison** is the

16

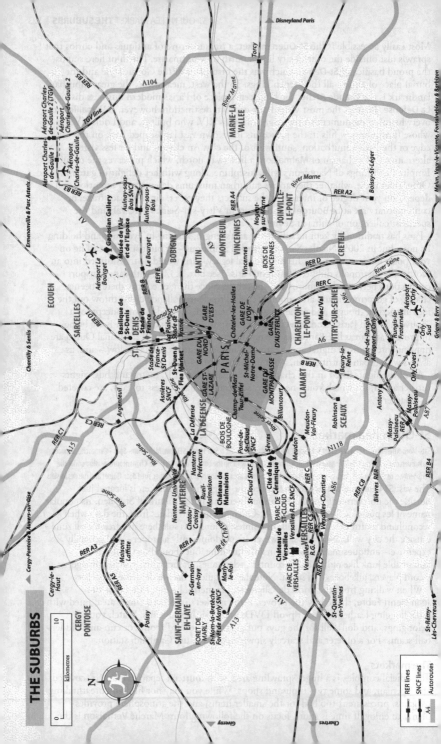

oldest in the complex, established in around 1920, and its maze-like, creeper-covered alleys are great fun to wander along, threading your way between stalls selling curios and bric-a-brac galore. Marché **Jules-Vallès** is smaller but similar, stuffed with books and records, vintage clothing, colonial knick-knacks and other curiosities. Marché **Malik** stocks mostly fashion – discount and vintage clothes and bags, as well as some couturier stuff – while the glazed roof of Marché **Dauphine** shelters an eclectic flea market mix of decorative antique furniture, vintage fashions, art, movie posters, rare books and comics, and a great vinyl/music section.

In the domed Marché **Malassis** little boutiques specialize in anything from maritime ephemera or jewellery to imaginatively restored eighteenth-century pieces and twentieth-century designer objets. For furnishings, the least expensive is Marché **Paul Bert-Serpette**, which offers furniture, china and the like, often unrestored and straight from the auction houses. Marché **Le Passage** has lots of fine furnishings and objets d'art, including new pieces by contemporary designers and aged gardenware – along with books, postcards and vintage clothes. The rest of the markets are seriously posh clusters of antiques shops, aimed more towards professionals than private clients. Marché **Biron** is the most luxurious of all, full of treasures from the seventeenth century onward. Marché **Antica** (mainly eighteenth- and nineteenth-century) and Marché **Cambo** are similar, the latter with an Art Deco area and some good Scandi stuff, while Marché **l'Entrepôt** houses large-scale antiques, from whole staircases to *boiserie* panelling and cast-iron gates. **L'Usine** and **Lécuyer** are restricted to dealers only.

Look out, too, for the **vintage village** courtyard space at 77 rue des Rosiers; the big hit here is **Habitat 64** (Sat & Sun 10am–6pm, Mon & Fri by appointment; ⓦhabitat.fr /vintage) an old warehouse selling some of the British store's iconic pieces from the Sixties, Seventies and Eighties.

EATING AND DRINKING   ST-OUEN MARKET

Chez Louisette Allée 10, Vernaison, 18ᵉ ⊕ 01 40 12 10 14; ⓜPorte de Clignancourt. An old-school *buvette* buried at the end of Marché Vernaison's Allée 10. The great gypsy jazz guitarist Django Reinhardt sometimes played here, but these days singers belt out Parisian *chanson* with keyboard backing every Sunday afternoon. The food, famously, is nothing special, and the fussed-up ambience won't be to all tastes, but it's a kitsch classic. Sat & Sun 10am–6pm, Mon 10.30am–5.30pm.

Ma Cocotte 106 rue des Rosiers, 18ᵉ ⊕ 01 49 51 70 00, ⓦmacocotte-lespuces.com; ⓜPorte de Clignancourt. Chichi, Philippe Starck-designed and -owned *Ma Cocotte* is a slightly incongruous presence on the shabby rue des Rosiers. The atmosphere is cosy if a little contrived, with an open kitchen, a cocktail bar and diners who want to see and be seen. Mains – bistro staples with modern twists, such as *coquillete* pasta with truffle butter and ham – start at around €20, though there are sharing plates, too,

starting at €14. Mon–Thurs noon–3pm & 7–10pm, Fri noon–3pm & 7–11pm, Sat 9am–11pm, Sun 9am–9.30pm.

La Recyclerie 83 bd Ornano, 18ᵉ ⊕ 01 42 57 58 49, ⓦlarecyclerie.com; ⓜPorte de Clignancourt. Where the cool kids off to market hang out, this vast, ramshackle old space, in an abandoned train station right by the métro, has a hint of Berlin or Brooklyn about it with its dilapidated decor and alternative vibe – it's all about recycling here, and yoga classes, plant sales, upcycling workshops and visits to urban farms are just some of the activities on offer. The weekend brunch (€20, €18 for veggies) is a good deal, including locavore dishes such as *pissaladière* or a Basque-style fricassee. Othewise grab a coffee or a fresh juice and settle down by the picture windows overlooking the old railway line – or, on sunny days, head out to the plant-shaded roof terrace. Mon–Wed noon–midnight, Thurs noon–1am, Fri & Sat noon–2am, Sun 11am–10pm.

St-Denis

For most of the twentieth century, **ST-DENIS**, 10km north of the centre of Paris and accessible by métro, was one of the most heavily industrialized communities in France, and a bastion of the Communist party. After the factories closed, unemployment spiralled and immigration radically altered the ethnic mix; for bourgeois Parisians, the political threat of the *banlieue rouge* ("red suburbs") became instead the social threat of what are now dubbed the *banlieue chaude* ("hot [or volatile] suburbs"). Visitors, however, are likely to find a poor but buoyant community, its pride buttressed by the town's twin attractions: the ancient **basilica of St-Denis** and the **Stade de France**, seat of the 1998 World Cup final.

Basilique de St-Denis

1 rue de la Légion d'Honneur, St-Denis • April–Sept Mon–Sat 10am–6.15pm, Sun noon–6.15pm; Oct–March Mon–Sat 10am–5pm, Sun noon–5.15pm; closed during weddings and funerals, and for extra services on feast days • €8.50, audioguide €4.50 • ⊕ 01 48 09 83 54, ⓦsaint-denis.monuments-nationaux.fr • ⓜ Basilique de St-Denis

The **Basilique de St-Denis** is the most important cathedral in France. This is where the French kings were both crowned (ever since Pepin the Short in 754) and buried (all but three since Hugues Capet, in 996); it is also where the Gothic architectural style was born. The building as it stands today was the twelfth-century masterpiece of unknown masons working under Abbot Suger, friend and adviser to kings. The west front and high, light-filled choir clearly made a deep impression on the bishops attending the dedication service – in the next half-century they went on to build most of the great Gothic cathedrals in France on its pattern. The innovative design can still be traced in the lowest storey of the choir, notably the ambulatory space, which allowed pilgrims to process easily around the relics held in the choir. The novel rib vaulting allowed the walls to be no more than an infilling between a stone skeleton, making huge, luminous windows possible. Today, the upper storeys of the choir are still airier than they were in Suger's day, having been rebuilt in the mid-thirteenth century, at the same time as the nave. A good way to appreciate the atmosphere in the basilica is during the

16

St-Denis Festival (usually throughout June; ⓦfestival-saint-denis.com), when it plays host to top-flight classical concerts, with an emphasis on choral music.

The necropolis

You enter the **necropolis** via a separate entrance in the south portal. Immediately on the left is the bizarre sight of the bare feet of **François 1ᵉʳ** and his wife Claude de France peeking out of their enormous Renaissance memorial. Beside the steps to the ambulatory lies **Charles V**, the first king to have his funeral effigy carved from life, on the day of his coronation in 1364. Alongside him is his wife Jeanne de Bourbon, clutching the sack of her own entrails to her chest – a reminder that royalty was traditionally eviscerated at death, the flesh boiled away from the bones and buried separately.

The **ambulatory** itself is a beautiful double-aisled design raised on the revolutionary pointed or ogival vaults, and richly lit by some of St-Denis' original stained glass, including the famous Tree of Jesse window immediately behind the altar. Just up the south steps and around to the right, a florid Louis XVI and a busty **Marie-Antoinette** – often graced by bouquets of flowers – kneel in prayer; the pious scene was sculpted in 1830, long after their execution.

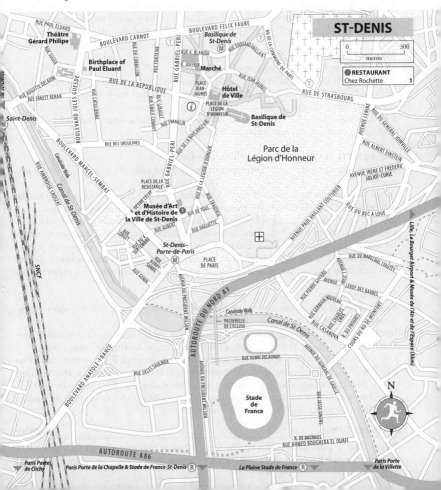

THE LEGEND OF ST DENIS

The first church at St-Denis was probably founded by an early (mid-third-century) Parisian bishop known by the name of St-Denis, or **St Dionysius** in English. The legend goes that after he was decapitated for his beliefs at Montmartre – supposedly so-called because it is the "Mount of the Martyr" – he picked up his own head and walked all the way to St-Denis, thereby indicating the exact spot where his abbey should be built. It's not in fact all that far – just over 5km – though as a friend of Edward Gibbon's once remarked, "The distance is nothing, it's the first step that counts".

On the north side of the ambulatory you pass the effigy of the sixth-century king **Clovis I**, a canny little German who wiped out Roman Gaul and turned it into France, with Paris for a capital. His effigy was actually executed some six hundred years after his death; alongside is another Merovingian, Childebert I, whose twelfth-century effigy is the earliest in the basilica. On the right of the northern steps, the tomb of **Henri II** and **Catherine de Médicis** was boldly designed by Primaticcio in the style of a Classical temple: kneeling on top are sculptures by Germain Pilon of the royal couple as living souls; down below, you can just see their soulless, decaying corpses. Just beyond is the memorial to **Louis XII** and **Anne de Bretagne**; again, if you look past the graceful Renaissance structure and allegorical figures you'll see the pain-wracked bodies of the royal couple.

Marché St-Denis

Place Jean-Jaurès • Tues, Fri & Sun 8am–2.30/3pm • ⓂBasilique de St-Denis

The **Marché St-Denis**, held in and around the main place Jean-Jaurès, has hundreds of stalls peddling vegetables at half the price of central Parisian markets, as well as cheap curios, clothes and fabrics. The covered *halles*, near the square just off rue Dupont, are a multiethnic affair where the produce on the butchers' stalls – ears, feet, tails and bladders – shows this is not rich folks' territory.

Musée d'Art et d'Histoire de la Ville de St-Denis

22bis rue Gabriel-Péri • Mon, Wed & Fri 10am–5.30pm, Thurs 10am–8pm, Sat & Sun 2–6.30pm • €5 • ☎ 01 42 43 05 10 • ⓂSt-Denis–Porte de Paris

About five minutes' walk south of the St-Denis basilica is the distinctly left-leaning **Musée d'Art et d'Histoire de la Ville de St-Denis**, housed in a former Carmelite convent. The quickest route is along rue de la Légion d'Honneur. The exhibits on display are not of spectacular interest, though the local archeology collection is good, and there are some intriguing paintings of industrial landscapes and an exhibition on the Communist poet Paul Eluard, native son of St-Denis. The one unique collection is of documents relating to the **Commune**: posters, cartoons, broadsheets, paintings, plus an audiovisual presentation.

Stade de France

Rue Francis de Pressensé • April–Aug daily; Sept–March Tues–Sun • Up to four English-language tours a day (1hr; €15) • ☎ 08 92 70 09 00, Ⓦ stadefrance.com • ⓂSt-Denis–Porte de Paris

Just beyond the métro stop St-Denis–Porte de Paris (or ten minutes further down rue Gabriel-Péri from the Musée d'Art et d'Histoire), a broad footbridge crosses the motorway and Canal St-Denis to the **Stade de France**, scene of France's first (and so far only) World Cup victory in 1998. At least €430 million was spent on the construction of this stadium, whose elliptical structure is best appreciated at night when lit up. If there isn't a match or a mega-event on, you can take a tour that explores the grounds, changing rooms, the VIP stands and a small museum.

INFORMATION   ST-DENIS

Tourist office St-Denis' tourist office is opposite the basilica at 1 rue de la République. It sells tickets for the St-Denis Festival (see p.227) and can provide maps of the town (April–Sept Mon–Sat 9.30am–1pm & 2–6pm,

Sun 10am–1 & 2–6pm; Oct–March Mon–Sat 9.30am–1pm & 2–6pm, Sun 10am–2pm; ☎01 55 87 08 70, Ⓦsaint-denis-tourisme.com; Ⓜ Basilique de St-Denis).

EATING

Chez Rochette 20 rue Gabriel-Péri ☎01 42 43 71 44; Ⓜ St-Denis–Porte de Paris. You'll find nothing fancy at this simple restaurant, near the museum, just good, old-fashioned French cooking – *terrines*, *poulet*, foie gras – at reasonable prices. Tues & Wed noon–3pm, Thurs–Sat noon–3pm & 7–10pm.

La Défense

Ⓜ/RER La Défense/Ⓜ Esplanade de la Défense

A thicket of glass and concrete towers, **La Défense**, just west of the city, is Paris's prestige **business district**. More than a hundred thousand people commute here daily during the week, and, with its shopping centres and cinemas it's often a popular and animated place at weekends, too – at least by day. Landmark buildings include the sleek elliptical **Tour EDF**, the **Tour Majunga**, with its radically "flowing" effect, and **Tour First** on the place des Saisons, which, at 231m, is France's tallest skyscraper (though still shorter than the Eiffel Tower). If buildings aren't your thing you may prefer the sixty-odd monumental **outdoor sculptures** – including works by Miró, Alexander Calder and César – scattered throughout the district.

The main artery of La Défense is the pedestrianized **Esplanade du Général de Gaulle**; you can pick up maps at **Info Défense**, an information centre on the main place de la Défense that also has a few exhibits about the development of the district (Mon–Fri 9am–6pm, Sat & Sun 10am–5pm; free; ☎01 47 74 84 24, Ⓦladefense.fr). The oldest work of art is nearby: Barrias's bronze **La Défense de Paris**, dating from the 1880s and depicting a soldier defending a young, rather powerful-looking woman who symbolizes Paris. It commemorates the defence of the city against the Prussians in 1870 and is the origin of the district's name.

La Grande Arche

Roof daily 10am–8pm • €10 • ☎01 49 07 27 55, Ⓦgrandearche.com • Ⓜ/RER La Défense/Ⓜ Esplanade de la Défense

Built in 1989 to honour the bicentenary of the Revolution, and in conscious tribute to the Arc de Triomphe, **La Grande Arche** is an astounding structure: a 112m, white

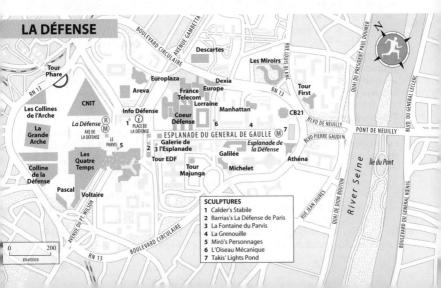

marble, hollow cube that's large enough to enclose Notre-Dame with ease. It closes the western axis of the Voie Triomphale (see p.62), albeit positioned at a slight angle so as to allow an uninterrupted view from its offices all the way to the Louvre's similarly askew Cour Carrée, 8km away. The architect was a little-known Danish professor, Johann Otto von Spreckelsen, who died before the arch's completion. The only thing that slightly mars its perfect form – or softens its brutality, depending on your point of view – is the lift scaffolding and a fibreglass "cloud" canopy, suspended within the hollow. There are excellent **views** from the steps that lead up to the base of the arch: down the Voie Triomphale to the city and along a second axis that leads through the Eiffel Tower and Tour Montparnasse; you can also take the glass elevator to the **roof** of the arch, where there is also a small, rather lacklustre museum of computers and video games.

For the most dramatic approach it's worth getting off a stop before the closest station (La Défense), métro Esplanade de la Défense, from where it's a twenty-minute walk.

Château de Malmaison

Rueil-Malmaison • April–Sept Mon & Wed–Fri 10.30am–12.30pm & 1.15–5.45pm, Sat & Sun 10.30am–12.30pm & 1.15–6.15pm; Oct–March Mon & Wed–Fri 10.30am–12.30pm & 1.30–5.15pm, Sat & Sun 10.30am–12.30pm & 1.15–5.45pm • €6.50 • ☎ 01 41 29 05 55, ⓦ chateau-malmaison.fr • ⓜ /RER La Défense, then bus #258 from the bus station (every 30min; 25min) towards St-Germain-en-Laye; from Le Château stop, walk 100m back up av Bonaparte, cross over and take the signposted side road (a 10min walk in all)

According to Napoleon's private secretary, the **Château de Malmaison**, 15km west of central Paris, was "the only place next to the battlefield where he was truly himself". It was the home, after all, of his beloved Joséphine de Beauharnais, who shaped it as a perfect example of the cool First Empire style. After their divorce – Joséphine failed to provide the emperor with an heir – she stayed on, receiving just two visits from the emperor there before her death in 1814.

Visitors today can see the stately **official apartments**, on the ground floor, which are preserved almost exactly as they were in Joséphine's day. The design fashions reflect imperial interests in Italy and Egypt – which Napoleon was busy conquering at the time Joséphine first began her interior design works here, in 1799. The cloth-hung Salle du Conseil, where Napoleon had ministerial meetings, feels like a luxurious version of a campaign tent; it's now overlooked by a reproduction of Gérard's heartbreakingly lovely portrait of Joséphine, the original of which hangs in the Hermitage. The dining room owes its decor to fashionable interest in Pompeii, and still contains the fabulous, eighty-piece gold dinner service used by the Empress. During the Nazi occupation, the imperial chair in the library was rudely violated by the fat buttocks of Reichsmarschall Goering, dreaming perhaps of promotion or the conquest of Egypt. On the top floor, a permanent **exhibition** shows off a more intimate side of the house's history. You can see Joséphine's collections and effects, including the most personal: her slippers, stockings, lace bonnet and petticoats, along with Napoleon's toothbrush.

The park and rose gardens

In Joséphine's time, Malmaison was renowned for its **gardens**, which nurtured scores of exotic species that had never before flowered in France, such as hibiscus, camellia and the heavenly magnolia soulangeana. They are still very lovely today. Behind the house extends a fine park in the English style, cut through by a picturesque stream and dotted with landmark trees – including a cedar of Lebanon planted by the imperial couple themselves, in 1800. On either side of the front courtyard stand two **roseries**, a distant echo of Malmaison's legendary collections from the latter half of the nineteenth century. (The question of whether there were roses here in Joséphine's own time, incidentally, is something of a historical mystery, but popular legend has it that the Empress cultivated scores of them herself.) The Roseraie moderne on the north side

16

LA DÉFENSE (P.229) >

features repeat-flowering varieties; the Roseraie ancienne, on the south side, has precious old varieties that flower just once, in June.

Versailles

RER Versailles-Château

Twenty kilometres southwest of Paris, the town of Versailles has grown up around the **Château de Versailles**, the vast palace built for Louis XIV. Consumed with envy of his finance minister's château at Vaux-le-Vicomte (see p.241), the king was determined to outdo him. He recruited the same design team – architect Le Vau, painter Le Brun and gardener Le Nôtre – and ordered something a hundred times the size. With its 700 rooms, 67 staircases and 352 fireplaces, Versailles is the apotheosis of French regal indulgence. While the self-aggrandizing decor of the "Sun King" is astonishing, its park and gardens are also a delight, and shouldn't be overlooked. That said, while it's possible to see the whole complex in one day, it's undeniably tiring, so it's best to pick and choose and plan with care (see p.234).

Château de Versailles

W chateauversailles.fr • RER Versailles-Château

Under its founder and master, Louis XIV, the **Château de Versailles** was the headquarters of every arm of the state, and the entire court of around 3500 nobles lived in the palace – in a state of unhygienic squalor, according to contemporary accounts. Construction began in 1664 and lasted virtually until Louis XIV's death in 1715, after which the château was abandoned for a few years before being reoccupied by Louis XV in 1722. It remained a residence of the royal family until the Revolution of 1789, when the furniture was sold and the pictures dispatched to the Louvre. Thereafter Versailles fell into ruin until Louis-Philippe established his giant museum of French Glory here; it still exists, though most is mothballed. In 1871, during the Paris Commune, the château became the seat of the nationalist government, and the French parliament continued to meet in Louis XV's opera building until 1879. Restoration only began in earnest between the two world wars, but today it proceeds apace, the château's management scouring the auction houses of the world in the search for original furnishings from Louis XVI's day. Ironically, they have been helped in the task by the efforts of the revolutionaries, who inventoried all the palace's furnishings before they were auctioned off in 1793–94.

Grands Appartements

Tues–Sun: April–Oct 9am–6.30pm; Nov–March 9am–5.30pm • €15, including audioguide, or included in the Passeport Versailles (see p.234); free for under-18s and EU residents under 26

The rooms you can visit without a guide are known as the **Grands Appartements**, and were used for all the king's official business – which meant all his daily life, as Louis XIV was an institution as much as a private individual. His risings and sittings, comings and goings, were minutely regulated and rigidly encased in ceremony, attendance at which was an honour much sought after by courtiers. The route leads past the **royal chapel**, a grand structure that ranks among France's finest Baroque creations. From there, a procession of gilded drawing rooms leads to the king's throne room and the dazzling **Galerie des Glaces** (Hall of Mirrors), where the Treaty of Versailles was signed after World War I. Under the golden barrel ceiling, with its paintings by Charles Le Brun showing the glories of Louis XIV, Georges Clemenceau finally won his notorious "war guilt" clause, which blamed the entire conflict on German aggression. The *galerie* is best viewed at the end of the day, when the crowds have departed and the setting sun floods it from the west, across the park. More fabulously rich rooms, this time belonging to the **queen's apartments**, line the northern wing, beginning with the queen's bedchamber, which has been restored exactly as it was in its last refit of 1787, with hardly a surface unadorned with gold leaf. At the end of the visit, the staircase leads down to the **Hall of Battles,** whose oversize canvases unashamedly blow the trumpet for France's historic military victories; be thankful that most of the rest of Louis-Philippe's historical museum is out of bounds.

The park and gardens

Gardens daily: April–Oct 8am–8.30pm; Nov–March 8am–6pm; park daily: April–Oct 7am–8.30pm; Nov–March 8am–6pm • Free, or €9/€8/€24 during spectacles (see below) • The petit train shuttles between the terrace in front of the château and the Trianons (€7.50 hop-on hop-off ticket for the full 5km loop); it runs about every 15min in summer

You could spend the whole day just exploring the **gardens** at Versailles. Beyond the great Water Parterres designed by André Le Nôtre, with their statues symbolizing the rivers of France, geometrically planned walks and gardens stretch out on all sides. There are countless statues of nymphs and gods, 50 fountains, 34 pools and of course the cruciform Grand Canal, on which entire naval battles were re-created for the amusement of the court. The outer limits of the estate are known as the **park**, and are made up of woods and fields grazed by sheep; the northernmost area is part of the Domaine de Marie-Antoinette (see below), and visitable on a separate ticket.

Domaine de Marie-Antoinette

Château de Versailles park • Tues–Sun: April–Oct noon–6.30pm; Nov–March noon–5.30pm • €10 (buy tickets from domaine entrance rather than at the palace entrance), or included in the Passeport Versailles, which has to be bought at palace entrance (see p.234); free for under-18s and EU residents under 26

Hidden away in the northern reaches of the park is the **Domaine de Marie-Antoinette** (Marie-Antoinette's estate), the queen's country retreat, centred on the Petit Trianon palace, where she could find some relief from the stifling atmosphere and etiquette of the court. Here she commissioned some dozen or so buildings, sparing no expense and imposing her own style and tastes throughout (and gaining herself a reputation for extravagance that wouldn't do her any favours in the long run). She also had a bucolic park created in the fashionable English style, and a miniature farm. The Swiss watchmakers Breguet have been responsible for much of the restoration of the estate, reviving a link with the queen that goes back to 1783 when Breguet's founder was commissioned to make her a watch with workings so complex that it was never completed in her lifetime.

16

Petit Trianon

The estate's centrepiece is the elegant and restrained Neoclassical **Petit Trianon** palace, built by Gabriel in the 1760s for Louis XV's mistress, Madame de Pompadour, and given to Marie-Antoinette by her husband Louis XVI as a wedding gift. The interior

---

VERSAILLES SPECTACLES

On the busiest days of the year, the Versailles gardens play host to what the French call a "*spectacle*": that is, the authorities turn the fountains on while piped classical music booms out all around. The dates are complex, and worth checking online, but broadly the **Grandes Eaux Musicales** run on weekends and bank holidays from April to October, with Tuesdays added in late May and June; they occur between 11am–noon & 3.30–5.30pm (or 11am–noon & 2.30–4pm on the Tuesday dates). The less exciting **Jardins Musicaux** features the piped music without the fountains, and takes place on Tuesdays, from April to mid-May and then from July to late October (10am–6.30pm). Tickets for the Grandes Eaux Musicales cost €9, or €8 for the Jardins Musicaux; on days they occur they are included in the Passeports Versailles (see p.234).

For the **Grandes Eaux Nocturnes**, the fountains and gardens are sumptuously lit up with colourful effects and lasers. This event runs on Saturdays from mid-June to mid-September, starting at 8.30pm and with a firework show at 10.50pm; the ticket costs a spectacular €24. It's preceded by a separate spectacle dubbed **La Sérénade**, in which musicians and dancers perform in the Galerie des Glaces (6.30pm, 6.50pm, 7.10pm, 7.30pm and 7.50pm; €17, €39 combined with the Grandes Eaux Nocturnes).

boasts a fine stone-and-wrought-iron staircase, sculpted wood panelling, period furniture and the intriguing *cabinet des glaces montantes*, the queen's elegant pale blue salon, fitted with sliding mirrors that could be moved by a sophisticated mechanism to conceal the windows, creating a more intimate space.

Grand Trianon

Included in the ticket for the Domaine de Marie-Antoinette is the Italianate, pink-marble **Grand Trianon** palace, a little to the west, designed by Hardouin-Mansart in 1687 as a "country retreat" for Louis XIV. Its two wings are linked by a colonnaded portico, with formal gardens to the rear. Napoleon stayed here intermittently between 1805 and 1813 and had the interior refurbished in Empire style. Nowadays it's often used by the French president when entertaining foreign dignitaries.

The formal gardens and Hameau de la Reine

West of the Petit Trianon are the formal gardens (**Jardins à la française**), dotted with pavilions such as the octagonal **Pavillon français** with its gold and marble interior and frieze of sculpted swans, ducks and other wildfowl – which would have been farmed on the estate. More impressive still is the deceptively plain-looking **Petit Théâtre**, built for the queen in 1778–79, where Marie-Antoinette would regularly perform, often dressed as a maid or shepherdess, before the king and members of her inner circle. To the east lies the impossibly bucolic **Jardin anglais**, with its little winding stream, grassy banks dotted with forget-me-nots and daisies, classical temple (Le Temple d'Amour), fake waterfall and grotto with belvedere. Further east again lies the equally enchanting, if rather bizarre, **Hameau de la Reine**, a play village and thatch-roofed farm where Marie-Antoinette could indulge her fashionable Rousseau-inspired fantasies of returning to the "natural" life.

ARRIVAL AND INFORMATION   CHÂTEAU DE VERSAILLES

By train To get to Versailles, take the RER line C5 from Champs de Mars or another Left Bank station to Versailles–Château (40min; €7.10 return); turn right out of the station then take the first left onto av de Paris, which leads to the palace – an 8min walk.

Opening times The château is open throughout the year, except on Mondays, public holidays and during occasional state events. We've given individual opening hours for each attraction within the account in this Guide.

Tickets and passes There are several types of ticket available. If you've got limited time, or are not keen on being on your feet for long periods, then you're probably best off buying separate tickets to the Grands Appartements of the château and Marie-Antoinette's estate (including the Trianons) according to what you want to see; we've quoted the price details for each attraction within our account. If you've got lots of time, or want to see everything, then it's worth going for a Passeport Versailles, a one- or two-day pass that gives access to all the main sights (€18 one day/€25 two consecutive days; €25/€30 on *spectacle* days). All tickets and passes – except for the *spectacles* (see p.233) – are free to under-18s and EU residents under 26, year round; head straight to Entrance A with proof of your status.

Crowds, queues and saving time Whatever the time of year, Versailles can get extremely crowded and the queues can be very long (lasting several hours at peak times – between 10am and 3pm, particularly on weekends and Tuesdays). There are certain things you can do to reduce your queuing time but unfortunately a degree of waiting is inevitable as security is strict. Buying tickets online at ⓦ chateauversailles.fr or ⓦ fnactickets.com is a good option; alternatively, pick them up from any branch of Fnac (see p.332) or at the Versailles town tourist office, near the entrance to the palace at 2bis av de Paris (April–Oct Mon 10am–6pm, Tues–Sun 9am–7pm; Nov–March Sun & Mon 11am–5pm, Tues–Sat 9am–6pm; ☏01 39 24 88 88, ⓦ versailles-tourisme.com). You can then head straight to Entrance A for admission. It's best to avoid the Grands Appartements at the busiest times; being packed in like sardines really diminishes the effect of some of the most popular spaces, such as the Hall of Mirrors. The ideal route to avoid the worst of the crowds would be to head for the gardens and park between 9am and noon, leaving the main palace to the tour buses, following that with the Trianon palaces and Marie-Antoinette's hamlet, and leaving the palace interior until last, ideally after 4.30pm or so.

Getting around Distances in the park are considerable. Shuttles run a 5km loop around the complex between the château and the Trianons (every 15min in summer; €7.50 hop-on hop-off ticket), with a soothing background of classical music; these can be a great help on hot or wet days or if you are covering a lot of ground. You can rent bikes at the Grille de la Reine, Porte St-Antoine and by the Grand Canal, and boats on the Grand Canal, next to a pair of café-restaurants. Electric vehicles are available for rent (€32/hour) for those with reduced mobility.

Guided tours Various guided tours (from €7), including English-language tours, are available, taking you to wings of the palace that can't otherwise be seen; some can be booked online in advance, while still more are bookable in the morning at the information point – turn up reasonably

early to be sure of a place – or via the Versailles town tourist office, near the entrance to the palace (see opposite). It's worth taking at least one tour, if only for the guides' well-informed commentaries – though some anecdotes should be taken with a pinch of salt.

Gardens Note that it is possible to visit the gardens only (see opposite).

Refreshments There are a number of snack and drinks carts, cafés and restaurants dotted around the grounds.

Versailles town

The town of **VERSAILLES** (Ⓦversailles-tourisme.com) sits right up against the château gates. Its centrepiece is **place Notre-Dame**, which has a lively food market (Tues, Fri & Sun 7am–2pm). The surrounding streets are full of buzzy cafés, and the little cobbled **rue du Bailliage** and adjoining **passage de la Geôle** are lined with antique shops (Ⓦantiques-versailles.com), selling anything from tin soldiers to books, paintings and ceramics. Versailles is a markedly conservative town, but it does preserve a building dear to the heart of Republicans, the **Salle du Jeu de Paume**, rue du Jeu de Paume. It was at this tennis court, built for the royals in 1686, that the representatives of the Third Estate set the Revolution in progress in 1789, and sealed the fate of the French monarchy; a small museum (April–Oct Tues–Sun 2–5.45pm; free) celebrates the event.

Potager du Roi

10 rue du Maréchal Joffre • Jan–March Tues & Thurs 10am–6pm; April–Oct Tues–Sun 10am–6pm; Nov & Dec Tues & Thurs 10am–6pm, Sat 10am–1pm • April–Oct Tues–Fri €4.50, Sat & Sun €7; Nov–March €3 • ☎ 01 39 24 62 62, Ⓦ potager-du-roi.fr • RER Versailles–Château

To reach the **Potager du Roi**, or king's kitchen-garden, turn right as you exit the Château de Versailles' main gate and it's a five-minute signposted walk away. Put aside any thoughts of allotments: this is a walled area the size of a small farm. It was run by Louis XIV's head gardener, Jean-Baptiste La Quintinie, who managed to produce strawberries and melons in March and asparagus in December, and gave the king gardening lessons. Today, a statue of the great man – La Quintinie, that is – stands on the raised terrace watching over his plot, a great sunken square of espaliered fruit trees and geometrically arranged vegetables in the lee of the stately church of St-Louis. Some of the 150 varieties of apples and pears, and fifty types of vegetables, are sold in the little farm shop.

Grand Ecurie du Roy

Av Rockefeller • **Horse shows** Feb–July Sat 6pm, Sun 3pm • €25 • **Training sessions** Sun 11.15am plus occasional extra days • €12 • ☎ 01 39 02 62 75, Ⓦ academequestre.fr • RER Versailles–Château

Opposite the main entrance to the Château de Versailles, the **Grand Ecurie du Roy**, or royal stables, housed six hundred horses under Louis XIV. It's now the home of the **Académie du Spectacle Equestre**, which puts on highly choreographed theatrical shows of horsemanship. You can also watch the horses being put through their paces at weekly morning **training sessions**.

Sèvres – Cité de la Céramique

2 place de la Manufacture, Sèvres • Daily except Tues 10am–5pm • €6 • ☎ 01 46 29 22 00, Ⓦ sevresciteceramique.fr • Ⓜ Pont de Sèvres, then cross the bridge and spaghetti junction on foot; the museum is the massive building facing the riverbank on your right – an alternative approach would be to take a métro to Ⓜ Boulogne-Pont de St-Cloud and head due south for about 2.5km through the Parc de St-Cloud

Around 10km southwest of Paris, the ceramic factory at **SÈVRES** has been manufacturing some of the world's most renowned **porcelain** since the eighteenth century. The original style, with its painted coloured birds, ornate gilding and rich polychrome enamels, was so beloved by Louis XV's mistress, Madame de Pompadour, that two new colours, *rose Pompadour* and *bleu de roi*, were named after the couple

16

in 1757. The compliment paid off: two years later, when the factory fell into financial trouble, the king bought up all the shares to guarantee its future, and it remained in royal hands until the Revolution. The site is now the **Cité de la Céramique**, which continues to operate as a factory while also housing one of the largest collections in the world, with fifty thousand pieces. Inevitably, displays centre on Sèvres ware, but there are also collections of Islamic, Chinese, Italian, German, Dutch and English pieces, and regular temporary exhibitions. Note there is very little information in English, so this is really an attraction for true fans and experts.

Mac/Val

Place de la Libération, Vitry-sur-Seine, 7.5km south of Paris • Tues–Fri 10am–6pm, Sat & Sun noon–7pm • €5 • ☎ 01 43 91 64 20, Ⓦ macval.fr • Ⓜ Porte de Choisy then bus #183 (the bus stop is right by the métro entrance on av de Choisy), direction Orly Terminal Sud, and get off at the Musée Mac/Val stop (a 15min journey)

The **Musée d'Art Contemporain du Val-de-Marne (Mac/Val)**, south of Paris in Vitry-sur-Seine, is a sleek, icebox-white slice of architectural contemporary cool, incongruously deposited in the suburbs. With its edgy exhibitions of French art since 1950, drawn from a distinguished, two-thousand-piece-strong collection, it consistently lures Parisians away from the centre for their modern-art fix. Artists exhibited here include Daniel Buren, Jean Dubuffet, Robert Doisneau, video artists Jean-Luc Vilmouth and Pierre Huyghe, and Christian Boltanski, known for his large-scale installations on themes related to the Holocaust. Temporary exhibitions also showcase international artists, such as the Danish artist Jesper Just, Indian Shilpa Gupta, British Mark Wallinger and Spanish Esther Ferrer. There's a well-stocked bookshop and a restaurant.

Le Bourget airport

5km east of St-Denis • Ⓜ La Courneuve\RER Le Bourget (from Gare du Nord); from either metro or RER station, take bus #152 to the museum

Until the development of Orly in the 1950s, **Le Bourget** airport, a short hop up the A1 motorway from St-Denis, was Paris's principal gateway, and is closely associated with the exploits of pioneering aviators – Lindbergh landed here after his epic first flight across the Atlantic. Today Le Bourget is used only for domestic flights, with a museum of powered flight, the **Musée de l'Air et de l'Espace** (Tues–Sun: April–Sept 10am–6pm; Oct–March 10am–5pm; €8–20 depending on how many interactive experiences you choose; ☎ 01 49 92 70 00, Ⓦ museeairespace.fr) occupying some of the older buildings.

Gagosian Gallery

26 av de l'Europe • Tues–Sat 11am–7pm • Free • ☎ 01 48 16 16 47, Ⓦ gagosian.com • RER from Gare du Nord to Le Bourget station, then bus #152 to Chemin de Notre Dame stop

In 2012, perhaps hoping to lure in rich collectors as they hop off their private jets, renowned international art dealer Larry Gagosian opened a huge art gallery in one of Le Bourget airport's old concrete hangars. The **Gagosian Gallery**, designed by star architect Jean Nouvel and ideal for large installations, exhibits work by artists such as Anselm Kiefer, John Calder and Jean Prouvé.

16

WATER LILIES AT GIVERNY

Day-trips from Paris

In the further reaches and beyond the boundaries of Ile-de-France lie exceptional towns and sights that are still accessible as day-trips from Paris, and are worth making the effort to visit. An excursion to Chartres can seem a long way to go for a building; but then you'd have to go a very long way indeed to find a building to beat it, and there are other attractions in the charming town. Of the châteaux that abound in this region, we describe only a select few: Chantilly, with its wonderful art collection and beautiful gardens; Vaux-le-Vicomte, the envy of Louis XIV; and Fontainebleau, the most elegant of Renaissance palaces. Monet's garden at Giverny, meanwhile, the inspiration for all the artist's water lily canvases, is perennially popular; it's bright and vibrant in spring, hauntingly melancholy in autumn.

17

Chantilly

People mostly visit **CHANTILLY**, a small town 40km north of Paris, to watch horses race and to see the astonishing collection of Italian art in the romantic **château**, which rises from the centre of a lake amid a forested park. The **horses** are hard to miss: scores of thoroughbreds can be seen thundering along the forest rides of a morning, and two of the season's classiest flat races are held here – the Jockey Club and the Prix de Diane, held on the first and second Sunday in June.

Domaine de Chantilly

Rue du Connétable • Nov–March (sometimes closed throughout Jan) daily except Tues 10.30am–5pm (grounds 6pm); April–Oct daily 10am–6pm (grounds 8pm); English-language guided tours of the Duc and Duchesse d'Aumale's private apartments daily 3.30pm (45min) • Château, grounds, horse museum & equestrian show €30; horse museum & equestrian show €21; château & equestrian show €16; tours of the Duc and Duchesse d'Aumale's private apartments €3; gardens only €7; mini train through grounds (hourly 11am–6pm) €5 • ☎ 03 44 27 31 80, W domainedechantilly.com

The **Chantilly estate** has been the powerbase of two of the most powerful clans in France: first to the Montmorencys, then, through marriage, to the Condés. The present, mostly late nineteenth-century **château** replaced a palace, destroyed in the Revolution, which had been built for the Grand Condé, who smashed Spanish military power on behalf of the infant king, Louis XIV, in 1643. It's a beautiful structure, surrounded by what's more a lake than a moat, looking out in a romantic manner over a formal arrangement of pools and **gardens** created by the busy André Le Nôtre, the designer of the gardens at Versailles (and indeed at every other seventeenth-century château with pretensions to grandeur). The château has an almost unrivalled **art collection** of Classical art, and its **stables**, practically as grand as the main building, devote more than a dozen rooms to an impressive **horse museum**.

Chantilly gardens

The **Chantilly gardens** were among Le Nôtre's favourites, and are well worth exploring, the water features, fountains and statues creating a truly elegant ensemble. In addition, there's a rustic **Anglo-Chinese garden**, created in 1773 – an artful faux-village, including five little half-beamed houses, that was said to have inspired Marie Antoinette to create her romantic Petit Trianon in Versailles – and a romantic nineteenth-century **"English" garden**, created over a part of Le Nôtre's garden that was destroyed during the Revolution. A small café, *Le Hameau*, in the Anglo-Chinese garden, offers good opportunities to sample the local, super-sweet speciality, **Chantilly cream** (March–Nov).

Musée Condé

The **Musée Condé**, which occupies the nineteenth-century **Grand Château**, harbours one of the greatest collections of art in France. Stipulated to remain exactly as organized by Henri d'Orléans, the son of France's last king and the donor of the château, the arrangement is madly crowded by modern standards, and yet immensely satisfying, as the pictures almost seem to spark ideas off each other. Some highlights can be found in the Rotunda – among them Poussin's *Massacre of the Innocents*, Raphael's *Madonna of Loreto* and Philippe de Champaigne's *Portrait of Richelieu* – and in the Sanctuary, where Italian Renaissance masterpieces include Raphael's *Three Graces* and Piero di Cosimo's allegorical *Simonetta Vespucci*. But the highlight must be the octagonal, red-walled Tribune, where Botticelli's resplendently fertile *Autumn* seems to rival Ingres' astoundingly sexy *Venus Anadyomene*, and works by Delacroix, Poussin and Van Dyck crowd in all around.

Cabinet des Livres

Among its 19,000 volumes, the **Cabinet des Livres** displays a perfect facsimile – and browsable, digitized version – of the fabulous manuscript **Les Très Riches Heures du Duc de Berry**, the original of which is also held here. This is the most celebrated of all the medieval Books of Hours, and the museum's single greatest treasure. The illuminated pages illustrating the months of the year with representative scenes from contemporary (early 1400s) rural life – such as harvesting and ploughing, sheep-shearing and pruning – are richly coloured and drawn with a delicate naturalism.

Appartements privés

The opulent **private apartments of the Princes de Condé**, on the first floor of the sixteenth-century wing known as the **Petit Château**, are bristling with superb furnishings, but there is a rare highlight: the exquisite *boiseries* panelling the walls of

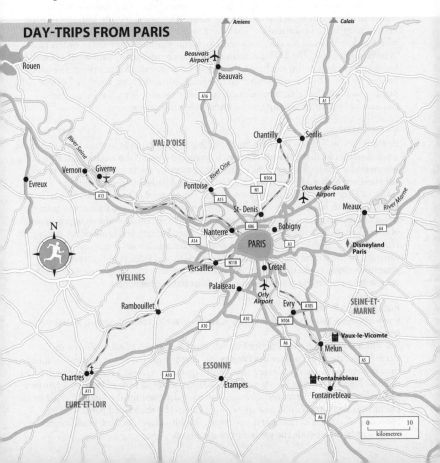

DAY-TRIPS FROM PARIS

17

> ### A MAN OF HONOUR
>
> Chantilly is perhaps most famous as the venue for a single notorious incident: the **suicide of Vatel**. The story is widely retold to illustrate the otherworldly moral code of the *ancien régime*. Maître d' to the nobility at the château, (supposed) inventor of Chantilly cream and orchestrator of financier Fouquet's fateful supper party in 1661 (see opposite), François Vatel was justifiably proud of his status. In April 1671, the Prince de Condé set him to organize a feast for three thousand guests, in honour of Louis XIV. On the opening evening, two tables went without meat thanks to unexpected arrivals. "I cannot endure such a humiliation," Vatel was heard to say, over and over again. At four in the morning, the distraught Vatel was seen wandering the corridors of the palace, where he met a fish supplier with two baskets of fish. "Is that all there is?" he asked, in horror, to which the man replied "Yes". The maître d' had in fact sent for supplies from all over France, though these had not yet arrived. Dishonoured, he played the Roman and ran upon his sword.

the **Singerie**, or Monkey Gallery, wittily painted with allegorical stories, all starring monkeys, in a pseudo-Chinese style.

Separate guided tours (€3) take you to the elegant but surprisingly intimate ground-floor **apartments of the Petit Château**, which belonged to the château's last private owners, the Duc and Duchesse d'Aumale. It was they who bequeathed the château to the Institut de France (see p.135), its present owners. The Duc d'Aumale had little reason to cling to it, in fact, as he was not actually a Condé, but the fifth son of King Louis-Philippe, and inherited the château through his godfather, Louis VI Henri, who had lost all six of his children – the eldest son was murdered on the orders of Napoleon, in 1804. The Duc d'Aumale's inheritance was doubly surprising as the old Condé was only induced to change his will by his mistress, a former prostitute named Sophia Dawes, who was also suspected of having murdered him, after the 74-year-old prince was found hanging from his bedroom window (not here, but in another château, at St-Leu), strung up by two knotted handkerchiefs.

Musée du Cheval

Five minutes' walk along the drive from the Château de Chantilly towards town stands the colossal stable block, the **Grandes Ecuries**, looking out towards the racetrack. The building was erected at the beginning of the eighteenth century by the incumbent Condé prince, who believed he would be reincarnated as a horse and wished to provide fitting accommodation for 240 of his future relatives. The **Musée du Cheval** boasts fifteen rooms and around two hundred objects from around the world devoted to the horse – from the history of domestication to the evolution of tack over the centuries, the changing depiction of the animal in art and literature, and its role in war, hunting and horseracing. Among the range of beautiful objects, check out the finely decorated carousel horses and venerable carriages. In the central ring a specialist team of riders and trainers put on spectacular **equestrian shows** combining music, elaborate choreography and horsemanship (check website for calendar), and, more frequently, short **training sessions**.

Potager des Princes

17 rue de la Faisanderie • March–Oct daily 10am–7pm, plus occasional days Feb–April, Nov & Dec; check website • €9.50 • ☎ 03 44 57 39 66, ⓦ potagerdesprinces.com

Set 400m down from the Grandes Ecuries, one block north of the main rue du Connétable, the lush **Potager des Princes**, or "kitchen garden of the princes", is more than merely meticulously planted herbs and vegetables – though it is that, certainly, in the best French tradition. There are also fountains set amid beds of flowers, a Japanese garden and bamboo maze, and a luscious orchard designed for the Grand Condé by the ubiquitous Le Nôtre. Children may be more excited by the animal park, with its collection of rare hens, ducks and pheasants, "rabbit village", ponies, donkeys and goats, gambolling beside the garden of exotic plants.

By train Trains depart daily for Chantilly Gouvieux station (every 30min–1hr; 25min) from Paris's Gare du Nord – on the main Grandes Lignes level, not the downstairs level serving the suburbs – on the line to Creil. Free buses to the town centre usually wait outside Chantilly station; you have to get off by the Grandes Ecuries and walk 500m to the château gates. It's arguably more pleasant to take a direct, 30min stroll along a signposted, beech-shaded footpath; turn right outside the station, then almost immediately left at the roundabout along the av des Aigles. You'll pass the racetrack about a third of the way along.

By car Chantilly is less than an hour's drive north of Paris on the A3 and/or A1 motorways; exit 7, signposted "Chantilly", takes you in quick succession via the D16 and D1017 onto the D924A, which you follow for 8km through the forest up to the chateau gate.

Tourist information ⓦ chantilly-tourisme.com.

Vaux-le-Vicomte

50km southeast of Paris • March–Nov daily 10am–6pm; fountains and other waterworks March–Oct second and last Sat of the month 3–6pm; candlelight illumination of state rooms and gardens early May to early Oct Sat 5pm–midnight • €16.50, with candlelight illumination €19.50; gardens only €8.50 • ⓣ 01 64 14 41 90, ⓦ vaux-le-vicomte.com

Of all the great mansions within reach of a day's outing from Paris, the Classical château of **Vaux-le-Vicomte** is the most architecturally harmonious, the most aesthetically pleasing and the most human in scale. It stands isolated in the countryside amid fields and woods, and its gardens make a lovely place to picnic.

The château was built between 1656 and 1661 for **Nicolas Fouquet**, Louis XIV's finance minister, by the finest design team of the day – architect Le Vau, painter-designer Le Brun and landscape gardener Le Nôtre. The result was magnificence and precision in perfect proportion, and a bill that could only be paid by someone who occasionally confused the state's accounts with his own. Fouquet, however, had little chance to enjoy his magnificent residence. On August 17, 1661, he invited the king and his courtiers to a sumptuous housewarming party. Three weeks later he was arrested – by d'Artagnan of Musketeer fame – charged with embezzlement, of which he was certainly guilty, and clapped into jail for the rest of his life. Thereupon, the king stripped the château of most of its furnishings, and carted off the design trio to build his own Versailles.

By 1875, the château had passed through a series of incompetent aristocratic hands and had fallen into a state of utter dereliction. It was bought by Alfred Sommier, a French industrialist, who made its restoration and refurbishment his life's work. It was finally opened to the public in 1968. Today, work continues on restoring more and more public rooms to their original grandeur.

The château and gardens

Seen from the entrance, the **château** is a rather austerely magnificent pile surrounded by an artificial moat. It's only when you go through to the south side, where the gardens decline in measured formal patterns of grass and water, clipped box and yew, fountains and statuary, that you can look back and appreciate the very harmonious and very French qualities of the building – the combination of steep, tall roof and bulbous central dome with classical pediment and pilasters.

The interior is opulent, and its main artistic interest lies in the work of **Le Brun**. He was responsible for the two fine **tapestries** in the entrance, made in the local workshops set up by Fouquet specifically to adorn his house, and subsequently removed by Louis XIV to become the famous Gobelins works in Paris (see p.175). Le Brun also painted numerous **ceilings**, notably in Fouquet's bedroom, the Salon des Muses, his *Sleep* in the Cabinet des Jeux, and the so-called "king's bedroom", whose decor is the first example of the ponderously grand style that became known as Louis XIV. Other points of interest are the cavernous **kitchens**, which have not been altered since construction, and a room displaying letters in the hand of Fouquet, Louis XIV and other notables. One, dated November 1794 (mid-Revolution), addresses the

17

incumbent Duc de Choiseul-Praslin as *tu*. "Citizen," it says, "you've got a week to hand over one hundred thousand pounds…", and signs off with "Cheers and brotherhood".

On Saturday evenings in summer the **state rooms** and gardens are **illuminated** with two thousand candles, as they probably were on the occasion of Fouquet's fateful party, with classical music in the gardens adding to the effect. The **fountains** and other waterworks can be seen in action on the second and last Saturday of the month (not in winter).

ARRIVAL AND DEPARTURE   VAUX-LE-VICOMTE

By train Services run from the Gare de Lyon as far as Melun (every 30min; 25min), from where an occasional shuttle-bus service (€8 return) covers the journey to the château (Sat & Sun April–Nov; serving some trains only; check ⓦ vaux-le-vicomte.com for up-to-date timetables). On weekdays, you'll have to take a taxi for the last 6km

(around €17 one way); there's a rank at the train station, with numbers to call if there are no taxis waiting.
By car Vaux-le-Vicomte is 6km east of Melun, which is itself 46km southeast of Paris; from Paris take the A4 or A6 then N104 and A5 (direction Troyes, exit 15 "Saint-Germain Laxis").

Fontainebleau

The **château of Fontainebleau**, 60km south of Paris, was once a mere hunting lodge in the magnificent **forest** that still surrounds it. Its transformation into an extravagantly luxurious palace only took place in the sixteenth century on the initiative of François I, who imported a colony of Italian artists to carry out the decoration, most notably Rosso Fiorentino, Primaticcio and Niccolò dell'Abate. The palace continued to enjoy royal favour well into the nineteenth century; Napoleon spent huge amounts of money on it, as did Louis-Philippe. And, after World War II, when it was liberated from the Germans by General Patton, it served for a while as Allied military HQ in Europe. The town itself now hosts the European campus of the prestigious INSEAD Business School.

The château

3km southwest of Fontainebleau-Avon train station • Daily except Tues: April–Sept 9.30am–6pm; Oct–March 9.30am–5pm • €11, €15.50 including guided tour of Grands Appartements; guided tours of the Petits Appartements €6.50; guided tours of the furniture museum €6.50; "Second Empire" guided tours, including the Musée Chinois, Napoleon's study and the Imperial Theatre €6.50; guided tours of the Imperial Theatre €5 • ☏ 01 60 71 50 70, ⓦ musee-chateau-fontainebleau.fr

The **buildings**, unpretentious and attractive despite their extent, have none of the unity of a purpose-built residence like Vaux-le-Vicomte. In fact, their chief appeal is the gloriously chaotic profusion of styles – a showcase of French architecture from the twelfth to the nineteenth centuries. From the expanse of the **Cour du Cheval Blanc**, built as a humble *basse cour* or working courtyard in the 1530s, you progress up a seventeenth-century horseshoe staircase into a confusion of wings, courtyards and gardens. At the very heart of the palace, the secretive and splendidly asymmetrical **Cour Ovale** conceals a twelfth-century fortress keep, jarringly but pleasingly flanked by fine Renaissance wings on either side.

The palace's highlights, however, are the sumptuous **interiors** worked by the Italians, chiefly the celebrated **Galerie François I**, which is resplendent in gilt, carved, inlaid and polished wood, and adorned down its entire length by intricate stuccowork and painted panels covered in vibrant Mannerist brushwork. The paintings' Classical themes all celebrate or advocate wise kingship, and had a seminal influence on the development of French aristocratic art and design.

Petits Appartements and museums

While the main rooms, the Grands Appartements, are suitably resplendent, utterly contrasting in style is the sober but elegant decor of Napoleon's **Petits Appartements**, the private rooms of the emperor, his wife and their intimate entourage. You have to buy a separate ticket to join the (obligatory) guided tour, but a tour of the **Musée Napoléon** – which displays a wide variety of souvenirs, some very personal, some official – is included in the main château ticket. The tour of the **Musée Chinois** shows off the Empress Eugénie's private collection of Chinese and Thai objets d'art in their original Second Empire setting; you also get to visit the Empress's breathtaking private theatre. There are two other museums – one highlighting some of Fontainebleau's fine seventeenth-century **paintings**, and the other a profusion of eighteenth- and nineteenth-century **furniture** – plus a recently restored **Imperial Theatre**, built between 1853 and 1856 for Napoleon and Eugénie and based upon Marie-Antoinette's little theatre in Versailles.

The gardens
The **gardens** – including among them André Le Nôtre's Grand Parterre, the largest formal garden in Europe – are equally splendid. In the summer months you could rent a boat on the Etang des Carpes, an ornamental lake with a Classical pavilion as its island centrepiece.

Forest of Fontainebleau

Though the château gardens are glorious, if you want to escape into the relative wilds, you should head for the surrounding **Forest of Fontainebleau**, which is crisscrossed with more than 1500km of walking and cycling trails. The main options are marked on Michelin map #106 (*Environs de Paris*) and detailed on ⓦ fontainebleau-tourisme.com, which also has information on rock climbing in the forest – Fontainebleau's many rocks are a favourite training ground for Paris-based *grimpeurs*.

ARRIVAL AND INFORMATION	**FONTAINEBLEAU**
By train SNCF trains run from the Gare de Lyon to Fontainebleau-Avon station (40min); line 1 bus ("Les Lilas"; 15min) takes you from the station to the château.	**By car** Driving to Fontainebleau from Paris is an option; it's 16km from the A6 autoroute (exit Fontainebleau). **Tourist information** ⓦ fontainebleau-tourisme.com.

Chartres

When King Philippe-Auguste visited **CHARTRES** to mediate between church and townsfolk after the riots of October 1210, the cathedral chapter noted that "he did not wish to stay any longer in the city but, so as to avoid the blasphemous citizens, stayed here only for one hour and hastened to return". Chartres' modern visitors often stay little longer, but if you've come all the way from Paris, a journey of 80km, the modest charms of the little market town at the cathedral's feet may persuade you to linger. One of the world's most astounding buildings, the cathedral is best experienced early or late in the day, when the low sun transmits the stained-glass colours to the interior stone and the quiet scattering of people leaves the acoustics unconfused.

Chartres cathedral

Cloître Notre-Dame • **Cathedral** Sept–June daily 8.30am–7.30pm; July & Aug Mon, Wed, Thurs & Sat 8.30am–7.30pm, Tues, Fri & Sun 8.30am–10pm • Free; crypt tours €3 • **North tower** May–Aug Mon–Sat 9.30am–12.30pm & 2–6pm, Sun 2–6pm; Sept–April Mon–Sat 9.30am–12.30pm & 2–4.30pm, Sun 2–5pm • €7.50 • ☏ 02 37 21 59 08, ⓦ cathedrale-chartres.org

Built between 1194 and 1260, Chartres' Gothic **cathedral** was one of the fastest ever constructed and, as a result, preserves a uniquely harmonious design. An earlier Romanesque structure burnt down in 1194, but the church's holiest **relic** – the **Sancta Camisia**, reputed to have been the robe Mary wore when she gave birth to Jesus – was discovered three days later, miraculously unharmed. It was a sign that the Virgin wanted her church lavishly rebuilt, at least so said the canny medieval fundraisers. Thereafter, hordes of **pilgrims** stopped here on their way south to the shrine of Santiago de Compostela in Spain, and the church needed to accommodate them with a sizeable crypt, for veneration of the relic, and a nave large enough to sleep hundreds – the sloping floor evident today allowed for it to be washed down more easily.

17

If those same pilgrims were to see the cathedral today, they would be deeply dismayed: since their time, the sculptures on the exterior portals have lost their bright paint and gilt, while the walls have lost the whitewash that once reflected the stained-glass windows. Worse still, the high altar has been brought down into the body of the church, among the hoi polloi, and chairs cover up the **labyrinth** on the floor of the nave (except on Fridays between Easter and October, when you can trace its 200m-long route all the way to the centre), whose diameter is the same size as that of the rose window above the main doors. Nonetheless, Chartres is still the **best-preserved** medieval cathedral in Eurospe, and one of the most intensely beautiful buildings in France, well worth the journey from the capital.

The exterior

Outside, hosts of **sculpted figures** stand like guardians at each entrance portal. Like the south tower and spire which abuts it, the mid-twelfth-century **Royal Portal** actually

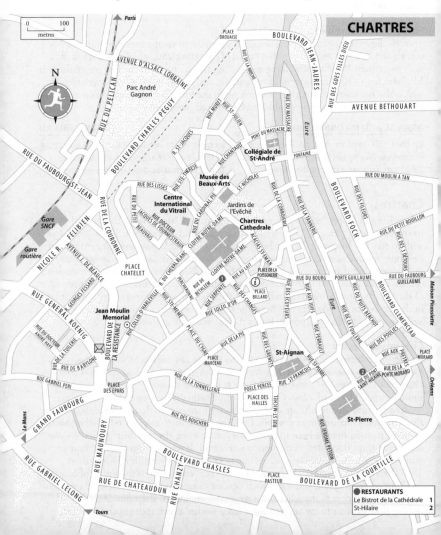

CHARTRES

RESTAURANTS
Le Bistrot de la Cathédrale 1
St-Hilaire 2

17

survives from the earlier Romanesque church, and it's interesting to compare its relatively stylized figures with the more completely Gothic sculptures on the north and south porches, completed half a century later.

The stained glass and choir screen

The geometry of Chartres cathedral is unique in being almost unaltered since its consecration, and virtually all of its magnificent **stained glass** is original – and unsurpassed – thirteenth-century work. Many of the windows in the nave were donated by craft guilds and merchants, whose symbols can often be seen in the bottommost pane. Some of the stories fit the donors' work, such as the carpenters' window showing Noah's ark. The superb, largely twelfth-century "**Blue Virgin**" window, in the first bay beyond the south transept, is filled with a primal image of the Virgin that has been adored by pilgrims for centuries.

The **choir screen**, which curves around the ambulatory, depicts scenes from the lives of Christ and the Virgin. Its sculptor, Jehan de Beauce, was also responsible for the design of the Flamboyant Gothic north spire.

The north tower and gardens

Crowds permitting, it's worth climbing the three hundred steps up the **north tower** for its bird's-eye view of the sculptures and structure of the cathedral. The **gardens** behind the cathedral, meanwhile, are a perfect spot for contemplation of the flying buttresses. You can pay for a tour of the crypt, but it's relatively unimpressive.

Centre International du Vitrail

5 rue du Cardinal Pie • Mon–Fri 9.30am–12.30pm & 1.30–6pm, Sat 10am–12.30pm & 2.30–6pm, Sun 2.30–6pm • €5.50 • ☎ 02 37 21 65 72, ⓦ centre-vitrail.org

Occasional exhibitions of stained glass – ancient and modern, from around the world – take place in the **Centre International du Vitrail**, a foundation devoted to sustaining and promoting the art form, and also offering workshops, classes and cathedral tours. The half-timbered building was once a medieval wine and grain store, and has a handsomely vaulted interior.

Musée des Beaux-Arts

29 rue Cloître Notre-Dame • May–Oct Wed–Sat 10am–12.30pm & 2–6pm, Sun 2–6pm; Nov–April Wed–Sat 10am–noon & 2–5pm, Sun 2–5pm • €3.40 • ☎ 02 37 90 45 80

The **Musée des Beaux-Arts**, in the rather gorgeous former episcopal palace just north of Chartres cathedral, punches somewhat over its weight. It has some beautiful tapestries and a room full of the works of French Fauvist Vlaminck, as well as the Spanish Baroque painter Zurbarán's *Sainte-Lucie*. There's also a number of Gallo-Roman stelae, a good Oceanic collection and some rather wonderful musical instruments made as exact replicas of those in the sculptures or windows of the cathedral.

River Eure and Collégiale de St-André

Behind the Musée des Beaux-Arts, rue Chantault leads past old townhouses to the **River Eure** and Pont du Massacre. You can follow this reedy river lined with ancient wash houses downstream along rue de la Tannerie, or upstream via rue du Massacre on the right bank. On the latter route, the cathedral appears from time to time through the trees; closer at hand, on the left bank, is the Romanesque **Collégiale de St-André**, a church now used for art exhibitions and concerts.

Chartres' medieval town

Chartres' **medieval town** spreads out southwest of the cathedral. At the top of rue du Bourg there's a turreted staircase attached to a house, and at the eastern end of place de la Poissonnerie, a carved salmon decorates a sixteenth-century building. The **food**

17

market takes place on place Billard and rue des Changes (Wed & Sat morning), and there's a **flower market** on place du Cygne (Tues, Thurs & Sat).

At the edge of the old town, on the corner of rue Collin-d'Harleville (to the right if you're coming up from the station), stands a memorial to **Jean Moulin**, Prefect of Chartres until he was sacked by the Vichy government in 1942. When the Germans occupied the town in 1940, Moulin refused to sign a document attributing Nazi atrocities to Senegalese soldiers in the French army. He later became De Gaulle's number one man on the ground, coordinating the Resistance, and died at the hands of Klaus Barbie in 1943.

Maison Picassiette

22 rue du Repos • April Mon & Wed–Sat 10am–noon & 2–5pm, Sun 2–5pm; May–Sept Mon & Wed–Sat 10am–noon & 2–6pm, Sun 2–6pm; Oct Sat 10am–noon & 2–6pm, Sun 2–6pm • €5.50 • ☎ 02 37 90 45 95

Crossing the river at the end of rue Tannerie and continuing southwest along rue du Faubourg Guillaume and rue des Rouliers will bring you, after around 1.5km, to an astonishing, idiosyncratic tourist attraction. Over almost thirty years, Raymond Isidore, a local road-mender and cemetery caretaker, decorated his **Maison Picassiette** inside and out, covering everything – from the walls to the stove to a small chapel – with mosaics, using shards of broken pottery and glass he found in the streets. "I took the things that other people threw away", as he put it, before he died in 1964. The result is a quirky yet moving example of rather beautiful folk art – it's well worth making the small detour to see it.

ARRIVAL AND INFORMATION   CHARTRES

By train Services run from the Gare du Montparnasse (hourly; roughly 1hr).

By car Chartres is 91km from Paris, around 1hr 15min by car. From the *périphérique*, follow the A6B autoroute, then follow the signs just after Villejuif and L'Haÿ-les-Roses that lead you via the E50 onto the A10 near Massy. Follow the signs onto the A11 near Orsay, and follow this to Chartres,

coming off at junction 2.

Tourist office The tourist office is at 8–10 rue de la Poissonnerie, a 5min walk from the train station by the cathedral (May–Sept Mon–Sat 9.30am–6.30pm, Sun 9.30am–5.30pm; Oct–April Mon–Sat 10am–6pm, Sun 10am–5pm; ☎ 02 37 18 26 26, ⊛ chartres-tourisme.com).
Website ⊛ chartres.fr.

EATING AND DRINKING

Le Bistrot de la Cathédrale 1 Cloître Notre-Dame ☎ 02 37 36 59 60. This wine bar and *bistrot* has a perfect spot right opposite the cathedral, and it doesn't waste it, with simple dishes like paté or risotto, a good selection of wines and a *terrasse*. *Menu du jour* on the blackboard, for around €23. Daily except Wed noon–2pm & 7–10pm.

St-Hilaire 11 rue du Pont St-Hilaire ☎ 02 37 30 97 57, ⊛ www.restaurant-saint-hilaire.fr. The genteel *St-Hilaire* serves refined regional cuisine – duck, lobster, foie gras – in a sweet little two-storey dining room near the river, a 10min walk from the cathedral. The €29.50 *menu* is good value. Tues–Sat noon–1.30pm & 7.30–9.30pm.

Giverny

Claude Monet considered his **gardens at Giverny** to be his greatest masterpiece. They're out in Normandy, 75km from Paris in the direction of Rouen, but they are well worth the trip in summer – though given their fame you certainly won't be alone.

Monet's gardens

84 rue Claude Monet • April–Oct daily 9.30am–6pm • €9.50; book advance online to avoid queuing • ☎ 02 32 51 28 21, ⊛ fondation-monet.fr

Monet lived in Giverny from 1883 till his death in 1926, painting and repainting the effects of the changing seasonal light on the **gardens** he laid out between his house and the river. Every month has its own appeal, but May and June, when the rhododendrons flower round the lily pond and the wisteria bursts into colour over the famous Japanese bridge, are the prettiest months to visit – though you'll have to contend with crowds photographing the water lilies and posing on the bridge. **Monet's house** stands at the top of the gardens, an idyllic pastel-pink building with green shutters. Inside, the rooms are all painted different colours, exactly as they were when Monet lived here, and are packed with family photos and paintings – in particular the painter's original collection of Japanese prints, including wonderful works by Hokusai and Hiroshige. Note, though, that you won't see any original Monet paintings.

Musée des Impressionnismes

99 rue Claude Monet • April–Oct daily 10am–6pm • €7 • ☎ 02 32 51 94 65, ⓦ mdig.fr

Just up rue Claude Monet from the artist's gardens is the **Musée des Impressionnismes**, which puts on exhibitions of works not just by Impressionists but by artists influenced by the movement. The museum owes its existence to the circle of American artists drawn to Giverny by Monet's fame, but its exhibitions have a broad remit: shows have included "Brussels, Impressionist Capital" and "Impressionism along the Banks of the Seine".

ARRIVAL AND DEPARTURE   GIVERNY

By train and bus Without a car, the easiest approach to Giverny is by train to the small town of Vernon, 6km north. Trains leave from Paris-St-Lazare (15 daily; 50min). At St-Lazare, follow signs to the mainline "Grandes Lignes" platforms, and get your ticket from the main office, signposted "Espace de Vente", or the yellow machines; the Ile-de-France counter is for suburban services only. A bus service, timed to meet the Paris trains, makes the 6km journey to the gardens (€8 return; 20min); there are only four daily from Vernon to Giverny so check the website (ⓦ fondation-monet

.fr) to try and time your arrival with one of the bus departures (they fill up quickly on busy days). Buses back from the gardens are more frequent. You can also take a taxi (€21), rent a bicycle at the station (€15 for the day; it's best to reserve in advance: ☎ 02 32 21 16 01) or simply walk (1hr): cross the river and turn right on the D5; take care as you enter Giverny to follow the left fork, otherwise you'll make a long detour to reach the garden entrance.

By car Giverny is an hour's drive from Paris; take the A13, direction Vernon/Giverny, to exit 14.

Disneyland Paris

Children will love Disneyland. What their minders will think of it is another matter, though a cartoon moment is still likely to cadge a smile from most grown-ups – and you can terrify yourself on a roller coaster at any age. At a distance of just 25km east of Paris, it's easy to visit as a day-trip. The complex is divided into three areas: Disneyland Park, the original Magic Kingdom, with most of the big rides; Walt Disney Studios Park, a more technology-based attempt to re-create the world of cartoon film-making, along with a few rides; and the restaurant complex of Disney Village. There's also the vast discount shopping mall – sorry, "village" – of La Vallée Outlet (see p.328); regular park shuttles connect it to the Disney hotels.

The **best time to go** is a term-time weekday, when you'll probably get round every ride you want, though queuing for and walking between rides is purgatorial in wet or very cold weather. At other times, long waits for the popular rides are common, though most of the very popular attractions offer the "Fastpass" prebooked time-slot scheme (see box, p.253).

If you're doing a lot of planning in advance, the official **website** ⓦdlpguide.com is worth a look. It has videos and reviews of rides, full restaurant listings, up-to-date minimum height regulations, and so on. In the run-up to the park's twenty-fifth anniversary in 2017, some of the most popular rides are being given a major makeover and may be closed for a period in 2016; the latest details are given on the website ⓦdlptoday.com.

18

It's very easy to visit Disneyland on a day-trip from central Paris; it's just forty minutes away on the RER (see p.254) and, if you decide in advance which rides you want to go on and use the Fastpass scheme, you can get to see and do a fair amount. The advantage of staying in the resort for a few days is that you can dip in and out and take things at a more leisurely pace, and you might be able to enjoy some perks such as having access to the park before it officially opens (see p.254).

There's not much that's French at Disneyland – for that, try the Parc Astérix (see p.351) – though Sleeping Beauty's Castle is partly based on an illustration in the medieval manuscript *Les Très Riches Heures du Duc de Berry* (see p.239), and there's the odd crêpe stand – otherwise, the food in the resort is almost always American, and often disappointing. The commentaries or scripts in the more theatrical attractions are usually in French, however, with translated summaries displayed on a board. In the most audience-focused attractions, you'll find an English-language headset to don.

Disneyland Park

The introduction to Disneyland Paris is **Main Street USA**, a mythical vision of a 1900s American town. It leads from Town Square, just beyond the entrance turnstiles, up to **Central Plaza**, the hub of the park. Clockwise from Main Street are Frontierland, Adventureland, Fantasyland and Discoveryland. The **castle**, directly opposite Main Street across Central Plaza, belongs to Fantasyland. A steam-train **Railroad** runs round the park with stations at each "land" and at the main entrance.

This guide reviews all but the most minor rides, with some warnings about suitability, though it's difficult to tell what one child will find exhilarating and another upsetting. For the youngest kids, **Fantasyland** is likely to hold the most thrills. There are no height restrictions here, and rides are mostly gentle. Each of the other three themed areas offers a landmark roller coaster and a theme; **Adventureland** sports tropical, pirate-themed sets, **Frontierland** is divided into the Wild West, while **Discoveryland** emphasizes technology and the Space Age. There aren't many green patches, though Adventureland has a few tree-shaded nooks and crannies, and you could try the seats by the river in Frontierland. Opportunities for afternoon naps, certainly, are limited; renting a pushchair (see p.255) for even an older child might be a good idea.

Main Street USA

Main Street is really just a giant mall for Disney sponsors. See if you can get down it without buying one of the following: a balloon; a hat with your name embroidered on it; an ice cream; silhouette portraits of the kids; the *Wall Street Journal* of 1902; a Donald Duck costume; a bag of muffins; or a complete set of Disney characters in ceramics, metal, plastic, rubber or wool. Leaving Main Street is quickest on foot (crowds permitting), although omnibuses, trams, horse-drawn streetcars and fire trucks are always on hand, plus the Disney *pièce de résistance*, the **Railroad**, for which Main Street Station has the longest queues.

RIDES AND ATTRACTIONS

The symbol ⓕ denotes that the ride uses Fastpass.

DISCOVERYLAND

L'Astroport Services Interstellaires A videogame arcade. Some games have an interactive element: you can distort a photo of your own face, for instance (then buy it). **Autopia** Miniature futuristic cars to drive on rails. Good fun, especially for little kids, but there's no possibility of any race-day stratagems. Minimum height to drive is 1.32m. **ⓕ Buzz Lightyear Laser Blast** An interactive cart ride through a black-light universe, inspired by *Toy Story 2*. You shoot at threatening space creatures, helping Buzz and his friendly three-eyed Martians save the galaxy. Good

for little kids.

Captain EO *Star Wars* meets the King of Pop in this 1986 3D film (17min; in English) produced by George Lucas, starring Michael Jackson on a mission to save the world – with the help of some snazzy song and dance routines. Some scenes may frighten younger children.

Les Mystères du Nautilus A stroll through a mock-up of the *Nautilus* submarine – Captain Nemo's vessel in *20,000 Leagues under the Sea*. What's supposed to impress you is the faithfulness of the decor to the original Disney set, though there is a fishy surprise inside.

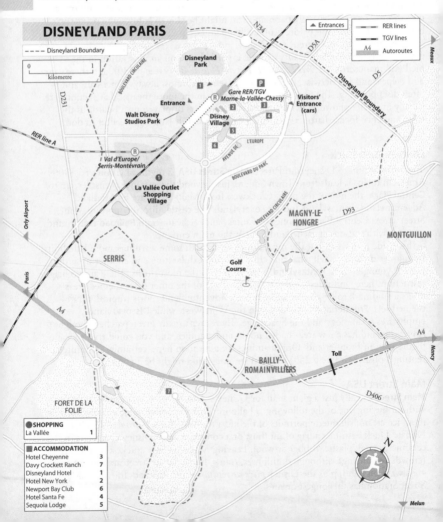

DISNEYLAND PARIS

▲ Entrances | RER lines | TGV lines | Autoroutes

– – – Disneyland Boundary

0   1
kilometre

Disneyland Park

Gare RER/TGV Marne-la-Vallée-Chessy

Entrance ▲

Walt Disney Studios Park

Disney Village

Visitors' Entrance (cars)

L'EUROPE

Val d'Europe/ Serris-Montévrain

RER line A

AVENUE DE

BOULEVARD DU PARC

La Vallée Outlet Shopping Village

BOULEVARD CIRCULAIRE

MAGNY-LE-HONGRE

D93

MONTGUILLON

SERRIS

Golf Course

A4

Paris

BAILLY-ROMAINVILLIERS

Toll

D406

A4   Nancy

FORET DE LA FOLIE

● **SHOPPING**
La Vallée   1

■ **ACCOMMODATION**

Hotel Cheyenne	3
Davy Crockett Ranch	7
Disneyland Hotel	1
Hotel New York	2
Newport Bay Club	6
Hotel Santa Fe	4
Sequoia Lodge	5

N34

D5A

D5

Disneyland Boundary

D231

Only Airport

Melun ▼

SHOWS AND PARADES

The all-dancing, all-costumed **Shows** and **Parades** in both Disneyland and Walt Disney Studio Park are huge affairs. Timing a visit to a popular ride to coincide with a big show is a clever idea if getting on all the big rides is your priority, though the parades are a memorable part of the Disney experience, especially for kids, so it's worth trying to catch at least one. Timetables are handed out with maps as you enter the park. One of the best parade vantage spots is on the queuing ramp for It's a Small World (see below), right by the gates through which the floats appear. From here, the parades progress, very slowly, to Town Square. The best seating is in front of the Fantasyland Castle, one of the points where the floats stop and the characters put on a performance. The parade floats represent all the top box-office Disney movies and characters, from Mickey and Minnie Mouse to the *Toy Story* team and the *Pirates of the Caribbean* crew. Everyone waves and smiles, and characters on foot shake hands with the kids who've managed to get to the front.

18

Orbitron The "rockets" on this ride go round and round fairly slowly and go up (at your control) to a daring thirty degrees above the horizontal. Suitable for small kids and for those who dislike more violent rides.

⊕ Space Mountain Mission 2 A thrilling space ride, this star attraction provides 1.3g of speed and a moment of weightlessness, all in an elaborately lit ambience, with meteor storms and rushing star clusters. Minimum height 1.32m, and pregnant women and people with health problems are advised not to ride.

⊕ Star Tours Giddy, simulated ride in a spacecraft (with sixty other people all in neat rows) piloted by friendly, incompetent C-3PO of *Star Wars* fame. The projection of what you're supposed to be careering through is actually from the film, which pleases fans. Minimum height 1.02m. Pregnant women and those with health problems are advised not to board. Note that it's due to close for a year from early 2016 for a makeover.

FANTASYLAND

Alice's Curious Labyrinth A giant maze with surprises. There are passages that only people under 1m can pass through without ducking and enough false turns and exits to make it a decent enough labyrinth. Takes maybe 10min, with the option to exit at the halfway point.

Blanche-Neige et les Sept Nains This *Snow White and the Seven Dwarfs* ride takes you through lots of menacing, moving trees, swinging doors and cackling witches, re-creating scenes from the classic Disney film. Can frighten smaller kids.

Le Carrousel de Lancelot A stately merry-go-round, whose every horse has its own individual medieval equerry in glittering paint.

Casey Jr – Le Petit Train du Cirque This charming little circus train chugs around rolling landscaped gardens behind Le Pays des Contes de Fées. Not too fast, not too slow, it's just right for little ones.

Dumbo the Flying Elephant Dumbo and his clones provide a safe, slow, aerial ride in which you can regulate the rise and fall of the revolving elephants with a lever. One of the most popular rides in Fantasyland, with queues to match, though it only lasts a measly 25 seconds.

It's a Small World This is a quintessential Disney experience; there's one in every Disneyland, and Walt considered it to be the finest expression of his corporation's philosophy. Your boat rides through a polystyrene and glitter world, where animated dolls in national/ethnic/tribal costumes dance beside their most famous landmarks or landscapes, singing the song *It's a Small World*. Some children seem to enjoy the sugar-coated fantasy.

Mad Hatter's Teacups Great big whirling teacups slide past each other on a chequered floor. Not a whizzy ride, so it suits younger ones, though it's disappointingly short.

Le Pays des Contes de Fée A boat ride through cleverly miniaturized fairy-tale scenes: *Alice in Wonderland, Pinocchio*, etc. Fine for little kids.

⊕ Peter Pan's Flight Very young children seem to really enjoy this jerky "flight" above Big Ben and the lights of London to Never-Never Land. Very popular.

Sleeping Beauty's Castle The castle stands at the entrance to Fantasyland, just off the Central Plaza at the end of Main Street. There's little to see inside other than a few bits of plasticky vaulting, stained glass and cartoon tapestries, though a huge animated dragon lurks in the dungeon.

Les Voyages de Pinocchio A rattling, swervy wagon ride through a string of beautifully re-created scenes from *Pinocchio*; some are dimly lit and faintly menacing.

ADVENTURELAND

Adventure Isle Not a ride, but a sort of playground of caves, bouncy bridges, huge boulders, trees, tunnels and waterfalls built on two small islands in the middle of Adventureland. Parents of over-tired children and those who need a break from the queues should not underestimate the thrill of just being able to wander around unfettered.

La Cabane des Robinson The 27m mock banyan tree at the top of Adventure Isle is one of Disneyland Paris's most obsessively detailed and most enjoyable creations, complete with hundreds of thousands of (false) leaves and blossoms. It's reached by walkways and a series of more than 170

18

steps, so it's best avoided by pram-pushers and toddler-haulers. Note that it is closed until Sept 2016 for renovation.

Indiana Jones and the Temple of Peril A fast roller coaster along rattling train tracks through a classic Indy landscape. Moderately intense and renowned for its 360-degree loop, though it's no Space Mountain. The minimum height for the ride is 1.40m. Children under around 8 years old, pregnant women and people with health problems should steer clear.

Le Passage Enchanté d'Aladdin A sedate meander on foot through a colourful, Oriental-style passageway takes you past animated scenes from *Aladdin*, featuring the genie, the flying carpet and some truly insistent theme music.

Pirates' Beach The ladders, walkways, climbing ropes and slides at this nautical-themed adventure playground give kids a great chance to run off steam, in the shadow of Captain Hook's pirate ship. It's divided into two different areas: one for 3–6s, the other for 7–9s.

Pirates of the Caribbean This satisfyingly long ride is one of the finest, consisting of an underground ride on water and down waterfalls, past scenes of evil piracy. The animated automata are the best yet – be warned that they set small children whimpering and crying immediately. Battles are staged across the water, skeletons slide into the deep, parrots squawk, chains rattle and a treasure-trove is revealed.

FRONTIERLAND

Big Thunder Mountain This popular roller coaster, mimicking a runaway mine train, is closed for major refurbishment and due to reopen at the end of 2016. As well as wicked twists and turns, sudden tunnels and hairy moments looking down on the water, the new ride also promises an "explosive surprise". No violent upside-down or corkscrew stuff. Minimum height 1.02m; not suitable for small children.

The Chapparal Theater Shows seasonal theatrical spectaculars featuring all the usual Disney suspects. Times are displayed outside and on the programme handed out with the main park map.

Legends of the Wild West A series of models, displays and mocked-up rooms commemorating characters and scenes from the gold-rush days of America's Wild West, all housed in Fort Comstock, a replica log-built stockade.

Phantom Manor *Psycho*-style house on the outside and Hammer Horror Edwardian mansion within. Holographic ghosts appear before cobweb-covered mirrors and ancestral portraits, but nothing actually jumps out and screams at you. Probably too frightening for young children nevertheless.

Pocahontas Indian Village This Native American-themed adventure playground is nicely sited by the water, providing a welcome spot for parents to sit down and recharge their batteries while their offspring play on the slides, bridges, climbing areas and tepees. For children aged 4–8.

River Rogue Keelboats A guided 10min keelboat ride around the lake. The attraction's relaunch a little while back was delayed for a full year when authorities decreed that the helmsmen would require full French boating licenses. At least you know you're in safe hands.

Rustler Roundup Shootin' Gallery There's a fee (€2) for this attraction, apparently because without some check people stay for hours and hours shooting infrared beams at fake cacti.

Thunder Mesa Riverboat Landing A rather pointless cruise around the lake, but the paddleboat steamer is carefully built to offer lots of antique-style curiosities, and it's fun to watch the roller coaster rattle around the rocks of Big Thunder Mountain.

Walt Disney Studios Park

The **Walt Disney Studios Park** complex has fewer mega-rides than its older, larger neighbour, and as a result tends to be less busy: the queues are often shorter and it's easier to meet characters as the area is smaller. And in some ways this side of the park is a more satisfying affair, focusing on what Disney was and is still renowned for – animation. You can try your hand at drawing, there are mock film and TV sets where you can be part of the audience, and the special effects and stunt shows are impressive in their way, although probably not as impressive as just going to the movies. This is also where you'll find the park's newest attraction, the family-friendly **Ratatouille** ride, plus three thrilling rides: the corkscrew-looping, heavy metal-playing white-knuckler of the **Rock 'n' Roller Coaster Starring Aerosmith**, the plummeting elevator of the **Twilight Zone Tower of Terror** and the swirling, "undersea" exhilarations of **Crush's Coaster**.

RIDES AND SHOWS

The symbol **⊕** denotes that the ride uses Fastpass.

Animagique Disney characters in full fluffy costumes act out classic scenes from Disney films.

Armageddon Special Effects Your group of fifty or so is ushered into a circular chamber decked out as a space station. As meteors rush towards the screens on all sides, the whole ship seems about to break up.

QUEUES AND FASTPASS

Energy-sapping, one-hour waits for the popular rides are pretty standard during school holidays and on summer weekends. Don't be fooled by the length of the visible queues; they often snake for a further 100m or more inside. Realistic **wait times** are posted at the entry to most rides (eg 20 minutes, 50 minutes). The free Disneyland app gives real-time waiting times for attractions but, frustratingly, neither of the parks offers free wi-fi access, which the app requires in order to work; the closest free access is available in some of the Disney Village restaurants and most of the hotels. Bring sun hats or umbrellas, and make sure your kids have all been to the toilet recently before you begin to queue as, once you're in, it can be hard to get out; keep snacks and drinks handy, too. A number of rides use the **Fastpass** scheme (free), well worth making use of; all you have to do is insert your entry card into a ticket machine by the entrance to the ride; the machine then spews out a time at which you should come back and join the much shorter Fastpass queue. You're limited to one reservation at a time, unless you have a **VIP Fastpass** (given to guests staying in certain hotel suites) or a **Premium Fastpass** (available for €60 from *Disneyland Hotel* and Disney's *Hotel New York*), which both offer unlimited access to all Fastpass lanes.

18

Less cynical children may find the whole experience overwhelming.

Art of Disney Animation You progress through two mini-theatres, one showing famous moments from Disney cartoons, the next with a "cartoonist" chatting to an on-screen animated creation, explaining to the creature how it came to look as it did. In the lobby area, children are taught to draw Mickey Mouse faces.

Cars Quatre Roues Rallye *Cars*-inspired ride on the lines of a destruction derby. The ride is real enough, though sedate – the hell-raising element is engineered using special effects.

CinéMagique A theatrical screening of a century of movie moments, with actors appearing to jump into and out of the on-screen action, helped by special effects.

Crush's Coaster The theme of this very popular coaster is taken from *Finding Nemo*. You're taken into a virtual underwater world on the back of a turtle, then into a minute-long roller-coaster section which isn't especially fast but features an unusual spinning mechanism. Minimum height 1.07m. Note that there's limited capacity and it doesn't use Fastpass, so be prepared to queue.

Disney Junior Live on Stage A lively, smiley stage show drawn from the TV series, featuring costumed characters aimed at littler ones: Mickey, the Little Einsteins, Handy Manny. Seating is on the floor.

❻ **Flying Carpets Over Agrabah** A good, solid fair-ground ride where the carpet-shaped cars wheel around the central lamp for a disappointingly short time. Very popular with smaller children, especially the lever that makes their carpet rise up and down.

Moteurs…Action! Stunt Show Spectacular Decked out like a Mediterranean village, a big arena is the scene for some spectacular stunts: jumping rally cars, sliding motorbikes, leaping jet skis, stuntmen falling from heights and so on. Various timed shows throughout the day.

❼ **Ratatouille: L'Aventure Totalement Toquée de Rémy** Disneyland's newest ride, opened in 2014 and costing a record 150 million euros, is based on the 2007 animated film about a rat who dreams of becoming a chef. You're "shrunk" to the size of rats and taken in trackless, GPS-guided ratmobiles on a frantic 3D chase through a kitchen, in which you dodge waiters' feet and falling ladles and experience real physical sensations, such as aromas of food. It's aimed at families, though younger children may find it overwhelming.

RC Racer A half-pipe roller coaster: you're shuttled back and forth and up and down an upended semicircle till you're begging to get off. Minimum height 1.20m.

❽ **Rock 'n' Roller Coaster Starring Aerosmith** A real heart-stopper, reaching 5g here at one point. There are corkscrews, loops and violent lurches, and the whole thing takes place in a neon-lit and hard rock-soundtracked darkness that makes it all the more alarming. It's all over in less than 2min. Minimum height 1.2m; entirely unsuitable for small children.

Slinky Dog Zigzag Spin This fairly gentle ride takes you round and round on an undulating track pulled by said Slinky Dog.

Stitch Live! A theatrical-type experience in which children talk and play with the virtual reality alien Stitch who, despite being on screen, manages to interact with the audience.

Studio Tram Tour: Behind the Magic An electric tram takes you on a circuit of various bits and pieces of film set. The high point is the halt among the Wild West rocks of Catastrophe Canyon – sit on the left for the scariest ride. It's due to undergo renovation sometime in 2016/17 and will be closed for a time; check on the website.

Toy Soldiers Parachute Drop Hanging in a group of bucket seats under a giant umbrella, you're repeatedly lifted up and dropped – not all that fast, but from fairly high up. Minimum height 0.81m.

18

◉ Twilight Zone Tower of Terror Exciting ride in which you "enjoy" the sensation of free-falling in the lift of a classic, crumbling Hollywood hotel. Not actually physically demanding, though the Twilight Zone video might scare some, and it does turn your stomach upside down. Minimum height 1.02m.

Disney Village

The **Disney Village** entertainment and restaurant complex, opposite the Marne-la-Vallée/Chessy RER and train stations, is basically a street lined with expensive shops and restaurants. The work of architect Frank Gehry, it looks like a circus tent that has had its top carried off by a bomb, with a pedestrian street driven through the middle of it. "Buffalo Bill's Wild West Show" (cowboys and Indians charging round a ring on horseback, with slapstick routines and dancing Disney characters) and rides on the PanoraMagique tethered balloon await you, alongside *Annette's Diner*, *Planet Hollywood*, the *Rainforest Café* and a host of other themed restaurants. You'll find French and Bavarian food at *King Ludwig's Castle* (two-course menu around €22). There's live outdoor music on summer nights, IMAX and multiplex cinemas and lots of sideshows.

When you're nearing exhaustion from so much enchantment, you can return to your **hotel** (see opposite) and have a sauna, jacuzzi or whirlpool dip and be in bed in time to feel fresh and fit to meet Mickey and Minnie again over breakfast. In the hotel area of the resort, you can play **golf** (27-hole course) and sail (in summer), though these activities can be expensive.

ARRIVAL AND DEPARTURE   DISNEYLAND PARIS

From London by train There are direct Eurostar trains to Disneyland, but it can sometimes be less expensive to change onto the TGV at Lille; all these trains arrive at Marne-la-Vallée/Chessy station, right outside the main entrance.

From the airports If you're coming straight from the airport, there are shuttle buses from both Charles de Gaulle and Orly, taking 45min from both airports (roughly every 45min 9am–7.30pm; see ⓦmagicalshuttle.fr/uk for timetables and pick-up points). Tickets cost €20 one way, but children under 12 pay €16, and under-3s go free. There is a Beauvais airport shuttle (ⓦsupershuttle.fr), but it takes more than 2hr 30min and costs around €145 for four passengers.

From Paris by train Take RER line A – from Châtelet-Les Halles, Gare-de-Lyon or Nation – to Marne-la-Vallée/Chessy station, which is right next to the train terminal, and opposite the main park gates (40min; €7.60 single, children under 10 half-price, under-4s free). You can get Mobilis travel cards that include Disneyland Paris (see p.27).

By car The park is a 32km drive east of Paris along the A4; take the Porte de Bercy exit off the *périphérique*, then follow "direction Metz/Nancy", leaving at exit 13 for *Davy Crockett Ranch* (see p.255) or exit 14 for Parc Disneyland and the hotels. From Calais follow the A26, changing to the A1, the A104 and finally the A4.

INFORMATION

Opening hours Depending on the season and whether it's a weekend, the parks open from 10am to anywhere between 7pm and 11pm at Disneyland Park, or between 6pm and 7pm at Walt Disney Studios. Depending on the season, staying in one of the Disney hotels might allow you two extra hours in the park in the morning.

Admission One-day one-park costs €39–57 for adults/ €33–51 children aged 3–11, depending on the season; one-day two-park tickets start from €51/€45. There are often two-for-one offers in August. See ⓦdlpguide.com for more information and tips on the best deals.

Contact details UK ☏ 0844 800 8898, France ☏ 01 60 30 60 30, ⓦdlpguide.com, ⓦdisneylandparis.com.

Tickets To avoid queuing, buy tickets online or from tourist offices (see p.40). The one-day one-park pass allows you to visit either the main Disneyland Park or the Walt Disney Studios Park, but you can't swap between them; you can come and go during the day, however.

Information At Disneyland Park, you enter underneath Main Street Station, on the internal railroad system; information is available at City Hall to the left. Information at Walt Disney Studios Park can be found at Studio Services, by the entrance.

Left luggage Luggage can be left in "Guest Storage" lockers near the park entrances (€1.50); there are also lockers at Marne-la-Vallée/Chessy station (from €5).

Disabled access The *Disabled Visitors Guide* is available from City Hall in Disneyland Park, or Studio Services in Walt Disney Studios Park; alternatively, visit ⓦdisneylandparis .co.uk/guest-services/guests-with-disabilities. Staff aren't allowed to lend assistance in getting into and out of the less accessible rides, but all toilets, shops and restaurants

OVERNIGHT PACKAGES

If you plan to stay at a Disneyland hotel, it's much cheaper to book a special accommodation and entry package. Visit an agent, or book through Disney, either online or on ☎ 0844 800 8898 in the UK, ☎ 0825 300 500 in France, or ☎ 00 33 1 60 30 60 53 from other countries.

are wheelchair accessible. You can rent wheelchairs (€15; €150 deposit) in Town Square, in Disneyland Park – the building on the right as you exit Main Street Station. Given the relative dearth of benches, visitors who can normally manage without a chair might appreciate having one.

Babies and small children You can rent pushchairs (€15; €150 deposit if you move between parks) from the same place as wheelchairs (see above). There are two Baby Care centres: next to *Plaza Gardens* restaurant in Disneyland Park, and beside Studio Services in Walt Disney Studios Park.

18

ACCOMMODATION

Disney's seven **themed hotels** are a mixed bag of kitsch designed by some of the world's leading architects – Michael Graves, Antoine Predock, Robert Stern and Frank Gehry. For all the dramatically themed exteriors and lobbies, the rooms are much the same inside: comfortable, huge and soulless. **Prices** vary hugely according to season and which package you book (see box above) – there are almost always offers. The prices we've given below are only a guide to what you might pay in high season for one night for a room accommodating two adults and two children, including entry tickets to the park. It's usually better value to book for two nights or more. All hotels except *Hotel New York* and *Disneyland Hotel* are too far away to walk to comfortably from the entrance with luggage, but free bright-yellow **shuttle buses** run to all the hotels from the bus station in the Central Plaza; the hotel name is shown on the front of each bus. Car drivers can go straight to their hotel (free parking) or to the Disneyland parking areas (€15/day).

HOTELS

Hotel Cheyenne Along with the *Sante Fe*, the *Cheyenne* is broken up into attractively small units: the film-set buildings of a Western frontier town, complete with wagons, cowboys, a hanging tree and scarecrows. With its Wild West theme and bunk beds in all the rooms, this is a good hotel for children – and it's usually relatively inexpensive. **€750–870**

Davy Crockett Ranch Self-catering bungalows and log cabins (4–6 people) in a wooded, Wild West–themed setting – there's even a high-wire tree-top assault course. The ranch is a 15min drive from the park, with no shuttle service laid on, so you'll need your own transport. **€800–970**

Disneyland Hotel Situated right over the entrance to the park with wings to either side, the large, frilly, pastel-pink *Disneyland Hotel* is decked out in glitzy Hollywood style. It's the most upmarket and best located by far. **€1500–1775**

Hotel New York Outside, the hotel is a plasticky, post-modern attempt at conjuring up the New York skyline, while the furnishings within are pseudo Art Deco with lots of apples. Comfortable, and towards the top of the range. **€1100–1200**

Newport Bay Club The largest of the hotels, with one thousand rooms, this "New England seaside resort circa 1900" spreads like a game of dominoes. Blue-and-white-striped canopies over the balconies fail to give it that cosy guesthouse feel, but some rooms have the benefit of looking out over the lake and the hotel has undergone an extensive makeover recently. **€1110**

Hotel Santa Fe Smooth, mercifully unadorned, imitation sun-baked mud buildings in various shapes and sizes. Between them are tasteful car wrecks, a cactus in a glass case, strange geological formations and other products of the distinctly un-Disney imagination of New Mexican architect Antoine Predock. Usually relatively inexpensive. **€750–870**

Sequoia Lodge Overlooking the lake and built around the theme of the "mountain lodge" typically found in the national parks of the western United States, but on a giant scale. **€1100–1170**

EATING AND DRINKING

There are opportunities to eat throughout both parks, as well as in Disney Village. As you'd expect, there's a lot of pricey American junk food, and although the "all-you-can-eat" buffet-style restaurants are not a bad deal, you can still end up paying three or four times the price of a meal outside the park. Consider booking ahead (at City Hall or Studio Services, or on ☎ 01 60 30 40 50), as all restaurants fill up quickly at lunch and dinner times. Adults can drink wine or beer at any of the park's restaurants. Officially, you're not supposed to bring in full-on picnics, but Goofy won't turn nasty if he sees you eating a sandwich.

L'HÔTEL, ST-GERMAIN

Accommodation

Accommodation is not, on the whole, Paris's strong point and it's becoming increasingly difficult to find good budget hotels. At the luxury end, things are sumptuous and stylish, and there are a fair few boutique hotels with cool design features. Unless you stumble upon a promotional deal, however, prices at the top end are stratospheric, and even in the better three- and four-star establishments, rooms are typically cramped for the price. If you stay at the back of the building, overlooking the courtyard, rooms can be dark, too, though at least you're spared potential street noise. There are, however, a few genuine gems, and many places where the welcome, the character or the location – and often, the views – easily outweigh the lack of space.

ESSENTIALS

Reservations The best hotels are typically booked up well in advance, especially in the spring and autumn peak seasons. It's wise to reserve a room as early as you can, particularly if you fancy staying in one of the more characterful places. You can generally book online but some hotels do require a phone call – all receptionists speak some English – and often a follow-up email so that they have requests in writing. In fact, it's always worth asking for a discount on the advertised rate; in August and from November to March (apart from Christmas) you may be able to negotiate reductions of ten to twenty percent or more.

Online reservation services The online agency ⓦ ratestogo.com offers discounts on last-minute bookings.

Tourist offices If you find yourself stuck on arrival, the main tourist office (see p.40) at rue des Pyramides and the branches at the Gare de Lyon, Gare du Nord and by Anvers métro station can find you a room in a hotel or hostel free of charge.

Hotel breakfasts Breakfast (*petit déjeuner*) is sometimes included (*compris*) in the room price but is normally extra (*en supplément*) – around €7–14 per person. Always make it clear whether you want breakfast or not when you take the room. Either way, it's usually a continental affair of croissants/baguette, fresh orange juice and coffee.

Stairs and lifts Many hotels, especially at the cheaper end of the scale, are shoehorned into very old buildings. What you gain in character you lose out on in amenities – many hotels don't have lifts, or have lifts only up to a certain floor – so if you have difficulty walking or carrying luggage, ask for a room on a lower floor.

Wi-fi Free wi-fi access is generally offered as standard in most hotels – though you may have to sit in reception to access it. The few hotels that do still charge for wi-fi should make this clear when booking.

19

HOTELS

One of the best central **areas for budget hotels** is the 10e, especially around place de la République, and the 11e, especially along rue du Grand Prieuré. Quieter districts, further out, where you can get some good deals are the 13e and 14e, south of Montparnasse, and the 17e and 20e, on the western and eastern sides of the city respectively. Our hotel recommendations are listed by area, following the same divisions used in the Guide. Most hotels have a selection of rooms – singles, doubles, twin-bedded and triples – at different prices, which can fluctuate widely throughout the year. In our listings we give advertised or online **prices for the cheapest double room in high season** – which will sometimes mean shared facilities – and also cite tariffs for **single rooms** where these are particularly good value.

THE ISLANDS

Hôtel de Lutèce 65 rue St-Louis-en-l'Ile, 4e ⓣ 01 43 26 23 52, ⓦ hoteldelutece.com; ⓜ Pont Marie; map pp.44–45. This narrow seventeenth-century townhouse, located on the most desirable island in France, has 23 tiny, pretty wood-beamed en suites. All have been renovated in a contemporary style, and come with modern bathrooms. €225

BOOKING A HOTEL ROOM

France's **star system** provides some clues as to the pretensions of a hotel, but little else – a two-star hotel might have lovely rooms but fail to be awarded a third star because its staff don't speak enough languages, or its foyer is small. As a rule of thumb, a double room in an old-fashioned two-star will cost between €80 and €150, depending on season and location, though don't expect much in the way of decor at the lower end of the scale. For something with a bit more class – whether that means a touch of design flair, slick service or in-room tech – you'll pay in the region of €130–250, again depending on location/season. At the luxury end of the scale the sky's the limit, with prices above €400 not uncommon – though online and off-season deals can chop a dramatic amount off the official price. It is possible to find a double room in a central location for around €50–70, though at this level you should expect a room with just a sink (*lavabo*) and a shared bathroom on the landing (*dans le palier*).

Within one hotel, **rooms** can vary hugely, and it's well worth asking what's available. Rooms at the back, overlooking an internal courtyard (*côté cour/jardin*) can be dark; rooms on the street (*côté rue*) tend to be larger and lighter, but noise can be a problem if there isn't double-glazing. Certain standard terms recur: *douche/WC* and *bain/WC* mean that you have a shower or bath as well as toilet in the room. A room with a *grand lit* (double bed) is usually cheaper than one with *deux lits* (two separate beds). Many hotels offer *de luxe* or *supérieure* rooms as well as those in a *standard* or *classique* class; a superior room in a less expensive hotel can often be better value than a standard one in a pricier establishment.

19

THE CHAMPS-ELYSÉES AND AROUND

Le 123 123 rue du Faubourg-St-Honoré, 8ᵉ ☎ 01 53 89 01 23, ⓦ astotel.com; Ⓜ St-Philippe-du-Roule; map pp.64–65. Friendly, stylish hotel – one of the generally good *Astotel* chain – a 5min walk from the Champs-Elysées. Rooms are a good size with high ceilings, laminate floors and modern furnishings, plus iPod docks. Some have balconies. **€240**

Hôtel d'Albion 15 rue de Penthièvre, 8ᵉ ☎ 01 42 65 84 15, ⓦ hotelalbion.net; Ⓜ Miromesnil; map pp.64–65. A small family-run hotel in a nineteenth-century townhouse, set around a quiet courtyard garden. Just a 10min walk from the Champs-Elysées, it's not fancy, but it's clean, comfortable and excellent value for the area. Many of the rooms have a view over the garden. **€150**

Hôtel Arioso 7 rue d'Argenson, 8ᵉ ☎ 01 53 05 95 00, ⓦ arioso-hotel.com; Ⓜ Miromesnil; map pp.64–65. About a 15min walk from the Champs-Elysées, this is a charming, comfy four-star boutique hotel set in a solid Haussmann-era block, run by courteous and helpful staff. The 28 rooms are small, especially the cheaper ones, and some pick up a bit of street noise, but all are cosily decorated with quality furnishings and decorative fabrics. Some of the more expensive rooms have jasmine-strewn balconies looking onto a pretty little tiled interior courtyard and their bathrooms are stocked with Occitane products. **€240**

Le Bristol 112 rue du Faubourg St-Honoré, 8ᵉ ☎ 01 53 43 43 00, ⓦ lebristolparis.com; Ⓜ Miromesnil; map pp.64–65. Among the city's most iconic hotels, *Le Bristol* opened in 1925 and has maintained its reputation for discreet, warm luxury with superb service. The 188-odd rooms, all very spacious, come with authentic antiques – including Gobelins tapestries – and the most expensive have private roof gardens. There's also a spa, swimming pool and three gourmet restaurants. **€900**

Hôtel Lancaster 7 rue de Berri, 8ᵉ ☎ 01 40 76 40 76, ⓦ hotel-lancaster.com; Ⓜ George-V; map pp.64–65. The 43 rooms in this elegantly restored nineteenth-century townhouse – the pied-à-terre for the likes of Garbo, Dietrich and Sir Alec Guinness – retain original features and are chock-full of Louis XVI and Rococo antiques, but with a touch of contemporary chic. A small interior Zen-style garden and impeccable service make for a relaxing stay, and there's an excellent Michelin-starred restaurant, too. **€500**

Hôtel Le Lavoisier 21 rue Lavoisier, 8ᵉ ☎ 01 53 30 06 06, ⓦ hotellavoisier.com; Ⓜ St-Augustin; map pp.64–65. A boutique hotel in a Haussmann-era townhouse, on a quiet side street around 15min walk from the Champs-Elysées. Rooms vary in size and style; some are decorated in neutral tones, with a comfortable, gentlemen's club kind of feel, while others are brighter and more decorative; those at the front have Juliet balconies. The comfortable reception area with sofas is a nice place to linger, but note that they charge €5 (per device per stay) for wi-fi. **€235**

Hôtel de Sers 41 av Pierre 1er de Serbie, 8ᵉ ☎ 01 53 23 75 75, ⓦ hoteldesers-paris.fr; Ⓜ George-V; map pp.64–65. This chic hotel, just off the Champs-Elysées, offers swish rooms with Italian-marble bathrooms, sleek decor and flashes of quirky colour; facilities include iPads and huge TVs. Some of the suites (from €800) on the top floor have fabulous panoramic terraces with views of the Eiffel Tower. Excellent offers and online deals can bring the rates right down. **€380**

THE TUILERIES AND LOUVRE

Hôtel Brighton 218 rue de Rivoli, 1ᵉʳ ☎ 01 47 03 61 61, ⓦ paris-hotel-brighton.com; Ⓜ Tuileries; map pp.74–75. Location is key at this elegant hotel, dating back to the late nineteenth century, with airy, high-ceilinged rooms. There are a range of options: "classic" rooms, which look over the courtyard, are fine if nothing special, while the "Tuileries" and "club" rooms, though small, have views of the gardens or the rue de Rivoli; the larger "deluxe" rooms are the best, particularly those on the upper floors, with magnificent vistas of the Tuileries gardens. **€280**

Costes 239 rue St-Honoré, 1ᵉʳ ☎ 01 42 44 50 00, ⓦ hotel costes.com; Ⓜ Tuileries; map pp.74–75. A favourite with media folk and fashionistas, this supercool hotel, marrying Second Empire style with up-to-date amenities, is post-modern decadence perfected. Beautiful people saunter through plush red-velvet interiors beneath dim lighting; service, however, is variable, and the cheapest rooms are very small indeed. The DJ bar and courtyard restaurant are destinations in themselves. **€500**

Le Relais Saint-Honoré 308 rue St-Honoré, 1ᵉʳ ☎ 01 42 96 06 06, ⓦ relaissainthonore.com; Ⓜ Tuileries; map pp.74–75. A charming little hotel, set in a stylishly renovated seventeenth-century townhouse on one of Paris's main fashion streets. The fifteen neat, tastefully furnished rooms are colourful and cheery, some with painted wooden beams and pretty floral fabrics; some are smaller than the others, while others have mezzanine areas. There's a suite suitable for families. **€250**

★ Hôtel Thérèse 5–7 rue Thérèse, 1ᵉʳ ☎ 01 42 96 10 01, ⓦ hoteltherese.com; Ⓜ Palais-Royal-Musée-du-Louvre; map pp.74–75. Very attractive boutique hotel, run by exceptionally helpful and courteous staff, on a quiet street within easy walking distance of the Louvre. Rooms are small and stylish, with luxury fabrics and cool furnishings; some of them overlook the leafy courtyard. Book in advance, as it's very popular, especially during the fashion shows. **€200**

THE GRANDS BOULEVARDS AND PASSAGES

Hôtel Chopin 46 passage Jouffroy, 9ᵉ; entrance on bd Montmartre, near rue du Faubourg-Montmartre ☎ 01 47 70 58 10, ⓦ hotelchopin-paris-opera.com; Ⓜ Grands Boulevards; map pp.74–75. A charming, quiet and old-fashioned hotel set in an atmospheric period building at the

TOP TEN FOR €100 OR LESS

Although Paris is expensive, there are still places where you don't have to spend a fortune. Here are our top choices for under €100 – and in some cases, less. Do bear in mind, though, that these represent the lowest prices in town – and in some cases for rooms with shared bathrooms – so be sure to keep your expectations realistic.

Hôtel Bonséjour Montmartre See p.263	**Hôtel de Nesle** See p.262
Cosmos Hôtel See p.265	**Hôtel du Nord** See p.265
Hôtel Eldorado See p.264	**Hôtel Port-Royal** See p.263
Hôtel du Loiret See p.260	**Solar Hôtel** See p.263
Hôtel Marignan See p.261	**Hôtel Tiquetonne** See p.259

19

end of a picturesque 1840s *passage*. The 36 rooms are clean and spruce, and good for the price, though the cheaper ones are on the small side and a little dark. **€106**

Hôtel Crayon 25 rue de Bouloi, 1er ☎01 42 36 54 19, Ⓦhotelcrayon.com; ⓂLouvre-Rivoli; map pp.74–75. Colourful, artist-owned hotel with a guesthouse feel. The 26 funky rooms are all different, with vibrant colour blocking and scattered with mismatched vintage and retro furniture. Check online for good deals. *Hôtel Crayon Rouge*, 150m away at 42 rue Croix des Petits Champs, is similar. **€240**

★**Hôtel Edgar** 31 rue d'Alexandrie, 2e ☎01 40 41 05 19, Ⓦedgarparis.com; ⓂSentier; map pp.74–75. It doesn't get much more designer than this, with fourteen small rooms conceived by artists, stylists, film-makers and creatives of every stripe. It's all presented with great joie de vivre, and whether you want the soft greys of "Cocoon", the boudoir chic of "Ma Nuit" or the kooky kiddy kitsch of "Dream", you'll find a niche. It's not all style over substance, either – the staff are friendly, rooms are comfy, with good bathrooms, and the street is quiet. **€235**

★**Hôtel Tiquetonne** 6 rue Tiquetonne, 2e ☎01 42 36 94 58, Ⓦhoteltiquetonne.fr; ⓂEtienne-Marcel; map pp.74–75. Located on a pedestrianized street a block away from lively rue Montorgueil, this excellent-value budget hotel in a 1920s building offers old-fashioned charm. Rooms have retro furnishings and are clean and well maintained: many are quite spacious, with larger-than-average bathrooms, though walls are thin. Non-en-suite rooms come with a sink and bidet; it costs €5 a go to use the shower on the landing, so it's worth spending €70 on an en-suite. **€55**

Hôtel Vivienne 40 rue Vivienne, 2e ☎01 42 33 13 26, Ⓦhotel-vivienne.com; ⓂGrands Boulevards/Bourse; map pp.74–75. A 10min walk from the Louvre, this family-run place does the essentials well: the 44 rooms are clean, good-sized and come with modern facilities; the cheapest are less impressive, though OK for the price, and have WC down the hall. Good online deals available. **€88**

BEAUBOURG AND LES HALLES

★**Hôtel du Cygne** 3–5 rue du Cygne, 1er ☎01 42 60 14 16, Ⓦcygne-hotel-paris.com; ⓂEtienne-Marcel; map p.86. This friendly hotel, harbouring twenty small,

cheerily decorated rooms, some of them with beamed ceilings, occupies a four-storey seventeenth-century townhouse with a dash of charm – there's no lift, just a narrow twisty staircase (staff will help with bags), and a cosy communal lounge. It's on a lively pedestrianized street in the heart of the Les Halles district, so can get a little noisy at night. Five singles are available for €95 a night in high season, and there are good online deals available. **€120**

Relais du Louvre 19 rue des Prêtres St-Germain l'Auxerrois, 1er ☎01 40 41 96 42, Ⓦrelaisdulouvre.com; ⓂPalais-Royal-Musée-du-Louvre; map p.86. An intimate hotel with 22 rooms set on a quiet backstreet opposite the church of St-Germain l'Auxerrois; you can admire the church's flying buttresses from the front-facing rooms. The rooms have rich fabrics, old prints, period furniture and paintings. There are also three comfy suites sleeping up to four. The relaxed atmosphere and charming service attract a repeat clientele. **€220**

★**Hôtel Saint-Merry** 78 rue de la Verrerie, 4e ☎01 42 78 14 15, Ⓦsaintmerrymarais.com; ⓂHôtel-de-Ville; map p.86. "Unique" is a much overused word, but perfectly appropriate when describing this quirky little hotel, where you can indulge your Gothic medieval fantasies in a former presbytery attached to the Eglise St-Merri. There are eleven rooms and one suite, all featuring dark-wood furniture, exposed stone walls and wrought iron; room 9, incorporating a flying buttress, no less, is the most popular, but there are a variety of sizes and standards. **€180**

THE MARAIS

★**Hôtel Bourg Tibourg** 19 rue du Bourg-Tibourg, 4e ☎01 42 78 47 39, Ⓦbourgtibourg.com; ⓂHôtel-de-Ville; map p.86. Oriental meets medieval meets bordello, with a dash of Second Empire, at this sumptuously designed little hotel related to the *Costes* (see opposite). Rooms are small, but cosseted with rich velvets, silks and drapes; some have their own mini balconies. With well-chosen books, classic movies and even a hotel playlist, this is a hip little romantic hideaway. **€260**

Hôtel de la Bretonnerie 22 rue Ste-Croix de la Bretonnerie, 4e ☎01 48 87 77 63, Ⓦbretonnerie.com; ⓂHôtel-de-Ville; map p.86. A charming, if slightly tired in places, hotel with 29 individually designed rooms, all decorated with quality fabrics, oak furniture and, in some cases, four-poster beds. The beamed attic rooms, and the split-level or dual-bathroom suites (from €250), are particularly appealing. The location's perfect for exploring the Marais, though front-facing rooms may suffer from street noise at night. **€180**

Caron de Beaumarchais 12 rue Vieille-du-Temple, 4ᵉ • 01 42 72 34 12, ⓦ carondebeaumarchais.com; ⓜ Hôtel-de-Ville; map p.97. Pretty hotel named after the eighteenth-century French playwright, who would have felt quite at home here: all the furnishings – the original engravings and Louis XVI furniture, not to mention the piano in the foyer – evoke the refined tastes of high-society pre-Revolution Paris. There are nineteen rooms; those overlooking the narrow courtyard are petite, while those on the street are more spacious, some with a small balcony, chandeliers and beams. **€175**

Hôtel Ecole Centrale 3 rue Bailly, 3ᵉ • 01 48 04 77 76, ⓦ paris-marais.fr; ⓜ Arts-et-Métiers; map p.94. Very friendly hotel in a Marais townhouse on a quiet cul-de-sac. Though rather garishly decorated, the rooms aren't a bad size, and those on the first and second floors – though they're the most basic – retain original features including wooden beams. The more expensive deluxe rooms in the attic have espresso makers, and two have jacuzzis. Various online discounts available, including last-minute and three-night offers, plus special weekend rates that include breakfast. **€145**

Hôtel Jeanne d'Arc 3 rue de Jarente, 4ᵉ • 01 48 87 62 11, ⓦ hoteljeannedarc.com; ⓜ St-Paul; map p.97. This old Marais townhouse, just off lovely place du Marché Ste-Catherine, has small, simple rooms, all of them different; some retain original features such as exposed brick walls. The triple at the top has nice views over the rooftops, and corner rooms have more light. Staff are friendly and helpful. You can consume your own snacks, drinks and meals in the quirky breakfast area, overlooking the pretty street. **€120**

Jules et Jim 11 rue des Gravilliers, 3ᵉ • 01 44 54 13 13, ⓦ hoteljulesetjim.com; ⓜ Arts-et-Métiers; map p.94. Very cool contemporary hotel with lots of hip design features – check out the reception desk made of books – and 23 quiet, swish rooms. There's a good bar opening onto the cobbled courtyard (it closes at 11pm, to avoid noise disturbing guests in courtyard rooms), and really welcoming staff. **€240**

Hôtel du Loiret 8 rue des Mauvais-Garçons, 4ᵉ • 01 48 87 77 00, ⓦ hotel-du-loiret.fr; ⓜ Hôtel-de-Ville; map p.97. If you're looking for location and quality at the lower end of the price spectrum, this 25-room hotel is a good choice. Most of the rooms are small but comfortable and clean, with shower and/or bath, and some have balconies. The higher rooms are larger, quieter and have views. **€100**

★**Hôtel de Nice** 42bis rue de Rivoli, 4ᵉ • 01 42 78 55 29, ⓦ hoteldenice.com; ⓜ Hôtel-de-Ville; map p.97. A well-run, cosy little establishment, with old-world charm and lots of quirky style: the 23 colourful rooms have Indian-cotton bed-spreads, carved wooden wardrobes, elaborate wallpaper and gilded mirrors. The rue de Rivoli is very busy, though double glazing helps to block out most of the traffic noise. **€165**

Hôtel Paris France 72 rue de Turbigo, 3ᵉ • 01 42 78 00 04, ⓦ paris-france-hotel.com; ⓜ Temple; map p.94. Welcoming hotel offering sizeable, comfortable rooms in a very convenient location, handy for the canal and the Louvre. The decor is understated and tasteful, with good bathrooms and great Eiffel Tower views from the upper floors. **€120**

★**Hôtel du Petit Moulin** 29–31 rue de Poitou, 3ᵉ • 01 42 74 10 10, ⓦ hoteldupetitmoulin.com; ⓜ St-Sébastien-Froissart/Filles-du-Calvaire; map p.97. Inside a former bakery – the lovely old exterior remains intact – this luxurious Christian Lacroix-designed boutique hotel is infused with the designer's hallmark *joie de vivre*. The seventeen rooms are a bold fusion of different styles, from elegant Baroque to Sixties kitsch via raunchy bordello; shocking pinks and lime greens give way to *toile de Jouy* prints, while pod chairs rub up alongside antique dressing tables and standalone bathtubs. **€225**

Hôtel Picard 26 rue de Picardie, 3ᵉ • 01 48 87 53 82, ⓦ Temple/République; map p.94. In a quiet Marais street, this family-run cheapie is very basic but a good budget option, particularly given its location. Rooms are spartan but the beds are comfy and staff are pleasant. The cheapest doubles have a washbasin, with a shower on the landing (an extra €3/shower). **€72**

Hôtel de la Place des Vosges 12 rue de Birague, 4ᵉ • 01 42 72 60 46, ⓦ hotelplacedesvosges.com; ⓜ Bastille; map p.94. A charming, well-priced hotel in a glorious building, dating back to 1605, very near the *place*. Rooms are contemporary in style, and small, but some have wooden floors, stone walls and wooden beams. **€150**

Hôtel St-Louis Marais 1 rue Charles-V, 4ᵉ • 01 48 87 87 04, ⓦ saintlouismarais.com; ⓜ Sully-Morland; map p.97. Formerly part of the seventeenth-century Célestins Convent, this characterful place retains its period feel, with stone walls, exposed beams and tiled floors. Some of the fifteen rooms are small, but the bathrooms are large and relatively luxurious. A major plus is the location, on a very quiet road, just a short walk from the Marais action, with the Left Bank easily accessible too. Avoid the less appealing annexe rooms. **€175**

TOP 5 BOUTIQUE BOLTHOLES

Auberge Flora See p.261
L'Hôtel See p.262
Hôtel Bourg Tibourg See p.259
Hôtel du Petit Moulin See p.260
Hôtel Thérèse See p.258

BASTILLE AND AROUND

★ **Auberge Flora** 44 bd Richard-Lenoir, 11ᵉ ☎ 01 47 00 52 77, ⓦ aubergeflora.fr; Ⓜ Bréguet-Sabin; map pp.110–111. A cute boutique hotel with 21 rooms from singles to "gourmande" options and suites, decorated on a loose theme according to which floor they're on (bohemia, vegetable plot or nature). The cheapest are tiny, but a good price, and all are colourful, quirky and comfortable, with lots of individual touches. Flora herself is also the chef at the restaurant below, offering deceptively simple, seasonal and delicious Mediterranean-influenced food. **€120**

Hôtel Marais Bastille 36 bd Richard-Lenoir, 11ᵉ ☎ 01 48 05 75 00, ⓦ maraisbastille.com; Ⓜ Bréguet-Sabin; map pp.110–111. Part of the *Best Western* chain and handily located for both the Marais and Bastille, this 37-room hotel has a swish, contemporary interior. The public spaces are a bit overdesigned, but the rooms, while small, are comfy and clean, done out in soothing hues with splashes of paintbox-bright colour and modern bathrooms. Good online deals available. **€179**

★ **Hôtel de la Porte Dorée** 273 av Daumesnil, 12ᵉ ☎ 01 43 07 56 97, ⓦ hoteldelaportedoree.com; Ⓜ Porte Dorée; map p.117. This welcoming, extremely child-friendly hotel is not as central as some offerings in its price range but it's very close to the Bois de Vincennes, right next to the métro, and Bastille is just 7min away by métro or a pleasant 20min stroll along the Promenade Plantée. Tastefully refurbished by an American-French family, the contemporary rooms, each with a private shower or bath, TV and comfy beds, have traditional features including ceiling mouldings and fireplaces, and some antique furnishings. Regular online deals offer significant reductions. **€119**

QUARTIER LATIN

Hôtel du Commerce 14 rue de la Montagne-Ste-Geneviève, 5ᵉ ☎ 01 43 54 89 69, ⓦ commerceparishotel .com; Ⓜ Maubert-Mutualité; map pp.122–123. This budget hotel is good value if you want to stay very centrally. They've made an effort with the decor, with bright colours everywhere, and while rooms are small and sometimes noisy, with a hostel-ish feel, they're clean, with comfortable beds. Prices range from washbasin-only cheapies (there's a €2 fee to use the shower in the hall) up to simple en suites (better value at around €78) and three- and four-bed rooms. No credit cards. **€58**

Hôtel Degrés de Notre-Dame 10 rue des Grands Degrés, 5ᵉ ☎ 01 55 42 88 88, ⓦ lesdegreshotel.com; Ⓜ St-Michel/Maubert-Mutualité; map pp.122–123. There are just ten rooms in this superbly idiosyncratic, homely hotel – it's not luxurious, but full of character. The building is ancient and the rooms – all with bathroom – are each very different, with prices corresponding to size. Unique, personal touches are everywhere: hand-painted murals, antique mirrors, ancient beams and curious nooks and crannies. Room 51 at the top

has great Notre-Dame views. **€110**

Hôtel Design de la Sorbonne 6 rue Victor Cousin, 5ᵉ ☎ 01 43 54 58 08, ⓦ hotelsorbonne.com; Ⓜ Cluny-La-Sorbonne; map pp.122–123. Brilliantly located hotel with photo exhibitions on each floor, eye-popping colour schemes and iMacs in each room. Above all, though, the rooms are cosy and comfortable, with good bathrooms, the staff are friendly and prices are reasonable for this standard. **€150**

Hôtel Esmeralda 4 rue St-Julien-le-Pauvre, 5ᵉ ☎ 01 43 54 19 20, ⓦ hotel-esmeralda.fr; Ⓜ St-Michel/Maubert-Mutualité; map pp.122–123. Dozing in an ancient house on square Viviani, this ancient hotel offers a deeply old-fashioned feel, with sixteen eccentrically decorated, simple en-suite rooms – a few of them with unrivalled views of Notre-Dame. It's not always perfectly tidy, the wallpaper can occasionally be alarming, and there are plenty of worn corners and few mod-cons but the staff are friendly and the location is incomparable. **€120**

Familia Hôtel 11 rue des Ecoles, 5ᵉ ☎ 01 43 54 55 27, ⓦ familiahotel.com; Ⓜ Cardinal-Lemoine/Maubert-Mutualité/Jussieu; map pp.122–123. Friendly, family-run hotel in the heart of the *quartier*. It's not luxurious, but it has charm – the small rooms are full of character, with beams, *toile de Jouy* wallpaper and pretty murals; some top-floor rooms have views of nearby Notre-Dame, and others have their own small balcony. The slightly more expensive *Minerva*, next door, has the same owners. **€130**

★ **Hôtel des Grandes Ecoles** 75 rue du Cardinal-Lemoine, 5ᵉ ☎ 01 43 26 79 23, ⓦ hotel-grandes-ecoles .com; Ⓜ Cardinal-Lemoine/Monge; map pp.122–123. A cobbled private lane leads through to a big surprise: a large and peaceful garden, right in the heart of the Quartier Latin, with the feel of a country house. The rooms are pretty in a modest way, with floral wallpaper and old-fashioned furnishings, and the welcome is homely and sincere. Reserve well in advance; it fills up fast. **€140**

Hôtel des Grands Hommes 17 place du Panthéon, 5ᵉ ☎ 01 46 34 19 60, ⓦ hoteldesgrandshommes.com; Ⓜ Maubert-Mutualité/RER Luxembourg; map pp.122–123. There's a certain magnificence in this old townhouse hotel: a number of the thirty rooms look out over the Panthéon and the decor and styling is distinctly luxurious, despite the occasional quirk (thin walls, small showers). But it's a friendly hotel at heart, with lovely service, and often offers up to 50 percent discounts on the official rate, both on their website and over the phone. Good value. **€190**

★ **Hôtel Marignan** 13 rue du Sommerard, 5ᵉ ☎ 01 43 54 63 81, ⓦ hotel-marignan.com; Ⓜ Maubert-Mutualité; map pp.122–123. This welcoming budget hotel, in the same family for three generations, is totally sympathetic to the needs of rucksack-toting foreigners, offering free laundry and ironing facilities plus a basic self-catering kitchen/diner. The thirty rooms are clean and comfortable, with options for up to five people; the cheapest have shared bathrooms.

19

19

Simple, but one of the best-value places in town – and breakfast is thrown in for free. No lift. **€91**

Hôtel Résidence Henri IV 50 rue des Bernardins, 5ᵉ ☎ 01 44 41 31 81, ⓦ residencehenri4.com; ⓜ Maubert-Mutualité; map pp.122–123. Set back from busy rue des Ecoles on a cul-de-sac, this hotel is discreet and elegant, with great service. There are eight standard doubles, as well as five larger suites with separate lounging areas. All are classically styled – some have original features like fireplaces – and all have miniature kitchenettes. **€230**

Hôtel St-Jacques 35 rue des Ecoles, 5ᵉ ☎ 01 44 07 45 45, ⓦ paris-hotel-stjacques.com; ⓜ Maubert-Mutualité/Odéon; map pp.122–123. This pretty hotel in the heart of the district combines original nineteenth-century features, including a wrought-iron staircase and decorative ceiling mouldings, with modern comforts. The rooms are pretty, some with flowery balconies and lovely views. Extra kudos: this is where Audrey Hepburn and Cary Grant stayed in the 1963 movie *Charade*. **€180**

Select Hôtel 1 place de la Sorbonne, 5ᵉ ☎ 01 46 34 14 80, ⓦ selecthotel.fr; ⓜ Cluny-La-Sorbonne; map pp.122–123. Situated right on the *place*, this fairly large (66-room), modern four-star hotel has a stylish feel, with exposed stone walls matched with contemporary furnishings – standard rooms are comfortable, if small. The more appealing rooms with views onto the square attract a hefty mark-up (€330). Efficiently run, with helpful staff. **€185**

ST-GERMAIN

Hôtel de l'Abbaye 10 rue Cassette, 6ᵉ ☎ 01 45 44 38 11, ⓦ hotelabbayeparis.com; ⓜ St-Sulpice; map pp.136–137. An atmosphere of calm presides over this elegant, prettily decorated hotel. Rooms are characterized by swathes of flowery fabric and brass fittings, all very tastefully done – perhaps best of all is its verdant courtyard garden and conservatory, where you can enjoy breakfast (often included in the rates, depending on season) or an evening *apéritif*. **€275**

La Belle Juliette 92 rue du Cherche-Midi, 6ᵉ ☎ 01 42 22 97 40, ⓦ labellejuliette.com; ⓜ Rue du Bac; map pp.136–137. Many of the rooms in this beautifully designed four-star boutique hotel look out onto one of the most charming roads on the Left Bank, populated with sweet cafés and shops. The decor brings high-concept arty touches to classic, late eighteenth-century elegance – the dark "starlit" halls can take a bit of getting used to. All rooms have iMacs, and there's a spa and garden. **€250**

Hôtel du Danube 58 rue Jacob, 6ᵉ ☎ 01 42 60 34 70, ⓦ hoteldanube.fr; ⓜ St-Germain-des-Prés; map pp.136–137. Elegant but very friendly hotel right in the heart of things. The teeny standard rooms are fine, but the *supérieures* (€250) are the ones to go for, if you can: unusually spacious, each with a pair of handsome, tall windows. It's popular, especially with Americans, so book well in advance. **€180**

★ **L'Hôtel** 13 rue des Beaux-Arts, 6ᵉ ☎ 01 44 41 99 00,

ⓦ l-hotel.com; ⓜ Mabillon/St-Germain-des-Prés; map pp.136–137. A small, quirky boutique hotel epitomizing louche Left Bank opulence, with twenty sumptuous rooms – the cheapest are tiny, but gorgeous – accessed by a spiral staircase. There's a tiny steam room/pool in the basement, an excellent restaurant and stylish bar. Oscar Wilde died here, "fighting a duel" with his wallpaper, and he's now remembered in a room with a "Wilde" theme. Rooms vary, so if you're not happy with yours, ask to see another. Continental breakfast included. **€325**

Hôtel Louis II 2 rue St-Sulpice, 6ᵉ ☎ 01 46 33 13 80, ⓦ hotel-louis2.com; ⓜ Odéon; map pp.136–137. Friendly, quiet boutique hotel with a lovely central location. Standard rooms are small but bright, with exposed beams and period furnishings. **€190**

Hôtel Michelet-Odéon 6 place de l'Odéon, 6ᵉ ☎ 01 53 10 05 60, ⓦ hotelmicheletodeon.com; ⓜ Odéon; map pp.136–137. A clean, comfortable and quiet choice – a bargain so close to the Jardin du Luxembourg. There are around forty rooms – those facing onto the *place*, especially the corner ones, are attractive. A few triples, quads and apartments are available (€185–225), making it a good deal for families. **€135**

★ **Hôtel de Nesle** 7 rue de Nesle, 6ᵉ ☎ 01 43 54 62 41, ⓦ hoteldenesleparis.com; ⓜ St-Michel; map pp.136–137. Bohemian hotel with lots of character in its themed rooms (some with shared facilities and others decorated with love-'em-or-hate-'em cartoon murals), its charming courtyard garden and its balcony terrace. Prices are low for the area, and the owner is a delight. Ideally, phone to reserve (it's best to have a little French). **€100**

Hôtel Odéon Saint-Germain 13 rue St-Sulpice, 6ᵉ ☎ 01 43 25 70 11, ⓦ hotelparisodeonsaintgermain.com; ⓜ St-Sulpice/Odéon; map pp.136–137. Old-fashioned luxury: antique furniture, some four-poster beds and elegant designer fabrics. The service is excellent, and the location splendid: right between the bd St-Germain and the Jardin du Luxembourg. **€220**

Relais Saint-Sulpice 3 rue Garancière, 6ᵉ ☎ 01 46 33 99 00, ⓦ relais-saint-sulpice.com; ⓜ St-Sulpice/St-Germain-des-Prés; map pp.136–137. Wonderfully located in a beautiful, aristocratic townhouse on a side street immediately behind St-Sulpice's apse, this is a discreetly classy hotel with well-furnished rooms – many overlook the leafy patio or the church's apse. All mod-cons, including a sauna off the dining room. **€199**

Hôtel de Verneuil 8 rue de Verneuil, 7ᵉ ☎ 01 42 60 82 14, ⓦ hotel-verneuil-saint-germain.com; ⓜ St-Germain-des-Prés; map pp.136–137. Ideally situated in a very quiet street between St Germain, the Louvre and the Musée d'Orsay, this boutique hotel exudes understated style and offers impeccable service. The smallest doubles are tiny but they're cosy – many retain period features, such as exposed beams – comfy and luxurious. **€230**

THE EIFFEL TOWER QUARTER

★**Hôtel du Champ-de-Mars** 7 rue du Champ-de-Mars, 7ᵉ ☎ 01 45 51 52 30, ⓦ hotelduchampdemars .com; ⓜ Ecole-Militaire; map pp.150–151. In a handsome area just off the rue Cler market, this good-value, quiet hotel has a comforting neighbourhood feel. The rooms are small but cosy, clean and colourful; a couple of them overlook pretty courtyards. Good value. **€160**

Hôtel du Palais Bourbon 49 rue de Bourgogne, 7ᵉ ☎ 01 44 11 30 70, ⓦ bourbon-paris-hotel.com; ⓜ Varenne; map pp.150–151. This substantial, handsome old three-star in the hushed, posh district near the Musée Rodin offers unusually spacious and prettily furnished double rooms. As befits a homely hotel, there are parquet floors and lots of period details – it's not luxurious, but has all the facilities you need. Family rooms are available, as well as a few miniature singles (€110). **€208**

MONTPARNASSE AND THE 14ᵉ

Hôtel Delambre 35 rue Delambre, 14ᵉ ☎ 01 43 20 66 31, ⓦ delambre-paris-hotel.com; ⓜ Edgar-Quinet; map pp.162–163. Beyond the appealing turquoise and gold exterior you'll find the odd colourful flourish in this reliable choice on the northern edge of Montparnasse towards St-Germain. Above all, though, the *Delambre* stands out for the friendly service and spotless, comfortable en-suite rooms, some of which have little balconies. **€120**

★**Solar Hôtel** 22 rue Boulard, 14ᵉ ☎ 01 43 21 08 20, ⓦ solarhotel.fr; ⓜ Denfert-Rochereau; map pp.162–163. This modern budget hotel maintains a determinedly ecological spirit, from its waste disposal to its water-saving. The rooms are unfussy, colourful and comfortable, a little like an upmarket hostel, each with private bathroom. Rates include a simple organic breakfast, which you can eat in the small garden, and use of bikes. **€89**

THE 15ᵉ

Hôtel de l'Avre 21 rue de l'Avre, 15ᵉ ☎ 01 45 75 31 03, ⓦ hoteldelavre.com; ⓜ La-Motte-Picquet-Grenelle; map pp.172–173. Within striking distance of the Eiffel Tower, this cheery, good-value hotel lies just off the rue du Commerce – but you could be forgiven for thinking you were in the provinces. The rooms – which do vary, so ask to see another if you don't like yours – have floral accents and wicker furniture, and some have balconies over the pretty courtyard garden. **€105**

Hôtel Printemps 31 rue du Commerce, 15ᵉ ☎ 01 45 79 83 36, ⓔ hotel.printemps.15e@wanadoo.fr; ⓜ Emile-Zola/La-Motte-Picquet-Grenelle; map pp.172–173. Cheap furnishings and ageing decor don't stop this being a reasonable budget choice given its neighbourhood location and friendly welcome; it's popular with backpackers. The nicer rooms have small balconies. You'll pay €10 more for a room with private facilities. **€50**

Splendid Hotel 54 rue Fondary, 15ᵉ ☎ 01 45 75 17 73, ⓦ splendid-hotel-paris.com; ⓜ Emile-Zola/La-Motte-Picquet-Grenelle; map pp.172–173. You won't get any luxury at this unfussy hotel set in a nineteenth-century townhouse on a quiet street. It's just a 15min walk from the Eiffel Tower – some rooms have views – yet offers a peaceful retreat from the bustle of the city. **€120**

THE 13ᵉ AND AROUND

La Manufacture 8 rue Philippe de Champagne, 13ᵉ ☎ 01 45 35 45 25, ⓦ hotel-la-manufacture.com; ⓜ Place d'Italie; map p.176. Even the smallest rooms of the sixty-odd choices at this comfortable, welcoming hotel are attractive, trimmed in bright colours, with wooden flooring; some have large bathrooms, some have balconies, and others look onto the handsome *mairie*. **€180**

★**Hôtel Port-Royal** 8 bd Port-Royal, 5ᵉ ☎ 01 43 31 70 06, ⓦ port-royal-hotel.fr; ⓜ Gobelins; map p.176. Actually located at the edge of the 5ᵉ arrondissement, at the rue Mouffetard end of the boulevard, near the métro, this is a one-star hotel at its best. The discreet address has been in the same family since the 1930s. The whole place is clean and comfy; some rooms have shared bathroom facilities (€2.50/timed shower) while en-suite double rooms (€95) are fairly large and attractive. No credit cards. **€68**

Hôtel Tolbiac 122 rue de Tolbiac, 13ᵉ ☎ 01 44 24 25 54, ⓦ hotel-tolbiac.com; ⓜ Tolbiac; map p.176. This big, friendly, well-run hotel is basic but a good budget option. The bed linen looks a little tired, but the rooms – from basic singles (€40) to doubles with sinks and shared facilities to en-suite doubles (€78) – are clean and not a bad size and there's double-glazing on all but the top floors. There's even a hotel dog and cat. **€60**

Le Vert-Galant 43 rue Croulebarbe, 13ᵉ ☎ 01 44 08 83 50, ⓦ vertgalant.com; ⓜ Gobelins; map p.176. On a quiet backwater overlooking the verdant square René-le-Gall, with a garden, this family-run hotel seems to belong to a provincial French town rather than Paris – and in the evening you can eat at the attached *Auberge Etchegorry*. The fifteen rooms are worn but clean and comfortable; some have French windows giving onto the garden. **€114**

MONTMARTRE

★**Hôtel des Arts** 5 rue Tholozé, 18ᵉ ☎ 01 46 06 30 52, ⓦ arts-hotel-paris.com; ⓜ Abbesses/Blanche; map p.182. Manages that rare combination of homeliness and efficiency, with courteous staff and welcoming accommodation. Rooms are fairly small but well maintained, quiet and very comfortable, with dashes of colour and style – and the topmost "superior" ones (€180) have Eiffel Tower views. The location – in the heart of the Abbesses quarter, opposite the classic 28 Studio art cinema (see p.182) – is fantastic. **€160**

★**Hôtel Bonséjour Montmartre** 11 rue Burq, 18ᵉ ☎ 01 42 54 22 53, ⓦ hotel-bonsejour-montmartre.fr;

19

19

Abbesses; map p.182. A budget hotel in a romantic location on an untouristy street on the slopes of Montmartre. Public spaces are drab, but the rooms, basic but clean and relatively spacious, offer one of Paris's best deals – standard simple doubles have just a sink (the shared showers and toilets are clean, with no extra charge to use them); oddly, rooms with private shower, but toilet along the hall, cost the same as full en suites (€105). The corner rooms have little balconies – a bargain. **€83**

Ermitage Hôtel 24 rue Lamarck, 18ᵉ ☎01 42 64 79 22, ⦿ermitagesacrecoeur.fr; Ⓜ Lamarck-Caulaincourt/ Château-Rouge; map p.182. One of the highest-altitude hotels in Paris, this discreet and charming family-run establishment has a deliciously old-fashioned feel with rooms that seem to be caught in time, decorated with antique objets d'art and lots and lots of florals. Just a stone's throw from the Sacré-Coeur, but it's best to approach via Ⓜ Anvers and the *funiculaire* to avoid the steep climb. They also offer apartments. **€135**

Hôtel Particulier Montmartre 23 av Junot, 18ᵉ ☎01 53 41 81 40, ⦿hotel-particulier-montmartre.com; Ⓜ Abbesses/Lamarck-Caulaincourt; map p.182. A hotel for a treat – or perhaps a retreat, given its secluded location in a garden off a private *passage* just back from one of Paris's most exclusive streets. Set in an elegant Neoclassical mansion, this discreet boutique hotel has just five rooms, all large and très designer – provocatively so, in some cases. You can often get discounts, especially during the week in summer. **€390**

THE 9ᵉ

9Hotel Opéra 14 rue Papillon, 9ᵉ ☎01 47 70 78 34, ⦿le9hotel.com/paris-opera; Ⓜ Poissonnière/Cadet/ Gare du Nord; map p.193. The small rooms are pretty minimalist but this boutique hotel offers style, comfort and a friendly, personal service. A good option if you need somewhere close to the Gare du Nord yet within easy reach of the charming *passages* and the big department stores. Great online discounts. **€125**

Hôtel Amour 8 rue Navarin, 9ᵉ ☎01 48 78 31 80, ⦿hotelamourparis.fr; Ⓜ Pigalle; map p.182. Bohemian designer hotel, with a deliberately sleazy Pigalle porn/ erotica theme. Every room is different – one is all black with disco balls above the bed – and some are more overtly "designer" than others, but all have iPod speakers and none has phone or TV. There's a spacious dining area, a bar and a cool clientele. **€230**

★**Hôtel Langlois** 63 rue St-Lazare, 9ᵉ ☎01 48 74 78 24, ⦿hotel-langlois.com; Ⓜ Trinité; map p.182. This genteel hotel feels as if it has scarcely changed in the last century, though it has all the facilities you'd expect of a three-star, plus excellent service. Each of the rooms is different, but they're all larger than average and handsome with high ceilings, antique furnishings, fireplaces and en-suite bathrooms, some of which are huge. **€185**

Lorette Opéra 36 rue Notre-Dame de Lorette, 9ᵉ ☎01 42 85 18 81, ⦿astotel.com; Ⓜ St-Georges; map p.182. With its handsome location by elegant place St-George, nicely situated between Opéra and Montmartre, this welcoming hotel feels refreshingly unlike a chain – it is part of the recommended *Astotel* group – and has a lot of individual style. The 84 clean, comfy and modern rooms are a good size; breakfast included. **€144**

★**Palm Opéra** 30 rue de Maubeuge, 9ᵉ ☎01 42 85 07 61, ⦿astotel.com; Ⓜ Cadet; map p.182. Fresh, upbeat hotel typical of the excellent *Astotel* group, with nicely designed, quiet and contemporary rooms, full of colour and light, and good bathrooms. Some have balconies and Eiffel Tower views. Delightful, welcoming staff, plus free snacks and drinks, and a family-friendly atmosphere. Rates include breakfast. **€145**

Perfect Hotel 39 rue Rodier, 9ᵉ ☎01 42 81 18 86, ⦿paris-hostel.biz; Ⓜ Anvers; map p.182. On a lively street lined with restaurants, this friendly, well-kept budget hotel – which also has four-bed hostel rooms (€33) – sees many return visitors. The rooms (en suites €86) are simple, clean and decent – as are the shared facilities – though, as you'd expect at this price, some are showing wear and tear and the walls are thin. Rates include simple breakfast. **€68**

THE 10ᵉ

Mercure Paris Terminus Nord 12 bd de Denain, 10ᵉ ☎01 42 80 20 00, ⦿accorhotels.com; Ⓜ Gare du Nord; map p.193. Large, professionally run three-star right opposite the Gare du Nord. It's reliable enough, and staff are great, but the rooms are variable, as are the prices, with doubles costing up to €260 according to demand. **€145**

BATIGNOLLES

★**Hôtel Eldorado** 18 rue des Dames, 17ᵉ ☎01 45 22 35 21, ⦿eldoradohotel.fr; Ⓜ Rome/Place de Clichy; map p.196. Idiosyncratic and enjoyable, this characterful 33-room hotel on a lively street has its own little restaurant and a sweet, flower-filled courtyard garden. The small rooms are worn in places but charmingly decorated, with bright colours offsetting vintage furnishings and the old hotel fittings that are fast disappearing from Paris. En-suite doubles are a bargain at €95, and there are a few single rooms (from €65 shared). **€78**

CANAL ST-MARTIN AND AROUND

Hôtel Beaumarchais 3 rue Oberkampf, 11ᵉ ☎01 53 36 86 86, ⦿hotelbeaumarchais.com; Ⓜ Filles-du-Calvaire/ Oberkampf; map p.198. Brightly decorated, with a little indoor garden for relaxing, this hotel's location on buzzy rue Oberkampf, right on the edge of the Marais and near the canal, means it's ideally situated for some of the most vibrant parts of the city. Rooms are small but functional. **€145**

★**Le Citizen Hotel** 96 quai de Jemmapes, 10ᵉ ☎01 83 62 55 50, ⦿lecitizenhotel.com; Ⓜ Jacques-Bonsergent; map p.198. With a perfect setting on the banks of the Canal

St-Martin, the *Citizen* is an ecofriendly, beautifully designed hotel with just twelve rooms, including one suite (€335) and one apartment. The soothing decor – light wood, clean lines and predominantly white, blue and grey tones – makes for nice airy rooms, all of which have great views of the canal. The cheaper rooms are compact; the more expensive are twice as big. Rooms come with iPads, and a home-made buffet breakfast is included; staff are lovely. It's worth checking the website for last-minute special deals. **€219**

Hôtel Gabriel 25 rue du Grand-Prieuré, 11ᵉ ☎01 47 00 13 38, ⓦhotelgabrielparis.com; ⓜOberkampf; map p.198. Beyond the unremarkable exterior is an elegant and tranquil hotel that combines an old-fashioned feel with modern design. Rooms are tiny, but very swish, with lots of cool contemporary furnishings and good bathrooms. Rates include breakfast, which you can eat in your room. **€190**

Le Général Hôtel 5–7 rue Rampon, 11ᵉ ☎01 47 00 41 57, ⓦlegeneralhotel.com; ⓜRépublique; map p.198. This cool boutique hotel, run by young staff and located on a peaceful road near the canal, has bright, airy, compact rooms with spotless bathrooms (complete with rubber ducks). Facilities include a sauna and fitness centre, espresso machines and iPod docks in the rooms; the breakfast area turns into a bar in the evenings. Book early for the lowest rates. **€190**

Hôtel des Métallos 50 rue de la Folie Méricourt, 11ᵉ ☎01 43 38 73 63, ⓦhoteldesmetallos.com; ⓜOberkampf; map p.208. The uncluttered, colourful decor of this modern establishment is simple and appealing. There's an eco slant, too – energy-saving lightbulbs, water-saving taps and environmentally friendly furniture. It can feel a bit pricey, but excellent online deals represent very good value. **€145**

★**Hôtel du Nord** 47 rue Albert Thomas, 10ᵉ ☎01 42 01 66 00, ⓦhoteldunord-leparivelo.com; ⓜJacques-Bonsergent/République; map p.198. A pretty ivy-strewn entrance leads into a cosy reception and 24 rooms, each of them different and all tastefully, if simply, decorated. The cheaper ones look onto the courtyard and tend to be a little smaller and darker. Four have a bath, the rest have showers, and a family room is available for €125. The friendly staff can lend out bikes. A genuinely charming budget choice. **€86**

MÉNILMONTANT

Cosmos Hôtel 35 rue Jean-Pierre-Timbaud, 11ᵉ ☎01 43 57 25 88, ⓦcosmos-hotel-paris.com; ⓜParmentier; map p.208. Contemporary budget hotel, excellently located

TOP 5 COOL STAYS
Hôtel Amour See p.264
Hôtel Crayon See p.259
Hôtel Edgar See p.259
Le Général Hôtel See p.265
Jules et Jim See p.260

for the bars and cafés of Oberkampf, offering clean, minimalist en-suite rooms. The styling is a little bland, the fittings occasionally a bit rough around the edges, and the bathrooms are minuscule – but beds are super-comfortable and it's a welcoming base (there's even a sleepy hotel cat padding around reception). The larger doubles (€80) are worth the extra for a longer stay, and the four-person room is a bargain at €98. **€70**

BAGNOLET

★**Mama Shelter** 109 rue de Bagnolet, 20ᵉ ☎01 43 48 48 48, ⓦmamashelter.com; ⓜAlexandre-Dumas; map p.211. The endless focus on hip and cool branding – "Mama says" this, "Mama says" that – can be a bit wearing, but the youthful *Mama Shelter*, owned by *Club Med* founders and designed by Philippe Starck, actually offers surprisingly good rates and can be a lot of fun. Free in-room movies and iMacs are standard, while a bar-restaurant (live music at weekends), sun terrace and top-notch service complete the package. The cheapest deals come via the website. **€119**

AUTEUIL AND PASSY

Hameau de Passy 48 rue de Passy, 16ᵉ ☎01 42 88 47 55, ⓦhameaudepassy.com; ⓜMuette/Passy; map p.216. Peaceful, modern hotel, set back from the main street, with a little garden area to one side. While the rooms are on the small side, they get lots of natural light and are attractively decorated. Rates include breakfast. Look out for good online deals. **€165**

Hotel Sezz 6 av Frémiet, 16ᵉ ☎01 56 75 26 26, ⓦhotelsezz.com; ⓜPassy; map p.216. Sleek boutique hotel hidden behind a nineteenth-century facade on a quiet street near the place de Passy. Rooms are minimal, veering on the austere, but splashes of colour provide a touch of warmth. The standard rooms are smallish; the suites come with huge bathtubs big enough for two, and all rooms have iPod docks, coffee machines and CD/DVD player. **€280**

APARTMENTS AND BED & BREAKFASTS

If you're staying for more than a few days, renting an **apartment** can transform a stay in Paris. Apartments tend to be more attractively styled than the average Parisian hotel, and they can make you feel that little bit like a local. **Apartment-hotels** – a hotel made up of mini-apartments each with its own self-contained kitchen – may be useful alternatives for families or visitors on an extended stay. Staying on a **bed and breakfast** basis in a private house is also worth considering if you want to get away from the more impersonal set-up of a hotel, and is a reasonably priced option. **Prices** for the following places are quoted per night, unless specified otherwise, and represent a **typical estimate** – prices will vary as new places appear on the lists, and in some cases may be much cheaper than quoted here.

19

Airbnb ⓦ airbnb.com. Allows owners of private houses to rent out rooms in their homes or apartments. Given the price of hotels in the city it's not surprising that Paris is one of the top Airbnb destinations – there are thousands of "hosts" in the city, some with beautiful apartments, many in trendier areas of town. Based on trust, and user feedback. Prices will vary as new properties are listed. €30

Alcôve & Agapes ⓦ bed-and-breakfast-in-paris.com. Personally run bed-and-breakfast organization with a good selection of private rooms on its books. Most accommodate couples, but some are able to welcome families, and some offer extras, such as French conversation, wine tasting or cookery classes. Minimum two or three nights. €95

Citadines ⓦ citadines.com. A Europe-wide chain of apartment-hotels. Most of its sixteen Paris establishments are centrally located and offer high-standard, comfortable accommodation – compact self-contained studios and apartments sleeping up to six, with well-equipped kitchens and bathrooms. All the amenities of a three-star hotel are offered, plus parking, laundry facilities and the option of breakfast. They sometimes have special offers and lower rates for long stays. €155

France Lodge 2 rue Meissonier, 17ᵉ ⓣ 01 56 33 85 80, ⓦ francelodge.fr. Bed-and-breakfast rooms, homestays and apartments inside and outside Paris. Reserve well in advance to be sure of something more special. They can also organize accommodation in furnished apartments; prices drop dramatically the longer you stay. Bed and breakfast €75, apartments by the week €630, apartments by the month €1300

Good Morning Paris 43 rue Lacépède, 5ᵉ ⓣ 01 47 07 28 29, ⓦ goodmorningparis.fr. Bed-and-breakfast accommodation (130 rooms in total) in private homes in central Paris. You have to stay at least two nights but there's no reservation fee – payment in full confirms your booking. €79

House Trip ⓦ housetrip.com. Very user friendly site listing around 1600 Parisian apartments, many of them rather stylish, available per night, with guest reviews and some gratifyingly low prices. €35

Lodgis 47 rue de Paradis, 10ᵉ ⓣ 01 70 39 11 11, ⓦ lodgis.com. A well-run estate agent with more than a thousand furnished studios and flats on its books. Most places are available by the week, but some will consider shorter stays. Per week €250

Only Apartments ⓦ only-apartments.com. More than six hundred apartments in Paris, searchable by area, size or price, with direct booking available with the owner. Most places prefer a booking of more than one night. €100

Paris B and B ⓣ 800 872 26 32, ⓦ parisbandb.com. US-based online bed-and-breakfast booking service. Quite luxurious rooms, plus apartments. Payment in US$ only. Minimum three-night stay. B&B US$90, apartments US$120

HOSTELS

The best **hostels** in Paris offer fantastic, central locations at prices that only a handful of budget hotels can match. The smarter, cleaner, quieter places tend to be run by institutions, and are often aimed at groups – these may have lockouts, with rooms closed for hours in the middle of the day. The funkier, livelier hostels are usually the independents, which are generally open 24hr, but they can be noisy, and standards and cleanliness can suffer in the face of the relentless party vibe. As a rule, double rooms in a hostel aren't a good deal, except in the newer places, where the spotless private rooms compare with those in the nicest budget hotels. In addition to those below, *Perfect Hotel*, a budget hotel with dorm rooms is an excellent option (see p.264).

GROUP AND INSTITUTIONAL HOSTELS

BVJ Opéra 1 rue de la Tour des Dames, 9ᵉ ⓦ bvjhotel .com; ⓜ Saint-Georges; map pp.74–75. The well-run *BVJ Opéra* in SoPi (South Pigalle) is the nicest in the BVJ group (they also have hostels in the Latin Quarter and near the Louvre), attracting a young student crowd from around the world. The historic building is lovely, and though the clean three- to ten-bed dorms have a somewhat institutional feel, the atmosphere is pretty peaceful. No curfew. Breakfast included. Dorms €30, doubles €70

Le Fauconnier 11 rue du Fauconnier, 4ᵉ ⓣ 01 42 74 23 45,

ⓦ mije.com; ⓜ St-Paul/Pont-Marie; map p.97. One of three hostels run by MIJE, all in the Marais. *Le Fauconnier* is in a superbly renovated seventeenth-century building with a courtyard. Dorms (single sex) sleep four to eight, and there are also some single (€55) and double rooms with shower; breakfast is included. 1am curfew. Dorms €33.50, doubles €82

Le Fourcy 6 rue de Fourcy, 4ᵉ ⓣ 01 42 74 23 45; ⓜ St-Paul; map p.97. Another good MIJE hostel, with the same rates as *Le Fauconnier* (see above). Housed in a beautiful mansion, this one has a small garden and an inexpensive restaurant. Doubles and triples are available, as well as dorms. 1am curfew. Dorms €33.50, doubles €82

Foyer International d'Accueil de Paris Jean Monnet 30 rue Cabanis, 14ᵉ ⓣ 01 43 13 17 00, ⓦ fiap.asso.fr; ⓜ Glacière; map pp.162–163. Huge (500-bed), efficient hostel in a fairly sedate area a couple of métro stops south of the Quartier Latin. Offers singles (€73), doubles and dorms sleeping up to seven. Facilities include a bar; rates include breakfast. No curfew. Dorms €33, doubles €90

TOP 5 ROOMS WITH A VIEW

Hôtel Brighton See p.258
Le Citizen Hotel See p.264
Hôtel Esmeralda See p.261
Palm Opéra See p.264
Hôtel Paris France See p.260

Foyer Tolbiac 234 rue Tolbiac, 13ᵉ ☎01 44 16 22 22, ⓦfoyer-tolbiac.com; ⓜGlacière; map p.176. Large place catering to working women aged 18–25 only, offering spartan but pleasant private rooms for long stays. Kitchens and shared bathrooms on every floor, wi-fi, activities and welcome parties. Single rooms per month €422

HI D'Artagnan 80 rue Vitruve, 20ᵉ ☎01 40 32 34 56, ⓦfuaj.org; ⓜPorte de Bagnolet; map p.211. On the eastern edge of the city near Bagnolet, which has some good bars, this reliable HI hostel is the largest in France, with 430 beds and lots of facilities including a small cinema, restaurant and bar, internet access and a swimming pool nearby; rooms must be vacated between 11am and 3pm. Rates quoted are for HI members. Dorms €26, doubles €63

Maubuisson 12 rue des Barres, 4ᵉ ☎01 42 74 23 45, ⓦmije.com; ⓜPont Marie/Hôtel-de-Ville; map p.97. A MIJE hostel in the same group as Le Fauconnier and nearby Le Fourcy (see above) in a magnificent medieval building on a quiet street. Shared use of the restaurant at Le Fourcy. 1am curfew. Breakfast included. Dorms only. Dorms €33.50

Maurice Ravel 6 av Maurice-Ravel, 12ᵉ ☎01 43 58 96 00, ⓦcisp.fr; ⓜPorte de Vincennes/Bel Air; map pp.110–111. Aimed at groups, this institutional hostel is some distance from central Paris, but near the lovely Bois de Vincennes. There are two restos, a bar and a cafeteria, a theatre, exhibition space and an outdoor swimming pool nearby. Rooms range from eight-bed dorms to twins and singles (€47.80); all share shower rooms. CISP has another hostel in a park near the Porte d'Italie, at the southern end of the 13ᵉ. No curfew. Dorms €26, twins €75

INDEPENDENT HOSTELS

★**3 Ducks Hostel** 6 place Etienne Pernet, 15ᵉ ☎01 48 42 04 05, ⓦ3ducks.fr; ⓜCommerce; map pp.172–173. Lively, long-established and popular hostel in a historic building, offering homely and colourful mixed and female-only (four- to eight-bed) dorms. Interior decor is funky, and the terrace and lively streetside bar are nice places to hang out. Rates include breakfast and there's a kitchen for guests' use. Dorms €41

★**Generator Hostel** 9–11 place du Colonel Fabien, 10ᵉ ☎01 70 98 84 00, ⓦgeneratorhostels.com; ⓜColonel-Fabien; map p.198. New, well-run and friendly hostel right by the métro in a safe neighbourhood, with spotless dorms (four- to ten-bed, with one eight-bed women-only option) and private bathrooms. As to be expected with the cut-above Generator group, facilities are excellent, with good bedding, lots of storage space, a friendly bar and handy café. There are some private doubles and quads with en-suite showers, which, while the hostel remains new, prove good value – particularly if you're travelling in a group. Dorms €33, doubles €70

Oops 50 av des Gobelins, 13ᵉ ☎01 47 07 47 00, ⓦoops-paris.com; ⓜGobelins; map p.176. This early "design hostel", opened in 2007, is decorated in bright colours and funky patterns. All dorms are en suite, there's free wi-fi, a/c and a basic breakfast included. You can get better value for private rooms elsewhere. The location is unexceptional, but it's just a couple of métro stops south of the Quartier Latin. Cash only. Dorms €43, doubles €115

Regent Hostel 37 bd de Rochechouart, 9ᵉ ☎01 48 78 24 00, ⓦleregent.com; ⓜAnvers; map p.182. Hostel and budget hotel in the heart of Montmartre. It could do with a lick of paint, but helpful staff and good facilities (kitchen, free lockers, breakfast included) make it a reliable option. Some en-suite doubles; those with shared showers have views of the Sacré-Coeur. Dorms €30, doubles €99

★**St Christopher's Canal** 159 rue de Crimée, 19ᵉ ☎01 40 34 34 40, ⓦst-christophers.co.uk/paris-hostels/canal; ⓜCrimée/Laumière; map p.200. Massive, slick hostel in an eye-catching, renovated former boat hangar overlooking the Bassin de la Villette – a great base, but some way from the centre. Dorms (including some women-only) feature curtained-off pod beds and are pleasant enough, and there's a lively bar, inexpensive restaurant, waterfront terrace, café, book exchange and dozens of activities on offer; prices fluctuate daily, but always include breakfast. There's another good St Christopher's hostel near Gare du Nord. Dorms €36, doubles €70

Le Village Hostel 20 rue d'Orsel, 18ᵉ ☎01 42 64 22 02, ⓦvillagehostel.fr; ⓜAnvers; map p.182. Reliable hostel in an attractively renovated nineteenth-century building with a view of the Sacré-Coeur from the terrace. Good facilities (sheets included; all rooms have shower, toilet and telephone; kitchen available). Rates include breakfast. Dorms €32, doubles €99

CAMPING

The least expensive option is, of course, camping. There's only one option anywhere near the centre; the other **campsites** in the region are way out of town. For a full list, contact the tourist office.

Paris Bois de Boulogne Indigo Campsite 2 Allée du Bord-de-l'Eau, 16ᵉ ☎01 45 24 30 00, ⓦcampingparis.fr; ⓜPorte Maillot then bus #244 to Moulins Camping; the bus doesn't run in the evening, but a shuttle bus is laid on in summer; map p.220. The most central campsite, with more than four hundred pitches, next to the Seine in the Bois de Boulogne, and usually booked out in summer. The ground is pebbly, but the site is well equipped and there are also gypsy caravans sleeping up to four and "cottages" (chalets, effectively) sleeping up to six. Tent/caravan or campervan for two people in high season €36.20, gypsy caravans €127, cottages €138

19

CAFÉ DE L'INDUSTRIE, BASTILLE

Cafés and restaurants

The French seldom separate the major pleasures of eating and drinking, and there are thousands of establishments in Paris where you can do both or either, as you wish. A restaurant may call itself a brasserie, *bistrot*, café or indeed restaurant; equally, a café can be a place to eat, drink, listen to music, dance or even watch theatre. To simplify matters, we've split our listings for each geographical area into two parts: under Cafés and wine bars, you'll find venues we recommend primarily for daytime or relaxed eating, with perhaps a snack, a sharing plate or light meal and drinks; under Restaurants, you'll find any establishment we recommend for a full meal. Most cafés and wine bars remain open until fairly late and are perfect for a beer, glass of wine or *digestif*; if you're looking for cocktails, pints or full-on nightlife, however, you'll need to head for the city's bars and clubs (see p.296).

Though many cafés are contemporary affairs – the kinds of cosmopolitan places you find in cities all over the world – happily the traditional Paris **café**, with zinc bar, tobacco-stained ceiling and globe lighting, still exists. Indeed, this type of place is a mainstay of Parisian society, where people come to gossip and discuss, pose and people-watch, or simply read a newspaper or a book. In addition to drinks, most cafés also serve **food**, from the simple pastries, *tartines* (open sandwiches) and toasted sandwiches often available in more basic places, to the dishes and full meals served in the larger cafés and **café-brasseries** – usually salads, *plats du jour* (daily specials), and perhaps a simple, limited- or no-choice two- or three-course *formule* menu. If you've a nostalgic hankering for the **café society** of old, head for boulevards Montparnasse and St-Germain, on the Left Bank, where the famed *Select, Coupole, Closerie des Lilas, Deux Magots* and *Flore* – erstwhile hangouts of Apollinaire, Picasso, Hemingway, Sartre, de Beauvoir et al – still have a place in the hearts of many Parisians (and probably even more tourists). Although they're pricier than other places it's hard not to be seduced by their historic charm.

Alongside cafés, we've listed **wine bars** or *bistrots à vin*. The most traditional of these offer simple platters of cheeses, charcuterie and regional dishes to go with their fine – but generally inexpensive – wines, while a more recent wave of places focuses on organic or natural wines and creative food that is among the most highly rated in the city, usually served in sharing plate style. Also included in this category you'll find **salons de thé** (tearooms), typically serving tea, pastries and light meals, and the best of the city's recent crop of artisan **coffee houses**, which have brought relief to the many visitors who have traditionally been shocked to find that those wonderful Parisian brasseries don't, as a rule, serve good coffee. Populated with the kind of hipster crowd you'd find in Shoreditch, Melbourne or Brooklyn, these so-called "third wave" coffee pit stops don't feel terribly Parisian, but if you're craving an expertly sourced and lovingly made brew they're useful to know about.

Most visitors come to Paris with a big appetite and high expectations. This is, after all, the city that invented the **restaurant**, and indeed fine dining. Certainly, Paris can still boast an abundance of Michelin-starred venues that cater for those in search of *haute gastronomie* and classic French cuisine, but the city is also responding to a change in trends. The so-called **bistronomy** movement, spearheaded in the 1990s by Yves Camdeborde of *La Régalade* (see p.289) – now run by Bruno Doucet, and with three locations – rejected the astronomical prices and over-fussy food of Michelin-starred cooking in favour of more experimental haute cuisine, focusing on zingy, fresh flavours (and even, shockingly, giving a starring role to vegetables), served in relatively casual settings. A new generation of committed restaurateurs and passionate chefs swiftly jumped on board, and today many of Paris's most talked about restaurants are the relatively relaxed, smaller, so-called **neo-bistros**, often in outlying neighbourhoods, where the focus is very much on the food, not the service or decor. These offer some of the most exciting cooking in town and are generally more affordable than the Old Guard places – that said, the most recent generation of rock-and-roll chefs have taken the city by storm, and though you can keep costs down by picking your way through a menu of sharing plates, prices are rising as the scene gets more and more creative. New-generation **chefs** to watch for include self-trained Inaki Aizpitarte of *Le Châteaubriand* (see p.294)

20

WAITERS, THE BILL AND TIPPING

Waiters in Paris are considered to be professionals, and are paid as such, so **tipping** is a matter of leaving a few coins, perhaps €3 or so, depending on the service. Many speak English and are eager to practise and/or show off, so try not to be offended if they shrug off your attempts in French. And never call a waiter *garçon*, whatever you were taught in school – *Monsieur, Madame/Mademoiselle* or *s'il vous plaît* or *excusez-moi* are de rigueur. To ask for **the bill**, the phrase is *l'addition, s'il vous plaît*.

and *Dauphin* (see p.293), David Toutain, who worked with Alain Passard at the famed *L'Arpège* (see p.288), and "Frenchie" Grégory Marchand, currently colonizing a street in the 2ᵉ with his New York/London/Paris fusion (see p.276).

Meanwhile, the cuisine at the **average Parisian restaurant** or simpler, more **local bistrot** can be surprisingly, and not unappealingly, conservative. Here you'll find *cuisine bourgeoise*, not *gastronomique* – homely meats in sauces, for the most part, with a fine chocolate mousse or perfect apple tart for dessert. Being comfortingly *correcte* is often judged as more important than gourmet flair in these places; some old-time brasseries and historic restaurants have become Parisian **institutions** whose owners and chefs rarely dare to meddle with a decor – or indeed a style of cooking – that has been enjoyed by locals and visitors for generations.

ESSENTIALS

Prices Prices will usually vary for consuming at the bar (*au comptoir*; the cheapest option), sitting down (*la salle*), or on the terrace (*la terrasse*; generally most expensive). Addresses in the smarter or more touristy arrondissements set costs soaring and you'll generally pay more on main squares and boulevards than on backstreets. At almost all cafés and bars, you're presented with a bill along with your drinks, which you settle when you leave. At most decent restaurants you may as much as €45 or more for a three-course meal, though the set *menus* (see below) cut costs. House wines are usually inexpensive, but a bottle of something interesting will generally add at least €20 to the bill, and potentially much more for a good bottle in a smart place. A fifteen percent service charge is legally included in your bill at all restaurants, bars and cafés, but you may want to leave an optional tip (see box, p.269).

Fixed-price menus The cheapest way to go is to opt for a fixed-price menu (simply called *le menu* in French, or often *formule* at lunchtime – the French word for "menu" in the English sense is *la carte*), though the choice is accordingly limited. Eating *à la carte* gives you access to everything on offer, though you'll pay a fair bit more; if you just want a main course it's worth looking out for the *plat du jour* (chef's daily special), which tend to be good value. Lunchtime *menus* are typically priced at less than €25 even at quite classy restaurants, and as little as €15 for two courses at good inexpensive places. Fine dining restaurants, too, typically offer a lunch *menu* for roughly half the price of the full evening experience, while the *menu dégustation* – a "tasting" menu – will be expensive but well worth trying for a splurge.

Opening hours The latest time at which you can walk into a restaurant and order is generally about 9.30 or 10pm, although it can be later. Once ensconced you can often remain

well into the night, but note that after 9pm or so, some restaurants serve only *à la carte* meals, which invariably works out more expensive than eating the set menu. Brasseries serve speedier meals, and at most hours of the day, often till midnight or 1am. Note that some restaurants may close for some of – or even all of – August. If you have an establishment in mind to visit during that month and haven't booked, it's always worth calling in advance to check they're open.

Reservations and dress code For the more upmarket or fashionable places, and at weekends, it's wise to reserve. Generally you will only need to do this a day or so in advance, but the most renowned places may require booking up to several weeks (or in some cases, months) before you wish to dine. Some more formal restaurants insist on men wearing jacket and tie.

FOOD AND DRINK

Vegetarian cuisine Traditionally Paris's gastronomic reputation was largely lost on vegetarians, who had to subsist on salads, omelettes and cheese. Nowadays, however, most places will often offer at least one or two non-meaty dishes, and even some of the newer gourmet restaurants are turning their attention to the fresh flavours and possibilities of vegetables. There are a number of exclusively veggie restaurants – *Soya* (see p.294) and *Potager du Marais* (see p.280) are recommended – along with *salons de thé* offering lighter dishes such as soups and quiches or flans (*tartes*); neo-bistros and hipper restaurants, along with the ethnic places, are also a good bet. It's also possible to put together a meal at even the most meat-oriented brasserie by choosing dishes from among the starters and soups. Useful French phrases to help you along are *Je suis végétarien(ne)* ("I'm a vegetarian") and *Il y a quelques plats sans viande?* ("Are there any non-meat dishes?").

Coffee and tea Historically, coffee in Paris has been hit and miss in terms of quality and flavour – sometimes good; often bland or burned. We've reviewed a few of the best new ("third wave") coffee houses, often helmed by expats hankering for the quality of brews they were used to at home, and listing flat whites and long blacks on their menus. In the traditional French cafés *un café* or *un express* is an

---

TOP 5 NEO-BISTROS

Le Châteaubriand See p.294
David Toutain See p.288
Le Galopin See p.295
Richer See p.293
Semilla See p.286

BREAKFAST AND BRUNCH

Given that most hotels typically charge around €7–14 for a pretty ordinary **breakfast**, heading out to a café or a brasserie is usually a far cheaper, and more satisfying, way to start your day. Even if they don't offer formal **petit déjeuner** as such, most cafés advertise **snacks** or *casse-croûtes* (quick bites), and **brasseries** can serve you coffee, *tartines* (baguettes and butter) and croissants. Meanwhile, **le brunch** has become a Sunday institution in gentrified and *bobo* (bourgeois-bohemian) areas such as the Marais, Bastille, Montmartre and eastern Paris; most places serve it from around noon to 4 or 5pm.

TOP BRUNCH SPOTS

Café de l'Industrie See p.281
Chez Casimir See p.292
Chez Prune See p.293

L'Entrepôt See p.289
Le Loir dans la Théière See p.280

espresso, *une noisette* an espresso with a dash of milk (similar to a macchiato) and *un crème* is a traditional French coffee with hot milk (you can get either a *grand crème* or a smaller, *petit crème*). In the morning you could also ask for *un café au lait* – espresso with hot milk. *Un déca* (decaffeinated coffee) and *chocolat chaud* (hot chocolate) is widely available. Drinkers of tea (*thé*), may have to settle for Lipton's teabags, served black, though *salons à thé* do serve more upmarket brands, such as *Mariage Frères* (see p.336). You can have a slice of lemon (*citron*) with it, or ask for milk, "*un peu de lait frais*". *Tisanes* or *infusions* are the generic terms for herbal teas. Common varieties include *verveine* (verbena), *tilleul* (lime blossom), *menthe* (mint) and *camomille*.

Soft drinks Boulangeries often stock chilled fizzy drinks – *limonade*, Coca, Orangina – as well as canned fruit juices. At cafés, bottled fruit juices and soft drinks are expensive. Better value is a freshly squeezed *citron pressé*: lemon juice served in the bottom of a long, ice-filled glass, with a jug of water and a sugar bowl. Particularly French are the various *sirops*, diluted with water to make cool, eye-catching drinks with traffic-light colours, such as *menthe* (peppermint) and *grenadine* (pomegranate). Bottles of mineral water (*eau minérale*) are widely drunk, from the best-selling, naturally sparkling Badoit to the most obscure spa product. Ask for *eau gazeuse* for sparkling, *eau plate* (pronounced "platt") for still. In most places tap water will be brought free to your table if you ask for *une carafe d'eau du robinet*.

Wine Wine is the thing to drink in Paris, and it's certainly a lot cheaper than the alternatives. The current vogue is for *vins du*

pays (country wines), with a blossoming interest in natural and organic (*bio*) wines – but you'll find the top-quality AOC (Appellation d'Origine Contrôlée) bottles on most menus. The annual release of the new red wine from the Beaujolais on November 15 is a much-heralded event – "*le Beaujolais Nouveau est arrivé*". A glass of house wine may also be included as part of a set-price meal – and on the most expensive tasting *menus* you may get different wines matched with each course. In less expensive restaurants you can usually get a fairly good house wine by the *pichet* (carafe) – ask for *un quart* or *un demi*, a quarter- or half-litre.

Beers While Belgian, German and Alsatian lagers are still in the majority, young Parisians are increasingly taking to craft brews, which are often to be found in the cooler bars (check ⓦ hoppyparis.com for a good rundown of the French scene). Most locals simply order *une pression*, or a glass of draught beer, but to be precise you could ask for *un demi* (25cl).

Apéritifs, brandies and liqueurs A *kir*, a white wine with a dash of *cassis* (blackcurrant liqueur), is a popular *apéritif*, sometimes with champagne instead of white wine – *un kir royal*. Another characteristically French *apéritif* is the aniseed-flavoured *pastis* – Pernod and Ricard are the most common brands – which turns cloudy when diluted with water and ice cubes (*glaçons*). As for the harder stuff, there are dozens of *eaux de vie* (brandies distilled from fruit) and liqueurs, in addition to the classic Cognacs or Armagnac. Measures are generous, but they don't come cheap; the same applies for imported spirits like whisky, usually referred to as *scotch*.

20

THE ISLANDS

CAFÉS AND WINE BARS

Berthillon 31 rue St-Louis-en-l'Ile, Ile St-Louis, 4ᵉ ⓣ 01 43 54 31 61, ⓦ berthillon.fr; ⓜ Pont Marie; map pp.44–45. *Berthillon* serves some of the best ice cream in Paris, in all sorts of tempting flavours – salted butter caramel is a highlight (€2.50 to take away; €4.50 in the pretty attached *salon de thé*). Wed–Sun 10am–8pm; closed Aug.

★ **Café St-Régis** 6 rue Jean du Bellay, Ile St-Louis, 4ᵉ ⓣ 01 43 54 59 41, ⓦ cafesaintregisparis.com; ⓜ Pont Marie; map pp.44–45. A characterful café-restaurant, nicely designed to pay homage to traditional old bistros – all gleaming white ceramic tiles, mirrored walls, dark wood, zinc bar and leather banquettes, with bustling waiters and a neighbourhood vibe. They serve a simple but tasty selection of French and American snacks and dishes

---

HAPPY EVER AFTERS: TOP 5 DESSERTS

Bistrot Paul Bert See p.282
Chez Janou See p.279
Drouant See p.276
Le Ratapoil du Faubourg See p.292
Le Verre Volé See p.294

---

all day – try a breakfast of Poîlane toast, butter and coffee (€3.50) or a Sunday brunch, or drop by for the good-value happy hour (7–9pm). Daily 7am–2am.

Taverne Henri IV 13 place du Pont-Neuf, Ile de la Cité, 1er ☎01 43 54 27 90; ⓜPont-Neuf; map pp.44–45. Bustling with a comfortable, old-fashioned atmosphere, this old-style wine bar is at its buzziest at lunchtime, when

it's full of quaffing lawyers and workers from the nearby Palais de Justice. You can get meat and cheese platters (from €15), as well as *tartines* (open sandwiches) with a choice of cheeses, hams, pâté and *saucisson* from €13, plus traditional *plats* (€15–16) such as *choux farci* (stuffed cabbage) or *coq au vin*. Mon–Sat noon–11pm.

RESTAURANT

Mon Vieil Ami 69 rue St-Louis-en-l'Ile, 4e ☎01 40 46 01 35, ⓦmon-vieil-ami.com; ⓜPont Marie; map pp.44–45. Owned by top Alsatian chef Antoine Westermann, this charming contemporary *bistrot* serves bold, zesty cuisine, with an emphasis on well-prepared vegetables; the wine list includes a fine selection of Alsatian vintages. Three-course *menu* €47.50; mains from €14. Wed–Sun noon–2.30pm & 7–11pm.

THE CHAMPS-ELYSÉES

CAFÉS AND WINE BARS

Aubrac Corner 37 rue Marbeuf, 8e ☎01 45 61 45 35, ⓦmaison-aubrac.com/aubrac-corner; ⓜFranklin-D.-Roosevelt; map pp.64–65. Can't afford the time or money for a meal at famed steakhouse *Maison de l'Aubrac* (see below)? Come to their neighbouring deli/café, where you can pick up terrific takeaway burgers (€10), baguettes filled with the finest cuts (from €7), *saucisson*, *rillettes* and countless carnivorous treats (*formules* from €9.90). Everything is impeccably sourced, most of it from the Auvergne. A bargain for this area. Mon–Fri 7.45am–8pm, Sat 10am–7pm.

Le Café Jacquemart-André 158 bd Haussmann, 8e ⓦmusee-jacquemart-andre.com; ⓜSt-Philippe-du-Roule/Miromesnil; map pp.64–65. Within the Musée Jacquemart-André (see p.69) but with independent access, this is among the city's most sumptuously appointed *salons de thé*. Huge tapestries adorn the walls, Louis XV consoles display posh pâtisserie, and ladies with parasols and gents in ruffs look down over a trompe l'oeil balustrade from a wonderful ceiling fresco by Tiepolo. Happily the café food lives up to the decor – you'll pay €11.50 for tea and a sumptuous pastry, and there are lunch menus from €18.50. Daily 11.45am–5.30pm.

Le Fouquet's 99 av des Champs-Elysées, 8e ☎01 40 69 60 50, ⓦlucienbarriere.com; ⓜGeorge-V; map pp.64–65. Dating from 1899, iconic *Le Fouquet's* (you pronounce the "t") is the favourite venue for celebrations after the annual César film awards and is such a well-established celebs' watering hole that it's been classified a Monument Historique. You can sit out on the *terrasse*, a prime spot for people-watching, or sink into a red velvet banquette in the plush café-brasserie. Coffee from €8 (€10 on the *terrasse*), mains around €30 – and what must surely be the most expensive *croque-monsieur* in the city at €28. Daily 8am–2am.

RESTAURANTS

Al Ajami 58 rue François-1er, 8e ☎01 42 25 38 44, ⓦajami.com; ⓜGeorge-V; map pp.64–65. This Lebanese restaurant is a branch of the venerable *Al Ajami* in Beirut. Meat dishes include croquettes of minced lamb pounded together with cracked wheat and grated onion, and there's plenty for vegetarians, too: tabbouleh and *chanklish* (goat's cheese in olive oil with tomato and onion), done to perfection; and exquisite *foul madamas* (an Egyptian dish of broad beans cooked with lemon and garlic) and *fattayer* (pastry triangles filled with spinach). *Menus* range from €17 for a weekday lunch to the €49 *dégustation*. Daily noon–midnight.

Lasserre 17 av Franklin-D.-Roosevelt, 8e ☎01 43 59 02 13, ⓦrestaurant-lasserre.com; ⓜFranklin-D.-Roosevelt; map pp.64–65. A classic, Michelin-starred haute cuisine restaurant with an old-school dining room, decorated with flower-draped balustrades and fine ceiling frescoes – on balmy summer nights the roof is rolled back to reveal the Paris sky. The food, from Ducasse alumni Adrien Trouilloud and pastry maestro Claire Heitzler, is generally traditional and beautifully executed: signature dishes include a sublime duck *à l'orange*, macaroni stuffed with black truffle and duck foie gras, and the ultimate crêpes Suzette. Evening *menu* €220, lunchtime *menus* €90 or €120. Tues–Sat 7–10pm, Thurs & Fri noon–2pm; closed Aug.

La Maison de l'Aubrac 37 rue Marbeuf, 8e ☎01 43 59 05 14, ⓦmaison-aubrac.com; ⓜFranklin-D.-Roosevelt; map pp.64–65. If you're hankering after a really good steak, this all-night restaurant is the place. The French in the know source their meat from the Auvergne, and the large photographs of prize-winning cattle from the restaurant's own farm leave you pretty sure as to what to expect from the quality of the beef here. While the fillet is

---

CLOCKWISE FROM TOP LEFT LE CHÂTEAUBRIAND (P.294); CAFÉ DE LA MOSQUÉE (P.283); L'ARPÈGE (P.288) >

GOURMET RESTAURANTS

While bistronomy and wine bar eating has shaken up the city's dining scene, the gourmet chefs continue to pull in diners eager to splash out on a quintessentially Parisian haute cuisine experience. Perhaps best known is **Alain Ducasse**, who swept like a tidal wave through the world of French cuisine in the early 1990s and has since become the chef with the most Michelin stars in the world; his headline restaurants include the three-starred *Le Meurice* (see opposite); *Le Jules Verne* (see p.289), halfway up the Eiffel Tower; and another at the *Plaza-Athénée* hotel near the Champs-Elysées, where in 2014 he made a brave decision – brave in the world of traditional haute cuisine, that is – to focus on contemporary dishes using fish and organic veg. Other gourmet chefs, all of whom currently hold three Michelin stars, include **Pascal Barbot** at *L'Astrance* (see p.286), known for his bold and innovative cuisine; **Pierre Gagnaire**, who has extended his experimental molecular cuisine beyond his titular flagship (see below) into a number of restaurants in Paris and around the world; **Alain Passard**, whose remarkable *L'Arpège* (see p.288) eschews most meat in favour of fish and vegetable dishes; Breton **Christian Le Squer** at *Le Cinq*; and **Anne-Sophie Pic** at the modern *La Dame de Pic*. In addition it's worth checking out **Hélène Darroze** (see p.286), who also has a Michelin-starred restaurant in London; **Adeline Grattard**, who combines French and Chinese cuisine at the much-lauded *Yam'Tcha* (see p.278); **Stephanie Le Quellec**, who is causing a stir at the sleek, contemporary *La Scène*; and **Guy Savoy**, mentor to Gordon Ramsay.

In the evening, prices at such places will average about €200, and there's no limit on the amount you can pay for top wines. To **cut costs**, book for a weekday lunch *menu* – it will still be pricey, but at least puts the food within reach of many. In addition, some of the star chefs have made their fine cuisine more accessible to a wider range of customers by opening up less expensive, more **casual**, but still high-quality establishments. Alain Ducasse, for example, also runs *Allard* (see p.285), *Aux Lyonnais* (see p.277) and *Le Relais du Parc* in the 16e. Hélène Darroze has her tapas-style *Salon d'Hélène*, while Pierre Gagnaire oversees the seafood restaurant *Gaya* (see p.286) and Guy Savoy has his rôtisserie, *L'Atelier Maître Albert* (see p.283).

20

tender, the flavour in the cheaper, more traditional French cuts such as *onglet* or *bavette* is fuller and richer, and the burger truly is a cut above. Choose from hearty dishes such as *pot-au-feu* or the *trilogie de viande* (*brochette*, steak *tartare* and a small burger). Mains from €20; lunch *menus* €26–36. Daily 24hr.

Mini Palais Av Winston Churchill, 8e ☎01 42 56 42 42, ⓦminipalais.com; ⓂChamps-Elysées-Clemenceau; map pp.64–65. The Grand Palais' restaurant lives up to its name with a large, sleek dining room and a stately colonnaded *terrasse* with fabulous views. Triple-Michelin-starred chef Eric Fréchon oversees the seasonal menu, a mix of French classics and international dishes such as tempura prawns or fettuccine with pesto, pine nuts and cockles; you can also just come for a snack (cheese platters €12), or a drink at the bar. Mains €17–39. Daily 10am–2am.

Miss Kô 49–51 av George-V, 8e ☎01 53 67 84 60, ⓦmiss-ko.com; ⓂGeorge-V; map pp.64–65. This Philippe Starck-designed fusion restaurant evokes a futuristic, pop-art Manga-esque world, with video screens flashing Asian TV channels up at you under a glass counter and neon lights recalling a Korean or Japanese food street. While the extensive Asian-French menu can be hit and miss (foie gras lollipops, anyone?), it's reasonably priced for the area – and notwithstanding the rock'n'roll vibe, kids love the place, so during the day it's a good family-friendly option. Mains, such as a bibimbap burger in curry bread, are €18–28, while sizeable sushi platters can cost as little as €12.50. Daily noon–2am.

Pierre Gagnaire Hôtel Balzac, 6 rue Balzac, 8e ☎01 58 36 12 50, ⓦpierre-gagnaire.com; ⓂGeorge-V; map pp.64–65. Eating at the highly acclaimed, three-Michelin-starred *Pierre Gagnaire* is a gastronomic adventure. The seven-course *menu dégustation* (€295) of modern French food might feature such dishes as oyster with cuttlefish, sailor clams and mussels in Kientzheim butter with crunchy fennel and black garlic (and that's just one course); the desserts are amazing. *A la carte* will set you back around €300, lunch €150; given that, the lunch menu at €85 isn't too expensive. Mon–Fri noon–1.30pm & 7.30–9.30pm; closed two weeks in Aug.

Le Relais de l'Entrecôte 15 rue Marbeuf, 8e ☎01 49 52 07 17, ⓦrelaisentrecote.fr; ⓂFranklin-D.-Roosevelt; map pp.64–65. The only dish served at this old-fashioned restaurant is *steak frites*, with a delicious, secret recipe sauce. The set price of €26.50 includes a salad starter – and seconds – but desserts, from a long list, including profite-roles and *crème brûlée*, are around €6–9 extra. No reservations, so you may have to queue, or arrive early – it's popular. There are two more branches: one in St-Germain and another near the Jardin du Luxembourg. Daily noon–2.30pm & 7–11.30pm.

Taillevent 15 rue Lamennais, 8ᵉ ☎01 44 95 15 01, ⓦ taillevent.com; ⓜ George-V; map pp.64–65. The Provençal-influenced cuisine of Alain Solivérès places the emphasis on the classic rather than the experimental; sample dishes on the rarely changing menu include steamed sea bass with leek, champagne and caviar sauce, and spiced roast duckling with verbena-scented fruit and vegetables. The decor is soothing and unobtrusive, and waiters are supremely charming. Eating *à la carte*, count on around €150; the tasting menu costs €218, and there's a set lunch for €88. Wine from around €30 a bottle up to €2000. Mon–Fri 12.30–2pm & 7.30–11pm; closed Aug.

LES TUILERIES

CAFÉS AND WINE BARS

Angélina 226 rue de Rivoli, 1ᵉʳ ☎01 42 60 82 00, ⓦ angelina-paris.fr; ⓜ Tuileries; map pp.74–75. This fabulously grand pâtisserie/*salon de thé*, dating from 1903 and still keeping its murals, gilded stuccowork and leather armchairs, does the best hot chocolate in town – one generous jugful with whipped cream on the side is enough for two (€8.20). The other speciality is the Mont Blanc, a chestnut cream, meringue and whipped cream dessert (€9.20). You could also treat yourself to breakfast (*à la carte*, or menus €20–29.50) or brunch (€39.50). There are other branches in town, but this is the original and best. Mon–Thurs 7.30am–7pm, Fri 7.30am–7.30pm, Sat & Sun 8.30am–7.30pm.

★ **Le Rubis** 10 rue du Marché-St-Honoré, 1ᵉʳ ☎01 42 61 03 34; ⓜ Pyramides; map pp.74–75. Very small and usually crowded, this is one of the city's oldest wine bars. It exudes old-world French charm with its zinc bar, faded sign, peeling paint and no-nonsense service, and is known for its wines – mostly from the Beaujolais and Loire regions – and hearty rustic food, such as home-made *rillettes* (a kind of pork pâté), charcuterie and herrings with potatoes. Mains around €10, omelettes from €6. Mon–Fri noon–11pm, Sat 9am–3pm.

RESTAURANTS

L'Ardoise 28 rue du Mont Thabor, 1ᵉʳ ☎01 42 96 28 18, ⓦ lardoise-paris.com; ⓜ Tuileries; map pp.74–75. A contemporary *bistrot* with a friendly atmosphere (the chef frequently pops out of the kitchen to greet diners) and a fresh take on the classics: think crab cakes with avocado purée or grilled lamb with celeriac *mousseline* and herb salad. With a three-course *menu* at €38, this is a good-value, reliable choice. Mon–Sat noon–2.30pm & 6.30–11pm, Sun 6.30–11pm.

Le Meurice Hôtel Meurice, 228 rue de Rivoli, 1ᵉʳ ☎01 44 58 10 55, ⓦ lemeurice.com; ⓜ Tuileries/Concorde; map pp.74–75. This sumptuous historic restaurant, decorated in Louis XVI style with a few flashes of contemporary style from Philippe Starck, is one of the most beautiful dining rooms in Paris. It is also one of the most highly sought-after, with three Michelin stars and Alain Ducasse at the helm presenting flawless contemporary French cuisine using seasonal, organic ingredients. The menu might not give away much, offering the likes of "vegetables and fruits"; "sea bream, beetroots, caviar"; "farm hen, black truffle"; even "hazelnuts, chestnuts" – but you can trust that whatever you choose will be exquisite. Lunch *menus* €85–130, *menu dégustation* €380, Sunday brunch €120. Mon–Fri 12.30–2pm & 7.30–10pm, Sun noon–2pm.

GRANDS BOULEVARDS

CAFÉS AND WINE BARS

Café de la Paix Corner of place de l'Opéra and bd des Capucines, 9ᵉ ☎01 40 07 36 36, ⓦ cafedelapaix.fr; ⓜ Opéra; map pp.74–75. The last survivor of the great nineteenth-century cafés that once lined the Grands Boulevards, this counts Zola, Maupassant, Tchaikovsky and Oscar Wilde among its former habitués. You can sit in the sumptuously gilded, frescoed restaurant or watch the world go by from the *terrasse*, with views of the Opéra Garnier – either way, it's a place for a special, quintessentially Parisian treat. Drinks start from €6 for an espresso; the *plat du jour* is €30 and the fine *soupe à l'oignon* €21. Daily 7am–11.30pm.

TRADITIONAL DISHES

Many visitors come to Paris hoping to sample traditional French dishes, from the rustic and regional to the more refined. Here are the best places for some classic dishes:

Andouillette *Robert et Louise* See p.281
Boeuf bourguignon *Chez Paul* See p.282
Boudin noir *Aux Lyonnais* See p.277
Crêpes *Crêperie Josselin* See p.289
Foie gras *Gallopin* See p.277
Mont Blanc *Angélina* See above
Mousse au chocolat *Chez Janou* See p.279

Pot-au-feu *L'Avant Goût* (see p.290), *Drouant* (see p.276)
Poulet rôti *L'Atelier Maître Albert* (see p.283), *Le Coq Rico* (see p.291)
Pounti *Rillettes* (see p.291)
Steak *Hugo Desnoyer* (see p.295), *La Maison de l'Aubrac* (see p.273), *Relais de l'Entrecôte* (see opposite).

Ladurée 16 rue Royal, 8ᵉ 📞01 42 60 21 79, 🌐laduree .com; Ⓜ️Madeleine/Concorde; map pp.74–75. This beautiful tearoom's melt-in-your-mouth *macarons* are legendary, but the light-as-air meringues and *millefeuilles* are just as good. When you're done with the pâtisserie, sit back and enjoy the luxurious interior of gilt-edged mirrors and ceiling. Tea and two *macarons* will set you back around €15. Other, equally grand branches throughout Paris. Mon–Thurs 8.30am–7.30pm, Fri & Sat 8am–8pm, Sun 10am–7pm.

Legrand Filles et Fils 7–11 Galerie Vivienne, 2ᵉ 📞01 42 60 07 12, 🌐caves-legrand.com; Ⓜ️Bourse; map pp.74–75. Attached to the classy wine and food emporium of the same name (see p.338), *Legrand* attracts a sober-suited, mature crowd with its reserved atmosphere, fine wines (glasses from around €6) and simple dishes, from soft-boiled egg (€9) to pan-roasted squid (€19). Mon noon–7pm, Tues–Thurs noon–7.30pm, Fri & Sat noon–8.30pm.

PASSAGES AND PALAIS-ROYAL

CAFÉS AND WINE BARS

Floquifil 17 rue de Montyon, 9ᵉ 📞01 42 46 11 19, 🌐floquifil.fr; Ⓜ️Grands Boulevards; map pp.74–75. There are no affectations in this good-looking, relaxed neighbourhood *bistrot à vins* – just excellent wines and country food with the odd contemporary twist. It's easy to linger a while, and difficult not to be charmed. Mains €14–20, lunchtime *plat* plus glass of wine and coffee €15. Mon–Fri 11am–midnight, Sat 6pm–midnight.

A Priori Thé 35 Galerie Vivienne, 2ᵉ 📞01 42 97 48 75, 🌐apriorithe.com; Ⓜ️Bourse; map pp.74–75. Unfussy *salon de thé* in a charming *passage*, with some tables in the arcade itself. You can get crumbly home-made scones or cheesecake (cakes around €5) and lots of varieties of tea, plus coffee, hot chocolate and light lunch dishes. Mon–Fri 9am–6pm, Sat 9am–6.30pm, Sun 12.30–6.30pm.

Racines 8 passage des Panoramas, 2ᵉ 📞01 40 13 06 41, 🌐racinesparis.com; Ⓜ️Grands Boulevards or Bourse; map pp.74–75. This pretty old *passage* (see p.82) has become quite the foodie hotspot – *Le Coinstot Vino* is another good option along here, but *Racines* has the edge: a cosy, neighbourhood, elbow-to-elbow *bistrot à vins* in a lovely old tile-floored wine shop. The short daily-changing menu offers a simple selection of home-cooked food – the likes of scallops, razor clams, charcuterie, pigeon, and always an excellent cheese platter – which they will pair with natural wines from the store. Starters €7–15, mains from €24. There's a second branch (*Racines 2*) at 39 rue de l'Arbre Sec in the 1ᵉʳ. Mon–Fri noon–2.30pm & 7.30–10.30pm.

Verlet 256 rue St-Honoré, 1ᵉʳ 📞01 42 60 67 39, 🌐cafesverlet.com; Ⓜ️Palais-Royal-Musée-du-Louvre; map pp.74–75. The intoxicating aroma of more than thirty types of coffee from all over the world greets you inside this long-established coffee merchant's and café, with its wood furnishings, leather benches and caddy-lined wall. If you're

RESTAURANT

Drouant 16–18 place Gaillon, 2ᵉ 📞01 42 65 15 16, 🌐drouant.com; Ⓜ️Opéra; map pp.74–75. Run by famed chef Antoine Westermann, *Drouant* has historic clout (it has been the headquarters of the Goncourt and Renaudot literary prizes since 1914) but offers a contemporary take on bourgeois cuisine. Main courses are single dishes, but it's the starters and desserts – four of each, served in small portions – that really showcase the chef's art. A vegetable-themed starter selection might include fresh truffle with potato salad or Jerusalem artichoke soup with toasted chestnuts and hazelnuts; you could also choose from a fish, classic or "international" selection. Meanwhile, if the *pot-au-feu* is on offer, snap it up – it's been voted the best in the city. Starters €27; mains plus sides from €25, weekday lunch *menu* €45, supper *menu* €47–59. Daily noon–2.30pm & 7pm–midnight.

having trouble deciding, opt for one of the rich and smoky house blends; there's a good selection of teas and snacks – including quiches – too. Mon–Sat 9.30am–6.30pm.

RESTAURANTS

★ Bistrot des Victoires 6 rue de la Vrillière, 1ᵉʳ 📞01 42 61 43 78; Ⓜ️Bourse; map pp.74–75. Just behind the chic place des Victoires, but very reasonably priced for the area, this charming, old-fashioned *bistrot* with zinc bar, mustard-coloured walls, globe lamps and velvet banquettes serves good standbys such as *confit de canard* and *poulet rôti* for around €10, as well as huge salads and *tartines* (€8.50) – try the hearty *savoyarde* (with bacon, potatoes and Emmental). Sunday brunch €15.50. Daily 9am–11pm.

L'Epi d'Or 25 rue Jean-Jacques Rousseau, 1ᵉʳ 📞01 42 36 38 12, 🌐faget-benard.com/jojo/epidor; Ⓜ️Louvre-Rivoli; map pp.74–75. Christian Louboutin is a fan of this perfect locals' *bistrot* that dishes up comforting, homely standards – from lentils with bacon or *escargots* to steaks and *tarte tatin* – in an Art Deco dining room. Mains from €14, *menus* from €19. Mon–Fri noon–2pm & 8–11pm, Sat 8–11pm.

Frenchie/Frenchie Bar à Vins/Frenchie to Go 5 rue du Nil, 2ᵉ 📞01 40 39 96 19; Frenchie Bar à Vins 6 rue du Nil, 2ᵉ 📞01 40 39 96 19; 🌐frenchie-restaurant.com; Frenchie to Go 9 rue du Nil, 2ᵉ 📞01 40 26 23 43, 🌐frenchietogo.com; Ⓜ️Sentier; map pp.74–75. When Grégory Marchand, who worked in New York and with Jamie Oliver at *Fifteen* in London (where he was known, predict-ably, as "Frenchie"), set up his tiny, simple eponymous restaurant, it quickly became the talk of the town. Using only the freshest ingredients, the menu features French classics with a twist, such as roasted lamb with chickpeas, zaatar and harissa (mains from €19; *menu* €68). The cheese plates, incongruously, focus on Brit cheeses from Neal's Yard Dairy. If you can't get a reservation (call between 3–5pm

Mon–Fri) try and bag a table at his *Bar à Vins* opposite, which doesn't take reservations and where you can join crowds of anglophone foodies enjoying interesting wines and snacking on sharing platters – though even here it's best to arrive early. During the day you can pick up lobster rolls (€22) and fish and chips (€14) at *Frenchie To Go*, the tiny coffee-shop-cum-deli a few doors down, which also offers a brunchy breakfast – granola (€6), bacon sandwiches on English muffins (€7), eggs Benedict (€12) and the like. Frenchie Mon–Fri 7–10.30pm; Frenchie Bar à Vins Mon–Fri 7–11pm; Frenchie To Go Mon–Fri 8.30am–4.30pm, Sat & Sun 9.30am–5.30pm.

Gallopin 40 rue Notre-Dame-des-Victoires, 2ᵉ ☎01 42 36 45 38, ⓦbrasseriegallopin.com; ⓂBourse; map pp.74–75. Endearing nineteenth-century brasserie, with all its original brass and mahogany fittings and beautiful painted glass. It's a popular, and not expensive, choice for classic French dishes including *escargots*, beef *tartare* and especially the foie gras *maison*, all of which are well above par. Weekday lunch *formule* €19, lunch and evening *menu* €29. Daily noon–11.30pm.

Higuma 32bis rue Ste-Anne, 1ᵉʳ ☎01 47 03 38 59, ⓦhiguma.fr; ⓂPyramides; map pp.74–75. The pick of the many basic Japanese canteens along and near this street, *Higuma* serves cheap and filling staples such as pork *katsu* curry and *gyosa* and *ramen* (noodle soup). Settle at the counter and watch the chefs at work, or sit in one of the two dining rooms. It's very popular; you may have to queue at lunchtime. From €7.50. Daily 11.30am–10pm.

Aux Lyonnais 32 rue St-Marc, 2ᵉ ☎01 58 00 22 06, ⓦauxlyonnais.com; ⓂBourse/Richelieu-Drouot; map pp.74–75. This gorgeous old *bistrot*, with its *belle époque* tiles, globe lights and mirrored walls, preserves a lovely old-fashioned ambience and serves classic Lyonnais cuisine under the direction of haute cuisine chef Alain Ducasse. Specialities include *quenelles* (delicate fish dumplings) and the house black pudding; the delicious Fin Gras du Mézenc beef, a rare find in Paris, needs to be ordered in advance. Three-course lunch/dinner *menus* €34/€35. Tues–Fri noon–2pm & 7.30–10pm, Sat 7.30–10pm.

Verjus 52 rue de Richelieu, 1ᵉʳ; wine bar 47 rue Montpensier, 1ᵉʳ; ⓂPyramides/Palais Royal; ☎01 42 97 54 40, ⓦverjusparis.com; map pp.74–75. This pretty, relaxed, American-owned dining room, tucked away above rue Montpensier, offers Modern European food on a seven-course *menu dégustation* (€68) that features such dishes as squid with squid ink gnocchi and salsify, or pigeon with kale, cabbage, whey, apple and pumpkin seed. If you haven't booked, or want to spend less, pop down the steps and around the corner to the postage-stamp-sized wine bar in the cellar at the back (no reservations), where you can perch on stools and tuck into sharing plates of buttermilk-fried chicken, broccoli with anchovies and the like. Surrounded almost exclusively by American and British foodies, with a cool playlist from Sinatra to New Orleans R&B, it's easy to forget you're actually in Paris, but the food (€8–15) is flawless. Restaurant Mon–Fri 7–11pm; wine bar Mon–Fri 6–11pm, food from 7pm.

BEAUBOURG AND LES HALLES

CAFÉS AND WINE BARS

Le Café des Initiés 3 place des Deux-Ecus, 1ᵉʳ ☎01 42 33 78 29, ⓦlecafedesinities.com; ⓂChâtelet-Les-Halles/Louvre; map p.86. A smart yet intimate and comfortable café with a popular *terrasse*. Locals gather round the zinc bar or tuck into tasty dishes such as grilled king prawns and steak *tartare* (from €14) and home-made apple crumble. It's also a good spot for an evening drink. Happy hour 5.30–8.30pm. Daily 7am–2am.

Le Cochon à l'Oreille 15 rue Montmartre, 1ᵉʳ ☎01 40 26 84 07; ⓂChâtelet-Les-Halles/Etienne-Marcel; map p.86. This classic little café-bar, with its stunning ceramic-tiled walls decorated with lively market scenes, dates from Les Halles' days as a market, and appears not to have changed since then. A nice Parisian spot with a vaguely bohemian feel, perfect for a coffee, glass of wine or light lunch. Mains around €16. Mon–Sat 9am–1am.

★ **Le Comptoir de la Gastronomie** 34 rue Montmartre, 1ᵉʳ ☎01 42 33 31 32, ⓦcomptoirdelagastronomie.com; ⓂLes Halles/Etienne-Marcel; map p.86. Gloriously old-fashioned deli (see p.335) serving fabulous baguettes – foie gras with fig chutney; smoked duck; house *terrines* – to take away (from €5.50); perfect for picnics. Or sit down to a

simple, beautifully executed, traditional *plat* (roast duck, cassoulet, onion soup and the like, from €16) in the traditional dining room attached (*formules* from €14.50). Deli Mon–Sat 6am–8pm; restaurant Mon–Thurs noon–11pm, Fri & Sat noon–midnight.

Dame Tartine 2 rue Brisemiche, 4ᵉ ☎01 42 77 32 22; ⓂRambuteau/Hôtel-de-Ville; map p.86. Overlooking the Stravinsky fountain, with outdoor seating under shady plane trees, this popular café is a handy pit stop in a heavily touristed area, offering cheap and tasty, open toasted sandwiches and soups, and a *menu* for children. Daily noon–11.30pm.

★ **Le Garde-Robe** 41 rue de l'Arbre Sec, 1ᵉʳ ☎01 49 26 90 60; ⓂLouvre-Rivoli; map p.86. Animated, cosy *bistrot à vins* that with its bare-board floors, retro wallpaper and globe lights manages to feel effortlessly stylish. Though the wines are superb, with many biodynamic and natural choices (around €5 per glass), part of the draw is the food, which you can eat at the counter or at a few tables at the back. A couple of simple and unusual lunchtime *menus* (€10–20) focus on organic ingredients, with tasty veggie choices; in the evenings the likes of cheese and charcuterie plates, *croques* and foie gras (from €12) take over. Mon–Fri 11am–3pm & 6.30pm–midnight, Sat 6.30pm–midnight.

20

TOP 5 HISTORIC CAFÉS

Angélina See p.275
Café de la Paix See p.275
Le Flore See p.285
Ladurée See p.276
Le Select See p.289

Le Petit Marcel 63 rue Rambuteau, 4ᵉ ☎ 01 48 87 10 20; Ⓜ Rambuteau; map p.86. A bustling place with a dash of *belle époque* style in its old mirrors and tiled floors and ceiling, with friendly staff and a tiny drinking space. There's a dining area, too, where you can get good-value, hearty dishes such as sausages with mustard, or a simple but tasty croissant and coffee breakfast. Mains from €13. Daily 8am–midnight.

RESTAURANTS

Au Pied de Cochon 6 rue Coquillière, 1ᵉʳ ☎ 01 40 13 77 00, Ⓦ aupieddecochon.com; Ⓜ Châtelet-Les-Halles; map p.86. Since opening its doors in 1946, *Au Pied de Cochon* has become a Les Halles institution – and it knows it. Still, this big old brasserie is worth a visit for extravagant middle-of-the-night pork chops, fresh lobster and, of course, pigs' trotters. *Menus* from €28.50. Daily 24hr.

★**Pirouette** 5 rue Mondétour, 1ᵉʳ ☎ 01 40 26 47 81, Ⓦ oenolis.com; Ⓜ Étienne Marcel; map p.86. This sleek restaurant has gained a name for serving beautifully presented, innovative French food in a relaxed, contemporary atmosphere, with fresh, bright flavours, lots of light choices and delicious veggie dishes. Menus change monthly, with mains starting at around €22; the two-course lunch *menu* is a bargain at €20, and there's a *menu dégustation* for €62. Reservations recommended. Mon–Sat 12.30–2.30pm & 7.30–10.30pm.

La Régalade Saint Honoré 123 rue St-Honoré, 1ᵉʳ ☎ 01 42 21 92 40; Ⓜ Louvre-Rivoli/Les Halles; map p.86. Tourists and locals flock to this pared-back, sober restaurant for Bruno Doucet's accomplished bistronomy cooking: the €38 three-course *menu* offers some of the city's best value, with dishes such as cod poached in chicken broth with beets and curried crème fraiche followed by Mont Blanc with green apple. Booking essential. Mon–Fri 12.30–2.30pm & 7.30–10.30pm.

La Robe et le Palais 13 rue des Lavandières St-Opportune, 1ᵉʳ ☎ 01 45 08 07 41, Ⓦ robe-et-palais .com; Ⓜ Châtelet; map p.86. Small, bustling *restaurant à vins* serving traditional cuisine and a *tête*-boggling selection of 250 wines *au compteur* (recommended for you by the staff and priced according to how much you consume) in a cosy space. Dishes range from the hearty (home-made foie gras, duck) to delicate (trout ceviche), all of it enjoyed by a happy local crowd. Reckon on around €50 a head for three courses without wine. Mon–Sat noon–2.30pm & 7.30–11pm.

★**La Tour de Montlhéry (Chez Denise)** 5 rue des Prouvaires, 1ᵉʳ ☎ 01 42 36 21 82; Ⓦ Louvre-Rivoli/ Châtelet; map p.86. An old-style, late-night, market *bistrot*, packed with regulars sitting elbow to elbow and tucking into rich, substantial French dishes, such as *daube* of beef, bone marrow, *tête de veau* or skate with *frites*, along with Loire wines from the barrel, in a convivial, unforgettable atmosphere. Mains around €25. Mon–Fri noon–3pm & 7.30pm–5am.

★**Yam'Tcha** 121 rue St-Honoré, 1ᵉʳ ☎ 01 40 26 08 07, Ⓦ www.yamtcha.com; Ⓜ Louvre-Rivoli; map p.86. Having grown out of its original site (see p.336), which now sells tea and serves *bao* buns to take away, Yam'Tcha's Chinese-French fusion restaurant moved to larger premises in 2015. The delicate, Michelin-starred food continues to dazzle and surprise – *menus découvertes* (€60/€120) might include roast duck breast with Szechuan-style aubergines, followed by melting meringue with moscatel grapes and lychee with shiso (similar to mint) sorbet. Book well – as far as a month – in advance. Tues 8–9.30pm, Wed–Sun noon–1.30pm & 8–9.30pm.

THE MARAIS

CAFÉS AND WINE BARS

Boot Café 19 rue du Pont aux Choux, 3ᵉ ☎ 06 26 41 10 66; Ⓜ St-Sébastien-Froissart; map p.94. Coffee shops don't get tinier than this cool Aussie-run hole-in-the-wall where they serve expert brews – and the odd unusual bite, including various takes on *congee* (Cantonese rice porridge). Grab a coffee to go – or bag one of the few chairs and prepare to be sociable. Daily 10am–6pm.

Café Charlot 38 rue de Bretagne, 3ᵉ ☎ 01 44 54 03 30, Ⓦ cafecharlotparis.com; Ⓜ Filles-du-Calvaire; map p.94. You'll need to fight for a seat on the *terrasse* of this white-tiled retro café (a former boulangerie), which bursts at the seams on weekends with locals and in-the-know tourists. The food – a mix of French and American standards – is not that special, but it's a great place for a drink and a spot of people-watching. Daily 7am–2am.

Caffè Marcovaldo 61 rue Charlot, 3ᵉ ☎ 09 80 44 86 49, Ⓦ marcovaldo.fr; Ⓜ Filles du Calvaire; map p.94. Pared down and laidback Italian coffee house/bar/bookshop, with mismatched furniture, stone floors and book-lined walls, where locals linger for hours with their laptops, their Italian coffees, their bio wines and their friends. Calzone, frittata and other simple Italian dishes dominate the short menu. Lots of author events and a pleasantly literary vibe. Mon–Thurs & Sun 11am–7pm, Fri & Sat 11am–11pm.

Loustic 40 rue Chapon, 3ᵉ ☎ 09 80 31 07 06; Ⓜ Arts-et-Métiers; map p.94. Just off rue Beaubourg on the Marais borders, this is one of the city's more established expat-run

20

coffee houses, the realm of a friendly Londoner. With the emphasis on expertly made, high-quality brews rather than on hipster style, it's a welcoming place, with a cosy Moroccan-style back room and a few small tables at the front where people relax and chat. Mon–Fri 8am–6pm, Sat 9am–7pm, Sun 10am–6pm.

Le Mary Celeste 1 rue Commines, 3ᵉ lemaryceleste .com; Filles-du-Calvaire; map p.94. With its high stools, exposed brick walls and cool vibe, this slick corner bar feels more New York than Paris, and it's where *bobo* (bourgeois-bohemian) Parisians and expats flock in their droves. A daily changing menu of inventive sharing plates (around €10), such as steamed oysters with chili, black vinegar and crispy shallots or foie gras tostada with blue cheese, radicchio and pickled plums, offers surprising and genuinely exciting food; the cocktails (specials around €12) are great, too. Daily 6pm–2am.

★**Merci** 111 bd Beaumarchais, 3ᵉ 01 42 77 79 28, merci-merci.com; St-Sébastien-Froissart; map p.94. There are three desirable eating options at this cool concept store (see p.338). The snug *Used Book Café* on the ground floor lets you curl up in a leather armchair with a good read – there are thousands of titles lining the walls – while sipping tea and tucking into pastries; the lower-floor *La Cantine de Merci*, with a little garden, is a family-friendly option that serves healthy, fresh light lunches; and the retro *Cinéma Café*, on street level, with a definite whiff of Parisian cool in its perfectly judged movie theming, offers simple charcuterie, salads and soup. Used Book Café & Cinéma Café Mon–Sat 10am–6.30pm; La Cantine de Merci Mon–Sat noon–6pm.

Le Progrès 1 rue de Bretagne, 3ᵉ 01 42 72 01 44; Filles-du-Calvaire; map p.94. Parisians prop up the zinc bar or bag the *terrasse* tables at this popular corner café, with its traditional mustard-coloured walls and mosaic floor. It's especially popular at *apéritif* time, but also makes a good spot for relaxing with a coffee and newspaper in the morning. Mon–Sat 8am–2am; closed three weeks in Aug.

RESTAURANTS

Ambassade d'Auvergne 22 rue de Grenier St-Lazare, 3ᵉ 01 42 72 31 22, ambassade-auvergne.com; Rambuteau; map p.94. Tourists love it, and for good reason: this is tasty, hearty Auvergnat cuisine that would

have made Vercingétorix proud, served in a cosy, traditional dining room. The starter of warm lentils and bacon could be a meal in itself, but for the ultimate in comfort food try the *saucisse* and *aligot* (creamy, cheesy potato; €16); the waiter brings the *aligot* to your table in a copper pan and demonstrates its gloriously silky texture by drawing it up high in the air on a spoon. Treats for afters include a vast help-yourself bowl of chocolate mousse and a fabulous cheese plate that includes the region's pungent Cantal. Daily 12.30–2pm & 7.30–10pm.

★**Chez Janou** 2 rue Roger Verlomme, 3ᵉ 01 42 72 28 21, chezjanou.com; Chemin Vert; map p.94. Fiercely popular Provençal restaurant that serves generous portions of traditional southern food – rabbit, risotto, *daube*, duck (mains from €16) – and more than eighty types of *pastis* in its warm, traditional dining room. Save room for dessert; the house chocolate mousse is legendary, served in a cavernous bowl from which you help yourself. Tables are crammed in, so unless you can bag one on the sunny *terrasse* you'll be getting cosy with your neighbours. Booking advised. Daily noon–3pm & 7pm–midnight.

Chez Omar 47 rue de Bretagne, 3ᵉ 01 42 72 36 26; Arts-et-Métiers; map p.94. You can't reserve at this perennially popular North African couscous restaurant, but it's no hardship to wait for a table at the bar, taking in the handsome old brasserie decor and brisk, spirited atmosphere. It's not gourmet food, but portions are copious and the couscous light and fluffy. The *merguez* (spicy sausage) variety costs €16, the *royale* (with three kinds of lamb) €25 – though if you go for the latter don't expect to have room for the sticky cakes afterwards. No credit cards. Mon–Sat noon–2.30pm & 7–11.30pm, Sun 7–11.30pm.

Pramil 9 rue Vertbois, 3ᵉ 01 42 72 03 60, pramil.fr; Temple/Arts-et-Métiers; map p.94. Elegant, petite restaurant with simple decor, serving an appetizing menu of classic and more unusual French dishes – cream of pumpkin and chestnut with foie gras "ice cream"; cauliflower cake; chocolate brownie with edamame – to foodie tourists. The wine list (from €22) is small but well chosen, and the set *menus* (dinner €33; lunch €24) are good value. At the end of the night the chef will usually come out and chat to diners, which gives the place a friendly feel. Tues–Sat noon–3pm & 7.30–10.30pm, Sun 7.30–10.30pm.

20

CENTRAL MARAIS

CAFÉS AND WINE BARS

L'As du Fallafel 34 rue des Rosiers, 4ᵉ 01 48 87 63 60; St-Paul; map p.97. The sign above the doorway of this falafel shop in the Jewish quarter reads *Toujours imité, jamais égalé* ("always copied, but never equalled"), a boast that few would challenge, given the queues outside. (It also says it's recommended by Lenny Kravitz, but that's another matter.) Falafels to take away start at €3 for ten, €6

in pitta with salad – or pay a bit more and sit in the buzzing dining room. Mon–Thurs & Sun noon–11.30pm, Fri noon–3pm.

La Caféothèque 52 rue de l'Hôtel-de-Ville, 4ᵉ 01 53 01 83 84, lacafeotheque.com; Pont Marie or Saint-Paul; map p.97. This arty, aromatic and airy third-wave coffee house, in a sunny spot by the Seine, provides the perfect setting to relax on plump

TOP 10 ALFRESCO EATING

Le Bistrot des Dames See p.293
Café de la Mosquée See p.283
L'Entrepôt See p.289
L'Heure Gourmande See p.285
Maison de l'Amérique Latine See p.286
Mini Palais See p.274
Le Moulin de la Galette See p.291
Les Philosophes See p.280
Relais de la Butte See p.291
Sardine See p.295

hessian-covered seating over a brew and make use of the free wi-fi. Coffee is taken seriously here, with daily specials and a three-cup *dégustation* option in addition to espressos, flat whites and the like. You can buy beans to go, too. Mon–Sat 10am–7pm, Sun noon–7pm.

L'Ebouillanté 6 rue des Barres, 4ᵉ ☎01 42 71 00 69, ⓦrestaurant-ebouillante.fr; ⓜHôtel-de-Ville; map p.97. In nice weather, this colourful, two-storey café spills onto a peaceful, cobbled street behind the church of St-Gervais. You can choose from an extensive choice of drinks, including home-made hot chocolate, as well as salads and crêpes (€14) – the food isn't amazing, but it's a pretty spot and a Marais classic on a sunny evening. Tues–Sun noon–10pm, till 7pm in winter.

L'Estaminet 39 rue de Bretagne, Marché des Enfants Rouges, 3ᵉ ☎01 42 72 28 12, ⓦlestaminetdesenfants rouges.com; ⓜFilles-du-Calvaire; map p.97. An inexpensive, charming corner café in this buzzing foodie market: sit at the paintbox-bright picnic tables outside to soak up the atmosphere and choose from tasty dishes including oysters (in season), charcuterie platters, gourmet salads, tarts, meaty French mains and world cuisine. *Plat du jour* €13, *formules* from €14. Breakfast served till noon. Free wi-fi. Tues–Sun 10am–8pm.

Le Loir dans la Théière 3 rue des Rosiers, 4ᵉ ☎01 42 72 90 61; ⓜSt-Paul; map p.97. A much-loved *salon de thé* decorated with arty posters and whimsical *Alice in Wonderland* murals (the name translates as "the dormouse in the teapot"). It's a popular place, nearly always full, and there a couple of comfy leather armchairs for lounging. The enormous (and delicious) home-made cakes are the thing to order (around €11 for tea and cake), but you can also get light meals and brunch. Daily 9.30am–7pm.

Marché des Enfants Rouges 39 rue de Bretagne, 3ᵉ; ⓜFilles-du-Calvaire; map p.97. A great picnic option – in addition to fresh fruit, veg and cheese, this venerable food market (see p.104) is the place to come for street food – rôtisserie, Japanese, couscous, crêpes, Lebanese, Italian, Creole – which you can eat at communal picnic tables. Tues, Wed & Thurs 8.30am–1pm & 4–7.30pm, Fri & Sat 8.30am–1pm & 4–8pm, Sun 8.30am–2pm.

Les Philosophes 28 rue Vieille du Temple, 4ᵉ ☎01 48 87 49 64, ⓦcafeine.com/philosophes; ⓜHôtel-de-Ville; map p.97. One of a number of *bistrots* on this stretch run by the same people, *Les Philosophes* has a corner *terrasse* brilliantly placed for people-watching, plus tasty, reasonably priced food – snacks and *plats* – matched by decent wines. It's a good spot for a cooked or continental breakfast, too. Daily 9am–2am.

Pozzetto 39 rue du Roi de Sicile, 4ᵉ ☎01 42 77 08 64, ⓦpozzetto.biz; ⓜHôtel-de-Ville; map p.97. Hugely popular ice-cream parlour, serving proper Italian *gelato* – try the moreish Sicilian pistachio flavour – made fresh every day; if you're having trouble choosing, ask for a free taster. You can get authentic Italian coffee here too. There's a newer branch around the corner at 26 rue Vieille du Temple, which also serves salads (open from 9am). Mon–Thurs 12.15–11pm, Fri & Sat 12.15pm–12.15am, Sun 12.15–10.45pm.

RESTAURANTS

Breizh Café 109 rue Vieille du Temple, 3ᵉ ☎01 42 72 13 77, ⓦbreizhcafe.com; ⓜSt-Paul; map p.97. A Breton restaurant serving delicious *galettes* (savoury buckwheat pancakes) and crêpes. Traditional fillings include ham and cheese, but this is a smartish place, so you can get more elaborate options such as salt cod or the Savoyarde, with Reblochon cheese and potatoes. Wash it all down with one of their many ciders and leave room for a sweet crêpe – Valrhona chocolate, perhaps, or ginger and salted caramel. Booking advised. Mains €5.50–12.50. Wed–Sat 11.30am–11pm, Sun 11.30am–10pm; closed three weeks in Aug.

Chez Hanna 54 rue des Rosiers, 4ᵉ ☎01 42 74 74 99, ⓦchezhanna-restaurant.fr; ⓜSt-Paul; map p.97. This simple restaurant is always packed with locals and in-the-know tourists for its reasonably priced Middle Eastern and Jewish delicacies – the falafel special, with super-fresh, warm falafel, sauce, hummus, fried aubergines and salad is huge, filling, delicious and a steal at €12; the *shawarma* (€16), made with tasty, spiced turkey, is also popular. Takeout falafel starts at €5. Tues–Sun 11.30am–midnight.

Pink Flamingo 105 rue Vieille du Temple, 3ᵉ ☎01 42 71 28 20, ⓦpinkflamingopizza.com; ⓜSt-Sébastien-Froissart; map p.97. The inventive, tasty pizzas (from €11.50) at the tiny Marais branch of this funky mini-chain – all graffitied walls and retro banquettes – include the Gandhi (*sag paneer*, *baba ganoush* and mozzarella) and the Bjork (smoked salmon, lumpfish caviar and crème fraîche). A fun, friendly budget option, with three other branches around town. Tues–Fri noon–3pm & 7–11.30pm, Sat & Sun noon–4pm & 7–11.30pm.

Le Potager du Marais 24 rue Rambuteau, 3ᵉ ☎01 57 40 98 57; ⓜRambuteau; map p.97. A small, welcoming vegetarian restaurant, rustically styled and with a menu featuring organic, gluten-free and vegan options. Dishes might include goat's cheese with honey, "crusty" quinoa burger or seitan Bourguignon, and there are scrumptious vegan desserts (*crème brûlée* with ginger, anyone?). Mains from €13. Wed–Sun noon–3pm & 7–11pm.

★**Robert et Louise** 64 rue Vieille du Temple, 3ᵉ ☎01 42 78 55 89, ⓦrobertetlouise.com; ⓜHôtel-de-Ville; map p.97. The welcome at this popular rustic *bistrot*, with

its exposed beams, is as warm and hearty as the meaty food. Start with foie gras or a blood sausage, then choose between at least three types of steak, lamb chops, duck confit or *andouillette* (tripe sausage). Lunch *menu* €14, three courses around €30. Booking advisable. Tues & Wed 7–11pm, Thurs–Sat noon–3pm & 7–11pm, Sun noon–11pm.

BASTILLE AND EAST

CAFÉS AND WINE BARS

L'Armagnac 104 rue de Charonne, 11ᵉ ☎01 43 71 49 43; ⓜCharonne; map pp.110–111. The red banquettes at this deliciously unpretentious, rather battered old-school café-bar, which has an appealingly lethargic air, are ideal for a reasonably priced coffee or drink at any time. Check out the lovely old mural on the back wall. Mon–Fri 7.30am–1.30am, Sat 10am–1am, Sun 10am–midnight.

★**Le Baron Rouge** 1 rue Théophile-Roussel, 12ᵉ ☎01 43 43 14 32; ⓜLedru-Rollin; map pp.110–111. Stallholders and shoppers from the nearby Marché Aligre gather at this glorious old spit-and-sawdust *bar à vins* for a light lunch or an *apéritif* during the day, especially on Sundays. If it's crowded, join the locals outside standing around the wine barrels and lunching on simple platters of *saucisson*, cheese or five different sizes of fresh oysters; try a half-dozen Cap Ferrat oysters washed down with a glass of Muscadet. Wines from €2, food from €7. Not to be missed. Mon 5–10pm, Tues–Fri 10am–2pm & 5–10pm, Sat 10am–10pm, Sun 10.30am–3.30pm.

Café des Anges 66 rue de la Roquette, 11ᵉ ☎01 47 00 00 63; ⓜBastille; map pp.110–111. This friendly corner café pulls a young, lively, hip crowd, filling up on good-value contemporary French dishes (from €11) – gourmet burgers (including a tasty duck confit version with onion chutney, Cantal and rocket), fish and chips, veggie lasagne, salads and quiches. It's popular for evening drinks. Mon–Sat 8am–2am, Sun 9am–2am.

★**Café de l'Industrie** 16 rue St-Sabin, 11ᵉ ☎01 47 00 13 53, ⓦcafedelindustrieparis.fr; ⓜBastille; map pp.110–111. The relaxed atmosphere and shabby neo-colonial/boho glamour – softly polished wood, huge potted plants, retro movie star photos and gypsy jazz soundtrack – attract a mixed crowd at this Bastille institution (there's another branch opposite, but this one has the edge). It's particularly popular at weekends when there's a good-value set brunch (until 5pm) for €17. The menu ranges from generous plates of pasta to more traditional French *bistrot* dishes, and while the food is not outstanding prices are low (mains €9–11; lunch *formule* €12). Daily 9am–2am.

Chezaline 85 rue de la Roquette, 11ᵉ ☎01 43 71 90 75; ⓜVoltaire; map pp.110–111. This gourmet deli has stirred up quite a buzz with its inexpensive, creative take on picnic food – eat in (if you're lucky enough to win one of the few tables) or take out baguettes (ham, artichoke and

pesto; roasted cod with tapenade), deli salads and daily changing specials, all from €5. Mon–Fri 11am–7pm.

Pause Café 41 rue de Charonne, corner of rue Keller, 11ᵉ ☎01 48 06 80 33; ⓜLedru-Rollin; map pp.110–111. Or maybe "Pose Café" – given the popularity of this cool and colourful café-*bistrot* with the *quartier*'s young crowd, who pack out the pavement tables at lunch and *apéritif* time. Service is predictably insouciant but there's a good atmosphere and an enviable location. The food won't win any prizes, but you can fill up on *plats du jour* including burgers and pasta (€12.50–14). Mon–Sat 8am–2am, Sun 9am–8pm (brunch noon–3pm).

La Ruche à Miel 19 rue d'Aligre, 12ᵉ ☎01 43 41 27 10; ⓜLedru-Rollin; map pp.110–111. The mouthwatering array of pistachio, almond, walnut and honey cakes at the entrance to this little Algerian teashop, on the rue d'Aligre market street, entices in many a passer-by. The best accompaniment to the cakes is the sugary fresh mint tea, served in the traditional way, on low brass tables. Around €10 for tea and two cakes; also couscous and tagines (from €12), plus hot breads. Tues–Thurs & Sun 8.30am–7.30pm, Fri & Sat 8.30am–11pm.

RESTAURANTS

★**Le 6 Paul Bert** 6 rue Paul Bert, 11ᵉ ☎01 43 79 14 32; ⓜFaidherbe-Chaligny; map pp.110–111. Brought to you by the same people as *Le Bistro Paul Bert* (see p.282) this elegant and relaxed place branches off in another direction entirely, with a focus on (large-ish) sharing platters of fresh, seasonal and contemporary food. The daily changing menu never misses, whether you go for suckling pig with salsify or octopus and chorizo torte, and there's a good selection of natural wines by the glass. Lunch *menus* €15/€19, four-course dinner €44. Reservations advised. Tues noon–2pm, Wed–Sat noon–2pm & 7.30–11pm.

A la Biche au Bois 45 av Ledru-Rollin, 11ᵉ ☎01 43 43 34 38; ⓜGare de Lyon; map pp.110–111. The queues leading out of the door tell you all you need to know about this traditional restaurant, which mixes charming service with keenly priced, well-produced food served in generous quantities. This is a carnivore's dream: don't miss the game dishes, the terrines, the wild duck and the huge, rich *coq au vin*. Four-course *menu* (including a fabulous array of cheeses) €39. Mon 7–11pm, Tues–Fri noon–2pm & 7–11pm.

20

Bistrot Paul Bert 18 rue Paul Bert, 11ᵉ ☎ 01 43 72 24 01; Ⓜ Faidherbe-Chaligny; map pp.110–111. This *bistrot* looks right, with its chalkboard menu, little tables, tiled floor and marbled mirrors, and it feels right, with a genuine neighbourhood buzz. Saturday lunchtime is a delight, with lively groups of friends and family taking their time over the seasonal food, from fried eggs with truffles via steak *au poivre* with crispy *frites*. Save room for dessert, such as the Paris-Brest puff pastry oozing hazelnut cream or the Grand Marnier soufflé. Three-course dinner *menu* €38. Reservations advised. Tues–Sat noon–2pm & 7.30–11pm.

Le Bistrot du Peintre 116 av Ledru-Rollin, 11ᵉ ☎ 01 47 00 34 39, Ⓦ bistrotdupeintre.com; Ⓜ Ledru-Rollin; map pp.110–111. It's difficult to resist this charming, traditional, rather shabby chic old *bistrot*, where small tables are jammed together beneath faded Art Nouveau frescoes, undulating mirrors and decorative panelling. There is a wide selection of cheese and charcuterie, with meaty *plats* from €12. Daily 7am–2am.

Bofinger 7 rue de la Bastille, 4ᵉ ☎ 01 42 72 87 82, Ⓦ bofingerparis.com; Ⓜ Bastille; map pp.110–111. This popular fin-de-siècle Alsatian brasserie, with its splendid, perfectly preserved coloured-glass dome, is a favourite with opera-goers and moneyed tourists. Specialities are seafood and steaming dishes of sauerkraut. *Menus* from €31. Mon–Fri noon–3pm & 6.30pm–midnight, Sat noon–3.30pm & 6.30pm–midnight, Sun noon–11pm.

Chez Paul 13 rue de Charonne, corner of rue de Lappe, 11ᵉ ☎ 01 47 00 34 57, Ⓦ chezpaul.com; Ⓜ Bastille; map pp.110–111. Housed in a wonky, dilapidated corner site, *Chez Paul* is a throwback to an older Bastille, with a long, handwritten menu, faded furnishings, black-and-white floor tiles and a mix of customers. Food is traditional (*pot-au-feu*, steak *au poivre*, *coq au vin* and so on, with a particularly good *boeuf bourguignon*) and affordable, and the ambience very congenial. Mains from €16; weekday lunch *menus* €18 and €21. Mon–Fri noon–3.30pm & 7pm–12.30am, Sat & Sun noon–12.30am.

L'Encrier 55 rue Traversière, 12ᵉ ☎ 01 44 68 08 16; Ⓜ Ledru-Rollin; map pp.110–111. The simple interior of exposed brick walls and timber beams complements the good-value, homely food served by pleasant staff in this small restaurant near the Viaduc des Arts. A good spot for well-executed dishes with a slight southwestern influence – *andouillette* (tripe sausage) with shallot chutney, say, or steak and morel mushrooms. *Menus* from €15.50 (lunch) or €20–35 (evening). Mon–Fri noon–2.15pm & 7.30–11pm, Sat 7.30–11pm.

★**Les Marcheurs de Planète** 73 rue de la Roquette, 11ᵉ ☎ 01 43 48 90 98, Ⓦ lesmarcheursdeplanete.com; Ⓜ Voltaire; map pp.110–111. Great restaurant/bar with a good old-fashioned Parisian atmosphere: chess tables; books and graphic novels to read; musical instruments dotted about; posters covering the walls (and ceiling); and

a friendly, wild-haired owner. More than 150 wines are on offer, plus top-notch cheeses and charcuterie, and rustic French food including *pot-au-feu* or steak, all at reasonable prices. Live music on Thursdays from around 10pm. Tues–Sun 5.30pm–2am; food served 7.30pm–midnight.

Paris-Hanoï 74 rue de Charonne, 11ᵉ ☎ 01 47 00 47 59, Ⓦ parishanoi.fr; Ⓜ Charonne; map pp.110–111. A perennially popular, cheap Vietnamese café that sees queues down the street at weekend lunchtimes for the inexpensive stir-fries, noodles and soups – try the *bun cha*, a noodle dish with veg, meatballs and caramelized peanuts. Around €15 a head for a full meal. No credit cards. Daily noon–2.30pm & 7–10.30pm; closed Aug.

Septime/Clamato 80 rue de Charonne, 11ᵉ ☎ 01 43 67 38 29, Ⓦ septime-charonne.fr; Ⓜ Charonne; map pp.110–111. A star in the city's neo-bistro firmament, *Septime* turns out inventive, delicate food – steamed cod with pickled turnips and *yuzu* sauce, say, or courgette with goat's cheese and rhubarb – on *dégustation* menus (€30 lunch; €65 dinner). It gets booked up weeks in advance, but the adjoining tapas bar, *Clamato*, which serves fish and seafood small plates, accepts walk-ins only (arrive early). Septime Mon & Tues 7.30–10pm, Wed–Fri 12.15–2pm & 7.30–10pm; Clamato Wed–Fri 7–11pm, Sat & Sun noon–11pm.

Le Souk 1 rue Keller, 11ᵉ ☎ 01 49 29 05 08, Ⓦ le-souk -paris.com; Ⓜ Ledru-Rollin; map pp.110–111. The exterior of this pretty Moroccan restaurant, with its hanging lanterns, rickety cupboards and heavy wooden doors, its jars of herbs and its pots piled high with colourful spices, transports you straight to the medina. They specialize in couscous, sweet and savoury tagines and brick-cooked meats, and prices are reasonable, with three-course *menus* at €16.50 and €22.50. Tues–Sun noon–2.30pm & 7pm–midnight.

Le Square Trousseau 1 rue Antoine Vollon, 12ᵉ ☎ 01 43 43 06 00, Ⓦ squaretrousseau.com; Ⓜ Ledru-Rollin; map pp.110–111. At once elegant – cream leather banquettes, marble columns, decorative ceiling – and cheerful, this *bistrot*, opposite a park and playground near the Marché Aligré, is as convenient for hungry families (chalk is supplied for decorating the paper tablecloths) as it is for a relaxed lunch. The menu features French dishes both traditional and modern, from chestnut and cep soup to cheeseburgers or lobster with *frites*. Mains from €20. Daily 8am–2am.

Le Train Bleu Gare de Lyon, 12ᵉ ☎ 01 43 43 09 06, Ⓦ le-train-bleu.com; Ⓜ Gare-de-Lyon; map pp.110–111. The jaw-dropping decor at *Le Train Bleu* – everything dripping with gilt, chandeliers hanging from lofty ceilings frescoed with scenes from the Paris–Lyon–Marseille train route – is from a bygone golden age, and to add to the spectacle, huge windows give onto the arriving and departing trains below. The traditional French cuisine has a hard time living up to all this, but is acceptable, if pricey (three-course *menu* €62, including half a bottle of wine). If you just want a glimpse, you could go for coffee and cake (around €21), or have a drink and snack in the comfy bar (which also serves breakfast). Daily 7.30am–10pm.

Au Vieux Chêne 7 rue du Dahomey, 11ᵉ ☎01 43 71 67 69, ⓦvieuxchene.fr; ⓜFaidherbe-Chaligny; map pp.110–111. A relaxed, traditional neighbourhood restaurant with fresh flowers on the tables and an unpretentious atmosphere. The simple, short menu does the classics well: try roast duck or veal, followed by a perfect plum tart. The two-/three-course set menus – €15/€19 lunch, €28/€33 dinner – are a steal.

THE QUARTIER LATIN

CAFÉS AND WINE BARS

Le 5ème Cru 7 rue du Cardinal Lemoine, 5ᵉ ☎01 40 46 86 34, ⓦ5ecru.com; ⓜCardinal-Lemoine; map pp.122–123. The shelves at this welcoming *bistrot à vins* are piled high with more than three hundred vintages, all from French artisan winemakers. Choose your bottle or let the friendly staff advise you, then join the locals in the cosy dining area and order slates of excellent charcuterie, cheese or more elaborate offerings, such as *ventrèche de thon* (tuna belly), all priced around €6–9. Lunchtime *formule* €15. Evening booking advisable. Mon noon–3pm & 7–11pm, Tues–Thurs noon–3pm & 7–11.30pm, Fri noon–3pm & 7pm–midnight, Sat 7pm–midnight.

★**Café de la Mosquée** 39 rue Geoffroy-St-Hilaire, 5ᵉ ☎01 43 31 38 20, ⓦla-mosquee.com; ⓜCensier-Daubenton; map pp.122–123. The *salon* has a lovely Arabic interior, where tasty tajines and authentic couscous are served for around €16 and up, but it's the tiled *terrasse* with its fig trees that's the real draw at the Paris mosque – the perfect spot to refuel with a glass of sweet mint tea and a honey-drenched cake. Watch out for weekend lunchtimes, though, when it's packed and rather chaotic. Female visitors can try a hammam-massage-meal option for €63. Daily 9am–midnight.

★**Café de la Nouvelle Mairie** 19 rue des Fossés-St-Jacques, 5ᵉ; ☎01 44 07 04 41; ⓜCluny-La Sorbonne/RER Luxembourg; map pp.122–123. Contemporary café-wine bar with a relaxed feel and a warm, convivial atmosphere. Small plates and sharing *assiettes* of cheese or charcuterie (€8–14) can be enjoyed all day, along with a fine selection of natural wines. Mon–Fri 8am–midnight.

La Fourmi Ailée 8 rue du Fouarre, 5ᵉ ☎01 43 29 40 99; ⓜMaubert-Mutualité; map pp.122–123. There's little surprising about the trad French food served in this quirky *salon de thé*, but with its background jazz and colourful surroundings – mosaic facade, cloudy sky trompe l'oeil, book-lined walls, giant flying ant (*fourmi ailée*) marionette – it's a popular stop for locals and tourists. Around €12–17 for a *plat* – including some Niçoise specialities – but you're best off plumping for a large slice of quiche (€10.50) or home-made cake (€7) and a cup of speciality tea. Daily

Mon–Fri noon–2pm & 8–10.30pm; closed last week in July and first two in Aug.

Waly Fay 6 rue Godefroy-Cavaignac, 11ᵉ ☎01 40 24 17 79, ⓦwalyfay.com; ⓜCharonne/Faidherbe-Chaligny; map pp.110–111. This West African restaurant has a cosy, stylish atmosphere, the dim lighting, white stone walls and dark timber beams creating an intimate ambience. Smart young Parisians come here to dine on fragrant, richly spiced stews, plantain fritters, jumbo prawns and other delicacies (mains €13–22). Daily 7pm–2am; closed two weeks in Aug.

noon–midnight; food served noon–3pm & 7–11pm.

★**Le Verre à Pied** 118bis rue Mouffetard, 5ᵉ ☎01 43 31 15 72, ⓦleverreapied.fr; ⓜMonge; map pp.122–123. An old-fashioned, charming and very authentic market bar where traders take their morning glass of wine at the bar and engage in lively conversation, or sit down to eat a simple *plat du jour* – *steak hâché, saucisson, entrecôte* – for around €12. Lunch *formule* €15. Tues–Sat 9am–9pm, Sun 9.30am–4pm.

RESTAURANTS

L'Atelier Maître Albert 1 rue Maître Albert, 5ᵉ ☎01 56≈81 30 01, ⓦateliermaitrealbert.com; ⓜMaubert-Mutualité; map pp.122–123. One of Michelin-starred chef-entrepreneur Guy Savoy's ventures, this rôtisserie specializes in big plates of spit-roast meats – primarily chicken, veal and beef – with lighter dishes such as a grilled scorpion fish, celery and mangetout casserole, or a delicious starter of sea bream *tartare* with radish. *Menus* €26/€31 (lunch) or €36 (dinner). Mon–Wed noon–2.30pm & 6.30–11pm, Thurs & Fri noon–2.30pm & 6.30pm–1am, Sat 6.30pm–1am, Sun 6.30–11pm.

L'Ecurie 58 rue de la Montagne-Ste-Geneviève, 5ᵉ ☎01 46 33 68 49; ⓜMaubert-Mutualité/Cardinal-Lemoine; map pp.122–123. Shoe-horned into a former stables on a lovely corner of the Montagne Ste-Geneviève, this ramshackle old family-run restaurant is bustling and full of character. Outside tables and the candlelit cellar below provide a few extra seats, but not many, so book ahead. Expect meat dishes served without flourishes – grilled with herbs and chips, mostly, with a choice of sauces – for less than €20, and simple, tasty country-style starters and puds for around €5. Lunch *menu* €13. Mon & Wed–Sat noon–3pm & 7pm–midnight, Tues & Sun 7pm–midnight.

Le Jardin des Pâtes 4 rue Lacépède, 5ᵉ ☎01 43 31 50 71; ⓜJussieu; map pp.122–123. In this light, airy, plant-filled space you can dine on delicious pasta, home-made with freshly ground organic grains and served with gourmet sauces. Try the chestnut pasta with duck, crème fraiche and mushrooms, or rice pasta with sautéed veg, soy sauce, ginger and tofu. Mains €11.50–14. Daily noon–2.30pm & 7–11pm.

20

LE SNACKING, TAKEAWAYS AND PICNICS

Paris is the perfect place for a picnic, and the city has plenty of places to sate "le snacking" demand. Even the simplest **boulangeries** (see p.334) are a good source of traditional takeaway food – most sell savoury quiches and tarts as well as breads and cakes – while you can compose a seriously gourmet picnic from the city's swankier food shops and delis (see pp.333–336). Although specializing in cooked meats like hams and pâtés, most **charcuteries** also stock a range of dressed salads and side dishes. You buy by weight, by the slice (*tranche*) or by the carton (*barquette*).

For **takeaway** hot food, **crêperie stands** sell *galettes* (savoury buckwheat pancakes) and *gaufres* (waffles) as well as sweet crêpes, while Middle Eastern falafel with salad is a great bet in the Jewish quarter of the Marais. Also worth checking out are the ubiquitous Chinese *traiteurs* and Turkish or North African **kebab shops**, the latter also serving couscous, which you can choose to have with *merguez* (spicy sausage), chicken or lamb, or *royale* – with all three.

TOP 5 TAKEAWAYS

Falafels at **L'As du Fallafel** See p.279
Deli salads at **Chezaline** See p.281
Foie gras baguettes at **Le Comptoir de la Gastronomie** See p.277

Lobster rolls at **Frenchie to Go** See p.276
Overstuffed sandwiches at **Pointe du Groin** See p.292

Perraudin 157 rue St-Jacques, 5ᵉ ☎01 46 33 15 75, ⓦrestaurant-perraudin.com; RER Luxembourg; map pp.123–124. Classic Left Bank *bistrot*, featuring solid, if unexciting, home cooking. The 1900s atmosphere is charming, though, thick with Parisian and international chatter floating above the packed-in, gingham-clad tables. Lunch/dinner *menus* €18.50/€34.50; mains around €14–30. Daily noon–2.30pm & 7–10.30pm; closed Aug.

Pho 67 59 rue Galande, 5ᵉ ☎01 45 25 56 69; ⓜMaubert-Mutualité; map pp.123–124. A beacon of Southeast Asian authenticity in this desperately touristy area. The chefs work away in an open kitchen, preparing a good range of reasonably priced Vietnamese dishes; go for the filling *pho* special (€14), made with tender French steak, or the three-course €17 menu. No credit cards. Mon 6.30–11pm, Tues–Sun noon–3pm & 6.30–11pm.

Le Reminet 3 rue des Grands-Degrés, 5ᵉ ☎01 44 07 04 24, ⓦlereminet.com; ⓜMaubert-Mutualité; map pp.123–124. This postage-stamp-sized *bistrot* is relaxed but very classy, all snowy-white tablecloths, gilded mirrors and chandeliers, with French windows opening out onto a leafy square. Traditional French ingredients are given intriguing twists: pressed foie gras with smoked eel, fried onions and an apple and bergamot coulis, for example. Three-course *menu* €49; *menu gastronomique* €65. Three-course *menu* €49; *menu gastronomique* €65. Daily noon–2.30pm & 7–10.30pm.

★**Ribouldingue** 10 rue St-Julien-le-Pauvre, 5ᵉ ☎01 46 33 98 80, ⓦribouldingue-restaurant.fr; ⓜMaubert-Mutualité; map pp.123–124. A meat- and offal-lover's paradise. Big servings are accompanied by hearty sides like nutmeg-rich *pommes dauphinoise*, and followed by gorgeous puddings – a delicious chestnut sorbet among them. The ambience, in a slightly quirky, wood-panelled dining room, is surprisingly stylish for this corner of the *quartier*. Menus €28/€34; lunchtime *plats* €16. Tues–Sat noon–2pm & 7–11pm.

Tashi Delek 4 rue des Fossés-St-Jacques, 5ᵉ ☎01 43 26 55 55; RER Luxembourg; map pp.123–124. Sober-looking but cheery Tibetan restaurant serving tasty Himalayan dishes ranging from robust, warming noodle soups to the addictive, ravioli-like beef *momok* and a salty, soupy yak-butter tea. It's good value, with evening *menus* at €17 and €22. Mon–Sat noon–2.30pm & 7–11pm; closed two weeks in Aug.

ST-GERMAIN

CAFÉS AND WINE BARS

★**L'Avant Comptoir** 9 carrefour de l'Odéon, 6ᵉ ☎01 44 27 07 97, ⓦhotel-paris-relais-saint-germain.com; ⓜOdéon; map pp.136–137. This hole-in-the-wall, with standing room for a handful only, is home to Yves Camdeborde's (see p.269) buzzy wine/tapas bar (bread, butter and pickles are served communally) where you can sample his innovative cooking at affordable prices (tapas from €2). The food (from the duck confit hot dog to the ham and artichoke waffles) is outstanding, as are the natural wines. Daily noon–11pm.

Bar du Marché 75 rue de Seine, 6ᵉ ☎01 43 26 55 15; ⓜMabillon; map pp.136–137. Perennially popular café, where the *serveurs* are cutely kitted out in flat caps and market trader dungarees and which gets a certain buzz from the rue de Buci market on the doorstep. *Plats* from €12, *tartines* from €7. Daily 8am–2am.

Café de la Mairie 8 place St-Sulpice, 6ᵉ ☎01 43 26 67 82; ⓜSt-Sulpice; map pp.136–137. A pleasant café on the sunny north side of the square, opposite St-Sulpice church and with lots of outside tables. Perfect for basking with a coffee or an *apéritif*. Mon–Sat 7am–2am, Sun 9am–9pm.

20

Au Chai de l'Abbaye 26 rue de Buci, 6ᵉ ☎ 01 43 26 68 26; ⓜ Mabillon; map pp.136–137. Bustling old café in the heart of St-Germain. Sink into a red leather banquette and tuck into a *tartine* made with Poilâne bread (from €7) – a perfect light lunch or accompaniment to an *apéritif*. There is also a selection of hot dishes and desserts. Mon–Sat 8am–2am, Sun 11am–11pm.

Coutume 47 rue Babylone, 7ᵉ ☎ 01 45 51 50 47, ⓦ coutumecafe.com; ⓜ Saint-François-Xavier; map pp.136–137. Quintessential third-wave coffee shop – all raw concrete and science-lab chic – with an Aussie at the helm and on-site roastery. The devotion to the bean borders on the obsessive here, which is, of course, how the MacBook-toting coffee fiends who pack the place out like it. Mon–Fri 8am–7pm, Sat & Sun 10am–7pm.

Le Flore 172 bd St-Germain, 6ᵉ ☎ 01 45 48 55 26, ⓦ cafedeflore.fr; ⓜ St-Germain-des-Prés; map pp.136–137. One of the city's iconic old literary brasseries, the great rival and immediate neighbour of the even more touristy *Les Deux Magots*. Sartre, de Beauvoir, Camus et al used to hang out here – and there's still the odd reading and debate. It's fun, but expect to pay a lot for the privilege of soaking up the history. Daily 7.30am–1.30am.

L'Heure Gourmande 22 passage Dauphine, 6ᵉ ☎ 01 46 34 00 40; ⓜ Odéon; map pp.136–137. Hidden away in a cobbled and tree-lined *passage* between rue Mazarine and rue Dauphine, this friendly *salon de thé* is best on warm days when you can escape the St Germain bustle and sit on the peaceful vine-draped *terrasse*, quietly enjoying a *coupe* of Berthillon ice cream (see p.271), a fresh juice or a huge slab of home-made cake (from €6). Mon 11.30am–3pm, Tues–Sun 11.30am–6.30pm.

Ladurée 21 rue Bonaparte, 6ᵉ ☎ 01 44 07 64 87, ⓦ laduree.com; ⓜ St-Germain-des-Prés; map pp.136–137. Left Bank outpost of *Ladurée*'s mini-empire (see p.276) with a lovely pale-green muralled conservatory at the back of the shop and a decadent Second Empire lounge upstairs. There's often a queue, particularly at weekends, but those famed *macarons* (€9.90 for four) and the sheer beauty of the surroundings make it worth the wait. Mon–Fri 8.30am–7.30pm, Sat 8.30am–8.30pm, Sun 10am–7.30pm.

La Palette 43 rue de Seine, 6ᵉ ☎ 01 43 26 68 15, ⓦ cafelapaletteparis.com; ⓜ Odéon; map pp.136–137. This former Beaux Arts student bar remains a place to be seen, but the atmosphere is relaxed. The decor features, of course, old oil paintings and paint-spattered palettes on the walls; the appealing outside *terrasse* is a big draw. There's a short menu of salads, *plats* and dishes to share. Mains €15–17; quiche €12. Mon–Sat 8am–2am.

RESTAURANTS

Allard 41 rue St-André-des-Arts, 6ᵉ ☎ 01 58 00 23 42, ⓦ restaurant-allard.fr; ⓜ Odéon; map pp.136–137.

Expect the menu at this proudly unreconstructed Parisian restaurant, opened in the 1930s and now part of the Alain Ducasse empire, to be meaty, comforting and old-fashioned – ox cheeks, veal sweetbreads, frogs' legs – rather than experimental, and you'll be very satisfied. The atmosphere is unimpeachably retro, the clientele moneyed and largely international. Mains from €30; lunch *menu* €34. Daily noon–2pm & 7.30–11.30pm; closed for lunch in Aug.

Bouillon Racine 3 rue Racine, 6ᵉ ☎ 01 73 20 21 12, ⓦ www.bouillon-racine.com; ⓜ Cluny-La Sorbonne; map pp.136–137. The bourgeois French cuisine isn't bad – nor is it outrageously expensive, especially if you go for the €15 weekday lunchtime *formule* – but it's the wildly extravagant Art Nouveau decor that's the real pull here, in one of just a few surviving *bouillons* (soup restaurants) that opened in the early 1900s. In the afternoons (3–7pm) it acts a *salon de thé*, so you can enjoy the ambience without having a full meal. Daily noon–11pm.

Le Comptoir du Relais St-Germain 9 carrefour de l'Odéon, 6ᵉ ☎ 01 44 27 07 97, ⓦ hotelrsg.com; ⓜ Odéon; map pp.136–137. Yves Camdeborde blazed the trail in introducing bistronomy to Paris; today his flagship restaurant offers a buzzy *bistrot* ambience during the day and at the weekends (no reservations), when you could order charcuterie, a *salade niçoise* (€18) or a simple *souris d'agneau* (€20) and watch St-Germain's finest sashay by. It's a more formal gourmet experience on weekday evenings, when there's a €60 tasting menu (reservations only). Mon–Fri noon–6pm (plus a single seating at 8.30pm for the tasting menu), Sat & Sun noon–11pm.

L'Epi Dupin 11 rue Dupin, 6ᵉ ☎ 01 42 22 64 56, ⓦ epidupin.com; ⓜ Sèvres-Babylone; map pp.136–137. This friendly modern *bistrot* in an untouristy corner is a great find, serving high-quality, seasonal food with imaginative touches but no pretension: perhaps chard fondue with mustard and beef, or scallop soup with sweet potato mousseline. The decor is relaxed, and the dining room usually full with locals. *Menus* €39 and €52; €28 at lunch. Mon 7–11pm, Tues–Fri noon–3pm & 7–11pm; closed Aug.

L'Epigramme 9 rue de l'Eperon, 6ᵉ ☎ 01 44 41 00 09; ⓜ Odéon; map pp.136–137. The emphasis in this tiny, welcoming and well-regarded restaurant – whitewashed stone walls, beamed ceiling, terracotta floor, open kitchen – is on contemporary French cooking (try the cod with polenta or the pistachio *crème brûlée*). When it's warm they throw the windows open to a pretty courtyard garden, and it can be difficult to drag yourself away. Good value – especially for the *menus* (€24/€38). Booking recommended. Tues–Sun noon–2.30pm & 7–10.30pm.

Ferrandaise 8 rue de Vaugirard, 6ᵉ ☎ 01 43 26 36 36, ⓦ laferrandaise.com; ⓜ Odéon; map pp.136–137. Don't be misled by the arty photos of Ferrandaise-breed cows on the flagstoned walls: it's about more than beef at this restaurant near the Jardin du Luxembourg. You might choose a hearty

20

beef cheek confit with lentil and mustard, but the regularly changing menu also lists such dishes as sea bream *tartare* with iced fennel cream, or mackerel fillets with guacamole. *Menus* €16/€37 lunch, €37 dinner. Mon 7.30–10.30pm, Tues–Thurs noon–2pm & 7.30–10.30pm, Fri noon–2pm & 7.30pm–midnight, Sat 7.30pm–midnight.

Gaya 44 rue du Bac, 7ᵉ 📞01 45 44 73 73, 🌐pierre -gagnaire.com; 🚇St-Germain-des-Prés; map pp.136–137. This sober, upscale mini-restaurant is a satellite of celebrity chef Pierre Gagnaire's empire, where classic French influences combine with Mediterranean-style focus in the freshest fish, seafood and veg dishes: creamed spider crab with Corsican pink grapefruit sorbet and spinach shoots, perhaps, or asparagus with tapioca, burrata, watercress and Mimolette cheese. For cuisine of this standard and originality, the prices aren't inflated: mains start at €30, with lunch *menus* at €48 (weekdays) and €65. Tues–Fri noon–2.30pm & 7–11pm, Sat noon–3pm & 7–11pm.

★**La Grande Crèmerie** 8 rue Grégoire de Tours, 6ᵉ 📞01 43 26 09 09, 🌐lagrandecremerie.fr; 🚇Odéon; map pp.136–137. They keep it simple but impeccable at this contemporary-rustic spot, serving the very best produce – white Italian ham with truffles, black pudding with toast, a Mason jar filled with a tasty sardine and seaweed combination – alongside natural and organic wines. The amazing food, the friendly staff and the warm space – all rough whitewashed stone, burnished copper, tin café chairs and distressed zinc – make this a godsend on this touristy stretch. Costs can mount, but the lunch *menu* at €19 (a *plat* and a glass of wine) is well worth it – especially if you choose a dish that comes with their creamy mash. Watch out for those irresistible add-ons, though – a side of mash alone costs €8.50. Tues–Sat noon–2pm & 7.30–11pm.

Hélène Darroze 4 rue d'Assas, 6ᵉ 📞01 42 22 00 11, 🌐helenedarroze.com; 🚇St-Sulpice/Sèvres-Babylone; map pp.136–137. Darroze herself now divides her time between here and London, but the earthy, robust food at her Michelin-starred Paris restaurant continues to impress. Beneath the *Salle à Manger* (lunch menu €58; lunch and dinner tasting *menus* from €98) – where typical offerings might be scallops with fava beans, xingar (ham) and peppers, or pigeon with foie gras and beetroot – the more informal *Salon d'Hélène* (lunch €28 and €49; dinner €65) offers imaginative tapas, drawing on Darroze's native Basque cuisine and on international influences and suppliers: chiffonnade of black ham, perhaps, or foie gras balls with truffles. Tues–Sat 12.30–2.30pm & 7.30–10.30pm.

★**Kitchen Galerie Bis** 25 rue des Grands-Augustins, 6ᵉ 📞01 46 33 00 85, 🌐kitchengaleriebis.com; 🚇St-Michel; map pp.136–137. Modern and minimalist, this sleek restaurant serves innovative and accomplished dishes, combining Mediterranean cuisine with Asian flavours: you might see grilled suckling pig with *tikka masala*, or confit quail with buckwheat, miso and galangal. Lunch *menus* €29/€36; the €55/€66 *menus découvertes* are a steal in this neighbourhood. Tues–Sat 12.30–3pm & 7.30–11pm.

Maison de l'Amérique Latine 217 bd St-Germain, 6ᵉ 📞01 49 54 75 10, 🌐mal217.org; 🚇Solférino; map pp.136–137. Although it's part of the Latin American cultural institute, there's not much Latino about this restaurant (other than a few Argentinian wines), which offers superior French cooking. It is at its best in summer, when the main draw is the romantic outdoor setting amid beautiful eighteenth-century gardens, candlelit in the evening. Set menus only (€40/€51/€59 lunch, €59 dinner). May–Sept Mon–Fri noon–2pm & 7–10pm; Oct–April Mon–Fri noon–2pm; closed late July and early Aug.

★**Semilla** 54 rue de Seine, 6ᵉ 📞01 43 54 34 50; 🚇Mabillon; map pp.136–137. The food at this standout modern *bistrot* – a light, airy space with an open kitchen – is fantastic; the inventive menu of fusion cuisine and updated French classics might feature such dishes as pumpkin fritters with roasted butternut squash cream and Brocciu cheese or mullet with fennel purée, pak choi and hazelnut oil. Great-value lunch *menu* €24; expect to pay around €60 in the evening. Bookings are taken up to 8.30pm; otherwise, wait at the bar for a table. Daily noon–3pm & 7–11pm.

La Tourelle 5 rue Hautefeuille, 6ᵉ 📞01 46 33 12 47; 🚇St-Michel; map pp.136–137. An old-fashioned *bistrot*, named after the stone *échauguette* tower outside, and packed into a low-ceilinged, intimate room. The short menu of meaty country dishes (mains €17) is simple and traditional in the best sense – they make terrines out of what wasn't finished the day before. The *menus* are good value (€23/€29). Mon–Fri noon–1.45pm & 7–9.45pm, Sat 7–9.45pm; closed Aug.

Vagenende 142 bd St-Germain, 6ᵉ 📞01 43 26 68 18, 🌐vagenende.com; 🚇Mabillon; map pp.136–137. This Art Nouveau beauty – all mirrors, marble pillars, chandeliers and dark wood that has been polished for decades to a lustrous glow – is a registered historic monument. Surprisingly unfussy, meaty brasserie dishes include *choucroute* and *pot-au-feu*, with some good seafood specials. Mains around €20; lunch *menus* €26/€32. Daily noon–midnight.

TROCADÉRO AND AROUND

RESTAURANTS

L'Astrance 4 rue Beethoven, 16ᵉ 📞01 40 50 84 40; 🚇Passy; map pp.150–151. Ignore the rather dull location – triple-Michelin-starred chef Pascal Barbot's *L'Astrance* produces some of the city's most exciting, delicate *nouvelle* cuisine in a non-stuffy atmosphere. The no-choice set menu

CLOCKWISE FROM TOP LEFT LADURÉE (P.276); CAFÉ DE LA MAIRIE (P.284); LA PALETTE (P.285); LE TRAIN BLEU (P.282) >

changes daily, but dishes might include foie gras and mushroom *millefeuille* with lemon *confit* and hazelnut oil, or turbot with miso butter and pear compote. The contemporary dining room is small, and bookings are notoriously hard to get. Lunch *menus* €70 and €150 (€230 with wine pairings included), dinner €230. Tues–Fri 12.15–3pm & 8–11pm.

Les Marches 5 rue de la Manutention, 16e ☎01 47 23 52 80; Ⓜléna; map pp.150–151. This cheery *bistrot* makes a handy lunch stop, with sunny tables on the pavement opposite the side wall of the Palais de Tokyo, and a menu of substantial *plats* (€14–17) – you might choose a poached egg and dandelion salad followed by steak *tartare* or *coq au vin*. Daily noon–2.30pm & 7.30–10.30pm; closed three weeks in Aug.

Monsieur Bleu Palais de Tokyo, 16e ☎01 47 20 90 47, Ⓦpalaisdetokyo.com; Ⓜléna/Alma-Marceau; map pp.150–151. The swishest of the restaurants inside the Palais de Tokyo (see p.159), chic *Monsieur Bleu* offers an experience – it's all about the stunning Art Deco room here, with its views over the Seine and Eiffel Tower. Food – contemporary comfort food and cocktails – is tasty; reckon on €50–65 *à la carte*. Daily noon–2am.

Tokyo Eat Palais de Tokyo, 16e ☎01 47 20 00 29, Ⓦpalaisdetokyo.com; Ⓜléna/Alma-Marceau; map pp.150–151. Service can be patchy and prices are somewhat inflated, but the fusion-tinged menu (mains €18–30), large, buzzy space – all pop colours, nightclub lighting and clashing shapes – and outdoor *terrasse* with views across to the Eiffel Tower make *Tokyo Eat* a handy pit stop in the Site de Création Contemporaine. Daily noon–midnight.

THE EIFFEL TOWER AND THE 7e

CAFÉS AND WINE BARS

★**Rosa Bonheur sur Seine** Near Pont Alexandre III, 7e ☎01 47 53 66 92, Ⓦrosabonheur.fr; Ⓜ Invalides; map pp.150–151. The ever-popular *Rosa Bonheur* (see p.295) has transferred its appealing, warm-hearted formula to this new offshoot café-bar, set on a large floating barge, with huge windows and deck seating, by the Berges de Seine. Whether you're after a quick coffee or a cocktail, want to pick at tapas (from €6) or feast on pizza from their riverside food truck, *Rosa* has pulled it off again, creating a relaxed, something-for-everyone vibe. There's quay-side seating for landlubbers. Mon & Tues 5.30pm–2am, Wed–Sun noon–2am; hours change according to season and weather.

RESTAURANTS

★**L'Arpège** 84 rue de Varenne, 7e ☎01 45 05 09 06, Ⓦalain-passard.com; Ⓜ Varenne; map pp.150–151. Alain Passard gives vegetables (all from his own *potager*) the spotlight in this three-Michelin-starred restaurant, which lacks the snootiness of many of its kind. He can turn a simple beetroot or tomato into a culinary symphony, singing with clean, sophisticated flavours, while dishes such as asparagus sushi with green tea, cauliflower hummus with lovage pesto, or blue lobster poached in wine are astounding. *Menus* €140 (lunch) and €240/€320 (dinner). Reservations essential. Mon–Fri noon–2.30pm & 7–10pm.

Au Bon Accueil 14 rue de Monttessuy, 7e ☎01 47 05 46 11, Ⓦaubonaccueilparis.com; Ⓜ Duroc/Vaneau; map pp.150–151. Huddled in the shadow of the Eiffel Tower, in an otherwise slightly dull area, this relaxed *bistrot* turns out well-executed dishes – a delicate cold soup of fava beans and white asparagus, say, followed by a perfectly cooked ox cheek braised in red wine. Lunch *menu* €35. Mon–Fri noon–2.30pm & 7–10.30pm; closed three weeks in Aug.

Le Cassenoix 56 rue de la Fédération, 15e ☎01 45 66 09 01, Ⓦle-cassenoix.fr; Ⓜ Dupleix; map pp.150–151. Cosy and friendly neighbourhood *bistrot*, conveniently near the Eiffel Tower, serving hearty portions of well-executed French food, both modern and traditional but always seasonal, with a good selection of wines by the glass. *Menu* €33 (lunch and dinner). Mon–Fri noon–2.30pm & 7–10.30pm.

Les Cocottes 135 rue St-Dominique, 7e Ⓦmaison constant.com; Ⓜ Ecole Militaire; map pp.150–151. This no-reservations canteen-style place is one of the more casual restaurants in southwestern chef Christian Constant's mini-empire. The menu focuses on mini-terrines and *cocottes* (cast-iron pots) of hearty, country food – potatoes stuffed with pig's trotters and caramelized, for example. Daily specials are often lighter, often spotlighting veg and seafood. Service can be patchy; it's better as a lunch option than for a romantic dinner. Two-/three-course weekday *formules* €23/€28; *cocotte* of the day €16. Daily noon–11pm.

★**David Toutain** 29 rue Surcouf, 7e ☎01 45 50 11 10, Ⓦdavidtoutain.com; Ⓜ Invalides; map pp.150–151. Genuinely innovative food, focusing on seasonal, perfectly judged flavours with lots of farm-fresh veg and delicate fish – typical offerings include beetroot rolls, scallops in Jerusalem artichoke *bouillon*, or smoked eel with black sesame sauce – in a light, modern-rustic space. Tasting *menus* €45 (lunch) and €72/€105 (dinner). Booking essential. Mon–Fri noon–2.30pm & 8–10pm.

La Fontaine de Mars 129 rue St-Dominique, 7e ☎01 47 05 46 44, Ⓦfontainedemars.com; Ⓜ La Tour-Maubourg; map pp.150–151. Heavy, pink-checked tablecloths, leather banquettes, attentive service: this restaurant, tucked under a colonnade with outdoor seating opposite an old stone fountain, offers a quintessentially French atmosphere. The food is reliable, meaty and southwestern: think snails, *magret de canard* and delicious

20

Basque *boudin* sausages. Starters €9–21, *plats* €17–33, *plats du jour* €22. Mon–Sat noon–3pm & 7.30–11pm, Sun 7.15–11pm.

Le Jules Verne Pilier Sud, Eiffel Tower, 7e ☎01 45 55 61 44, ⊕lejulesverne-paris.com; Ⓜ Bir-Hakeim; map pp.150–151. Dining halfway up the Eiffel Tower is a draw in itself, but luckily Alain Ducasse's contemporary French food and the smart decor match the setting. It's best at dinner (€190/€230), but cheaper for a weekday lunch (a mere €105). Reserve months in advance (online only), dress up, and don't count on getting a window table. Daily noon–1.30pm & 7–9.30pm.

Le P'tit Troquet 28 rue de l'Exposition, 7e ☎01 47 05 80 39; Ⓜ Ecole Militaire; map pp.150–151. This tiny family *bistrot* has a discreetly nostalgic feel, with its marble

TOP 5 COFFEE HOUSES
La Caféothèque See p.279
Caffè Marcovaldo See p.278
Coutume See p.285
Holybelly See p.293
Verlet See p.276

tables and ornate zinc bar. The cuisine, served to the diplomats of the *quartier* and lots of happy American tourists, focuses on traditional meaty dishes, but has some surprises – an endive *tatin* with apple and goat's cheese, for example. Three-course *menu* €35, *plats* €21. Reservations recommended. Mon & Sat 6.30–10pm, Tues–Fri noon–2pm & 6.30–10pm.

MONTPARNASSE AND THE 14e

CAFÉS AND WINE BARS

L'Entrepôt 7–9 rue Francis-de-Pressensé, 14e ☎01 45 40 60 70, ⊕lentrepot.fr; Ⓜ Pernety; map pp.162–163. Lively, innovative arts cinema with a spacious, relaxed café and a courtyard where you can enjoy lunchtime *menus* of tasty home-cooked food (€16.50 and €21), a great Sunday brunch (€30), and *plats du jour* – *poulet fermier*, scallops, beef *tartare* and the like – for under €20. Frequent evening gigs. Mon–Sat noon–2.30pm & 7–11pm, Sun 11.45am–2.45pm & 7–11pm.

Le Select 99 bd du Montparnasse, 6e ☎01 73 20 27 60, ⊕leselectmontparnasse.fr; Ⓜ Vavin; map pp.162–163. If you want to visit one of the great historic Montparnasse cafés – as frequented by Picasso, Matisse, Henry Miller, Ernest Hemingway and F. Scott Fitzgerald – make it this. It's the most traditional of them all, the prices aren't *too* shocking, the brasserie food isn't bad – and it's on the sunny side of the street. Mon–Thurs & Sun 7am–2am, Fri & Sat 7am–3am.

RESTAURANTS

Crêperie Josselin 67 rue du Montparnasse, 14e ☎01 43 20 93 50; Ⓜ Edgar-Quinet/Montparnasse; map pp.162–163. Montparnasse is traditionally the Breton quarter of Paris (the station is on the direct line to northern France), and this crêperie – heavy wood furniture, lace, rustic porcelain – couldn't be any more traditionally Breton. The authentic, buttery crêpes (€5–10), with jugs of cider to wash them down, are commonly agreed to be the best in the city, so it's always crowded. No reservations; no cards. Tues–Fri noon–3pm & 6–11pm, Sat noon–midnight, Sun noon–11pm; closed Aug.

A Mi Chemin 31 rue Boulard, 14e ☎01 45 39 56 45; Ⓜ Denfert-Rochereau; map pp.162–163. Resolutely local *bistrot* in the charming rue Daguerre neighbourhood, serving food that's unshowy but spot on. The menu lists classics such as roast veal and Breton couscous, with a

few fragrant, well-spiced North African choices and an unusually long selection of desserts. Around €40 a head. Tues–Sat 12.30–2pm & 7.30–11pm.

La Régalade 49 av Jean-Moulin, 14e ☎01 45 45 68 58; Ⓜ Alésia; map pp.162–163. Diners at this renowned *bistrot* – the original in the *Régalade* group, established by Yves Camdeborde and now under the aegis of Bruno Doucet – are packed cheek-by-jowl, and service can be frustratingly slow, but overall it still delivers. The three-course €37 *prix fixe* is good value – a hearty *amuse bouche* of help-yourself home-made terrine, then a beautifully composed meat or fish dish, rounding off, perhaps, with a signature Grand Marnier soufflé – will leave you satisfied. Mon 7–11pm, Tues–Fri noon–2pm & 7–11pm.

La Rotonde 105 bd du Montparnasse, 6e ☎01 43 26 48 26, ⊕www.rotondemontparnasse.com; Ⓜ Vavin; map pp.162–163. One of the grand old Montparnasse establishments, frequented in its time by the full roll-call of prewar artists and writers, plus Lenin and Trotsky. Today, with a plush decor of red velvet and brass, it offers reliable (if slightly pricey) French food almost around the clock. Starters such as onion soup or snails cost €7–23, mains such as rump steak or lamb shoulder €15–45, with a wide selection of seafood (including oysters from €6.50). Daily 7.30am–1am.

Le Timbre 3 rue Ste-Beuve, 6e ☎01 45 49 10 40, ⊕restaurantletimbre.com; Ⓜ Vavin/Notre-Dame-des-Champs; map pp.162–163. "The Postage Stamp" deserves its name: operating from one minuscule corner of a tiny dining room, chef Charles Danet produces delicious modern and light French food on no-choice *prix fixe* menus. You might have marinated mackerel with avocado and grapefruit or kale soup with egg, followed by a perfect lamb sweetbread with white asparagus – and finish with a heavenly chocolate mousse. *Menus* €26 at lunch, €34–49 at dinner. Reservations advised. Tues–Sat noon–3pm & 7–11pm.

20

THE 15e AND AROUND

RESTAURANTS

Afaria 15 rue Desnouettes, 15e ☎01 48 42 95 90, ⊛restaurant-afaria.fr; Ⓜ Convention; map pp.172–173. Tasty French food with hearty Basque accents in this popular, if pricey, restaurant. *Plats* (€16–24) might include delicious duck breast or skate poached with tomato and Parmesan-crusted vegetables; they also offer tapas such as a Basque *croque-monsieur* or a *crème brûlée* of chorizo and parmesan. Weekday lunch *menus* from €23. Tues–Sat noon–2.30 & 7–11pm.

Le Café du Commerce 51 rue du Commerce, 15e ☎01 45 75 03 27, ⊛lecafeducommerce.com; Ⓜ Emile-Zola; map pp.172–173. This popular brasserie, which opened in 1921, is still a buzzing, characterful place to eat, with the tables set on three storeys of galleries running round a central patio. Honest, high-quality meat is the speciality, with steaks from Limousin cows bought whole; around €16–20 for a main course, with a bargain €15.80 two-course lunch *menu*. Daily noon–3pm & 7pm–midnight.

La Veraison 64 rue de la Croix Nivert, 15e ☎01 45 32 39 39, ⊛laveraison.com; Ⓜ Cambronne; map pp.172–173. The open kitchen at this terrific, contemporary neighbourhood *bistrot* turns out excellent modern French food, the likes of foie gras ravioli, beetroot gazpacho and duckling with sticky rice fritters, in a laidback little space always brimming with happy locals. Tues–Sat 7.30–10pm.

THE 13e AND AROUND

RESTAURANTS

★ **L'Avant Goût** 26 rue Bobillot, 13e ☎01 53 80 24 00, ⊛lavantgout.com; Ⓜ Place d'Italie; map p.176. Unassuming, small Butte-aux-Cailles restaurant with a big reputation for good French cuisine – try the rich, spicy signature *pot-au-feu* – and wines to match. Decor is colourful and unfussy, crowded with a happy clientele relaxing on bright red leather banquettes. Superb-value lunch *menu* €15, evening *menu* €36. Tues–Sat noon–2pm & 7.30–10pm; closed three weeks in Aug.

★ **Chez Gladines** 30 rue des Cinq-Diamants, 13e ☎01 45 80 70 10, ⊛gladines.com; Ⓜ Corvisart; map p.176. This Basque-run corner *bistrot* – one of a chain of five in the city – is always warm, welcoming and packed. Excellent wines and hearty Basque and southwest dishes – the mashed/fried potato with Cantal is a must, perfect with the *magret de canard*, and there are snails, charcuterie plates and giant warm salads for €8. Around €20 for a (very) full meal. No credit cards. Mon & Tues noon–3pm & 7pm–midnight, Wed–Fri noon–3pm & 7pm–1am, Sat noon–4pm & 7pm–1am, Sun noon–4pm & 7pm–midnight.

Coco de Mer 34 bd St-Marcel, 5e ☎06 20 26 77 67, ⊛cocodemer.fr; Ⓜ St-Marcel; map p.176. Actually located down at the southeastern end of the 5e, this Seychellois restaurant lets you enjoy Indian Ocean food – curried octopus, fish in passion fruit sauce – while wriggling your toes on a carpet of real sand. Full meals around €37, plus wine. Mon 7.30pm–midnight, Tues–Sat noon–3pm & 7.30pm–midnight.

Indochine 86 av de Choisy, 13e ☎01 44 24 28 08; Ⓜ Tolbiac; map p.176. This is a better-than-average Vietnamese option in the heart of Paris's Chinatown, with tasty *banh xeo* pancakes, zingy fresh *pho* and *bun bo hue* soups, plus vermicelli, stir-fries and grilled specialities – you'll eat well for less than €20. Mon, Tues & Thurs–Sun noon–3.30pm & 7–10.30pm.

Lao Lane Xang 102 av d'Ivry, 13e ☎01 58 89 00 00; Ⓜ Tolbiac; map p.176. Bustling restaurant offering reasonably priced Thai, Vietnamese and a relative novelty: Laotian cuisine. Try the popular toasted rice salad, served in a lettuce leaf, or the *panaché* of Laotian specialities, including delicious pork sausage. Mon, Tues & Thurs noon–3pm & 7–11pm, Fri noon–3pm & 7–11.30pm, Sat & Sun noon–4pm & 7–11.30pm.

Le Temps des Cerises 18–20 rue de la Butte-aux-Cailles, 13e ☎01 45 89 69 48, ⊛letempsdescerisescoop.com; Ⓜ Place d'Italie/Corvisart; map p.176. Welcoming place – it's run as a workers' co-op – with elbow-to-elbow seating and a daily choice of hearty French dishes that range from *cassoulet* to fish stew. Drinks include organic coffee and Breton cola. *Menus* €20 and €24.50, plus €13 and €16 on weekday lunchtimes. Food served Mon–Sat 11.45am–2.30pm & 7–11.30pm; coffee and bar food between meal times.

MONTMARTRE AND THE 9e

CAFÉS AND WINE BARS

Café des Deux Moulins 15 rue Lepic, 18e ☎01 42 54 90 50; Ⓜ Blanche; map p.182. Though still proudly sporting its *Amélie* poster (she waited tables here in the film), and welcoming a number of movie fans, this retro café remains a down-to-earth neighbourhood hangout – burly *ouvriers* in the morning, boho hipsters in the evening – with a classic 1950s interior. *Plats* €13, charcuterie or cheese platter €12. Daily 7.30am–2am.

La Guêpe 14 rue des Trois Frères, 18e ☎01 46 06 15 11; Ⓜ Abbesses/Anvers; map p.182. This contemporary tapas bar, a cut above the raft of so-so, tourist-oriented restaurants along this stretch, is a useful standby when you want a convivial, no-fuss evening. For just €3–6 per dish choose from a creative selection – cuttlefish croquettes, mackerel *rillettes*, gazpacho of the day. Wine prices to match. Tues–Sun 6pm–2am; closed Aug.

Le Progrès 1 rue Yvonne Le Tac, 18e ☎01 42 64 07 37;

Ⓜ Abbesses/Anvers; map p.182. With generous picture windows overlooking a bustling crossroads at the heart of Abbesses, this simple, relaxed café, serving reasonably priced meals and salads (€13–18), transforms into a lively bar at night. Daily 9.30am–2am.

Le Refuge 72 rue Lamarck, 18ᵉ; Ⓜ Lamarck–Caulaincourt; map p.182. If you're shocked by the tourist crowds of Montmartre, a refuge is exactly what this classic café – right by the Lamarck-Caulaincourt métro – provides. The decor hasn't changed much in a hundred years, and the clientele is resolutely local. Offers simple, reasonably priced dishes, including onion soup for €6. Daily 7am–2am.

Relais de la Butte 12 rue Ravignan, 18ᵉ ☏ 01 42 23 24 34; Ⓜ Abbesses; map p.182. On a quiet spot halfway up the butte, this otherwise unremarkable restaurant has one of the best *terrasses* in the city, clustered on a tiny tree-shaded, cobbled *place* with lovely views down over Paris. The drinks aren't too expensive when you consider the sheer buzz of sitting out here, and if you choose a simple salad or cheese plate you can eat reasonably well. Daily 9am–midnight.

★ **Le Village** 36 rue des Abbesses, 18ᵉ ☏ 01 42 54 99 59, Ⓦ bistrotlevillage.com; Ⓜ Abbesses; map p.182. This friendly, non-sceney little bar-café knocks the posier sidewalk cafés on Abbesses into a cocked hat. The *terrasse* is teeny – though it breathes out and extends across the sidewalk after dark – but the interior is a retro delight, with gleaming ceramic wall tiles, high stools, huge mirrors and a zinc bar held up by all manner of local *habitués*. Equally good for a morning coffee, a quick lunch – *croques*, salads, omelettes – or a late-night Cognac, and perfect for watching the world go by. Daily 7am–2am.

RESTAURANTS

Le Coq Rico 98 rue Lepic, 18ᵉ ☏ 01 42 59 82 89, Ⓦ lecoqrico.com; Ⓜ Abbesses/Blanche; map p.182. It's all about the birds at Antoine Westermann's chic, relatively formal Montmartre outfit, from the huge rôtisserie that turns out moist whole grilled chickens, to the duck *rillettes*, giblet platters, roast pigeon and poultry soups; even the desserts showcase organic eggs. Mains €20–40. Daily noon–2.30pm & 7–11pm.

Cul de Poule 53 rue des Martyrs, 9ᵉ ☏ 01 53 16 13 07; Ⓜ Pigalle; map p.182. With a nod to quirky decor this small restaurant is not one of the hipper options in this foodie' hood, but the menu does offer something a bit different, with a fusion tinge to dishes like crispy polenta with beetroot and walnuts or marinated spare ribs with miso aubergine. It's all done well, and there's an appealing, easy-going neighbourhood vibe. Menus €28/€32. Daily noon–2.30pm & 8–11pm.

Le Grand 8 8 rue Lamarck, 18ᵉ ☏ 01 42 55 04 55; Ⓜ Anvers; map p.182. It's hard to believe that you're just footsteps away from the Sacré-Coeur scrum at this friendly,

pared-down neighbourhood *bistrot*, which serves simple food done just right, using market-fresh produce (white asparagus with parmesan cream, for example, or Aveyron lamb with seasonal veg) with a light touch. Prices are good for the area (*menus* €28/€34) – book in advance for a table by the back window, and savour the view over the city. Wed–Sat 7.30–10.40pm, Sun noon–2.40pm & 7.30–10.40pm.

Le Mono 40 rue Véron, 18ᵉ ☏ 01 46 06 99 20; Ⓜ Abbesses; map p.182. Welcoming, casual Togolese restaurant with *soukous* on the stereo and African art on the walls. Mains (around €13) focus on grilled fish or meat with sour, hot sauces and rice or cassava. The selection starter plate gets you a tasty array; for dessert, think rum-flambéed bananas. Mon, Tues & Thurs–Sun 7pm–midnight; closed Aug.

Le Moulin de la Galette 83 rue Lepic, 18ᵉ ☏ 01 46 06 84 77, Ⓦ lemoulindelagalette.fr; Ⓜ Abbesses; map p.182. Though the food is standard – pumpkin soup, knuckle of pork in mustard sauce, burgers – the chance to eat in one of the last surviving Montmartre windmills is reason enough to make the climb to this popular venue. Add in the charming staff and a pleasant garden arbour out back, and you could do much worse. Two-course lunch menu €23 (until 5pm), or around €40–60 at dinner. Daily noon–11.30pm.

Refuge des Fondus 17 rue des Trois Frères, 18ᵉ ☏ 01 42 55 22 65; Ⓜ Abbesses; map p.182. The €21 *menu* at this raucous restaurant gets you a hearty fondue – *bourguignonne* (meat) or *savoyarde* (cheese) – an aperitif, a dessert and your personal *biberon*, or baby bottle – don't ask – of wine. This concept is unflaggingly popular with a raucous young crowd, who squeeze onto the banquettes and enthusiastically add to the graffiti on the walls. No credit cards. Daily 7pm–2am; closed Sun & Mon July & Aug.

Le Relais Gascon 6 rue des Abbesses, 18ᵉ ☏ 01 42 58 58 22, Ⓦ lerelaisgascon.fr; Ⓜ Abbesses; map p.182. This noisy two-storey restaurant (upstairs is cosier) provides a welcome blast of straightforward Gascon heartiness in a touristy area. The enormous hot salads, all served with hot garlicky potatoes, cost around €13.50, and there are good-value *plats* and lunch *menus*. Daily noon–midnight.

★ **Les Rillettes** 33 rue de Navarin, 9ᵉ ☏ 01 48 74 02 90, Ⓦ lesrillettes.fr; Ⓜ St-Georges/Pigalle; map p.182. The husband and wife team create a wonderful, warm-hearted atmosphere in this charming small restaurant – she front

20

TOP 5 SALONS DE THÉ

A Priori Thé See p.276
Le Barbouquin See p.294
Le Café Jacquemart-André See p.272
La Fourmi Ailée See p.283
L'Heure Gourmande See p.285

of house, he producing amazing food from their tiny open kitchen. As the name suggests, this is country cooking, with a short menu of simple, beautifully executed – and not heavy – dishes, largely from the Auvergne, such as *pounti*

(a savoury, eggy, cake-like concoction made with cheese, ham, sausage, spinach and plums), sausage cooked in a hay pot or black pork with red peppers – everything is delicious. Mains from €20. Tues–Sat 7–11pm.

THE 10ᵉ AND GOUTTE D'OR

CAFÉS AND WINE BARS

Le Petit Chateau d'Eau 34 rue du Chateau d'Eau, 10ᵉ ☎01 42 08 72 81; ⓜJacques-Bonsergent; map p.193. Lovely, peaceful old café-bar with zinc bar, gorgeous ceramic tiles on the walls, fresh flowers on the tables and a laidback local crowd enjoying coffee, wine and small plates, including a Comté platter (€7) or veg samosas (€4). Mon–Fri 8am–midnight, Sat 9am–5pm.

★**La Pointe du Grouin** 8 rue de Belzunce, 10ᵉ ⓦlapointedugrouin.com; ⓜGare du Nord; map p.193. This lively, hip, slightly nuts café-wine bar-restaurant, on a small square moments from the Gare du Nord, has a strong Breton accent. There's a €10 minimum spend, you need to convert your euros into "grouin" tokens in a vending machine in order to pay, and you order at the bar. Once you've got the hang of it, it's a treat – great, inexpensive food, Breton cider, and natural wines that you choose from the cellar. Breton cakes, salads and tasty small plates are served all day, but don't miss the €4 lunchtime sandwiches made from home-baked bread and overstuffed with such delights as Rennes chicken with mustard cream and rocket. Things get lively at night, with a merry crowd belting out tunes on the piano. Mon–Fri 10am–midnight.

Le Réveil du Dixième 35 rue du Château-d'Eau, 10ᵉ ☎01 42 41 77 59; ⓜChâteau-d'Eau; map p.193. Nothing revolutionary here, just a welcoming wine bar, opposite a covered market, serving glasses of wine (€5), small dishes including herring, cheese plates and snails, big salads and honest *plats* (around €15) including *confit de canard*. Mon–Sat 8am–midnight; closed Aug.

★**Vivant Cave/Vivant Table** 43 rue des Petites-Ecuries, 10ᵉ ☎01 42 46 43 55, ⓦvivantparis.com; ⓜBonne Nouvelle/Château-d'Eau; map p.193. Pierre Jancou, an evangelist of the natural wine movement, offers a superb selection at this pretty little *restaurant à vins*, while the short grazing menu of small plates features simple, impeccably sourced, seasonal produce – oysters, white asparagus, foie gras and the like. If you want a fuller meal, head to the adjoining *Vivant Table*, where farm-fresh, seasonal ingredients are employed in delicious bistronomy

(two-/three-course *menus* €28/€34) in a glorious old dining room bedecked in decorative *faience* tiles. Cave: Mon–Fri 6pm–1am; Table: Mon–Fri noon–2pm & 7pm–midnight, Sat 7pm–midnight.

RESTAURANTS

★**Chez Casimir** 6 rue de Belzunce, 10ᵉ ☎01 48 78 28 80; ⓜGare du Nord; map p.193. This deliciously retro local *bistrot*, with a peaceful corner location opposite a church, is a godsend so close to the Gare du Nord – though not if you're in a rush. Two-/three-/four-course lunch *menus* (€24/€28/€32) are great value, listing hearty *cuisine bourgeoise*: haddock carpaccio, pork with *choucroute*, plums with mascarpone, amazing cheese platters. The Sunday "brunch" (€25) – a smorgasbord of dishes from fish soup to pork casserole – is an adventure, during which you choose your own wine from the cellar. The chef-owner, Thierry Breton, offers a Breton-flavoured *menu* at the slightly pricier, excellent *Chez Michel*, two doors down, at no. 10 (☎01 44 53 06 20), and a creative wine bar experience at *La Pointe du Grouin* next door (see above). Mon–Fri noon–2pm & 7.30–10.30pm, Sat & Sun 10am–7pm.

Flo 7 cour des Petites-Ecuries, 10ᵉ ☎01 47 70 13 59, ⓦbrasserieflo-paris.com; ⓜChâteau-d'Eau; map p.193. Hidden down what was once Louis XIV's stableyard, this opulent Alsatian brasserie is so handsome that even the crammed-in tourist/business clientele and the patchy service from old-time waiters in aprons can't spoil the experience. Focusing on fish and seafood, the food is not cheap, but you're paying for the setting and there are reasonably priced *menus* from €29. Mon–Thurs & Sun noon–3pm & 7–11pm, Fri & Sat noon–3pm & 7pm–midnight.

Pooja 91 passage Brady, 10ᵉ ☎01 48 24 00 83, ⓦpoojarestaurant.com; ⓜStrasbourg-St-Denis/ Château-d'Eau; map p.193. In a glazed *passage* that offers Paris's own slice of the Indian subcontinent, *Pooja* is slightly pricier and sometimes slightly more creative than its many neighbours, and has more outside (well, *passage*-side) seating. Lunch *formule* €12; evening *menus* €18–26. Daily noon–3pm & 7–11pm.

Le Ratapoil du Faubourg 72 rue de Faubourg Poissonnière, 10ᵉ ☎01 42 46 30 53, ⓦratapoildufaubourg .fr; ⓜPoissonnière; map p.193. One of the new breed of accomplished restaurants populating the 10ᵉ, *Ratapoil* is a modern *bistrot* serving unfussy contemporary-country food – red mullet *tartare*, mussels, roast pigeon with morels – on

TOP 5 BISTROTS À VIN

Au Passage See p.294
L'Avant Comptoir See p.284
Le Garde-Robe See p.277
Le Verre Volé See p.294
Vivant Table See p.292

20

daily changing, good-value lunch (€18/€22) and dinner *dégustation* (three/four/six dishes €30/€40/€60) *menus* that give a starring role to fresh veg, fish and seafood. Don't miss the chocolate and salted caramel dessert. Mon–Sat noon–2.30pm & 7.30–11pm.

★**Richer** 2 rue Richer, 9ᵉ 🕿01 48 24 44 80, 🌐lericher .com; 🚇Poissonier/Bonne Nouvelle; map p.193. They serve astoundingly good food in this light, bright, modern dining room, a fresh update on the traditional all-day Parisian brasserie. It's as welcoming to business people, *bon viveurs* and weary tourists alike, offering coffee, wine and tapas all day, along with simple breakfasts – but it's the short, seasonal menu that knocks your socks off, using dazzlingly fresh ingredients in innovative ways. Starters (€9) might include crispy ravioli of beef cheek with a salty broth of peanut and smoked eel, while typical mains (around €18) include steamed hake with beetroot purée, horseradish and Thai basil. No reservations. *L'Office*, a more intimate place a few doors down on rue Richer, and *52*, around the corner at 52 rue du Faubourg St-Denis, both of which are run by the same people, are also worth checking out. Daily 8am–1am; full meals noon–2.30pm & 7.30–10.30pm.

BATIGNOLLES

CAFÉS AND RESTAURANTS

Le Bistrot des Dames 18 rue des Dames, 17ᵉ 🕿01 45 22 13 42, 🌐eldoradohotel.fr; 🚇Place de Clichy; map p.196. The food at this bric-a-brac-strewn *bistrot*, on one of Batignolle's most appealing streets, is largely French with Mediterranean and Asian touches – scallop risotto with crab; Thai salad with prawns – but the main draw is the cosy conviviality and the pretty, green courtyard garden. Starters €8–16, mains €16–23. Summer daily noon–2am; winter Mon–Fri noon–3pm & 7pm–2am, Sat & Sun 12.30pm–2am.

Fuxia 69 place du Docteur Félix-Lobligeois, 17ᵉ 🕿01 42 28 07 79, 🌐fuxia.fr; 🚇Rome/Brochant; map p.196. It may be one of a small French chain of upmarket Italian café-delis, but the corner location here is appealing, with an airy interior and lots of outdoor tables on this pedestrianized *place* in the heart of Batignolles. The food is unfussy, filling and fresh, with plenty for vegetarians. Choose from the blackboard list of pasta and salad specials (€12–15), or perhaps a *bruschette* platter (€15). Daily 9am–2am.

Wepler 14 place de Clichy, 18ᵉ 🕿01 45 22 53 24, 🌐wepler.com; 🚇Place de Clichy; map p.196. As palatial brasseries go, *Wepler*, now more than a hundred years old, has remained a beacon of conviviality amid the traffic-choked place de Clichy. Honest brasserie food (*menus* from €24.50), with an oyster bar and classic seafood platters (from €35). Daily 8am–12.30am.

CANAL ST-MARTIN AND AROUND

CAFÉS AND WINE BARS

L'Atmosphère 49 rue Lucien-Sampaix, 10ᵉ 🕿01 40 38 09 21, 🌐latmosphere.fr; 🚇Gare-de-l'Est; map p.198. Laid-back, vaguely boho bar-restaurant with decent, good-value *plats* (onion soup; gorgonzola and goat cheese ravioli with peas; sea bream stuffed with lime) for €7–20. On a pleasant corner beside the Canal St-Martin, it's equally appealing in summer, when tables spill out onto the towpath, and winter, when it's a haven of cosy corners and mulled wine. Mon–Sat 9.30am–2am, Sun 9.30am–midnight.

Chez Prune 36 rue Beaurepaire, 10ᵉ 🕿01 42 41 30 47; 🚇Jacques-Bonsergent; map p.198. Named after the owner's grandmother (a bust of whom is inside), this funky, laidback café-bar is the quintessential canalside haunt, gently buzzing with an artsy crowd enjoying everything from a morning coffee to a lazy Sunday brunch (noon–4pm) or a charcuterie platter (€11) and glass of wine at night when full meals aren't served. International lunchtime dishes (lasagne, tandoori, etc) around €14. Mon–Sat 8am–2am, Sun 10am–2am.

Dauphin 131 av Parmentier, 11ᵉ 🕿01 55 28 78 88, 🌐restaurantledauphin.net; 🚇Goncourt; map p.198. Behind an unassuming shop front, this hot destination is all cool simplicity with its white marble counters and tabletops, dark wood chairs, mirrors and twinkling candles. If you can't afford a meal at *Châteaubriand* (see p.294) – or even if you can – this is a great and gratifyingly unpretentious spot to enjoy the food of stellar chef Inaki Aizpitarte in tapas portions, from duck charcuterie or oysters with watercress and chilli to scallops with parsley butter and blood orange. Eat in the bar (no reservations), with a quick glass of wine, or at one of the few tables at the back (reservations taken). Tues–Sat 5.30pm–2am.

Holybelly 19 rue Lucien Sampaix, 10ᵉ 🌐holybel.ly; 🚇Jacques Bonsergent; map p.198. Get your flat white or long black fix at this third-wave coffee house, which has a definite whiff of Melbourne with its airy ceramic-tiled interior, its short but on-point coffee list, its pancakes and its eggy brunches – plus a few seasonal French lunch dishes for good measure. Mon, Thurs & Fri 9am–5pm (food till 3pm), Sat & Sun 10am–5pm (food till 4pm).

★**La Patache** 60 rue de Lancry, 10ᵉ 🕿01 42 08 40 51; 🚇Jacques Bonsergent; map p.198. A cosy vibe, low lighting and sharing boards of top-quality regional produce make this an atmospheric stop for a drink and a bite to eat. Its candlelit corners really come into their own in the colder months, when you can hole up and nurse a well-priced bottle of wine with a comforting *plat* of sausage and lentils or roast lamb (dishes around €15). Mon–Fri 5pm–2am, Sat & Sun 3pm–2am.

20

RESTAURANTS

L'Auberge Pyrénées Cévennes 106 rue de la Folie Méricourt, 11ᵉ ☎01 43 57 33 78; ⓜRépublique; map p.198. Make sure you come hungry to this cosy, family-run place, serving enormous portions of hearty country cuisine. Highly recommended are the house terrine for starters, the boar stew and the *cassoulet*. Three-course *menu* €31. Mon–Fri noon–2pm & 7–11pm, Sat 7–11pm.

★ **Le Châteaubriand** 129 av Parmentier, 11ᵉ ☎01 43 57 45 95, ⓦlechateaubriand.net; ⓜGoncourt; map p.198. In 2006, Basque chef Inaki Aizpitarte helped change the face of the Paris dining scene with this innovative *bistrot*, which remains one of the city's finest addresses and one of the most highly regarded restaurants in the world. The daily changing menu features amazing ceviches and concoctions such as squid salad with sea asparagus, onions, redcurrants and wakame powder or oyster soup with red fruits and beetroot. It's not obscenely expensive, either: the five-course *menu dégustation* costs €70. Reservations are essential for the first seating, but aren't taken for the second seating, which starts at 9.30pm; if you don't bag a place, head to Aizpitarte's tapas bar, *Dauphin*, next door (see p.293). The incongruously traditional name, incidentally, is simply carried over from the establishment that existed here before Aizpitarte moved in. Tues–Sat 7.30–10.30pm.

Chez Imogène Corner rue Jean-Pierre-Timbaud and rue du Grand-Prieuré, 11ᵉ ☎01 48 07 14 59, ⓦcreperie -imogene.fr; ⓜOberkampf; map p.198. A great crêperie in a beamed dining room: you could start with a home-made blini and smoked salmon, followed by a *savoyarde* crêpe (filled with two cheeses, potato, onion and ham), and finish with a sweet crêpe, perhaps fromage blanc with apple. *Menus* from €10.50 at lunch, €19 at dinner, with a good kids' *menu* at €8.80. Mon 7–11pm, Tues–Sat noon–2.30pm & 7–11pm.

★ **Au Passage** 1bis passage de Saint-Sebastien, 11ᵉ ☎01 43 55 07 52, ⓦrestaurant-aupassage.fr; ⓜSt-Sébastien-Froissart; map p.198. Quiet, subtle, market-fresh food served in a bright, noisy, bare-bones dining room – part tapas/wine bar, part restaurant. Small plates (€4–15) focus on seasonal ingredients in simple, contemporary dishes, with lots of fish and veg – asparagus with goat's cheese, for example, or cod with aioli. Larger *plats* from €18. Reservations recommended; walk-ins after 9.30pm. Mon–Sat 7pm–1.30am.

Soya 20 rue de la Pierre Levée, 11ᵉ ☎01 48 06 33 02; ⓜGoncourt/Parmentier; map p.198. A cool loft-style converted warehouse housing an inventive organic vegetarian restaurant. The creative fusion cuisine, which is predominantly vegan and gluten-free, ranges from Asian seaweed pâté to tasty couscous and Lebanese stew (mains from €17) – the fresh juices are delicious, too. Mon–Fri noon–3.30pm & 7–11pm, Sat 11.30am–11pm, Sun 11.30am–4pm.

★ **Le Verre Volé** 67 rue de Lancry, 10ᵉ ☎01 48 03 17 34, ⓦleverrevole.fr; ⓜJacques Bonsergent; map p.198. This wine shop doubles as a simple, cool venue for amazing food, with an appreciative local crowd filling the formica tables crammed into the small space. The short menu lists beautifully executed modern and traditional dishes (from €25) along with cheaper, simpler offerings such as black pudding or sausage with lentils, and amazing desserts at just €6. Their wine selection is impeccable, of course, focusing on natural and biodynamic varieties – staff can select one for you, depending on your tastes and your meal – you pay the over-the-counter price plus €7 corkage fee. Reservations recommended. Restaurant daily 12.30–2pm & 7.30–10.30pm.

BELLEVILLE AND MÉNILMONTANT

CAFÉS AND WINE BARS

L'Autre Café 62 rue Jean-Pierre-Timbaud, 11ᵉ ☎01 40 21 03 07, ⓦlautrecafe.com; ⓜParmentier; map p.208. Amid the throng of bars on this popular nightlife stretch, this attractive fin-de-siècle café-bar-restaurant offers something slightly different, welcoming all comers and giving off an easy, effortless vibe. It's spacious, with high ceilings, a long zinc bar and comfy leather banquettes, drinks are reasonably priced, and the food isn't bad either, especially if you stick to the blackboard specials, which might include *boeuf bourguignon* (around €10). A great place to enjoy a lazy breakfast (€8.50) or to while away time browsing the newspapers or taking advantage of the free wi-fi. Daily 8am–2am.

Aux Deux Amis 45 rue Oberkampf, 11ᵉ ☎01 58 30 38 13; ⓜOberkampf; map p.208. You'd never guess it from the outside, but this ordinary-looking neighbourhood café on the lower stretch of the rue Oberkampf is one of the neighbourhood's hot tickets – it packs out quickly so it's best to get there by 7pm and be prepared to elbow your way to the bar. Everyone is here for the fresh and inventive small plates (from €10; typical dishes might include veal *tartare* with anchovy mayonnaise or an earthy braised squid) and Spanish tapas, all of which can be paired with the fine selection of natural wines. Prices are reasonable, and the vibe generally friendly. Tues–Sat noon–2am.

La Bague de Kenza 106 rue St-Maur, 11ᵉ ☎01 43 14 93 15, ⓦlabaguedekenza.com; ⓜParmentier; map p.208. Welcoming, colourful *salon de thé*, linked to a tempting North African pâtisserie (see p.335) and serving hearty soups and couscous (€8–15). Mon–Thurs, Sat & Sun 10am–9pm (tea room from 10am), Fri 2–9pm.

Le Barbouquin 1 rue Denoyez, 20ᵉ ☎09 84 32 13 21; ⓜBelleville; map p.208. Sitting on the corner of Denoyez, a graffiti-emblazoned backstreet dotted with artists' workshops, this relaxed café is a soothing way-station for a coffee, a fresh mint and ginger tea (€4.50) or a fresh juice. Light food includes savoury tarts and wraps, while the soundtrack wanders from *chanson* to rap. Pluck a book from the shelves, settle in an armchair and relax. Tues noon–6pm, Wed–Fri 10am–6pm, Sat & Sun 10.30am–6pm.

La Mère Lachaise 78 bd Ménilmontant, 20ᵉ ☎ 01 73 20 24 44, 🌐 lamerelachaise.fr; Ⓜ Père-Lachaise; map p.208. The sunny *terrasse* of this bar-restaurant, popular with students and *bobos* (bourgeois-bohemians), makes a good place for a drink after a visit to Père-Lachaise, or check out the cosy interior bar with its retro-chic decor. The restaurant serves classic dishes and cheeseburgers (mains €13–20, menus from €15). Mon–Sat 8am–2am, Sun 11am–1am.

Rosa Bonheur Parc des Buttes-Chaumont, 2 allée de la Cascade, 19ᵉ ☎ 01 42 00 00 45, 🌐 rosabonheur.fr; Ⓜ Botzaris/Jourdain; map p.208. Set inside a former *guinguette* – an open-air café or dance hall – this popular bar (see p.302) is also a nice place for a relaxing drink and snack or light meal – deli dishes and tapas from €3 – during the day. Thurs & Fri noon–1am, Sat & Sun 10am–1am.

RESTAURANTS

Astier 44 rue Jean-Pierre-Timbaud, 11ᵉ ☎ 01 43 57 16 35, 🌐 restaurant-astier.com; Ⓜ Parmentier; map p.208. This lovely old *bistrot* is a stalwart in this gentrifying area, turning out reliable classics – including roast duck, rabbit and a fabulous foie gras *royale* – in a pleasingly old-fashioned dining room. The cheese board is legendary, so leave space if you can. *Menus* from €35. Mon–Fri 12.30–2.30pm & 7–10.30pm, Sat 12.30–2.30pm & 7–11pm, Sun 12.30–2.30pm & 7–10.30pm.

★**Le Baratin** 3 rue Jouye-Rouve, 20ᵉ ☎ 01 43 49 39 70; Ⓜ Pyrénées/Belleville; map p.208. At first glance there's not much to distinguish *Le Baratin* from any Parisian *bistrot à vins*: the chalkboard menu, tiled floor and black-and-white photos are all in place. But the genuine neighbourhood feel, the stellar cooking and the fine organic wines – matched with your meal by the waiter – elevate it above the competition. The €19 three-course lunch *menu* changes daily but might include a thick bean

TOP 5 NORTH AFRICAN
La Bague de Kenza See p.294
Café de la Mosquée See p.283
Chez Omar See p.279
La Ruche à Miel See p.281
Le Souk See p.282

soup, melt-in-the-mouth veal cheeks and a quivering crème caramel; in the evenings, count on around €45 a head. It's best to book. Tues–Fri noon–2.30pm & 7.30pm–1am, Sat 7.30pm–1am.

★**Le Galopin** 34 rue Sainte-Marthe, 10ᵉ ☎ 01 47 06 05 03, 🌐 le-galopin.com; Ⓜ Belleville/Goncourt; map p.216. With its bare brick walls, stone floor and simple wooden chairs, this pared-down neighbourhood place epitomizes the neo-bistro scene, offering a seven-course dinner *menu* of small, delicate plates (€54). The relaxed atmosphere belies the skill behind Romain Tischenko's innovative cooking: mains might include cauliflower soup with salmon roe, squid with peppers and pork *jus* or sea bass with celery and butternut squash. Book ahead. Mon–Fri 7.30–10.30pm.

Jambo 23 rue Sainte-Marthe, 10ᵉ ☎ 01 42 45 46 55; Ⓜ Colonel Fabian; map p.208. With a sunshine-yellow frontage and cosy interior filled with African art, this pan-African restaurant goes out of its way to make you welcome. €28 gets you three courses; dishes range from a sour-sharp Masai soup to samosas from Zanzibar and Rwandan beef stew. Tues–Sat 7.30–10.30pm.

La Sardine 32 rue Sainte-Marthe, 10ᵉ ☎ 01 42 49 19 46, 🌐 barlasardine.com; Ⓜ Colonel Fabien or Goncourt; map p.208. Colourful, contemporary café-restaurant in a foodie corner of Belleville. The *terrasse* is a draw on sunny days, and the short menu of home-made food is gratifyingly inexpensive. Weekly lunchtime *plats* (salt cod, chilli, steak *tartare*, burgers) are good value at €11.50; they also offer a popular weekend brunch from €13 and Spanish-style tapas (Serrano ham, roasted peppers and the like) from €3.50. Mon–Fri 9am–2am, Sat & Sun 10am–2am.

20

AUTEUIL AND PASSY

RESTAURANTS

La Gare 19 chaussée de la Muette, 16ᵉ ☎ 01 42 15 15 31, 🌐 restaurantlagare.com; Ⓜ La Muette; map p.216. This former Passy train station has been turned into an elegant restaurant-bar, which boasts a huge, sunny dining room and an attractive *terrasse*. It's best at lunchtime, when it offers modern French/Mediterranean food – goat's cheese and chorizo tart; grilled prawns with polenta – on good-value weekday *menus* (€25/€29). Daily noon–11.30pm.

Hugo Desnoyer 28 rue du Docteur-Blanche, 16ᵉ ☎ 01 46 47 83 00, 🌐 hugodesnoyer.fr; map p.216. A carnivore's dream – a few tables in a butcher's shop where

you can dine on the finest cuts – mainly veal and beef, prepared simply and to perfection. It's not cheap, though – reckon on around €65 a head. Shop Tues–Sat 8.30am–7.30pm; food served 11am–3pm.

La Table Lauriston 129 rue Lauriston, 16ᵉ ☎ 01 47 27 00 07, 🌐 latablelauriston.com; Ⓜ Trocadéro; map p.216. The staid, well-heeled crowd in this relaxed neighbourhood restaurant enjoy well-executed *cuisine bourgeoise*: Burgundy snails, Basque octopus salad and Chateaubriand with morels are typical. You'll easily spend €50–60 per person. Mon–Sat noon–2.30pm & 7–10.30pm; closed Aug.

NEW MORNING JAZZ CLUB

Bars, clubs and live music

Paris's fame as the quintessential home of decadent, hedonistic nightlife has endured for centuries, and there remain plenty of places to drink and to dance, whatever your tastes. Bars run the gamut from genuinely bohemian dives to swanky posers' paradises, with a newer breed of hipster cocktail bars with a speakeasy vibe adding to the mix. Following some years of stagnation, the club scene is currently lively, with a variety of cool promoters offering eclectic, mixed programmes in venues from superclubs to refitted old theatres and riverboats. Where the city truly excels, however, is in its array of live music, from world music and rock to jazz and *chanson*.

The city has no rival in Europe for the variety of **world music** to be discovered: Algerian, West and Central African, Caribbean and Latin American sounds are represented in force, along with hip-hop, both imported and domestic. **Jazz** fans are in for a treat, too, with all styles from New Orleans to avant-garde filling venues almost nightly; **gypsy jazz** (*jazz manouche*), pioneered by Django Reinhardt, is also in vogue. French **chanson**, meanwhile – a tradition long associated with Paris, particularly during the war years through cabaret artists like Edith Piaf, Maurice Chevalier and Charles Trenet, and in the 1960s with poet-musicians as diverse as Georges Brassens, Jacques Brel and Serge Gainsbourg – remains as cool, and as popular, as ever. For something entirely different, a truly nostalgic taste of the entertainments of the past, you could head out of town altogether, and make for one of the old suburban eating-drinking-dancing venues known as **guinguettes**.

ESSENTIALS

Information To find out what's on, get hold of one of the city's listings magazines (see p.40). The online ⓦ lylo.fr offers a pretty good rundown of gigs in the city, searchable by genre, but if you want more in-depth coverage, try ⓦ parisbouge.com and the arts and music magazine *Nova* (ⓦ novaplanet.com). You can also pick up flyers in the city's trendier shops, music stores, bars and cafés.

Tickets Concert tickets, whether rock, jazz or *chanson* (or indeed classical), can be bought at the venues themselves, online, or through agents such as Fnac (see p.332). It can also be worth checking ⓦ billetreduc.com for cut-price tickets at the more mainstream venues.

BARS

The following listings review the city's livelier venues for **night-time drinking**, places that stay open late and maybe have DJs or occasional live music. Also included are the more vibrant, late-opening **cafés**, Alsatian/German-type **beer cellars** and a scattering of modish **cocktail bars**, many of which have a speakeasy vibe. You'll find lower-key and more relaxed cafés and *bars à vins*, geared more to eating than nightlife, listed in the "Cafés and restaurants" chapter (see pp.268–295), while full-on nightclubs, with entry fees and proper sound systems, are reviewed separately under "Clubs" (see p.302).

THE CHAMPS-ELYSÉES AND AROUND

Pershing Lounge Pershing Hall, 49 rue Pierre Charron, 8ᵉ ☎ 01 58 36 58 36, ⓦ pershinghall.com; ⓜ George-V; map pp.64–65. The swanky *Pershing Hall Hotel*'s lounge bar is an upscale retreat from the bustle of the city, with its 30m-high vertical garden, planted with exotic vegetation. Cocktails are priced to match the setting (€20 and upwards). Daily 6pm–1am.

Sir Winston 5 rue de Presbourg, 16ᵉ ☎ 01 40 67 17 37, ⓦ sirwinston.fr; ⓜ Kléber/Charles-de-Gaulle-Etoile; map pp.64–65. Churchill's eyes would surely have lit up on perusing the drinks menu at this vaguely British Empire themed bar-restaurant, with its fifty kinds of whisky and martini cocktails (from €10). There are plenty of cosy corners for chilling out, with leather chesterfields and snug booths; evenings see DJ sets with a world music slant (from 11pm). Mon–Wed & Sun 9am–2am, Thurs–Sat 9am–4am.

GRANDS BOULEVARDS AND AROUND

Bar Costes Hôtel Costes, 239 rue St-Honoré, 1ᵉʳ ☎ 01 42 44 50 00, ⓦ hotelcostes.com; ⓜ Concorde/Tuileries; map pp.74–75. Though its star is waning a little, this hotel bar – haunt of fashionistas, movie stars and media folk – is still a decadently romantic place for an *apéritif* or late-night drinks amid the sexy red velvet, swags and columns, set around an Italianate courtyard draped in ivy and atmospherically lit at night. Dress up, and be prepared for the too-cool-for-school

staff. Cocktails from around €20; DJs get going at around 9pm. Mon–Wed & Sun 5pm–2am, Thurs–Sat 7pm–3am.

★**La Conserverie** 37bis rue du Sentier, 2ᵉ ☎ 01 40 26 14 94, ⓦ laconserveriebar.com; ⓜ Bonne-Nouvelle; map pp.74–75. This stylishly converted, relaxed little *atelier* on a quiet backstreet mixes some extremely original cocktails and expertly made martinis. The food goes beyond the usual charcuterie platters, with Modern European, fusion and Eastern dishes that you can consume on low, soft sofas at candlelit tables. Cocktails around €12; regular DJ nights and occasional live bands. Mon & Tues 7pm–midnight, Wed–Fri 7pm–2am, Sat 8pm–2am.

Delaville Café 34 bd de la Bonne Nouvelle, 10ᵉ ☎ 01 48 24 48 09, ⓦ delavillecafe.com; ⓜ Bonne-Nouvelle; map pp.74–75. The grand staircase, gilded mosaics and marble columns hint at this bar's former incarnation as a bordello. It draws in crowds of pre-clubbers, who sling back a mojito or two before moving on to one of the area's clubs. High-profile DJ nights Thurs–Sun. Daily 9am–2am.

Lockwood 73 rue d'Aboukir, 2ᵉ ⓜ Sentier/Grands Boulevards; ⓦ lockwoodparis.com; map pp.74–75. Ticking all the hipster boxes, and part of a group that includes a number of cool Sydney bars, this artisan café/coffee house transforms into a cocktail bar after dark, its candlelit brick-walled cellar filled with cool young expats and locals quaffing creative whisky cocktails and chatting over the retro playlist. Mon–Sat 9am–2am.

21

BEAUBOURG AND LES HALLES

Le Fumoir 6 rue de l'Amiral-Coligny, 1er ☎01 42 92 00 24, Ⓦlefumoir.com; ⓂLouvre-Rivoli; map p.86. Sedate, long-established cocktail bar where chatter from the thirty-something crowd rises above the mellow jazz soundtrack and the genteel clatter of cocktail shakers. There's a book-lined dining area, and you can browse the international press. Cocktails from €11. Daily 11am–2am.

Kong 5th floor, 1 rue du Pont-Neuf, 1er ☎01 40 39 09 00, Ⓦkong.fr; ⓂPont-Neuf; map p.86. Your face will need to fit and your clothes look right in this über-designer Philippe Starck-fashioned bar/restaurant. The decor is pop art meets Oriental kitsch, with images of gorgeous models glaring at you as you sip your €16 cocktail. The (pricey) restaurant upstairs is under an impressive glass roof, with views over the Seine, and there is also a cosier, Baroque-styled smoking room, which feels quite at odds with the rest of the surroundings. Club nights Fri & Sat. Daily 6pm–2am.

Au Trappiste 4 rue St-Denis, 1er ☎01 42 33 08 50; ⓂChâtelet; map p.86. Proudly announcing itself as the "royaume de la bière", this is a temple for beer lovers. More than 140 draught beers, mainly from Belgium, include Belgian Blanche Riva; Jenlain, France's best-known *bière de garde*; and Kriek from the Mort Subite (Sudden Death) brewery – ask for a taster if you can't decide – plus *moules frites*, bistro food and *tartines* to soak it all up. Mon–Thurs & Sun 11am–2am, Fri & Sat 11am–4am.

THE MARAIS

★ Andy Wahloo 69 rue des Gravilliers, 3e ☎01 42 71 20 38, Ⓦandywahloo-bar.com; ⓂArts-et-Métiers; map p.94. This very popular bar, decked out in quirky retro-meets-Arabic decor, is fairly quiet during the week but gets packed to the gills at weekends with a hip but friendly and mixed crowd. They serve excellent cocktails, including a few originals (among them the Wahloo julep, which adds tobacco liqueur and bitter cherry to the traditional rum/mint/sugar concoction; €15). There is also a small selection of hot food and salads, served until midnight. Thurs–Sat nights see DJs play a wide range of dance music, including hip-hop, Moroccan rock and Algerian raï. Tues–Sat 6pm–2am.

La Belle Hortense 31 rue Vieille du Temple, 4e ☎01 42 74 59 70, Ⓦcafeine.com/belle-hortense; ⓂSt-Paul; map p.97. You can sip a glass while reading or chatting in this friendly little wine/champagne bar-cum-bookshop with book-lined walls and a zinc bar. There's a snug room with sofas at the back, though you'll be lucky to get a seat there later on. Daily 5pm–2am.

Les Etages 35 rue Vieille du Temple, 4e ☎01 42 78 72 00; ⓂSt-Paul or ⓂHôtel-de-Ville; map p.97. Charming, laidback bar – a tad bohemian with its overstuffed armchairs, paper lanterns, fairy lights and secret corners.

Simple meals – sweet or savoury tarts plus salad – are served during the day, while evenings see the place fill with a lively crowd enjoying creative cocktails. Daily noon–2am.

La Perle 78 rue Vieille du Temple, 3e ☎01 42 72 69 93, Ⓦcafelaperle.com; ⓂSt-Paul; map p.97. An extremely popular, casually retro and often noisy café-bar that maintains a *très cool* reputation and is always packed with an arty, *bobo* (bourgeois-bohemian) crowd knocking back cheap beer or excellent rosé and spilling onto the pavement in the warmer months. Daily 8am–2am.

★ Sherry Butt 20 rue Beautreillis, 4e ☎09 83 38 47 80, Ⓦsherrybuttparis.com; ⓂSt-Paul/Bastille; map p.94. Much less pretentious than some of its fashionable equivalents on the Left Bank, this New York-style cocktail bar is nevertheless a shrine to all things cool. The cocktail menu is innovative, listing drinks such as the Sassy Green (Scotch, pistachio and wasabi syrup, lime juice and sage leaves) – and staff will create drinks based on your tastes. Dark leather sofas and low lighting provide a laidback, intimate and relaxing atmosphere. Tues–Sat 6pm–2am, Sun & Mon 8pm–2am.

Stolly's 16 rue Cloche-Perce, 4e ☎01 42 76 06 76, Ⓦcheapblonde.com/stollys.html; ⓂSt-Paul; map p.97. The antithesis of Parisian cool, this rowdy no-nonsense, Anglo bar is an institution. You can watch broadcasts of major sporting events while enjoying pints of Guinness, Newcastle Brown Ale and "Cheapblonde" beer or a wide selection of spirits and cocktails (from €8). Happy hour 5–8pm. Daily 4.30pm–2am.

BASTILLE AND AROUND

Le Lèche-Vin 13 rue Daval, 11e ☎01 43 55 06 70; ⓂBastille; map pp.110–111. Appealing, rough around the edges little bar, dotted with kitschy religious decor. The statue of Mary with a cross in the window sets the tongue-in-cheek scene; the pics in the toilet, on the other hand, are far from pious. Gets packed very quickly at night with a young, cosmopolitan crowd. Daily 6pm–2am.

Moonshiner 5 rue Sedaine, 11e ☎09 50 73 12 99; ⓂBréguet-Sabin; map pp.110–111. Deliciously hidden away behind the cold room in an otherwise unremarkable pizzeria, this speakeasy-style bar is a good spot to snuggle down on a leather sofa with a well-mixed gin, vodka and (especially) whisky cocktail. Try if you dare the "Back to Basil" gin fizz with olive oil and basil. Daily 6pm–2am.

QUARTIER LATIN

Le Bateau Ivre 40 rue Descartes, 5e ☎01 44 07 22 64; ⓂCardinal-Lemoine; map pp.122–123. Small, dark and ancient, this studeny dive bar is just clear of the Mouffetard tourist zone, though it attracts a fair number of Anglos in the evenings for its beer specials, friendly vibe and good prices (cocktails from €5). Daily 6pm–2am.

Le Piano Vache 8 rue Laplace, 5ᵉ ☎ 01 46 33 75 03, ⓦ lepianovache.fr; ⓜ Cardinal-Lemoine; map pp.122–123. Venerable, easy-going *boîte* with poster-lined walls and dim lighting, crammed with students setting the world to rights. Mon–Sat 6pm–2am.

Le Reflet 6 rue Champollion, 5ᵉ ☎ 01 43 29 97 27; ⓜ Cluny-La Sorbonne; map pp.122–123. Cool without even trying, this bar-café has a nostalgic flavour of the *Nouvelle Vague* with its scruffy black decor, lights rigged up on a gantry, peeling movie posters, and Dylan, Coltrane and Cohen LP sleeves adorning the walls. It's a friendly spot, perfect for a drink at the tightly packed tables before or after a movie at one of the many arts cinemas on this street. Daily 11am–2am.

Le Violon Dingue 46 rue de la Montagne-Ste-Geneviève, 5ᵉ ☎ 01 43 25 79 93; ⓜ Maubert-Mutualité; map pp.122–123. This long, dark, student pub has no pretensions to being cool – it's noisy and popular, packed with young travellers, with English-speaking bar staff and cheap drinks. Tues–Sat 7pm–5am.

ST-GERMAIN

Bar du Marché 75 rue de Seine, 6ᵉ ☎ 01 43 26 55 15; ⓜ Mabillon; map pp.136–137. A good place to sit and chat, this former market café is a place for animated conversation rather than banging techno, beer and *kir* rather than cocktails. Daily 8am–2am.

Castor Club 14 rue Hautefeuille, 6ᵉ ☎ 09 50 64 99 38; ⓜ Odéon; map pp.136–137. An excellent and relatively laidback cocktail bar, not too sceney, despite its trendy speakeasy-cum-hunting-lodge decor. Come for the well-crafted cocktails (around €13 – try the Chirac 95, made with Calvados) and impeccably cool playlist of American country, rockabilly, soul and jazz. Tues–Sat 7pm–2am.

★ **Chez Georges** 11 rue des Canettes, 6ᵉ ☎ 01 43 26 79 15; ⓜ Mabillon; map pp.136–137. This spirited wine bar – all nicotine-stained walls and fading posters – is a neighbourhood institution. The predominantly (but not entirely) young, largely local crowd come for the cheap drinks and cheesy music, and it gets good-naturedly rowdy later on in its vaulted cellar bar – where the fight for space means there's dancing on the tables. Tues–Sat 2pm–2am; closed Aug.

La Mezzanine de l'Alcazar 62 rue Mazarine, 6ᵉ ☎ 01 53 10 19 99, ⓦ alcazar.fr; ⓜ Odéon; map pp.136–137. Both decor and clientele are *très design* at this swish cocktail bar, set on a mezzanine level overlooking Terence Conran's *Alcazar* restaurant. The prices are only slightly above average for the area, however – around €14 for a cocktail, with champagne at €85 a bottle. Occasional DJ nights and events. Tues–Sat 7pm–2am.

La Palette 43 rue de Seine, 6ᵉ ☎ 01 43 26 68 15, ⓦ cafelapaletteparis.com; ⓜ Odéon; map pp.136–137. A traditional café-bar (see p.285) that brims with a chatty

TOP 10 BARS: DJS AND DANCEFLOORS

21

Andy Wahloo See p.298
Café Chéri(e) See p.301
Le Carmen See p.300
Le Comptoir Général See p.301
Delaville Café See p.297
La Féline See p.301
Glass See p.300
Nüba See p.304
Panic Room See p.301
Piston Pélican See p.301

crowd till late, and has a terrific outdoor *terrasse*, in a peaceful spot away from the roaring traffic. Great for a relaxed *apéro* or two. Mon–Sat 8am–2am.

Prescription 23 rue Mazarine, 6ᵉ ☎ 09 50 35 72 87, ⓦ prescriptioncocktailclub.com; ⓜ Odéon; map pp.136–137. This tiny bar is a firm favourite on the cool cocktail scene, with a glamorously plush interior behind its artfully blank facade and some creative cocktails (around €14, or €45 for the "Old Cuban", a concoction of rum, champagne, ginger and mint served in a teapot for four to share) on its retro-style menu. Chic and restrained earlier in the evening, but pretty lively later on, with frequent DJ nights. Mon–Thurs 7pm–2am, Fri & Sat 7pm–4am, Sun 8pm–2am.

THE 7ᵉ

★ **Rosa Bonheur sur Seine** Near Pont Alexandre III, 7ᵉ ☎ 01 47 53 66 92, ⓦ rosabonheur.fr; ⓜ Invalides; map pp.150–151. The riverside sibling of the iconic *Rosa Bonheur* (see p.302), this cool café-bar on a barge is the best spot for a relaxed drink on the Berges du Seine, offering cocktails (from €7), beer and wine, tapas (from €6) and pizza to a friendly, mixed crowd. Of the other Berges du Seine bars, *Flow*, further west, is pricier and posier, with deckchair seating, while *Faust*, under the bridge, is largely for scenesters prepared to splash some serious cash. Mon & Tues 5.30pm–2am, Wed–Sun noon–2am, but hours change according to season and weather.

MONTPARNASSE AND SOUTHERN PARIS

La Folie en Tête 33 rue Butte-aux-Cailles, 13ᵉ ☎ 01 45 80 65 99, ⓦ lafolieentete.wix.com; ⓜ Corvisart; map pp.162–163. It's a bit set back from the main Butte-aux-Cailles action, but this vibrant, alternative bar, littered with bric-a-brac, is a classic of the *quartier*, with world music, laidback underground beats or *chanson* on the sound system. Happy hour 5–8pm. Mon–Sat 5pm–2am.

Le Merle Moqueur 11 rue Butte-aux-Cailles, 13ᵉ; ⓜ Place d'Italie/Corvisart; map pp.162–163. Classic little shop-front-style Butte-aux-Cailles bar, which saw the Paris debut of Manu Chao. Nowadays it chiefly serves up

21

1980s French rock CDs and home-made flavoured rums to a merry crowd of young Parisians. Happy hour 5–8pm. Daily 5pm–2am.

Le Rosebud 11bis rue Delambre, 14e ✆ 01 43 35 38 54; Ⓜ Vavin; map pp.162–163. Sartre and his crew used to drink at this hushed, faintly exclusive bar just off the boulevard Montparnasse; today the white-jacketed barmen, who seem to date from the same era as the decor, serve up wonderful, traditional cocktails (around €13) to a thirty-something-plus clientele. Daily 7pm–2am; closed Aug.

MONTMARTRE AND NORTHERN PARIS

★ **Le Carmen** 34 rue Duperré, 9e ✆ 01 45 26 50 00, Ⓦ le-carmen.fr; Ⓜ Pigalle; map p.182. This beautiful cocktail bar occupies the grand, high-ceilinged reception rooms of Georges Bizet's old house. You'll feel like you're at the ball from *La Traviata*, except the music is provided by edgy DJs, and everyone's drinking designer cocktails (bespoke, and stunning; they start at €15 – which isn't bad, given that a beer is €10). There's a sofa in a giant birdcage and alternative events from classical piano soirées to artistic performances – as well as gigs and parties. Daily midnight–6am.

Au Clair de la Lune 1 rue Ramey, 18e; Ⓜ Jules-Joffrin; map p.182. Scruffily hip bar – all Art Deco styling, neon lights, table football and shabby posters – a million miles away, in spirit, from the touristy Montmartre hubbub. Picture windows allow you to watch the rough-edged street scene on rue Clignancourt. Daily 8am–2am.

★ **Chez Camille** 8 rue Ravignan, 18e; Ⓜ Abbesses; map p.182. Cool and charming little neighbourhood bar in a pretty spot on the slopes of the Butte. With a simple list of drinks, and an effortlessly stylish, retro decor – creamy walls, ceiling fans, a few old mirrors, mismatched school tables – it pulls a local crowd of all ages who could as easily be enjoying a quiet chat as spontaneously dancing to anything from Elvis to raï. Happy hour 6–8pm; DJ nights first and third Thurs of the month. Mon–Sat 6pm–1.30am, Sun 6pm–midnight.

Chez Jeannette 47 rue du Faubourg St-Denis, 10e ✆ 01 47 70 30 89, Ⓦ chezjeannette.com; Ⓜ Château-d'Eau; map p.193. A cool corner café-bar that acts as a nexus for the bobos of the 10e. Beneath the high ceilings, the decor is genuine prewar vintage, but the crowd is up to the minute: all iPads and asymmetric haircuts. Daily 9am–2am.

★ **Cyrano** 3 rue Biot, 17e ✆ 01 45 22 53 34; Ⓜ Place de Clichy; map p.196. This old café-bar, with its superb *belle époque* gold mosaics and giant mirrors, its neighbourhood clientele and its dapper patron presiding over the whole set-up, is a Clichy institution. A lively crowd of theatrical types gathers here (and at its neighbour, *L'Entracte*, two doors along) in the evenings. Mon–Fri 8.30am–2am, Sat 4pm–2am, Sun 6pm–midnight.

Le Fantôme 36 rue de Paradis, 10e ✆ 09 66 87 11 20; Ⓜ Poissonière; map p.182. Combining retro arcade games,

formica decor and garish 80s pop-culture references with carefully crafted cocktails and posh pizza, this youthful place is bang on trend, and attracts a lively crowd most evenings. Mon–Fri 11am–2am, Sat 6pm–2am.

La Fourmi 74 rue des Martyrs, 18e ✆ 01 42 64 70 35; Ⓜ Pigalle/Abbesses; map p.182. The long bar, tall windows and artfully distressed high-ceilinged room of this popular venue provide a warm and welcoming space for a lively, trendy Parisian crowd. Be prepared to fight your way to the bar, and don't expect to be served quickly, but it's worth the wait to enjoy cheap drinks, buzzy vibe and good electro-lounge music, with DJs at the weekend. Mon–Thurs 9am–2am, Fri & Sat 9am–4am, Sun 10am–2am.

★ **Glass** 7 rue Frochot, 9e ✆ 09 80 72 98 83, Ⓦ glassparis.com; Ⓜ Pigalle; map p.182. Don't be put off by the grotty surroundings; this little bar with its knowing take on hipster Americana is at the heart of the "So Pi" phenomenon, a hub of cool in this seedily gentrifying neighbourhood. The whisky-based cocktails (€10), organic hot dogs and craft beers hit the spot with the young, up-for-it crowd, while DJs spin anything from Balearic beats to Krautrock. Sun–Thurs 7pm–4am, Fri & Sat 7pm–5am.

Au Rendez-Vous des Amis 23 rue Gabrielle, 18e ✆ 01 46 06 01 60; Ⓜ Abbesses; map p.182. Halfway up the Butte, this unpretentious corner hangout – attached to a restaurant – attracts a local following, and is especially popular with a young non-sceney crowd. Live gypsy jazz Fri and Sat. Daily 8.30am–2am.

Le Sans Souci 65 rue Jean-Baptiste Pigalle, 9e ✆ 01 53 16 17 04; Ⓜ Pigalle; map p.182. This old-style corner café, with a certain retro panache in its marble fittings and copper bar, is a key meeting-point for the cool kids of the quarter. It's friendly – and fairly low-key until the DJs get going and the crowds build up. Mon–Sat 9am–2am.

CANAL ST-MARTIN, OBERKAMPF AND AROUND

★ **Bar Ourcq** 68 quai de la Loire, 19e ✆ 01 42 40 12 16, Ⓦ barourcq.free.fr; Ⓜ Laumière; map p.200. With its sky blue facade and windows looking out onto the *quai*, this canalside bar really comes into its own in the warmer months when you can sit out on the quayside, or borrow the bar's set of pétanques. It's cosy inside, too, with sofas and cushions. DJ sets early evenings Thurs–Sun plus late Fri & Sat. Tues–Thurs 3pm–midnight, Fri & Sat 3pm–2am, Sun 3–10pm.

Café Charbon 109 rue Oberkampf, 11e ✆ 01 43 57 55 13; Ⓜ St-Maur/Parmentier; map p.208. The place that pioneered the rise of the Oberkampf bar scene is still going strong and continues to draw in a young, fashionable, mixed crowd day and night for its attractively restored *belle époque* decor – all high ceilings, huge mirrors, comfy booths and dangling lights – and the long happy hour (daily 4.30–8pm). Food served, too. Sun–Thurs 9am–2am, Fri & Sat 9am–4am.

Le Cannibale 93 rue Jean-Pierre-Timbaud, 11ᵉ ☎01 49 29 95 59, ⓦcannibalecafe.com; ⓜCouronnes; map p.208. This handsome *belle époque* former brasserie, with a faded retro charm, is better for drinks than food. Locals chill out to an eclectic soundtrack – both recorded and from DJs – and there's usually live music (often *chanson*, jazz funk or Cuban) on Sun. Mon–Fri 8am–2am, Sat & Sun 9am–2am.

★ **Le Comptoir Général** 80 quai de Jemmapes, 10ᵉ ☎01 44 88 24 48, ⓦlecomptoirgeneral.com; ⓜRépublique ou Goncourt; map p.198. Tucked away like a secret off a lane behind the canal, this rambling space is a "ghetto museum" during the day (see p.199), while at night, the whole place transforms into a supercool garage-style bar. The two bars, huge space, friendly staff and impeccably cool playlist – from Velvet Underground to soukous – keep the lively, mixed crowd happy. Occasional live African music, too. Donation for entry requested. Daily 11am–2am.

Le Kitch 10 rue Oberkampf, 11ᵉ; ⓜFilles-du-Calvaire/ Oberkampf; map p.198. Living up to its name, this little bar brims with eclectic jumble – a ceramic Bambi here, a garden gnome there. Punters pile in for the excellent-value happy hour (5.30–9pm), when cocktails are just €5 (go with tradition and order the minty green Shrek) – it's crowded, noisy and fun. Tues–Sun 5.30pm–2am.

Panic Room 101 rue Amelot, 11ᵉ ☎01 58 30 93 43, ⓦpanicroomparis.com; ⓜFilles-du-Calvaire; map p.198. Wildly popular DJ bar with a cool young set knocking back cocktails – just €6 during happy hour (6.30– 9pm) – and dancing to electronica. You can bring your own snacks. Mon–Sat 6.30pm–2am.

★ **Point Ephémère** 200 quai de Valmy, 10ᵉ ☎01 40 34 02 48, ⓦpointephemere.org; ⓜJaurès; map p.198. A great atmosphere pervades this young, creative space, run by an arts collective and showcasing music (see p.305), dance and visual arts in a former boathouse on the banks of the canal. There's always interesting multilingual conversation going on around the bar, and you can get decent street food in the restaurant looking out onto the canal. Mon–Sat noon–2am, Sun noon–9pm (later if there's a concert).

BELLEVILLE, MÉNILMONTANT AND BAGNOLET

Café Chéri(e) 44 bd de la Villette, 19ᵉ ☎01 42 02 02 05; ⓜBelleville; map p.208. A shabby-cool DJ bar, with scruffy red interior and popular terrace, where local hipsters sit at their laptops during the day, or drop in for drinks after work and stay long into the night. Drinks are reasonably priced. Music, from hip-hop to indie, Thurs–Sat nights. Daily 11am–2am.

Caves Joséphine 25 rue Moret, 11ᵉ ☎01 48 07 16 70, ⓦcafejosephine.fr; ⓜMénilmontant; map p.208. Just off the top end of rue Oberkampf, this sophisticated little speakeasy-type bar serves wine, whiskies, champagne and

cocktails (from €10), plus platters of cheese and charcuterie and interesting offerings including tuna *rillettes* with wasabi (€5–11). Mon–Wed 6pm–3am, Thurs–Sat 6pm–4.30am.

La Féline 6 rue Victor Letalle, 20ᵉ ⓦlafelinebar.com; ⓜMénilmontant; map p.208. Ménilmontant dive bar packed with a high-spirited mix of rockabilly kids, wild-eyed punks, old rockers and hip tourists. There's live music – garage rock, punk, ska – plus burlesque and DJ nights, but above all this is a deliciously unpretentious place to hang out and have a really good time. Tues–Sat 6pm–2am.

Aux Folies 8 rue de Belleville, 20ᵉ ☎06 28 55 89 40, ⓦaux-folies-belleville.fr; ⓜBelleville; map p.208. Once a café-théâtre hosting the likes of Edith Piaf and Maurice Chevalier, the charmingly shabby *Aux Folies* offers a slice of old Belleville life; its *terrasse* and brass bar, with mirrored tiles and neon lights, are packed with a mixed, cosmopolitan crowd enjoying cheap beer, cocktails and mint tea. Occasional live music. Daily 7am–2am.

Lou Pascalou 14 rue des Panoyaux, 20ᵉ ☎01 46 36 78 10, ⓦcafe-loupascalou.com; ⓜMénilmontant; map p.208. A friendly place with a zinc bar and sunny terrace, this relaxed hangout is a good find. Be sure to try their delicious mint tea – over a game of chess if you fancy. You can also choose from a wide range of reasonably priced beers, bottled and on tap. Good music, too, including gypsy jazz, Latin singers and *chanson*. Happy hour 5–8pm. Daily 9am–2am.

Le Perchoir 14 rue Crespin du Gast, 11ᵉ ☎01 48 06 18 48, ⓦleperchoir.fr; ⓜMénilmontant; map p.208. The drinks may be pricey for the neighbourhood (cocktails €12), and you may have to queue to get in, but this popular seventh-floor cocktail bar has real pulling power – in summer you can languish on the huge rooftop terrace, enjoying amazing city views. Mon–Fri 6pm–midnight, Sat 2pm–midnight.

★ **Piston Pélican** 15 rue de Bagnolet, 20ᵉ ☎01 43 71 15 76, ⓦpistonpelican.com; ⓜAlexandre-Dumas; map p.211. This friendly local joint, with its chipped mirrors, old posters and pop culture memorabilia, has an appealingly eclectic soundtrack, featuring rock, cabaret, world music and the odd drum'n'bass anthem. There's free live music – anything from *chanson* to reggae – from 9pm Thurs–Sat, often followed by a DJ. They do have cheese and *saucisson* platters, but you are also encouraged to bring your own nibbles and "picnic". Happy hour daily 5–8pm. Mon–Sat 5pm–2am, Sun 2–11pm.

> **TOP 5 COCKTAIL BARS** **21**
>
> **Castor Club** See p.299
> **La Conserverie** See p.297
> **Lockwood** See p.297
> **Prescription** See p.299
> **Sherry Butt** See p.298

21

★ **Rosa Bonheur** Parc des Buttes-Chaumont, 2 av des Cascades, 19e ☎ 01 42 00 00 45, ⓦ rosabonheur.fr; ⓜ Botzaris/Jourdain; map p.208. Tucked away in the Parc des Buttes-Chaumont, the pretty *Rosa Bonheur* is set inside a former *guinguette* – an open-air café or dance hall. A very mixed crowd of Parisians of all ages comes to drink, dance and nibble on tapas here in a relaxed setting amid the birds and the trees. It gets packed in summer. Entrance to the park after closing is exclusively via 7 rue Botzaris. Thurs & Fri noon–1am, Sat & Sun 10am–1am.

CLUBS

Once awash with wall-to-wall techno, the **club scene** in Paris today is dominated by edgier, esoteric programmes put on at smaller venues, and where deep house once ruled, you can find hip-hop, r'n'b, electro-lounge, rock, reggae and more. The clubs listed below are among the most popular, but the music and the general vibe really depend on who's running the "*soirée*" on a particular night. Some clubs showcase occasional live acts, too. It's also worth checking the listings for **live music** venues (see p.297), which tend to hold DJ sessions after hours, and the **LGBT** club listings (see p.359). Note too that lots of **bars** (see pp.297–302) bring in DJs, especially on weekend nights. Venues rarely warm up before 1am or 2am, whatever their opening hours.

CHAMPS-ELYSÉES AND AROUND

Showcase Below Pont Alexandre III, 8e ☎ 01 45 61 25 43, ⓦ showcase.fr; ⓜ Champs-Elysées–Clemenceau; map pp.64–65. This superclub, in a former boat hangar facing onto the river, has a fantastic sound system and an up-for-it crowd – and though you should dress up to get in, it's less pretentious than it once was. Techno, deep house and bass are the order of the day. Entry up to €20, but check the Facebook page for promo codes. *Faust*, across the bridge on the other side of the river, is a swish new restaurant, bar and club run by the same people. Fri & Sat 11.30pm–6am.

Zig Zag Club 32 rue Marbeuf, 8e ⓦ zigzagclub.fr; ⓜ Franklin-D-Roosevelt; map pp.64–65. One of the city's newer electronica clubs, with a fantastic Funktion One sound system and big-name and underground DJs filling the huge dancefloor with a wild crowd (capacity 1200). Entry from €12. Fri & Sat 11.30pm–7am.

GRANDS BOULEVARDS AND PASSAGES

★ **Rex Club** 5 bd Poissonnière, 2e ☎ 01 42 36 10 96, ⓦ rexclub.com; ⓜ Bonne-Nouvelle; map pp.74–75. The iconic *Rex* is the clubbers' club: spacious and serious about music, which is strictly electronic, notably techno, played through a top-of-the line sound system. Refreshingly unpretentious, with big-name DJs. Entry up to €20. Thurs–Sat 11.30pm–7am.

★ **Social Club** 142 rue Montmartre, 2e ☎ 01 40 28 05 55, ⓦ parissocialclub.com; ⓜ Bourse/Grands Boulevards; map pp.74–75. Despite the forbidding black decor, this unpretentious club offers one of the best nights out in Paris, packed with a mixed clientele from local students to lounge lizards. Here, it's all about the music, with everything from G-House to Trap and hip-hop on the playlist, and regular live bands (see p.304) – the mint vodka is the drink *de rigueur*. Friday is gay night. Entry free €20. Club nights Thurs–Sat 11pm–6am.

BASTILLE AND AROUND

Badaboum 2bis rue des Taillandiers, 11e ☎ 01 48 06 50 70, ⓦ badaboum-paris.com; ⓜ Bastille; map pp.110–111. Relatively intimate club, concert venue and cocktail bar/street food restaurant rolled into one, in a converted warehouse. Music focuses on digital EDM, but can stray as far as zouk and hip-hop, with live bands earlier on. Entry €10–15. Cocktail bar Wed–Sat 7pm–2am; club hours vary according to event, but roughly Mon–Wed & Sun 7.30pm–midnight, Thurs 7pm–5am, Fri & Sat 7.30pm–6.30am.

★ **Concrete** 69 Port de la Rapée, 12e ⓦ concreteparis.fr; ⓜ Gare de Lyon; map p.115. Moored on a boat on the Seine, out near the Gare de Lyon, this is one of the hottest spots on the clubbing scene, putting on all-night and all-day techno parties and featuring the biggest-name DJs. Fri–Sun hours vary.

ST-GERMAIN

Le Montana 28 rue St-Benoît, 6e; ⓜ St-Germain-des-Prés; map pp.136–137. This small, exclusive and distinctly beautiful mini-club is achingly jet-set, and so celebrity-packed it doesn't need a publicly listed phone number. You'll have to look the part to get in, and feel the part to enjoy it. No entry fee, but expensive drinks. Mon–Sat 11pm–5am.

EIFFEL TOWER QUARTER

YOYO Palais de Tokyo, 13 av du Président-Wilson, 16e ⓦ yoyo-paris.com; ⓜ Iéna; map pp.150–151. Housed in the huge basement of the Palais de Tokyo, this is one of the city's top dance clubs, serving up a top-notch mix of hip-hop, soul, house anthems and electro to a seriously cool crowd. Days vary, 11pm–6am.

THE 13e

★ **Batofar** Opposite 11 quai François Mauriac, 13e ☎ 01 53 60 17 00, ⓦ batofar.org; ⓜ Quai de la Gare; map p.176.

21

Though you're spoiled for choice for cool nightlife spots along this stretch of the river – other excellent floating options just here include *Le Petit Bain*, a modernist bar/gallery/performance space; *La Dame de Canton*, a world music venue on a beautiful Chinese junk; and *El Alamein*, a dilapidated barge putting on great *chanson* and jazz – this is one of the originals and still one of the best. An old lighthouse boat moored at the foot of the Bibliothèque Nationale, it offers a club, live music space and restaurant, with an eclectic playlist of alternative electro, techno, hip-hop, whatever – and the odd experimental funk night or the like thrown in. Entry from €8. Opening times vary.

Nüba 34 quai d'Austerlitz, 13ᵉ ⓦ nuba-paris.fr; Ⓜ Gare d'Austerlitz; map p.176. This swish waterside restaurant-bar-club, on the top floor of the Cité de la Mode et du Design, really comes into its own in summer when its vast rooftop deck is opened and you can sip your cocktail looking out over the Seine while a DJ plays an electro or dance set. The vibe matches the venue – chilled, cool and welcoming to all. Tues–Sat 6pm–5am, Sun noon–2am, plus daytime events.

MONTMARTRE AND PIGALLE

La Machine du Moulin Rouge 90 bd de Clichy, 18ᵉ ☎ 01 53 41 88 89, ⓦ lamachinedumoulinrouge.com; Ⓜ Blanche; map p.182. Next to the fabled *Moulin Rouge*, this friendly club has a concert space hosting international names – from Skrillex to Of Mice and Men – plus a dedicated basement dancefloor known as "La Chaufferie",

a garden terrace and a funky bar. EDM is the order of the day here, but a touch of hedonism lifts it above the usual monster club. Entry €13–20. Times vary but generally Fri & Sat 11pm–6am, often with gigs before.

Le Rouge 77 rue Jean-Baptiste Pigalle, 9ᵉ ☎ 01 42 85 00 70, ⓦ rpigalle.com; Ⓜ Pigalle; map p.182. *Le Rouge* cashes in on its days as an old Pigalle cabaret – the red velvet and gilt decor seems to have changed little since the Roaring Twenties – with electro DJs, hip live bands and a rumbustuous line in gay nights. Club nights 11pm–5am.

EASTERN PARIS

Glaz'art 7–15 av de la Porte de la Villette, 19ᵉ ☎ 01 40 36 55 65, ⓦ glazart.com; Ⓜ Porte de la Villette; map p.202. Artsy, alternative-leaning venue that's serious about its music – a hugely eclectic range of club nights and live acts covering everything from pagan metal to dub. It's spacious, and in summer there's a glorious outdoor "beach". Entry €5–20. Times vary, but weekend club nights usually 11pm–5am.

Le Nouveau Casino 109 rue Oberkampf, 11ᵉ ☎ 01 43 57 57 40, ⓦ nouveaucasino.net; Ⓜ Parmentier; map p.208. Next to *Café Charbon* (see p.300), this excellent venue puts on an interesting line-up of live gigs that makes way for a relaxed, dancey crowd later on, with music ranging from electro-pop or techno to funk. There's a good sound system and ventilation, but not much space. Entry €6–15, depending on whether you reserve online and when you arrive. Fri & Sat midnight–5am.

ROCK AND WORLD MUSIC

Paris is a fantastic place to see **world music**, with artists from throughout Africa, in particular, making regular appearances. Most of the **venues** listed here are primarily devoted to live acts, though some double up as clubs on certain nights or after hours. A few will have live music all week, but the majority host bands on just a couple of nights. Note that the most interesting **clubs** (see p.302) tend to host gigs earlier on, and that some bars (see p.297) have occasional live music, too. It's also worth checking the **jazz venues** (see opposite), as these often branch into other genres such as world music and folk – *New Morning* (see p.307) is a classic example.

GRANDS BOULEVARDS AND PASSAGES

★Social Club 142 rue Montmartre, 2ᵉ ☎ 01 40 28 05 55, ⓦ parissocialclub.com; Ⓜ Bourse/Grands Boulevards; map pp.74–75. This smallish but high-profile club (see p.302) has one of the most intriguing live music programmes in the city – folk, bluegrass and African acts find space alongside Scandi rappers and indie darlings. Opening times vary.

BASTILLE

Café de la Danse 5 passage Louis-Philippe, 11ᵉ ☎ 01 47 00 57 59, ⓦ cafedeladanse.com; Ⓜ Bastille; map pp.110–111. Reliable, unpretentious venue for the best contemporary rock, world, folk and jazz music played in an intimate space with dancing room and a bar. Entry €12–30. Opening times vary.

Café de la Plage 59 rue de Charonne, 11ᵉ ☎ 06 68 17 56 78, ⓦ lecafedelaplage-paris.com; Ⓜ Ledru-Rollin; map pp.110–111. This friendly bar stages a wide variety of live music and club nights. The emphasis is on latin, but you could also catch ska gigs, Indonesian concerts or New Orleans funk. Shows start 9 or 10pm. Tues–Sat 6pm–2am.

MONTMARTRE AND PIGALLE

La Cigale 120 bd de Rochechouart, 18ᵉ ☎ 01 49 25 81 75, ⓦ lacigale.fr; Ⓜ Pigalle; map p.182. Opened in 1887 and formerly playing host to the likes of Mistinguett and Maurice Chevalier, this rather gorgeous 1400-seater Pigalle theatre has become a leading venue for world music and French and continental European bands. The adjoining *La Boule Noir* (ⓦ www.laboule-noire.fr) is smaller, with a more indie vibe. Opening times vary.

21

Le Divan du Monde 76 rue des Martyrs, 18ᵉ ☎ 01 40 05 06 99, ⓦ divandumonde.com; Ⓜ Pigalle; map p.182. In a café whose regulars once included Toulouse-Lautrec, this venue offers a vibrant music programme, largely show-casing French and European acts ranging from pornogrind via techno to avant-garde metal, rap and reggae, with dancing till dawn at the weekends. Opening times vary.

EASTERN PARIS

Le 104 5 rue Curial, 19ᵉ ☎ 01 53 35 50 00, ⓦ 104.fr; Ⓜ Riquet; map p.200. It's always worth checking out the schedule at this innovative arts centre (see p.201) to find pop gigs, indie rock, *chanson* sets and contemporary *bals de danse*. Opening times vary.

★**L'Alimentation Générale** 64 rue Jean-Pierre-Timbaud, 11ᵉ ☎ 01 43 55 42 50, ⓦ alimentation -generale.net; Ⓜ Parmentier; map p.208. Despite its name, this is not the local grocer's shop – confusingly, there is a real *alimentation générale*, further up the road, with the same street number, so don't be deterred – but one of Oberkampf's most popular nightlife spots, with a global line-up of live music ranging from Afro rock to Balkan beats and trance. A DJ usually takes over later and there's some room for dancing. There's usually a cover charge of €5–10 that includes the first drink, but it's often free before 11pm. Food – tapas, burgers, cheese plates – is available. Daily 6pm–2am.

Le Bataclan 50 bd Voltaire, 11ᵉ ☎ 01 43 14 00 30, ⓦ le-bataclan.com; Ⓜ Oberkampf; map p.198. Historic pagoda-styled ex-theatre venue (the Velvet Underground played a legendary gig here, recorded on their *Le Bataclan '72* album) with an eclectic line-up covering anything from international and local dance and rock – Pete Doherty, Fleet Foxes and Death Cab for Cutie, for example – to *chanson*, comedy and techno nights. The Follivores and Crazyvores gay club nights are popular. Opening times vary.

★**La Bellevilloise** 19–21 rue Boyer, 20ᵉ ☎ 01 46 36 07 07, ⓦ labellevilloise.com; Ⓜ Gambetta/Ménilmontant; map p.208. There's always something interesting going on at this former workers' co-operative, dating back to 1877, now a dynamic bar, club, concert venue and exhibition space. It also hosts film festivals, community events and vintage and organic markets. Its cool bar-restaurant, *La Halle aux Oliviers*, with real olive trees dotted about

beneath a glass roof, makes an attractive place for a drink, dinner (from €16 for mains such as spinach and ricotta ravioli or steak and chips), or jazz brunch on Sunday (€29). The excellent basement club and live music venue hosts bands, playing anything from Afro jazz to Balkan beats, *chanson* to swing. Opening times vary, but generally: Wed & Thurs 7pm–1am, Fri 7pm–2am, Sat 6pm–2am, Sun 11.30am–midnight.

La Flèche d'Or 102bis rue de Bagnolet, corner of rue des Pyrénées, 20ᵉ ☎ 01 44 64 01 02, ⓦ flechedor.fr; Ⓜ Porte de Bagnolet/Alexandre-Dumas (it's a 15min walk from both); map p.211. Housed in the old Charonne train station on the defunct *petite ceinture* railway, this bar and live music venue has a punkish atmosphere, with throngs of bikers, clubbers, musos and students drawn by the eclectic music programme – indie pop, ska, rock, *chanson* and punk, with international names including the likes of Laura Marling and Nadine Shah. Opening times vary.

★**L'International** 5 rue Moret, 11ᵉ ☎ 01 42 02 02 05, ⓦ linternational.fr; Ⓜ Menilmontant; map p.208. With two stages and at least two free gigs a night, this friendly *café-concert*, related to the record shop opposite (see p.333), is a staple on the Oberkampf scene, showcasing the best new, indie and edgy acts – mostly French, but not exclusively – in all genres, from rap to electro. DJs take over later on. Happy hour daily 6–9pm. Daily 6pm–2am; shows usually 9pm & 11pm.

Maroquinerie 23 rue Boyer, 20ᵉ ☎ 01 40 33 35 05, ⓦ lamaroquinerie.fr; Ⓜ Gambetta; map p.208. Cool arts centre with a smallish concert venue downstairs. The line-up encompasses anything from folk and jazz to metal and hip-hop, with international names and a good selection of French musicians. A classy restaurant (daily 7.30–11.30pm) offers a small menu of modern food (from chestnut gnocchi to pulled pork in focaccia with kimchee) from €12. Opening times vary.

★**Point Ephémère** 200 quai de Valmy, 10ᵉ ☎ 01 40 34 02 48, ⓦ pointephemere.org; Ⓜ Jaurès/Louis Blanc; map p.198. Run by an arts collective in a disused boat-house, this superbly dilapidated cultural venue (see p.301) is a nexus for alternative and underground performers of all kinds. There are gigs most nights, covering anything from electro to Afro jazz via folk rock. Mon–Sat noon–2am, Sun noon–9pm (later if there's a concert).

JAZZ AND CHANSON

Traditional French **chanson** is alive and well in Paris, as is **jazz**, with clubs plying all styles from Dixieland to avant-garde. **Gypsy jazz** (*jazz manouche*), pioneered by Django Reinhardt, remains in vogue; carrying on the tradition are musicians such as Romane and the Ferré brothers. Other jazz names to look out for are saxophonist Didier Malherbe; violinist Didier Lockwood; British-born but long-time France resident, guitarist John McLaughlin; pianist Alain Jean-Marie; clarinettist Louis Sclavis; and accordionist Richard Galliano, who updates the French *musette* style. *Bistrots* and bars can be a good place to catch gypsy jazz, as well as *chanson*; look out for flyers and posters in the venues themselves. In addition to the places listed here, it's also worth checking out the world and rock venues listed above for occasional *chanson* or jazz concerts.

21

JAZZ IN PARIS

Jazz has long enjoyed an appreciative audience in France, especially since the end of World War II, when the intellectual rigour and agonized musings of bebop struck an immediate chord of sympathy in the existentialist hearts of the *après-guerre*. Charlie Parker, Dizzy Gillespie, Miles Davis – all were being listened to in the 1950s, when in Britain their names were known only to a tiny coterie of fans.

Gypsy guitarist **Django Reinhardt** and his partner, violinist Stéphane Grappelli, whose work represents the distinctive and undisputed French contribution to the jazz canon, had much to do with the genre's popularity. But it was also greatly enhanced by the presence of many front-rank black American musicians, for whom Paris was a haven of freedom after the racial prejudice of the States. Among them were the soprano sax player **Sidney Bechet**, who set up a legendary partnership with French clarinettist Claude Luter, and Bud Powell, whose turbulent exile partly inspired the tenor man played by Dexter Gordon in the film *Round Midnight*.

GRANDS BOULEVARDS AND PASSAGES

★**Au Limonaire** 18 Cité Bergère, 9ᵉ ☎01 45 23 33 33, ⓦlimonaire.free.fr; ⓜGrands Boulevards; map pp.74–75. Tiny, cosy backstreet wine bar/"*bistro chantant*", perfect for Parisian *chanson* nights, showcasing young singers, zany music/poetry performances and boozy singalongs. Reserving a table for dinner guarantees you a seat for the show at 10pm (Sun 7pm); otherwise you'll be crammed up against the bar, if you can get in at all. Daily 6pm–midnight.

LES HALLES

Le Baiser Salé 58 rue des Lombards, 1ᵉʳ ☎01 42 33 37 71, ⓦlebaisersale.com; ⓜChâtelet; map p.86. The "salty kiss" is a small, crowded, upstairs room with live music every night – usually jazz, but also world music, funk, flamenco and soul (from around €12). There are free jazz jam sessions on Mon, and the downstairs bar is great for chilling out. Daily 5.30pm–6am, with most sets starting at 7 & 9.30pm.

Duc des Lombards 42 rue des Lombards, 1ᵉʳ ☎01 42 33 22 88, ⓦducdeslombards.com; ⓜChâtelet/Les-Halles; map p.86. This modern venue is a high-profile place to hear jazz piano, blues and fusion, with big names from Ahmad Jamal to Jamie Cullum. Admission varies but is rarely below €23. Nightly 7pm–3am, shows 7.30 & 9.30pm, free jam sessions 11.30pm Fri & Sat.

Le Sunset/Le Sunside 60 rue des Lombards, 1ᵉʳ ☎01 40 26 46 60, ⓦsunset-sunside.com; ⓜChâtelet-Les-Halles; map p.86. Two clubs in one: *Le Sunside* on the ground floor features mostly traditional, acoustic jazz, whereas the *Sunset* cellar is a venue for electric and fusion. Both usually host two shows per night. Performers have been as diverse as Benny Golson, Didier Lockwood, Brad Mehdau, Kenny Barron and Avishai Cohen. Entry €15–30. Daily 8pm–2.30am.

MARAIS

Péniche Le Marcounet Moored on the quai de l'Hôtel de Ville by the Pont Marie, 4ᵉ ☎06 60 47 38 52, ⓦpeniche-marcounet.fr; ⓜPont Marie; map p.97. A romantic and quirky way to experience live jazz, swing, blues and flamenco – on a canal boat. Enjoy an *apéritif* on deck then head below to the concert area. Entry free–€10. Tues–Sat 6pm–midnight, Sun 11am–4pm (concerts Tues–Thurs, plus sometimes Fri & Sat; musical brunch Sun from noon).

BASTILLE

L'Atelier Charonne 21 rue de Charonne, 11ᵉ ☎01 40 21 83 35, ⓦateliercharonne.com; ⓜLedru-Rollin/Bastille; map pp.110–111. This sleek bar-restaurant is a good place to hear gypsy jazz, with nightly gigs from French and international artists. Booking ahead for a dinner concert (from €34.90 for two courses; €39.90 at weekends) reserves you a table with a view of the stage. There's also a separate bar area with limited views. Concerts 9pm Mon–Sat; Sun sees a *jazz manouche* jam session from 7.30pm. Mon–Sat 8pm–midnight, Sun 7pm–midnight.

QUARTIER LATIN

Caveau de la Huchette 5 rue de la Huchette, 5ᵉ ☎01 43 26 65 05, ⓦcaveaudelahuchette.fr; ⓜSt-Michel; map pp.122–123. An atmospheric, historic old cellar bar – self-styled "*temple du swing*" – that offers a wonderful slice of old Parisian life in an overwhelmingly touristy street. There are live concerts, usually Dixieland, boogie woogie, blues or swing, and energetic dancing from the enthusiastic crowd. Sun–Thurs €13, Fri & Sat €15. Sun–Wed 9.30pm–2.30am, Thurs–Sat 9.30pm–dawn.

★**Aux Trois Mailletz** 56 rue Galande, 5ᵉ ☎01 43 25 96 86, ⓦlestroismailletz.fr; ⓜSt-Michel; map pp.122–123. This corner café-resto transforms into a convivial piano bar (after 6pm); even later (after 8.30pm) a good jazz/cabaret bar sets up in the basement, featuring anything from outrageous cabaret to fabulous world music artists. Daily 6pm–5am.

MONTPARNASSE

Au Magique 42 rue de Gergovie, 14ᵉ ☎ 01 45 42 26 10, ⓦ aumagique.com; ⓜ Pernety; map pp.162–163. Unpretentious restaurant-bar and "*chanson* cellar" with traditional French *chanson* performances from local and lesser-known performers. Entry around €5; drinks are reasonably priced. Wed–Sat 8pm–2am; concerts usually 9pm.

MONTMARTRE, PIGALLE AND THE 9ᵉ

Autour de Midi…et Minuit 11 rue Lepic, 18ᵉ ☎ 01 55 79 16 48, ⓦ autourdemidi.fr; ⓜ Blanche; map p.182. Its prime Montmartre location means it is inevitably touristy, but this cosy cellar jazz club is an amiable place to sit back and enjoy a variety of jazz acts, from swing via bebop to gypsy jazz. Jam sessions Tues and Wed. Tues–Sat, hours vary.

Casino de Paris 16 rue de Clichy, 9ᵉ ☎ 01 49 95 99 99, ⓦ casinodeparis.fr; ⓜ Trinité; map p.182. This decaying, once-plush casino in one of the seediest streets in Paris is a quirky venue for all sorts of performances – from *chanson* to electronic pop via cabaret and poetry. Most performances start 8.30pm.

★**Au Lapin Agile** 22 rue des Saules, 18ᵉ ☎ 01 46 06 85 87, ⓦ au-lapin-agile.com; ⓜ Lamarck-Caulaincourt; map p.182. A legendary club famously painted and patronized by Picasso, Utrillo and other leading lights of the early twentieth-century Montmartre scene, the "nimble rabbit" – in an adorable shuttered building with a pretty garden – is now an intimate *chanson* club much beloved by tourists. Visitors sit packed in on benches round the walls of the old back room, listening – and occasionally

joining in with – *chanson*, cabaret and poetry. €28 including one drink, students €20 (except Sat). Tues–Sun 9pm–1am.

Les Trois Baudets 64 bd de Clichy, 18ᵉ ☎ 01 42 62 33 33, ⓦ lestroisbaudets.com; ⓜ Blanche/Pigalle; map p.182. With a proud place on the Pigalle nightlife scene, this refitted 1940s theatre specializes in developing young, upcoming French singer-songwriters of all stripes, so concerts are something of a lucky dip. The venue is intimate (200 seats), and there's a lively bar/restaurant. Concert nights 7pm–midnight.

THE 10ᵉ

★**New Morning** 7–9 rue des Petites-Ecuries, 10ᵉ ☎ 01 45 23 51 41, ⓦ newmorning.com; ⓜ Château-d'Eau; map p.193. Although relatively understated, housed in a former printing press, this established place attracts some of the big international jazz names and a very knowledgeable crowd. Often standing room only. Excellent blues and world music, too, from klezmer to dancehall. Entry around €23. Usually daily 8pm–1.30am (concert times vary).

FURTHER AFIELD

Instants Chavirés 7 rue Richard-Lenoir, Montreuil ☎ 01 42 87 25 91, ⓦ instantschavires.com; ⓜ Robespierre. Highly respected avant-garde, experimental and improvised jazz joint close to the Porte de Montreuil. A place where musicians go to hear each other play. Entry €10–17. Concerts 8.30pm.

GUINGUETTES

Though Paris has a number of contemporary riverside bars and venues, for the ultimate retro experience you need to head out of the centre to a traditional riverbank **guinguette**. You can usually eat homely French food at these places, but the real draw is the band. Depending on the venue you'll find families, older couples and trendy young things from the city swaying with varying degrees of skill to foxtrots, tangos and lots of well-loved accordion numbers – especially nice on a Sunday afternoon.

Chalet du Lac Facing the Lac de St-Mandé, Bois de Vincennes, 12ᵉ ☎ 01 43 28 09 89, ⓦ chaletdulac.fr; ⓜ St-Mandé-Tourelles. Tango tea dances in the afternoons (Mon, Thurs & Sat 2.30–7pm, €6; Sun 3–8pm, €12) and other types of dance, such as latin and swing, in the evenings (7/8pm–midnight or later; €7–20; check the programme for listings). The restaurant serves brasserie classics.

Chez Gégène 162bis quai de Polangis, Joinville-le-Pont ☎ 01 48 83 29 43, ⓦ chez-gegene.fr; RER Joinville-le-Pont. Just the other side of the Bois de Vincennes from the *Chalet du Lac*, this is a genuine *guinguette* established in the 1900s, though today the band mixes in pop anthems with the accordion tunes.

There's a decent restaurant, but the time to come is on Saturday nights (9pm–2am) and Sunday afternoons (3–7pm), when a live band plays ballroom music and traditional French numbers. Entry €12 for non-diners, €45 with a meal. April–Dec.

Guinguette de l'Ile du Martin-Pêcheur 41 quai Victor-Hugo, Champigny-sur-Marne ☎ 01 49 83 03 02, ⓦ guinguette.fr; RER A2 to Champigny-sur-Marne. Traditional and charming rural *guinguette* situated on a shady island in the River Marne. Entry free, dinner around €30. March–May, Sept & Oct Sat 7.30pm–1.30am, Sun noon–6pm; June–Aug Fri 7.30pm–midnight, Sat 7.30pm–1.30am, Sun noon–6pm; Nov & Dec Sat 7.30pm–1.30am.

21

CINÉMATHÈQUE

Film, theatre and dance

Cinema-lovers in Paris have a choice of around three hundred films showing in any one week, taking in contemporary French movies, classics from all eras and international offerings. The city also has vibrant theatre and dance scenes, with innovative, cutting-edge domestic productions jostling with the best shows touring or transferring from across Europe. The famous cabarets, unfortunately – places such as the *Lido* and *Moulin Rouge* – thrive off group bookings for an expensive dinner-and-show formula, and retain none of the bawdy atmosphere depicted in Toulouse-Lautrec's sketches or Baz Luhrmann's film. Listings for all films and stage productions are detailed in *Pariscope* (see p.40), *L'Officiel de Spectacles* and other weeklies, with brief résumés or reviews.

FILM

Paris is truly a cinephiliac's city – one of the few capitals in the world in which you can enjoy not only entertainment but also a wonderful film education from the programmes of regular (never mind specialist) cinemas. **Independent movie houses**, especially in the Quartier Latin, continue to resist the popcorn-touting clout of the big chains, UGC and Gaumont, by screening classic and contemporary films, retrospectives, seasons and all-nighters. Most of these, gratifyingly, are **v.o.** (*version originale*). The unappealing alternative, **v.f.** (*version française*) – which means the film has been dubbed into French – is mostly used for blockbusters, screened in the big chains rather than the independents.

PROGRAMMES AND TICKETS

Séances (programmes) start between 1 and 3pm at many places, though sometimes as early as 10am, and can continue until 10.30pm or so. Tickets rarely need to be bought in advance, and they're not expensive by European standards. We've quoted standard prices below, which usually start at around €9; the cheapest tickets are at the smaller, independent cinemas. There are often considerable discounts for off-peak *séances*, and almost all venues have reductions for students and the unemployed. If you're in town in March, watch out for Printemps du Cinéma (ⓦprintempsducinema.com), when, for a few days, cinemas across the city charge a flat rate of €3.50.

CINÉMATHÈQUES AND CULTURAL INSTITUTIONS

Cultural institutions and embassies often have their own cinema programmes and screenings: the Pompidou Centre (see p.86) runs particularly good seasons. In addition, some of the city's foreign institutes host occasional screenings, so if your favourite director is a Hungarian, a Swede or a Korean, check what's on at those countries' cultural centres. These are listed in *Pariscope* along with other cinema clubs and museum screenings under "*Séances exceptionnelles*", and are usually cheaper than ordinary cinemas.

★**Cinémathèque Française** 51 rue de Bercy, 12ᵉ ☎01 71 19 33 33, ⓦcinematheque.fr; Ⓜ Bercy. This is the best venue in Paris for movie buffs. Along with a museum of cinema (see p.116), you get a choice of around two dozen different films and shorts every week, including retrospectives and silent, and many of which would never be shown commercially – all in an incredible building designed by Frank Gehry. Closed Tues. Tickets €6.50.

Forum des Images 2 rue du Cinéma, Porte St-Eustache, Forum des Halles, 1ᵉʳ; ☎01 44 76 63 00, ⓦforumdesimages.fr; Ⓜ Châtelet-Les Halles/Châtelet. Classic movies, themed seasons, director-led events and festivals, with at least four films (or projected videos) screened a day on its five screens. The Salle des Collections (see p.344) offers individual terminals with digital access to the (huge) archive and some wonderfully obscure titles. Tickets €5; entry to Salle des Collections included.

CINEMAS

★**L'Arlequin** 76 rue de Rennes, 6ᵉ ☎01 45 44 28 80, ⓦarlequin.cine.allocine.fr; Ⓜ St-Sulpice. Owned by Jacques Tati in the 1950s, then by the Soviet Union as the Cosmos cinema until 1990, L'Arlequin is a lovely Left Bank temple to film, showing indie movies, world classics and obscure titles. Tickets €9.60.

Le Champo 51 rue des Ecoles, 5ᵉ ☎01 43 54 51 60, ⓦlechampo.com; Ⓜ Cluny-La-Sorbonne/Odéon. Boho little Latin Quarter cinema at the foot of rue Champollion. Runs themed *v.o.* seasons over a week or more, featuring Oshima, perhaps, or Bernardo Bertolucci. Tickets €9.

★**L'Entrepôt** 7–9 rue Francis-de-Pressensé, 14ᵉ ☎01 45 40 07 50, ⓦlentrepot.fr; Ⓜ Pernety. This Montparnasse alternative cinema has been keeping cine-addicts happy for years with its three screens dedicated to the obscure, the subversive and the brilliant, as well

22

HOME-GROWN FILM

Cinemas and film foundations all over Paris help promote and support the French film industry. The **Fondation Jérôme Seydoux-Pathé** has its headquarters in a Renzo Piano-directed renovation of the old Cinéma Rodin – whose facade was sculpted by Rodin, no less – at 73 av des Gobelins, 13ᵉ; Ⓜ Place de Italie/Les Gobelins (Tues–Fri 1–7pm, Sat 10am–7pm; ☎01 83 79 18 96, ⓦfondation-jeromesey doux-pathe.com). It is primarily a research centre, but also has an exhibition space for temporary shows of posters, stills, programmes and the like, a small gallery of cinematographic equipment from 1896 onwards and a screening room showing silent movies with live accompaniment. Meanwhile, in 2012 the director Luc Besson opened the **Cité Européene du Cinéma** in a former power plant at 20 rue Ampère in the suburb of St-Denis (Ⓜ Carrefour Pleyel; 1hr 30min "behind the scenes" tours €14.90; ⓦciteducinema.org). As a studio complex where film-makers can produce an entire film without having to move off site, the aim, much like at Pinewood Studios in the UK, is to support the work of the French film industry both creatively and financially.

22

FILM FESTIVALS

The **International Festival of Women's Films**, usually held in March or early April, is organized by the Maison des Arts in the southeastern suburb of Créteil, on place Salvador Allende (☎01 49 80 38 98, ⓦfilmsdefemmes.com; ⓜCréteil-Préfecture). At roughly the same time of year, Magic Cinéma, in the suburb of Bobigny, northeast of the city (rue du Chemin-Vert, Bobigny; ⓦmagic-cinema.fr; ⓜBobigny/Pablo-Picasso) runs the festival **Bande(s) à Part au Cinéma**; it concentrates on art-house and new movies (ⓦbandesapart.fr). In the city itself, in early July, a number of the independent cinemas give themselves over for a week to the **Festival Paris Cinéma** (ⓦpariscinema.org), featuring previews of the year to come and celebrations of individual countries' and directors' work; there are usually a couple of alfresco screenings, too.

August offers more alfresco cinephilia. At the **Festival de Cinéma en Plein Air** (ⓦcinema .arbo.com) movies are shown most nights at the Parc de la Villette (ⓜPorte de Pantin), usually at around 10pm, unless it's raining. Entry is free, but you have to pay €7 if you want to rent a deckchair; most people arrive at 7.30pm or so, with a bottle and blanket, and hang out until the sun goes down. The lovely **Cinéma au Clair de Lune** (ⓦforumdesimages.fr), meanwhile, screens films on a set theme, often linked to Paris, in various locations in parks and squares, or projected onto the sides of buildings; films start at 9.30pm, as long as it's not raining, and entry is free.

Other movie events worth looking into include **Quinzaine des Réalisateurs** in May (see p.321) and the **Fête du Cinéma** in June/July (see p.321).

as events and seasons ("Cinema and philosophy", for example). Tickets €8.

L'Escurial Panorama 11 bd de Port-Royal, 13e ☎01 47 07 28 04, ⓦescurial.cine.allocine.fr; ⓜGobelins. Combining plush seats, a big screen, and more art than commerce in its programming policy, this cinema is likely to be showing a French classic on the small screen and the latest offering from a big-name director – French, Japanese or American – on the panoramic screen (never dubbed). Tickets €9.

★**La Filmothèque du Quartier Latin** 9 rue Champollion, 5e ☎01 43 26 70 38, ⓦlafilmotheque.fr; ⓜCluny-La-Sorbonne. Art-house cinema specializing in creative and thoughtful retrospectives, themed seasons and lectures; it has a particular love affair with classic and rediscovered Hollywood movies – the small screening rooms are named after Audrey Hepburn and Marilyn Monroe. Tickets €9.

Grand Action 5 rue des Ecoles, 5e ☎01 43 54 47 62, ⓦlegrandaction.com; **Le Desperado**, 23 rue des Ecoles, 5e ☎01 43 25 72 07, ⓦactioncinemas.com (both ⓜCardinal-Lemoine/Maubert-Mutualité); **Action Christine**, 4 rue Christine, 6e ☎01 43 25 85 78; ⓜOdéon/St-Michel. The Action group focuses on new prints of old classics and screens contemporary films from around the world. Grand Action €9; Le Desperado and Action Christine €8; *carnet* of twelve tickets for all three €45.

★**Le Louxor** 170 bd de Magenta, 10e ☎08 92 68 05 79, ⓦcinemalouxor.fr; ⓜBarbès-Rochechouart. This legendary 1920s moviehouse reopened in 2013 after 25 years dormant. The imposing neo-Egyptian architecture has been restored to its former glory, with three screens showing art-house and mainstream films, as well as hosting festivals and film courses, and a lovely cinema bar. Tickets €9.

Lucernaire 53 rue Notre-Dame-des-Champs, 6e ☎01 45 44 57 34, ⓦlucernaire.fr; ⓜNotre-Dame-des-Champs/Vavin. Arts complex with three screening rooms, theatres, art gallery, bookshop, bar and restaurant. Shows classic art movies and undubbed contemporary releases from around the world. Tickets €8.

Luminor Hôtel de Ville 20 rue du Temple, 4e ☎01 42 78 47 86, ⓦluminor-hoteldeville.com; ⓜHôtel-de-Ville. Interesting and varied range of art-house movies, documentaries, premieres and festivals in a restored and reconditioned 1914 movie house. Tickets €8.50.

Max Linder Panorama 24 bd Poissonnière, 9e ☎08 92 68 50 52, ⓦmaxlinder.cine.allocine.fr; ⓜGrands Boulevards. This Art Deco cinema, with a large screen, always shows films in the original language and has state-of-the-art surround sound. It offers a mixed programme of arty and more mainstream offerings. Tickets €9.50.

MK2 Bibliothèque 128–162 av de France, 13e ☎08 92 69 84 84, ⓦmk2.com; ⓜBibliothèque/Quai de la Gare. Behind the Bibliothèque Nationale, this member of the excellent, citywide MK2 chain is an architecturally cutting-edge cinema with a very cool café and fourteen screens showing *v.o.* movies and a range of French films – mostly new, some classic – along with retrospectives and seasons. Tickets €11.

MK2 Quai de Seine 14 quai de la Seine, 19e ☎08 92 69 84 84, ⓦmk2.com; ⓜJaurès/Stalingrad. You could come to this cinema for the setting alone. It's on the banks of the canal de l'Ourcq, and opposite another MK2 cinema (the Quai de Loire) – both offer a mixed programme that appeals to art-house lovers as well as blockbuster fans. Tickets €11.

Le Nouvel Odéon 6 rue de l'Ecole de Médecine, 6ᵉ ☎ 01 46 33 43 71, ⓦ nouvelodeon.com; ⓜ Odéon/Cluny-La Sorbonne. The renovated Racine Odéon is now an elegant minimalist treat, with an enticing programme featuring some splendid little-seen classics from French and international cinema among its art-house selection. Tickets €9.50.

★ **La Pagode** 57bis rue de Babylone, 7ᵉ ☎ 01 45 55 48 48, ⓦ etoile-cinemas.com/pagode; ⓜ Saint-François-Xavier. The most beautiful of the city's cinemas, built in Japanese style at the end of the nineteenth century to be a rich Parisienne's party place. The wall panels of the Salle Japonaise auditorium are embroidered in silk, golden dragons and elephants hold up the candelabra, and a battle between warriors rages on the ceiling. Shows a mix of art films and documentaries, as well as commercial movies in *v.o.* Lovely garden bar, too. Tickets €9.80.

★ **Reflet Médicis** 3 rue Champollion, 5ᵉ ☎ 01 43 54 42 34, ⓦ lesecransdeparis.fr; ⓜ Cluny-La-Sorbonne.

Three screens showing rare movies and classics, including frequent retrospectives covering directors, both French and international, and world cinema (always *v.o.*). Tickets €9.30.

Rex 1 bd Poissonnière, 2ᵉ ☎ 01 45 08 93 89, ⓦ legrand rex.com; ⓜ Bonne-Nouvelle. A glamorous 1930s cinema with an Art Deco facade, though more often than not the programme features blockbusters – dubbed, if the film is foreign. There's a ceiling of glowing stars and a kitsch, Hollywood-meets-Baroque cityscape inside its colossal (2650-seater), three-storey Grande Salle, which is also used for major concerts. Tickets €10.

★ **Studio 28** 10 rue Tholozé, 18ᵉ ☎ 01 46 06 36 07, ⓦ cinemastudio28.com; ⓜ Blanche/Abbesses. In its early days, after one of the first showings of Buñuel's *L'Age d'Or*, this cinema was done over by extreme right-wing Catholics who destroyed the screen and the paintings by Dalí and Ernst in the foyer. It still hosts avant-garde premieres, followed occasionally by discussions with the director, though nowadays it focuses mainly on the best new releases. The courtyard bar/café is a delight. Tickets €8.50.

THEATRE

Looking at the scores of métro posters in Paris, you might think bourgeois farces starring gurning celebs form the backbone of French theatre. To an extent, that's true, though the classics – Molière, Corneille and Racine – are also regularly performed, and well worth a try if your French is up to it. You can get by with quite basic French at one of the plays by the postwar generation of francophone dramatists, such as Anouilh, Genet, Camus, Ionesco and Samuel Beckett. For non-French-speakers, the most rewarding theatre in Paris is likely to be the genre-busting, radical kind best represented by **Ariane Mnouchkine** and her **Théâtre du Soleil**, based at the Cartoucherie in Vincennes. The best time of all for theatre-lovers to come to Paris is for the **Festival d'Automne** from mid-September to late December (see p.322), an international celebration of all the performing arts, which attracts high-calibre stage directors from around the world. For a useful rundown of the city's theatre and dance scene, including listings, check out the monthly arts journal **La Terrasse**, available from venues and bars and online at ⓦ journal-laterrasse.fr. And for discounted tickets – usually for the more mainstream shows – check ⓦ billetreduc.com.

CAFÉ-THEATRE

Café-théâtre, a revue, monologue or mini-play performed in a place where you can drink, and sometimes eat, is in reality probably less accessible to non-Parisians than a Racine tragedy at the Comédie Française – the humour or dirty jokes, wordplay, and allusions to current fads, phobias and politicians can leave even a fluent French-speaker in the dark. To give it a try, head for one of the main venues concentrated around the Marais. The spaces are small, though you have a good chance of getting in on the night during the week, and tickets are likely to be cheaper than at standard theatres.

Blancs Manteaux 15 rue des Blancs-Manteaux, 4ᵉ ☎ 01 48 87 15 84, ⓦ blancsmanteaux.fr; ⓜ Hôtel-de-Ville/Rambuteau. Revues, plays, stand-up comedy and *chanson*. As well as hosting established names, it encourages new talent and has launched a number of French stars. Tickets €20.

Café de la Gare 41 rue du Temple, 4ᵉ ☎ 01 42 78 52 51, ⓦ cdlg.org; ⓜ Hôtel-de-Ville/Rambuteau.

Founded in 1969, this place retains a reputation for novelty and specializes in stand-up comedy and comic plays. Tickets €10–25.

Point Virgule 7 rue Ste-Croix-de-la-Bretonnerie, 4ᵉ ☎ 01 42 78 67 03, ⓦ lepointvirgule.com; ⓜ Hôtel-de-Ville/St-Paul. With a policy of giving new and up-and-coming performers a chance to shine, this popular venue also offers an eclectic variety of comic acts. Tickets €10–20.

22

PARIS ON FILM

Parisians have had a passionate love affair with cinema since the day the **Lumière** brothers projected their "Cinematograph" at the Parisian *Grand Café du Boulevard des Capucines* in 1895. The 1930s were the golden age of French cinema, with stars of musicals and theatres being showcased in casually censored film vehicles that helped create the French reputation for naughtiness, and *auteurs* scripting, directing and producing moody classics with a gritty, humanist edge. **Jean Renoir**, son of the Impressionist painter Auguste, was among them; check out his *Le Crime de Monsieur Lange* (1935), an affecting Socialist romance set in a print shop in the then-crumbling Marais. The movement known as Poetic Realism grew up around Renoir and the director Marcel Carné, who made the Canal St-Martin area famous in *Hôtel du Nord* (1938), a film that starred Arletty, a great populist actress of the 1930s and 40s. Arletty and Poetic Realism reached their apogee in Carné's wonderful *Les Enfants du Paradis* (1945), set in the theatrical world of nineteenth-century Paris, with a script by the poet Jacques Prévert.

Postwar, Renoir continued to make great films: his *French CanCan* (1955) is *the* film about the *Moulin Rouge* and the heyday of Montmartre. Like the vast majority of prewar films, however, even those with a Parisian setting, it was shot in the studio. An exception to this was Claude Autant-Lara's wartime comedy *La Traversée de Paris* (1956), which follows Jean Gabin smuggling black-market goods across the city. From 1959, however, the directors of the revolutionary **Nouvelle Vague** ("New Wave") took their new, lightweight cameras out onto the streets, abandoning the big studio set pieces in favour of a fluid, avant-garde style in real-life locations. Among seminal works, **Les Quatre Cents Coups** (1959), by François Truffaut, and **A Bout de Souffle** (1959), by Jean-Luc Godard, showcase the city streets to thrilling, kinetic effect. Other key Nouvelle Vague Paris movies include *Paris Vu Par* (*Six in Paris*; 1965), a collection of shorts by the key figures of the genre; and the quirky *Zazie dans le Métro* (1961), which is only outdone for its Parisian locations by Agnès Varda's *Cléo de 5 à 7* (1962), which depicts two hours in the life of a singer as she moves through the city – mainly around Montparnasse.

Following the success of Claude Berri's *Jean de Florette* (1986), French cinema concentrated on "heritage" movies. Few did Paris any favours, although there were a couple of exceptions: Jean-Pierre Jeunet's *Un long dimanche de fiançailles* (2004) re-created the city – including the market pavilions of Les Halles – during World War I, while Bernardo Bertolucci's *Innocents*, or *The Dreamers* (2003), was set in the radical Paris of 1968. In contrast, the **Cinéma du Look** movement captured a cool, image-conscious version of Paris in films like Léos Carax's *Les*

22

Amants du Pont-Neuf (1991), though its bridge was actually a set in the south of France; Jean-Jacques Beineix's *Diva* (1981), which takes in the Bouffes du Nord theatre (18ᵉ); Luc Besson's *Nikita* (1990), with its classic scene in the railway restaurant *Le Train Bleu* (12ᵉ); and Besson's *Subway* (1985), filmed largely in the Auber métro station (15ᵉ).

In the **1990s**, Paris was depicted in a more meditative and less frenetic style. Krzysztof Kieslowski's *Three Colours: Blue* (1993) featured Juliette Binoche as the quintessential melancholy Parisian – and had her swimming in the Pontoise swimming pool (5ᵉ). The premise of Cédric Klapisch's *Chacun cherche son chat* (1995) – *When the Cat's Away* – was the perfect excuse to explore the Bastille quarter in its full, mid-1990s swing. Far edgier is Mathieu Kassovitz's **La Haine** (1996), a savage portrayal of exclusion and racism in the *banlieu*. In the **new millennium**, Kassovitz also had international hits as an actor in the Jeunet-directed *Amélie* (2001) – which relaunched Montmartre as an international tourist destination – and in Gaspar Noé's shocking *Irréversible* (2002), which follows two bourgeois-bohemian Parisians drawn into a nightmare underworld. Equally dark is *Caché* (2005), Austrian director Michael Haneke's haunting story of voyeurism, race and murder set in the Butte-aux-Cailles (13ᵉ), while Cédric Klapisch's *Paris* (2008), a touching ensemble piece seen largely from Romain Duris's Montmartre balcony window, is lighter in tone. Pawel Pawlikowski's psychological thriller *The Woman in the Fifth* (2011), meanwhile, depicts a lonely, empty city in two contrasting locations – a seedy hotel and an elegant Left Bank apartment – but it's back to the suburbs again for Celine Sciamma's *Girlhood* (2014), which, with its almost exclusively black cast and focus on female characters, takes a long-overdue, fresh take on the coming-of-age-in-the-*banlieu* genre.

For **non-French films** with Paris locations, look no further than Vincente Minnelli's musical *An American in Paris* (1951), featuring Gene Kelly and Leslie Caron dancing on the *quais* of the Seine – a scene hilariously homaged in Woody Allen's *Everyone Says I Love You* (1996). Other gems include Billy Wilder's *Love in the Afternoon* (1957); Stanley Donen's musical *Funny Face* (1957) and his comic thriller *Charade* (1963), both starring Audrey Hepburn; Roman Polanski's nightmarish *Frantic* (1988); Richard Linklater's romantic sequel to *Before Sunrise* (1995), *Before Sunset* (2004), featuring Ethan Hawke and Julie Delpy living out a one-night Parisian fantasy; Doug Liman's upmarket thriller *The Bourne Identity* (2002); Woody Allen's sweetly romantic *Midnight in Paris* (2011), whose protagonist roams through a nostalgic dreamworld of 1920s Paris, and, equally bittersweet, Martin Scorsese's love letter to the city, and to cinema itself, *Hugo* (2011). The darkly funny British *Le Week-End* (2013), meanwhile, scripted by Hanif Kureishi, turned the romantic dream upside down in its account of two jaded spouses struggling to rekindle their love in the City of Light.

22

BUYING TICKETS

Booking well in advance is essential for new productions and all shows by the superstar directors. Prices are mostly in the range of €20–40; inexpensive previews are advertised in *Pariscope* and the other listings magazines, and there are discounts at some places for students. Most theatres are closed on Sunday and Monday, and during August. The easiest place to get tickets to see a stage performance in Paris is from one of the Fnac shops (see p.332) or online at W fnac.com, W theatreonline.com or W billetreduc.com (which offers discounts). Same-day tickets with a fifty percent discount (minus a small commission) are available from half-price ticket kiosks (W kiosquetheatre.com) on place de la Madeleine, 8e; opposite no. 15, on the Esplanade de la Gare du Montparnasse, 14e; and on the place des Ternes, 17e (all branches Tues–Sat 12.30–8pm, Sun 12.30–4pm). Queues can be long, however, and tickets are likely to be for the more commercial plays.

VENUES

★ **Bouffes du Nord** 37bis bd de la Chapelle, 10e ☎ 01 46 07 34 50, W bouffesdunord.com; M La Chapelle/Gare du Nord. Groundbreaking theatre director Peter Brook resurrected the derelict Bouffes du Nord in 1974 and was based here until 2011, mounting experimental works, most famously his nine-hour *Mahabharata* in 1985. The gorgeous old theatre's two current French directors, Olivier Mantei and Olivier Poubelle, are continuing Brook's innovative approach.

★ **Cartoucherie** Rte du Champ-de-Manœuvre, 12e; M Château-de-Vincennes. This ex-army barracks is home to several cutting-edge theatre companies: the Théâtre du Soleil (see p.311); the French-Spanish troupe, Théâtre de l'Epée de Bois (☎ 01 48 08 39 74, W epeedebois.com); the Théâtre de la Tempête (☎ 01 43 28 36 36, W la-tempete.fr); and the Théâtre de l'Aquarium (☎ 01 43 74 99 61, W theatredelaquarium.net).

Comédie Française Place Colette, 1er ☎ 01 44 58 15 15, W comedie-francaise.fr; M Palais-Royal. Venerable national theatre that's *the* venue for the French classics: chiefly tragedies and comedies by Molière, Racine and Corneille, but also twentieth-century greats. There are three sites: the Théâtre du Vieux-Colombier, 21 rue du Vieux-Colombier, 6e; the mini Studio-Théâtre, under the Louvre, accessed via the Carrousel, 1er; and the head-quarters, next to the Palais Royal on place Colette, 1er – the Salle Richelieu or "Maison de Molière", as it's dubbed.

Maison des Arts de Créteil (mac) Place Salvador-Allende, Créteil ☎ 01 45 13 19 19, W maccreteil.com; M Créteil-Préfecture. As well as hosting the International Festival of Women's Films (see box, p.310), mac also serves as a lively suburban theatre with a good variety of shows, including for kids; Exit, a festival in March/April

of multicultural and cutting-edge performances, always throws up something interesting.

MC93 9 bd Lénine, Bobigny ☎ 01 41 60 72 60, W mc93 .com; M Bobigny Pablo Picasso. MC93 – Maison de la Culture de la Seine-Saint-Denis – succeeds with its challenging productions, and regularly features foreign directors.

Ménagerie du Verre 12/14 rue Léchevin, 11e ☎ 01 43 38 33 44, W menagerie-de-verre.org; M Parmentier. Multidisciplinary studio devoted to experimental theatre and contemporary dance; their annual festival, Etrange Cargo (March), is always worth a look.

★ **Odéon Théâtre de l'Europe** Place de l' Odéon, 6e ☎ 01 44 85 40 40, W theatre-odeon.eu; M Odéon. This Neoclassical state-funded theatre puts on only European plays – mainly contemporary, although there are some modern interpretations of the classics – as well as *version originale* productions by well-known foreign companies. During May 1968, the theatre was occupied by students and became an open parliament with the backing of its directors.

Le Tarmac 159 av Gambetta, 20e ☎ 01 43 64 80 80, W letarmac.fr; M Saint-Fargeau/Gambetta. Specializing in works from the Francophone world, this passionate and innovative theatre hosts diverse performances from countries such as Guadeloupe, Senegal, Cameroon and Canada.

Théâtre des Amandiers 7 av Pablo-Picasso, Nanterre ☎ 01 46 14 70 00, W nanterre-amandiers.com; RER Nanterre-Préfecture and theatre shuttle bus. Renowned for innovative, challenging and avant-garde productions of classic and contemporary works, including many plays performed in *v.o.*

Théâtre de la Bastille 76 rue de la Roquette, 11e ☎ 01 43 57 42 14, W theatre-bastille.com; M Bastille. One of the best places for new work and fringe productions – in both theatre and dance.

Théâtre du Châtelet Place du Châtelet, 1er ☎ 01 40 28 28 40, W chatelet-theatre.com; M Châtelet. The vogue for musicals is strong in Paris, and the Théâtre du Châtelet is the best place to see them, bringing over Broadway and West End hits, from *Singin' in the Rain* to *My Fair Lady*.

Théâtre de la Huchette 23 rue de la Huchette, 5e ☎ 01 43 26 38 99, W theatre-huchette.com; M St-Michel. More than sixty years on, this intimate little theatre, seating ninety, is still showing Ionesco's *La Cantatrice Chauve* (*The Bald Prima Donna*; 7pm) and *La Leçon* (8pm), two classics of the Theatre of the Absurd, from Tues–Sat.

★ **Théâtre National de Chaillot** Palais de Chaillot, place du Trocadéro, 16e ☎ 01 53 65 30 00, W theatre -chaillot.fr; M Trocadéro. With a beautiful interior and a lobby looking out on to one of the most famous vistas in the world, the Chaillot theatre is worth a trip for the venue alone. It puts on an exciting programme of innovative works, including many foreign productions.

Théâtre National de la Colline 15 rue Malte Brun, 20ᵉ ☎ 01 44 62 52 52, ⓦ colline.fr; ⓜ Gambetta. Dedicated to supporting emerging writers, and known for its modern and cutting-edge productions.

Théâtre Paris Villette 11 av Jean-Jaurès, 19ᵉ ☎ 01 40 03 72 23, ⓦ theatre-paris-villette.fr; ⓜ Porte de Pantin.

Occupying a grand Neoclassical former abattoir in the creative hub of La Villette, this exciting new venue has two stages featuring challenging and fresh new work for kids and adults.

Théâtre de l'Opprimé 78 rue du Charolais, 12ᵉ ☎ 01 43 40 44 44, ⓦ theatredelopprime.com; ⓜ Reuilly-Diderot. A small theatre, inspired by the ideas of Brazilian director Augusto Boal, that puts on mostly contemporary plays.

22

DANCE

Paris is a key player in the nation's dance scene, and regularly hosts the best **contemporary** practitioners. Names worth looking out for include Compagnie Maguy Marin and troupes from Régine Chopinot, Jean-Claude Gallotta, Catherine Diverrès and Angelin Preljocaj. As for **ballet**, the principal stage is at the Opéra Garnier, home to the Ballet de l'Opéra National. It still bears the influence of Rudolf Nureyev, its charismatic, controversial director from 1983 to 1989, and frequently revives his productions. Plenty of space and critical attention are also given to **tap**, **tango**, **folk** and **jazz dancing**, and to international traditional dance troupes. The free monthly arts journal **La Terrasse** (ⓦ journal-laterrasse.fr), available at bars, cafés and arts venues, is a good resource for dance news and events.

VENUES

Centre Mandapa 6 rue Wurtz, 13ᵉ ☎ 01 45 89 01 60, ⓦ centre-mandapa.fr; ⓜ Glacière. Mainly hosts (and gives lessons in) classical Indian dance, but also showcases other music and dance traditions, from Asia and elsewhere.

★**Centre National de la Danse** 1 rue Victor Hugo, Pantin ☎ 01 41 83 98 98, ⓦ cnd.fr; ⓜ Hoche/RER Pantin. Converted from a disused 1970s monolith in the suburb of Pantin into an airy, high-tech space, the national centre for dance is the base for hundreds of French dance companies, and promotes dance through training, workshops and exhibitions. Plus performances, masterclasses, and a huge archive and multimedia library.

Maison des Arts de Créteil (mac) Place Salvador-Allende, Créteil ☎ 01 45 13 19 19, ⓦ maccreteil.com; ⓜ Créteil-Préfecture. Innovative dance and physical theatre in this always interesting theatre/arts venue.

Ménagerie du Verre 12/14 rue Léchevin, 11ᵉ ☎ 01 43 38 33 44, ⓦ menagerie-de-verre.org; ⓜ Parmentier. Creative multidisciplinary studio/performance space encouraging innovation in conceptual dance and physical theatre, with regular shows and a well-regarded annual festival, Etrange Cargo, in March.

★**Opéra Garnier** Place de l'Opéra, 9ᵉ ☎ 08 92 89 90 90, ⓦ opera-de-paris.fr; ⓜ Opéra. This extravagantly decorated opera house is the main home of the Ballet de l'Opéra National and the place to see ballet classics.

Pompidou Centre Entrance rue Beaubourg, 4ᵉ ☎ 01 44 78 16 25, ⓦ centrepompidou.fr; ⓜ Rambuteau. Hosts contemporary performances by visiting companies.

Regard du Cygne 210 rue de Belleville, 20ᵉ ☎ 01 43 58 55 93, ⓦ leregarducygne.com; ⓜ Place des Fêtes/Jourdain. A studio promoting innovative dance in all styles. One of the centre's best-known events is its series of "Sauvages", in which virtually anyone can perform and exchange ideas with other artists and professional dancers.

Théâtre des Abbesses 31 rue des Abbesses, 18ᵉ ☎ 01 42 74 22 77, ⓦ theatredelaville-paris.com; ⓜ Abbesses. Sister company to the Théâtre de la Ville (see p.316), with a slightly more offbeat programme, including international dance.

Théâtre de la Bastille 76 rue de la Roquette, 11ᵉ ☎ 01 43 57 42 14, ⓦ theatre-bastille.com; ⓜ Bastille. As well as new and traditional theatre, this venue also hosts dance and mime performances by young dancers and choreographers.

Théâtre des Champs-Elysées 15 av Montaigne, 8ᵉ ☎ 01 49 52 50 50, ⓦ theatrechampselysees.fr; ⓜ Alma-Marceau. This prestigious venue regularly hosts major foreign troupes and stars from around the world.

DANCE FESTIVALS

Major dance festivals – many of which incorporate theatre, mime and experimental and classical music – include **Faits d'Hiver** throughout January (ⓦ faitsdhiver.com); **Exit festival** in March/April in Créteil (ⓦ maccreteil.com); **Etrange Cargo** at the Ménagerie du Verre, usually held in spring (ⓦ menagerie-de-verre.org); **Les Etés de la Danse** in July (ⓦ lesetesdeladanse .com), held in various venues; **Paris Quartier d'Eté** from mid-July to early August (ⓦ quartierdete.com), which sometimes takes to the streets; and the mighty **Festival d'Automne**, which fills the city with dance fans from mid-September to December (ⓦ festival-automne.com).

Théâtre du Châtelet Place du Châtelet, 4ᵉ ☎ 01 40 28 28 40, ⓦ chatelet-theatre.com; Ⓜ Châtelet. Though mainly used for classical concerts and musicals, it also hosts top-notch international visiting ballet companies as well as commercial and contemporary dance acts.

Théâtre de la Cité Internationale 17 bd Jourdan, 14ᵉ ☎ 01 43 13 50 50, ⓦ theatredelacite.com; RER Cité Universitaire. Three spaces staging an innovative and sometimes provocative programme of theatre, music, dance and circus.

★**Théâtre National de Chaillot** Palais de Chaillot, place du Trocadéro, 16ᵉ ☎ 01 53 65 30 00, ⓦ theatre-chaillot.fr; Ⓜ Trocadéro. Dance from some of France's leading choreographers, as well as regular slots by foreign ballet companies, all add up to a varied and imaginative programme.

★**Théâtre de la Ville** 2 place du Châtelet, 4ᵉ ☎ 01 42 74 22 77, ⓦ theatredelaville-paris.com; Ⓜ Châtelet. The biggest contemporary dance venue in the city, specializing in mainstream and avant-garde productions by French companies as well as working with some of Europe's best choreographers.

PHILHARMONIE DE PARIS

Classical music and opera

Classical music, as you might expect in this Neoclassical city, is alive and
well – and was given even more of a boost in 2015 after the city's top orchestra,
the Orchestre de Paris, took up residence at Jean Nouvel's state-of-the-art
2400-seat Philharmonie de Paris auditorium in La Villette. The Paris Opéra,
meanwhile, with its two homes, puts on a fine selection of opera and ballet,
from core repertoire to new commissions. There's an energetic contemporary
music scene, too, with a major point of focus at IRCAM, near the Pompidou
Centre, and smaller venues elsewhere. The city also hosts a good number of
music festivals; the Chopin and St-Denis festivals, the Fête de la Musique and
Paris Quartier d'Eté (see pp.321–322) are particularly worthwhile.

ESSENTIALS

Tickets Ticket prices for classical concerts depend on the seat, venue and event; opera, ballet and celebrity performers attract higher prices, while churches and museums tend to be relatively inexpensive. You might pay anything from €5 for a recital in a small church, or a restricted-view seat in a big venue to €150 for a stalls seat in a big-name opera, but most seats cost €15–40. Tickets can almost always be bought online; for big names you may find overnight queues at the actual box office.

Listings and information Listings mag *L'Officiel des Spectacles* (ⓦ offi.fr), excellent monthly magazine *Diapason* (ⓦ diapasonmag.fr), devoted to the music scene, and *Opéra* (ⓦ opera-magazine.com), with its emphasis on opera, can be bought at *tabacs* or browsed online. Listings can also be found in *Pariscope*, the free arts mag *La Terrasse* (ⓦ journal -laterrasse.fr), or online at ⓦ concertclassic.com.

CLASSICAL MUSIC

Besides the **Orchestre de Paris**, Paris's other main orchestra is the **Orchestre National de France**, under the baton of Daniele Gatti. **Early music** has a dedicated following; the most respected Baroque ensemble is William Christie's Les Arts Florissants (ⓦ arts-florissants.com), renowned for exciting renditions of Rameau's operas and choral works by Lully and Charpentier. **Contemporary** and **electronic** work flourishes, too. Regular concerts are given at IRCAM, a vast laboratory of acoustics and "digital signal processing", funded by the state and long headed by renowned composer Pierre Boulez, a pupil of Olivier Messiaen, the grand old man of modern French music who died in 1992. Although Boulez no longer conducts the acclaimed Ensemble Intercontemporain (ⓦ ensembleinter.com), based at the Philharmonie de Paris, it still bears its creator's stamp and is committed to performing new work. The following venues host regular concerts, but many other museums and churches – including Notre-Dame cathedral (see p.46) – put on occasional events, including gospel concerts; check *Pariscope* (see p.40).

AUDITORIUMS AND THEATRES

Bouffes du Nord 37bis bd de la Chapelle, 10ᵉ ☎01 46 07 34 50, ⓦ bouffesdunord.com; ⓜ La Chapelle/Gare du Nord; map p.193. This excellent and rather beautiful theatre, famously brought back to life by Peter Brook (see p.314), is also known for its superb chamber music recitals.

Conservatoire National Supérieur de Musique et de Danse de Paris 209 av Jean-Jaurès, 19ᵉ ☎01 40 40 46 47, ⓦ conservatoiredeparis.fr; ⓜ Porte de Pantin; map p.202. Debates, masterclasses and free performances from the Conservatoire's students, based in the Parc de la Villette.

IRCAM (Institut de Recherche et Coordination Acoustique/Musique) 1 place Igor-Stravinsky, 4ᵉ ☎01 44 78 48 43, ⓦ ircam.fr; ⓜ Hôtel-de-Ville; map p.86. IRCAM hosts regular experimental concerts on site and also in the nearby Pompidou Centre and at the Théâtre des Bouffes du Nord.

Maison de Radio France 116 av-du-Président-Kennedy, 16ᵉ ☎01 56 40 15 16, ⓦ radiofrance.fr; ⓜ Passy; map p.216. The radio station France Musique schedules an excellent range of classical music, plus operas and contemporary music, on site (at both the recently renovated Salle 104 and a brand-new, 1461-seat auditorium) and at venues around town – some are free.

Philharmonie 2 221 av Jean-Jaurès, 19ᵉ ☎01 44 84 44 84 ⓦ philharmoniedeparis.fr; ⓜ Porte de Pantin; map p.202. The old Cité de la Musique concert hall, renamed and now rather in the shadow of the adjacent Philharmonie de Paris, still stages concerts in its two auditoriums (capacity 900 and 250), covering anything from traditional Korean music to the Ensemble Intercontemporain, with the occasional airing of instruments from the on-site Musée de la Musique (see p.204).

Philharmonie de Paris 221 av Jean-Jaurès, 19ᵉ ☎01 44 84 44 84, ⓦ philharmoniedeparis.fr; ⓜ Porte de Pantin; map p.202. Designed by celebrated architect Jean Nouvel, the city's long-awaited new concert hall finally opened in 2015. The state-of-the-art structure – a massive (capacity 2400), aluminium-clad angular building, with a zigzagging ramp leading up to the roof – has been likened by some to a huge spaceship. If the exterior seems forbidding by day, at night it looks more inviting, lit up and sparkling, drawing concert-goers up a long elevator to the main entrance. The interior is creamy-warm and soft, with curved balconies dipping down towards the stage; acoustics are excellent and the ambience is intimate. The resident Orchestre de Paris, under conductor Paavo Järvi (due to step down in 2016), and the Ensemble Intercontemporain promise an exciting programme of music-making. The city needed a concert hall of this calibre, but whether it can fulfil its aim of drawing in new audiences from the nearby *banlieues*, as well as luring traditional audiences from the leafy west of Paris, remains to be seen.

Salle Gaveau 45 rue la Boétie, 8ᵉ ☎01 49 53 05 07, ⓦ sallegaveau.com; ⓜ Miromesnil; map pp.64–65. This atmospheric and intimate concert hall, built in 1907, is a major venue for piano recitals by world-class players, and also stages chamber music recitals and full-scale orchestral works.

★**Théâtre des Champs-Elysées** 15 av Montaigne, 8ᵉ ☎01 49 52 50 50, ⓦ theatrechampselysees.fr; ⓜ Alma-Marceau; map pp.64–65. Two-thousand-seater

Modernist theatre, seeping history, with sculptures by Bourdelle and paintings by Vuillard. Opened in 1913, it was the location of the premiere of Stravinsky's *Rite of Spring*, whose modernity scandalized Paris. Now home to the Orchestre National de France and Orchestre de Chamber de Paris (w orchestredechambredeparis.com), it also hosts international orchestras, superstar conductors and ballet troupes, and has a vigorous operatic programme. Tickets for seats with no view at all are a bargain, but you can pay up to €150 or so for star performers.

Théâtre du Châtelet 1 place du Châtelet, 1er ☎ 01 40 28 28 40, w chatelet-theatre.com; Ⓜ Châtelet; map p.86. Prestigious concert hall with a varied programme of high-profile operas, concerts and solo recitals, as well as musical shows (see p.314).

CHURCHES AND MUSEUMS

Auditorium du Louvre Musée du Louvre (Pyramide entrance), 1er ☎ 01 40 20 55 00, w louvre.fr; Ⓜ Louvre-Rivoli/Palais-Royal-Musée-du-Louvre; map p.50. Lunch-time and evening concerts of chamber music, contemporary works and young artists. Tickets from €6.

Eglise de la Madeleine Place de la Madeleine, 8e ☎ 01 42 50 96 18, w eglise-lamadeleine.com; Ⓜ Madeleine; map pp.74–75. Organ recitals, chamber concerts and choral performances; some free, some ticketed, with prices at around €20.

Musée National du Moyen Age 6 place Paul Painlevé, 5e ☎ 01 53 73 78 16, w musee-moyenage.fr; Ⓜ Cluny-La-Sorbonne; map pp.122–123. Regular concerts of little-known medieval music (tickets €12), as well as short choral concerts on Sundays at 4pm and Mondays at 12.30pm (from €4).

Musée d'Orsay 1 rue de Bellechasse, 7e ☎ 01 40 49 47 50, w musee-orsay.fr; Ⓜ Solférino/RER Musée d'Orsay; map pp.136–137. Varied and high-quality programme of recitals and concerts, often themed to link with temporary exhibitions. Tickets €14–35.

St-Eustache 2 impasse Saint-Eustache, 1er ☎ 01 42 36 31 05, w saint-eustache.org; Ⓜ Les Halles; map p.86. This beautiful Gothic church is known for its music, and offers a consistently good programme of chamber music, choral pieces and awe-inspiring (free) organ recitals.

St-Julien-le-Pauvre 1 rue St-Julien-le-Pauvre, 5e ☎ 01 42 26 00 00; Ⓜ St-Michel; map pp.122–123. Mostly chamber music, Chopin and choral recitals. Tickets from €13.

St-Séverin 3–4 rue des Prêtres St-Séverin, 5e ☎ 01 48 24 16 97, w saint-severin.com; Ⓜ Cluny-La-Sorbonne; map pp.122–123. Atmospheric fifteenth-century church offering varied programmes, with tickets from €15.

Sainte-Chapelle 8 bd du Palais, 1er ☎ 01 42 77 65 65; Ⓜ Cité; map pp.44–45. A fabulous setting for mainly Mozart, Bach and Vivaldi classics. Tickets €34–44.

23

OPERA

The venerable Opéra National de Paris has two homes: the **Palais Garnier** and the less appealing **Opéra Bastille**. The more popular productions sell out within days of **tickets** (€5–230) becoming available – note that they go online first. For last-minute tickets, join the queue early at the venues – they go on sale at 11.30am at the Palais Garnier and 2.30pm at Bastille. Unfilled seats are also sold at a discount (€30 or less) to people under the age of 28, 30min before the curtain goes up, and, at the Opera Bastille some standing-room tickets are sold for €5, 1hr 30min before each show. Major multipurpose **performance venues** such as the Palais des Congrès (w viparis.com), the Olympia rock venue (w olympiahall.com), and even the Stade de France stadium (w stadefrance.fr) occasionally stage large-scale opera and musical events – these are usually well advertised.

VENUES

Opéra Bastille Place de la Bastille, 12e w operade paris.fr; Ⓜ Bastille; map pp.110–111. Opened in 1989, this opera house hasn't been entirely successful. The design is unlovable and opinions differ over the acoustics. The stage, at least, is well designed and allows the auditorium uninterrupted views, prices are generally a little lower than at the Palais, and there's no doubting the high calibre of the Bastille orchestra.

Opéra Comique 5 rue Favart, 2e ☎ 08 25 01 01 23, w opera-comique.com; Ⓜ Richelieu-Drouot; map pp.74–75. The venerable Opéra Comique, under its dynamic director Jérôme Deschamps, offers something different – the rich, yet largely forgotten (in some cases with good reason) French opera genre, "opéra comique", of the nineteenth century,

reviving such obscure composers as Hérold and Auber with successful and surprising results.

Opéra Garnier Place de l'Opéra, 9e w operaparis.fr; Ⓜ Opéra; map pp.74–75. An evening in this opulent nineteenth-century opera house, used for ballets and smaller-scale opera productions, is unforgettable. While views from some of the side seats can be poor, the acoustics are excellent.

Péniche Opéra 46 quai de la Loire, 19e ☎ 01 53 35 07 77, w penicheopera.com; Ⓜ Laumière/Jaurès; map p.200. Opera – from operetta to contemporary works – up close and personal on this cute barge. It may lack the grandeur of the big halls, but the immediacy, emotion and sheer atmosphere more than make up for it.

NUIT BLANCHE

Festivals and events

Paris hosts an impressive roster of festivals and events. The city's most colourful jamborees are Bastille Day, on July 14, and the summer-long Paris Plages, but throughout the year there's invariably something on. If it's not one of the big exhibitions, it'll be one of the arts events subsidized by the ever-active town hall or culture ministry. The tourist office can give details of all the mainstream events; otherwise check listings in Paris magazines (see p.40) such as *Pariscope*, or look up "Fêtes et festivals" at ⓦparisinfo.com. Many Parisian *quartiers* such as Belleville, Ménilmontant and Montmartre have open-door weeks when artists' studios are open to the public – keep an eye open for posters and flyers. The following listings give a selection of the most important or entertaining festivals and events in the Paris calendar.

JANUARY/FEBRUARY

Paris Face Cachée (end Jan/early Feb) One-off adventures all over the city that allow you to experience places that are usually closed to the public, or to revisit public spaces from an unusual angle – from meeting the city's river workers to taking behind-the-scenes architectural tours (ⓦ parisfacecachee.fr).

Chinese New Year (mid-Feb) Various celebrations in different neighbourhoods; the main parade weaves through the heart of Chinatown around av d'Ivry in the 13e (ⓦ parisinfo.com).

MARCH

Printemps des Poètes (mid-March) A fortnight featuring thousands of readings, debates, lectures and workshops on the art of *la poésie* (ⓦ printempsdespoetes.com).

Festival de Films des Femmes (mid- to late March) Major women's international film festival (see p.310) held at Créteil, in the southeastern suburbs (ⓦ filmsde femmes.com).

Banlieues Bleues (late March to early April) International festival of jazz and roots music in the towns of Seine-St-Denis – including Aubervilliers, Pantin, St-Ouen and many others (ⓦ banlieuesbleues.org).

APRIL

Marathon International de Paris (early/mid-April) The Paris Marathon departs from the Champs-Elysées and arrives on the avenue Foch 42km later. There's also a half-marathon in March and a 20km run in October, starting at the Eiffel Tower (ⓦ parismarathon.com; ⓦ semideparis .com; ⓦ 20kmparis.com).

MAY

Fête du Travail (May 1) May Day. Everything closes and there are marches and festivities in eastern Paris and around place de la Bastille.

Printemps des Rues (mid-May) Free street theatre and experimental performances in the 18e and around the Canal St-Martin in the 10e (ⓦ leprintempsdesrues.com).

Nuit des Musées (usually third Sat in May) Most of Paris's museums stay open till around midnight, many putting on workshops, talks and concerts (ⓦ nuitdesmusees.culture.fr).

Quinzaine des Réalisateurs (mid-May) Public screenings in the Forum des Images of films from the Cannes alternative film festival (ⓦ quinzaine-realisateurs.com).

Internationaux de France de Tennis (late May and first week June) The French Open tennis championships, on the clay courts of Stade Roland Garros (ⓦ roland garros.com).

Festival Jazz à St-Germain (last week in May) Left Bank jazz festival, featuring big names and new talent from around the world, performing in all manner of venues (ⓦ festivaljazzsaintgermainparis.com).

JUNE

Festival de St-Denis (throughout June) Classical and world music festival with opportunities to hear music in the Gothic St-Denis basilica (ⓦ festival-saint-denis.com).

Weather Festival (early June) House and techno festival with mainstream and underground artists, a 24hr party over the weekend and various afterparties on the Monday (ⓦ weatherfestival.fr).

Fête du Vélo (early June) Cyclists unite, taking to the streets for mass bike rides, picnics and festivities during this France-wide celebration (ⓦ feteduvelo.fr).

La Goutte d'Or en Fête (early to mid-June) Music festival that has extended beyond its rap, reggae and raï roots to embrace music from around the world, with local and international performers, and carnival parades, in the Goutte d'Or district (ⓦ gouttedorenfete.org).

Paris Jazz Festival (early June to late July) Big jazz and world music names give concerts – many of them free – in the Parc Floral at the Bois de Vincennes (ⓦ parisjazzfestival.fr).

Journées d'Architectures à Vivre (second and third weekend of June) More than 450 houses across the country are opened up to the public, with presentations from the architects who designed them (ⓦ journeesavivre.fr).

Festival de Chopin (mid-June to July) Chopin recitals by candlelight or on weekend afternoons, held in the Orangerie de Bagatelle, in the Bois de Boulogne (ⓦ frederic -chopin.com).

Fête de la Musique (June 21) Free concerts in open and public spaces throughout the city; orchestras play in the Palais Royal courtyard, buskers take to the streets and big music venues stage free concerts (ⓦ fetedelamusique .culture.fr).

Gay Pride (late June) France's biggest LGBT Pride march – aka Marche des Fiertés – starting in Montparnasse and ending at Place de Bastille, sees around 650,000 people hit the streets (ⓦ marche.inter-lgbt.org).

Fête du Cinéma (last Sun in June to first Wed in July) A wide range of screenings from classics to the cutting-edge in French and foreign cinema. All tickets cost just €3.50 (ⓦ feteducinema.com).

JULY

Bastille Day (July 14 and evening before) The 1789 surrender of the Bastille is celebrated with parades of tanks down the Champs-Elysées, fireworks and concerts. On the evenings of the 13th and 14th, there's dancing in the streets around Bastille to good French bands, and "Bals des Pompiers" parties rage inside every fire station – rue Blanche and rue du Vieux Colombier are known to be among the best (ⓦ parisinfo.com).

Paris Quartier d'Eté (mid-July to mid-Aug) A broad range of cinema, dance, music, circus and theatre events around the city, in formal venues and public spaces (ⓦ quartierdete.com).

24

Paris Plages (mid-/late July to mid-/late Aug) Wildly popular scheme in which 3km of the Seine *quais* – between the Louvre and Pont de Sully – are transformed into beaches, complete with sand, parasols and deck chairs and outdoor activities. There's also a "beach" at the Bassin de la Villette, where you can muck about in kayaks and pedal boats as well as swim, sail, play volleyball, or simply relax and enjoy a drink, and another on the Left Bank, in front of the Bibliothèque Nationale (13°). All daily 9am–midnight (W paris.fr).

Arrivée du Tour de France (third or fourth Sun in July) The biggest event of the French sporting calendar: the Tour de France cyclists cross the finishing line on the Champs-Elysées (W letour.fr).

Festival de Cinéma en Plein Air (end July to end Aug) Thousands turn up at dusk every night for one of the city's favourite film festivals (see p.310), screening free, open-air, classic and independent movies at the Parc de la Villette (W cinema.arbo.com).

AUGUST

Cinéma au Clair de Lune (early Aug) Alfresco movies, usually relating to Paris, projected onto giant screens in various venues (see p.310), from Montmartre to Parc Montsouris – for free (W forumdesimages.fr).

Rock en Seine (late Aug) Major three-day music festival – artists have included Alt J, Chemical Brothers and the Libertines – in a lovely Seine-side park on the western edge of the city (W rockenseine.com).

SEPTEMBER

Jazz à la Villette (early to mid-Sept) Legendary greats and local conservatory students perform in the various venues in the Parc de la Villette, with a related programme of movie screenings (W jazzalavillette.com).

Fête de l'Humanité (second or third weekend in Sept) Sponsored by the French Communist Party and *L'Humanité* newspaper, this huge three-day event, north of Paris at La Courneuve, mixes excellent French and international music with political and cultural debates. There are more than 450 stands – food, books, art – and a big firework display (W fete.humanite.fr).

Biennale des Antiquaires (mid-Sept) The city's largest antiques show, held over ten days at the Grand Palais, with everything from coins and stamps to art, furniture and jewellery (W sna-france.com).

Festival d'Automne (mid-Sept to late Dec) Major festival of contemporary theatre, music, dance and avant-garde arts, held in around 25 city venues (W festival-automne.com).

Technoparade (mid-Sept) Heralding Paris Electronic Week, which celebrates electronic music in all its forms, this parade attracts hundreds of thousands. The route changes each year, culminating in a major afterparty with dozens of

DJs (W technoparade.fr and W pariselectronicweek.fr).

Journées du Patrimoine (third weekend in Sept) France-wide "heritage days" where normally off-limits buildings are opened to a curious public. Special museum events and workshops, too (W journeesdupatrimoine .culture.fr).

OCTOBER

Festival de l'Imaginaire (Oct–Dec) Musical performances, screenings and workshops showcasing traditional cultures from around the world (W festivaldelimaginaire.com).

Fêtes des Vendanges (early Oct) Five-day festival in Montmartre, celebrating the grape harvest of the local vineyard with talks, exhibitions, concerts, tastings, artisan food stalls, a parade and fireworks, and an associated programme of poetry events (W fetedesvendangesde montmartre.com).

Nuit Blanche (first Sat in Oct) Wildly popular citywide event, from 7pm to 7am, that brings together musicians, artists, circus acts and all sorts to create an unforgettable night of stunning spectacles – underwater dancers in vertical tanks, a giant crescent moon being hoisted onto the St-Eustache church, live chemical reactions in glass beakers projected onto the side of the Hôtel de Ville. (W paris.fr).

Foire Internationale d'Art Contemporain (FIAC) (third week in Oct) International contemporary art fair taking place over several days at the Grand Palais and outdoor spaces such as the Jardin des Tuileries and Berges de Seine (W fiac.com).

NOVEMBER

Festival les Inrocks (early Nov) International indie rock – in all its forms, from folk to electronica – at a range of venues. Previous acts have included The Jesus and Mary Chain, Lykke Li and Palma Violets (W lesinrocks.com).

Paris Photo (mid-Nov) Held at the Grand Palais, this four-day event is one of the world's largest and most impressive photography events, showing international work from early images to modern masterpieces (W paris photo.com).

Beaujolais Nouveau Day (late Nov) Oenophiles flock to the streets to taste the first Beaujolais nouveau *vin de primeur*, released for sale on the third Thursday in Nov.

DECEMBER

Noël (Dec 24–25) Christmas Eve is a huge affair, much more important than the following day. Notre-Dame, the Eglise de la Madeleine and the Basilique du Sacré-Coeur hold midnight Mass services.

Le Nouvel An (Dec 31) New Year's Eve means dense crowds of out-of-towners on the Champs-Elysées, fireworks at the Champs de Mars and super-elevated restaurant prices everywhere.

24

AGNÈS B

Shops and markets

Paris is almost as fabled for shopping as it is for gastronomy and romance. From the flagship "concept stores" of Europe's glitziest couture houses to the humblest of neighbourhood bakeries, you'll find throughout the city an obsession with quality and style, and a fierce pride in detail. Supermarkets and chains have made small advances in the city, but Parisians, for the most part, remain loyal to local traders and independently owned shops. Whether you can afford to buy or not, some of the most entertaining experiences of a trip to Paris are to be had for free just browsing in small boutiques, their owners proudly displaying their cache of offbeat items, particular passions and mouthwatering treats.

25

WHERE TO SHOP IN PARIS

The smartly renovated nineteenth-century covered **arcades**, or *passages*, in the **2e and 9e arrondissements** offer distinctive and unusual shopping possibilities, from toy shops and independent designers to antique book stores and wine cellars. On the streets proper, the square kilometre around **place St-Germain-des-Prés** is hard to beat – for window-shopping at least; to the north of the square, the narrow streets are lined with antique shops and arts and interior design stores, while to the south, and in particular along **rue du Cherche Midi**, are designer clothing brands and the famed Le Bon Marché department store. St-Germain is also good for classy food outlets. The other major department stores, Galeries Lafayette and Printemps, are on **Boulevard Haussmann**, which also boasts some good independent shops and concept stores in the surrounding streets.

The **Marais** (focused on rues Vieille du Temple, Poitou and Charlot) and the hip **Bastille** *quartier* have filled up with dinky little boutiques, arty interior design stores, specialist shops and galleries, many of them quite pricey; northeastern Paris (**Oberkampf** and the **Canal St-Martin**) and Bercy are heading that way, but for now remain more affordable. **Montmartre** (in particular around Abbesses and rue des Martyrs) is a good hunting ground for independent fashion and upmarket food; for Parisian **haute couture**, the traditional bastions are avenue Montaigne, rue François-1er, and the upper end of **rue du Faubourg-St-Honoré** in the 8e, while **Les Halles** is good for high-street fashion.

Place de la Madeleine is the place to head for seriously luxury **food** stores, such as Fauchon and Hédiard, while the Latin Quarter is bookshop and graphic novel terrain. For essentials, cheap supermarket chains include Dia. Other last-minute or convenience shopping is probably best done at Fnac shops (for books and records), the big department stores (for high-quality merchandise) and Monoprix (for basics).

ESSENTIALS

Opening hours Many shops in Paris stay open all day Monday to Saturday. Most tend to close comparatively late – 7 or 8pm as often as not. Some smaller businesses close for up to two hours at lunchtime, somewhere between noon and 3pm.

Sunday trading Most shops are closed on Sunday and some on Monday as well. An exception is made for the shops in the major tourist zones, which gives these areas – some of which are also pedestrianized on that day – a pleasant, relaxed buzz. Sunday zones include the Butte Montmartre, around Abbesses (18e); the Marais, between place des Vosges and rue des Francs-Bourgeois (3e–4e); the Viaduc des Arts (12e); rue d'Arcole, on the Île de la Cité (4e); boulevard St-Germain (6e); rue de Rivoli (1er); the Carrousel du Louvre (1er) and the Champs-Elysées (8e). Note too that many food shops, especially boulangeries, are open on Sunday morning.

VAT It's worth researching VAT reimbursement for non-EU citizens (see p.39).

CLOTHES, SHOES AND ACCESSORIES

Milan, New York and London are fierce contenders, but Paris remains the world capital of **fashion**. As a tourist, you may not be able to get into the haute couture shows, but there's nothing to prevent you trying on fabulously expensive creations – as long as you can brave the intimidatingly chic assistants and the awesome chill of the marble portals. But if it's actual shopping you're interested in, there are plenty of good areas to browse and affordable, interesting shops to discover. **Sales** are held twice a year, generally beginning in mid-January and mid-July and lasting about a month, while ends of lines and old stock from the couturiers are sold year-round in "stock" **discount** shops (see p.328), or at La Vallée Outlet, inside the frontiers of Disneyland (see p.328).

DEPARTMENT STORES AND HYPERMARKETS

Le BHV Marais 52–64 rue de Rivoli, 4e ⓦ bhv.fr; ⓜ Hôtel-de-Ville; map p.97. Just two years younger than Le Bon Marché and noted for its homewares, artists' materials and menswear, with the womenswear and shoe departments in particular worth a look. The store is less elegant in appearance than some of its rivals, but the range is good. Mon, Tues & Thurs–Sat 9.30am–8pm, Wed 9.30am–9pm.

★ **Le Bon Marché** 24 rue de Sèvres, 7e ⓦ lebonmarche .com; ⓜ Sèvres-Babylone; map pp.136–137. The world's oldest department store, founded in 1852 and now run by the luxury goods empire LVMH. It's smaller, calmer and classier than Galeries Lafayette and Printemps, and has an excellent kids' department and a legendary food hall (see box, p.334). Mon–Wed & Sat 10am–8pm, Thurs & Fri 10am–9pm.

Galeries Lafayette 40 bd Haussmann, 9ᵉ ⓦgaleries lafayette.com; ⓜHavre-Caumartin; map pp.74–75. The store's forte is high fashion, with two floors given over to the latest creations by leading designers; the fourth floor has a huge selection of lingerie, the basement is for shoes, and there's a large children's clothes section on the fifth floor. Then there's a host of big names in men's and women's accessories, a huge parfumerie and a branch of *Angélina salon de thé*, all under a superb 1912 dome. Just down the road at no. 35 is Lafayette Maison/Gourmet, its five floors split between quality kitchenware, linens and furniture, and luxury food and wine. Mon–Sat 9.30am–8pm, Thurs till 9pm; Lafayette Gourmet Mon–Sat 8.30am–9.30pm.

★**Printemps** 64 bd Haussmann, 9ᵉ; ⓜHavre-Caumartin; Carrousel du Louvre, 99 rue de Rivoli, 1ᵉʳ; ⓜLouvre-Rivoli; ⓦdepartmentstoreparis.printemps .com; map pp.74–75. The beautiful *belle époque* store on Haussmann is in a glorious building full of decorative flourishes; Printemps' iconic sixth-floor brasserie sits right underneath the stunning stained-glass dome. With a big range of high-end brands, the store is actually divided into three – the women's store, devoted to fashion, shoes and accessories; the beauty/home store, which includes children's gear and food (and has a rooftop terrace restaurant with panoramic views); and the seven-storey men's store. The branch in the Carrousel du Louvre (the only luxury department store that opens on Sunday) focuses on leather goods, make-up, jewellery and watches. Bd Haussmann Mon–Sat 9.35am–8pm, Thurs till 8.45pm; Carrousel du Louvre daily 10am–8pm.

Tati 4–18 bd Rochechouart, 18ᵉ; ⓜBarbès; map p.182; 174 rue du Temple, 3ᵉ; ⓜTemple; map p.94; ⓦtati.fr. Budget department store chain with a distinctive pink-gingham logo, selling reliable and cheap clothing, among a host of other items, from toiletries to trainers. A staple for bargain-hunters, with other branches across the city. Bd Rochechouart Mon–Fri 10am–7pm, Sat 9.30am–7pm; rue du Temple Mon–Fri 9.30am–7.30pm, Sat 10am–7pm.

HIGH FASHION AND FRENCH CHIC

agnès b. 6 & 10 rue du Vieux Colombier, 6ᵉ; ⓜSt-Sulpice; map pp.136–137; 2, 3 & 6 rue du Jour, 1ᵉʳ ⓜChâtelet-Les-Halles; map p.86; ⓦeurope.agnesb .com. Born in Versailles, this queen of understatement (it's pronounced "ann-yes bay") favours cool, simple staples – matelot shirts, straw hats and the like. While the line has expanded into watches, sunglasses and cosmetics, her clothing for men, women and kids remains chic, timeless and relatively affordable. Rue du Vieux Colombier (both branches) Mon–Sat 10am–7.30pm; 3 & 6 rue du Jour Oct–April Mon–Sat 10am–7.30pm; May–Sept Mon–Fri 10.30am–7.30pm, Sat 10am–7.30pm; 4 rue du Jour Oct–April Mon–Sat 10am–7pm; May–Sept Mon–Sat 10.30am–7.30pm.

Ba&sh 22 rue des Francs-Bourgeois, 3ᵉ ⓦba-sh.com; ⓜSt-Paul; map p.97. Barbara Boccara and Sharon Krief produce modern, chic and easy-to-wear women's clothes in quality materials such as silk and cashmere. Their hallmarks are slouchy tops and short tunic dresses, with most items in the €120–200 range. There are other branches at 215 St Honoré and 21 rue Etienne Marcel (both 1ᵉʳ), 59 rue Bonaparte (6ᵉ) and 80 rue des Sts-Pères (7ᵉ). Mon–Sat 11am–7.30pm, Sun noon–7pm.

Chanel 31 rue Cambon, 1ᵉʳ ⓦchanel.com; ⓜMadeleine/Opéra; map pp.74–75. Karl Lagerfeld is currently at the helm of the iconic brand, which retains the elegance and classic style of Coco's conception while continuing to offer new, modern interpretations of the classic suits and little black dresses. Mon–Sat 10am–7pm.

Comptoir des Cotonniers 30 rue de Buci, 6ᵉ; ⓜMabillon; map pp.136–137; 33 rue des Francs-Bourgeois, 4ᵉ; ⓜSt-Paul; map p.97; 41 rue des Abbesses, 18ᵉ; ⓜAbbesses; map p.182; ⓦcomptoirdes cotonniers.com. Hugely popular, upmarket French chain stocking well-cut, elegant women's basics that nod to contemporary fashions without being faddish. Trousers, shirts and dresses from around €110. There are around thirty branches in Paris; these three represent a good range. Rue de Buci Mon–Sat 11am–8pm; rue des Francs-Bourgeois Mon 11am–7.30pm, Tues–Sun 11am–8pm; rue des Abbesses Mon 11am–7pm, Tues–Fri 10.30am–7.30pm, Sat 10.30am–8pm.

Isabel Marant 16 rue de Charonne, 11ᵉ ⓦisabel marant.com; ⓜBastille/Ledru-Rollin; map pp.110–111. Parisian Marant has an international reputation for her feminine and flattering clothes, including elegantly tapered trousers, wedged trainers, and ruffled, floaty tops and dresses, and her more affordable line, Etoile. There are other branches at 1 rue Jacob (6ᵉ), 47 rue de Saintonge (3ᵉ) and 151 av Victor Hugo (16ᵉ). Mon 11am–7pm, Tues–Sat 10.30am–7.30pm.

Kabuki 25 rue Etienne-Marcel, 1ᵉʳ ⓦkabukiparis .tumblr.com; ⓜEtienne-Marcel; map pp.74–75. A one-stop concept store for all your Balenciaga, Balmain and Givenchy needs, along with a number of other couture designers. There's a men's store two doors down. Mon–Sat 11am–7pm.

Lanvin 15 (men) & 22 (women, children and accessories) rue du Faubourg-St-Honoré, 8ᵉ ⓦlanvin .com; ⓜConcorde; map pp.64–65. One of the first French fashion houses, Lanvin epitomizes classic French elegance, although the designs of the originally Breton label often incorporate idiosyncrasies such as taffeta trench coats, satin capes, and removable cuffs and collars. Mon–Sat 10.30am–7pm.

25

Maison Fabre Jardins du Palais Royal 128–129, Galerie de Valois, 1er ⓦ maisonfabre.com; ⓂPalais-Royal-Musée-du-Louvre; map pp.74–75. Gloves to die for, from another era: butter-soft leather, with a classic chic that could only be French. Prices start at around €90; for a special treat you could order a bespoke pair. Mon–Sat 11am–7pm.

★**Maje** 49 rue Vieille du Temple, 4e; ⓦ maje.com; Ⓜ St-Paul; map p.97. This Paris-based but now international brand offers utterly Parisian clothes: relaxed, slightly bohemian, cool and always elegant. This is a sizeable store, offering a good choice; there are many other branches around town. Mon–Sat 10.30am–7.30pm, Sun 1–7pm.

★**Paul & Joe** 62–66 rue des Sts-Pères, 7e; ⓂSèvres-Babylone; map pp.136–137; ⓦ paulandjoe.com. The clothes here are quintessentially French: quirky but not overly showy, playful but not overly radical – for men and women alike. As long as you've got a slim, French-style figure to match, Paul & Joe will magically transform you into a chic Parisian. There are seven branches in Paris, including Paul & Joe Sister, the slightly more youthful offshoot. Mon–Sat 10am–7pm.

Saint Laurent 32 (men) & 38 (women) rue du Faubourg-St-Honoré, 8e; ⓂConcorde; map pp.64–65; 6 place St-Sulpice (women), 6e; ⓂSt-Sulpice/Mabillon; map pp.136–137; ⓦ ysl.com. Though the man himself has gone, his pioneering designs and brand live on, currently under the direction of LA-based Hedi Slimane. Classic monochrome chic remains the staple for men while womenswear swings from rock'n'roll to ultra-feminine according to the season. All branches Mon 11am–7pm, Tues–Sat 10.30am–7pm.

Sandro 47 rue des Francs-Bourgeois, 4e; ⓂHôtel-de-Ville; map p.97; discount "stock" shop 26 rue de Sévigné, 4e; ⓂHôtel-de-Ville; map p.97; ⓦ sandro-paris.com. With more than forty outlets around the city, most of them in the main shopping areas, you won't need to look far to find this chic French brand, whose stock in trade is classic separates in block colours and feminine shorts, minis and tailored trousers. Their men's gear is a tad more casual. Rue des Francs-Bourgeois daily 10am–8pm; rue de Sévigné Mon–Sat 10am–7.30pm, Sun 11am–7pm.

Sonia by Sonia Rykiel 6 rue de Grenelle, 6e ⓦ soniaby.com; ⓂSt-Sulpice; map pp.136–137. This less expensive (roughly €120–350) offshoot of the Rykiel brand is younger, fresher and more everyday in feel, but still features the signature Gallic stripes, flounces and slogan Ts and enjoys playful use of colour. There's another good branch at 37 rue de Poitou (3e). Mon–Sat 10.30am–7pm.

Sonia Rykiel 175 bd St-Germain, 6e; ⓂSt-Germain-des-Prés; map pp.136–137; 70 rue du Faubourg Saint-Honoré, 8e; ⓂConcorde; map pp.64–65; ⓦ soniarykiel.com.

CLOTHES SHOPPING IN THE FASHION CAPITAL

For designer prêt-à-porter, the **department stores** Galeries Lafayette and Printemps (see p.325) have unrivalled selections; if you're looking for a one-stop hit of Paris fashion, this is probably the place to come.

For couture and seriously expensive designer wear, head to the wealthy, manicured streets around the **Champs-Elysées**, especially rue François-1er, avenue Montaigne, avenue George V and **rue du Faubourg-St-Honoré**. Younger designers have colonized the lower reaches of the last street, between rue Cambon and rue des Pyramides. In the heart of this area, luxurious **place Vendôme** abounds in top-end jewellery.

A notch or two down in terms of price is the compact area around **St-Sulpice** métro, on the Left Bank. You'll find a host of upscale French clothing brands in **St-Germain** on rues du Vieux Colombier, de Rennes, Madame, de Grenelle and du Cherche-Midi; the chichi department store, Le Bon Marché, is a stone's throw away on rue de Sèvres.

On the eastern side of the city, around the **Marais** and **Bastille**, the clothes, like the residents, are younger, cooler and more relaxed. Chic boutiques line the Marais' main shopping street, **rue des Francs-Bourgeois**, and there are good indie options on rues Charlot, de Saintonge, de Turenne and de Poitou. Young, cool designers and some good secondhand outlets congregate on Bastille's **rue de Charonne** and **rue Keller**. The further east you head, via the trendy Canal St-Martin (especially along rue Beaurepaire and rue de Marseille) and toward multicultural Belleville and Ménilmontant, the more alternative the shops become.

Also at the more alternative end of the spectrum, there's a selection of the hipper high-street names and one-off designer boutiques at the foot of Montmartre spreading down south of Pigalle – try rues des Martyrs, des Trois Frères, de la Vieuville, Houdon and Durantin. **Rue Etienne-Marcel** is good for high-end boutiques, while there are plenty of cheaper offerings in the **Forum des Halles** mall and surrounding roads, and a clutch of discount clothes shops in the southern arrondissements.

Unmistakeably Parisian designer who brought out her first line when the *soixante-huitards* threw Europe into social revolution, and whose early customers included Brigitte Bardot and Audrey Hepburn. Her elegant multicoloured designs – especially those stripy sweaters – are still all the rage. Both branches Mon–Sat 10.30am–7pm.

★**Spree** 16 rue de la Vieuville, 18ᵉ ⓦspree.fr; ⓜAbbesses; map p.182. A gallery-like concept store whose hip, feminine clothing collection is led by designers such as Isabel Marant and Christian Wijnants. Often a few vintage pieces, too, plus bigger-brand lines (Comme des Garçons, for instance), accessories, homeware and furniture. Clothing mostly €200–500. Sun & Mon 3–7pm, Tues–Thurs 11am–7.30pm, Fri & Sat 10.30am–7.30pm.

Vanessa Bruno 25 rue St-Sulpice, 6ᵉ; ⓜOdéon; map pp.136–137; 12 rue de Castiglione, 1ᵉʳ; ⓜTuileries; map pp.64–65; 100 rue Vieille du Temple, 3ᵉ; ⓜSaint-Sébastien-Froissart; map p.97; ⓦvanessabruno.com. Typically sophisticated, effortlessly beautiful women's fashions from the Parisian model turned designer, with a hint of hippie chic and lots of pretty draped tailoring. Around €260 for a top or skirt. Rue St-Sulpice & rue de Castiglione Mon–Sat 10am–7pm; rue Vieille du Temple Mon 12.30–7.30pm, Tues–Sat 10.30am–7.30pm, Sun 2–7pm.

Zadig & Voltaire 1 rue du Vieux Colombier, 6ᵉ; ⓜSt-Sulpice; map pp.136–137; discount outlet range 22 rue du Bourg-Tibourg, 4ᵉ; ⓜHôtel-de-Ville; map p.97; ⓦzadig-et-voltaire.com. The women's clothes at this upmarket chain focus on urban chic, with tailored pieces, dark tones, skinny pants and textured fabrics, and sporty and tailored styles for men. Tops from around €130. There are more than twenty branches. Rue du Vieux Colombier Mon–Sat 10.30am–7.30pm; rue du Bourg-Tibourg Mon–Fri 11am–7pm, Sat 11am–7.30pm, Sun 2–7.30pm.

BOUTIQUES AND STREETWEAR

Le 66 66 av des Champs-Elysées, 8ᵉ ⓦle66.fr; ⓜFranklin-D.-Roosevelt; map pp.64–65. High-end trainers and streetwear labels such as Evisu, Raf Simons, American Retro and Acne for men and women. Jeans from €100, T-shirts from €50. Mon–Fri 11am–8pm, Sat 11am–8.30pm, Sun 1–8pm.

★**Antoine et Lili** 95 quai de Valmy, 10ᵉ; ⓜRépublique; map p.198; 51 rue des Francs-Bourgeois, 4ᵉ; ⓜSt-Paul; map p.97; 90 rue des Martyrs, 18ᵉ; ⓜAbbesses; map p.182; ⓦantoineetlili.com. Quirky Parisian institution, with a flagship store on Quai de Valmy whose three neighbouring candy-coloured frontages (one for women's clothes, one for kids, and one for homeware) light up the Canal St-Martin. There are several branches across the city, each as colourful. The women's and children's clothes and accessories, best described as ethnic revisited, have a dose

of kitsch and an emphasis on fun. Dresses and trousers start at around €100. Shoes and colourful homeware, too. Quai de Valmy Mon–Fri 10.30am–7.30pm, Sat 10am–8pm, Sun 11am–7pm; rue des Francs-Bourgeois Mon–Fri 10.30am–7.30pm, Sat 10.30am–8pm, Sun 11am–7.30pm; rue des Martyrs Mon 11am–2pm & 3–8pm, Tues–Fri 11am–8pm, Sat 10am–8pm, Sun 11am–1pm & 2–7pm.

★**APC** 38 rue Madame, 6ᵉ; ⓜSt-Sulpice; map pp.136–137; 3 bd des Filles du Calvaire, 3ᵉ; ⓜSt-Sébastien-Froissart; map p.94; APC Surplus 20 rue André del Sarte, 18ᵉ; ⓜBarbès-Rochechouart; map p.182; ⓦapc.fr. This chain is perfect for young, urban basics. Simple cuts and fabrics create a minimal, Parisian look – with tops from €85. The main shop is on rue Madame, but there are seven branches and counting, with a handy outlet on Filles du Calvaire in the Marais, and APC Surplus selling discounted over-stock items. Rue Madame Mon–Sat 11am–7.30pm; bd des Filles du Calvaire Mon–Sat 10am–7.30pm; APC Surplus Mon–Sat noon–7.30pm.

Autour du Monde 12 rue des Francs-Bourgeois, 4ᵉ ⓦbensimon.com; ⓜSt-Paul; map p.97. Bensimon, known for their cute canvas sneakers in eye-popping colours (from around €30) also sell casual clothes at this bright, youthful store. A second branch at no. 8, a few doors down, extends the brand into homeware. Mon–Sat 11am–7pm, Sun 1.30–7pm.

Colette 213 rue St-Honoré, 1ᵉʳ ⓦcolette.fr; ⓜTuileries; map pp.74–75. This cutting-edge concept store, combining high fashion, design and cool gadgetry – and complete with photo gallery and exhibition space – makes high couture accessible to the fashionista masses. When you've finished sizing up the Pucci undies, Stella McCartney womenswear and Valentino jackets, you could settle for a pair of funky reading glasses or a selfie stick – gift items start at around €6. Mon–Sat 11am–7pm.

La Fausse Boutique 32 rue Pierre Fontaine, 9ᵉ; ⓜBlanche; map p.97; 19 rue des Ecouffes, 4ᵉ; ⓜSt-Paul; map p.97; ⓦlafausseboutique.com. Unique, edgy and playful one-offs from French and international designers, with separates for men and women, from simple vests to glamorous capes, funky sneakers to statement jewellery, plus gifts. Rue Pierre Fontaine Mon–Sat noon–7.30pm; rue des Ecouffes daily 12.30–7.30pm.

★**Sessùn** 34 rue de Charonne, 11ᵉ ⓦsessun.com; ⓜLedru-Rollin; map pp.110–111. The bright and spacious boutique on this trendy shopping street sells all the womenswear you could want, from pretty prints and elegant winter coats to cosy knits and basic Ts. Prices start at around €100 – good value given the quality. Mon–Sat 11am–7pm.

Swildens 18 rue du Vieux Colombier, 6ᵉ; ⓜSt-Sulpice; map pp.136–137; surplus store 22 rue de Poitou, 3ᵉ; ⓜSt-Sébastien-Froissart; map p.97; ⓦswildens.fr.

Juliette Swildens designs well-cut clothes for women and teens with a hint of vintage styling. Typical are off-the-shoulder smocks, slouchy sweatshirts, tailored blazers and layered knits (prices around €130–300). There are other branches at 16 rue de Turenne (4e), 9 rue Guichard (6e) and 16 bd des Filles du Calvaire (11e). Rue du Vieux Colombier Mon–Fri 10.30am–7pm; rue de Poitou Mon–Sat 11am–7.30pm, Sun 2–7pm.

DISCOUNTED DESIGNER FASHION

A number of dedicated "stock" shops (short for *déstockage*) sell end-of-line and last year's collections at thirty- to fifty-percent reductions, while the best of the many consignment stores – *dépôts-vente* – sell preloved couture and designer clothes for hundreds of euros off retail. The best times of year to join the scrums are after the new collections have come out in January and October.

Défilé de Marques 171 rue de Grenelle, 7e ⓦmondepotvente.com; ⓜLa Tour-Maubourg; map pp.136–137. Wide choice of designer clothing for women – last season's lines returned unsold from the big-name boutiques, plus some vintage. Labels from Chanel to YSL via Alexander McQueen and Prada, for around €300–700 for jackets, half that for shoes, or as little as €50 for accessories. Tues–Sat 1–8pm.

Madame de 65 rue Daguerre, 14e ⓦmadamede.fr; ⓜDenfert-Rochereau; map pp.162–163. There's a good mix in this *depot-vente*, from last season's Isabel Marant to some vintage couture, all of it in great nick. Tues–Fri 11am–7.30pm, Sat 11am–6.30pm.

Réciproque 89, 92, 93–97 & 101 rue de la Pompe, 16e ⓦreciproque.fr; ⓜPompe; map p.216. This *dépôt-vente* spreads along the street, offering pre-owned haute couture from names including Christian Lacroix, Moschino and Manolo Blahnik. There are three womenswear shops – no. 93 concentrates on evening wear; no. 95 couture, casualwear, sportswear and accessories; no. 101 accessories, bags, jewellery and swimsuits. No. 92 is the mens' store, and no. 89 sells gifts and jewellery. No. 97 is for deposits. Tues–Fri 11am–7pm, Sat 10.30am–7pm.

La Vallée Inside Disneyland Paris boundary ⓦlavallee village.com; map p.250. Outlet shopping village, best for discounted designer labels, with more than one hundred names including Armani, Burberry, Calvin Klein and the like. Mon–Fri & Sun 10am–7pm, Sat 10am–8pm.

SECONDHAND AND VINTAGE

The vintage scene is going from strength to strength in Paris, from the *dépôts-vente* selling last-season's clothes to smaller thrift-store-type outlets, often referred to as *friperies*. In addition to the places reviewed here, try the flea markets at Porte de Montreuil (see p.339) and St Ouen (see p.223).

Casablanca 17 rue Moret, 11e ⓣ09 80 56 54 75; ⓜCouronnes; map p.208. Cool vintage store – with its own little dog – near Oberkampf, with lots of Thirties, Forties and mid-century gear and a particularly good line in natty men's suits. A visiting barber offers vintage haircuts. Mon–Sat 2–7pm.

Chezel 59 rue Condorcet, 9e; ⓜPigalle; map p.182. One of the best of three or four (the others come and go) little vintage fashion shops on this street. Prices from €30 to easily five times that for a classic – some serious designer-wear finds its way here. Tues–Fri noon–7.30pm, Sat 11.30am–7.30pm.

Free "P" Star 52 & 61 rue de la Verrerie, 4e; ⓜHôtel-de-Ville; map p.86; 20 rue de Rivoli, 4e; ⓜSt-Paul; map p.97; ⓦfreepstar.com. Small chain of very popular vintage clothing shops, with racks of Lacoste polo shirts, 1970s floral dresses, inexpensive Levis, army surplus, Twenties flapper gear, leather jackets and more. Many items €10–30. 52 & 61 rue de la Verrerie Mon–Sat 11am–9pm, Sun 2–9pm; rue de Rivoli Mon–Sat 10am–9pm, Sun noon–9pm.

★**Kiliwatch** 64 rue Tiquetonne, 2e ⓦespacekiliwatch .fr; ⓜEtienne-Marcel; map pp.74–75. You'll have no problem coming up with an original outfit in this vast store, where vintage duds meet cheap'n'chic streetwear: match cool trainers/sneakers with army surplus, lumber-jack shirts, 70s boho gear and a great selection of vintage women's shoes. It's also *the* place to buy jeans, with loads of brands. Mon 10.30am–7pm, Tues–Sat 10.30am–7.30pm.

Kilo Shop 69–71 rue de la Verrerie, 4e; ⓜHotel-de-Ville; map p.86; 125 bd St-Germain, 6e; ⓜMabillon; map pp.136–137; ⓦkilo-shop.fr. A popular concept – everything is sold by weight (€20–60/kg) so you can pile up your basket with retro casual gear (Levis, combat jackets, lacy shirts, Eighties sweats) and tot up costs on the scales provided. Rue de la Verrerie Mon 2–7.45pm, Tues–Fri 11am–7.45pm, Sat 11am–8pm, Sun 2–7.45pm; bd St-Germain Mon–Sat 11am–7.45pm, Sun 1–7.45pm.

Mamz'Elle Swing 35 bis rue du Roi de Sicile, 4e; ⓜSt-Paul; map p.97. True to its name, this cute little Marais store specializes in Fifties and Fifties-style frocks, with a variety of styles from simple cotton daywear to fancy netted cocktail dresses, plus lingerie and accessories. Mon–Sat 2–7pm, Sun 3–7pm.

★**Violette & Léonie** 114 rue de Turenne, 3e ⓦviolette leonie.com; ⓜFilles-du-Calvaire/St-Sébastien-Froissart; map p.94. This secondhand shop looks so smart you'd think it was a designer boutique, and its decent range of stock, from high-end labels to H&M and Zara, is in great condition. Mon 1–7.30pm, Tues–Sat 11am–7.30pm, Sun 2–7pm.

25

SHOES

In addition to the places reviewed below, see Autour du Monde (see p.327) for funky and inexpensive tennis shoes beloved of the city's young *bobos* (bourgeois bohemians).

Annabel Winship 29 rue du Dragon, 6ᵉ ⓦannabel winship-shop.com; ⓂSt-Sulpice; map pp.136–137. Quirky and playful, these feminine women's shoes – emblazoned with flowers, Union Jacks, glam lightning bolts and colourful piping – are designed by an English expat and guaranteed to make you smile. Mon–Sat 11am–7pm.

Christian Louboutin 38–40 rue de Grenelle, 7ᵉ ⓦchristianlouboutin.com; ⓂRue du Bac; map pp.136–137. The iconic red-soled shoes are the object of every female fashionista's desires; according to the designer, men love them too. This sumptuous little boutique is a shrine to his creations; there are other branches, all on the right bank, including at rue Jean-Jacques Rousseau (1ᵉʳ) and 68 rue du Faubourg-St-Honoré (8ᵉ). Mon–Sat 10.30am–7pm.

Freelance 30 rue du Four, 6ᵉ; ⓂMabillon; map pp.136–137; 54 rue Montmartre, 2ᵉ; ⓂSentier; map pp.74–75; ⓦfreelance.fr. From leather to feathers, these very popular, free-spirited shoe shops attract young and funky Parisians, though you can expect to pay from €200 upwards. Both branches Mon–Fri 10am–7pm, Sat 10am–7.30pm.

K Jacques 16 rue Pavée, 4ᵉ ⓦkjacques.fr; ⓂSt-Paul; map p.97. This iconic St Tropez brand has been crafting simple strappy leather sandals since the 1930s and still defines quintessential South of France boho chic, as worn by Bardot, Picasso and Kate Moss. Mon–Sat 10am–7pm, Sun 1–6pm.

Repetto 22 rue de la Paix, 2ᵉ ⓦrepetto.fr; ⓂOpéra; map pp.74–75. This long-established supplier of ballet shoes, which has shod dancers from Margot Fonteyn to Sylvie Guillem, has branched out to produce attractive ballerina pumps in assorted colours as well as a range of heels, much coveted by the fashion crowd – and at a price. Many branches throughout town. Mon–Sat 9.30am–7.30pm.

LINGERIE

It's no cliché to say that lingerie is a national obsession, and Paris offers a dazzling selection of outlets where you can stock up on *sous-vêtements*. For the widest choice you're best off at the department stores, but there are also some standout boutiques.

Aubade 33 rue des Francs-Bourgeois, 3ᵉ ⓦaubade .com; ⓂSt-Paul; map p.97. Aubade lingerie is traditionally considered the height of refinement, glamour and seduction: lacy and sexy yet discreet and elegant. This store features corsets, basques and other items in addition to perfectly designed bras that cost upwards of €90. Mon 1.30–7.30pm, Tues–Sat 10.30am–7.30pm, Sun noon–7pm.

Cadolle 4 rue Cambon, 1ᵉʳ ⓦcadolle.fr; ⓂConcorde; map pp.64–65. This family has produced couture lingerie and corsets since 1889 – at this ready-to-wear boutique you can pick up an exquisite bra and camiknickers for a mere €200 or so. Mon & Tues 10am–6.30pm, Wed–Sat 11am–7pm; closed Aug.

Fifi Chachnil 34 rue de Grenelle, 7ᵉ ⓦfifichachnil.com; ⓂRue du Bac; map pp.136–137. Soft lighting and sumptuous furnishings make this decadent boutique feel more like a boudoir than a shop. Part-fantasy, part-Parisian chic, Chachnil's vintage-inspired, frou-frou creations strike a careful balance between saucy and elegant. Mon–Sat 11am–7pm.

Princesse Tam Tam 4 rue de Sèvres, 6ᵉ ⓦprincesse tamtam.com; ⓂSt-Sulpice; map pp.136–137. In the market since the 1930s, French lingerie brand Princesse Tam Tam offers a comprehensive range, from vintage-style silk slips (€70) to sportier, more contemporary styles from around €15. There are many branches in Paris, and in all the main department stores. Mon–Fri 10am–7.30pm, Sat 11am–7pm.

★**Sabbia Rosa** 71–73 rue des Sts-Pères, 6ᵉ; ⓂSt-Germain-des-Prés; map pp.136–137. This gorgeous jewel-box of a store sells supermodel scanties – they all

---

BEST PARISIAN PARFUMERIES

Annick Goutal 12 place St-Sulpice, 6ᵉ ⓦannick goutal.com; ⓂSt-Sulpice; map pp.136–137. Though Goutal has passed on, the business is still in the family, continuing to produce her exquisite perfumes, all made from natural essences and presented in old-fashioned, ribbed-glass bottles. This is the original branch. From €79 for 50ml eau de toilette. Mon–Sat 10am–7pm.

Belle de Jour 7 rue Tardieu, 18ᵉ ⓦbelle-de-jour.fr; ⓂAbbesses/Anvers; map p.182. Deeply old-fashioned shop selling perfume bottles, both new and vintage. From €10 for an inexpensive mini gift-bottle to €500 (or more) for the serious antiques – which range

from eighteenth-century to desirable Art Nouveau numbers. Tues–Fri 10.30am–1pm & 2–7pm, Sat 10.30am–1pm & 2–6pm.

Editions de Parfums Frédéric Malle 37 rue de Grenelle, 7ᵉ ⓦfredericmalle.com; ⓂRue du Bac; map pp.136–137. All the perfumes at this deliciously serious boutique are from *créateurs*, which means professional parfumeurs working under their own name through this "publishing house". A 50ml bottle costs more than €100, but you're buying a genuine work of art, and getting seriously expert advice too. Mon noon–7pm, Tues–Sat 11am–7pm; closed two weeks in Aug.

25

shop here – at supermodel prices. The retro, boudoir-style space is the perfect setting for the beautiful, luxurious lingerie, made in France using natural materials – lots of shimmering silk – in vibrant, bold colours. Mon–Sat 10am–7pm.

ACCESSORIES AND JEWELLERY

Anthony Peto 56 rue Tiquetonne, 2ᵉ Ⓦanthonypeto.com; ⓂEtienne-Marcel; map pp.74–75. A friendly, largely men's *chapelier*, loaded with fedoras, top hats, panamas and the like in wool and cotton plaid, tweed, velour and fur. Most of the fancier hats run at around €100. Mon–Sat 11am–7pm.

Bird on the Wire 2 rue de Lesdiguières, 4ᵉ Ⓦsuicidalshop.fr; ⓂBastille; map p.94. Accessories, jewellery, stationery and homewares from around the world are sold at this quirky gift store. You could come away with a peacock-shaped key holder, a colourful notebook, a vintage-style suitcase or candles with campfire or apple-picking aromas. Tues–Sat noon–7pm.

Delphine Pariente 19 rue de Turenne, 4ᵉ; ⓂSt-Paul; map p.94; 101 rue de Turenne, 3ᵉ; ⓂFilles-du-Calvaire; map p.94; 10 rue des Filles du Calvaire, 3ᵉ; ⓂFilles-du-Calvaire; map p.94; Ⓦdelphinepariente.fr. After working with Jean-Paul Gaultier and Christian Lacroix, Delphine Pariente opened her boutiques in the Marais selling delicate gold- and silver-plated necklaces, bangles, rings and earrings, many engraved or employing a witty use of words. Prices from €50. All branches daily 11am–7pm.

Entrée des Fournisseurs 8 rue des Francs-Bourgeois, 4ᵉ Ⓦentreedesfournisseurs.fr; ⓂSt-Paul; map p.97. Set back from the main road, this cheery spot has everything you might need to make clothes yourself, including buttons, ribbons, fabrics, patterns and knitting equipment. Mon–Sat 10.30am–7pm.

Harpo 19 rue Turbigo, 1ᵉʳ Ⓦharpo-paris.com; ⓂEtienne-Marcel; map pp.74–75. Specializing in Native American turquoise and silver jewellery, this popular shop sells necklaces, bracelets, rings, clasps, bolo ties, moccasins and accessories from the Soutwestern states of the USA. Much under €100. Mon–Fri 9am–6.45pm, Sat 11am–6.45pm.

Hermès 24 rue du Faubourg-St-Honoré, 8ᵉ; ⓂConcorde; map pp.64–65; 17 rue de Sèvres, 6ᵉ; ⓂSèvres-Babylone; map pp.136–137; Ⓦhermes.com. This superluxe fashion and accessories store is the place to come for an iconic "Birkin" or "Kelly" bag or the ultimate silk scarf – at a price. Check out the rue de Sèvres concept store, housed in an Art Deco swimming pool. Rue du Faubourg-St-Honoré Mon–Sat 10am–6.30pm; rue de Sèvres Mon–Sat 10am–7pm.

Hervé Chapelier 1bis rue du Vieux-Colombier, 6ᵉ; ⓂSt-Sulpice; map pp.136–137; 390 rue Saint-Honoré, 1er; map pp.74–75; Ⓦwww.hervechapelier.com. Often imitated, rarely matched, these classic nylon bags and purses with their distinctive, bold two-tone colour schemes never go out of fashion. Purses from €40. Mon–Fri 10.15am–1pm & 2–7pm, Sat 10.15am–7.15pm.

Louis Vuitton 101 av des Champs-Elysées, 8ᵉ Ⓦlouisvuitton.com; ⓂGeorge V; map pp.64–65. You'll have to contend with the crowds but this colossal flagship store offers you the best of LV – a "bag bar", jewellery emporium and men's and women's ready-to-wear collections. Mon–Sat 10am–8pm, Sun 11am–7pm.

Marie-Hélène de Taillac 8 rue de Tournon, 6ᵉ Ⓦmariehelenedetaillac.com; ⓂOdéon; map pp.136–137. Beautiful contemporary jewellery, mixing vivid, bold-coloured precious stones with deep, antique-looking gold in eye-catching designs. Expensive: even a tiny pair of earrings is more than €500. Mon–Sat 11am–7pm.

Marie Mercié 23 rue St-Sulpice, 6ᵉ Ⓦmariemercie.com; ⓂSt-Sulpice; map pp.136–137. This grande dame of *chapellerie* sells a glamorous and whimsical collection of plaid, straw, felt and fur hats for all (fancy) occasions – at €250 and up. Mon–Sat 11am–7pm.

Maroquinerie Saint Honoré 334 rue St-Honoré, 1ᵉʳ; ⓂPyramides/Tuileries; map pp.74–75. An unexpected find on one of the city's most exclusive shopping streets, this bargain shop sells French-made leather handbags (around €90 and above). Mon–Sat 10.30am–6.30pm.

L'Oeuf 9 & 14 rue Clauzel, 9ᵉ Ⓦloeufparis.com; ⓂSt-Georges; map p.182. Fashion-forward concept store selling accessories: anything from feather earrings to old-school Casio watches in bright colours, plus keyrings, jewellery, bags and "South Pigalle" branded gear. No. 14 focuses on shoes. Both Tues–Sun 11.30am–8pm.

ART, STATIONERY AND PHOTOGRAPHY

Dubois 20 rue Soufflot, 5ᵉ Ⓦdubois-paris.com; ⓂCluny-La Sorbonne; map pp.122–123. In the same great apothecary-style building since the 1860s, the Dubois family still offers an excellent selection of art supplies, notebooks and pens. Mon 10am–1pm & 2–6.30pm, Tues–Sat 9.30am–7pm.

Papier Plus 9 rue du Pont-Louis-Philippe, 4ᵉ Ⓦpapierplus.com; ⓂSt-Paul; map p.97. Top-quality, colourful stationery, including notebooks, travel journals, photo albums and artists' portfolios. Mon–Sat noon–7pm.

Photo Rent 6 bd Beaumarchais, 11ᵉ Ⓦphotorent.fr; ⓂChemin-Vert; map pp.110–111. New and secondhand photographic equipment. If they don't have what you're looking for, try the other camera shops on the same street. Mon 9am–12.30pm & 2–6pm, Tues–Fri 9am–12.30pm & 2–6.45pm, Sat 10am–12.30pm & 2–6.45pm.

25

Sennelier 3 quai Voltaire, 7ᵉ ⓦ magasinsennelier.com; ⓜ St-Germain-des-Prés; map pp.136–137. Serious, old-fashioned art suppliers, with beautiful and reasonably priced sketchbooks. Other branches at 4bis rue de la Grande Chaumière (6ᵉ) and 6 rue Hallé (14ᵉ). Mon 2–6.30pm, Tues–Sat 10am–12.45pm & 2–6.30pm.

BOOKS

Paris has a gratifying number of bookshops compared to other European cities – the most atmospheric areas for **book shopping** are the Seine *quais*, with their rows of new and secondhand bookstalls perched against the river parapet, and the narrow streets of the Quartier Latin. For a particularly good **gay bookshop** in the Marais, turn to our chapter on LGBT Paris (see p.358).

ENGLISH-LANGUAGE BOOKS

Abbey Bookshop 29 rue de la Parcheminerie, 5ᵉ ⓦ abbeybookshop.wordpress.com; ⓜ St-Michel; map pp.122–123. An overstuffed warren of a place, this Canadian bookshop, round the corner from Shakespeare and Company, is packed ceiling to floor with used British and North American fiction and travel guides. Helpful staff, soothing classical music – and free coffee. Mon–Sat 10am–7pm.

★**Galignani** 224 rue de Rivoli, 1ᵉʳ ⓦ galignani.com; ⓜ Concorde; map pp.74–75. Reputedly the first English bookshop established on the Continent, opened (on a different site) way back in the early 1800s. Not all the stock is English-language, but what there is is top notch, including fiction, fine art and children's books. Mon–Sat 10am–7pm.

Shakespeare and Company 37 rue de la Bûcherie, 5ᵉ ⓦ shakespeareandcompany.com; ⓜ St-Michel; map pp.122–123. A cosy and very famous literary haunt (see p.121), run by Americans and staffed by earnest young Hemingway wannabes. They offer the biggest selection of secondhand English-language books in town, and lots of new stock, especially Paris-related – on busy days you may have to wait to get in. There's a reading room upstairs where you can sit for as long as you like, frequent readings and signings (arrive early) and a new café in an adjacent building. Daily 10am–11pm.

WH Smith 248 rue de Rivoli, 1ᵉʳ ⓦ whsmith.fr; ⓜ Concorde; map pp.74–75. The Parisian outlet of the British chain stocks a wide range of new books, newspapers, magazines and DVDs (albeit at a price), plus a small selection of gifts. Mon–Sat 9am–7pm, Sun 12.30–7pm.

FRENCH BOOKS

Fnac Forum des Halles, Niveau 2, Porte Pierre-Lescot, 1ᵉʳ; ⓜ/RER Châtelet-Les-Halles; map p.86; 74 av des Champs-Elysées, 8ᵉ; ⓜ Franklin-D.-Roosevelt; map pp.64–65; ⓦ fnac.com. Fnac is France's leading retail chain for books, CDs, games and electronics – as well as for concert and sports events tickets. There are nine branches in Paris. The shops offer supermarket-style discounting, but the range of books and music extends into the higher brow. Lots of comics, guidebooks and maps. Forum des Halles Mon–Sat 10am–8pm; Champs-Elysées Mon–Sat 10am–11.45pm, Sun noon–11.45pm.

Gallimard 15 bd Raspail, 7ᵉ ⓦ gallimard.fr; ⓜ Sèvres-Babylone; map pp.136–137. Most French publishers operate their own flagship bookshops, and Gallimard's is one of the greats, with a full selection of their own and other titles – particularly strong on art, literature and travel. Mon–Sat 10am–7.30pm.

Gibert Jeune 6 place St-Michel, 5ᵉ ⓦ gibertjeune.fr; ⓜ St-Michel; map pp.122–123. There's a fair English-language and discounted selection at this branch of the classic Quartier Latin student/academic bookshop. A vast selection of French books can be found in the other seven branches, which are dotted all around the *place*, and easily spotted with their distinctive yellow awnings. A real institution. Mon–Sat 9.30am–7.30pm.

Gibert Joseph 26 bd St-Michel, 6ᵉ ⓦ gibertjoseph.com; ⓜ St-Michel; map pp.122–123. Neighbour and rival of the very similar Gibert Jeune group, with new and secondhand English books for sale at this branch. Mon–Sat 10am–8pm.

ART, DESIGN, PHOTOGRAPHY AND FILM BOOKS

Artazart 83 quai de Valmy, 10ᵉ ⓦ artazart.com; ⓜ Jacques Bonsergent; map p.198. Very cool Canal St-Martin store, with books, magazines and gifts devoted to contemporary graphic art, design and photography, plus regular book signings, exhibitions and events. Mon–Fri 10.30am–7.30pm, Sun 2–8pm.

★**Artcurial** 7 Rond-Point des Champs-Elysées, 8ᵉ ⓦ librairie.artcurial.com; ⓜ Franklin-D.-Roosevelt; map pp.64–65. In an astonishingly grand townhouse that also houses an auctioneers, this is a swanky setting for excellent art books, including French and foreign editions. Mon–Fri 9am–7pm, Sat 10.30am–7pm, Sun 1–7pm; closed two weeks in Aug.

La Chambre Claire 14 rue St-Sulpice, 6ᵉ ⓦ la-chambre-claire.fr; ⓜ Odéon; map pp.136–137. Photography specialist selling art titles, style guides and instruction manuals, with coffee-table books and some English-language offerings. Tues–Sat 11am–7pm.

La Hune 18 rue de l'Abbaye, 6ᵉ ⓦ groupe-flammarion.com; ⓜ St-Germain-des-Prés; map pp.136–137.

The main selling point of this general French bookstore – apart from its history as a Left Bank arts institution – is the art, design, fashion and photography collection on the mezzanine. Sun–Thurs 11am–8pm, Fri & Sat 11am–10pm.

★ **La Librairie du Cinéma du Panthéon** 15 rue Victor Cousin, 5ᵉ ⓦ cinereflet.com; Ⓜ Cluny-La Sorbonne; map pp.122–123. Superb store devoted to cinema, with shelves of books, not all in French – biographies, technical manuals, screenplays, theory, coffee-table titles – plus magazines, posters, cards and DVDs. There are also books on literature, music, psychology and art, plus comics, all with some relationship to cinema. Mon–Fri 1–8pm, Sat 11am–8pm.

Librairie le Moniteur Cité de l'Architecture et du Patrimoine, place du Trocadéro, 16ᵉ ⓦ www.librairie dumoniteur.com; Ⓜ Trocadéro; map pp.150–151. Well-curated little store dedicated to architecture books, contemporary and historical, with some in English. Mon, Wed & Fri–Sun 11am–7pm, Thurs 11am–8pm.

COMICS (BANDES DESSINÉES)

Album 8 rue Dante, 5ᵉ; Ⓜ Maubert-Mutualité; map pp.122–123; 84 bd St-Germain, 5ᵉ; Ⓜ Cluny-La Sorbonne; map pp.122–123; ⓦ album.fr. Album offers a good range of indie and mainstream material; the Dante branch in particular (on a street with at least six comics shops) has a serious collection of French BDs, some of them rare editions with original artwork. Rue Dante Mon–Fri 10.30am–7.30pm, Sat 10am–8pm; bd St-Germain Mon–Sat 10am–8pm, Sun noon–7pm.

Le Pied de Biche 86 rue de Charonne, 11ᵉ

ⓦ lepieddebiche.com; Ⓜ Charonne; map pp.110–111. Cool little indie store with a lovingly curated cache of underground, cult and international titles, plus regular in-store events and exhibitions. Tues–Fri 11.30am–8pm, Sat 11am–8pm.

Thé-Troc 52 rue Jean-Pierre-Timbaud, 11ᵉ; Ⓜ Parmentier; map p.208. The friendly owner of this old-school treasure-trove publishes *The Fabulous Furry Freak Brothers* in French and English, and sells underground comic books and memorabilia, secondhand records and assorted junk. The attached *salon de thé* (until 7pm) is comfy, colourful and restful. Mon–Sat 10am–noon & 2–8pm.

TRAVEL BOOKS AND MAPS

★ **Latitude Littéraire** 48 rue Ste-Anne, 2ᵉ ⓦ latitude -litteraire.fr; Ⓜ Pyramides; map pp.74–75. This slick, stylish and sprawling bookshop, offshoot of the travel agency/travel goods store on the same street, is devoted to travel writing, with guides in English and translation, plus travel literature, note books, maps and accessories. Mon–Sat 9.30am–7pm.

Librairie Ulysse 26 rue St-Louis-en-l'Île, 4ᵉ ⓦ ulysse.fr; Ⓜ Pont Marie/Sully-Morland; map pp.44–45. Tiny bookshop, piled from floor to ceiling with thousands of new and secondhand travel writing and run by a friendly English-speaking owner. Tues–Fri 2–8pm, mornings & Sat by appointment.

Le Monde des Cartes 50 rue de la Verrerie, 4ᵉ ⓦ ign.fr; Ⓜ Hôtel-de-Ville; map p.86. The official (and best) source for maps of France, and indeed the entire world, plus guidebooks, satellite photos, old and new maps of Paris – and, sign of the times, Satnavs. Mon–Sat 11am–7pm.

MUSIC

The 11ᵉ, especially around Bastille, Ménilmontant and the Canal St-Martin, is a good place to look for specialist record shops selling vinyl. For mainstream releases, Fnac (see above) usually has the best prices.

Crocodisc/Crocojazz 40–42 rue des Ecoles, 5ᵉ; 64 rue de la Montagne-Sainte-Geneviève, 5ᵉ; both Ⓜ Maubert-Mutualité; ⓦ crocodisc.com; map pp.122–123. The rue des Ecoles shop has been selling new and used records at low prices for decades. You'll dig up everything here, except classical – reggae, Latin, punk, film music, gospel, country, you name it, with a particularly good world music selection. Crocojazz, on rue de la Montagne-Sainte-Geneviève, focuses on jazz from bebop to crooners. Rue des Ecoles Tues–Sat 11am–7pm; rue de la Montagne-Sainte-Geneviève Tues–Sat 11am–1pm & 2–7pm; closed first two weeks in Aug.

International Records 12 rue Moret, 11ᵉ ⓦ linternationalrecords.com; Ⓜ Menilmontant; map p.208. Offshoot of the splendid little live music venue off Oberkampf (see p.305), this store is a great hunting ground for indie music of all stripes – chillwave to krautrock, drone to dub – on vinyl and CD used and new. Mon–Thurs noon–8pm, Fri & Sat noon–10pm.

Patate Records 57 rue de Charonne, 11ᵉ ⓦ patate -records.com; Ⓜ Charonne; map pp.110–111. Jamaican specialist, packed with vinyl, CDs and DVDs covering everything from dancehall to dub and piled high with flyers for reggae and world music gigs. Tues–Sat 1–7pm.

FOOD AND DRINK

Paris has resisted the march of mega-stores with admirable resilience. Almost every *quartier* still has its charcuterie, boulangerie and weekly market, while some **streets**, such as rue Daguerre in the 14ᵉ, rue des Martyrs in the 9ᵉ, rue Cler in the 7ᵉ and rue de Bretagne in the 3ᵉ, are lined with grocers', butchers' shops, delis, pâtisseries, cheese shops

25

and wine merchants. We have reviewed the best of the **specialist food shops** – many of which are fairly expensive – and the grand **food halls** (see box below), but you should also hit the city's **street markets** (see p.339), where you can pick up gourmet picnic foods for a snip. Useful **supermarkets** include Franprix, Monoprix and Ed l'Epicier; this last is particularly cheap. **Health food** and organic shops are also easy to find; look for the many branches of Naturalia and Biocoop.

BREAD

La Flute Gana 226 rue des Pyrénées, 20ᵉ ⓦ gana.fr; ⓜ Gambetta; map p.208. Although Ganachaud *père* has long left the business, his three daughters continue his work, and the baguettes – and the cakes, especially the almond pastries – at this neighbourhood store are still out of this world, at prices that put the trendier boulangeries to shame. Tues–Sat 7.30am–8pm.

★ **Gontran Cherrier** 22 rue Caulaincourt, 18ᵉ ⓦ gontran cherrierboulanger.com; ⓜ Abbesses; map p.182. Cherrier produces some of the most creative boulangerie and pâtisserie in Paris – while the baguettes and sweet pastries are amazing, disciples will trek across the city for his squid-ink and nigella-seed buns filled with smoked swordfish and *jamon* (trust us, they're phenomenal). You can also buy green (rocket and courgette), red (paprika) or brown (molasses and coriander) buns to make sandwiches. Mon, Tues & Thurs–Sat 7.30am–8pm, Sun 8am–7.30pm.

★ **Le Grenier à Pain** 38 rue des Abbesses, 18ᵉ ⓦ legrenierapain.com; map p.182. The long lines outside this unassuming Montmartre bakery tell the story – this excellent small chain offers outstanding bread, tarts and pastries at astonishingly low prices. Their baguettes frequently win "Best in Paris" awards, their buttery croissants, fruit tarts and quiches are irresistible, and their nut- or fruit-packed loaves could feed a family for days, but it's the mini *ficelles* and *fougasses* – packed with cheese and olives – that steal the show, for less than a euro. Thurs–Mon 7.30am–8pm.

Du Pain et Des Idées 34 rue Yves Toudic, 10ᵉ ⓦ dupain etdesidees.com; ⓜ Jacques Bonsergent; map p.198. Christophe Vasseur, a former fashion-industry sales executive, now produces heavenly baguettes, brioches, pastries and the signature *pain des amis*, a nutty sourdough bread, in a store that exudes retro Parisian chic. Don't miss the croissants flavoured with green tea or rosewater. Mon–Fri 6.45am–8pm.

Poilâne 8 rue du Cherche-Midi, 6ᵉ; ⓜ Sèvres-Babylone; map pp.136–137; 38 rue Debellyme, 3ᵉ; ⓜ Filles-du-Calvaire; map p.94; 48 bd de Grenelle, 15ᵉ; ⓜ Dupleix; map pp.172–173; ⓦ poilane.com. A classic, source of the famous "Pain Poilâne" – a sourdough bread baked using traditional methods (albeit ramped up on an industrial scale) as conceived by the late, legendary Monsieur Poilâne himself. The shops also have dining areas serving an interesting selection of *tartines*, pies and salads. Rue du Cherche-Midi Mon–Sat 8.30am–7pm, Sun 9.30am–3.30pm; rue Debellyme Wed–Sun 8.30am–7pm; bd de Grenelle Tues–Sun 7.15am–8.15pm.

Sacha Finkelsztajn/Boutique Jaune 27 rue des Rosiers, 4ᵉ ⓦ laboutiquejaune.com; ⓜ St-Paul/Hôtel-de-Ville; map p.97. This Ashkenazi family-owned bakery has been here since 1946, producing the best *boreks* and blinis, strudels and *latkes* – plus great *challah* bread and cheesecake – to be found in the Marais. There's a deli counter, too. Mon 11am–7pm, Wed & Thurs 10am–7pm, Fri–Sun 10am–7.30pm; closed Aug.

GOURMET GROCERIES

Any list of iconic Parisian food shops has to start with these three:

Fauchon 24–26 & 30 place de la Madeleine, 8ᵉ ⓦ fauchon.fr; ⓜ Madeleine; map pp.74–75. The luxury brand's flagship store (no. 24–26) sells extravagantly beautiful groceries, pâtisserie, charcuterie, wines both French and foreign – at exorbitant prices. The quality is assured by blind testing, which all suppliers have to submit to. Don't miss their sublime eclairs, the brie with truffles, or the *macarons*. No. 30 is perfect for foodie gifts – tea, jam, truffles, chocolates, exotic vinegars, mustards and so forth. No. 24–26 Mon–Sat 8am–8pm; no. 30 Mon–Sat 8am–9pm.

La Grande Epicerie 38 rue de Sèvres, 7ᵉ ⓦ lagrande epicerie.com; ⓜ Sèvres-Babylone; map pp.136–137. This offshoot of the famous Bon Marché department store is a fabulous emporium of fresh and packaged foods, with a focus on what's new and unusual as well as all the traditional favourites. Popular among choosy Parisians, expats (for its country-specific goodies, from Yorkshire tea to Marmite) and foodie tourists alike. Mon–Sat 8.30am–9pm.

Hédiard 21 place de la Madeleine, 8ᵉ ⓦ hediard.fr; ⓜ Madeleine; map pp.74–75. The aristocrat's grocer since the 1850s, with sales staff as deferential as servants – as long as you don't try to reach for items yourself. You may not be able to stretch to their caviar, champagne or foie gras, but the coffees, spices and conserves make fabulous gifts. Mon–Sat 9am–8pm.

PÂTISSERIE

La Bague de Kenza 106 rue St-Maur, 11e Ⓦ labague
dekenza.com; Ⓜ Parmentier; map pp.110–111. The
window of this Algerian pâtisserie is groaning with
enticing little cakes made of dates, orange, pistachios, figs,
almonds and other tasty ingredients plus hot Algerian
breads and savoury pastries. There's a *salon de thé* attached
(see p.294). Mon–Thurs, Sat & Sun 9am–9pm, Fri
1.30–9pm.

Les Fées Pâtissières 21 rue Rambuteau, 4e
Ⓦ lesfeespatissieres.com; Ⓜ Rambuteau; map p.97.
Contemporary, whimsical and very feminine Marais
pâtisserie with a twist – dainty, bite-sized creations that
verge on the avant-garde. Tues–Sat 11am–8pm, Sun
11am–7pm.

Mesdemoiselles Madeleines 37 rue des Martyrs, 9e
Ⓦ mllesmadeleines.com; Ⓜ Pigalle; map p.182. Pamper
your inner Proust and head to this sleek boutique devoted
solely to the little cakes of the author's youth. These are
not Madeleines as Marcel would know them, though – try
the Faustine, made with fresh fennel and topped with
blackcurrant; the Hortense, crowned with a lemon curd
dome; or the René, a savoury treat of black olive tapenade,
carrots and cumin. Tues–Sun 9.30am–7pm.

★**Pâtisserie Stohrer** 51 rue Montorgueil, 2e
Ⓦ stohrer.fr; Ⓜ Sentier; map pp.74–75. Pâtisserie,
chocolate and deli delights have been produced in this
lovely little shop since 1730. The window display is irresistible: from delectable chocolate eclairs to towering vol-aux-
vents and quail stuffed with foie gras. Daily 7.30am–8pm,
closed first two weeks in Aug.

★**Pierre Hermé** 72 rue Bonaparte, 6e Ⓦ pierreherme
.com; Ⓜ St-Sulpice; map pp.136–137. The *macarons*
made by this pastry demigod are widely considered to be
the best in Paris, if not France. While the more unusual
flavour pairings, such as foie gras and chocolate, may
sound risky, Hermé hasn't earned his stellar reputation for
nothing. There are various branches around town. Sun &
Mon–Wed 10am–7pm, Thurs & Fri 10am–7.30pm, Sat
10am–8pm.

Popelini 29 rue Debellyme, 3e; Ⓜ Filles-du-Calvaire;
map p.94; 44 rue des Martyrs, 9e; Ⓜ St-Georges; map
p.182; Ⓦ popelini.com. Done with *macarons*? Time to
move on to a new Parisian bite-sized treat and head to this
contemporary shop dedicated to *choux à la crème* (choux
buns). The delicate morsels of crisp pastry filled with
rich *crème pâtissière* in flavours such as bitter chocolate,
pistachio, and the irresistible salted caramel, are divine –
to look at and to eat. Rue Debellyme Tues–Sat 11am–
7.30pm, Sun 10am–6pm; rue des Martyrs Tues–Sat
11am–7pm, Sun 10am–3pm.

Sébastien Gaudard 22 rue des Martyrs, 9e; Ⓜ Notre-
Dame-de Lorette; map p.182; 1 rue des Pyramides,
1er; Ⓜ Tuileries; map pp.74–75; Ⓦ sebastiengaudard.fr.

Beautiful old pâtisserie whose elegant array of pastries
and tarts, from *Paris-Brests* to *vacherin*, harks back to a
golden era of classic pâtisserie. The newer, smaller Tuileries
branch includes a *salon de thé*. Rue des Martyrs Tues–Fri
10am–8pm, Sat 9am–8pm, Sun 9am–7pm; rue des
Pyramides Tues–Sat 10am–8pm, Sun 9am–7pm.

CHOCOLATE AND SWEETS

Chocolaterie Jacques Genin 133 rue de Turenne, 3e
Ⓦ jacquesgenin.fr; Ⓜ République; map p.94. After
years supplying chocolates to Paris's top restaurants,
Genin opened his own very fancy shop in 2008.
A wonderful selection of chocolates, caramels, nougats
and ganaches; flavours include Earl Grey, raspberry and
Szechuan pepper. There's a small *salon de thé* at the back
for a seriously posh pitstop, and another branch in the 7e
at 27 rue de Varenne. Tues–Fri & Sun 11am–7pm, Sat
11am–8pm.

Debauve et Gallais 30 rue des Sts-Pères, 7e Ⓦ debauve
-et-gallais.fr; Ⓜ St-Germain-des-Prés/Sèvres-Babylone;
map pp.136–137. This beautiful shop specializing in
chocolate and elaborate sweets has been around since
chocolate was taken as a medicine and an aphrodisiac,
and is designated a *Monument Historique*. There's a smaller
branch at 33 rue Vivienne (2e). Mon–Sat 9am–7pm.

Joséphine Vannier 4 rue Pas de la Mule, 4e
Ⓦ chocolats-vannier.com; Ⓜ Bastille; map p.94. This
creative chocolatier sells chocolate shaped into anything
from accordions and violins to hiking boots, stilettos, Eiffel
Towers and Arcs de Triomphe – exquisite and daft creations,
almost too realistic to eat. Tues–Sat 11am–1pm &
2–7pm, Sun 2.30–7pm.

CHARCUTERIE, CAVIAR, TRUFFLES AND
SNAILS

Caviar Kaspia 17 place de la Madeleine, 8e Ⓦ kaspia.fr;
Ⓜ Madeleine; map pp.74–75. Blinis, smoked salmon and
Beluga caviar, all of which can also be sampled in the plush
upstairs restaurant. Mon–Sat 10am–1am; closed Aug.

★**Le Comptoir de la Gastronomie** 34 rue Montmartre,
1er Ⓦ comptoirdelagastronomie.com; Ⓜ Les Halles/
Etienne-Marcel; map p.86. The walls of this lovely old-
fashioned shop are stacked high with foie gras, *saucisses*,
hams, *terrines*, preserves, oils and wine. The deli does a fine
line in baguettes to take away, and there's also a superb little
restaurant (see p.277). Mon–Sat 6am–8pm.

Aux Ducs de Gascogne 111 rue St-Antoine, 4e Ⓦ ducs
degascogne.com; Ⓜ St-Paul; map p.97. This postage-
stamp-sized place specializes in foie gras, as well as
enticing – and expensive – deli goods from charcuterie and
little salads to caviar. Daily 10am–8pm.

La Maison de l'Escargot 79 rue Fondary, 15e Ⓦ maison
-escargot.com; Ⓜ Dupleix; map pp.172–173. As the
name suggests, this is the place for snails: they even sauce

25

them and re-shell them while you wait. Tues–Sat 9.30am–7pm; closed mid-July to Sept.

Maison de la Truffe 19 place de la Madeleine, 8e ⓦ maison-de-la-truffe.com; ⓜ Madeleine; map pp.74–75. Truffles, of course, both *noires*, from France, and *blanches*, from Italy – prices can be upwards of €1500 per 400g. Also sells roe, foie gras and similar delicacies. There's an attached restaurant (lunch Mon–Fri, *menus* from €29), but you might want to bring a second credit card. Mon–Sat 10am–10pm.

CHEESE

Androuet 134 rue Mouffetard, 5e ⓦ androuet.com; ⓜ Censier-Daubenton; map pp.122–123. One of a selection of fine cheese shops on the rue Mouffe market street, all offering wonderful selections, beautifully displayed. There are around seven branches of this highly regarded chain in Paris. Tues–Fri 9.30am–1pm & 4–7.30pm, Sat 9.30am–7pm, Sun 9.30am–1pm.

★**Barthélémy** 51 rue de Grenelle, 7e; ⓜ Rue du Bac; map pp.136–137. Exquisite, historic store packed to the rafters with carefully ripened and meticulously stored seasonal cheeses. Knowledgeable staff will help you choose. Tues–Thurs 8.30am–1pm & 3.30–7.15pm, Fri & Sat 8.30am–1.30pm & 3–7.15pm; closed Aug.

Fromagerie Alléosse 13 rue Poncelet, 17e ⓦ fromage-alleosse.com; ⓜ Ternes; map pp.64–65. A connoisseur's selection, including Brie from Champagne, creamy Brillat-Savarin, nutty-flavoured Mont d'Or and an enormous variety of goat's cheeses. Tues–Fri 9am–1.15pm & 3–7pm, Sat 9am–7pm, Sun 9am–1pm.

OIL, SPICES, JAMS AND CONDIMENTS

Les Abeilles 21 rue Butte-aux-Cailles, 13e ⓦ lesabeilles.biz; ⓜ Corvisart/Place d'Italie; map p.176. Honey from all over France and further afield, sold from a barrel by an experienced beekeeper, plus honey-infused oils, vinegars, soaps and cakes. Try the prized – and pricey – Miel de Paris – harvested from beehives across the city. Tues–Sat 11am–7pm.

★**G. Detou** 58 rue Tiquetonne, 2e; ⓜ Etienne-Marcel; map pp.74–75. Friendly neighbourhood-style épicerie that gets packed to the gills on Saturdays. Kilos of spices, nuts and chocolate, plus *confiserie*, *marrons glacés*, jars and tins, mustards, *confit*, foie gras and the like. Mon–Sat 8.30am–6.30pm.

Maille 6 place de la Madeleine, 8e ⓦ maille.com; ⓜ Madeleine; map pp.74–75. Founded in 1747, Maille is best known for its Dijon mustard, but it also makes scores of other varieties, with specials including such flavours as pesto, rocket and white wine, or cocoa and raspberry, plus flavoured vinegars and rustic, hand-painted mustard pots. Mon–Sat 10am–7pm.

COFFEE AND TEA

★**L'Arbre à Café** 10 rue de Nil, 10e ⓦ larbreacafe.com; ⓜ Sentier; map pp.74–75. A trailblazer in Paris's much-lauded coffee renaissance, this little shop offers the haute cuisine of beans, with an impeccable selection bought direct from small biodynamic and organic estates – from Ethiopia to Hawaii – and roasted on demand. Tues–Fri 12.30–7.30pm, Sat 10am–7pm.

Brûlerie Daval Cour Damoye, 12 rue Daval, 11e ☎ 01 48 05 29 46; ⓜ Bastille; map pp.110–111. Tucked away in an adorable cobbled passageway (see p.112), this rickety and aromatic little coffee roastery hasn't changed for generations. It's packed to the gills with huge hessian sacks spilling over with beans; make your choice, of beans or blended coffees, and wait as they're painstakingly measured out on old-fashioned scales by the redoubtable Madame. They sell loose tea, too. Tues–Sun 10am–1pm & 3–7pm (though you may find them open between 1 & 3pm).

Mariage Frères 30 rue du Bourg-Tibourg, 4e ⓦ mariage-freres.com; ⓜ Hôtel-de-Ville; map p.97. Hundreds of teas, prettily packed in tins, line the floor-to-ceiling shelves of this historic tea emporium that's been trading since 1854. There's also a classy *salon de thé* (serving from 3pm). Also at 32 and 35 rue du Bourg Tibourg, and other branches throughout the city. Daily 10.30am–7.30pm.

Verlet 256 rue St-Honoré, 1er ⓦ verlet.fr; ⓜ Palais-Royal-Musée-du-Louvre; map pp.74–75. An old-fashioned *torréfacteur* (coffee merchant), selling both familiar and less common varieties of coffee and tea from around the world. There's also a tearoom, perfect for a pick-me-up. Mon–Sat 9.30am–7pm.

Yam'Tcha 4 rue Sauval, 1er ⓦ www.yamtcha.com; ⓜ Les Halles; map p.86. The famed gourmet restaurant has moved (see p.278), but the original pocket-sized site now holds a teahouse from the same team, selling delicate teas and accessories from China and Taiwan and serving chef Adeline Grattard's delicious steamed *bao* buns to take away. Wed–Sun 11.30am–7.30pm.

WINE AND BEER

Nicolas, nysa and Le Repaire de Bacchus are the most reliable of the chains, but it's really worth speaking to the knowledgeable staff in the independent shops reviewed here; you'll be more likely to go home with some gems. As for natural wines, you're spoiled for choice, with an increasing number of places offering a good range of biodynamic, sulphite-free and organic options.

La Cave des Papilles 35 rue Daguerre, 14e ⓦ lacavedespapilles.com; ⓜ Denfert Rochereau; map pp.162–163. More than a thousand organic and natural wines, hand-selected from small-scale producers by the charming owners, along with champagnes, whiskies, cognacs, armagnacs and brandies. Mon 3.30–8.30pm,

25

Tues–Fri 10am–1.30pm & 3.30–8.30pm, Sat 10am–8.30pm, Sun 10am–1.30pm.

Les Caves Augé 116 bd Haussmann, 8ᵉ ⓦcavesauge.com; ⓜSt-Augustin; map pp.64–65. This old-fashioned, wood-panelled shop is the oldest *cave* in Paris, dating back to 1850, and sells around six thousand French and foreign wines and champagne, many of them organic or natural. Mon–Sat 10am–7.30pm.

★**La Dernière Goutte** 6 rue Bourbon Le Château, 6ᵉ ⓦladernieregoutte.net; ⓜMabillon; map pp.136–137. A much-loved neighbourhood wine shop. Owner Juan Sanchez hand-picks a selection of wines from small and mid-sized French producers, mainly organic and biodynamic. On Friday and Saturday they also host informal wine tastings, often led by the wine-makers themselves. Mon 3.30–8pm, Tues–Sat 10.30am–1.30pm & 3–8pm, Sun 11am–7pm.

Lavinia 3–5 bd de la Madeleine, 8ᵉ ⓦlavinia.fr; ⓜMadeleine; map pp.74–75. Vast wine and spirits store with a modern interior displaying thousands of bottles from more than 43 countries, and a wine cellar that holds some of the rarest bottles in the world. The attached wine library and bar/restaurant allow you to read up, then

drink up. Mon–Sat 10am–8.30pm.

Legrand Filles et Fils 7–11 Galerie Vivienne, 2ᵉ ⓦcaves-legrand.com; ⓜBourse; map pp.74–75. This fancy wine merchant, dating back more than a hundred years, has an extensive cellar and also sells quality truffles, foie gras and chocolates. There's a wine bar/restaurant, too (see p.276). Mon 11am–7pm, Tues–Fri 10am–7.30pm, Sat 10am–7pm.

Soif d'Ailleurs 38 rue Pastourelle, 3ᵉ ⓦsoifdailleurs.com; ⓜArts-et-Metiers; map p.94. There's something a little naughty – perhaps even sacrilegious – about buying wines from Syria, the USA, Croatia or England in Paris – but the quality and expertise in this contemporary wine shop has made it a favourite with the city's connoisseurs. Mon–Sat 11am–9pm, Sun 11am–6pm.

De Vinis Illustribus 48 rue de la Montagne-Ste-Geneviève, 5ᵉ ⓦdevinis.fr; ⓜMaubert-Mutualité; map pp.122–123. Connoisseur Lionel Michelin set up shop in this ancient wine cellar in 1994. He still specializes in very old and very rare vintages but is just as happy selling you a €9 bottle of Coteaux du Languedoc and orating eloquently on its tannins. Tues–Sat 2–7pm.

HOMEWARE AND KITCHENWARE

In addition to the selection of shops below, it's worth checking out the art and design **museums** and the streets around Bastille, where a high concentration of stores specialize in particular periods. Also try the **kitchen departments** at Le BHV Marais (see p.324) and Lafayette Maison (see p.324) for cookware and cutlery.

★**Astier de Villatte** 173 rue St-Honoré, 1ᵉʳ ⓦastierdevillatte.com; ⓜPalais Royal; map pp.74–75. Delightful, unusual shop modelling the arty, shabby elegance of its carefully selected ceramics, homeware, candles and gifts in a beautiful space of parquet floorboards, dark wood cabinets and peeling-plaster walls (pieces from around €35). Mon–Sat 11am–7pm.

★**CSAO** 9 rue Elzévir, 3ᵉ ⓦcsao.fr; ⓜSt-Paul; map p.97. They sell everything from recycled plastic bracelets to woven baskets in this stylish and colourful African store/gallery – it stands for Compagnie du Sénégal et de l'Afrique de l'Ouest. A great spot for colourful cushions and fabrics, kitchen goods, lamps, crockery and table linen, most of it from reclaimed, refashioned and upcycled materials. Tues–Sat 10am–7pm, Sun 2–7pm.

Dominique Picquier 10 rue Charlot, 3ᵉ ⓦdominiquepicquier.com; ⓜFilles-du-Calvaire/St-Sébastien-Froissart; map p.94. "A tribute to nature in the city" is how this textile designer describes her beautiful fabrics printed with striking graphic patterns. Picquier also does an attractive range of retro-influenced accessories, including tote bags and purses (from €45), often focusing on city landmarks. Tues–Fri 11am–7.30pm, Sat 2.30–7.30pm.

E. Dehillerin 18–20 rue Coquillière, 1ᵉʳ ⓦe-dehillerin.fr; ⓜChâtelet-Les-Halles; map p.86. This nineteenth-century institution, in business since 1820, is laid out like a

traditional ironmonger's: narrow aisles, no fancy displays, prices buried in catalogues, but good-quality stock of knives, slicers, peelers, presses and a great selection of copper and pewter pans, many of restaurant quality, at reasonable prices. Mon 9am–12.30pm & 2–6pm, Tues–Sat 9am–6pm.

Gab & Jo 28 rue Jacob, 6ᵉ ⓦgabjo.fr; ⓜSt-Germain-des-Prés; map pp.136–137. Colourful, intriguing and original – everything in this concept store, from soap to furniture to candles to books, is designed and made in France. Mon–Sat 11am–7pm.

★**Merci** 111 bd Beaumarchais, 3ᵉ ⓦmerci-merci.com; ⓜSt-Sébastien-Froissart; map pp.110–111. Flowers, bed linen, throws, kitchenware, fragrances and clothes (some specially created for the store by leading designers such as Stella McCartney) are all available from this hip and original concept store. This stuff is not cheap, but all profits go to charity. Three good eating options, too (see p.279). Mon–Sat 10am–7pm.

A. Simon 48–52 rue Montmartre, 2ᵉ; ⓜEtienne-Marcel; map pp.74–75. A huge collection of anything and everything for professional and home cooks, including a wide range of cast-iron and copper cookware, and fine glassware. Bovida, at no. 36, and MORA, at no. 13, are the big rivals on the street, but this place has the edge. Mon–Sat 8.30am–6.30pm.

ANTIQUES AND COLLECTIBLES

★**Boîtes à Musique Anna Joliet** Jardin du Palais Royal, 9 rue de Beaujolais, 1er; ⓜPalais-Royal-Musée-du-Louvre; map pp.74–75. A delightful, minuscule boutique selling every style of music box, from inexpensive self-winding toy models to grand cabinets costing thousands of euros. Parisians have long loved mechanical instruments, and many of these play old favourites such as *La Vie en Rose* and *Chim Chim Cheree*. Prices from around €50. Mon–Sat noon–7pm; closed three weeks in Aug.

Deyrolle 46 rue du Bac, 7e ⓦdeyrolle.com; ⓜRue du Bac; map pp.136–137. Extraordinary, historic palace of taxidermy – as much a sight as a shop (see p.143) – full of quirky treasures. Downstairs offers garden and inexpensive homewares; upstairs you can spend from €10 for a pinned iridescent butterfly or a fossil or €35 for a vintage pharmacy bottle filled with squid ink to €50,000 for a (naturally

deceased) zebra. Mon 10am–1pm & 2–7pm, Tues–Sat 10am–7pm.

Louvre des Antiquaires 2 place du Palais-Royal, 1er ⓦlouvre-antiquaires.com; ⓜPalais-Royal-Musée-du-Louvre; map pp.74–75. An enormous antiques and furniture hypermarket where you can pick up anything from a Mycenaean seal ring to an Art Nouveau vase – for a price. Tues–Sun 11am–7pm; closed July & Aug.

Lulu Berlu 2 rue du Grand-Prieuré, 11e ⓦluluberlu .com; ⓜOberkampf; map p.198. This sunshine-yellow store is crammed with twentieth-century toys and curios, most in their original packaging. There's a particularly good collection of 1970–90s favourites, including *Doctor Who*, *Star Wars*, *Planet of the Apes* and *Batman* figures. Mon–Sat 11am–7.30pm.

MARKETS

Paris's **markets** are a grand spectacle. Most of the food markets are resolutely French, their produce forming an enduring tie between the city and that great national obsession: *terroir*, or land/region. But you'll also find ethnic markets: African on the fringes of the 18e arrondissement and in the 11e, for example, and Southeast Asian in the 13e. There are regular food markets in all the arrondissements – a list can be found at ⓦparis.fr (search for "marchés"). Other street markets – among them the **puces de St-Ouen**, covered in our "Suburbs" chapter (see p.223) – are dedicated to secondhand goods (the *marchés aux puces*), clothes and textiles, flowers, birds, books and stamps.

BOOKS AND STAMPS

Marché du Livre Ancien et d'Occasion 104 rue Brancion, 15e ⓦgippe.org; ⓜPorte de Vanves; map pp.172–173. Around fifty stalls selling secondhand and antiquarian books. Best in the morning. Sat & Sun 9am–6pm.

Marché aux Timbres Junction of avs Marigny and Gabriel, on the north side of place Clemenceau in the 8e; ⓜChamps-Elysées-Clemenceau; map pp.64–65. The stamp market in Paris, attracting professional dealers as well as individual sellers. You can also buy postcards and phonecards. Thurs, Sat, Sun & hols 9am–7pm.

CLOTHES AND FLEA MARKETS

Porte de Montreuil Av de Porte de Montreuil, 20e; ⓜPorte de Montreuil; map p.110–111. Cheap new clothes now dominate what used to be the city's best market for secondhand clothes; it's cheapest on Mondays when weekend leftovers are sold off. Also old furniture, household goods and assorted flea market finds. Sat, Sun & Mon 7am–5pm.

★**Puces de St-Ouen** 18e; map p.224. By far the biggest and most visited of Paris's flea markets, situated on the northern outskirts (see p.223).

Puces de Vanves Av Georges Lafenestre/av Marc Sangnier, 14e ⓦpucesdevanves.fr; ⓜPorte de Vanves; map pp.162–163. Bric-a-brac and Parisian knick-knacks, with professionals dealing alongside weekend amateurs.

Sat & Sun 7am–1pm, or till around 3pm on av Georges Lafenestre.

FLOWER MARKETS

Marché Place Lépine Ile de la Cité, 4e; ⓜCité; map pp.44–45. On Sundays, the flower market – officially called Marché aux Fleurs Reine-Elizabeth-II – is augmented with caged birds and pets. Daily 8.30am–7pm; shorter hours in winter.

Marché Place de la Madeleine 8e; ⓜMadeleine; map pp.74–75. Flowers and plants. Mon–Sat 8am–7.30pm; shorter hours in winter.

Marché Place des Ternes 8e; ⓜTernes; map pp.64–65. Flowers and plants. Tues–Sun 8am–7.30pm; shorter hours in winter.

FOOD MARKETS

★**Marché d'Aligre** Place d'Aligre, 12e; ⓜLedru-Rollin; map pp.110–111. Historic street and covered food market in the square; one of the cheapest and most popular in Paris. Tues–Sat 9am–1pm & 4–7.30pm, Sun 9am–1.30pm.

Marché Bastille Bd Richard-Lenoir, 11e; ⓜRichard-Lenoir; map pp.110–111. Huge, authentic Parisian street market, with lots of regional produce. Thurs & Sun 7am–2.30pm.

★**Marché Belleville** Bd de Belleville, 11e; ⓜBelleville; map p.208. Lively, noisy neighbourhood market selling a

25

good range of fresh produce, with lots of ethnic food. Tues & Fri 7am–2.30pm.

Marché Biologique des Batignolles Bd des Batignolles between nos. 27 and 35, 17ᵉ; ⓜ Rome; map p.196. One of the city's main haunts for organic produce. Sat 9am–3pm.

Marché Brancusi Place Brancusi, 14ᵉ; ⓜ Gaîté; map pp.162–163. Excellent organic market. Sat 8am–2pm.

Marché Cler Rue Cler, 7ᵉ; ⓜ La Tour-Maubourg; map pp.136–137. Fancy delis and food stores line the street, joined by gourmet and produce stalls, with antiques and junk at the weekend. Tues–Fri, plus Sat & Sun mornings.

Marché Convention Rue de la Convention, 15ᵉ; ⓜ Convention; map pp.172–173. One of the largest markets in Paris, with a wide selection of fresh produce plus clothing on Thurs. Tues, Thurs & Sun 7am–2.30pm.

Marché Daumesnil Place Félix Eboué and bd de Reuilly, 12ᵉ; ⓜ Bel Air; map pp.110–111. Large fresh-produce market that also offers clothes and household goods. Tues & Fri 7am–2.30pm.

Marché Dejean Rue Dejean 18ᵉ; ⓜ Chateau Rouge; map p.182. Predominantly West African foods and household items in the Goutte d'Or. Tues–Sat & Sun morning.

★**Marché Edgar-Quinet** Bd Edgar-Quinet, 14ᵉ; ⓜ Edgar-Quinet; map pp.162–163. Two separate markets: food and arts and crafts. The food market is superb, with a vast range of fresh produce, from seafood and artisan cheese to fresh crêpes and home-made pizza.

Food Wed & Sat 7am–2.30pm, art and crafts Sun roughly 10am–dusk.

Marché des Enfants Rouges 39 rue de Bretagne, 3ᵉ; ⓜ Filles-du-Calvaire; map p.97. Covered food market abounding in eating outlets (see p.280) and fresh produce. Tues, Wed & Thurs 8.30am–1pm & 4–7.30pm, Fri & Sat 8.30am–1pm & 4–8pm, Sun 8.30am–2pm.

Marché Monge Place Monge, 5ᵉ; ⓜ Place Monge; map pp.122–123. Fabulous (and quite pricey) produce set around the pretty Monge fountain; organic stalls on Sun. Wed, Fri & Sun 7am–2.30pm.

Marché Montorgueil Rue Montorgueil, 1ᵉʳ; ⓜ Etienne-Marcel; map pp.74–75. Market stalls, artisan produce and gourmet food stores spread along this foodie street. Tues–Fri, plus Sat & Sun mornings.

Marché Mouffetard Rue Mouffetard, 5ᵉ; ⓜ Place Monge; map pp.122–123. Lively (and extremely touristy) market street with open-air stalls joining permanent food and wine stores. Tues–Sun mornings.

★**Marché Raspail/Marché Bio** Bd Raspail, 6ᵉ; ⓜ Rennes; map pp.136–137. The city's main organic market, also selling herbal remedies and artisan produce. Sun 9am–3pm.

★**Marché Saxe-Breteuil** Av de Saxe, 7ᵉ; ⓜ Ségur; map pp.150–151. Often regarded as the city's most beautiful market, in the shadow of the Eiffel Tower. Fresh produce plus clothing and household goods. Thurs & Sat 7am–2.30pm.

JOSEPHINE BAKER POOL

Activities and sports

If you've had enough of following crowds through museums or wandering through the city in the blazing sun or pouring rain, then it may be time to do what the Parisians do. There are ice rinks to glide over, libraries to settle down in and some genuinely beautiful swimming pools to dive into. Hammams, or Turkish baths, are particularly popular here, and range from the chichi to the steamingly authentic. You could also learn the tricks of the gourmet chef at a cookery school, or simply play a few rounds of boules. There's a world-leading array of spectator sports on offer, too, from football to horse racing, not to mention the triumphal arrival of the Tour de France in July. Information on municipal facilities is available from the Hôtel de Ville (see ⓦparis.fr) or at the *mairies* of each arrondissement. For details of sporting events, try the sports paper *L'Equipe* (ⓦlequipe.fr).

26

BOULES

The classic French game, **boules** (or pétanque), is a common sight on balmy summer evenings in many of the city's parks and gardens. You could check ⓦ paris.fr for a list of boules courts organized by arrondissement, but you'll certainly see it played at the Arènes de Lutèce (see p.132), Jardin du Luxembourg (see p.141) and the Bois de Vincennes (see p.116). The principle is the same as British bowls but the terrain is always rough – usually gravel or sand, and never grass – and the area much smaller. The metal ball is also smaller than a bowling ball, usually thrown upwards from a distance of about 10m, with a strong backspin in order to stop it skidding away from the wooden marker (*cochonnet*). Though traditionally the social equivalent of darts or perhaps pool, the game is becoming far less male-dominated; there are café or neighbourhood teams and endless championships.

COOKERY COURSES

Paris is, of course, the perfect place to get to grips with French gastronomy and wine. There are a large number of institutions offering **courses**.

Atelier des Chefs Various venues ⓦ atelierdeschefs.fr. A variety of classes (in French) in a number of venues. Probably the best option is the fun 30min session in which you prepare a quick lunch (a burger, perhaps, or crispy chicken with tarragon pesto), for €17. Other options include 2hr pâtisserie classes (€76) or "grande cuisine" *cordon bleu* sessions (4hr; €150).

Atelier des Sens 40 rue Sedaine, 11ᵉ ☎ 01 40 21 08 50, ⓦ atelier-des-sens.com; ⓜ Bastille. This unstuffy school has three kitchens in Paris and offers a host of courses (including many on weekday evenings and Sundays) ranging from "pâtisserie" and "dim sum" to events focusing on individual French regions, seasonal ingredients or molecular cuisine. They do run courses in English, but you'll be able to choose from a much wider selection if you can opt for a class in French. Sessions are capped at twelve

people; most cost about €68 for 2hr or €92 for 3hr.

Le Cordon Bleu 8 rue Léon-Delhomme, 15ᵉ ⓦ lcbparis .com; ⓜ Vaugirard/Convention. This international chain of cookery schools offers bilingual demonstrations of how to prepare French regional cuisine, followed by tastings (morning or afternoon sessions; from €45), plus half- to four-day hands-on workshops on everything from bread-baking and fruit tarts to food and wine pairing (some in English; from €48).

Le Foodist ☎ 06 71 70 95 22, ⓦ lefoodist.com. Lively, informative English-language classes and demonstrations in the Latin Quarter (they tell you where when you book), with added extras – prepare and then eat your pâtisserie with a cup of tea while listening to a storyteller (2hr 30min–3hr; from €85), or start your class with a market visit (from €135). Also wine and cheese pairing classes.

CYCLING

The French are truly mad about cycling and in response to its ongoing enthusiasm for the city's Vélib' bike rental scheme (see p.30) Paris now has around 400km of dedicated **cycle lanes**. Cyclists have access to more than 2km of car-free waterside pedalling at the Berges de Seine area (see p.152), which has three Vélib' stations of its own (ⓦ lesberges.paris.fr), but if you would rather cycle in a greener environment you may prefer the Bois de Boulogne or the Bois de Vincennes, both of which have extensive bike tracks. You can pick up Vélib' bikes by the entrances to all the major parks, which also offer bicycles for

---

CYCLING EVENTS

The biggest event of the French sporting year is the grand finale of the **Tour de France** (ⓦ letour.fr), which ends in a sweep along the Champs-Elysées in the third or fourth week of July with the French president himself presenting the *maillot jaune* (the winner's yellow jersey). Though exciting, this is largely a ceremonial occasion; only very rarely does Paris witness memorable scenes such as those of 1989, when American Greg Lemond snatched the coveted *maillot jaune* on the final day. Other classic long-distance bike races that begin or end in Paris include the week-long **Paris–Nice** event in March (ⓦ letour.com), covering more than 1100km; the **Paris–Roubaix** in April, instigated in 1896, which, with its brutally cobbled route is reputed to be the most exacting one-day race in the world (also ⓦ letour.com); and the 600km **Bordeaux–Paris** in May, the world's longest single-stage race, first held in 1891 (ⓦ bordeauxparis.com).

Major cycling events, including time trials, are held at the spanking new **national velodrome**, in the suburbs at Saint-Quentin-en-Yvelines, around 25km west of the city (ⓦ velodrome-national.com).

children (see p.352). The **Paris Respire** scheme (see p.345) closes off certain roads on Sundays and public holidays year-round, which brings out the cyclists and rollerbladers in force. Keen cyclists might also want to visit the city during one of the major **cycling events** (see opposite).

GYMS, EXERCISE CLASSES, YOGA AND DANCE

You'll find any number of aerobics classes, dance workouts and anti-stress fitness programmes in Paris, along with yoga, t'ai chi and martial arts. Many **gyms** organize their activities in courses or require a minimum month's or year's subscription, but if your latest meal has left you feeling the need to shed a few kilos, here are some options. Note too that gym facilities and classes are offered at the Aquaboulevard waterpark (see p.346).

26

Ashtanga Yoga Paris 40 av de la République, 11ᵉ ☎01 45 80 19 96, ⓦashtangayogaparis.fr; ⓜCouronnes/Parmentier. A bilingual yoga studio run by a Franco-Canadian couple offering a range of classes, including ashtanga, yin and vinyasa yoga, in two good-sized rooms. A one-hour beginner's class is €20, or it's €50 for a week-long pass, with classes held daily, most of them in the evening. Bring your own mat or rent one for €2 (€5/week). You can just turn up for a class, but if you're coming before 8am or after 8pm, or at the weekend, call or email first to get the door code.

Centre de Danse du Marais 41 rue du Temple, 4ᵉ ☎01 42 77 58 19, ⓦparis-danse.com; ⓜHôtel-de-Ville. More than forty dance disciplines are on offer here, from rock'n'roll, tap and Bollywood to African, flamenco and more – with classes for all standards and one-off visitors welcome. Each session costs €18 (€66 for four, €74 for five), though you must become a member for insurance purposes (€12). Mon–Fri 9am–9pm, Sat 9am–8pm, Sun 9am–7pm.

Espace Sportif Pontoise 19 rue de Pontoise, 5ᵉ ☎01 55 42 77 88, ⓦcarilis.fr/centre/espace-sportif

-pontoise; ⓜMaubert-Mutualité. Gym, exercise classes, swimming and squash; €4.80 entry, or €11.10 for a weekday evening pass with access to pool, gym and sauna. Mon, Tues, Thurs & Fri 7am–8.30am, 12.15–1.30pm & 4.30–11.45pm, Wed 7am–8.30am, 11.30am–7.30pm & 8.15–11.45pm, Sat 10am–7pm, Sun 8am–7pm; extended hours during school hols.

Gym Suedoise ☎01 45 00 18 22, ⓦgymsuedoise.com. Hour-long "Swedish gym" classes combine aerobics, stretching and simple dance steps. You don't have to be experienced or hyper-fit (or speak French), and can just show up, without booking, to any one of the dozens of inexpensive classes held all over Paris – in school gyms, community centres and even nightclubs. Check the website for your nearest class. €10 per class; no cash – cards only.

Rasa Yoga 21 rue Saint-Jacques, 5ᵉ ☎01 43 54 14 59, ⓦrasa-yogarivegauche.com; ⓜCluny-La Sorbonne. A bright, white and welcoming yoga studio on the Left Bank with plenty of classes (€22) in English. There's a wide range of disciplines on offer, for all levels, plus various massages from €50.

HAMMAMS

Turkish baths, or **hammams**, are one of the unexpected delights of Paris. More luxurious than the standard Swedish sauna, but less soothingly upmarket than a spa, these are places to linger, meet up and chat – some of them can get quite raucous, but that's all part of the fun. You can usually pay extra for a massage and a *gommage* – an exfoliation – followed by mint tea or a cool drink to recover. You're often given a strip of linen and modest towel on entry, and usually some slippers, but bring your own swimsuit for mixed men-and-women sessions.

Hammam Medina Center 43–45 rue Petit, 19ᵉ ☎01 42 02 31 05, ⓦhammam-medina.com; ⓜLaumière. A bit far from the centre, but it's one of the most authentically bustling hammams in the city, attracting locals for traditional mud treatments. €44 hammam and *gommage*; €59 with massage. Women: Mon–Fri 11am–10pm & Sun 9am–7pm; mixed: Sat 10am–9pm.

Hammam de la Mosquée 39 rue Geoffroy-St-Hilaire, 5ᵉ ☎01 43 31 38 20, ⓦla-mosquee.com; ⓜCensier-Daubenton. This lovely mosque (see p.131) includes an old-fashioned public bath, for women only, where locals come to relax and chat. It has an atmospheric, vaulted cooling-off room and a marble-lined steam chamber. Good value at €18, though towels are extra (€4), and you can also

have a reasonably priced massage and brisk *gommage* (€12 for a 10min session of either); a €43 package, which gets you entrance, traditional Moroccan "black soap", *gommage*, a 10min massage and a mint tea. Leave time to enjoy mint tea and honey cakes in the tiled courtyard café (see p.283). Daily except Tues 10am–9pm.

O'Kari Hammam 22 rue Dussoubs, 2ᵉ ☎01 42 36 94 66, ⓦo-kari.com; ⓜRéaumur Sébastopol. Very soothing (during off-peak hours at least), women-only hammam in a pretty little building. Packages start at €59 for an hour including steam, *gommage*, shampoo and a home-made lemonade. They also have a good range of face and hair masks, all made from natural products. Mon–Wed, Fri & Sat 10am–8pm, Thurs 10am–10pm.

26

ICE-SKATING

In winter, a big **outdoor rink** is set up on place de l'Hôtel de Ville, 4ᵉ (Dec–end Feb Mon & Thurs noon–10pm, Tues, Wed & Sun 10am–10pm, Fri & Sat 10am–midnight; free; ⓜHôtel-de-Ville), which is particularly impressive after dark; there's a small section cordoned off for young children and beginners. You can rent skates (*patins*) for around €6 (bring your passport).

PERMANENT RINKS

Patinoire de Bercy Bercy Arena, 8 bd de Bercy, 12ᵉ ☎01 82 73 16 23, ⓦbercyarena.paris/patinoire/; ⓜBercy. Especially lively on Friday and Saturday nights, when the place practically transforms into a disco on ice. Admission €4, €6 on Fri and Sat evenings; skate rental €3. Hours vary, but usually Wed 3–6pm, Fri 9.30pm–12.30am, Sat 3–6pm & 9.30pm–12.30am, Sun 10am–noon & 3–6pm.

Patinoire Pailleron 32 rue Edouard Pailleron, 19ᵉ

☎01 40 40 27 70, ⓦpailleron19.com; ⓜBolivar. In the same sports complex as the lovely Art Deco swimming pool (see p.346), this rink is particularly popular with families. Admission €4; skate rental €3. Mon & Tues noon–1.30pm & 4.15–8.30pm, Wed 2.45–9.30pm, Thurs noon–1.30pm & 4.15–10.30pm, Fri noon–1.30pm & 4.15pm–midnight, Sat 12.30pm–midnight, Sun 10am–noon (families only) & noon–6pm; hours are extended during the school holidays, when there are special family sessions.

LIBRARIES

Paris's **libraries** provide the perfect environment for a quiet moment, and some have beautiful interiors. For English-language books, the American Library's collection is unrivalled. As befits a city of cinephiliacs, there are also a couple of film libraries where watching a movie on the spot is as easy as taking out a book. Some of the collections below require non-residents without a library card to buy day-passes (around €3); take photo ID. You can find information on the city's municipal libraries, searchable by arrondissement, at ⓦparis-bibliotheques.org.

American Library in Paris 10 rue du Général-Camou, 7ᵉ ☎01 53 59 12 60, ⓦamericanlibraryinparis.org; ⓜEcole-Militaire. Hundreds of American magazines and newspapers and thousands of English-language books, plus readings, talks, children's story hours and other events. Day-pass €15, weekly €30. Free wi-fi access; otherwise book a (free) slot in advance on one of their computers. Used book sales on the first Sat & Sun of the month. Tues–Wed, Fri & Sat 10am–7pm, Thurs 10am–10pm, Sun 1–7pm.

Bibliothèque des Femmes Marguerite Durand 79 rue Nationale, 13ᵉ ☎01 53 82 76 77; ⓜOlympiades. A feminist library with books, journals, photos, posters and original manuscripts and letters. Free membership with photo ID. Tues–Sat 2–6pm.

Bibliothèque Forney Hôtel de Sens, 1 rue du Figuier, 4ᵉ ☎01 42 78 14 60; ⓜPont Marie. Medieval building filled with volumes on fine and applied arts. Tues, Fri & Sat 1–7.30pm, Wed & Thurs 10am–7.30pm.

Bibliothèque Historique de la Ville de Paris (BHVP) Hôtel Lamoignon, 24 rue Pavée, 4ᵉ ☎01 44 59 29 40; ⓜSt-Paul. Sixteenth-century mansion housing centuries of texts and picture books on the city. Mon–Sat 10am–6pm.

Bibliothèque Mazarine Institut de France, 23 quai de Conti, 6ᵉ ☎01 44 41 44 06, ⓦbibliotheque-mazarine .fr; ⓜSt-Michel. History of France and of religion. The setting, in a magnificent seventeenth-century building, with fine views across the Seine to the Louvre, is a real lure. Free admission for five consecutive days. Mon–Fri 10am–6pm; closed first two weeks in Aug.

Bibliothèque Nationale François Mitterrand Quai François-Mauriac, 13ᵉ ☎01 53 79 59 59, ⓦbnf.fr; ⓜQuai de la Gare/Bibliothèque François Mitterrand. The huge national library (see p.178), with two levels, one for the public, the other for accredited researchers. Hosts a large number of exhibitions. €3.50 for a day-pass; bring ID. Public reading rooms Mon 2–7pm, Tues–Sat 9am–7pm, Sun 1–7pm; closed first week of Sept.

Bibliothèque Ste-Geneviève 10 place du Panthéon, 5ᵉ ☎01 44 41 97 97; RER Luxembourg. Reference library with beautiful murals in the foyer and a gorgeous reading room with a vaulted ceiling supported by openwork iron arches and narrow cast-iron columns. You have to register; bring ID and a photo. Mon–Sat 10am–10pm, with reduced hours during academic hols.

BPI Centre Pompidou, 3ᵉ ⓦbpi.fr; ⓜRambuteau. The vast Bibliothèque Publique d'Information collection includes the foreign press, videos and a language lab where you can brush up on your French. Free. Mon & Wed–Fri noon–10pm, Sat & Sun 11am–10pm.

Cinémathèque Française 51 rue de Bercy, 12ᵉ ☎01 71 19 32 32, ⓦcinematheque.fr; ⓜLedru-Rollin. The library in the excellent Cinémathèque (see p.116) includes magazines, books, stills, posters, videos and DVDs. Free with museum entry or €3.50 for a day-pass. Mon & Wed–Fri 10am–7pm, Sat 1–6.30pm.

Salle des Collections Forum des Images, 2 rue du Cinéma, Porte St-Eustache, Forum des Halles, 1ᵉʳ ☎01 44 76 62 00, ⓦforumdesimages.fr; RER Châtelet-Les-Halles/Châtelet. For the price of a movie (€5) at the

Forum des Images cinémathèque (see p.309) you can also settle down in front of a monitor to watch daily screenings and select from thousands of film clips, newsreels, documentaries, soaps and the like, many of them related to Paris, along with extracts from world classic movies from 1896 to the present. Tues–Fri 1–9pm, Sat & Sun 2–9pm.

ROCK CLIMBING

Mur Mur Pantin 55 rue Cartier Bresson, Pantin ☎01 48 46 11 00, ⓦmurmur.fr; ⓜAubervilliers/RER Pantin. The Paris suburbs lay claim to one of the world's largest indoor climbing arenas, with some 13,000 square metres of wall space, as well as a special section for honing your ice-climbing skills. €15, or €9 on weekdays before 2pm for return visits. They have a second branch in Issy-les-Moulineaux, in the southwestern suburbs. Mon–Thurs 9.30am–11pm, Fri 9.30am–midnight, Sat 9.30am–8pm, Sun 9.30am–6.30pm.

26

ROLLERBLADING AND SKATEBOARDING

A hugely popular activity in Paris, **rollerblading** takes over entire streets most Friday nights from 10pm, when expert skaters – up to 15,000 on fine evenings – meet on the esplanade of the Gare Montparnasse in the 14ᵉ (ⓜMontparnasse) for a demanding **three-hour circuit** of the city; check out ⓦpari-roller.com for details of this and other roller events. A more sedate outing – and a better choice for families – takes place on Sundays, departing at 2.30pm from the place de la Bastille and returning at 5.30pm (ⓦrollers-coquillages.org). Popular areas for **rollerblading and skateboarding** include the concourse of the Palais de Chaillot (ⓜTrocadéro) and the flat areas beside the place de la Bastille and place du Palais-Royal; on Sunday, when a number of roads throughout the city are closed to cars as part of the "**Paris Respire**" scheme, rollerbladers come out in force (see ⓦparis.fr for the list of routes, complete with maps). The best place to find more **information** and **rent blades** (around €8 for a half-day, including helmet and padding) is Nomades, 37 bd Bourdon, 4ᵉ (Tues–Fri 11.30am–7.30pm, Sat 10am–7pm, Sun noon–6pm; ☎01 44 54 07 44, ⓦnomadeshop.com; ⓜBastille), which also holds its own events.

SQUASH, TABLE TENNIS AND TENNIS

Squash Dedicated squash centres include Squash Montmartre, 14 rue Achille-Martinet, 18ᵉ (Mon–Fri 10am–11pm, Sat & Sun 10am–8pm; ☎01 76 41 06 87, ⓦsquash montmartre-paris.com; ⓜLamarck-Caulaincourt), which charges around €21 for 40min; book in advance. Alternatively, the Espace Sportif Pontoise (see p.343) has squash courts at €31/hr.

Table tennis The Mairie provides outdoor table-tennis tables in many of the smaller parks and outdoor spaces in Paris. It's up to you to bring a racquet and balls. Check ⓦparis.fr for a list, organized by arrondissement.

Tennis Private clubs demand steep membership fees, but most of the city's forty or so municipal courts are in quite good shape. One of the nicest places to play is in the Jardin du Luxembourg, which has six open-air asphalt courts (☎01 43 25 79 18; ⓜSt-Placide). You can book city courts online at ⓦtennis.paris.fr (open-air €9/hr, covered €17/hr), but in practice, it's often fine to just turn up with your kit and wait on the spot – usually no more than an hour, except at busy times.

RUNNING

For **running**, the Jardin du Luxembourg, Tuileries and Champ de Mars are particularly popular with Parisians; all provide decent, varied, though short runs, and are more or less flat. The 2km riverside stretch Berges du Seine (see p.152) is also a good bet – you could even sign up for runners' coaching sessions at ⓦlesberges.paris.fr. The "**Paris Respire**" scheme, which bans cars from certain roads on Sundays and public holidays year-round, can make city jogging more pleasant (see above). If you want to run for longer distances or tackle hills, head for the Parc des Buttes-Chaumont in the 19ᵉ or Parc Montsouris in the 14ᵉ, or, best of all, the Bois de Boulogne and the Bois de Vincennes, which are the largest open spaces (though both are cut through by a number of roads). And if you fancy keeping fit while sightseeing at the same time, contact **Paris Running Tour**, who provide guides to run with you – on your own or in small groups – on a variety of circuits (from 1hr; from €65; ⓦparisrunningtour.com).

THE PARIS MARATHON

The **Paris Marathon** is held in early/mid-April over a route from place de la Concorde to Vincennes. If you want to join in, check out ⓦparismarathon.com, where you can register to run. A half-marathon is held in March (ⓦsemideparis.com), and "Les 20km de Paris" takes place in mid-October, beginning at the Eiffel Tower (ⓦ20kmparis.com).

SWIMMING

A swim in most of Paris's excellent **municipal pools** usually costs just €3. If you plan to go swimming a lot, the €24 *carnet* of ten tickets is good value. The **opening hours** of most municipal pools vary, with early morning sessions, lunchtime sessions and evening sessions on offer, with longer hours during the school holidays; we've listed the non-school holiday hours here, so at other times you should check with the *mairie* of the relevant arrondissement. **Privately run pools**, even if they're city-owned, are usually more expensive and will keep their own hours.

Les Amiraux 6 rue Hermann-Lachapelle, 18ᵉ ☎ 01 46 06 46 47; ⓜSimplon. This 33m-long municipal pool is a handsome 1920s building – as featured in the film *Amélie* – surrounded by tiers of changing cabins. €3; €24 for ten swims. Mon 5–8pm, Tues & Thurs 7–8.30am & 11.30am–1.30pm, Wed 7–8.30am & 11.30am–6pm, Fri 7–8.30am, 11.30am–1.30pm & 4.30–7pm, Sat 7am–6pm, Sun 8am–6pm; longer hours during school hols.

Aquaboulevard 4 rue Louis-Armand, 15ᵉ ☎ 01 40 60 10 00, ⓦaquaboulevard.com; ⓜBalard/Porte de Versailles/RER Bd-Victor. Huge waterpark with pools, slides and wave machines, plus a private fitness pool and state-of-the-art gym. Day-pass €23/€29 at weekends (€15 all week for children aged 3–11). Mon–Thurs 9am–11pm, Fri 9am–midnight, Sat 8am–midnight, Sun 8am–11pm.

Butte-aux-Cailles 5 place Paul-Verlaine, 13ᵉ ☎ 01 45 89 60 05; ⓜPlace d'Italie. Housed in a spruced-up 1920s brick building with an Art Deco ceiling, this is one of the most pleasant municipal pools in the city. In summer the main 33m indoor pool is joined by two 25m heated outdoor pools. €3; €24 for ten swims. Tues 7–8am, 11.30am–1pm & 5–8.15pm, Wed–Fri 7–8am & 11.30am–5.15pm, Sat 7–8am & 10.30am–5.15pm, Sun 8am–5.15pm; longer hours during school hols.

Les Halles Suzanne Berlioux 10 place de la Rotonde, Niveau 3, Porte du Jour, Forum des Halles, 1ᵉʳ ☎ 01 42 36 98 44, ⓦcarilis.fr/centre/centre-sportif-suzanne -berlioux; ⓜChâtelet/RER Châtelet-Les-Halles. Very centrally located, this 50m pool sports a glass wall looking through to a tropical garden, and stays open conveniently late. €4.50; €40 for ten swims. Mon 7–8.15am & 10am–11pm, Tues, Thurs & Fri 11.30am–10pm, Wed 11.30am–11pm, Sat & Sun 9am–7pm; longer hours during school hols.

Henry-de-Montherlant 30 bd Lannes, 16ᵉ ☎ 01 40 72 28 30; ⓜRue de la Pompe. Two pools, one 25m and one 15m, plus a terrace for sunbathing, a solarium – and the Bois de Boulogne close by. €3; €24 for ten swims. Tues 7–8.30am, 11.30am–1.30pm & 4.45–10pm, Wed 7–8.30am & 11.30am–6pm, Thurs & Fri 7–8.30am & 11.30am–1.30pm, Sat 7am–6pm, Sun 8am–6pm; longer hours during school hols.

Jean Taris 16 rue Thouin, 5ᵉ ☎ 01 55 42 81 90; ⓜMonge. A 25m pool in the centre of the Quartier Latin, and a student favourite. There's a small pool for children. €3; €24 for ten swims. Tues 7–8.30am & 11.30am–1.30pm, Wed 7–8.30am & 11.30am–6pm, Thurs 7–8.30am & 11.30am–1.30pm, Fri 7–8.30am, 11.30am–1.30pm & 5–8.30pm, Sat 7am–6pm, Sun 8am–6pm; longer hours during school hols.

Joséphine Baker Quai François-Mauriac, 13ᵉ ☎ 01 56 61 96 50; ⓜQuai de la Gare. Eye-catching floating 25m, four-lane pool, moored on the Seine by the Bibliothèque Nationale and with a number of cool floating bars and clubs just along the river. There's a retractable roof for when it rains, as well as a jacuzzi, sauna and a large paddling pool for children. It can get crowded. Winter €3, summer €5; €24 for ten swims. Mon 7–8.30am & 1–9pm, Tues & Thurs 7–8.30am & 1–11pm, Wed & Fri 7–8.30am & 1–9pm, Sat 11am–8pm, Sun 10am–8pm.

Pailleron 32 rue Edouard Pailleron, 19ᵉ ☎ 01 40 40 27 70, ⓦpailleron19.com; ⓜBolivar. A 1930s Art Deco marvel, 33m long, surrounded by tiers of changing rooms and arched over by a gantrywork roof, this is hugely popular and can get packed, especially during school holidays. €3.10, or €4.80 after 8pm; €24 for ten swims. Mon & Thurs 11.30am–8.30pm, Tues 11.30am–10.30pm, Wed 7am–8.30pm, Fri 7–8.30am & 11.30am–midnight, Sat 9am–midnight, Sun 9am–6pm; longer hours during school hols.

Pontoise 19 rue de Pontoise, 5ᵉ ☎ 01 55 42 77 88, ⓦcarilis.fr/centre/espace-sportif-pontoise; ⓜMaubert-Mutualité. Its excellent central location, Art Deco architecture, beautiful blue mosaic interior and 33m-long pool make this one of the top draws in the city. Juliette Binoche memorably swam here in the Kieslowski film *Three Colours: Blue*. €4.80; €38 for ten swims; €11.10 for evening entry with access to sauna and gym. Mon & Fri 7–8.30am, 12.15–1.30pm & 4.30–8pm, Tues 7–8.30am, 12.15–1.30pm & 4.30–7pm, Wed 7–8.30am & 11.30am–7.30pm, Thurs 7–8.30am, 12.15–1.30pm & 4.30–7.15pm, Sat 10am–7pm, Sun 8am–7pm; longer hours during school hols.

SPECTATOR SPORTS

Paris St-Germain (PSG), one of France's richest and most powerful **football** teams, is the only major-league club in the city. The capital's teams also retain a special status in the **rugby** and **tennis** worlds, and **horse racing** is a serious pursuit. Probably the biggest deal, however, is **cycling**, with a number of major events to look out for.

ATHLETICS

Bercy Arena 8 bd Bercy, 12ᵉ ☎ 01 40 02 60 60, ⓦ bercy
.fr; Ⓜ Bercy. This stadium hosts all manner of sporting
events as well as stadium gigs from the likes of Madonna
and U2. It holds 17,000 people, so you've a fair chance of
getting a ticket at the door, championships excepted.
Otherwise, tickets are sold through Fnac (see p.332) and
the stadium's website.

FOOTBALL AND RUGBY

Parc des Princes 24 rue du Commandant-Guilbaud,
16ᵉ; ⓦ leparcdesprinces.fr; Ⓜ Porte de St Cloud.
The capital's main stadium for domestic football events
(*le foot*), and home ground to the first-division PSG. The
next-door Stade Jean-Bouin, home to the Stade Français
rugby club, hosts most of their home matches.

Stade de France Rue Francis de Pressensé, St-Denis
☎ 08 92 70 09 00, ⓦ stadefrance.com; Ⓜ St-Denis–
Porte de Paris. Specially built to host the 1998 World
Cup (see p.374) – which France then went on to win –
this huge stadium out in the suburbs is the venue for
international football matches and Six Nations rugby
union matches.

HORSE RACING

Major races The week starting the last Sunday in June
sees nine big racing events, at Vincennes, Longchamp,
St-Cloud and Chantilly (see p.238), but the biggest horse

race is the Grand Prix de l'Arc de Triomphe (ⓦ prixarc
detriomphe.com), held on the first week in October at
Longchamp in the Bois du Boulogne. In May the Auteuil
racecourse, also in the Bois du Boulogne, hosts the Great
Paris Steeplechase (ⓦ grandsteeple.com), the poshest of
all French equestrian competitions. Auteuil is off the route
d'Auteuil (Ⓜ Porte d'Auteuil), and Longchamp is off the
route des Tribunes (Ⓜ Porte Maillot and then bus #244, or
free shuttle buses on major race days). See *Paris-Turf*
(ⓦ paris-turf.com) for details of horse racing events.

Trotting races These races, with the jockeys in chariots,
are held at the Vincennes racecourse, in the Bois de
Vincennes (ⓦ letrot.com/courses-spectacle).

TENNIS

Roland Garros Between the Parc des Princes and
the Bois de Boulogne, av Gordon-Bennett, 16ᵉ ☎ 01 47
43 48 00, ⓦ rolandgarros.com; Ⓜ Porte d'Auteuil. The
French equivalent of Britain's Wimbledon complex (with
clay courts), Roland Garros hosts the French Tennis Open,
one of the four major events that together comprise the
Grand Slam, in the last week of May and first week of June.
Tickets need to be reserved online months in advance
(usually in late Feb, with last-minute offers from mid-May),
but you can sometimes pick up tickets for unseeded matches
at Roland Garros itself on the day of the tournament. There's
also a heavily oversubscribed, official online ticket exchange,
Viagogo (ⓦ rolandgarros.viagogo.com).

26

CAROUSEL, JARDIN D'ACCLIMATATION

Paris for children

The French are welcoming to children on the whole, and Paris's vibrant atmosphere, with its street performers, pavement cafés and merry-go-rounds, is certainly family-friendly. Disneyland aside (see p.248), there are plenty of attractions and activities to keep kids happy, from circuses to rollerblading. Museum-hopping with youngsters in Paris can be as tedious as in any other big city, but remember that while the Louvre and Musée d'Orsay cater to more acquired tastes, the Musée des Arts et Métiers, the Pompidou Centre, Parc de la Villette and some of the other attractions listed here will interest children and adults alike. Travelling with a child also provides the perfect excuse to enjoy some of the simpler pleasures of city life – the playgrounds, ice creams and toy shops that Paris seems to offer in abundance.

ESSENTIALS

Peak times It's worth remembering that the peak times for children's activities are Wednesday afternoons, when primary school children have free time, and Saturdays; Wednesdays continue to be child-centred even during the school holidays.

Listings The most useful sources of information for current shows, exhibitions and events are the special sections in the listings magazines: "Enfants" in *Pariscope* and "Pour les jeunes" in *L'Officiel des Spectacles* (☉ offi.fr). The bimonthly Paris with Kids, the English edition of *Paris Mômes (môme* being French for "kid"), provides the lowdown on current festivals, concerts, films and other activities for children up to age 12; it's available for free from the tourist office, or look up the website, ☉ parismomes.fr. The tourist office also has ideas for families and children's outings on its website ☉ parisinfo.com. It's worth checking the festivals calendar (see pp.320–322) for annual events such as Paris Plage,

Bastille Day, the Tour de France and the Fête de la Musique.

Discounts Many cafés, bars or restaurants offer *menus enfants* (special children's set menus) or are often willing to cook simpler food on request, and hotels tack only a small supplement for an additional bed or cot onto the regular room rate. Throughout the city the RATP (Paris Transport) charges half-fares for 4–10s; under-4s travel free on public transport.

Babysitting Many hotels can organize babysitting; just check when you book. Otherwise, reliable babysitting agencies include Baby Sitting Services, 1 place Paul Verlaine, Boulogne Billancourt 92100 (☎ 01 46 21 33 16, ☉ babysittingservices.fr). You can also try individual notices at the American Church, 65 quai d'Orsay, 6ᵉ (Ⓜ Invalides; ☉ acparis.org), the Alliance Française, 101 bd Raspail, 6ᵉ (Ⓜ St-Placide; ☉ alliancefr.org), or CIDJ, 101 quai Branly, 15ᵉ (Ⓜ Bir-Hakeim; ☎ 01 44 49 12 00, ☉ cidj.com).

PARKS, GARDENS AND ZOOS

Younger kids in particular are well catered for by the parks and gardens within the city. Although there aren't, on the whole, any open spaces for spontaneous games of football, baseball or cricket, most parks have an enclosed playground with swings, climbing frames and a sandpit, while there's usually a netted enclosure for older children to play casual **ball games**. The most standard forms of entertainment in parks and gardens are puppet shows and **Guignol**, the French equivalent of Punch and Judy; these usually last about 45 minutes, cost around €3 and take place on Wednesday, Saturday and Sunday afternoons (more frequently during school holidays). Children under 8 seem to appreciate these shows most, with the puppeteers eliciting an enthusiastic verbal response from them; even though it's all in French, the excitement is contagious and the stories are easy enough to follow.

MAJOR PARKS

Jardin d'Acclimation Bois de Boulogne, by Porte des Sablons ☎ 01 40 67 90 82, ☉ jardindacclimatation .fr; Ⓜ Les Sablons/Porte Maillot; map p.220. The Jardin d'Acclimatation, dating back to 1860, is a cross between a funfair, playground, farm and amusement park, with temptations including bumper cars, merry-go-rounds, pony and camel rides, distorting mirrors, adventure playgrounds, a paddling pool and a fine puppet theatre installed in a renovated Second Empire stable block. The Jardin was created by Napoléon III in 1860 and has an appealing old-fashioned charm; some of its rides, such as the magical mini-canal ride ("*la rivière enchantée*"), date back to the park's beginnings, as does the little train with open-air carriages that you can take to get to the park; it departs from near Ⓜ Porte Maillot – cross over the *boulevard périphérique* (every 15min: Mon, Tues, Thurs & Fri noon–6pm, from 10am Wed, Sat & Sun and during hols; €5.90 return, includes admission). New attractions such as a zip wire and an adventure course have been installed recently, designed to appeal to older children, but note that these are only open on Wed, Sat, Sun & hols noon–5pm; the same is true of the pony and camel rides and the puppet shows. Entry to the park for adults and children €3, under-3s free; rides and attractions €2.90, or buy a *carnet*

of 15 tickets for €35. Daily: May–Sept 10am–7pm; Oct–April 10am–6pm.

Parc de la Villette Av Jean-Jaurès, 19ᵉ ☎ 01 40 03 75 75, ☉ lavillette.com; Ⓜ Porte de Pantin/Porte de la Villette; map p.202. As well as the Cité des Enfants (see p.354) and wide-open spaces to run around or picnic in, the Parc de la Villette has a series of twelve themed gardens, some specially designed for kids. All are linked by a walkway called the Promenade des Jardins, indicated on the park's free map. Most popular with children are the Jardin du dragon, with its huge slide in the shape of a dragon, and the Jardin des dunes et des vents (April–Oct daily 10am–8pm; Nov–March Wed, Sat, Sun & school hols 10am till dusk; under-13s only and their accompanying adults), with sandpits, large air-filled cushions that roll like waves and are great for bouncing on, climbing frames, zip wires and tunnels. The park also holds regular workshops and activities for children, such as music, baking and gardening. Full details are given on the website or at the information centre at the Porte de Pantin entrance. Admission free. Daily 6am–1am.

Parc Floral Bois de Vincennes, Esplanade du Château de Vincennes ☎ 01 49 57 24 81, ☉ www.parcfloral deparisjeux.com; Ⓜ Château-de-Vincennes, then bus #112 or a 10min walk past the Château de Vincennes.

27

PARIS WITH BABIES AND TODDLERS

You will have little problem in getting hold of **essentials for babies** in Paris. Familiar brands of baby food are available in the supermarkets, as well as disposable nappies (*couches à jeter*), and the like. After hours, you can get most goods from late-night pharmacies, though they are slightly more expensive.

Getting around with a pushchair poses the same problems as in most big cities. The métro is especially awkward, with its endless flights of stairs (and few escalators). Buses are much easier, with seats near the front for passengers with young children.

Unfortunately, many of the lawns in Parisian **parks** are out of bounds ("*pelouse interdite*"), so sprawling on the grass with toddlers and napping babies is often out of the question. That said, more and more parks are now opening the odd grassy area to the public, and there are two central spaces that offer complete freedom to sit on the grass: place des Vosges and Parc des Buttes-Chaumont.

Finding a place to **change and feed** a baby is especially challenging. While most of the major museums and some department stores have areas within the women's toilets equipped with a shelf and sink for changing a baby, most restaurants do not. Breast-feeding in public, though not especially common among French women, is, for the most part, tolerated if done discreetly. Few restaurants have high-chairs available for babies and toddlers.

The excellent playground at the Parc Floral has a relatively new attraction, Evasion Verte (see below), as well as slides, swings, ping-pong, quadricycles, mini-golf modelled on Paris monuments (adults €10, children €7.50), an electric car circuit, and a little train touring all the gardens (April–Oct daily 1–5pm). Tickets for the paying activities are sold at the playground between 2 and 5.30pm weekdays and until 7pm at weekends; activities stop fifteen minutes afterwards. Note that many of these activities are available only in the afternoon from March/April to Sept on Wed and weekends, daily during the school holidays. Also in the park is a children's theatre, the Théâtre Astral, which has mime, clowns and other not-too-verbal shows for small children aged 3 to 8, for which you're best off booking ahead online, as they're popular with school groups (usually Wed & Sun 3pm; school hols Mon–Fri & Sun 3pm; €8; ⓦ theatreastral.com). There is also a series of pavilions with child-friendly educational exhibitions (free), which look at nature in Paris; the best is the butterfly garden (mid-May to mid-Oct Mon–Fri 1.30–5.15pm, Sat & Sun 1.30–6pm). Parc Floral is free except June–Sept Wed, Sat & Sun when entry is €5, €2.50 for 7–26-year-olds (under-7s are always free). Daily: April to mid-Sept 9.30am–8pm; mid-Sept to mid-Oct 9.30am–7pm; mid-Oct to March 9.30am–5/6pm.

Evasion Verte Parc Floral ⓦ evasion-verte.fr. The Parc Floral's "Green Escape" attraction allows you to explore the treetops by walking along rope ladders, swinging on ropes from tree to tree and suchlike. You're attached to a harness and given a brief introduction; you then choose one of four walkways of varying height and difficulty. All children have to be accompanied by an adult. Children aged 6 and under 1.30m in height €14, adults and children over 1.30m in height €18; ticket valid for 2hr. Generally, open Wednesdays, weekends and school holidays in the afternoon, but check online for the latest opening times.

OTHER PARKS, SQUARES AND GARDENS

Arènes de Lutèce Rue des Arènes, 5ᵉ ⓦ paris.fr; ⓜ Place Monge; map pp.122–123. This great public park, built on what used to be a Roman theatre, has a fountain, sandpit and jungle gyms (also see p.132). Daily 7.30 or 8am till dusk.

Berges de Seine ⓦ lesberges.paris.fr; ⓜ Invalides; map pp.150–151. This pedestrianized stretch of the river (see box, p.152) has floating gardens, a climbing wall, P'tit Vélib' bikes for hire (June–Sept Wed, Sat & hols 2–6pm; €4/1hr; see p.352) and various open-air games for children, such as a giant snakes-and-ladders board painted on the ground.

Buttes-Chaumont 19ᵉ ⓦ paris.fr; ⓜ Buttes-Chaumont/Botzaris; map p.208. Built on a former quarry, these grassy slopes are perfect for rolling down and offer great views. Unusually for Paris there are no "keep off the grass" signs. You'll also find several playgrounds, a lake, waterfall, pony rides (Wed & Sat 3–6pm) and Guignol shows (see p.349). Daily 7.30 or 8am till dusk.

Champs-de-Mars 7ᵉ ⓦ paris.fr; ⓜ Ecole-Militaire; map pp.150–151. Large playground, merry-go-round and pedal cars. Puppet shows Wed, Sat & Sun at 3.15pm & 4.15pm.

Jardin du Luxembourg 6ᵉ ⓦ senat.fr/visite/jardin; ⓜ St-Placide/Notre-Dame-des-Champs/RER Luxembourg; map pp.136–137. Within the elegant Jardin du Luxembourg (see p.140) are a large playground for under-12s and one for under-6s, an old-fashioned merry-go-round and swing boats, sandpits, pony rides and toy-boat rental (Wed & Sun). A 45min marionette show takes place

EATING OUT WITH CHILDREN

Restaurants in Paris are usually good at providing small portions or allowing children to share dishes. A number of places listed in the "Cafés and restaurants" chapter (see pp.268–295) offer a **menu enfant**, including *Chez Imogène* (see p.294), *Merci* (see p.279) and *Dame Tartine* (see p.277), which last also has the advantage of outside tables in a traffic-free environment. Other family-friendly options include *Miss Kô* (see p.274), just off the Champs-Elysées, and *Le Square Trousseau* (see p.287), opposite a park and playground in the Bastille area.

Wed at 3.15pm & 4.30pm, Sat & Sun at 11am & 3.30pm. Daily 7.30 or 8am till dusk.

Jardin des Plantes 57 rue Cuvier, 5ᵉ Ⓜjardindes plantes.net; ⓂJussieu/Monge; map pp.122–123. The wonderful botanical gardens contain a small zoo, called the Ménagerie (April–Sept Mon–Sat 9am–6pm, Sun 9am–6.30pm; Oct–March daily 9am–5pm; €9, under-26s €7, under-4s free), a playground, hothouses and plenty of greenery (see p.130). Daily: April–Aug 7.30am–8pm; Sept–March 8am–dusk.

Jardin du Ranelagh Av Ingres, 16ᵉ Ⓜparis.fr; ⓂMuette; map p.217. Marionettes, playground, sandpits and pony rides (weekends & hols). Daily 7.30 or 8am till dusk.

Jardin des Tuileries Place de la Concorde/rue de Rivoli, 1ᵉʳ ☎01 40 20 90 43; ⓂPlace de la Concorde/Palais-Royal-Musée-du-Louvre; map pp.64–65. Pony rides (Wed, weekends & hols), vintage merry-go-round, marionettes, trampolines, toy sailing boats (Wed & Sun) and funfair in July & Aug (see p.70). Daily 7.30 or 8am till dusk.

Parc Georges-Brassens Rue des Morillons, 15ᵉ Ⓜparis .fr; ⓂConvention/Porte de Vanves; map pp.172–173. Access the park at the entrance across from 86 rue Brancion. Climbing rocks, puppets (Ⓦwww.marionnettes-parc -brassens.fr), artificial river, playground and scented herb gardens (see p.174). Daily dawn till dusk.

Parc Monceau Bd de Courcelles, 17ᵉ Ⓜparis.fr; ⓂMonceau; map pp.64–65. There's a lake where you can feed the ducks, a playground and a rollerblading circuit (see p.68). Daily 7.30 or 8am till dusk.

Parc Montsouris Bd Jourdan, 14ᵉ Ⓜparis.fr; ⓂGlacière/RER Cité-Universitaire; map pp.162–163. Puppet shows by the lake (Wed & Sat 3.30pm & 4.30pm, Sun 11.30am, 3.30pm, 4.30pm & 5.30pm), a number of playgrounds and a waterfall (see p.169). Daily 9am till dusk.

Parc Zoologique Junction of av Daumesnil and route de la Ceinture du Lac, 12ᵉ ☎08 11 22 41 22, Ⓦparc zoologiquedeparis.fr; ⓂPorte Dorée; map p.117. Paris's main zoo (see p.118), recently restored, is sure to appeal with its lions, zebras, giraffes, manatees and enormous tropical hothouse. Admission €22, 3–11-year-olds €14, 12–25-year-olds €16.50. Mid-March to mid-Oct Mon–Fri 10am–6pm, Sat, Sun & hols 9.30am–7.30pm; mid-Oct to mid-March daily 10am–5pm.

Place des Vosges 4ᵉ; ⓂBastille/Chemin Vert/St-Paul; map p.94. The oldest square in Paris (see p.95) has two popular sandpits, a small playground and plenty of space to run around in. Daily 7.30 or 8am till dusk.

FUNFAIRS, MERRY-GO-ROUNDS AND THEME PARKS

Funfairs Three big funfairs (*fêtes foraines*) are held in Paris each year. The season kicks off in late March with the Foire du Trône in the Bois de Vincennes (running until late May), followed by the funfair in the Tuileries gardens late June to late August, with more than forty rides, including a giant Ferris wheel, and ending up with the Fête à Neu-Neu, held near the Bois de Boulogne from early September to mid-October. Look up "Fêtes Populaires" under "Agendas" in *Pariscope* (see p.40) for details if you're in town at these times.

Merry-go-rounds There's usually a merry-go-round at the Forum des Halles, in place de l'Hôtel de Ville and beneath the Tour St-Jacques at Châtelet, with carousels for smaller children on place de la République, at the Rond-Point des Champs-Elysées by avenue Matignon, at place de la Nation, and at the base of the Montmartre funicular in place St-Pierre and at place des Abbesses.

Musée des Arts Forains 53 av des Terroirs de France, 12ᵉ ☎01 43 40 16 15, Ⓦarts-forains.com; ⓂCour

St-Émilion; see p.116. Located within one of the old Bercy wine warehouses on the edge of the Parc de Bercy, the privately owned funfair museum has working merry-go-rounds as well as fascinating relics from nineteenth-century fairs. Visits, which consist of a 90min guided tour and cost €16 (children €8), are by advance reservation only, either by phone or online.

PARC ASTÉRIX

Parc Astérix Plailly, 38km north of Paris off the A1 autoroute ☎08 26 46 66 26, Ⓦparcasterix.fr. Disneyland Paris (see pp.248–255) has put all Paris's other theme parks into the shade, though Parc Astérix – better mind-fodder, less crowded and cheaper – is well worth considering. Interesting historical-themed sections including Ancient Greece, Roman Empire, Gallic Village, Middle Ages and Old Paris are sure to spark curiosity in your children. A Via Antiqua shopping street, with buildings

27

from every country in the Roman Empire, leads to a Roman town where gladiators play comic battles and dodgem chariots line up for races. In another area, street scenes of Paris show the city changing from Roman Lutetia to the present-day capital. All sorts of rides are on offer, including the Trace du Hourra, a bobsled that descends very fast from high above. Dolphins and sea lions perform tricks for the crowds; there are parades and jugglers; restaurants for every budget; and most of the actors speak English. The easiest way to get here is to take the shuttle bus from the Louvre, which runs in the summer and can be booked online; check website for times (€22). Alternatively, take the half-hourly shuttle bus (9am–6/7pm; €8.50, under-12s €7.50) from RER Roissy-Charles-de-Gaulle (line B). Admission €46 (children aged 3–11 €38, under-3s free), though the website often has special offers. Parking €10. Check the website or phone for opening times, as they vary, but generally April–June daily 10am–6pm; July & Aug daily 10am–7pm; Sept & Oct Sat & Sun 10am–6pm; also closed for several days in May.

CIRCUSES, THEATRE, MAGIC AND CINEMA

Language being less of a barrier for smaller children, the younger your kids, the more likely they are to appreciate Paris's many special **theatre** shows and **films**. There's also **mime** and the **circus**, which need no translation.

CIRCUS (CIRQUE)

Unlike funfairs, **circuses** are taken seriously in France, coming under the heading of culture as performance art (and there are no qualms about performing animals). Some circuses have permanent venues, of which the most beautiful in Paris is the nineteenth-century Cirque d'Hiver Bouglione (see below). You'll find details of the seasonal ones under "Cirques" in the "Pour les Jeunes" section of *L'Officiel des Spectacles* and under the same heading in the "Enfants" section of *Pariscope*, and there may well be visiting circuses from Warsaw or Moscow.

Cirque Diana Moreno-Bormann 1 place Skanderbeg, 19ᵉ ☎ 06 10 71 83 50, ⓦ www.cirque-diana-moreno .com; bus #65 (direction Mairie d'Aubervilliers). A traditional circus, with lion-tamers, camels, zebras, acrobats, jugglers, trapeze artists – the lot. From €10, children under 4 free. Shows Wed, Sat & Sun 3pm.

Cirque d'Hiver Bouglione 110 rue Amelot, 11ᵉ ☎ 01 47 00 28 81, ⓦ cirquehiver.com; ⓜ Filles-du-Calvaire. From mid-October to early March, this splendid Second Empire building, decorated with pilasters, bas-reliefs and sculpted panels, is the setting for dazzling acrobatic feats, juggling, lion-taming and much else – the Christmas shows are extremely popular. (It hosts TV and fashion shows the rest of the year.) Tickets from €25. See website for show times.

Cirque Micheletty 115 bd Charles-de-Gaulle, Villeneuve-La-Garenne ☎ 01 47 99 40 40, ⓦ journee -au-cirque.com; ⓜ RER Les Grésillons then bus #177. This dream day out allows you to spend an entire day at the circus (€37, children aged 3–11 from €30, including show and lunch). In the morning you are initiated into the arts of juggling, walking the tightrope, clowning and make-up. You have lunch in the ring with your artist tutors, then join the spectators for the show, after which, if you're lucky, you might be taken round to meet the animals. You can, if you

---

SWIMMING, ROLLERBLADING AND OTHER FAMILY ACTIVITIES

One of the most fun things a child can do in Paris – and as enjoyable for the minders – is to have a wet and wild day at **Aquaboulevard** (see p.346), a giant leisure complex with a landscaped wave pool, slides and a grassy outdoor park. In addition, many municipal **swimming pools** (see p.346) in Paris have dedicated children's pools.

Cycling and **rollerblading** can also be fun for the whole family (see p.342). Sunday is the favoured day to be en famille on wheels in Paris, when the central quais of the Seine and the Canal St-Martin are closed to traffic. One of the most thrilling wheelie experiences is the **mass rollerblading** (see p.345) that takes place on Friday nights and Sunday afternoons (the Sunday outings tend to be family affairs and the pace is a bit slower). Paris à Vélo C'est Sympa (see p.30) has a good range of kid-sized bikes as well as baby carriers and tandems, and they also offer bicycle tours of Paris. In 2015 the popular Vélib' scheme was extended to children – **P'tit Vélib'**; bikes in four different sizes, including a balance bike for toddlers, can be hired at six locations, such as the Bois de Boulogne and the Berges de Seine, mostly on weekends and Wednesdays only. They're generally free for the first half-hour, then €2 for a subsequent two hours, but check the website ⓦ en.velib.paris.fr for the latest details.

Boules (see p.342) and **billiards** are both popular in Paris and might amuse older kids and teenagers.

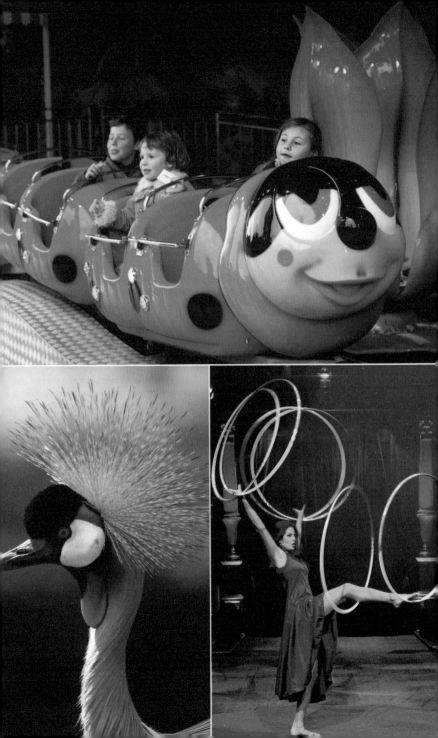

27

prefer, just attend the show at 2pm (from €15, under-12s €10), but you'd better not let the kids know what they've missed. Jan–June, Sept & Oct 10am–5pm on varying days (see website).

Cirque Pinder Pelouse Reuilly Bois de Vincennes, 12ᵉ ☎ 01 45 90 21 25, ⓦ cirquepinder.com; ⓜ Porte de Charenton/Porte Dorée. This travelling circus has been entertaining French audiences since 1854 with acts featuring performing lions, elephants and camels, clowns and trapeze artists. From €11. Early Nov to early Jan.

THEATRE AND MAGIC

The "Spectacles" section under "Enfants" in *Pariscope* lists details of magic, mime, dance and music shows. Several theatres, in addition to the Théâtre Astral in the Parc Floral (see p.349), specialize in shows for children, and a few occasionally have shows in English. Le Point Virgule, 7 rue Ste-Croix-de-la-Bretonnerie, 4ᵉ (☎ 01 42 78 67 03, ⓦ lepointvirgule.com; ⓜ Hôtel-de-Ville), in the Marais has an excellent reputation for occasional programming for kids, while Théâtre Dunois, 7 rue Louise Weiss, 13ᵉ (☎ 01 45 84 72 00, ⓦ theatredunois.org), and Théâtre

Paris-Villette, 211 av Jean-Jaurès, 19ᵉ (☎ 01 40 03 74 20, ⓦ theatre-paris-villette.fr), are dedicated almost solely to children's theatre. If your kids are really into magic they should visit the Musée de la Magie (see p.107), where a magician performs throughout the day.

Le Double-Fond 1 place du Marché Ste-Catherine, 4ᵉ ☎ 01 42 71 40 20, ⓦ doublefond.com; ⓜ St-Paul; map p.97. The magicians' venue hosts a special children's magic show (€10), though there's a lot of chat in French along with the sleight of hand. Sat 2.30pm & 4.30pm, Sun 4.30pm.

CINEMA

There are many cinemas (see pp.309–311) showing cartoons and children's films, but if they're foreign they are usually dubbed into French. The Cinémathèque Française (see p.309) screens films for children on Wednesday and Sunday afternoons, and the Forum des Images (see p.309) shows films on Wednesday and Saturday, followed by an afternoon tea. At La Villette (see p.204), the Géode IMAX cinema will appeal to most children.

MUSEUMS

Cité des Enfants Cité des Sciences, Parc de la Villette, 30 av Corentin-Cariou, 19ᵉ ☎ 08 92 69 70 72, ⓦ cite-sciences.fr; ⓜ Porte de la Villette; map p.202. The Cité des Enfants, the Cité des Science's special section for children, with sessions for 2–7s and 5–12s, is totally engaging. Kids can touch, smell and feel inside things, play about with water (it's best to bring a change of clothes), construct buildings on a miniature site (complete with cranes, hard hats and barrows), experiment with sound and light, manipulate robots, race their own shadows, and superimpose their image on a landscape. They can listen to different languages by inserting telephones into the appropriate country on a globe, and put together their own television news. Everything, including the butterfly park, is on an appropriate scale, and the whole area is beautifully organized and managed (if you haven't got a child, it's worth borrowing one just to get in here). The rest of the museum is also pretty good for kids, particularly the planetarium, the various film shows, the Argonaute

submarine and the frequent temporary exhibitions designed for the young. In the Parc de la Villette, there's lots of wide-open green space and a number of playgrounds. Admission to the Cité des Enfants costs €7 (€9 for over-25s); as sessions are very popular, advance booking online is recommended, or you can book a place (for weekday sessions only) by phone. Sessions last 1hr 30min; check online for times.

Le Musée en Herbe 21 rue Hérold, 1ᵉʳ ☎ 01 40 67 97 66, ⓦ musee-en-herbe.com; ⓜ Les Halles/Palais-Royal; map pp.74–75. Fun, interactive art exhibitions, using jigsaws, dressing-up clothes and the like, designed for children from as young as 2; recent exhibitions have included the world of Tintin and the works of Niki de Saint Phalle and the Nouveaux Réalistes. They also run popular art workshops that chime in with the exhibitions – some are for toddlers (aged 2 and a half to 4; €10), others for children aged from 5 to 12 (€10). General admission €6. Daily 10am–7pm, Thurs till 9pm.

CHILDREN'S WORKSHOPS

Many museums organize children's **workshops** on Wednesdays, Saturdays and daily throughout the school holidays. The **Musée d'Art Moderne de la Ville de Paris** (see p.158) has special exhibitions and workshops in its children's section (entrance 14 av de New-York). Other museums with sessions for kids include the **Musée Carnavalet** (see p.96), **Musée d'Orsay** (see p.144), **Musée de la Mode et du Textile** (see p.61), **Musée des Arts Décoratifs** (see p.61), **Institut du Monde Arabe** (see p.132), **Musée du Quai Branly** (see p.152) and the **Petit Palais** (see p.67). For the current programme of workshops, look under "Animations" in the "Pour les Jeunes" section of *L'Officiel des Spectacles*.

TOP TEN CHILD-FRIENDLY PARIS SIGHTS

One of the best treats for children of every age from 2 upwards is probably the Cité des Enfants (see opposite) within the Cité des Sciences, and the Cité des Sciences museum itself, in the Parc de la Villette. However, lots of Paris's main attractions, although not exclusively aimed at children, have much to offer young visitors; here are our top ten recommendations.

Les Arts Décoratifs The collections of cutting-edge furniture and the temporary fashion and design exhibitions here may well appeal to some teenagers. See p.61

Catacombs Older children may relish the creepiness of the catacombs, stacked with millions of bones from the city's old charnel houses and cemeteries. See p.168

Cinéaqua An impressive aquarium in the Jardins du Trocadéro, with thousands of exotic fish – and sharks too – in giant fishtanks. See p.157

Eiffel Tower Children love the drama of this magnificent structure; try and book tickets well in advance, or join the shorter queue for the ascent on foot – children from around age 5/6 should manage the steps up. See p.148

Grande Galerie de l'Evolution in the Jardin des Plantes Includes a children's discovery room, the Galerie des Enfants, on the first floor with child-level microscopes, glass cases with live caterpillars and moths, and a burrow of Mongolian rodents. See p.131

Jardin d'Acclimatation Children could easily spend a whole day in this enchanting playpark in the Bois de Boulogne. See p.349

Musée de la Magie Lots of hands-on fun on offer here – operate quirky automata, experiment with optical illusions and enjoy a magic show. See p.107

Musée de la Musique A wonderful way to introduce children to musical instruments from the past and present, helped by audioguides with English-language commentary (and excerpts of music) specially for kids. There are regular free workshops and concerts for children too. See p.204

Pompidou Centre Children will enjoy ascending the escalator and seeing what's on at the Galerie des Enfants; and the piazza in front of the main entrance often draws mime artists, buskers, jugglers and acrobats. See p.86

Sewers Entered through a large square manhole, and some 500m down, *les égouts* are dank, damp, dripping, claustrophobic and filled with echoes. It's a fascinating way to explore the city. See p.152

27

SHOPS

The fact that Paris is filled with beautiful, enticing, delicious and expensive things all artfully displayed is not lost on most children. Toys, gadgets and clothing are all bright, colourful and appealing, while the sheer amount of ice cream, chocolate, biscuits and sweets of all shapes and sizes is almost overwhelming. The only goodies you are safe from are high-tech toys, of which France seems to offer a particularly poor range. A good place to head is **rue Vavin**, just north of boulevard Montparnasse, in the St-Germain district, and **rue de la Villette**, in the Parc des Buttes-Chaumont area, both of which have a good concentration of children's shops.

ENGLISH-LANGUAGE BOOKS

Chantelivre 13 rue de Sèvres, 6ᵉ ⓦ chantelivre.com; ⓜ Sèvres-Babylone; map pp.136–137. A huge selection of everything to do with and for children, including good picture books for the younger ones, an English section, and a play area. Mon 1–7pm, Tues–Sat 10.30am–7.30pm; closed mid-Aug.

Galignani 224 rue de Rivoli, 1ᵉʳ ⓦ galignani.com; ⓜ Tuileries; map pp.74–75. This long-established English bookshop (see p.332) stocks a decent range of children's books. Mon–Sat 10am–7pm.

Shakespeare and Company 37 rue de la Boucherie, 5ᵉ ⓦ shakespeareandcompany.com; ⓜ Maubert-Mutualité; map pp.122–123. There's a comfy children's classics

area upstairs at this famous bookstore (see p.332). Daily 10am–11pm.

WH Smith 248 rue de Rivoli, 1ᵉʳ ⓦ whsmith.fr; ⓜ Concorde; map pp.74–75. The first floor of this British bookseller (see p.332) has a very good children's section. Mon–Sat 9am–7pm, Sun 12.30–7pm.

TOYS AND GAMES

In addition to the shops below, be sure to check out the superb selection of toys at Le Bon Marché department store (see p.324).

Amuzilo 34 rue Dauphine, 6ᵉ ⓦ amuzilo.com; ⓜ Odéon; map pp.136–137. Small, friendly toy shop with a nice selection of wooden toys (some handcrafted in

France) for toddlers; marionettes, dolls' house furniture and games for primary-school-aged children. Mon 3–7.30pm, Tues–Sat 11am–7.30pm, Sun 2–6pm.

Le Bonhomme de Bois 141 rue d'Alésia, 14ᵉ ⓦ bonhommedebois.com; ⓜ Alésia; map pp.162–163. Perfect little shop with classic wooden cars and dolls, and plush, colourful, floppy-eared stuffed animals. Mon–Sat 10am–7.30pm.

Le Ciel Est à Tout le Monde 10 rue Gay-Lussac, 5ᵉ ☎ 01 46 33 53 91; RER Luxembourg; map pp.122–123. Once a kite shop, now specializing in traditional wooden toys, mobiles, kids' cutlery and other accessories, mostly aimed at babies and young children. Mon 1–7pm, Tues–Sat 10.30am–7pm.

Les Cousins d'Alice 36 rue Daguerre, 14ᵉ ⓜ Gaîté/Edgar-Quinet; map pp.162–163. *Alice in Wonderland* decorations, toys, games, puzzles and mobiles, plus a general range of books. Tues–Sat 10am–7.30pm; closed Aug.

Au Nain Bleu 252 blvd Saint-Germain, 7ᵉ ⓦ aunainbleu.com; ⓜ Solférino; map pp.136–137. Around since the 1830s, this shop is expert at delighting children with wooden toys, dolls and faux-china tea sets galore. Mon–Sat 10.30am–6.30pm.

Pain d'Epices 29 passage Jouffroy, 9ᵉ ⓦ paindepices.fr; ⓜ Grands Boulevards; map pp.74–75. Fabulous dolls' house necessities from furniture to wine glasses. Mon 12.30–7pm, Tues–Sat 10am–7pm, Thurs till 9pm.

Puzzles Michèle Wilson 116 rue du Château, 14ᵉ ⓦ puzzles-et-jeux.com; ⓜ Pernéty; map pp.162–163. Beautiful wooden jigsaw puzzles of paintings and Paris scenes, with workshop on the premises. Tues–Sat 10.30am–1pm & 2–7pm.

Si Tu Veux 68 galerie Vivienne, 2ᵉ ⓦ situveuxjouer.com; ⓜ Bourse; map pp.74–75. Well-made traditional toys plus toy-making kits and ready-made costumes. Mon–Sat 10.30am–7pm.

Tout s'arrange 27 rue Delambre, 14ᵉ ⓦ toutsarrange.fr; ⓜ Vavin; map pp.162–163. A delightfully idiosyncratic miniature boutique selling inexpensive tiny treasures (jewellery, decorations, micro-dollies) handmade using objects found or recycled by the owner, who also makes toys and bags. Tues–Sat 10.30am–7pm.

CLOTHES

Besides the specialist shops listed here, most of the big department and discount stores have children's sections (see p.324). Of the latter, Tati is the cheapest, while Monoprix has decent prices and quality.

Alice à Paris 9 rue de l'Odéon, 6ᵉ ⓦ aliceaparis.com; ⓜ Odéon; map pp.136–137. Beautiful, elegant clothes to make your children perfect little Parisians. From babies upward, but best for toddlers and older children. Expensive, but not overpriced. Mon 2–7pm, Tues–Sat 11am–7pm.

Bonpoint 50 rue Etienne-Marcel, 2ᵉ ⓦ bonpoint.com; ⓜ Etienne-Marcel; map pp.74–75. Insanely expensive but utterly elegant outfits for the 0- to 6- to going-on-24-year-old. These are elegant, well-designed clothes mixing traditional children's outfitting with contemporary touches. Prices in the €50–100 range. A half-dozen other branches around the city, and available at Le Bon Marché (see p.324). Mon–Sat 10am–7pm.

Du Pareil au Même 122 rue du Faubourg-St-Antoine, 12ᵉ ⓦ dpam.com; ⓜ Ledru-Rollin; map pp.110–111. Beautiful kids' clothing at very good prices. Gorgeous floral dresses, cute jogging suits and brightly coloured basics. Branches all over Paris. Mon–Sat 10am–7pm.

Les P'tits Bo'Bo 7 rue Clauzel, 9ᵉ; ⓜ St-Georges; map p.182. A treasure-trove of secondhand but top-quality children's clothing for newborns to 12-year-olds, stocking leading "bourgeois-bohemian" brands like Bonpoint, Bonton, IKKS and Luco, plus internationals Burberry and Finger in the Nose. Also sells used toys and accessories. Tues–Sat 11am–7pm.

27

GAY PRIDE MARCH

LGBT Paris

Paris has long had a strong gay presence – boosted in recent times by the fact that the city's mayor for thirteen years, Bertrand Delanoë, was openly gay. The focal point of the scene over the past few decades has been the Marais, whose central street, rue Ste-Croix-de-la-Bretonnerie, has visibly gay-oriented businesses at almost every other address, including the bulk of the nightlife venues, but there are other LGBT-friendly pockets scattered throughout the city, and the community is well catered for by rights and support organizations and an active press. The high spot on the calendar is the huge annual Gay Pride parade, which normally takes place on the last Saturday in June (ⓦmarche.inter-lgbt.org).

USEFUL CONTACTS

Centre LGBT de Paris 63 rue Beaubourg, 3ᵉ Ⓦ centre lgbtparis.org; Ⓜ Arts-et-Métiers/Rambuteau. The website is a good source of information on special events, and the office is the first port of call for information and advice – legal, social, psychological and medical. Centre Mon–Fri 3.30–8pm, Sat 1–7pm; different services keep different hours (check website).

Inter-LGBT ☎ 01 71 08 68 45, Ⓦ inter-lgbt.org; Ⓜ St-Sébastien-Froissart. Actively campaigns for gay rights and organizes the annual Pride march.

MAG 106 rue de Montreuil, 11ᵉ ☎ 01 43 73 31 63, Ⓦ mag-paris.fr; Ⓜ Nation. The Mouvement d'Affirmation des Jeunes Gais et Lesbiennes, Bi et Trans, a group aimed at young people that organizes a drop-in welcome service (Fri 6–10pm, Sat 4–9pm) as well as occasional parties, picnics, and cinema and theatre nights.

Paris Gay Village Ⓦ parisgaivillage.com. Voluntary association that acts as an alternative tourist office, with inexpensive monthly guided walks and museum visits ("gay Louvre" and "Left Bank lesbians", for example) and a free one-hour welcome-to-gay-Paris service.

BOOKS AND WEBSITES

Barbieturix Ⓦ barbieturix.com. Excellent lesbian resource, with news, reviews, interviews and articles, plus good club and bar listings.

Citegay Ⓦ citegay.fr. One of the best national websites (in French), with lots of links, features and contacts.

Les Mots à la Bouche 6 rue Ste-Croix-de-la-Bretonnerie, 4ᵉ ☎ 01 42 78 88 30, Ⓦ motsbouche.com; Ⓜ Hôtel-de-Ville; map p.97. The city's main gay and lesbian bookshop, with exhibition space and meeting rooms and a good selection, from graphic novels to biographies to art books, with some literature in English. Lots of free listings maps and club flyers to pick up, and there will usually be someone around who can speak English. Mon–Sat 11am–11pm, Sun 1–9pm.

Têtu Ⓦ tetu.com. The glossiest and most readable of France's gay (and to a lesser extent, lesbian) monthlies – the name means "headstrong" – with lifestyle articles, listings and reviews.

NIGHTLIFE

In terms of **nightlife**, Paris's "gay village" is the Marais, centred on rue Ste-Croix-de-la-Bretonnerie, rue des Archives and spreading up past the Pompidou Centre towards métro Etienne-Marcel. There are also a few gay bars and clubs on **rue Sainte-Anne** in the 1ᵉʳ and clustered around the **Bonne Nouvelle** métro on rue Poissonnière in the 2ᵉ. The selection below only scratches the surface. **Lesbian bars** congregate along rue du roi de Sicile – in addition to those listed below, check the *Rosa Bonheur* bars (see p.288 & p.295), which although mixed, have a strong lesbian following. As everywhere, the reputation of wild hedonism in gay **clubs** has spread beyond the gay community and attracted heterosexuals in search of a good time. Consequently, straights are welcome in some gay establishments, especially when in gay company. Don't forget that many if not most mainstream clubs run gay *soirées* – the Follyvores/Crazyvores nights at the excellent *Bataclan* club are particularly popular (see p.305) – but the best thing is to keep an eye on flyers and ask around in bars. **Entry prices** are generally around €10–20, depending on the size of the venue and the popularity of the individual *soirée*.

BARS – MAINLY WOMEN

3W-Kafé 8 rue des Ecouffes, 4ᵉ ☎ 01 48 87 39 26; Ⓜ Hôtel-de-Ville; map p.97. Swish lipstick-lesbian lounge-café. It's the haunt of sophisticated professionals earlier on, but warms up considerably at weekends, when the cellar bar gets moving. Prices are high. The owners also run *Les Jacasses*, opposite, a lower-key wine bar which does decent tapas, bruschette and the like. Sun & Mon 7pm–midnight, Tues–Fri 7pm–4am, Sat 7am–6pm.

La Champmeslé 4 rue Chabanais, 2ᵉ ☎ 01 42 96 85 20, Ⓦ lachampmesle.fr; Ⓜ Pyramides; map pp.74–75. Long-established lesbian address, particularly popular among thirty-somethings, though it packs everyone in for occasional cabaret nights. A good place to begin exploring the scene. Mon–Sat 4pm–4am.

Le So What! 30 rue du Roi de Sicilie, 4ᵉ ☎ 01 42 71 24 59; Ⓜ St-Paul; map p.97. A lesbian bar aimed at a more mature crowd. Friendly ambience, with good DJ sets, and club nights at the weekend. Check the Facebook page for listings. Thurs 8pm–2am, Fri & Sat 8pm–5am.

BARS – MAINLY MEN

Café Cox 15 rue des Archives, 3ᵉ ☎ 01 42 72 08 00, Ⓦ cox.fr; Ⓜ Hôtel-de-Ville; map p.97. Muscular types, up for a seriously good time, pack out this loud, well-established bar – an essential fixture on the Marais circuit – which has an extended happy hour (Mon–Sat 6–10pm, Sun 6pm–2am). Daily 5pm–2am.

★**Le Duplex** 25 rue Michel-le-Comte, 3ᵉ ☎ 01 42 72 80 86, Ⓦ duplex-bar.com; Ⓜ Rambuteau; map p.97. Arty little bar that's popular with intellectual and media types for its relaxed and chatty atmosphere. Friendly rather than cruisey, with occasional art exhibitions. Happy hour 8–10pm. Mon–Thurs & Sun 8pm–2am, Fri & Sat 8pm–4am.

Le Free DJ 35 rue Ste-Croix-de-la-Bretonnerie, 4ᵉ ☎ 01 48 04 95 14, Ⓦ freedj.fr; Ⓜ Hôtel-de-Ville; map p.97.

28

This stylish DJ bar draws the young and *très looké* – beautiful types. It's friendly, though, and features some big sounds (house, disco-funk) in the basement club at the weekends. Daily 6pm–4am.

L'Open Café 17 rue des Archives, 4ᵉ Ⓦopencafe.fr; ⓂHôtel-de-Ville; map p.97. *L'Open* is *the* most famous gay bar in Paris and, as such, it's expensive and quite touristy, but still good fun, with not-bad café food and lots of *terrasse* seating for observing the scene on the streets. An essential stop on the circuit. Mon–Thurs & Sun 11am–2am, Fri & Sat 11am–3am.

Le Raidd 23 rue du Temple, 4ᵉ Ⓦraiddbar.com; ⓂHôtel-de-Ville; map p.97. One of the city's biggest, glossiest bars, famous for its beautiful staff, topless waiters and go-go boys' shower shows. Daily 5pm–2am.

CLUBS

Le Club 18 18 rue du Beaujolais, 1ᵉʳ ☎01 42 97 52 13, Ⓦclub18.fr; ⓂPalais Royal; map pp.74–75. The oldest gay club in Paris, but still fashionable, especially among a friendly, fresh-faced crowd. Tiny, too, which is part of the fun. Entry €10, which includes a drink. Fri & Sat midnight–6am.

CUD 12 rue des Haudriettes, 3ᵉ; ⓂRambuteau; map p.97. The "Classic Up and Down" is just that: bar upstairs, club below. A good venue for low-key, relaxed dancing with no queues, door policies or overpriced drinks. More for bears than boys, though it's pretty mixed. Really hots up around 2am as it's one of the few places in the Marais open till the wee hours. Free; check events on the Facebook page. Daily 11.30pm–7am.

Queen 102 av des Champs-Elysées, 8ᵉ ☎01 53 89 08 90,

Ⓦqueen.fr; ⓂGeorge V; map pp.64–65. The gay club of the 1980s has bounced back after a period in the doldrums, though it's now much more of a mixed venue, catering to all sexualities. The friendly, gay-focused Sunday nights are the best of the lot. Entry costs vary, but its location on the Champs-Elysées means it's pricey. Opens 11.30pm; closing hours vary according to the night.

Le Rive Gauche 1 rue du Sabot, 6ᵉ ☎01 40 20 43 23, Ⓦlerivegauche.com; ⓂSt-Germain-des-Prés; map pp.136–137. Fashionable among gorgeous young *gamines* on the Saturday girls-only nights (€15), this pocket club is a historic 1970s address (preserving some of its gold mirror-mosaic decor). Daily 11pm–5am.

Scream 18 rue du Faubourg du Temple, 11ᵉ ☎06 17 27 68 98, Ⓦscream-paris.com; ⓂRepublique; map p.198. Popular gay club pumping out house/techno in one room and poppier sounds in the second, smaller space. The up-for-it crowd looks good and is generally friendly. €10 including a drink before 1am, €15 after 1am (no drink). Sat from 11pm.

★**Le Tango** 13 rue au Maire, 3ᵉ ☎01 42 72 17 78, Ⓦboite-a-frissons.fr; ⓂArts-et-Métiers; map p.94. Unpretentious (and inexpensive) gay and lesbian club in a retro 1930s dance hall, with a traditional Sunday-afternoon tea dance/*bal* from 6pm, featuring slow dances as well as anything from tango to camp disco classics. Friday and Saturday nights also begin with couples of all sexual orientation dancing every kind of traditional *danse à deux*, until the legendary "Madison" line dance at 12.30am, after which it's pure fetish costume and disco – and no techno allowed. Also does themed nights and singles nights. €6–9. Fri & Sat 10.30pm–5am, Sun 6–11pm.

28

Contexts

History

Early humans – and for many millennia their Neanderthal cousins alongside them – first lived in the Paris region some 600,000 years ago, when deer, boar, bear and auroch roamed the banks of a half-kilometre-wide river. The waters slowly shifted southward before settling in the current bed of the Seine in around 30,000 BC (leaving behind today's Marais or "marsh"). The discovery of 14,000-year-old reindeer-hunter campsites at Pincevent, Verberie and Etiolles, in the Paris basin, suggests that modern humans arrived relatively recently. The oldest encampment yet uncovered, dating back to about 7600 BC, was found by the river in the southwest corner of the modern 15^e arrondissement; it seems to have been a site for sorting flint pebbles. At Bercy, several well-preserved dugout canoes probably date from a marshy fishing and hunting settlement of around 4500 BC.

The Parisii

Mud and water were clearly still major features of the area when the **Gauls** or **Celts** began to settle, probably in the third century BC, as the Roman rendition of their name for the city, **Lutetia** or Lucotetia, is drawn from *luco*, a Celtic root word for "marshland". The local Quarisii or **Parisii** tribe built an oppidum or Iron Age fort on the eastern part of what is now the Ile de la Cité. The island was originally part of a miniature archipelago of five islets, with two further islets lying to its east (these became the modern Ile St-Louis; another, easternmost island was only joined to the Right Bank at boulevard Morland in 1843). The fort of the Parisii commanded a perfect site: defensible and astride the most practicable north–south crossing point of an eminently navigable river.

Roman Paris

When Julius Caesar's conquering armies arrived in 52 BC, they found a thriving and populous settlement – the Parisii had managed to send a contingent of some eight thousand men to stiffen the Gallic chieftain Vercingétorix's doomed resistance to the invaders. Romanized Lutetia prospered, thanks to its commanding position on the Seine trade route, the river's *nautes*, or boatmen – remembered in the carved pillar now in the Musée du Moyen Age (see p.125) – occupying an important position in civic society. And yet the town was fairly insignificant by **Roman** or even Gaulish standards, with a population no larger than the Parisii's original eight-thousand-strong war band; other Gallo-Roman cities, by contrast, had populations of twenty to thirty thousand. The Romans established their basilica on the Ile de la Cité, but the town lay almost

Third century BC	52 BC		Around 275
A tribe known as the Parisii begins to settle on the Ile de la Cité.	When Julius Caesar's conquering armies arrive they find a thriving settlement of some eight thousand people.		St Denis brings Christianity to Paris. He is martyred for his beliefs at Montmartre.

entirely on the Left Bank, on the slopes of the Montagne Ste-Geneviève. Though no monuments of their presence remain today, except the baths by the Hôtel de Cluny and the amphitheatre in rue Monge, their street plan, still visible in the north–south axes of rue St-Martin and rue St-Jacques, determined the future growth of the city.

Roman rule in Gaul disintegrated under the impact of **Germanic invasions** around 275 AD, at about the same time St-Denis (see box, p.228) established **Christianity** in the Paris region. Roman Lutetia itself, however, or "Paris", as it was beginning to be called, held out for almost two hundred years. The Emperor Julian was headquartered in the city for three years from 358, during his campaign against the German and Frankish tribes – the latter so-called after the Latin word for "ferocious" – making Paris the de facto capital of the Western Empire. Julian found the climate agreeable, with mild winters and soft breezes carrying the warmth of the ocean, and noted that the water of the Seine was "very clear to the eye".

Franks and Capetians

The marauding bands of **Attila the Hun** were repulsed in 451, supposedly thanks to the prayerful intervention of Geneviève, who became the city's patron saint. (Popular legend has it that Attila had massacred eleven thousand virgins in Cologne, on his way to Paris, and that there weren't enough virgins in the city to make it worth his while.) In any case, the city finally fell to **Clovis the Frank** in 486, the leader of a group of Germanic tribes who traced their ancestors back to Merowech, the son of a legendary sea monster – hence the name of the **Merovingian** dynasty Clovis founded. (This sea-monster story has, if anything, more respectable historical roots than the conspiratorial theory that the Merovingians were the descendants of Jesus and Mary Magdalene.) It was the first but by no means the last time the city would fall to German troops.

Clovis's own conversion to Christianity hastened the Christianization of the whole country. In 511 Clovis's son Childebert commissioned the cathedral of St-Etienne, whose foundations can be seen in the Crypte Archéologique under the square in front of Notre-Dame. He also imported the relics of St Vincent to a shrine on the Left Bank. The site slowly grew to become the great monastery at St-Germain-des-Prés, while St-Denis, to the north of the city, became the burial site of the Merovingians from Dagobert I onwards, in the early seventh century.

The endlessly warring, fratricidally minded Merovingians were gradually supplanted by the hereditary Mayors of the Palace, the process finally confirmed by the coronation of Pépin III, "the Short", in St-Denis, in 754. Pépin's heir, Carolus Magnus or "**Charlemagne**", who gave his name to the new Carolingian dynasty, conquered half of Europe and sparked a mini-Renaissance in the early ninth century. Unfortunately for Paris, he chose to live far from the city. Paris's fortunes further plummeted after the break-up of Charlemagne's empire, being repeatedly sacked and pillaged by the **Vikings** from the mid-840s onwards. Finally, in the 880s, **Eudes**, the Comte de Paris, built strong fortifications on the Ile de la Cité, and the Vikings were definitively repulsed. Yet Paris lay largely in ruins, a provincial backwater without power, influence or even a significant population. Only the Right Bank, which lacked the wealthy monasteries of the main city, had escaped the Vikings' depredations. It was to emerge as the heart of a reborn city.

486	768	845–85
The city falls to Clovis the Frank. His dynasty, the feuding Merovingians, governs Paris for the next two hundred years or so.	Charlemagne is proclaimed king at St-Denis. Over the next forty years he conquers half of Europe – but spends little time in Paris.	Vikings repeatedly sack Paris.

The medieval heyday

In 987, Eudes' descendant Hugues Capet was crowned king, but the early rulers of the new **Capetian dynasty** rarely chose to live in Paris, despite the association of the monarchy with the city. Regrowth, therefore, was slow, and by 1100, the city's population was only around three thousand. One hundred years later, however, Paris had become the largest city in the Christian world (which it would remain until overtaken by London in the eighteenth century), as well as its intellectual and cultural hub. By the **1320s**, the city's population had swollen again to around a quarter of a million. This unparalleled success rested on the city's valuable river-borne trade and the associated expansion of the **merchant classes**, coupled with thriving **agriculture** in the wider Paris region. Vines and cereals grew to the south, while swathes of rich woodland lay to the east and west, and in the north, between the city and the hill of Montmartre. The economic boom was matched by the growth of the city's university, and protected by the novelty of a relatively strong – and largely Paris-based – monarchy, which gradually brought the surrounding regions under its overlordship. Between them, Louis VI, Louis VII and Philippe-Auguste ruled with confidence for almost all the twelfth century.

Walls and Watermen

To protect his burgeoning city, **Philippe-Auguste** (1180–1223) built the **Louvre fortress** whose excavated remains are now on display beneath the Louvre museum. He also constructed a vast **city wall**, which swung north and east to encompass the Marais, and south to enclose the Montagne Ste-Geneviève – a line roughly traced by the inner ring of modern Paris's 1er–6e arrondissements (though the abbey at St-Germain-des-Prés remained *extra muros*). European contemporaries saw the fortifications as a wonder of the world (even if by Rabelais' time "a cow's fart" would have brought down the walls on the Left Bank), a vital guarantee of the city's security and a convincing proof of the monarchy's long-term ambitions to construct an imperial capital. Famously appalled by the stench of the city's mud as a young man, Philippe-Auguste even began to pave some of the city's streets, though most remained filthy, hopelessly rutted and crowded with people and animals – Louis VI's heir had even been killed when de-horsed by a runaway pig in 1131.

LEFT AND RIGHT: A TALE OF TWO RIVERBANKS

During the medieval era, the city's commercial activity naturally centred on the place where goods came in to the city – a trade monopolized by the powerful Watermen's guild of Paris. The chief landing place was the place de Grève, a strip of marshy ground which lay where the Hôtel de Ville now stands, on the Right Bank. The Left Bank's intellectual associations were formed equally early, as students came to study at the two great monasteries of Ste-Geneviève and St-Germain-des-Prés. Europe's pre-eminent scholar, Peter Abélard – famously the lover of Héloïse and the victim of violent castration – taught in Paris in the early twelfth century, and in 1215 a papal licence allowed the official formation of what gradually became the renowned University of Paris, eventually to be known as the **Sorbonne**, after Robert de Sorbon, founder of a college for poor scholars in 1257. By 1300 there were around three thousand students on the Left Bank of the city, protected by ecclesiastical rather than city law. At this time, the Latin used both inside and outside the schools gave the student district its name of the "Latin Quarter".

987	1200s	1330s to 1430s
Hugues Capet, one of the counts of Paris, is elected king of Francia and makes Paris his capital.	Paris experiences an economic boom, its university becomes the centre of European learning and King Philippe-Auguste constructs a vast city wall.	The French and English nobility struggle for power in the Hundred Years' War. One year in four is a plague year and Paris's population falls by half.

The administration of the city remained in the hands of the monarchy until 1260, when **Louis IX** (St Louis) ceded a measure of responsibility to the *échevins* or leaders of the Paris Watermen's guild (see box, p.363). The city's government, when it has been allowed one, has been conducted ever since from the place de Grève/place de l'Hôtel de Ville, and the guild's motto, Sec Fluctuat Nec Mergitur ("Battered, but not sinking"), was later adopted by the city itself.

A city adrift

From the **mid-fourteenth** to **mid-fifteenth centuries**, Paris shared the same unhappy fate as the rest of France, embroiled in the long and destructive **Hundred Years' War**, which pitted the French and English nobilities against each other in a power struggle whose results were misery for the French peasant classes, and penury for Paris. A break in the Capetian line led to the accession of Philippe VI, the first of the **Valois dynasty**, but the legitimacy of his claim on the throne was contested by Edward III of England. Harried by war, the Valois monarchs spent much of their troubled reigns outside their capital, whose loyalty was often questionable. Infuriated by the lack of political representation for merchant classes, the city mayor, or Prévôt des Marchands, **Etienne Marcel**, even let the enemy into Paris in 1357.

Charles V, who ruled from 1364, tried to emulate Philippe-Auguste by constructing a new Louvre and a new city wall that increased Paris's area by more than half again (roughly incorporating what are now the modern 9e–11e arrondissements, on the Right Bank), but the population within his walls was plummeting due to disease and a harsh climate in Europe generally, as well as warfare and political instability. The **Black Death**, which arrived in the summer of 1348, killed some eight hundred Parisians a day, and over the next 140 years one year in four was a plague year. In the fourteenth century, the state and populace alike easily found scapegoats for such ills. Leading knights of the wealthy Templar order were burnt at the stake on the tip of the Ile de la Cité in 1314, and they were followed to their deaths by hundreds of **Jews** falsely accused of poisoning the city's wells. France's Jews were definitively expelled from the kingdom in 1394. Paris had lost two of its most economically productive minorities. Harvests repeatedly failed – icebergs even floated on the Seine in 1407 – and politically, things were no better. Taxes were ruinous, trade almost impossible and government insecure.

In 1422 the Duke of Bedford based his overlordship of northern France in Paris. **Joan of Arc** made an unsuccessful attempt to drive the English out in 1429, but was wounded in the process at the Porte St-Honoré, and the following year the English king, Henry VI, had the cheek to have himself crowned king of France in Notre-Dame. Meanwhile, the Valois kings fled the city altogether for a life of pleasure-seeking irrelevance in the gentle Loire Valley, a few days' ride to the southwest.

Renaissance

In the course of the hundred years leading up to the mid-fifteenth century, Paris's population more than halved. It was only when the English were expelled – from Paris in 1437 and from France in 1453 – that the economy had the chance to recover from

1429	1528	1572
Joan of Arc attempts to drive the English out of Paris. It is not until 1437 that Charles VII regains control of his capital.	François I transfers the royal court from the Loire to his new palace at the Louvre.	On St Bartholomew's Day, August 25, some 3000 Protestants gathered in Paris are massacred at the instigation of the ultra-Catholic Guise family.

decades of devastation. Even so, it was many more years before the Valois monarchs felt able to quit their châteaux and hunting grounds in the Loire and return to the city. Finally, in 1528, **François I** decided to bring back the royal court to Paris, aiming, like Philippe-Auguste before him, to establish a new Rome. Work began on reconstructing the Louvre and building the Tuileries palace for **Catherine de Médicis**, and on transforming Fontainebleau and other country residences into sumptuous Renaissance palaces. An economic boom brought peasants in from the countryside in their thousands, and the city's population surpassed its medieval peak by the 1560s. Centralized planning coughed into life to cope with the influx; royal edicts banned overhanging eaves on houses, and a number of gates were removed from Charles V's walls to improve street congestion. But Paris remained, as Henri II put it, a city of "mire, muck and filth".

The wars of religion

In the second half of the century, war interrupted the early efforts at civic improvement – this time **civil war** between Catholics and Protestants. Paris, which swung fanatically behind the Catholic cause – calls for the establishment of a new Jerusalem quickly replaced the old Roman ideals – was the scene of one of the worst atrocities ever committed against French Protestants. Some three thousand of them were gathered in Paris for the wedding of Henri III's daughter, Marguerite, to Henri, the Protestant king of Navarre. On August 25, 1572, **St Bartholomew's Day**, as many as three thousand Protestants were massacred at the instigation of the noble "ultra-Catholic" Guise family. When, through this marriage, Henri of Navarre became heir to the French throne in 1584, the Guises drove his father-in-law, Henri III, out of Paris. Forced into alliance, the two Henris laid siege to the city in May 1590 – Henri III claiming to love the city more than he loved his own wife (which, given he was a notorious philanderer among both men and women, was almost certainly true). Parisians were quickly reduced – and it wasn't to be for the last time – to eating donkeys, dogs and rats. Five years later, after Henri III had been assassinated and some forty thousand Parisians had died of disease or starvation, Henri of Navarre entered the city as king **Henri IV**. "Paris is worth a Mass", he is reputed to have said, to justify renouncing his Protestantism in order to soothe Catholic sensibilities.

Henri's inheritance

The Paris that Henri IV inherited was not a very salubrious place. It was **overcrowded**: no domestic building had been permitted beyond the limits of Philippe-Auguste's twelfth-century walls because of the guilds' resentment of the unfair advantage enjoyed by craftsmen living outside the jurisdiction of the city's tax regulations. The swollen population had caused an **acute housing shortage** and a terrible strain on the rudimentary water supply and drainage system. It is said that the first workmen who went to clean out the city's cesspools in 1633 fell dead from the fumes. It took seven months to clean out 6420 cartloads of filth that had been accumulating for two centuries. The overflow ran into the Seine, whence Parisians drew their drinking water.

1607	1661–1715	1789
The triumphant monarch Henri IV builds the Pont-Neuf and sets about creating a worthy capital.	Louis XIV transfers the court to Versailles, but this doesn't stop the city growing in size, wealth and prestige.	Long-standing tensions explode into revolution. Ordinary Parisians, the "sans-culottes", storm the Bastille prison on July 14.

BOULEVARDS AND AVENUES

Aside from his grand palace at Versailles, just outside Paris (see p.232), Louis XIV's most significant architectural legacy was perhaps the demolition of Charles X's old fortifications to make way for the new **boulevards** – which took their name from the bulwarks, or giant earthen ramparts, that they replaced – and the creation of long, tree-lined **avenues** such as the Champs-Elysées, which was laid out in 1667 by the landscape designer Le Nôtre. Avenues and boulevards were to become the defining feature of Paris's unique cityscape.

Planning and expansion

As the **seventeenth century** began, Henri IV's government set to work in Paris, regulating street lines and facades, and laying out the splendidly harmonious place Royale (later renamed the place des Vosges) and place Dauphine. Most emblematic of all the new construction work, however, was the **Pont-Neuf**, the first of the Paris bridges not to be cluttered with medieval houses. It was a potent symbol of Paris's renewal and architectural daring. After Henri IV was assassinated in 1610 – while caught in his carriage in a seventeenth-century traffic jam on rue de la Ferronnerie – his widow built the **Palais du Luxembourg**, the first step in the city's colonization of the western Left Bank – previously the province of abbeys and churches.

The tradition of grandiose public building initiated by Henri IV perfectly symbolized the bureaucratic, centralized power of the newly self-confident state. The process reached its apogee in the seventeenth century under **Louis XIV**, whose director of architecture promised to fill the city "with so many magnificent buildings that the whole world will look on in wonder". Under the unifying design principles of grace and **Classicism**, the places Vendôme and Victoire were built, along with the sublime Cour Carrée of the Louvre, and half a dozen Italianate Baroque domes.

Grandiose building projects were commissioned as often without royal patronage as with it. The aristocratic *hôtels*, or private mansions, of the **Marais** were largely erected during the seventeenth century, to be superseded early in the **eighteenth century** by the **Faubourg St-Germain** as the fashionable quarter of the rich and powerful. Despite the absence of the court, Paris only grew in size, wealth and prestige, until the writer Marivaux could claim, with some truth, in 1734 that "Paris is the world, and the rest of the earth nothing but its suburbs". By the 1770s and 1780s, conversational *salons*, Masonic lodges, coffee houses or "cafés" and newspapers had opened by the hundreds to serve the needs of the burgeoning **bourgeoisie**, while the Palais Royal became the hub of fashionably decadent Europe – a gambling den, brothel, mall and society venue combined. In 1671, however, Louis repaired with his entire court to a new and suitably vast palace at **Versailles**, declaring it was "the spot where I can most be myself". The monarchy would not return until Louis' grandson, Louis XVI, was brought back at pike-point in 1789.

The poor

Meanwhile, the centre of the city remained a densely packed and unsanitary warren of **medieval lanes and tenements**. And it was only in the years immediately preceding the 1789 Revolution that any attempt was made to clean it up. The buildings crowding the bridges were dismantled as late as 1786. Pavements were introduced for the first time

1793	1799	1820s
The revolutionaries banish the monarchy and execute Louis XVI. A dictatorship is set up, headed by the ruthless Robespierre.	Army general Napoleon Bonaparte seizes control in a coup and, in 1804, crowns himself emperor in Notre-Dame.	Paris acquires gas lighting and its first omnibus.

and attempts were made to improve the drainage. A further source of pestilential infection was removed with the emptying of the overcrowded cemeteries into the catacombs. One grave-digger alone claimed to have buried more than ninety thousand people in thirty years, stacked "like slices of bacon" in the charnel house of the Innocents, which had been receiving the dead of 22 parishes for eight hundred years.

In 1786 Paris received its penultimate ring of fortifications, the so-called **wall of the Fermiers Généraux**, which roughly followed the line of modern Paris's inner and outer ring of arrondissements. The wall had 57 *barrières* or toll gates (one of which survives in the middle of place Stalingrad), where a tax was levied on all goods entering the city. At its outer edge, beyond the customs tolls, new houses of entertainment sprang up, encouraging a long tradition of Parisians crossing the boundaries of the city proper in search of drink, dancing and other kinds of transgression. It was a tradition that would culminate – and largely die – with the early twentieth-century artistic boom-towns of Montmartre and Montparnasse.

The Revolution

The **Revolution of 1789** was provoked by a financial crisis. Louis XVI had poured money into costly wars and the only way to increase revenue was to tax the clergy and nobility. He couldn't easily impose his will despotically so, for the first time since 1614, he recalled the **Estates General** – a kind of tax-raising parliament made up of representatives of the country's three "estates", or orders: the clergy (the First Estate), the nobility (the Second) and the rest (the Third). In May 1789 each of the three orders presented its grievances to the Crown; the bourgeois delegates representing the Third Estate were particularly resentful and outspoken. Responding to rising tension, Louis XVI began posting troops around Versailles and Paris, as though preparing for a coup to reverse his actions.

Fear of attack by royal troops propelled the Parisian people from the sidelines into the heart of the action. The Parisian electoral assembly entered the Hôtel de Ville, declared itself the municipal government or **Commune**, and set up a bourgeois militia, later to become known as the National Guard. It was supposed to keep order in an agitated city, but actually joined in when a band of ordinary Parisians stormed the **Bastille** prison on July 14. The Parisian working classes, known as the **sans-culottes**, literally "the people without breeches", now became major players in the unfolding drama. As the king gathered troops at Versailles, the deputies of the Third Estate proclaimed themselves the **National Assembly** and threatened to unleash a popular explosion in Paris. The king was forced to recognize the new parliament, which in August 1789 passed the **Declaration of the Rights of Man**, sweeping away the feudal privileges of the old order. Rumours were rife of counter-revolutionary intrigues at the court in **Versailles**, and in October a group of Parisians marched on Versailles and forced the king to return to Paris with them; they installed him in the Tuileries, where he was basically kept prisoner. In 1791 he attempted to flee abroad, but was stopped at Varennes and humiliatingly brought back to Paris.

As France was drawn into a succession of wars with neighbouring states, radical clamours for the overthrow of the king grew. The National Assembly was divided, but in August 1792 the *sans-culottes* rose up again, imprisoned the king and set up an

1830

After three days of fighting, known as *les trois glorieuses*, Louis-Philippe is elected constitutional monarch.

1848

In June, revolution erupts once again. Louis Napoléon Bonaparte, Napoleon's nephew, is elected president. In 1851 he declares himself Emperor Napoléon III.

insurrectionary Commune at the Hôtel de Ville. Under pressure from the Commune, the Assembly agreed to disband and order elections for a new **Convention** to draw up a new, republican, constitution. Later that month the Convention abolished the monarchy, set up a republic and convicted the king of treason. He was guillotined on place de la Révolution (now place de la Concorde) in January 1793. Europe was in uproar.

The Terror

The Convention, under the radical **Jacobin** faction, set up a war dictatorship. The Committee of Public Safety, headed by the chillingly ruthless Maximilien **Robespierre**, began the extermination of "enemies of the people", a period known as the *Grande Terreur*. Among the first casualties was **Marie-Antoinette**, who went with calm dignity to the guillotine in October 1793. Over the next few months some further 2600 individuals were executed, including many of the more moderate revolutionaries such as **Danton** whose last words as he went to his death were typical of his proud spirit: "Above all, don't forget to show my head to the people; it's well worth having a look at." **The Terror** finally ended in July 1794 when Robespierre, now widely perceived as a tyrant, was himself arrested by members of the Convention; he suffered the fate he had meted out to so many.

Power was thereafter put into the hands of a more temperate – but fatally weak – five-man **Directory**. The longed-for strong leader quickly emerged in the form of the celebrated General **Napoleon Bonaparte**, who had put down a Royalist insurrection in Paris in October 1795 with the minimum of fuss. In November 1799 he overthrew the Directory in a **coup d'état**. He appointed himself first consul for life in 1802 and **emperor** in 1804.

Napoleon

Napoleon is best known for his incessant **warmongering**, but he also upheld the fundamental reforms of the Revolution. His rights-based Code Civil, or Code Napoléon, long outlasted Napoleon's empire and has been a major influence on legal systems in many other countries. He established the system of education which still endures today, and created an efficient **bureaucracy** that put Paris in still firmer control of the rest of the country. He wanted to make Paris the "capital of capitals", but focused more on public works than monuments: he lined the Seine with two and a half miles of stone *quais*, built three bridges and created canals and reservoirs, providing Paris with its modern water supply. He also built the arcs de Triomphe and Carrousel, extended for the Louvre, and drew up plans for a temple to the Grande Armée – which later became the church of the Madeleine. He laid out the long and straight rue de Rivoli and rue de la Paix and devised new street-numbering (still in place) – odd on one side, even on the other; where streets ran parallel to the Seine, the numbering followed the flow of the river; in other streets, numbering started at the end nearest the river.

By 1809 Napoleon's conquered territory stretched from southern Italy to the Baltic, an empire much greater than that achieved by Louis XIV or even Charlemagne, but the **invasion of Russia** in 1812 was a colossal disaster. Out of four hundred thousand men (half of whom were conscripts from Napoleon's empire), barely twenty thousand made it back home. In March 1814 an army of Russians, Prussians and Austrians marched

1850s and 1860	1863	1870
Baron Haussmann literally bulldozes the city into the modern age, creating long, straight boulevards and squares. The poor are driven out to the suburbs.	At the Salon des Refusés, Manet's proto-Impressionist painting *Déjeuner sur l'Herbe* scandalizes all of Paris.	Hundreds die of starvation as the city is besieged by the Prussians.

into Paris – the first time foreign troops had invaded the city since the English in 1429. Napoleon was forced to abdicate and **Louis XVIII**, brother of the decapitated Louis XVI, was installed as king. In a last desperate attempt to regain power, Napoleon escaped from exile on the Italian island of Elba and reorganized his armies, only to meet final defeat at **Waterloo** on June 18, 1815. Louis XVIII was restored to power.

Restoration and barricades

For the rest of the **nineteenth century** after Napoleon's demise, France was occupied fighting out the contradictions and unfinished business left behind by the Revolution of 1789. Aside from the actual conflicts on the streets of the capital, there was a tussle between the class that had risen to wealth and power as a direct result of the destruction of the monarchy and the survivors of the old order, who sought to make a comeback in the 1820s under the **restored monarchy** of Louis XVIII and Charles X. This conflict was finally resolved in favour of the new bourgeoisie. When Charles X refused to accept the result of the 1830 National Assembly elections, **Adolphe Thiers** – who was to become the veteran conservative politician of the nineteenth century – led the opposition in revolt. Barricades were erected in Paris and there followed three days of bitter street fighting, known as **les trois glorieuses**, in which 1800 people were killed (they are commemorated by the column on place de la Bastille). The outcome of this **July Revolution** was parliament's election of **Louis-Philippe** in August 1830 as constitutional monarch, or *le roi bourgeois*, and the introduction of a few liberalizing reforms, most either cosmetic or serving merely to consolidate the power of the wealthiest stratum of the population.

As the demands of the disenfranchised poor continued to go unheeded, so their radicalism increased, exacerbated by **deteriorating living and working conditions** in the large towns, especially Paris, as the Industrial Revolution got under way. There were, for example, twenty thousand deaths from cholera in Paris in 1832, and 65 percent of the population in 1848 were too poor to be liable for tax. Eruptions of discontent invariably occurred in the capital, with insurrections in 1832 and 1834. When Thiers ringed Paris and its suburbs with a defensive wall (thus defining the limits of the modern city), his efforts soon appeared misdirected. In 1848, the lid blew off the pot. Barricades went up in February, and the **Second Republic** was quickly proclaimed. It looked for a time as if working-class demands might be at least partly met, but in the face of agitation in the streets, the more conservative Republicans lost their nerve, and the nation showed its feelings by returning a spanking reactionary majority in the April elections.

Revolution appeared the only alternative for Paris's radical poor. On June 23, 1848, working-class Paris – Poissonnière, Temple, St-Antoine, the Marais, Quartier Latin, Montmartre – rose in revolt. In what became known as the **1848 Revolution**, men, women and children fought side by side against fifty thousand troops. In three days of fighting, nine hundred soldiers were killed. No one knows how many of the *insurgés* – the insurgents – died. Fifteen thousand people were arrested and four thousand sentenced to prison terms. **Louis Napoléon Bonaparte**, the nephew of Napoleon I, was elected president in November 1848, but within three years he brought the tottering republic to an end by announcing a coup d'état. Twelve months later, he had himself crowned Emperor **Napoléon III**.

1871

Paris surrenders in March, but the Prussians withdraw after just three days. In the aftermath, workers rise up and proclaim the Paris Commune. It is speedily and bloodily suppressed by French troops.

1889

The all-new Eiffel Tower steals the show at the Exposition Universelle, or "Great Exhibition".

Baron Haussmann

The nearly twenty years of the **Second Empire** brought rapid **economic growth** alongside virulent repression designed to hold the potentially revolutionary underclasses in check. It also brought **Baron Haussmann**, who undertook a total **transformation of the city**. In love with the straight line and grand vista, he drove 135km of broad new streets through the cramped quarters of the medieval city, linking the interior and exterior boulevards, and creating long, straight north–south and east–west cross-routes.

In 1859, all the land up to Thiers' wall of 1840 was incorporated into the city of Paris. A contemporary journalist railed "they have sewn rags onto the dress of a queen", but it was a brave and possibly brilliant decision – and a move that subsequent governments have consistently failed to emulate, leaving Paris's future suburbs to swell energetically but chaotically, then wallow in unregulated and unadorned semi-squalor. Between 1860 and the outbreak of World War I, the population of Paris "beyond the walls", or the **banlieue** as it became known, tripled in size, becoming the home of 1.5 million almost-Parisians. (The city proper had been surpassed in population by London in the eighteenth century; after 1900 it was overtaken by New York too, with Berlin, Vienna and St Petersburg catching up fast.)

The dark side

Haussmann's demolitions were at least in part aimed at workers, and the poor. Barracks were located at strategic points – like the place du Château-d'Eau, now République, controlling the turbulent eastern districts – and the broad boulevards were intended to facilitate cavalry manoeuvres and artillery fire, with angled intersections that would allow troops to outflank any barricades. In other ways, however, **the poor** within the city were largely left to fend for themselves. Some 350,000 Parisians were displaced. The prosperous classes moved into the new western arrondissements, abandoning the decaying older properties. These were divided and subdivided into ever-smaller units as landlords sought to maximize their rents. Sanitation was nonexistent. Water standpipes were available only in the street. Migrant workers from the provinces, sucked into the city to supply the vast labour requirements, crammed into the old villages of Belleville and Ménilmontant. Many, too poor to buy furniture, lived in barely furnished digs or *demi-lits*, where the same bed was shared by several tenants on a shift basis. Cholera and TB were rife. Until 1870 refuse was thrown into the streets at night to be collected the following morning. When in 1884 the Prefect of the day required landlords to provide proper containers, they retorted by calling the containers by his name, Poubelle – and the name has stuck as the French word for "dustbin".

The Siege and the Commune

In September 1870, Napoléon III surrendered to Bismarck at the border town of Sedan, less than two months after France had declared war on the well-prepared and superior forces of the **Prussian** state. The humiliation was enough for a Republican government to be instantly proclaimed in Paris. The Prussians advanced and by September 19 were laying **siege** to the capital. Minister of the Interior Léon Gambetta was flown out by hot-air balloon to rally the provincial troops but further balloon

1895	1900	1914
Parisians are the first people anywhere in the world to see the jerky cinematic documentaries of the Lumière brothers.	The Métropolitain underground railway, or "métro", is unveiled.	War with Germany calls time on the "*belle époque*". In September, the Kaiser's armies are just about held off by French troops shuttled from Paris to the front line, only fifteen miles away.

HAUSSMANN'S HARMONIOUS CITY

In half a century, from 1853, much of Paris was rebuilt, transforming an overgrown and insanitary medieval capital into an **urban utopia**. Napoléon III's government provided the force, while banks and private speculators provided the cash. The poor, meanwhile, were either used for labour or cleared out to the suburban badlands.

The presiding genius was the emperor's chief of works, **Baron Haussmann**. In his brave new city, every apartment building was seven storeys high. Every facade was built in creamy limestone, often quarried from under the city itself, with Neoclassical details sculpted around the windows. Every second and fifth floor had its wrought-iron balcony and every lead roof sloped back from the streetfront at precisely 45 degrees. It would all have been inhumanly regular if it hadn't been for the ground-floor shops, which have provided Paris's streets with a more varied face ever since.

The basic Haussmann design proved astonishingly resilient. In the Art Nouveau period, sinuous curves and contours crept across the faces of apartment buildings, and Art Deco and Modernism provided their own, stripped-down facelifts, but still, underneath the new styles, many Parisian buildings followed the basic Haussmann pattern. The result is a city of rare and enduring harmony.

messengers ended up in Norway or the Atlantic. The few attempts at military sorties from Paris turned into yet more blundering failures. Meanwhile, the city's restaurants were forced to change menus to fried dog, roast rat or peculiar delicacies from the zoos, and death from disease or starvation became an ever more common fate.

The government's half-hearted defence of the city – more afraid of revolution within than of the Prussians – angered Parisians, who clamoured for the creation of a 1789-style Commune. The Prussians, meanwhile, were demanding a proper government to negotiate with. In January 1871, those in power agreed to hold elections for a new National Assembly with the authority to surrender officially to the Prussians. A large monarchist majority, with the conservative Adolphe Thiers at its head, was returned, and on March 1, Prussian troops marched down the Champs-Elysées and garrisoned the city for three days while the populace remained behind closed doors in silent protest. On March 18, amid growing resentment from all classes of Parisians, Thiers' attempt to take possession of the National Guard's artillery in Montmartre (see box, p.186) set the barrel alight. The **Commune** was proclaimed from the Hôtel de Ville and Paris was promptly subjected to a second siege by Thiers' government, which had fled to Versailles, followed by the remaining Parisian bourgeoisie.

The Commune lasted just 72 days, and implemented no lasting reforms. It succumbed to Thiers' army on May 28, 1871, after a week of street-by-street warfare – the so-called *semaine sanglante*, or "Bloody Week" – in which some 25,000 men, women and children were killed, including thousands in random revenge shootings by government troops.

The belle époque

The Commune left great landmarks such as the Tuileries palace and Hôtel de Ville as smoking ruins, but within six or seven years few signs of the fighting remained.

1920s	1940
In the aftermath of war, the decadent *années folles* (or "mad years") of the 1920s rescue Paris's international reputation for hedonism.	In May and June, the government flees Paris, and Nazi soldiers are soon marching down the Champs-Elysées. Four years of largely collaborative fascist rule ensue.

Visitors remarked admiringly on the teeming streets, the expensive shops and energetic nightlife. Charles Garnier's Opéra was opened in 1875. Aptly described as the "triumph of moulded pastry", it was a suitable image of the frivolity and materialism of what the British called the "naughty" Eighties and Nineties, and the French called the **belle époque**, or "Age of Beauty". In 1889 the **Eiffel Tower** stole the show at the great Exposition. For the 1900 repeat, the Métropolitain or "**métro**" was unveiled.

The years up to World War I were marked by the unstable but thoroughly conservative governments of the **Third Republic**. On the extreme right, fascism began to make its ugly appearance with Maurras' proto-Brownshirt organization, the Camelots du Roi. Despite – or maybe in some way because of – the political tensions, Paris emerged as the supremely inspiring environment for artists and writers – the so-called Bohemians – both French and foreign. It was a constellation of talents such as Western culture has rarely seen. **Impressionism**, **Fauvism** and **Cubism** were all born in Paris in this period, while French **poets** like Apollinaire, Laforgue, Max Jacob, Blaise Cendrars and André Breton were preparing the way for Surrealism, concrete poetry and Symbolism. **Cinema**, too, first saw the light in Paris, with the jerky documentaries of the Lumière brothers and George Méliès' fantastical features both appearing in the mid-1890s.

War and Depression

As a city, Paris escaped **World War I** relatively lightly, with only a brief Zeppelin bombardment in 1916, and heavy shelling from the Germans' monstrous, long-range "Big Bertha" cannon mercifully restricted to the early part of 1918. The human cost was rather higher: one in ten Parisian conscripts failed to return. But Paris remained the world's art – and party – capital after the war, with an injection of foreign blood and a shift of venue from Montmartre to Montparnasse. Indeed, the **années folles** (or "mad years") of the 1920s were among Paris's most decadent and scintillating, consolidating a long-standing international reputation for hedonistic, often erotic, abandon that has sustained its tourism industry for the best part of a century. Meanwhile, work on the dismantling of Thiers' outmoded fortifications progressed with aching slowness from 1919 until 1932 – after which the cleared space languished as a wilderness of shantytowns, or *bidonvilles*, until the construction of the *boulevard périphérique* ring road in the 1960s.

As **Depression** deepened in the 1930s and Nazi power across the Rhine became more menacing, however, the mood changed. Politicized thuggery grew rife in Paris, and the Left united behind the banner of the Popular Front, winning the **1936 elections** with a handsome majority. Frightened by the apparently revolutionary situation, the major employers signed the Matignon Agreement with Socialist Prime Minister Léon Blum. It provided for wage increases, nationalization of the armaments industry, a forty-hour week, paid annual leave and collective bargaining on wages. These reforms were pushed through Parliament, but when Blum tried to introduce exchange controls to check the flight of capital the Senate threw the proposal out and he resigned. The Left returned to opposition, where it remained, with the exception of coalition governments, until 1981.

1942	1944	1961
Parisian Jews are rounded up – by other Frenchmen – and shipped off to Auschwitz.	Liberation arrives on August 25, with General de Gaulle motoring up the Champs-Elysées to the roar of a vast crowd.	As France's brutal repression of its Algerian colony reaches its peak, at least two hundred Algerians are murdered by police during a civil rights demonstration.

Fascism and Resistance

The outbreak of war was followed with stunning swiftness by the **Fall of France**. After sweeping across the low countries, the German army broke across the Somme in early June. The French government fled south to Bordeaux, declaring Paris an "open city" in an attempt to save it from a destructive siege. By 14 June, Nazi troops were parading down the Champs-Elysées. During the **occupation** of Paris in **World War II**, the Germans found some sections of Parisian society, as well as the minions of the Vichy government, only too happy to hobnob with them. For four years the city suffered fascist rule with curfews, German garrisons and a Gestapo HQ. Parisian Jews were forced to wear the Star of David and in 1942 were rounded up – by other Frenchmen – and shipped off to Auschwitz.

The **Resistance** was very active in the city, gathering people of all political persuasions into its ranks, but with Communists and Socialists, especially of East European Jewish origin, well to the fore. The job of torturing them when they fell into Nazi hands – often as a result of betrayals – was left to their fellow citizens in the fascist militia. Those who were condemned to death – rather than the concentration camps – were shot against the wall below the old fort of Mont Valérien above St-Cloud.

As Allied forces drew near to the city in 1944, the FFI (armed Resistance units) called their troops onto the streets. Alarmed at the prospect of the Left seizing power in his absence, the free French leader, **Général de Gaulle**, urged the Allies to let him press on towards the capital. To their credit, the Paris police also joined in the uprising, holding their Ile de la Cité HQ for three days against German attacks. On August 23, Hitler famously gave orders that Paris should be physically destroyed, but the city's commander, Von Choltiz, delayed just long enough. **Liberation** arrived on August 25 in the shape of General Leclerc's tanks, motoring up the Champs-Elysées to the roar of a vast crowd.

Revolts and demonstrations

Postwar Paris has remained no stranger to political battles in its streets. Violent demonstrations accompanied the Communist withdrawal from the coalition government in 1947. In the Fifties the Left took to the streets again in protest against the colonial wars in Indochina and Algeria. And, in 1961, in one of the most shameful episodes in modern French history, some two hundred Algerians were killed by the police during a civil rights demonstration – a "**secret massacre**", which remained covered by a veil of total official silence until the 1990s.

In the extraordinary month of **May 1968**, a radical, libertarian, leftist movement gathered momentum in the Paris universities. Students began by occupying university buildings in protest against old-fashioned and hierarchical university structures (see box, p.124), but the extreme reaction of the police and government helped the movement to spread until it represented a mass revolt against institutional stagnation that ended up with the occupation of hundreds of factories across the country and a general strike by nine million workers.

Yet this was no revolution. The vicious battles with the paramilitary CRS police on the streets of Paris shook large sectors of the population – France's silent majority – to the core. Right-wing and "nationalist" demonstrations – orchestrated by de Gaulle – left

1968	1969	1973
In May, left-wing students occupying university buildings are supported by millions of striking and marching workers.	President de Gaulle loses a referendum, and retires, wounded, to his country house.	Paris's first skyscraper, the Tour Montparnasse, tops out at 56 hideous storeys. The *périphérique* ring road is completed in April.

public opinion craving stability and peace, and a great many workers were satisfied with a new system for wage agreements. Elections called in June returned the Right to power, the occupied buildings emptied and the barricades in the Latin Quarter came down. For those who thought they were experiencing The Revolution, the defeat was catastrophic.

But French institutions and French society had changed – de Gaulle didn't survive a referendum in 1969. His successor, **Georges Pompidou**, only survived long enough to begin the construction of the giant Les Halles development, and the expressways along the *quais* of the Seine. In 1974, he was succeeded by the conservative **Valéry Giscard d'Estaing**, who appointed one Jacques Chirac as his prime minister. In 1976, Chirac resigned, but made a speedy recovery as Mayor of Paris less than a year later.

Corruption and cohabitation

When **François Mitterrand** became president in 1981, hopes and expectations were initially high. By 1984, however, the flight of capital, inflation and budget deficits had forced a complete volte-face, and the Right won parliamentary elections in 1986, with **Chirac** beginning his second term as prime minister, while also continuing as Paris's mayor (he occupied the latter office continuously from 1977 to 1995). This was France's first period of "cohabitation": the head of state and head of government belonging to opposite sides of the political fence. Paris, meanwhile, pursued its own course, with the town halls of all twenty of the city's arrondissements remaining under right-wing control through much of the 1980s. It was a period of widespread corruption, but it didn't stop the city's mayor, **Jacques Chirac**, winning the election as **president** and taking office in May 1995.

That summer, **bombs** thought to have been planted by an extremist Algerian Islamic group exploded across Paris. There were further bomb threats throughout the autumn. The tense atmosphere was compounded by widespread discontent and a wave of massive strikes protesting against Prime Minister Alain Juppé's proposed sweeping **economic liberalization**, seen by many as a threat to the founding values of the French republic. Chirac and his successors would face similar protests again and again, ultimately frustrating every attempt to alter the course of the French economy.

Cataclysms, demonstrations and heat waves

When France won the **World Cup** in July 1998, change seemed to be in the air. The victory at the new Stade de France in the ethnically mixed Paris suburb of St-Denis, with a multiethnic team, prompted a wave of popular patriotism. For once, support for "les bleus" seemed to override all other colour distinctions, and some even thought that Parisians might start being interested in football. Both notions, however, would soon be proved ephemeral.

After the smooth **introduction of the euro** on January 1, 2002, came the shocking success of the far-Right candidate **Jean-Marie Le Pen** in the first round of the presidential election of spring 2002. On May 1, some 800,000 people packed the boulevards of Paris in the biggest **demonstration** the capital had seen since the student protests of 1968. Two weeks later, in the run-off, Chirac duly triumphed, winning 90 percent of the vote in Paris.

1998	**2001**	**2002**
In July, a multiracial French team wins the World Cup at the new Stade de France, in the suburb of St-Denis.	Unassuming Socialist candidate, Bertrand Delanoë, is elected Mayor of Paris in March.	Parisians find themselves paying a little extra for their coffees and baguettes with the introduction of the euro, on January 1.

THE MODERN FACE OF PARIS

Paris changed little up to the late 1960s – all the action took place out in the suburbs. Even the 1970s brown-glass skyscraper of the **Tour Montparnasse** only inspired a law limiting buildings taller than 37m in the city centre. And the demolition of the ironwork marketplace of Les Halles resulted in a conservationist outcry – though it didn't prevent the construction of its replacement, the ugly curved-glass pit of the **Forum des Halles** shopping centre, itself recently revamped and covered over with a giant glass roof, the so-called Canopée (see p.90). The only postmodern success was the **Pompidou Centre**. Critics called it a giant petrol refinery, but Parisians were soon happily referring to it as Beaubourg – or "Prettytown" – after the name of the ancient district in which it was built.

Owing largely to the **Grands Projets** of Socialist president François Mitterrand, Paris changed more in the 1980s and 1990s than it had since the era of Eiffel, with I.M. Pei's glass **Pyramide** in the Louvre's courtyard, Jean Nouvel's **Institut du Monde Arabe** and the **Cité de la Musique** at La Villette all becoming well-loved classics. However, there were also some less successful projects: the **Bibliothèque Nationale** was deemed woefully inadequate for its purpose, while the **Grande Arche de la Défense** feels overweening rather than triumphal. As for the unhappy **Bastille Opéra**, it has been compared to a hospital, an elephant and even, according to Parisophile Edmund White, "a cow palace in Fort Worth".

The twenty-first century has seen the construction of fewer landmark buildings. The two most recent structures couldn't be more different. Jean Nouvel's huge, aluminium-clad **Philharmonie** concert hall in La Villette (see p.204), which feels like a leftover from the Grands Projets era, is brooding, dark and angular, while Frank Gehry's **Fondation Louis Vuitton** (see p.221) in the 16ᵉ, is a light, airy, deconstructed glass building that looks as though it might float off (or possibly collapse) at any moment.

Paris's **skyline** could undergo a much more radical shift in future: in 2011 the city council changed the law so that buildings of up to 180m can be built, and the go-ahead has been given for the construction of a number of skyscrapers, albeit on the city's periphery. The Tour Triangle is taking (triangular) shape at the Porte de Versailles in the 15ᵉ, while Renzo Piano (who built the Pompidou Centre) is designing a 160m tower of steel and glass boxes in the 17ᵉ, at the Porte de Clichy, which will house the Palais de Justice, currently sited in antiquated buildings on the Ile de la Cité. Even **high-rise flats** are being given the go-ahead; two tower blocks, 50m tall, were recently erected in the 13ᵉ, for example. Given that the mayor, Anne Hidalgo, is against a "heritage vision" of Paris and all in favour of a "living, dynamic" city, it seems likely that many more such structures will see the light of day.

With such a mandate, Chirac and his reformed and renamed UMP party decided to take on the public sector: first pensions and unemployment benefits, then worker-friendly hiring and firing rights, and finally the world-leading health service. Again, hundreds of thousands came out onto the streets in protest. More trouble came when Chirac declared in March 2003 that he would veto any UN resolution that contained an ultimatum leading to **war in Iraq**. The cherished but often fragile Franco-American relationship collapsed, catastrophically, and American tourists seemed to vanish from the capital. That **summer** was as heated in reality as politically. Parisian temperatures in the first half of August regularly topped 40°C (104°F) – more than 10°C above the average maximum for the time of year – and **climate change** finally forced its way onto the mainstream agenda.

2002

On April 21, far-Right candidate Jean-Marie Le Pen knocks Socialist Lionel Jospin into third place in the first round of presidential elections. Incumbent president Jacques Chirac wins the second round.

2002

Mayor Bertrand Delanoë launches Paris's new image by turning three kilometres of riverbank expressway into a summer beach: "Paris Plage" is an immense success.

Delanoë and the greening of Paris

Climate change and green issues were high on the agenda of the new mayor of Paris, **Bertrand Delanoë**, who was elected in 2001. (Incidentally, the fact that this was the first time the Left had won control of the capital since the bloody uprising of the Paris Commune in 1871 was far more of a shock to most Parisians than the fact that he was openly gay). Delanoë tackled traffic congestion and created **bus lanes, cycle lanes and pedestrianized areas** (including a 2km stretch of the Seine). He also introduced the tremendously popular hop-on, hop-off community bicycles, **Vélib'** ("free bike") and **Autolib'**, electric rental cars; all-new **tramway lines** began threading through the suburbs and encircling the ring road. His other popular measures, **Paris Plage** ("Paris Beach"), in which 3km of the riverbank roads are turned into a public beach each summer, and **Nuit Blanche** ("Sleepless Night"), a city-wide all-night party of live music and performance art in October, are now established events on the city's calendar.

"Sarko"

In 2004, a new political force emerged in the hyperenergetic if diminutive shape of **Nicolas Sarkozy** – a kind of Margaret Thatcher meets JFK, bent on giving France a dose of neoliberal or "Anglo-Saxon" capitalism. In 2005 and again in 2006 – when students once again occupied the Sorbonne – waves of passionate strikers flooded the city streets, but the more dramatic **civil unrest** began after two teenagers died fleeing what they thought was police pursuit in Clichy-sous-Bois, a run-down area in the Paris *banlieue*. Local **car-burnings** and confrontations with police quickly spread to other Parisian suburbs and then beyond. Night after night, for three weeks, youths across France torched cars, buses, schools, and police and power stations – anything associated with the state. As Interior Minister, "Sarko" demanded that the neighbourhoods were cleaned with power-hoses.

Such right-wing posturing seemed to pay off, and, on May 16, 2007, Nicolas Sarkozy became President. Then came the **global financial crisis** of 2008–09. Suddenly, the "Anglo-Saxon" form of market-led, laissez-faire capitalism seemed exactly what French socialists had always said it was: a debt-fuelled castle built on sand. In response, Sarkozy performed an astonishing political about-turn, pledging to wield the power of the state to ensure stability. Strong-state *dirigisme* was back. National reform, again, would have to wait.

The Charlie Hebdo massacre

Seduced by promises of budgetary rigour and social justice, and somewhat disenchanted with the brash bling of Sarkozy, in 2012 voters chose Socialist candidate **François Hollande** as their new president. However, Hollande's inept handling of the economy and rising unemployment levels saw his ratings tumble dramatically from 65 to 13 in a couple of years (making him the least popular president since the start of the Fifth Republic in 1958). The country seemed to be in the grip of a general malaise, from which it was brutally shaken on January 7, 2015, when two self-confessed jihadists, brothers Saïd and Chérif Kouachi, stormed into the offices of the satirical magazine **Charlie Hebdo**, in the 11ᵉ arrondissement, and shot dead twelve people,

2003	2005
Following Chirac's spat with George W. Bush over Iraq, US tourists temporarily vanish from the capital. In the summer, temperatures soar above 40°C (100°F).	In late October, disaffected youths riot in the impoverished Paris suburb of Clichy-sous-Bois. Right-wing interior minister, Nicolas Sarkozy, declares a state of emergency.

THE NEW GREATER PARIS: THE FUTURE METROPOLIS

While France has long lavished money on its capital, adorning the city centre with grand buildings and cultural institutions, the *banlieue*, or suburbs, have festered as they have grown, kept at arm's length from the centre by the administrative and physical barricade of the *périphérique* ring road. Currently, a large part of the suburban population, including many immigrants and their families, living in troubled *cités* (housing estates), are effectively excluded from the city centre. The high-paying, white-collar jobs of the shopping, banking and governmental districts just don't seem to be available to black youths from the "9–3" – as the depressed *département* of Seine St-Denis, officially numbered 93, is known.

In an attempt to break down these barriers, the government is creating a new city authority, the **Metropole du Grand Paris (MGP)**, due to come into effect In 2016–17. It will include the three administrative *départements* of the Petite Couronne ("Little Crown"), the suburban districts immediately encircling Paris, containing some four million people – twice as many as Paris proper. This plan to expand Paris beyond its current boundaries arose from an earlier initiative, the "Grand Paris", launched in 2009. Central to the plan and the creation of a greater Paris is the construction of a new high-speed suburban transport network, **Grand Paris Express**, with 200km of new lines and 72 new stations, linking key suburbs and airports. Billions of euros more will be spent on improving and extending existing métro lines.

Another key concern of the "Grand Paris" is housing. Rising house prices, together with desirable new towns to the south and west of the city, are sucking away Paris's lifeblood: its **population**. There are now 2.1 million people living "intra-muros", or in Paris proper, down from 2.8 million in the late 1950s. Retirees make up fifteen percent of the population, while twenty per cent of flats in the historic centre are second homes. Parisians are regularly alarmed by horrifying statistics such as the fact that the city has lost roughly a quarter of its small food stores in the last decade, or that bakeries are nowhere to be found near the Champs-Elysées. (They may be comforted to learn, however, that a city with "only" 159 cheese shops is not yet facing a crisis.) Intent on preventing the "museumification" of Paris, the Mairie has bought up private apartment buildings in the historic centre, to be rented out as **social housing**, while the suburbs have been promised thousands of new and affordable flats and houses.

Whether these plans to erase the boundaries between the rich centre and its poorer suburbs will go far enough to create a more up-to-date metropolis on the lines of New York or London remains to be seen. What is clear is that, with climate change, social unrest and economic disturbances all lapping at the city's walls, Paris cannot remain an island forever.

including well-known cartoonists and journalists. Long known for its controversial cartoons satirizing religion, including Islam, *Charlie Hebdo* journalists were no strangers to death threats, but the scale and nature of this attack was horrific and shocking. It was seen as an attack on freedom of speech and cherished Republican values; and the murdered cartoonists, among them Jean Cabut and Georges Wolinski, were well-loved, household names.

Paris was still reeling from this atrocity when, the following day, Amédy Coulibaly, a close friend of the Kouachi brothers, shot dead a police officer and four people he'd taken hostage in a kosher supermarket in the Porte de Vincennes district. The two incidents provoked a huge outpouring of grief and protest; on January 11, up to two million people, including forty world leaders, took to the streets in a "**unity rally**" and marched through Paris, congregating at the place de la République. People expressed their solidarity with the victims with cries of *Je suis Charlie, je suis Ahmed* (the Muslim

2007	2009
As Nicolas Sarkozy becomes president, Mayor Delanoë continues his greening of Paris: bus and cycle lanes appear everywhere, as do the new Vélib' rental bikes. Smokers are banished from cafés and restaurants.	Paris contemplates its future with an exhibition of architectural visions for the green mega-city of the future, dubbed "Le Grand Paris".

police officer shot dead as he lay wounded on the ground) and *Je suis juif*, and ordinary French citizens reaffirmed their identity and support for the Republican ideals of "Liberté, Egalité and Fraternité". In the months following the shootings, there was a rallying round François Hollande, who was deemed to have responded to the attacks in a statesmanlike way, and he saw his ratings rise again. Meanwhile, much soul-searching goes on, as France reflects on how to counter the rise of **homegrown terrorism** (the three gunmen were born and raised in the Paris area) and the disturbing resurgence of anti-Semitism.

Madame La Maire

Only nine months in the job when the *Charlie Hebdo* shootings took place, Paris's newly elected and first woman mayor, the Socialist **Anne Hidalgo**, found herself rapidly thrust into the limelight, having to speak for a city in shock and mourning. Born to Spanish migrants and brought up on a housing estate outside Lyon, *Madame la maire*, as Hidalgo insists on being called, much to the annoyance of French grammarians (the correct spelling is *le maire*), cites as her chief concerns immigration, housing and breaking down inequalities between Paris's affluent west and poorer east. She's also committed to taking her predecessor Delanoë's green policies further, creating a more cycle-friendly environment, and planning to reclaim for pedestrians more of the riverbank, as well as the city's famous squares, place de la Bastille and place de la Nation. Whether she will achieve her proposal to build council housing down the middle of avenue Foch, aka "Billionaire's Row", in western Paris, remains to be seen, but with a reputation for steely determination, it looks as though she could well push through some radical changes in the capital.

2012	2014	2015
Disenchanted with Sarkozy, French voters elect Socialist François Hollande as president, but rue their choice when Hollande fails to tackle the country's economic woes.	Paris elects its first woman mayor, Anne Hidalgo.	Paris is rocked by the mass shootings by two jihadist militants of twelve people, including eight journalists, at the offices of *Charlie Hebdo* magazine.

Books

HISTORY AND POLITICS

Anthony Beevor & Artemis Cooper *Paris After the Liberation: 1944–1949.* Gripping account of a crucial era in Parisian history, featuring de Gaulle, the Communists, the St-Germain scene and Dior's New Look. Five strange, intense years that set the tone for the next fifty.

Larry Collins and Dominique Lapierre *Is Paris Burning?* (out of print). Classic history-as-thriller account of the race to save Paris from the destruction threatened by the retreating Nazis.

Alistair Horne *The Fall of Paris* and *Seven Ages of Paris.* Highly regarded historian Alistair Horne's *The Fall of Paris* is a very readable and humane account of the extraordinary period of the Prussian siege of Paris in 1870 and the ensuing struggles of the Commune. His *Seven Ages of Paris* is a compelling (if rather old-fashionedly fruity) account of significant episodes in the city's history.

★**Andrew Hussey** *Paris, The Secret History.* Delves into some fascinating and little-known aspects of Paris's history, including occultism, freemasonry and the seedy underside of the city. Hussey is concerned above all with ordinary Parisians, and their frequent clashes with authority. His recent book, *The French Intifada: The Long War between France and Its Arabs,* made a timely appearance just after the *Charlie Hebdo* shootings and is indispensable reading for an understanding of the background to the simmering tensions between France and its Arab population.

★**Colin Jones** *Paris: Biography of a City.* Jones focuses tightly on the actual life and growth of the city, from the Neolithic past to the future. Five hundred pages flow by easily, punctuated by thoughtful but accessible boxes on characters, streets and buildings whose lives were especially bound up with Paris's, from the Roman *arènes* to Zazie's métro. The best single book on the city's history.

Peter Lennon *Foreign Correspondent: Paris in the Sixties* (out of print). Irish journalist Peter Lennon went to Paris in the early 1960s unable to speak a word of French. He became a close friend of Samuel Beckett and was a witness to the May 1968 events.

Lucy Moore *Liberty: The Lives and Times of Six Women in Revolutionary France.* Follows the fervid lives of six influential women through the Revolution, taking in everything from sexual scandal to revolutionary radicalism.

Orest A. Ranum *Paris in the Age of Absolutism.* A truly great work of city biography, revealing how and why seventeenth-century Paris rose from medieval obscurity to become the foremost city in Europe under Louis XIV.

★**Graham Robb** *Parisians.* This playful, joyfully readable but magnificently researched book tells the story of Paris from 1750 to today, through the eyes of the people who have played key roles in its turbulent life. Among other scenes, Robb shows us Marie-Antoinette fleeing the Tuileries, Napoleon losing his virginity in the Palais Royal, Hitler's day-trip conquerer's tour, and the nasty build-up to the suburban riots of 2005.

Duc de Saint-Simon *Memoirs.* Written by an insider, this compelling memoir of life at Versailles under Louis XIV is packed with fascinating, gossipy anecdotes.

Gillian Tindall *Footprints in Paris.* In this beautifully written and personal micro-history of the Quartier Latin, Tindall reconstructs the intimate lives of a handful of the quarter's residents, both celebrated and obscure, creating an evocative portrait of the city in the nineteenth and twentieth centuries.

CULTURE AND SOCIETY

★**Marc Augé** *In the Metro.* A philosophically minded anthropologist descends deep into métro culture and his own memories of life in Paris. A brief, brilliant essay in the spirit of Roland Barthes.

Walter Benjamin *The Arcades Project.* An all-encompassing portrait of Paris covering 1830–70, in which the *passages* are used as a lens through which to view Parisian society. Never completed, Benjamin's magnum opus is a kaleidoscopic assemblage of essays, notes and quotations, gathered under such headings as "Baudelaire", "Prostitution", "Mirrors" and "Idleness".

James Campbell *Paris Interzone.* The feuds, passions and destructive lifestyles of Left Bank writers in 1946–60 are evoked here. The cast includes Samuel Beckett, Boris Vian, Alexander Trocchi, Eugène Ionesco, Jean-Paul Sartre, Simone de Beauvoir, Vladimir Nabokov and Allen Ginsberg.

Rupert Christiansen *Paris Babylon: Grandeur, Decadence and Revolution 1869–1875.* Written with verve and dash, Christiansen's account of Paris at the time of the Siege and the Commune is exuberant and original. Worth reading for its evocative and insightfully chosen contemporary quotations alone – it begins with a delightful 1869 guidebook to "Paris Partout!"

Richard Cobb *Paris and Elsewhere.* Selected writings on postwar Paris by the acclaimed historian of the Revolution, with a personal and meditative tone.

Adam Gopnik *Paris to the Moon.* Intimate and acutely observed essays from the Paris correspondent of the *New Yorker* on society, politics, family life and shopping. Probably the most thoughtful and enjoyable book by an expat in Paris.

★ **Julien Green** *Paris*. Born in Paris in 1900, Green became one of the city's defining writers. This bilingual edition presents twenty-odd short, meditative and highly personal essays on different aspects of *quartiers* of Paris, from Notre-Dame and the 16ᵉ to "stairways and steps" and the lost cries of the city's hawkers. Proust meets travel-writing.

★ **Eric Hazan** *The Invention of Paris*. Utterly compelling psychogeographical account of the city, picking over its history *quartier* by *quartier* in a thousand *aperçus* and anecdotes. It's a weighty book, but a zesty, lefty bias nicely brings out the passions behind the rebellions and revolutions.

J.K. Huysmans *Parisian Sketches*. Published in 1880, Huysmans' fantastical, intense prose pieces on contemporary Paris drip with decadence, and cruelly acute observation. Rhapsodies on "Landscapes" and "Parisian characters" are matched by an exhilaratingly vivid account of the Folies Bergère. If Manet had been a novelist, he might have produced this.

Ian Littlewood *A Literary Companion to Paris* (out of print). A thorough account of which literary figures went where, and what they had to say about it.

Gertrude Stein *The Autobiography of Alice B. Toklas*. The most accessible of Stein's works, written from the point of view of her long-time lover, is an amusing account of the artistic and literary scene of Paris in the 1910s and 1920s.

Tad Szulc *Chopin in Paris: The Life and Times of the Romantic Composer*. Not much on music, but explores Chopin's relationship with his friends – Balzac, Hugo, Liszt among them – and his lover, George Sand, and their shared life in Paris.

Judith Thurman *Colette: Secrets of the Flesh*. An intelligent and entertaining biography of Colette (1873–1954), highly successful novelist, vaudeville artist, libertine and flamboyant *bon viveur*.

Sarah Turnbull *Almost French: A New Life in Paris*. Funny but mostly painful account of a young *australienne* falling in love, moving to Paris and desperately failing to fit in. Acute observation lifts it above chick-lit travel status. A must for would-be expats.

★ **Edmund White** *The Flâneur*. An American expat novelist muses over Parisian themes and places as diverse as the Moreau museum, gay cruising and the history of immigration, as well as the art of being a good *flâneur* – a loiterer or stroller.

William Wiser *The Twilight Years: Paris in the 1930s*. Breathless account of the crazy decade before the war, all jazz nights, scandals, and the social lives of expat poets and painters.

ART AND ARCHITECTURE

André Chastel *French Art*. The great French art historian tries to define what is distinctively French about French art in this insightful and superbly illustrated three-volume work.

Ross King *The Judgement of Paris: The Revolutionary Decade That Gave the World Impressionism*. High-octane account of the fierce battles in the 1860s and 1870s between the "finishers", the Classical painters of the academic Salons, and the upstart "sketchers" who tried to supplant them with their impressionistic canvases. Focuses on the culture and political atmosphere of the times as much as the art.

Michel Poisson *The Monuments of Paris*. Arrondissement-by-arrondissement survey of Paris's chief buildings, with attractive line drawings and brief notes. Short on contemporary architecture but otherwise fairly comprehensive.

Sue Roe *In Montmartre*. A vivid, intimate portrait of the intertwined lives and rivalries of the young Picasso, Matisse, Derain, Vlaminck and Modigliani in the seedy Montmartre of 1900–1910.

Anthony Sutcliffe *Paris – An Architectural History*. Excellent overview of Paris's changing cityscape, as dictated by fashion, social structure and political power.

CHILDREN'S BOOKS

Miroslav Sasek *This is Paris*. A kind of illustrated child's travel guide, with enticing facts about the city and beautiful, quirky watercolours and drawings. First published in 1959, but still a brilliant companion (or preparation) for a trip with children.

FICTION

IN ENGLISH

Helen Constantine (ed) *Paris Tales*. Twenty-two (very) short stories and essays, each chosen for their evocation of a particular place in Paris. From Balzac in the Palais Royal and Colette in Montmartre cemetery, to Perec on the Champs-Elysées and Jacques Réda on the rue du Commerce. In a similar vein, *Paris Metro Tales* is a literary tour of Paris by underground – literally – with a map provided to take you to the correct métro station and the next story's location.

Charles Dickens *A Tale of Two Cities*. Paris and London during the 1789 Revolution and before. The plot is pure, breathtaking Hollywood, but the streets and the social backdrop are very much for real.

Ernest Hemingway *A Moveable Feast*. Hemingway's memoirs of his life as a young man in Paris in the 1920s. Includes fascinating accounts of meetings with literary celebrities Ezra Pound, F. Scott Fitzgerald and Gertrude Stein, among others.

Henry Miller *Tropic of Cancer; Quiet Days in Clichy*. Semi-autobiographical, rage- and sex-fuelled roar through the 1930s Parisian demi-monde; or, "a gob of spit in the face of Art", as the narrator puts it.

George Orwell *Down and Out in Paris and London*. Documentary account of breadline living in the 1930s – Orwell at his best.

Jean Rhys *Quartet*. A beautiful and evocative story of a lonely young woman's existence on the fringes of 1920s Montparnasse society. In the same vein are the subsequent *After Leaving Mr Mackenzie* and *Good Morning, Midnight*, both exploring sexual politics and isolation in the atmospheric streets, shabby hotel rooms and smoky bars of interwar Paris, all in Rhys's spare, dream-like style.

FRENCH (IN TRANSLATION)

★**Honoré de Balzac** *The Père Goriot*. Biting exposé of cruelty and selfishness in the contrasting worlds of the fashionable faubourg St-Germain and a down-at-heel but genteel boarding-house in the Quartier Latin. Balzac's equally brilliant *Wild Ass's Skin* is a strange moralistic tale of an ambitious young man's fall from grace in early nineteenth-century Paris.

Muriel Barbery *The Elegance of the Hedgehog*. This whimsical, philosophically minded novel, set among the eccentric characters of a Parisian apartment block, sold over a million copies in France. Deftly exposes the pretensions and aspirations of the upper middle classes.

André Breton *Nadja*. First published in 1928, *Nadja* is widely considered the most important and influential novel to spring from the Surrealist movement. Largely autobiographical, it portrays the complex relationship between the narrator and a young woman in Paris.

Louis-Ferdinand Céline *Death on Credit*. Disturbing semiautobiographical novel recounting working-class Paris through the eyes of an adolescent at the beginning of the twentieth century. Much of it takes place in the passage Choiseul, and its claustrophobic atmosphere is vividly evoked.

Blaise Cendrars *To the End of the World*. An outrageous, bawdy tale of a randy septuagenarian Parisian actress, having an affair with a deserter from the Foreign Legion.

Colette *Chéri*. Considered Colette's finest novel, *Chéri* brilliantly evokes the world of a demi-monde Parisian courtesan who has a doomed love affair with a man at least half her age.

Didier Daeninckx *Murder in Memoriam*. A thriller involving two murders: one of a Frenchman during the massacre of the Algerians in Paris in 1961, the other of his son twenty years later. The investigation by an honest detective lays bare dirty tricks, corruption, racism and the cover-up of the massacre.

★**Gustave Flaubert** *Sentimental Education*. A lively, detailed 1869 reconstruction of the life, manners, characters and politics of Parisians in the 1840s, including the 1848 Revolution.

Victor Hugo *Les Misérables*. A long but eminently readable novel by the master. Set among the Parisian poor and low-life in the first half of the nineteenth century, it's probably the greatest treatment of Paris in fiction – unless that title goes to Hugo's haunting (and shorter) *Notre-Dame de Paris*, a novel better known in English as *The Hunchback of Notre-Dame*.

Claude Izner *Murder on the Eiffel Tower*. 1889: a young bookseller falls in love and investigates a series of curious murders. One of the best of a new series of detective stories from the team of bookish sisters known as "Claude Izner".

François Maspero *Cat's Grin* (out of print). Moving and revealing, semiautobiographical novel about a young teenager living in Paris during World War II, with an adored elder brother in the Resistance.

★**Guy de Maupassant** *Bel-Ami*. Maupassant's *chef-d'oeuvre* is a brilliant and utterly sensual account of corrupt Parisian high society during the *belle époque*. Traces the rake's progress of the fascinating journalist and seducer, Georges Duroy.

Karim Miské *Arab Jazz*. Set in the multicultural 19e arrondissement, this brilliant debut crime thriller from a French-Mauritian film-maker explores the theme of fundamentalism – Islamic, Jewish and Christian – with a light and humorous touch and a colourful cast of characters.

Daniel Pennac *Monsieur Malaussène* (out of print). The last in the "Belleville Quintet" of quasi-detective novels set in the working-class east of Paris is possibly the most disturbing, centred on a series of macabre killings. Witty, experimental and chaotic, somewhat in the mode of Thomas Pynchon.

Georges Perec *Life: A User's Manual*. An extraordinary literary jigsaw puzzle of life, past and present, human, animal and mineral, extracted from the residents of an imaginary apartment block in the 17e arrondissement.

Jean-Paul Sartre *The Age of Reason*. The first in Sartre's *Roads to Freedom* trilogy is probably his most accessible work. A philosophy teacher in wartime Paris's Montparnasse struggles to find both the money for his girlfriend's abortion and the answers to his obsession with freedom.

Georges Simenon *Maigret at the Crossroads* – or any other of the Maigret crime thrillers. The Montmartre and seedy criminal locations are unbeatable. If you don't like crime fiction, go for *The Little Saint*, the story of a little boy growing up in the rue Mouffetard when it was a down-at-heel market street.

★**Emile Zola** *Nana*. The rise and fall of a courtesan in the decadent times of the Second Empire. As the quintessential realist, Zola is *the* novelist for bringing the seedy, seething reality of nineteenth-century Paris alive. Paris is also the setting for Zola's *L'Assommoir, The Masterpiece, Money, Thérèse Raquin* and *The Debacle*.

French

There's probably nowhere harder to speak or learn French than Paris. Like people from most capital cities, many Parisians speak a kind of hurried slang. Worse still, many speak fairly good English – which they may assume is better than your French. Generations of keen visitors have been offended by being replied to in English after they've carefully enunciated a well-honed question or menu order. Then there are the complex codes of politeness and formality – knowing when to add Madame/Monsieur is only the start of it. Despite this, the essentials are not difficult to master and can make all the difference. Even just saying "Bonjour Madame/Monsieur" and then gesticulating will usually get you a smile and helpful service, even if your efforts to speak French come to nothing. The *Rough Guide Phrasebook: French* and the *Rough Guide Audio Phrasebook and Dictionary: French* (ebook) give more detail.

Pronunciation

One easy rule to remember is that consonants at the end of words are usually silent. Pas plus tard (not later) is thus pronounced "pa-plu-tarr". But when the following word begins with a vowel, you run the two together: pas après (not after) becomes "pazapray".

Vowels are the hardest sounds to get right. Roughly:

a as in hat

e as in get

é between get and gate

è like the ai in pair

eu like the u in hurt

i as in machine

o as in hot

o/au as in over

ou as in food

u as in a pursed-lip, clipped version of toot

More awkward are the combinations in/im, en/em, on/om, un/um at the end of words, or followed by consonants other than n or m. Again, roughly:

in/im like the "an" in anxious

an/am, en/em like "on" said with a nasal accent

on/om like "on" said by someone with a heavy cold

un/um like the "u" in understand

Consonants are much as in English, except that ch is always sh, h is silent, th is the same as t, ll is sometimes pronounced like the y in "yes" when preceded by the letter "i" as in "fille" and "tilleul", w is v, and r is growled (or rolled).

WORDS AND PHRASES

THE TOP TWELVE

yes	oui
no	non
please	s'il vous plaît
thank you	merci
excuse me	pardon/excusez-moi
sorry	pardon, Madame/ Monsieur
hello	bonjour
goodbye	au revoir
good morning/afternoon	bonjour
good evening	bonsoir
OK/agreed	d'accord

I (don't) understand	Je (ne) comprends (pas)

KEY WORDS AND PHRASES

French nouns are divided into masculine and feminine. This causes difficulties with adjectives, whose endings have to change to suit the gender of the nouns they qualify. If in doubt, stick to the masculine form, which is the simplest – it's what we have done in the glossary below.

today	aujourd'hui
yesterday	hier
tomorrow	demain
in the morning	le matin
in the afternoon	l'après-midi

in the evening	le soir
now	maintenant
later	plus tard
at one o'clock	à une heure
at three o'clock	à trois heures
at ten-thirty	à dix heures et demi
at midday	à midi
man	un homme
woman	une femme
here	ici
there	là
this one	ceci
that one	cela
open	ouvert
closed	fermé
big	grand
small	petit
more	plus
less	moins
a little	un peu
a lot	beaucoup
half	la moitié
cheap	bon marché/pas cher
expensive	cher
good	bon
bad	mauvais
hot	chaud
cold	froid
with	avec
without	sans

TALKING TO PEOPLE

When addressing people you should always use Monsieur for a man, Madame for a woman, Mademoiselle for a girl – plain "bonjour" by itself is not enough. This isn't as formal as it seems, and it has its uses when you've forgotten someone's name or want to attract someone's attention. "Bonjour" can be used well into the afternoon, and people may start saying "bonsoir" surprisingly early in the evening, or as a way of saying goodbye.

How are you?	Comment allez-vous?/ Ça va?
Fine, thanks	Très bien, merci
I don't know	Je ne sais pas
I see!	Ah bon!
Do you speak English?	Vous parlez anglais?
How do you say... in French?	Comment dit-on... en français?
What's your name?	Comment vous appelez-vous?
My name is...	Je m'appelle...
I'm English/ Irish/ Scottish/	Je suis anglais(e)/ irlandais(e)/ écossais(e)/
Welsh/ American/ Australian/ Canadian/ a New Zealander	gallois(e)/ américain(e)/ australien(ne)/ canadien(ne)/ néo-zélandais(e)
Can you speak more slowly?	S'il vous plaît, parlez moins vite?
Let's go	Allons-y
See you tomorrow	A demain
See you soon	A bientôt
goodnight	bonne nuit

EMERGENCIES

Leave me alone	Laissez-moi tranquille
Please help me	Aidez-moi, s'il vous plaît
Help!	Au secours!

QUESTIONS AND REQUESTS

The simplest way of asking a question is to start with "s'il vous plaît" (please), then name the thing you want in an interrogative tone of voice. For example:

Where is there a bakery?	S'il vous plaît, la boulangerie?
Which way is it to the Eiffel Tower?	S'il vous plaît, pour aller à la Tour Eiffel?
We'd like a room for two	S'il vous plaît, une chambre pour deux
Can I have a kilo of oranges?	S'il vous plaît, un kilo d'oranges?
where?	où?
how?	comment?
how many?	combien?
how much is it?	c'est combien?
when?	quand?
why?	pourquoi?
at what time?	à quelle heure?
what is/which is?	quel est?

GETTING AROUND AND DIRECTIONS

metro/subway station	métro
Where is the nearest metro?	Où est le métro le plus proche?
bus	bus
bus (coach)	car
bus station	gare routière
bus stop	arrêt
car	voiture
train/taxi/ferry	train/taxi/ferry
boat	bateau
plane	avion
railway station	gare
platform	quai
What time does it leave /arrive?	Il part/arrive à quelle heure?

a ticket to…	un billet pour…	sheets	draps
single ticket	aller simple	blankets	couvertures
return ticket	aller retour	quiet	calme
validate your ticket	compostez votre billet	noisy	bruyant
valid for	valable pour	hot water	eau chaude
ticket office	vente de billets/billetterie	cold water	eau froide
how many kilometres?	combien de kilomètres?	Is breakfast included?	Est-ce que le petit déjeuner est compris?
how many hours?	combien d'heures?		
on foot	à pied	I would like breakfast	Je voudrais prendre le petit déjeuner
Where are you going?	Vous allez où?		
I'm going to…	Je vais à…	I don't want breakfast	Je ne veux pas le petit déjeuner
I want to get off at…	Je voudrais descendre à…		
the road to…	la route pour…	youth hostel	auberge de jeunesse
near	près/pas loin		
far	loin		

MONTHS, DAYS AND DATES

left	à gauche	January	janvier
right	à droite	February	février
straight on	tout droit	March	mars
on the other side of	de l'autre côté de	April	avril
on the corner of	à l'angle de	May	mai
next to	à côté de	June	juin
behind	derrière	July	juillet
in front of	devant	August	août
before	avant	September	septembre
after	après	October	octobre
under	sous	November	novembre
to cross	traverser	December	décembre
bridge	pont	Monday	lundi
to park the car	garer la voiture	Tuesday	mardi
car park	un parking	Wednesday	mercredi
no parking	défense de stationner/ stationnement interdit	Thursday	jeudi
		Friday	vendredi
petrol station	poste d'essence	Saturday	samedi
		Sunday	dimanche

ACCOMMODATION

a room for one /two people	une chambre pour une personne/deux personnes	August 1	le premier août
		March 2	le deux mars
		July 14	le quatorze juillet
with a double bed	avec un grand lit	November 23, 2014	le vingt-trois novembre, deux mille quatorze
a room with a shower	une chambre avec douche		
a room with a bath	une chambre avec baignoire	**NUMBERS**	
for one/two/three night(s)	pour une/deux/trois nuit(s)	1	un
		2	deux
Can I see it?	Je peux la voir?	3	trois
a room in the courtyard	une chambre sur la cour	4	quatre
a room over the street	une chambre sur la rue	5	cinq
first floor	premier étage	6	six
second floor	deuxième étage	7	sept
with a view	avec vue	8	huit
key	clé	9	neuf
to iron	repasser	10	dix
do laundry	faire la lessive	11	onze
		12	douze
		13	treize

14	quatorze	60	soixante
15	quinze	70	soixante-dix
16	seize	75	soixante-quinze
17	dix-sept	80	quatre-vingts
18	dix-huit	90	quatre-vingt-dix
19	dix-neuf	95	quatre-vingt-quinze
20	vingt	100	cent
21	vingt-et-un	101	cent un
22	vingt-deux	200	deux cents
30	trente	1000	mille
40	quarante	2000	deux mille
50	cinquante	1,000,000	un million

FOOD AND DRINK TERMS

BASICS

déjeuner	Lunch
dîner	Dinner
menu	Set menu
carte	Menu
à la carte	Individually priced dishes
entrées	Starters
les plats	Main courses
une carafe d'eau/de vin	A carafe of tap water/ wine
eau minérale	Mineral water
eau gazeuse	Fizzy water
eau plate	Still water
carte des vins	Wine list
un quart/demi de rouge /blanc	A quarter/half-litre of red/ white house wine
un (verre de) rouge/blanc	A glass of red/white wine
Je voudrais réserver une table pour deux personnes, à vingt heures et demie	I'd like to reserve a table, for two at 8.30pm
Je prendrai le menu à trente euros	I'm having the €30 menu
Monsieur/Madame!	Waiter! (never say "garçon")
l'addition, s'il vous plaît	The bill, please
une pression	A glass of beer
un café	Coffee (espresso)
un café americain	Black coffee
un crème	White coffee
un café au lait	Big bowl of milky breakfast coffee
un cappuccino	Cappuccino
une noisette	An espresso with a dash of hot milk

COOKING TERMS

Chauffé	Heated
Cuit	Cooked
Cru	Raw
Emballé	Wrapped

À emporter	Takeaway
Fumé	Smoked
Salé	Salted/savoury
Sucré	Sweet

ESSENTIALS

Beurre	Butter
Bio	Organic
Bouteille	Bottle
Couteau	Knife
Cuillère	Spoon
Fourchette	Fork
Huile	Oil
Lait	Milk
Oeufs	Eggs
Pain	Bread
Poivre	Pepper
Sel	Salt
Sucre	Sugar
Verre	Glass
Vinaigre	Vinegar

SNACKS

Crêpe	Pancake (sweet)
...au citron	...with lemon
...à la confiture	...with jam
...au miel	...with honey
...aux œufs	...with eggs
...au sucre	...with sugar
Galette	Buckwheat (savoury) pancake
Un sandwich/une baguette	Sandwich
...jambon	ham sandwich
...fromage	cheese sandwich
...mixte	ham and cheese sandwich
Croque-Monsieur	Grilled cheese and ham sandwich
Croque-Madame	Croque-Monsieur with an egg on top

Oeufs	eggs
...au plat	fried eggs
...à la coque	boiled eggs
...durs	hard-boiled eggs
...brouillés	scrambled eggs
Omelette	Omelette
...nature	plain omelette
...aux fines herbes	omelette with herbs
...au fromage	cheese omelette

SOUPS (SOUPES)

Bisque	Shellfish soup
Bouillabaisse	Marseillais fish soup
Bourride	Thick fish soup
Potage	Thick vegetable soup
Velouté	Thick soup, usually with fish or poultry

STARTERS (ENTRÉES, OR HORS D'OEUVRES)

Assiette de charcuterie	Plate of cold meats
Crudités	Raw vegetables with dressings
Hors d'œuvres variés	Combination of the above

FISH (POISSON), SEAFOOD (FRUITS DE MER) AND SHELLFISH (CRUSTACES OR COQUILLAGES)

Anchois	Anchovies
Anguilles	Eels
Bar	Sea bass
Barbue	Brill
Brème	Bream
Brochet	Pike
Cabillaud	Cod
Calmar	Squid
Carrelet	Plaice
Claire	Type of oyster
Colin	Hake
Coquilles St-Jacques	Scallops
Crabe	Crab
Crevettes grises	Shrimps
Crevettes roses	Prawns
Daurade	Sea bream
Escargots	Snails
Flétan	Halibut
Friture	Whitebait
Gambas	King prawns
Hareng	Herring
Homard	Lobster
Huîtres	Oysters
Langouste	Spiny lobster
Langoustines	Saltwater crayfish (scampi)
Limande	Lemon sole

Lotte de mer	Monkfish
Loup de mer	Sea bass
Louvine, loubine	Similar to sea bass
Maquereau	Mackerel
Merlan	Whiting
Morue	Dried, salted cod
Moules (marinière)	Mussels (with shallots in white wine sauce)
Raie	Skate
Rouget	Red mullet
Sandre	Pike-perch
Saumon	Salmon
Seiche	Squid
Sole	Sole
Thon	Tuna
Truite	Trout
Turbot	Turbot

FISH: DISHES AND RELATED TERMS

Aïoli	Garlic mayonnaise served with salt cod and other fish
Béarnaise	Sauce made with egg yolks, white wine, shallots and vinegar
Beignets	Fritters
La douzaine	A dozen
Frit	Fried
Fumé	Smoked
Fumet	Fish stock
Gigot de mer	Large fish baked whole
Grillé	Grilled
Hollandaise	Butter & vinegar sauce
A la meunière	In a butter, lemon and parsley sauce
Mousse/mousseline	Mousse
Quenelles	Light dumplings

MEAT (VIANDE) AND POULTRY (VOLAILLE)

Agneau (de pré-salé)	Lamb (grazed on salt marshes)
Andouille, andouillette	Tripe sausage
Bavette	Beef flank steak
Boeuf	Beef
Boudin blanc	Sausage of white meats
Boudin noir	Black pudding
Caille	Quail
Canard	Duck
Caneton	Duckling
Contrefilet	Sirloin roast
Coquelet	Cockerel
Dinde	Turkey
Entrecôte	Ribsteak
Faux filet	Sirloin steak

Foie	Liver
Foie gras	Fattened (duck/goose) liver
Gigot (d'agneau)	Leg (of lamb)
Grillade	Grilled meat
Hachis	Chopped meat or mince hamburger
Langue	Tongue
Lapin, lapereau	Rabbit, young rabbit
Lard, lardons	Bacon, diced bacon
Lièvre	Hare
Merguez	Spicy, red sausage
Mouton	Mutton
Museau de veau	Calf's muzzle
Oie	Goose
Onglet	Cut of beef
Os	Bone
Pièce de boeuf	Steak
Porc	Pork
Poulet	Chicken
Poussin	Baby chicken
Ris	Sweetbreads
Rognons	Kidneys
Rognons blancs	Testicles
Sanglier	Wild boar
Tête de veau	Calf's head (in jelly)
Tournedos	Thick slices of fillet
Tripes	Tripe
Veau	Veal
Venaison	Venison

MEAT AND POULTRY: DISHES AND RELATED TERMS

Aile	Wing
Blanquette de veau	Veal in cream and mushroom sauce
Boeuf bourguignon	Beef stew with red wine, onions and mushrooms
Canard à l'orange	Roast duck with orange and wine sauce
Carré	Best end of neck, chop or cutlet
Cassoulet	Casserole of beans and meat
Choucroute garnie	Sauerkraut served with sausages or cured ham
Civet	Game stew
Confit	Meat preserve
Coq au vin	Chicken with wine, onions and mushrooms, cooked till it falls off the bone
Côte	Chop, cutlet or rib
Cou	Neck
Cuisse	Thigh or leg

Daube, estouffade, hochepot, navarin and ragout	Stews of different kinds
En croûte	In pastry
Epaule	Shoulder
Farci	Stuffed
Au feu de bois	Cooked over a wood fire
Au four	Baked
Garni	With vegetables
Gésier	Gizzard
Grillé	Grilled
Magret de canard	Duck breast
Marmite	Casserole
Médaillon	Round piece
Mijoté	Stewed
Museau	Muzzle
Pavé	Thick slice
Rôti	Roast
Sauté	Lightly cooked in butter
Steak au poivre (vert/rouge)	Steak in a black (green/red) peppercorn sauce
Steak tartare	Raw chopped beef, topped with a raw egg yolk

FOR STEAKS

Bleu	Almost raw
Saignant	Rare
A point	Medium
Bien cuit	Well done
Très bien cuit	Very well cooked
Brochette	Kebab

GARNISHES AND SAUCES

Beurre blanc	Sauce of white wine and shallots, with butter
Chasseur	White wine, mushrooms and shallots
Diable	Strong mustard seasoning
Forestière	With bacon and mushroom
Fricassée	Rich, creamy sauce
Mornay	Cheese sauce
Pays d'Auge	Cream and cider
Piquante	Gherkins or capers, vinegar and shallots
Provençale	Tomatoes, garlic, olive oil and herbs

VEGETABLES (LEGUMES), HERBS (HERBES) AND SPICES (EPICES)

Ail	Garlic
Algue	Seaweed
Anis	Aniseed
Artichaut	Artichoke
Asperges	Asparagus

Avocat	Avocado
Basilic	Basil
Betterave	Beetroot
Carotte	Carrot
Céleri	Celery
Champignons, cèpes, chanterelles	Mushrooms of various kinds
Chou (rouge)	(Red) cabbage
Chou-fleur	Cauliflower
Ciboulette	Chives
Concombre	Cucumber
Cornichon	Gherkin
Echalotes	Shallots
Endive	Chicory
Epinards	Spinach
Estragon	Tarragon
Fenouil	Fennel
Flageolets	White beans
Gingembre	Ginger
Haricots	Beans
...verts	String/French beans
...rouges	Kidney beans
...beurres	Butter beans
Laurier	Bay leaf
Lentilles	Lentils
Maïs	Corn
Menthe	Mint
Moutarde	Mustard
Oignon	Onion
Pâtes	Pasta
Persil	Parsley
Petits pois	Peas
Pignons	Pine nuts
Piment	Pimento
Poireau	Leek
Pois chiche	Chickpeas
Pois mange-tout	Snow peas
Poivron (vert, rouge)	Sweet pepper (green, red)
Pommes (de terre)	Potatoes
Primeurs	Spring vegetables
Radis	Radishes
Riz	Rice
Safran	Saffron
Salade verte	Green salad
Sarrasin	Buckwheat
Tomate	Tomato
Topinambour	Jerusalem artichoke
Truffes	Truffles

VEGETABLES: DISHES AND RELATED TERMS

Beignet	Fritter
Farci	Stuffed
Forestière	With mushrooms
Gratiné/au gratin	Browned with cheese
/gratin de	or butter
Jardinière	With mixed diced vegetables
A la parisienne	Sautéed in butter (potatoes); with white wine sauce and shallots
Parmentier	With potatoes
Sauté	Lightly fried in butter
A la vapeur	Steamed

FRUITS (FRUITS) AND NUTS (NOIX)

Abricot	Apricot
Amandes	Almonds
Ananas	Pineapple
Banane	Banana
Brugnon	Nectarine
Cacahouète	Peanut
Cassis	Blackcurrants
Cerises	Cherries
Citron	Lemon
Citron vert	Lime
Figues	Figs
Fraises (des bois)	Strawberries (wild)
Framboises	Raspberries
Fruit de la passion	Passion fruit
Groseilles	Redcurrants and gooseberries
Mangue	Mango
Marrons	Chestnuts
Melon	Melon
Myrtilles	Bilberries
Noisette	Hazelnut
Noix	Nuts
Orange	Orange
Pamplemousse	Grapefruit
Pêche (blanche)	(White) peach
Pistache	Pistachio
Poire	Pear
Pomme	Apple
Prune	Plum
Pruneau	Prune
Raisins	Grapes

FRUIT: RELATED TERMS

Beignets	Fritters
Compote de...	Stewed...
Coulis	Sauce
Flambé	Set aflame in alcohol
Frappé	Iced

DESSERTS (DESSERTS) AND PASTRIES (PÂTISSERIE)

Bavarois	Mousse or custard – the term refers to the mould

Bombe	Ice cream dessert, moulded	Mousse au chocolat	Chocolate mousse
Brioche	Sweet, high-yeast breakfast roll	Palmiers	Caramelized puff pastries
Charlotte	Custard and fruit in lining of almond fingers	Parfait	Frozen mousse, sometimes ice cream
Coupe	Serving of ice cream	Petit suisse	Smooth mixture of cream and curds
Crème Chantilly	Vanilla-flavoured and sweetened whipped cream	Petits fours	Bite-sized cakes/ pastries
Crème fraîche	Sour cream	Sablé	Shortbread biscuit
Crème pâtissière	Thick, eggy pastry filling	Savarin	Filled, ring-shaped cake
Crêpe	Pancake	Tarte	Tart
Crêpe suzette	Thin pancake with orange juice and liqueur	Tartelette	Small tart
Financier	Almond cake	Truffes	Truffles, chocolate or liqueur variety
Galette	Buckwheat pancake	Yaourt, yogourt	Yoghurt
Glace	Ice cream		
Île flottante/oeufs à la neige	Soft meringues floating on custard		
Macarons	Macaroons		
Madeleine	Small sponge cake		
Marrons Mont Blanc	Chestnut purée and cream on a rum-soaked sponge cake		

CHEESE (FROMAGE)

There are more than four hundred types of French cheese, most of them named after their place of origin. *Chèvre* is goat's cheese and *brebis* is cheese made from sheep's milk. *Le plateau de fromages* is the cheeseboard, and bread – but not butter – is served with it.

Glossary

arrondissement one of any of the twenty districts of Paris

banlieue suburb

berge riverside

biologique or bio organic

chemin path

consigne left-luggage office

défense de… It is forbidden to…

dégustation tasting (wine or food)

fermeture closing period

gare station; "routière" – bus station; "SNCF" – train station

hôtel hotel, but also a townhouse or mansion

jours fériés public holidays

marché market

navette shuttle

nocturne late-night opening

place square

plan city map; "du métro" – métro map

porte gateway or door

poste post office

quartier district

rez-de-chaussée ground floor

roman Romanesque (as opposed to "romain", which means "Roman")

soldes sales

sortie exit

tabac bar or shop selling stamps, cigarettes, etc

tarif price of admission; **tarif réduit** reduced price (for children, students etc)

villa a small residential street

zone bleue restricted parking

zone piétonne pedestrian zone

Small print and index

A ROUGH GUIDE TO ROUGH GUIDES

Published in 1982, the first Rough Guide – to Greece – was a student scheme that became a publishing phenomenon. Mark Ellingham, a recent graduate in English from Bristol University, had been travelling in Greece the previous summer and couldn't find the right guidebook. With a small group of friends he wrote his own guide, combining a highly contemporary, journalistic style with a thoroughly practical approach to travellers' needs.

The immediate success of the book spawned a series that rapidly covered dozens of destinations. And, in addition to impecunious backpackers, Rough Guides soon acquired a much broader readership that relished the guides' wit and inquisitiveness as much as their enthusiastic, critical approach and value-for-money ethos.

These days, Rough Guides include recommendations from budget to luxury and cover more than 120 destinations around the globe, as well as producing an ever-growing range of ebooks.

Visit **roughguides.com** to find all our latest books, read articles, get inspired and share travel tips with the Rough Guides community.

Rough Guide credits

Editors: Melissa Graham, Neil McQuillian
Layout: Nikhil Agarwal
Cartography: Rajesh Chhibber
Picture editor: Aude Vauconsant
Proofreader: Diane Margolis
Managing editor: Monica Woods
Assistant editor: Sharon Sonam
Production: Jimmy Lao

Cover design: Nicole Newman, Aude Vauconsant,
Nikhil Agarwal
Editorial assistant: Freya Godfrey
Senior pre-press designer: Dan May
Programme manager: Gareth Lowe
Publisher: Keith Drew
Publishing director: Georgina Dee

Publishing information

This fifteenth edition published January 2016 by
Rough Guides Ltd,
80 Strand, London WC2R 0RL
11, Community Centre, Panchsheel Park,
New Delhi 110017, India
Distributed by Penguin Random House
Penguin Books Ltd, 80 Strand, London WC2R 0RL
Penguin Group (USA), 345 Hudson Street, NY 10014, USA
Penguin Group (Australia), 250 Camberwell Road,
Camberwell, Victoria 3124, Australia
Penguin Group (NZ), 67 Apollo Drive, Mairangi Bay,
Auckland 1310, New Zealand
Penguin Group (South Africa), Block D, Rosebank Office
Park, 181 Jan Smuts Avenue, Parktown North, Gauteng,
South Africa 2193
Rough Guides is represented in Canada by DK Canada, 320
Front Street West, Suite 1400,Toronto, Ontario M5V 3B6
Printed in Singapore
© Rough Guides 2016
Maps © Rough Guides

416pp includes index
A catalogue record for this book is available from the
British Library
ISBN: 978-0-24119-924-4
The publishers and authors have done their best to
ensure the accuracy and currency of all the information
in **The Rough Guide to Paris**, however, they can accept
no responsibility for any loss, injury, or inconvenience
sustained by any traveller as a result of information or
advice contained in the guide.
1 3 5 7 9 8 6 4 2

Help us update

We've gone to a lot of effort to ensure that the fifteenth
edition of **The Rough Guide to Paris** is accurate and up-
to-date. However, things change – places get "discovered",
opening hours are notoriously fickle, restaurants and
rooms raise prices or lower standards. If you feel we've got
it wrong or left something out, we'd like to know, and if
you can remember the address, the price, the hours, the
phone number, so much the better.

Please send your comments with the subject line
"Rough Guide Paris Update" to mail@uk.roughguides
.com. We'll credit all contributions and send a copy of the
next edition (or any other Rough Guide if you prefer) for
the very best emails.

Find more travel information, connect with fellow
travellers and plan your trip on ⓦ roughguides.com.

ABOUT THE AUTHORS

Ruth Blackmore is a freelance editor and writer, and longstanding contributor to the Rough Guides to Paris and France. She grew up in South Wales and lives in Dorset with her young family.

Samantha Cook is a London-based writer and editor who has been nipping across the Channel to Paris on a regular basis since the age of seven. Her other books as author include Rough Guides to London; Vintage London; Kent, Sussex & Surrey; Budget Accommodation in Britain; New Orleans; and Chick Flicks.

Acknowledgements

Ruth Blackmore Many thanks to my editors Neil McQuillian and Melissa Graham for their thorough and careful editing. Special thanks to those who helped with my updating of this edition, especially Dylan, Hannah, Rosa, Jules and Ute.

Samantha Cook This edition of the *Rough Guide to Paris* was a delight to work on. A big part of that was down to

editors Neil and Melissa, who applied both eagle-eyed precision and a wry sense of fun to the project, and to co-author Ruth, who shared her deep knowledge and tons of experience with grace, generosity and humour. Huge thanks too, to Natasha for the commission, and above all to Greg "flâneur" Ward, without whom none of it would be possible – or even half as much fun.

Readers' updates

Thanks to all the readers who have taken the time to write in with comments and suggestions (and apologies if we've inadvertently omitted or misspelt anyone's name):

Anne Freimanis; Val and John Horridge; Emily Logie; Colin Morison; Mike Richmond; John Rivaldi; Chris Wildt.

Photo credits

All photos © Rough Guides except the following:
(Key: t-top; c-centre; b-bottom; l-left; r-right)

p.1 Jon Arnold/AWL Images
p.2 Sylvain Sonnet/Getty Images
p.7 Fred de Noyelle/Godong/Robert Harding Picture Library (tl); Peter Phipp/Getty Images (b)
p.8 Eurasia/Robert Harding Picture Library
p.9 Bertrand Gardel/Corbis (t); Andrea Innocenti/Robert Harding Picture Library (c)
p.10 Bertrand Rieger/Corbis
p.11 Owen Franken/Corbis (t)
p.12 Cogoli Franco/4Corners (t); Hans-Peter Merten/Robert Harding Picture Library (b)
p.14 Thomas Craig/SuperStock (tl); Fabien Campoverde/Musée national Picasso-Paris (tr); Sophie Boegly/Sophie Boegly (b)
p.15 Mehdi Fedouach/Getty Images (t); Hemis/Alamy Images (c); Tuul & Bruno Morandi/Corbis (b)
p.17 Benjamin Leterrier/Corbis (tl); Godong/Robert Harding Picture Library (tr)
p.20 Neil Farrin/Corbis
p.42 Tristan Deschamps/SuperStock
p.49 Stuart Dee/Robert Harding Picture Library
p.55 Stuart Dee/Robert Harding Picture Library (b)
p.62 Travelshots/SuperStock
p.81 Bernard Jaubert/Robert Harding Picture Library (t)
p.85 Fernand Ivaldi/Getty Images
p.103 Fabien Campoverde/Musée national Picasso-Paris (tl); Hemis/Alamy (b)
p.119 Ben Johnson/Corbis
p.129 Arnaud Chicurel/Corbis (b)
p.147 Massimo Borchi/Corbis
p.160 Sylvain Sonnet/Corbis

p.167 John Kellerman/Alamy Images (b)
p.189 Photononstop/SuperStock (tl)
p.197 Hideo Kurihara/Alamy Images
p.206 Hemis/Alamy Images
p.214 Huften and Crow/Corbis
p.222 John Kellerman/Alamy Images
p.231 John Kellerman/Alamy Images
p.237 Maremagnum/Getty Images
p.248 Howard Sayer/Alamy Images
p.273 Damien Lamargue/Le Chateaubriand (tl)
p.287 Glenn Harper/Alamy Images (tl); Hemis (br)
p.303 LOOK Die Bildagentur der Fotografen GmbH/Alamy Images (tl); Tuul & Bruno Morandi/Corbis (b)
p.312 Swim Ink 2, LLC/Corbis (tl); Etoile Cinémas (tr)
p.313 AF archive/Alamy Images (tl); John Springer Collection/Corbis (tr)
p.317 Charles Platiau/Corbis
p.329 Sueddeutsche Zeitung Photo/Alamy Images (tl); Alistair Philip Wiper/Corbis (bl)
p.341 Maurizio Borgese/SuperStock
p.353 Horacio Villalobos/Corbis (bl); Bertrand Guay/AFP/Getty Images (br)
p.357 Lucas Dolega/epa/Corbis
p.360 John Harper/Corbis

Front cover and spine Art Nouveau métro sign © Jon Boyes/incamerastock/Corbis
Back cover Banks of the Seine © Hemis/AWL Images (t); Pol Bury's spheres in the courtyard of the Palais Royal © Daniel Auduc/Photononstop/Corbis (br); Bonnat chocolate bars © Andia/Latitude (bl)

Index

Maps are marked in grey

Map index

Listings key

■ Accommodation

● Café/wine bar/restaurant

■ Bar/club/live music/LGBT bar

● Shopping

City plan

The **city plan** on the pages that follow is divided as shown:

N

0	250
	metres

Map symbols

– – – Chapter division boundary	✈ Airport	✡ Synagogue
Motorway	Ⓜ Metro	Basilica
Major road	Ⓡ RER Paris	✝ Cathedral
Minor road	Ⓣ Tram stop	◆ Place of interest
Pedestrian road	Boats	Building
Steps	Ⓟ Parking	Church
Railway	✉ Post office	Stadium
— Ferry route	ⓘ Tourist information	Cemetery
– – – Footpath	Hospital	Park
River	⊙ Statue	
⌣ Bridge	Chateau	

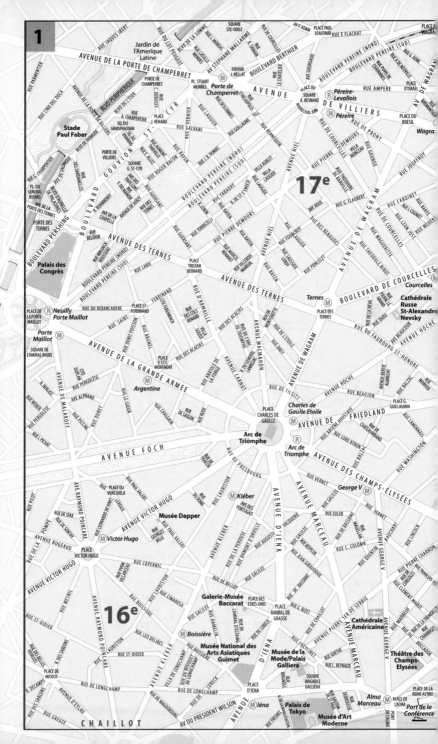

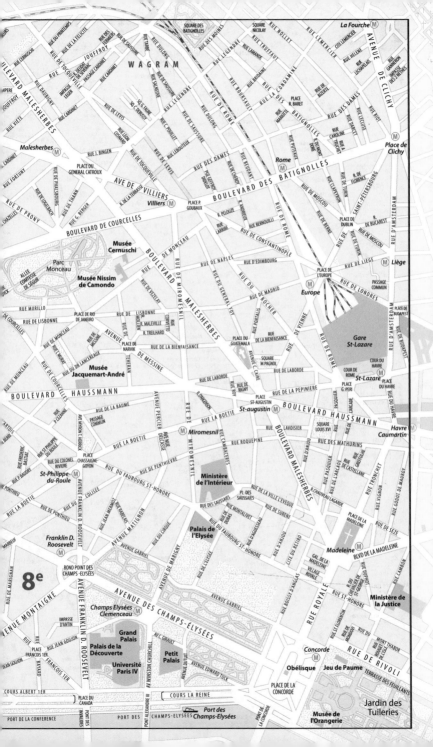

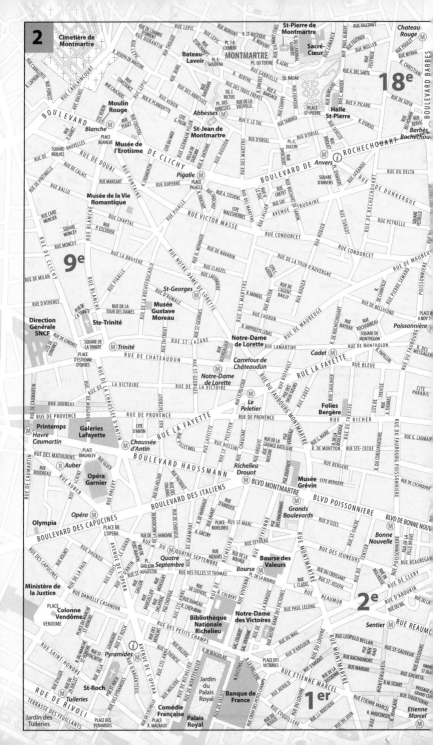

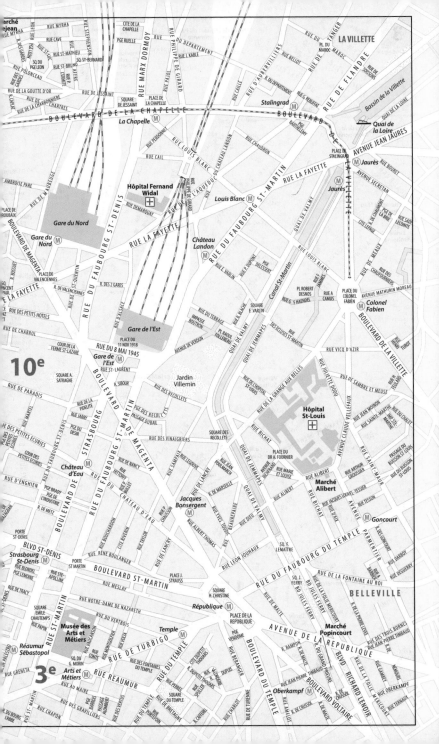

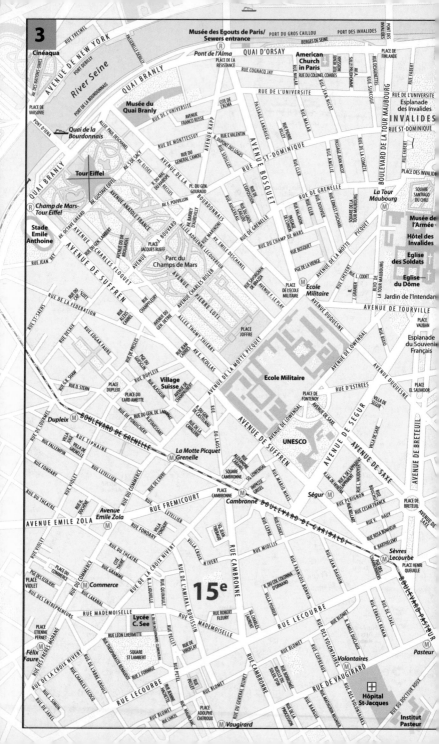

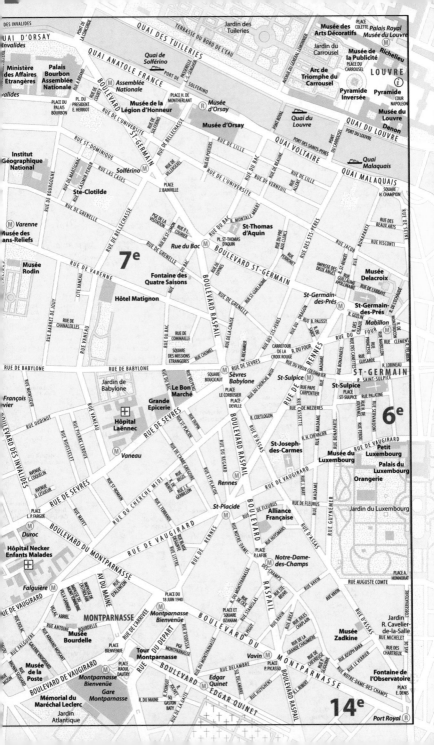

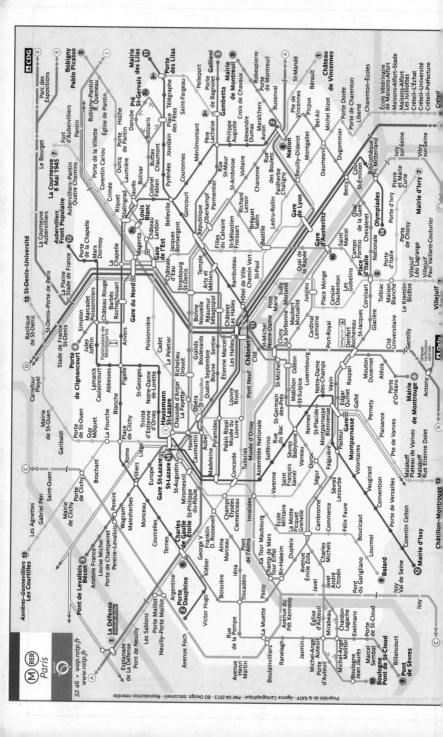